John A. Grim is Professor of Religion at Buc
University. He is the author of *The Shaman:
Patterns of Siberian and Ojibway Healing* and
coeditor of *Worldviews and Ecology*.

Indigenous Traditions and Ecology

Publications of the Center for the Study of World Religions
Harvard Divinity School

General Editor: Lawrence E. Sullivan
Senior Editor: Kathryn Dodgson
Associate Editor: Eric Edstam

Religions of the World and Ecology

Series Editors: Mary Evelyn Tucker and John Grim

Cambridge, Massachusetts

Indigenous Traditions and Ecology

The Interbeing of Cosmology and Community

edited by

JOHN A. GRIM

distributed by
Harvard University Press
for the
Center for the Study of World Religions
Harvard Divinity School

Cover art: Penan-Kelabit community in Sarawak, Borneo, resisting logging on their homeland (photo courtesy of Mutang Urud). A *t'nalak* (abaca cloth weaving) of the T'boli people of Mindanao, Philippines, depicting the *tofi* (frog) pattern associated with the creation moment of the human in T'boli cosmology (photo courtesy of John A. Grim).

Cover design: Patrick Santana

Library of Congress Cataloging-in-Publication Data

Indigenous traditions and ecology : the interbeing of cosmology and community / edited by John A. Grim.
    p. cm. — (Religions of the world and ecology)
    Includes bibliographical references and index.
    ISBN 0-945454-27-9 (hardcover : alk. paper)
    ISBN 0-945454-28-7 (paperback : alk. paper)
    1. Indigenous peoples—Religion. 2. Indigenous peoples—Ecology. 3. Ethnophilosophy. 4. Cosmology. 5. Environmental degradation—Religious aspects. 6. Environmental ethics. I. Grim, John. II. Series.

GN470.2.I53 2001
306'.08—dc21

2001017257

Acknowledgments

The series of conferences on religions of the world and ecology took place from 1996 through 1998, with supervision at the Harvard University Center for the Study of World Religions by Don Kunkel and Malgorzata Radziszewska-Hedderick and with the assistance of Janey Bosch, Naomi Wilshire, and Lilli Leggio. Narges Moshiri, also at the Center, was indispensable in helping to arrange the first two conferences. A series of volumes developing the themes explored at the conferences is being published by the Center and distributed by Harvard University Press under the editorial direction of Kathryn Dodgson and with the skilled assistance of Eric Edstam.

These efforts have been generously supported by major funding from the V. Kann Rasmussen Foundation. The conference organizers appreciate also the support of the following institutions and individuals: Aga Khan Trust for Culture, Association of Shinto Shrines, Nathan Cummings Foundation, Dharam Hinduja Indic Research Center at Columbia University, Germeshausen Foundation, Harvard Buddhist Studies Forum, Harvard Divinity School Center for the Study of Values in Public Life, Jain Academic Foundation of North America, Laurance Rockefeller, Sacharuna Foundation, Theological Education to Meet the Environmental Challenge, and Winslow Foundation. The conferences were originally made possible by the Center for Respect of Life and Environment of the Humane Society of the United States, which continues to be a principal cosponsor. Bucknell University, also a cosponsor, has provided support in the form of leave time from teaching for conference coordinators Mary Evelyn Tucker and John

Grim as well as the invaluable administrative assistance of Stephanie Snyder. Her thoughtful attention to critical details is legendary. Then President William Adams of Bucknell University and then Vice-President for Academic Affairs Daniel Little have also granted travel funds for faculty and students to attend the conferences. Grateful acknowledgment is here made for the advice from key area specialists in shaping each conference and in editing the published volumes. Their generosity in time and talent has been indispensable at every step of the project. Throughout this process, the support, advice, and encouragement from Martin S. Kaplan has been invaluable.

The volume editor wishes also to acknowledge participants in the conference whose contributions do not appear in this volume: Nelly Arvelo-Jimenez, Mary Des Chene, William Fisher, Teresia Hinga, Donna House, Jiger Janabel, Kenneth Kensinger, Oren Lyons, Pashington Obeng, Jacob Olupona, Theodore MacDonald, Suresh Ale Magar, Rex Mansmann, Joel Martin, David Maybury-Lewis, Russell Peters, Mary Steedly, Jake Swamp, Ines Talamantez, Mutang Urud, Piers Vitebsky, Victor Yellow Hawk White. Appreciation also goes to Igor Krupnik of the Smithsonian Institution who although unable to attend, recommended participants. The cover photograph, taken by Mutang Urud, was used on the cover of the original conference program and is used here again with permission. Thanks also to research assistant Ryan Neenan and to Ben Marsh in the geography department at Bucknell University for their assistance in preparing the overview maps of indigenous peoples for this volume. Martin L. White prepared the index. Gratitude is extended to David Kinsley, Lee Irwin, and Joel Martin for their careful reading of the manuscript. The editor gratefully acknowledges the insightful term of Thich Nhat Hahn, namely, "interbeing," which is used here to accentuate the reciprocal relations between natural and human worlds.

Contents

Complex Cosmologies

Embedded Worldviews

Preface

LAWRENCE E. SULLIVAN

Religion distinguishes the human species from all others, just as human presence on earth distinguishes the ecology of our planet from other places in the known universe. Religious life and the earth's ecology are inextricably linked, organically related.

Human belief and practice mark the earth. One can hardly think of a natural system that has not been considerably altered, for better or worse, by human culture. "Nor is this the work of the industrial centuries," observes Simon Schama. "It is coeval with the entirety of our social existence. And it is this irreversibly modified world, from the polar caps to the equatorial forests, that is all the nature we have" (*Landscape and Memory* [New York: Vintage Books, 1996], 7). In Schama's examination even landscapes that appear to be most free of human culture turn out, on closer inspection, to be its product.

Human beliefs about the nature of ecology are the distinctive contribution of our species to the ecology itself. Religious beliefs—especially those concerning the nature of powers that create and animate—become an effective part of ecological systems. They attract the power of will and channel the forces of labor toward purposive transformations. Religious rituals model relations with material life and transmit habits of practice and attitudes of mind to succeeding generations.

This is not simply to say that religious thoughts occasionally touch the world and leave traces that accumulate over time. The matter is the other way around. From the point of view of environmental studies, religious worldviews propel communities into the world with fundamental predispositions toward it because such religious world-views are primordial, all-encompassing, and unique. They are *primordial* because they probe behind secondary appearances and stray thoughts to rivet human attention on realities of the first order: life at its source, creativity in its fullest manifestation, death and destruction at their origin, renewal and salvation in their germ. The revelation of first things is compelling and moves communities to take creative action. Primordial ideas are prime movers.

Religious worldviews are *all-encompassing* because they fully absorb the natural world within them. They provide human beings both a view of the whole and at the same time a penetrating image of their own ironic position as the beings in the cosmos who possess the capacity for symbolic thought: the part that contains the whole—or at least a picture of the whole—within itself. As all-encompassing, therefore, religious ideas do not just contend with other ideas as equals; they frame the mind-set within which all sorts of ideas commingle in a cosmology. For this reason, their role in ecology must be better understood.

Religious worldviews are *unique* because they draw the world of nature into a wholly other kind of universe, one that appears only in the religious imagination. From the point of view of environmental studies, the risk of such religious views, on the one hand, is of disinterest in or disregard for the natural world. On the other hand, only in the religious world can nature be compared and contrasted to other kinds of being—the supernatural world or forms of power not always fully manifest in nature. Only then can nature be revealed as distinctive, set in a new light startlingly different from its own. That is to say, only religious perspectives enable human beings to evaluate the world of nature in terms distinct from all else. In this same step toward intelligibility, the natural world is evaluated in terms consonant with human beings' own distinctive (religious and imaginative) nature in the world, thus grounding a self-conscious relationship and a role with limits and responsibilities.

In the struggle to sustain the earth's environment as viable for future generations, environmental studies has thus far left the role of religion unprobed. This contrasts starkly with the emphasis given, for example, the role of science and technology in threatening or sustaining the ecology. Ignorance of religion prevents environmental studies from achieving its goals, however, for though science and technology share many important features of human culture with religion, they leave unexplored essential wellsprings of human motivation and concern that shape the world as we know it. No understanding of the environment is adequate without a grasp of the religious life that constitutes the human societies which saturate the natural environment.

A great deal of what we know about the religions of the world is new knowledge. As is the case for geology and astronomy, so too for religious studies: many new discoveries about the nature and function of religion are, in fact, clearer understandings of events and processes that began to unfold long ago. Much of what we are learning now about the religions of the world was previously not known outside of a circle of adepts. From the ancient history of traditions and from the ongoing creativity of the world's contemporary religions we are opening a treasury of motives, disciplines, and awarenesses.

A geology of the religious spirit of humankind can well serve our need to relate fruitfully to the earth and its myriad life-forms. Changing our habits of consumption and patterns of distribution, reevaluating modes of production, and reestablishing a strong sense of solidarity with the matrix of material life—these achievements will arrive along with spiritual modulations that unveil attractive new images of well-being and prosperity, respecting the limits of life in a sustainable world while revering life at its sources. Remarkable religious views are presented in this series—from the nature mysticism of Bashō in Japan or Saint Francis in Italy to the ecstatic physiologies and embryologies of shamanic healers, Taoist meditators, and Vedic practitioners; from indigenous people's ritual responses to projects funded by the World Bank, to religiously grounded criticisms of hazardous waste sites, deforestation, and environmental racism.

The power to modify the world is both frightening and fascinating and has been subjected to reflection, particularly religious reflection, from time immemorial to the present day. We will understand ecology better when we understand the religions that form the rich soil of memory and practice, belief and relationships where life on earth is rooted. Knowledge of these views will help us reappraise our ways and reorient ourselves toward the sources and resources of life.

This volume is one in a series that addresses the critical gap in our contemporary understanding of religion and ecology. The series results from research conducted at the Harvard University Center for the Study of World Religions over a three-year period. I wish especially to acknowledge President Neil L. Rudenstine of Harvard University for his leadership in instituting the environmental initiative at Harvard and thank him for his warm encouragement and characteristic support of our program. Mary Evelyn Tucker and John Grim of Bucknell University coordinated the research, involving the direct participation of some six hundred scholars, religious leaders, and environmental specialists brought to Harvard from around the world during the period of research and inquiry. Professors Tucker and Grim have brought great vision and energy to this enormous project, as has their team of conference convenors. The commitment and advice of Martin S. Kaplan of Hale and Dorr have been of great value. Our goals have been achieved for this research and publication program because of the extraordinary dedication and talents of Center for the Study of World Religions staff members Don Kunkel, Malgorzata Radziszewska-Hedderick, Kathryn Dodgson, Janey Bosch, Naomi Wilshire, Lilli Leggio, and Eric Edstam and with the unstinting help of Stephanie Snyder of Bucknell. To these individuals, and to all the sponsors and participants whose efforts made this series possible, go deepest thanks and appreciation.

Series Foreword

MARY EVELYN TUCKER and JOHN GRIM

The Nature of the Environmental Crisis

Ours is a period when the human community is in search of new and sustaining relationships to the earth amidst an environmental crisis that threatens the very existence of all life-forms on the planet. While the particular causes and solutions of this crisis are being debated by scientists, economists, and policymakers, the facts of widespread destruction are causing alarm in many quarters. Indeed, from some perspectives the future of human life itself appears threatened. As Daniel Maguire has succinctly observed, "If current trends continue, we will not."[1] Thomas Berry, the former director of the Riverdale Center for Religious Research, has also raised the stark question, "Is the human a viable species on an endangered planet?"

From resource depletion and species extinction to pollution overload and toxic surplus, the planet is struggling against unprecedented assaults. This is aggravated by population explosion, industrial growth, technological manipulation, and military proliferation heretofore unknown by the human community. From many accounts the basic elements which sustain life—sufficient water, clean air, and arable land—are at risk. The challenges are formidable and well documented. The solutions, however, are more elusive and complex. Clearly, this crisis has economic, political, and social dimensions which require more detailed analysis than we can provide here. Suffice it to say, however, as did the *Global 2000 Report:* ". . .once such global environmental problems are in motion they are difficult to reverse. In fact few if any of the problems addressed in the *Global 2000*

Report are amenable to quick technological or policy fixes; rather, they are inextricably mixed with the world's most perplexing social and economic problems."[2]

Peter Raven, the director of the Missouri Botanical Garden, wrote in a paper titled "We Are Killing Our World" with a similar sense of urgency regarding the magnitude of the environmental crisis: "The world that provides our evolutionary and ecological context is in serious trouble, trouble of a kind that demands our urgent attention. By formulating adequate plans for dealing with these large-scale problems, we will be laying the foundation for peace and prosperity in the future; by ignoring them, drifting passively while attending to what may seem more urgent, personal priorities, we are courting disaster."

Rethinking Worldviews and Ethics

For many people an environmental crisis of this complexity and scope is not only the result of certain economic, political, and social factors. It is also a moral and spiritual crisis which, in order to be addressed, will require broader philosophical and religious understandings of ourselves as creatures of nature, embedded in life cycles and dependent on ecosystems. Religions, thus, need to be reexamined in light of the current environmental crisis. This is because religions help to shape our attitudes toward nature in both conscious and unconscious ways. Religions provide basic interpretive stories of who we are, what nature is, where we have come from, and where we are going. This comprises a worldview of a society. Religions also suggest how we should treat other humans and how we should relate to nature. These values make up the ethical orientation of a society. Religions thus generate worldviews and ethics which underlie fundamental attitudes and values of different cultures and societies. As the historian Lynn White observed, "What people do about their ecology depends on what they think about themselves in relation to things around them. Human ecology is deeply conditioned by beliefs about our nature and destiny—that is, by religion."[3]

In trying to reorient ourselves in relation to the earth, it has become apparent that we have lost our appreciation for the intricate nature of matter and materiality. Our feeling of alienation in the modern period has extended beyond the human community and its patterns of material exchanges to our interaction with nature itself. Especially in technologically sophisticated urban societies, we have become removed from the recognition of our dependence on nature. We no longer know who we are as earthlings; we no longer see the earth as sacred.

Thomas Berry suggests that we have become autistic in our interactions with the natural world. In other words, we are unable to value the life and beauty of nature because we are locked in our own egocentric perspectives and shortsighted needs. He suggests that we need a new cosmology, cultural coding, and motivating energy to overcome this deprivation.[4] He observes that the magnitude of destructive industrial processes is so great that we must initiate a radical rethinking of the myth of progress and of humanity's role in the evolutionary process. Indeed, he speaks of evolution as a new story of the universe, namely, as a vast cosmological perspective that will resituate human meaning and direction in the context of four and a half billion years of earth history.[5]

For Berry and for many others an important component of the current environmental crisis is spiritual and ethical. It is here that the religions of the world may have a role to play in cooperation with other individuals, institutions, and initiatives that have been engaged with environmental issues for a considerable period of time. Despite their lateness in addressing the crisis, religions are beginning to respond in remarkably creative ways. They are not only rethinking their theologies but are also reorienting their sustainable practices and long-term environmental commitments. In so doing, the very nature of religion and of ethics is being challenged and changed. This is true because the reexamination of other worldviews created by religious beliefs and practices may be critical to our recovery of sufficiently comprehensive cosmologies, broad conceptual frameworks, and effective environmental ethics for the twenty-first century.

While in the past none of the religions of the world have had to face an environmental crisis such as we are now confronting, they remain key instruments in shaping attitudes toward nature. The unintended consequences of the modern industrial drive for unlimited economic growth and resource development have led us to an impasse regarding the survival of many life-forms and appropriate management of varied ecosystems. The religious traditions may indeed be critical in helping to reimagine the viable conditions and long-range strategies for fostering mutually enhancing human-earth relations.[6]

Indeed, as E. N. Anderson has documented with impressive detail, "All traditional societies that have succeeded in managing resources well, over time, have done it in part through religious or ritual representation of resource management."[7]

It is in this context that a series of conferences and publications exploring the various religions of the world and their relation to ecology was initiated by the Center for the Study of World Religions at Harvard. Coordinated by Mary Evelyn Tucker and John Grim, the conferences involved some six hundred scholars, graduate students, religious leaders, and environmental activists over a period of three years. The collaborative nature of the project is intentional. Such collaboration maximizes the opportunity for dialogical reflection on this issue of enormous complexity and accentuates the diversity of local manifestations of ecologically sustainable alternatives.

This series is intended to serve as initial explorations of the emerging field of religion and ecology while pointing toward areas for further research. We are not unaware of the difficulties of engaging in such a task, yet we have been encouraged by the enthusiastic response to the conferences within the academic community, by the larger interest they have generated beyond academia, and by the probing examinations gathered in the volumes. We trust that this series and these volumes will be useful not only for scholars of religion but also for those shaping seminary education and institutional religious practices, as well as for those involved in public policy on environmental issues.

We see such conferences and publications as expanding the growing dialogue regarding the role of the world's religions as moral forces in stemming the environmental crisis. While, clearly, there are major methodological issues involved in utilizing traditional philosophical and religious ideas for contemporary concerns, there are also compelling reasons to support such efforts, however modest they may be. The world's religions in all their complexity and variety remain one of the principal resources for symbolic ideas, spiritual inspiration, and ethical principles. Indeed, despite their limitations, historically they have provided comprehensive cosmologies for interpretive direction, moral foundations for social cohesion, spiritual guidance for cultural expression, and ritual celebrations for meaningful life. In our search for more comprehensive ecological worldviews and more effective environmental ethics, it is inevitable that we will draw from the symbolic and conceptual resources of the religious traditions of the world. The effort to do this is not without precedent or problems, some of which will be signaled below. With this volume and with this series we hope the field of reflection and discussion regarding religion and ecology will begin to broaden, deepen, and complexify.

Qualifications and Goals

The Problems and Promise of Religions

These volumes, then, are built on the premise that the religions of the world may be instrumental in addressing the moral dilemmas created by the environmental crisis. At the same time we recognize the limitations of such efforts on the part of religions. We also acknowledge that the complexity of the problem requires interlocking approaches from such fields as science, economics, politics, health, and public policy. As the human community struggles to formulate different attitudes toward nature and to articulate broader conceptions of ethics embracing species and ecosystems, religions may thus be a necessary, though only contributing, part of this multidisciplinary approach.

It is becoming increasingly evident that abundant scientific knowledge of the crisis is available and numerous political and economic statements have been formulated. Yet we seem to lack the political, economic, and scientific leadership to make necessary changes. Moreover, what is still lacking is the religious commitment, moral imagination, and ethical engagement to transform the environmental crisis from an issue on paper to one of effective policy, from rhetoric in print to realism in action. Why, nearly fifty years after Fairfield Osborne's warning in *Our Plundered Planet* and more than thirty years since Rachel Carson's *Silent Spring,* are we still wondering, is it too late?[8]

It is important to ask where the religions have been on these issues and why they themselves have been so late in their involvement. Have issues of personal salvation superseded all others? Have divine-human relations been primary? Have anthropocentric ethics been all-consuming? Has the material world of nature been devalued by religion? Does the search for otherworldly rewards override commitment to this world? Did the religions simply surrender their natural theologies and concerns with exploring purpose in nature to positivistic scientific cosmologies? In beginning to address these questions, we still have not exhausted all the reasons for religions' lack of attention to the environmental crisis. The reasons may not be readily apparent, but clearly they require further exploration and explanation.

In discussing the involvement of religions in this issue, it is also appropriate to acknowledge the dark side of religion in both its institutional expressions and dogmatic forms. In addition to their oversight with regard to the environment, religions have been the source of enormous manipulation of power in fostering wars, in ignoring racial and social injustice, and in promoting unequal gender relations, to name only a few abuses. One does not want to underplay this shadow side or to claim too much for religions' potential for ethical persuasiveness. The problems are too vast and complex for unqualified optimism. Yet there is a growing consensus that religions may now have a significant role to play, just as in the past they have sustained individuals and cultures in the face of internal and external threats.

A final caveat is the inevitable gap that arises between theories and practices in religions. As has been noted, even societies with religious traditions which appear sympathetic to the environment have in the past often misused resources. While it is clear that religions may have some disjunction between the ideal and the real, this should not lessen our endeavor to identify resources from within the world's religions for a more ecologically sound cosmology and environmentally supportive ethics. This disjunction of theory and practice is present within all philosophies and religions and is frequently the source of disillusionment, skepticism, and cynicism. A more realistic observation might be made, however, that this disjunction should not automatically invalidate the complex worldviews and rich cosmologies embedded in traditional religions. Rather, it is our task to explore these conceptual resources so as to broaden and expand our own perspectives in challenging and fruitful ways.

In summary, we recognize that religions have elements which are both prophetic and transformative as well as conservative and constraining. These elements are continually in tension, a condition which creates the great variety of thought and interpretation within religious traditions. To recognize these various tensions and limits, however, is not to lessen the urgency of the overall goals of this project. Rather, it is to circumscribe our efforts with healthy skepticism, cautious optimism, and modest ambitions. It is to suggest that this is a beginning in a new field of study which will affect both religion and ecology. On the one hand, this process of reflection will inevitably change how religions conceive of their own roles, missions, and identities, for such reflections demand a new sense of the sacred as not divorced from the earth itself. On the other hand, environmental studies can recognize that religions have helped to shape attitudes toward nature. Thus, as religions themselves evolve they may be indispensable in fostering a more expansive appreciation for the complexity and beauty of the natural world. At the same time as religions foster awe and reverence for nature, they may provide the transforming energies for ethical practices to protect endangered ecosystems, threatened species, and diminishing resources.

Methodological Concerns

It is important to acknowledge that there are, inevitably, challenging methodological issues involved in such a project as we are undertaking in this emerging field of religion and ecology.[9] Some of the key interpretive challenges we face in this project concern issues of time, place, space, and positionality. With regard to time, it is necessary to recognize the vast historical complexity of each religious tradition, which cannot be easily condensed in these conferences or volumes. With respect to place, we need to signal the diverse cultural contexts in which these religions have developed. With regard to space, we recognize the varied frameworks of institutions and traditions in which these religions unfold. Finally, with respect to positionality, we acknowledge our own historical situatedness at the end of the twentieth century with distinctive contemporary concerns.

Not only is each religious tradition historically complex and culturally diverse, but its beliefs, scriptures, and institutions have themselves been subject to vast commentaries and revisions over time. Thus, we recognize the radical diversity that exists within and among religious traditions which cannot be encompassed in any single volume. We acknowledge also that distortions may arise as we examine earlier historical traditions in light of contemporary issues.

Nonetheless, the environmental ethics philosopher J. Baird Callicott has suggested that scholars and others "mine the conceptual resources" of the religious traditions as a means of creating a more inclusive global environmental ethics.[10] As Callicott himself notes, however, the notion of "mining" is problematic, for it conjures up images of exploitation which may cause apprehension among certain religious communities, especially those of indigenous peoples. Moreover, we cannot simply expect to borrow or adopt ideas and place them from one tradition directly into another. Even efforts to formulate global environmental ethics need to be sensitive to cultural particularity and diversity. We do not aim at creating a simple bricolage or bland fusion of perspectives. Rather, these conferences and volumes are an attempt to display before us a multiperspectival cross section of the symbolic richness regarding attitudes toward nature within the religions of the world. To do so will help to reveal certain commonalities among traditions, as well as limitations within traditions, as they begin to converge around this challenge presented by the environmental crisis.

We need to identify our concerns, then, as embedded in the constraints of our own perspectival limits at the same time as we seek common ground. In describing various attitudes toward nature historically, we are aiming at *critical understanding* of the complexity, contexts, and frameworks in which these religions articulate such views. In addition, we are striving for *empathetic appreciation* for the traditions without idealizing their ecological potential or ignoring their environmental oversights. Finally, we are aiming at the *creative revisioning* of mutually enhancing human-earth relations. This revisioning may be assisted by highlighting the multiperspectival attitudes toward nature which these traditions disclose. The prismatic effect of examining such attitudes and relationships may provide some necessary clarification and symbolic resources for reimagining our own situation and shared concerns at the end of the twentieth century. It will also be sharpened by identifying the multilayered symbol systems in world religions which have traditionally oriented humans in establishing relational resonances between the microcosm of the self and the macrocosm of the social and natural orders. In short, religious traditions may help to supply both creative resources of symbols, rituals, and texts as well as inspiring visions for reimagining ourselves as part of, not apart from, the natural world.

Aims

The methodological issues outlined above were implied in the overall goals of the conferences, which were described as follows:

1. To identify and evaluate the *distinctive ecological attitudes,* values, and practices of diverse religious traditions, making clear their links to intellectual, political, and other resources associated with these distinctive traditions.

2. To describe and analyze the *commonalities* that exist within and among religious traditions with respect to ecology.

3. To identify the *minimum common ground* on which to base constructive understanding, motivating discussion, and concerted action in diverse locations across the globe; and to highlight the specific religious resources that comprise such fertile ecological ground: within scripture, ritual, myth, symbol, cosmology, sacrament, and so on.

4. To articulate in clear and moving terms *a desirable mode of human presence with the earth;* in short, to highlight means of respecting and valuing nature, to note what has already been actualized, and to indicate how best to achieve what is desirable beyond these examples.

5. To outline the most significant areas, with regard to religion and ecology, in need of *further study;* to enumerate questions of highest priority within those areas and propose possible approaches to use in addressing them.

In this series, then, we do not intend to obliterate difference or ignore diversity. The aim is to celebrate plurality by raising to conscious awareness multiple perspectives regarding nature and human-earth relations as articulated in the religions of the world. The spectrum of cosmologies, myths, symbols, and rituals within the religious traditions will be instructive in resituating us within the rhythms and limits of nature.

We are not looking for a unified worldview or a single global ethic. We are, however, deeply sympathetic with the efforts toward formulating a global ethic made by individuals, such as the theologian Hans Küng or the environmental philosopher J. Baird Callicott, and groups, such as Global Education Associates and United Religions. A minimum content of environmental ethics needs to be seriously considered. We are, then, keenly interested in the contribution this series might make to discussions of environmental policy in national and international arenas. Important intersections may be made with work in the field of development ethics.[11] In addition, the findings of the conferences have bearing on the ethical formulation of the Earth Charter that is to be presented to the United Nations for adoption within the next few years. Thus, we are seeking both the grounds for common concern and the constructive conceptual basis for rethinking our current situation of estrangement from the earth. In so doing we will be able to reconceive a means of creating the basis not just for sustainable development, but also for sustainable life on the planet.

As scientist Brian Swimme has suggested, we are currently making macrophase changes to the life systems of the planet with microphase wisdom. Clearly, we need to expand and deepen the wisdom base for human intervention with nature and other humans. This is particularly true as issues of genetic alteration of natural processes are already available and in use. If religions have traditionally concentrated on divine-human and human-human relations, the challenge is that they now explore more fully divine-human-earth relations. Without such further exploration, adequate environmental ethics may not emerge in a comprehensive context.

Resources: Environmental Ethics Found in the World's Religions

For many people, when challenges such as the environmental crisis are raised in relation to religion in the contemporary world, there frequently arises a sense of loss or a nostalgia for earlier, seemingly less complicated eras when the constant questioning of religious beliefs and practices was not so apparent. This is, no doubt, something of a reified reading of history. There is, however, a decidedly anxious tone to the questioning and soul-searching that appears to haunt many contemporary religious groups as they seek to find their particular role in the midst of rapid technological change and dominant secular values.

One of the greatest challenges, however, to contemporary religions remains how to respond to the environmental crisis, which many believe has been perpetuated because of the enormous inroads made by unrestrained materialism, secularization, and industrialization in contemporary societies, especially those societies arising in or influenced by the modern West. Indeed, some suggest that the very division of religion from secular life may be a major cause of the crisis.

Others, such as the medieval historian Lynn White, have cited religion's negative role in the crisis. White has suggested that the emphasis in Judaism and Christianity on the transcendence of God above nature and the dominion of humans over nature has led to a devaluing of the natural world and a subsequent destruction of its resources for utilitarian ends.[12] While the particulars of this argument have been vehemently debated, it is increasingly clear that the environmental crisis and its perpetuation due to industrialization, secularization, and ethical indifference present a serious challenge to the world's religions. This is especially true because many of these religions have traditionally been concerned with the path of personal salvation, which frequently emphasized otherworldly goals and rejected this world as corrupting. Thus, as we have noted, how to adapt religious teachings to this task of revaluing nature so as to prevent its destruction marks a significant new phase in religious thought. Indeed, as Thomas Berry has so aptly pointed out, what is necessary is a comprehensive re-evaluation of human-earth relations if the human is to continue as a viable species on an increasingly degraded planet. This will require, in addition to major economic and political changes, examining worldviews and ethics among the world's religions that differ from those that have captured the imagination of contemporary industrialized societies which regard nature primarily as a commodity to be utilized. It should be noted that when we are searching for effective resources for formulating environmental ethics, each of the religious traditions have both positive and negative features.

For the most part, the worldviews associated with the Western Abrahamic traditions of Judaism, Christianity, and Islam have created a dominantly human-focused morality. Because these worldviews are largely anthropocentric, nature is viewed as being of secondary importance. This is reinforced by a strong sense of the transcendence of God above nature. On the other hand, there are rich resources for rethinking views of nature in the covenantal tradition of the Hebrew Bible, in sacramental theology, in incarnational Christology, and in the vice-regency (*khalifa Allah*) concept of the Qur'an. The covenantal tradition draws on the legal agreements of biblical thought which are extended to all of creation. Sacramental theology in Christianity underscores the sacred dimension of material reality, especially for ritual purposes.[13] Incarnational Christology proposes that because God became flesh in the person of Christ, the entire natural order can be viewed as sacred. The concept of humans as vice-regents of Allah on earth suggests that humans have particular privileges, responsibilities, and obligations to creation.[14]

In Hinduism, although there is a significant emphasis on performing one's *dharma,* or duty, in the world, there is also a strong pull toward *moksa,* or liberation, from the world of suffering, or *samsāra.* To heal this kind of suffering and alienation through spiritual discipline and meditation, one turns away from the world (*prakṛti*) to a timeless world of spirit (*puruṣa*). Yet at the same time there are numerous traditions in Hinduism which affirm particular rivers, mountains, or forests as sacred. Moreover, in the concept of *līlā,* the creative play of the gods, Hindu theology engages the world as a creative manifestation of the divine. This same tension between withdrawal from the world and affirmation of it is present in Buddhism. Certain Theravāda schools of Buddhism emphasize withdrawing in meditation from the transient world of suffering (*saṃsāra*) to seek release in *nirvāṇa*. On the other hand, later Mahāyāna schools of Buddhism, such as Hua-yen, under-score the remarkable interconnection of reality in such images as the jeweled net of Indra, where each jewel reflects all the others in the universe. Likewise, the Zen gardens in East Asia express the fullness of the Buddha-nature (*tathāgatagarbha*) in the natural world. In re-cent years, socially engaged Buddhism has been active in protecting the environment in both Asia and the United States.

The East Asian traditions of Confucianism and Taoism remain, in certain ways, some of the most life-affirming in the spectrum of world religions.[15] The seamless interconnection between the divine, human, and natural worlds that characterizes these traditions has been described as an anthropocosmic worldview.[16] There is no emphasis on radical transcendence as there is in the Western traditions. Rather, there is a cosmology of a continuity of creation stressing the dynamic movements of nature through the seasons and the agricultural cycles. This organic cosmology is grounded in the philosophy of *ch'i* (material force), which provides a basis for appreciating the profound inter-connection of matter and spirit. To be in harmony with nature and with other humans while being attentive to the movements of the *Tao* (Way) is the aim of personal cultivation in both Confucianism and Taoism. It should be noted, however, that this positive worldview has not prevented environmental degradation (such as deforestation) in parts of East Asia in both the premodern and modern period.

In a similar vein, indigenous peoples, while having ecological cos-mologies have, in some instances, caused damage to local environ-ments through such practices as slash-and-burn agriculture. Nonethe-less, most indigenous peoples have environmental ethics embedded in their worldviews. This is evident in the complex reciprocal obli-gations surrounding life-taking and resource-gathering which mark a community's relations with the local bioregion. The religious views at the basis of indigenous lifeways involve respect for the sources of food, clothing, and shelter that nature provides. Gratitude to the creator and to the spiritual forces in creation is at the heart of most indigenous traditions. The ritual calendars of many indigenous peoples are carefully coordinated with seasonal events such as the sound of returning birds, the blooming of certain plants, the movements of the sun, and the changes of the moon.

The difficulty at present is that for the most part we have developed in the world's religions certain ethical prohibitions regarding homicide and restraints concerning genocide and suicide, but none for biocide or geocide. We are clearly in need of exploring such comprehensive cosmological perspectives and communitarian environmental ethics as the most compelling context for motivating change regarding the destruction of the natural world.

Responses of Religions to the Environmental Crisis

How to chart possible paths toward mutually enhancing human-earth relations remains, thus, one of the greatest challenges to the world's religions. It is with some encouragement, however, that we note the growing calls for the world's religions to participate in these efforts toward a more sustainable planetary future. There have been various appeals from environmental groups and from scientists and parliamentarians for religious leaders to respond to the environmental crisis. For example, in 1990 the Joint Appeal in Religion and Science was released highlighting the urgency of collaboration around the issue of the destruction of the environment. In 1992 the Union of Concerned Scientists issued the statement "Warning to Humanity," signed by over 1,000 scientists from 70 countries, including 105 Nobel laureates, regarding the gravity of the environmental crisis. They specifically cited the need for a new ethic toward the earth.

Numerous national and international conferences have also been held on this subject and collaborative efforts have been established. Environmental groups such as World Wildlife Fund have sponsored interreligious meetings such as the one in Assisi in 1986. The Center for Respect of Life and Environment of the Humane Society of the United States has also held a series of conferences in Assisi on

Spirituality and Sustainability and has helped to organize one at the World Bank. The United Nations Environmental Programme in North America has established an Environmental Sabbath, each year distributing thousands of packets of materials for use in congregations throughout North America. Similarly, the National Religious Partnership on the Environment at the Cathedral of St. John the Divine in New York City has promoted dialogue, distributed materials, and created a remarkable alliance of the various Jewish and Christian denominations in the United States around the issue of the environment. The Parliament of World Religions held in 1993 in Chicago and attended by some 8,000 people from all over the globe issued a statement of Global Ethics of Cooperation of Religions on Human and Environmental Issues. International meetings on the environment have been organized. One example of these, the Global Forum of Spiritual and Parliamentary Leaders held in Oxford in 1988, Moscow in 1990, Rio in 1992, and Kyoto in 1993, included world religious leaders, such as the Dalai Lama, and diplomats and heads of state, such as Mikhail Gorbachev. Indeed, Gorbachev hosted the Moscow conference and attended the Kyoto conference to set up a Green Cross International for environmental emergencies.

Since the United Nations Conference on Environment and Development (the Earth Summit) held in Rio in 1992, there have been concerted efforts intended to lead toward the adoption of an *Earth Charter* by the year 2000. This *Earth Charter* initiative is under way with the leadership of the Earth Council and Green Cross International, with support from the government of the Netherlands. Maurice Strong, Mikhail Gorbachev, Steven Rockefeller, and other members of the Earth Charter Project have been instrumental in this process. At the March 1997 Rio + 5 Conference a benchmark draft of the *Earth Charter* was issued. The time is thus propitious for further investigation of the potential contributions of particular religions toward mitigating the environmental crisis, especially by developing more comprehensive environmental ethics for the earth community.

Expanding the Dialogue of Religion and Ecology

More than two decades ago Thomas Berry anticipated such an exploration when he called for "creating a new consciousness of the multiform religious traditions of humankind" as a means toward renewal of the human spirit in addressing the urgent problems of contemporary society.[17] Tu Weiming has written of the need to go "Beyond the Enlightenment Mentality" in exploring the spiritual resources of the global community to meet the challenge of the ecological crisis.[18] While this exploration has also been the intention of both the conferences and these volumes, other significant efforts have preceded our current endeavor.[19] Our discussion here highlights only the last decade.

In 1986 Eugene Hargrove edited a volume titled *Religion and Environmental Crisis*.[20] In 1991 Charlene Spretnak explored this topic in her book *States of Grace: The Recovery of Meaning in the Post-Modern Age*.[21] Her subtitle states her constructivist project clearly: "Reclaiming the Core Teachings and Practices of the Great Wisdom Traditions for the Well-Being of the Earth Community." In 1992 Steven Rockefeller and John Elder edited a book based on a conference at Middlebury College titled *Spirit and Nature: Why the Environment Is a Religious Issue*.[22] In the same year Peter Marshall published *Nature's Web: Rethinking Our Place on Earth*,[23] drawing on the resources of the world's traditions. An edited volume titled *Worldviews and Ecology*, compiled in 1993, contains articles reflecting on views of nature from the world's religions and from contemporary philosophies, such as process thought and deep ecology.[24] In this same vein, in 1994 J. Baird Callicott published *Earth's Insights*, which examines the intellectual resources of the world's religions for a more comprehensive global environmental ethics.[25] This expands on his 1989 volumes, *Nature in Asian Traditions of Thought* and *In Defense of the Land Ethic*.[26] In 1995 David Kinsley issued a book titled *Ecology and Religion: Ecological Spirituality in a Cross-Cultural Perspective*,[27] which draws on traditional religions and contemporary movements, such as deep ecology and ecospirituality. Seyyed Hossein Nasr wrote his comprehensive study *Religion and the Order of Nature* in 1996.[28] Several volumes of religious responses to a particular topic or theme have also been published. For example, J. Ronald Engel and Joan Gibb Engel compiled a monograph in 1990 titled *Ethics of Environment and Development: Global Challenge, International Response*[29] and in 1995 Harold Coward edited the volume *Population, Consumption and the Environment: Religious and Secular Responses*.[30] Roger Gottlieb edited a useful source book, *This Sacred Earth: Religion, Nature, Environment*.[31] Single volumes on the world's religions and ecology were published by the Worldwide Fund for Nature.[32]

The series Religions of the World and Ecology is thus intended to expand the discussion already under way in certain circles and to invite further collaboration on a topic of common concern—the fate of the earth as a religious responsibility. To broaden and deepen the reflective basis for mutual collaboration was an underlying aim of the conferences themselves. While some might see this as a diversion from pressing scientific or policy issues, it was with a sense of humility and yet conviction that we entered into the arena of reflection and debate on this issue. In the field of the study of world religions, we have seen this as a timely challenge for scholars of religion to respond as engaged intellectuals with deepening creative reflection. We hope that these volumes will be simply a beginning of further study of conceptual and symbolic resources, methodological concerns, and practical directions for meeting this environmental crisis.

Notes

1. He goes on to say, "And that is qualitatively and epochally true. If religion does not speak to [this], it is an obsolete distraction." Daniel Maguire, *The Moral Core of Judaism and Christianity: Reclaiming the Revolution* (Philadelphia: Fortress Press, 1993), 13.

2. Gerald Barney, *Global 2000 Report to the President of the United States* (Washington, D.C.: Supt. of Docs. U.S. Government Printing Office, 1980–1981), 40.

3. Lynn White, Jr., "The Historical Roots of Our Ecologic Crisis," *Science* 155 (March 1967):1204.

4. Thomas Berry, *The Dream of the Earth* (San Francisco: Sierra Club Books, 1988).

5. Brian Swimme and Thomas Berry, *The Universe Story* (San Francisco: Harper San Francisco, 1992).

6. At the same time we recognize the limits to such a project, especially because ideas and action, theory and practice do not always occur in conjunction.

7. E. N. Anderson, Ecologies of the Heart: Emotion, Belief, and the Environment (New York and Oxford: Oxford University Press, 1996), 166. He qualifies this statement by saying, "The key point is not religion per se, but the use of emotionally powerful symbols to sell particular moral codes and management systems" (166). He notes, however, in various case studies how ecological wisdom is embedded in myths, symbols, and cosmologies of traditional societies.

8. *Is It Too Late?* is also the title of a book by John Cobb, first published in 1972 by Bruce and reissued in 1995 by Environmental Ethics Books.

9. Because we cannot identify here all of the methodological issues that need to be addressed, we invite further discussion by other engaged scholars.

10. See J. Baird Callicott, *Earth's Insights: A Survey of Ecological Ethics from the Mediterranean Basin to the Australian Outback* (Berkeley: University of California Press, 1994).

11. See, for example, The Quality of Life, ed. Martha C. Nussbaum and Amartya Sen, WIDER Studies in Development Economics (Oxford: Oxford University Press, 1993).

12. White, "The Historical Roots of Our Ecologic Crisis," 1203–7.

13. Process theology, creation-centered spirituality, and ecotheology have done much to promote these kinds of holistic perspectives within Christianity.

14. These are resources already being explored by theologians and biblical scholars.

15. While this is true theoretically, it should be noted that, like all ideologies, these traditions have at times been used for purposes of political power and social control. Moreover, they have not been able to prevent certain kinds of environmental destruction, such as deforestation in China.

16. The term "anthropocosmic" has been used by Tu Weiming in *Centrality and Commonality* (Albany: State University of New York Press, 1989).

17. Thomas Berry, "Religious Studies and the Global Human Community," unpublished manuscript.

18. Tu Weiming, "Beyond the Enlightenment Mentality," in *Worldviews and Ecology,* ed. Mary Evelyn Tucker and John Grim (Lewisburg, Pa.: Bucknell University Press, 1993; reissued, Maryknoll, N.Y.: Orbis Books, 1994).

19. This history has been described more fully by Roderick Nash in his chapter entitled "The Greening of Religion," in The Rights of Nature: A History of Environmental Ethics (Madison: University of Wisconsin Press, 1989).

20. *Religion and Environmental Crisis,* ed. Eugene Hargrove (Athens: University of Georgia Press, 1986).

21. Charlene Spretnak, *States of Grace: The Recovery of Meaning in the Post-Modern Age* (San Francisco: Harper San Francisco, 1991).

22. *Spirit and Nature: Why the Environment Is a Religious Issue,* ed. Steven Rockefeller and John Elder (Boston: Beacon Press, 1992).

23. Peter Marshall, *Nature's Web: Rethinking Our Place on Earth* (Armonk, N.Y.: M. E. Sharpe, 1992).

24. *Worldviews and Ecology,* ed. Mary Evelyn Tucker and John Grim (Lewisburg, Pa.: Bucknell University Press, 1993; reissued, Maryknoll, N.Y.: Orbis Books, 1994).

25. Callicott, *Earth's Insights.*

26. Both are State University of New York Press publications.

27. David Kinsley, *Ecology and Religion: Ecological Spirituality in a Cross-Cultural Perspective* (Englewood Cliffs, N.J.: Prentice Hall, 1995).

28. Seyyed Hossein Nasr, *Religion and the Order of Nature* (Oxford: Oxford University Press, 1996).

29. *Ethics of Environment and Development: Global Challenge, International Response,* ed. J. Ronald Engel and Joan Gibb Engel (Tucson: University of Arizona Press, 1990).

30. *Population, Consumption, and the Environment: Religious and Secular Responses,* ed. Harold Coward (Albany: State University of New York Press, 1995).

31. This Sacred Earth: Religion, Nature, Environment, ed. Roger S. Gottlieb (New York and London: Routledge, 1996).

32. These include volumes on Hinduism, Buddhism, Judaism, Christianity, and Islam.

Introduction

JOHN A. GRIM

The ethical code of my own Anishinabeg community of the
White Earth Reservation in northern Minnesota keeps
communities and individuals in line with natural law.
"Minobimaatisiiwin"—it means both the 'good life' and
'continuous rebirth'—is central to our value system. In
minobimaatisiiwin, we honor women as the givers of lives,
we honor our *Chi Anishinabeg,* our old people and ancestors who hold the knowledge. We honor our children as the
continuity from generations, and we honor ourselves as a
part of creation. Implicit in *minobimaatisiiwin* is a continuous habitation of place, an intimate understanding of
the relationship between humans and the ecosystem and of
the need to maintain this balance.[1]

While no one person can possibly speak for the diversity of
peoples and traditions signified by the term "indigenous," still, the
quote above from the Anishinabe leader, Winona LaDuke, provides an
entry into many of the issues discussed in this volume. Her statement
also foreshadows several of the problems raised by any study of indigenous religious traditions and contemporary ecological concerns.
Foremost among the values indicated in her remarks, and echoed by
the contributors to this volume, is the description by different indigenous peoples, in remarkably diverse ways, of a central, seamless, organizing orientation, or lifeway. Winona LaDuke's observation brings
the social, ecological, and spiritual frames into alignment in a way

that distinguishes but does not separate indigenous human communities, the natural world, and the realms of the holy beings.

Minobimaatisiiwin introduces an Anishinabe discourse that gathers together ethical concerns of social justice, political insights regarding gender, ecological knowledge of local place, and religious awareness of a relational balance that pervades the constantly changing world. As a coherent and central conversation, *minobimaatisiiwin* does not emphasize rational development for humans exclusively. Nor does it posit a transcendental self that autonomously gathers objective sense data so as to know the world. Nor does it present a transcendent realm of the sacred beyond the circle of human-animal-earth habitations. At the heart of this statement, and, indeed, a primary agenda in this volume, is the effort to express the coherence of diverse indigenous discourses about lifeways and ecologies. Each particular lifeway is an ongoing creative practice that is simultaneously rational, affective, intentional, and ethical.

The statement by Winona LaDuke also gives us an introduction to this volume on indigenous traditions and ecology, in which a complex mix of political, economic, ecological, and spiritual features are explored by native and non-native contributors. The multiplicity of perspectives corresponds to the thematic approaches used to organize the essays in this volume, suggesting that, of course, there is no one "indigenous" view on religion and ecology. Moreover, inseparable from considerations of indigenous religions and contemporary environmental issues are the current crises of survival for these peoples. Thus, these articles explore spiritual relationships established between native peoples and their homelands. Yet, they also question any study of indigenous religions that ignores such issues as the grinding poverty leading to environmental deterioration, or the degrading marginality from vital economic exchanges, or the disempowering loss of political control in community affairs.

Challenges to the Lifeway Concept

Two problematic perspectives need to be addressed in opening with an emphasis on the "lifeway" concept that draws attention to the seamless cosmology-cum-economy character of indigenous societies. First, the stress on the interrelatedness of diverse aspects of individual, community, and natural life suggests that the "balance" or harmony of an indigenous lifeway is a homeostatic condition. Several early studies of indigenous traditions and ecology, such as Roy Rappaport's insightful account of ritual pig killing among the Tsembaga Maring in Papua New Guinea, described that religious system as a type of feedback mechanism assuring human adaptation to a changing environment.[2] Though well beyond earlier studies, in which evolutionary theory was used to interpret this perceived lifeway equilibrium of indigenous peoples as an "inferior" or "primitive" development, these foundational studies in cultural ecology suggested a closed system accommodating internal and external pressures as the religious ideal. The essays in this volume modify and expand that approach, emphasizing contestations and negotiations within indigenous communities especially in relation to modernization. They pointedly address the compelling questions of how indigenous communities, within the theoretical frames of their traditional lifeways, manage local lands under intense development pressures from global and national development schemes. This first challenge embedded within the lifeway concept, then, is the need to understand the roles of indigenous religions in their efforts to maintain a spiritual balance with larger cosmological forces while creatively accommodating current environmental, social, economic, and political changes.

The Andean activist Eduardo Grillo Fernandez described this challenging road leading through both development and decolonization, saying:

> ... in the Andean culture the nurturing of harmony is not the responsibility of a human community that arrogates to itself the universal representation to take decisions and implement them. Harmony in the Andes can only emerge from the communion of the human community with the community of the *sallqa* [nature's flora] and with the community of *huacas* [deities]. And even then, it is not a matter of a decision taken by an assembly with opinions of the member communities. Harmony, in order to be constantly nurtured, must be revealed starting from the specific circumstances because it must not correspond to the will of the collectivity of the living world but to its physiology. The form of the harmony to be nurtured is not in the surface of the appearance but hidden inside the living world. It is as the sculptor in stone of Cajamarca said when someone asked him for the models that inspired his works: 'In the insides of the stone is the form.'[3]

In this quest for nurturance of indigenous Andean cultural life, Grillo points toward deeper realms than the "collectivity" or institutional realms often associated with "religion." Rather than "beyond," however, he motions toward the within of things. Grillo calls for attention to a traditional form of perception that balances inner and outer cosmological realities. Through the insights of elders and the revelations of dreamers and visionaries, these small-scale native communities manage acceptable forms of modernization, mount resistance to development schemes in which they have no voice, and successfully transmit ethnic identity despite centuries, in some cases, of continuing oppression. This is an imaginative act no less daunting than that looming ahead of Western industrial societies as they confront the termination of the petroleum era.

A second observation is that as an analytical concept lifeways may make an "other" of native religions, leading to stereotypes, an orientalism of expectations, and an exploitative romanticism. This point requires some consideration of indigenous ways of knowing. A synecdochic mode of knowing operative in indigenous traditions may affirm the use of one material item, such as the feathers of certain birds, or one way of ritual action, such as dancing, to make present the whole of the lifeway. A Western linear, rational analysis of these articles and actions may interpret them as holistic symbols that represent the holy. This interpretation overlooks the lifeway context of an interactive community of beings in the world. Hence, an outsider wishing to appropriate the experience of the holy within indigenous religions seizes on a ritual article or action, as well as excerpted and often misunderstood explanations of native practitioners. This romantic exploitation of indigenous religions typically accentuates a perceived native ecological wisdom as having been genetically transmitted. However, even a brief example, such as that from the Gitksan peoples of central British Columbia, reveals complex human-earth-spirit linkages needed to access traditional indigenous environmental knowledge.

> Each Gitksan house is the proud heir and owner of an *adáox*. This is a body of orally transmitted songs and stories that act as the house's sacred archives and as its living, millennia-long memory of important events of the past. This irreplaceable verbal repository of knowledge consists in part of sacred songs believed to have arisen *literally from the breaths of the ancestors*. Far more than musical representations of

history, these songs serve as vital time-traversing vehicles. They can transport members across the immense reaches of space and time into the dim mythic past of Gitksan creation *by the very quality of their music and the emotions they convey.*

Taken together, these sacred possessions—the stories, the crests, the songs—provide a solid foundation for each Gitksan house and for the larger clan of which it is a part. According to living Gitksan elders, each house's holdings confirm its ancient *title to its territory and the legitimacy of its authority over it.*

In fact, so vital is the relationship between each house and the lands allotted to it for fishing, hunting, and food-gathering that the *daxgyet,* or spirit power, of each house and the land that sustains it are one.[4]

Rather than conceptually reducing cultural life among indigenous peoples to a social construction, the term lifeway seeks to bridge the depersonalizing distance of observer and observed. The second challenge in the lifeway concept, then, is to open interpretive possibilities for understanding an integrated environmental vision that transmits spiritual states of knowing and moral ways of being in the world. The task is to reflect on the interbeing of cosmology and community from the perspective of indigenous peoples.

Lifeway and Terms in the Study of Religion

If the lifeway concept provides us with a helpful theory of cosmological totalities operative in indigenous traditions, it is not without its totalizing ambiguities. That is, the terminology available for discussing indigenous religious traditions and ecology is fraught with tensions and contradictions. Who are "indigenous" peoples? In a straightforward manner indigenous means anything produced, growing, or living naturally in a particular region or environment. Yet, there are semantic and political difficulties involved in determining who is "indigenous." To a large extent these issues are beyond the scope of this discussion, but it is significant to note that the United Nations continues to grapple with these issues. The United Nations Declaration on the Rights of Indigenous Peoples, prepared for approval by the separate nation-states during the Decade of Indigenous Peoples (1994–2004), has posed this question largely within international law and human rights contexts.[6] In these international forums, "indigenous" refers to ethnic groups with clear cultural, linguistic, and kinship bonds who have been so marginalized by modern nation-states that their inherent dignity and coherence as societies are in danger of being lost.

One objection to such definitions from India, for example, is that mainstream peoples of the nation-state of India have been in that region for millennia. Hence, they are also "native" or "indigenous." In this argument, to make such distinctions as calling minority groups "indigenous" is unnecessary, irrelevant, and harmful to national sovereignty. Two points might be emphasized, namely, nation-state sovereignty and the fear of secession by indigenous groups underlies much of the political rhetoric in the debate about who is "indigenous." Second, anxieties to create a national consciousness have engendered a drive to "normalize" local native lifeways and bring them into the mainstream culture. Criticisms of these normalizing and civilizing processes are given by several authors in this volume. Along with "indigenous," there are other problematic terms, such as "religion," "tradition," and "ecology," to name just a few.

Is the term "religion" so hopelessly caught up in sacred and profane dichotomies and Western institutional histories that it is meaningless in discussing indigenous lifeways? The sacred-secular split is largely absent in indigenous lifeways, or, if present, operates in a different ontological setting in which numinous realities may emerge suddenly from ordinary reality. The term "tradition" also seems to mirror some of the homeostatic, changeless presumptions discussed above. Furthermore, "ecology" as a science studying the interrelationships of organisms in biosystems is quite different from the use of the term ecology as a broad conceptual referent for human-earth interactions. There are novel and distinctive responses to these questions about terms, and they are tied to larger issues of discourse analysis and its subsequent critique of Enlightenment rationality. Rather than jettison these terms, as well as Western rationality and science as the embodiment of a colonial epistemology, the following essays explore ways of re-reasoning, and re-imaging, the natural world that have been present and are emerging in indigenous settings. In that sense, many analytical terms are contested in these essays, but they are also used as limited concepts that can guide our thinking about indigenous traditions. In thinking about indigenous religions it is appropriate to acknowledge that they provide alternative epistemologies to Western classical, medieval, enlightenment, and postmodern modes of rational analysis. Contemporary indigenous lifeways and ecological cultures are not "pure" thought systems; rather, they are distinct hybrids creatively influenced by the regional, national, and global regimes they have encountered and resisted.

The Mix of Perspectives on Indigenous Religions and Ecology

It is helpful to step back a bit and briefly consider some of the approaches found in these essays. From comparative religions has come some understanding of the shared characteristics of many indigenous myths, rituals, symbol systems, and concern for and deep love of local places. The power and beauty of these cultural insights into the fecund mystery of nature have impressed non-native observers since first encounters. For some time now the history of religions has investigated changes over time in indigenous lifeways regarding mythic narrations, ritual practices, and sacred symbols and sites. This diachronic analysis corrected, to some extent, the synchronic tendencies to see indigenous traditions as static and unchanging. Anthropology especially refocused the study of indigenous traditions on particular cultural sources of meaning and worldview values that inform other aspects of small-scale society life.

With the growing attention to ecological concerns from the 1970s, the study of indigenous religions could no longer ignore the overt marginalization of indigenous societies within and from mainstream cultures. Foremost among the observations that emerged was a Marxian analysis associated with political economy. In this perspective the power of production of colonial systems was understood as having been used to marginalize and exploit indigenous peoples and lands, as well as to impose its own rational analytical scientific knowledge systems over native ways of knowing. Ironically, the indigenous regard for the inherent spiritual connections of the life community was dismissed as superstitious, mythic, or false logic by both Marxist and colonial capitalist systems. Centuries-old forms of traditional environmental knowledge were largely ignored by dominating outsiders. Where possible, indigenous peoples adapted traditional ways of knowing into the new modes of productive life available to them as peasants, laborers, and outcaste peoples.

Prior to any academic recognition of the coherence of indigenous lifeways or indigenous technical knowledge systems, native peoples themselves allowed outsiders access to those insights. Often those privileges were given because indigenous activists mounted resistance to the hegemonic intrusions of mainstream cultures, and they sought the support of those outsiders. Indeed, responsible intellectuals in mainstream cultures who have been interested in indigenous lifeways have been drawn to those positions as much by the depth of resistance and capacities of articulation by indigenous peoples as by academic presentations of ideas, ethics, or religious practices. Certainly, creative exchange has occurred among both indigenous and non-native intellectuals, but the former have seldom received recognition or credit. In this volume the contributors draw attention to that unique mix in indigenous lifeways in which the cultural production of knowledge, especially in the forms labeled "religion," not only opens questions about the deeper motivations of indigenous economics, but also affirms conversations in indigenous settings regarding the moral context of bioregional relations between humans and other-than-humans.

With the increasing globalization of capitalist economics in the late twentieth century, indigenous peoples have come under another wave of intense pressures to assimilate into mainstream cultures and to open their homelands for resource exploitation. The insidious character of this most recent assault on indigenous homelands lies in the argument from the multinational corporations, seconded by nation-states, that rampant development is simply normative rational planning. The counter-arguments raised in this volume indicate that indigenous peoples have alternative development models that value homelands differently than capitalist sustainability models can adequately present. Even as native peoples use those lands and living beings for food, habitat, and trade, they embody alternative models of sustainable life.

The effort to subvert indigenous lifeways by development agendas has been the subject of a broad-based analysis called political ecology. The dynamics of this perspective have been much more receptive to considering indigenous religions and other cultural knowledge systems as contributing more to production than earlier Marxist-oriented political economy analyses conceded. Political ecology has shown interest in the ambiguity of knowledge-based terms without necessarily rejecting them. This mode of exploration has given close attention to understanding the social fabrication of society and nature, along with the ways in which images of nature also construct self and society.

This focus on the imaginative act in all societies, whereby local environments become central to ethnic identity, connects directly to considerations of indigenous religions. In their study entitled *Liberation Ecologies,* Richard Peet and Michael Watts expressed their understanding of these issues in this manner:

> Each society carries what we refer to as an "environmental imaginary," a way of Imaging nature, including visions of those forms of social and individual practice which are ethically proper and morally right with regard to nature. . . . this imaginary is typically expressed and developed through regional discursive formations, which take as central themes the history of social relations to a particular natural environment. Environmental imaginaries are frequently, indeed usually, expressed in abstract, mystical, and spiritual lexicons. However, they contain some degree of the reasoned approaches which display or "work out" the consequences of environmental actions referred to earlier as "prior knowledges." Liberation ecology proposes studying the processes by which environmental imaginaries are formed, contested, and practiced in the course of specific trajectories of political-economic exchange. . . . perhaps most importantly, through the concept of environmental imaginary, liberation ecology sees nature, environment, and place as *sources* of thinking, reasoning, and imagining: the social is, in this quite specific sense, naturally constructed.[7]

This volume, and the series "Religions of the World and Ecology," can be said to be sympathetic with this call for the study of "liberation ecologies." Many of the essays here explore environmental imaginaries in ways that expand this concept to include interior spiritual perceptions of the natural world actively shaping indigenous thought and personhood in different regional traditions.

The Study of Religion and Environmental Imagination

While leaving specific case studies and examples to the essays below, it is helpful to isolate ways in which the study of indigenous religions activates environmental imagination both in those communities and increasingly in mainstream societies. First, indigenous religions as lifeways that have strong ethnic identity attractors in the local ecology continue to resist intruding ways of life that seek to colonize and erase them. Whether considering the historical "Cargo Cults" of the Pacific region, the "Ghost Dance" phenomenon of the North American plains, or the "Mau-Mau" uprisings of East Africa, each of these social movements manifested strong religious expressions whose inner dynamics connected deeply into the local ecology. The sharp critique by native spokespeople and scholars to the appropriation of indigenous religions is directly related to this role of "religion" as at the core of indigenous cultural identity. In the long history of colonial and neocolonial theft of material and cultural life, indigenous lifeways have remained the source of deepest resistance to dominance by outsiders.

Second, indigenous religions continue in many settings to be the primary source of numinous experiences that initiate creative life in indigenous communities. This continues apart from, and often in relation to, resistance-oriented agendas of community and self-preservation. This heightened intimacy with the world is variously expressed in the following essays, sometimes in the language of spirits as "persons," or in seeing the world as "vital," or in describing the lifeway as "animist." It is this deepened connection with the natural world that is described as the cosmological perspective of particular lifeways.

Third, study of environmental imaginaries among indigenous religions opens contemporary dialogues between indigenous traditions and contemporary intellectual currents in ways that may be mutually beneficial. Intellectual currents, such as postcolonialism, poststructuralism, legal and literary theories, gender studies, critical theories of science, environmental history, political economy and political ecology, have been fortuitously linked to indigenous movements. In several essays below, the roles of indigenous intellectuals and activists detail how ideas and conceptual systems were integrated into indigenous resistance. Finally, it is crucial that these interpretive discourses not be simplistically used to make native epistemologies palatable for nonindigenous readers. Indigenous peoples are not well served if a term such as "environmental imaginaries" becomes a language-oriented reinscription that writes over their authentically lived and experienced world.

Fourth, the interdependent effects of traditional governance systems, economic markets, and social movements often find overt expression in the organizational and institutional expressions of religions. Thus, the study of indigenous religious organizations and institutions provides extraordinary insights into the ways in which traditional environmental knowledge has been encoded, negotiated, and contested. Directly challenging views that see traditional knowledge as static or unchanging, this view emphasizes the dynamic character of indigenous lifeways as individuals and communities image themselves in relation to local bioregions.

One classic example of this type of revisioning that both affirmed traditional knowledge and challenged it with new insights is the North American Plains Indians affirmation of the dream or vision quest.[8] Sent alone to a place often acknowledged as sacred to tribal, familial, or personal memory, an individual fasts for a vision according to traditional canons. In reporting a vision, an individual follows time-honored procedures, and the visionary is, in turn, subject to the authenticating critique of traditional symbols and patterns of visions. These interactions often involve topographic features, such as sacred sites, and possibly animals and plants experienced as "persons." The traditional frames for understanding provide stability for the visionary, yet new insights and experiences are common. The vision accommodates transmitted views of visionary exchange, but it also provokes creative symbolic thought and novel ways of interpretation. In the historical and mythical narrations of native peoples, some visions initiated migrations to new lands, or legitimated a people's movement into a region.[9]

Finally, it is evident that several of the essays in this work do not overtly address "religion." To some extent this is a function of the manner in which the conference from which these essays derive was organized. This volume emerged from a November 1997 conference at Harvard University's Center for the Study of World Religions. Unlike the nine other conferences that focused on one particular intercultural religion, the "Indigenous Traditions and Ecology" conference involved indigenous participants from every continent. The intention was to assemble a diverse group of indigenous and non-native scholars and environmental activists sensitive to indigenous issues who could speak insightfully about the environmental implications of indigenous peoples' religions. It was also hoped that some of the participants would actually give voice to indigenous environmental perspectives rather than presume scientific ecology was the only paradigm for discussing human-earth interactions. The organizers presumed that any discussion of homelands by indigenous peoples would involve questions of sovereignty, political economy, and political ecology. They also assumed that neither the conference nor the volume of essays would be exhaustive but that both would be suggestive of further work to be done.

An Overview of the Articles

The thematic organization of the essays lays out some of the observations of these introductory remarks. The opening section, "Fragmented Communities," draws attention to both the intense development pressures that threaten to fracture indigenous communities and the intense symbol systems that foster commitment and creativity. Articles by Darrell Posey and Tom Greaves shed light on traditional indigenous environmental knowledge and technique as intellectual property. Posey describes field experiences of shamanic initiations among the Kayapo peoples of Brazil to highlight the nonlineal and mythic character of indigenous environmental knowledge and the manner in which those ways of knowing are largely unavailable to Western categories of linear, historical analysis. Posey also explores the possibilities and inadequacies of arguments to protect indigenous knowledge from the standpoint of "intellectual property rights." These efforts to protect indigenous communities have floundered both conceptually and legally, largely because of the individualistic and entrepreneurial orientations in copyright law, but also because of the complex and costly procedures for filing cases nationally and internationally.

Greaves draws out the struggles over indigenous lands, resources, and values by examining "five major theaters," namely, economic rights, sovereignty, management of intellectual and cultural property, sacred meanings, and the struggle by native peoples to control their futures. The complex examples in each of these "theaters" subtly accentuate the pervasive and ambiguous presence of environmental concerns and racism in native peoples' efforts to preserve ethnic identity, cultural heritage, and homeland.

Pradip Prabhu provides the reader with an overview of the green political storm raging around India's "Scheduled Tribes," as many of the indigenous peoples are designated by the Constitution of India. In his historical, cultural, and economic discussions he analyzes the contemporary realities of traditional environmental knowledge among several native peoples of India, as well as the commercialization of that knowledge evident in development schemes. Prabhu compares earlier colonial exploitative laws to the "greenwashing" national legislation, which promotes protected environmental areas while disenfranchising indigenous peoples from power and self-control in their own homelands.

Stephanie Fried examines the impact on the *adat,* native peoples of Kalimantan Borneo, of linked ideological, material, and political exploitation by Chinese Christian missionaries, multinational logging companies, and the politics of Suharto's Golkar Party. She describes the often ambiguous interactions of these exploitative forces within Indonesian Borneo on the traditional Kaharingan religion of *adat* peoples. Embedded within her remarks is the suggestion that attentiveness to religions accompanying modernization, such as Christianity and Islam, is a significant feature of any study of indigenous traditions and ecology.

The next section, titled "Complex Cosmologies," attempts to cut across stereotyping and romanticizing tendencies in discussions of indigenous environmental concerns to emphasize the inherent complexity of these traditions. These articles suggest the manifold approaches to reality active among diverse native societies. Jack Forbes opens this section by investigating the use of such terms as "nature" and "culture." He provides a sampling of both Euro-American and indigenous linguistic perspectives on these terms. He presents linguistic considerations from several Native American languages as parallels to the nature-culture dualism so prominent in Cartesian rationality. In his discussion of "nature," Forbes translates several linguistic referents with the phrase "away from people," drawing attention to different indigenous understandings of geographical space determined by forces other than those stemming from the human. Neither wild nor undomesticated, the meditative, subsistence, and solitary implications of being "away from people" cast instructive light on the "wilderness" controversies in environmental thought. This direction of thought also provides fruitful sources for nuancing the holistic concerns of indigenous "religions" without losing the categories for distinguishing difference in the world so evident in those traditions.

The next article discusses Southeast Asian environmental concerns in Sarawak, or east Malaysian Borneo. Mention should be made of extensive efforts by indigenous peoples in other settings of this region, such as East Timor, to assert ecological and political sovereignty. In his article Peter Brosius questions the appropriateness of the use of the word "sacred" in discussing indigenous ecologies. He suggests that the term, sacred, is linked to the "grammar of conquest," and that unexamined uses of the term, sacred, may actually be counterproductive for indigenous peoples. Concentrating on the Penan of Sarawak, Brosius investigates the local and biographical character of Penan religious ideas related to the environment. Penan experiences of rivers, ridge site camps, and ridge burials stand in sharp contrast to Western ideas of the sacred conveniently adapted by outsiders for the exploitation of Penan homelands.

Leslie Sponsel examines the historical ecology of Hawai'i, identifying four assumptions operating in this volume. These four positions regarding indigenous societies are: 1) significant knowledge of local ecosystems; 2) sustainable economies; 3) conservation practices; and 4) a profound spiritual ecology. Sponsel examines the backlash reaction to the promotion of an indigenous spiritual ecology and appropriately acknowledges that the romanticized stereotypes of indigenous spiritual ecology entirely miss the diversity of indigenous relationships with local bioregions. Focusing on the Hawai'ian islands, he discusses the environmental impact of both Polynesian and Euro-American settlers. His sobering assessments of the global trends toward ecological disequilibrium bring a special force to his understanding that any practical solutions of the current environmental crises must take cognizance of approaches by indigenous societies to the four assumptions mentioned above.

Manuka Henare foregrounds Mäori cosmological values that have clear ecological implications. Drawing on the nineteenth-century speech of a Mäori elder, Henare explores Mäori terminology for concepts helpful in understanding native sustainable development. He draws on the metaphor of the *koru,* or unfolding frond of a plant, to liken Mäori cosmology to a philosophy of vitalism. His presentation also suggests parallels and connections to process thought in his analysis of the ecological character of Mäori thought. As much as Henare amplifies the intellectual aspects of Mäori thought, he also emphasizes their pragmatics in linkages with local lands and environmental values imaged in the spiraling growth of the fern frond.

The Mayan anthropologist Victor Montejo reexamines Mayan religiosity as fostering interconnected realizations. Reaching beyond the alternating fads for interpreting Mayan religions, he argues that Mayan spirituality is a quest for a holistic perspective in which the human, environmental, and supernatural realms become interconnected. He reexamines the ecological metaphors in Mayan mythology for the deeper meanings that ground economic and political life in ethical relationships with the land.

The third section, "Embedded Worldviews," presents articles that focus on specific traditions and the ways in which environmental values are deeply implanted in indigenous cultural life. Each of these regional studies explores dimensions of the religious, symbolic life of particular indigenous peoples. These articles bring the reader into a diversity of challenges faced by native peoples, and the ways in which their symbolic and ritual life provides resources for addressing those challenges. Ogbu Kalu draws on worldview analysis to investigate the interactions of development schemes and traditional values in West Africa. In turning toward African traditional religions, Kalu probes ethical and theological responses to the ecological crises, and the ironies that flow from inappropriate development strategies. Kalu assesses the benefits and limits of indigenous worldviews, such as that found in the Ife divination system of proverbs, for transmitting cultural identity in the struggle with modernization.

Simeon Namunu continues this analysis in terms of his home region of Misima Island in Papua New Guinea. Namunu develops the ecological implications of *gut pela sindaun,* a Melanesian conceptualization for the traditional knowledge of life. Likening this concept to the Western idea of "worldview," Namunu draws out the ways in which spirits, body painting, and traditional symbols manifest an exchange relationship at the heart of his peoples' interactions with the nonhuman world. The diminishment of this traditional system among the governing indigenous elite of Papua New Guinea figures prominently in the growth of extractive enterprises in his country. Recovery of ecological ideals evident in the Constitution of Papua New Guinea will not come from such an elite, according to the author, but by the reassertion of traditional religious and aesthetic values that provide openings both to modernization and indigenous forms of democratization.

Victoria Tauli-Corpuz continues this regional focus on environmental knowledge, writing of her Igorot peoples of Northern Luzon, Philippines. Her work explores Igorot lifeway, or *Sinang-adum ay Pammati,* as well as colonial religious attitudes toward those customary indigenous laws that knit together the human and natural worlds, spirit beings, and the ancestors. Focusing on rice cultivation, ritual prayers, and pest control, Tauli-Corpuz suggests that Igorot religions wove together a complex system of ecological balance, which is today breaking apart under extreme pressures.

The Nahua scholar Javier Galicia Silva demonstrates how rural indigenous agricultural life has actually been an ongoing field of resistance to dominant colonial exploitative practices. Maize agriculture, especially, continues to transmit core worldview values of the ancient Mesoamerican indigenous civilizations. Silva describes the techniques of Nahuatl agriculture and the living cosmovision in which mythic narratives, gardens, and mountains interact to fructify those practices.

Continuing the Mesoamerican focus, María Elena Bernal-García presents a close reading of the significance of the sacred mountain to indigenous peoples of the region according to sixteenth-century myths and histories. Recognizing the relationships between mythic metonyms, such as "mountain-plain" in the *Popol Vuh,* and the spatial metaphors in the indigenous landscape, Bernal-García lays out her reading of the sequence of transformations with which native Mesoamerican cultures related to the earth as the sacred mountain of bountiful reality.

Next, Angel García Zambrano discusses the historical process by which specific flora, specifically the famous calabash gourd, and cacti figured in the rituals of settlement performed by indigenous peoples as recorded in colonial Mexico. His work underscores the formal and functional relationships between native peoples and regions that focused on certain plants known from the ancient myths as the embodiment of their ethnic identity.

The final essay in this section, by Werner Wilbert, focuses on Warao spiritual ecology. He provides a detailed study of the ethnography and geography of the Warao peoples of the Orinoco River Delta. Wilbert's work describes the types of soil, plant, and animal knowledge that has enabled these peoples to live in relative equilibrium within their riverine delta homeland. Given recent archaeological evidence, he conjectures that the Warao have lived in this manner from an undetermined period well before the historic period. Most importantly, Wilbert endeavors to present Warao taxonomies and ecological concepts so that the reader might understand how the Warao interpret their environment. His perspicacious and empathetic presentation enables a reader to understand the basis on which Warao make judgments about what levels of pollution and loss of bioregional life are acceptable in the struggle for economic gain and political sovereignty.

The fourth section, titled "Resistance and Regeneration," presents articles that detail the clashes, compromises, and modes of reinventing indigenous communities and their worldviews in the era of increased market and media globalization. There is a decided circumpolar focus on North America in the opening essay, but reference should also be made to Eurasian Saami and Tungusic peoples, as well as to other North American Inuit and Athapaskan peoples, such as the Gwich'in. These peoples have all drawn on their worldview values to mount significant environmental resistance to development projects they have judged harmful to themselves and their homelands. Several crucial issues in this section are hydroelectric damming, co-opting tradition, and indigenous agricultural knowledge.

In his overview of the James Bay Cree resistance to hydroelectric damming by the Quebec provincial power company, HydroQuebec, Harvey Feit details the ways in which Cree leaders have skillfully translated indigenous cosmological concepts and subsistence practices into mainstream metaphors, such as the image of the "garden." Juxtaposing such diverse ideas and customs as Western property ownership and Cree stewardship of hunting territories, he explores their differences and brings the reader into the ways that the Cree have understood and echoed those differences to educate non-Cree about their way of life. Feit shows how Cree elders have for some time been deeply involved in the conversations involving conceptual analyses and political activities in international debate about indigenous resistance to outsider development schemes.

Smithu Kothari's article deepens this analysis from the standpoint of indigenous *swaraj,* self-rule, in light of the national development policies of the overtly Hindu governing alliance, namely, the Bharatiya Janata Party (BJP). Kothari also identifies four central elements that stand at the core of South Asian indigenous traditions, namely, the centrality of forests, the primacy of the collective, the regeneration of language, and the need for political and economic autonomy. Threaded through these issues, Kothari maintains, are *adivasi,* or indigenous, self-awakening and regeneration. Though challenged to define their relations to the modern world, indigenous peoples, according to Kothari, seek to modernize in ways that are distinctive—neither simply imitative of the democratic, individ-ualizing nation-state nor marred by the self-loathing of traditional wisdom too often inculcated by successive dominating states.

Opening her work with a strong emphasis on ethnographic differ-ence in Australia, Diane Bell presents a historical analysis of what happened to the land after European settlement in Australia and why. Following the legal implications of the principle of *terra nullius* in Euro-Australian relations with Aboriginal peoples, she also turns a reflexive eye on her own anthropological community. From her own field experiences she brings a sharper awareness of the mutual mean-ings of kin and country for Australian indigenous peoples. Her discussions of gender knowledge and confidentiality in Aboriginal women's struggles for voice in the political and legal maze of Australian justice have striking implications for the study of religion and ecology.

Tom and Ellen Trevorrow, active in the Ngarrindjeri Lands and Progress Association and principal organizers of the Camp Coorong Race Relations Cultural Education Centre, give first-person accounts of the government inquiry conducted by the Hindmarsh Island Royal Commission. Their perspective reorients the placename of the inquiry to *Kumarangk,* namely, the Ngarrindjeri women's name for this island to which a bridge has been proposed by outside developers. Their dis-cussions accentuate the poignant injustice that indigenous people face when legal experts use "tradition" itself as a criteria with which to subvert the claims of a people battered by centuries of colonial and governmental oppression.

Tirso Gonzales and Melissa Nelson extend this discussion of envi-ronmental issues in North America, or Turtle Island as many indige-nous nations call the continent, by giving an overview of legacies of "internal colonialism" on Native North American reservations. Stressing that "land is everything" for native peoples, they relate vari-ous innovative ways in which indigenous individuals, communities, and organizations are involved in environmental issues. They describe an active Internet organization, the Indigenous Environmental Net-work (IEN), and its efforts to link up with other grassroots indigenous groups, especially through its annual "Protecting Mother Earth" conferences. They also discuss two case studies, namely, the Mescalero Apache struggle over locating a nuclear waste depository on their New Mexico reservation, and the proposed location of a low-level radioactive waste dump on a sacred site of five local California Indian tribes, collectively called the Quechan peoples, in Ward Valley. The striking differences in these two case studies stress the underlying political economic and cultural realities on American Indian reservations, as well as the ways in which the marginalization of indigenous peoples from both local and national markets shadows both of these case studies. This marginalization results in degraded reservation environments in which "sovereignty from above" subverts indigenous efforts to reestablish ecological equilibrium. The authors emphasize re-indigenizing activism in which de-colonizing becomes a spiritual, emotional, physical, linguistic, and social act.

The final section, titled "Liberative Ecologies," presents articles describing environmental pedagogies flowing from indigenous thought that have implications for dominant societies. These contributors offer insights that may help dominant societies unlearn some things and become open to other ways of knowing the world. Ann Fienup-Riordan's paper on the Yup'ik peoples of Alaska presents striking narratives of the resentment engendered among these Inuit peoples by wildlife management policies in which they have little or no voice. Her work explores Yup'ik cosmological concerns for the effects of personal thought on the community—both human and nonhuman. The Yup'ik affirm the value of hunting as the human act which initiates the return of even larger flocks of geese from year to year. Such a traditional value conflicts with the material, empirical, and individual concerns of science-based conservation research. Thus, scientific wildlife management assumptions about over-hunting collide directly with Yup'ik views that geese intentionally return in response to respectful hunting. Moreover, Yup'ik peoples avoid the types of direct human-animal contact that occur in wildlife management tagging, saying that it diminishes the flocks of geese. Her descriptions of emerging co-management practices suggest that some insertion of Yup'ik spiritual concerns into ecological policies is possible. Perhaps more importantly, these collaborative exchanges may also enable the Yup'ik to learn more about science and "Fish and Game" biologists to appreciate the human dimensions of traditional values and the need for indigenous participants to have significant local control in game management.

In addressing the pressures on indigenous, or *adivasi,* peoples of South Asia, Pramod Parajuli develops the concept of "ecological ethnicities" in terms of their communities and their flourishing cosmological visions, intellectual thought, and political activism. Parajuli presents a historical model in which indigenous peoples are seen as becoming more resistant to national development programs and global economic schemes. He proposes that in several geographical settings in South Asia the ethnosemiotics of oppressed indigenous peoples stand as viable alternative development models for social action against the dominant semiotics of market-based capital.

In considering several indigenous ecological perspectives in Papua New Guinea, Mary MacDonald emphasizes place, relationships, and work. Walking with an old friend from the Kewa peoples of the Southern Highlands, MacDonald notes the substantial spatial modes of memory active in their conversation. Linking this "tastescape" and spatial memory with a "give-and-take" ethic, she highlights the attentiveness of indigenous peoples to subtle memories of interaction with place. The sense knowledge encoded in this ecological patterning is further developed by the ritual work connected with gardens. Each of these indigenous realities—place, relationships, and work—is now undergoing profound changes in which resource extraction, the introduction of monetary economies, and the allure of modernization are creating crises in the transmission of traditional knowledge.

Gregory Cajete's overview article on North America provides the reader with a personal narrative from his own Puebloan perspective. His focus on orientation to place highlights the central purposes of indigenous education as an experiential quest to know "that place that Indian peoples talk about." Emphasizing art, hunting, and planting as the source of mythic tribal expressions, Cajete explores the indigenous ecological education embedded in Puebloan lifeways.

The indigenous Andean agronomist Julio Valladolid withdrew from his academic post to work more closely with Quechua and Aymara peasant farmers. He and anthropologist Frédérique Apffel-Marglin describe the work of the indigenous agricultural organization PRATEC in fostering indigenous agricultural ritual knowledge and techniques based on ancient ways of "seeing" and "feeling." Apffel-

Marglin's essay critiques the intellectual position that indigenous techniques based on mythic cosmologies lack adequate objectivity by affirming their collective data gathering and concerns for bioregional health. Valladolid extends this analysis by critiquing the individualizing, objectivizing, and homogenizing tendencies of modern agriculture. He points out the concerns for diversity and variability in indigenous, community-oriented agriculture as well as its intellectual foundation in the "impenetrable" character of all life as unique beings in the process of change.

Conclusion

While the plurality of cultural systems and the diversity of environmental knowledge within and between cultures mark this volume, a Western philosophical reflection on the relation of the many (read: multicultural perspectives) to the one (read: universal, rational, globality) is not the central issue posed here. The sovereignty of indigenous peoples and the conservation of endangered bioregions with their animals and plant habitats—the survival of life—are more prominent issues. These concerns cannot be reduced to a question of theoretical models in which formalist rational patterns are used to interpret religious activities or in which highly specialized sociolinguistic ethnographies are used to describe peoples as types to be catalogued. Along with those methods as perspectives for interpretation of indigenous life, the imaginative act has been highlighted as a significant cognitive arena. Here, questions regarding the indigenous understandings of place, knowledge, and sovereignty vie with the conceptual subtleties and power relations posed by the contemporary intellectual scene. Indeed, the relationship of such different cognitive acts as dreams to sensory and sonic ways of knowing in these diverse traditions challenges scholarly understanding. This is so because traditional environmental knowledge relates to animal-plant-mineral life in ways that even contemporary "co-management" strategies cannot easily comprehend.

The relationship between the act of imaging oneself, understanding reality, and surviving development pressures found recent poignant expression in the deaths of three environmental activists in Colombia. Between 25 February and 4 March 1999, three activists, Lahe'ena'e

Gay, Terence Freitas, and Ingrid Washinawatok, were killed by guerrilla soldiers of the Revolutionary Armed Forces of Colombia (FARC). While these guerillas killed the activists to make a statement, they had no idea of the international reactions to their brutal act, nor did they have a clear sense of indigenous rights. It was said of the three murdered activists that "All of them were defending human rights. They [were] environmentalists, activists who [were] working on the international level."[10] Ingrid Washinawatok herself spoke of her understanding of indigenous rights, saying:

> Since the time that human beings offered thanks for the first sunrise, sovereignty has been an integral part of indigenous people's daily existence. With the original instructions from the Creator, we realize our responsibilities, and those are the laws that lay the foundation for our society. These responsibilities are manifested through our ceremonies. These ceremonies are not just motions we go through. It is a process that reaffirms our connection to the Creator and all of creation. Sacred is not separate from responsibility and daily existence. From the mundane to the momentous, sovereignty is an integral part of the foundation that anchors our culture, society and organizational structures.[11]

By recalling the words of this heroic woman, and by remembering her companions, an effort is made here to draw attention to the imaginative act constellated in "responsibility," "ceremony," and "creation." Such a vision of religion and ecology is what Thomas Berry has called a shared dream experience. He writes:

> . . . only out of imaginative power does any grand creative work take shape. Since imagination functions most freely in dream vision, we tend to associate creativity also with dream experience. The dream comes about precisely through uninhibited spontaneities. In this context we might say: In the beginning was the dream. Through the dream all things were made, and without the dream nothing was made that has been made.
>
> While all things share in this dream, as humans we share in this dream in a special manner. This is the entrancement, the magic of the world about us, its mystery, its ineffable quality. What primordial source could, with no model for guidance, imagine such a fantastic world as that in which we live—the shape of the orchid, the coloring of the fish in the sea, the winds and the rain, the variety of sounds that flow over the earth, the resonant croaking of the bullfrogs, the songs of

the crickets, and the pure joy of the predawn singing of the mocking-bird?

... All of these derive from the visionary power that is experienced most profoundly when we are immersed in the depths of our own being and of the cosmic order itself in the dreamworld that unfolds within us in our sleep, or in those visionary moments that seize upon us in our waking hours.

We need to remember that this process whereby we invent ourselves in these cultural modes is guided by visionary experiences that come to us in some transrational process from the inner shaping tendencies that we carry within us, often in revelatory dream experience. Such dream experiences are so universal and so important in the psychic life of the individual and of the community that techniques of dreaming are taught in some societies.[12]

Indigenous peoples are among the last cultural groups to teach techniques of dreams and visions and ways to activate an ecological imagination. Our shared experiences are not simply culturally differentiated dreams, but common cosmological concerns. Coursing through these essays are underlying cosmological visions that have been identified here as lifeways.

The study of these lifeways does not elevate precapitalist models as panaceas for today's complex problems, which are rooted in global demographies, widespread environmental crises, and increasing economic inequalities. Yet, studies of indigenous traditions do remind us of alternative visions and possibilities that exist among peoples who have imagined themselves more intimately into their worlds. Many within mainstream societies feel the allure of this cosmological act of dreaming. An aspect of their journey is the deeper moralization of issues until now understood simply as political, economic, or religious. By "deeper moralization" is meant a creative behavior that not only responds to the concerns of place, knowledge, and sovereignty of indigenous peoples, but also collaboratively explores visions of flourishing life. While it is possible to agree that "creativity begins with the familiar,"[13] it is also evident that creativity flows forth in the dream of the earth.

The deaths of the three activists model the depth of their commitments to a dream they shared with the U'wa people, namely, that these people might move beyond military oppression by guerilla or national militaries, and beyond material exploitation of oil in their homelands by petroleum multinationals. It is a modeling that bears on the issue of the "indigenous." We are all indigenous to the planet. In this volume we have chosen to construe the term so that certain small-scale societies might be emphasized. That emphasis can easily be misread as ethnocentrism, or an assertion of what one scholar calls the "ecological indian." Just as the activists shared a dream across their ethnic identities, so the concern for indigenous homelands crosses beyond simply political, environmental, or social justice issues. The articles in this volume speak to the tensions and ambiguities within indigenous societies as they encounter, adopt, resist, accommodate, and transform global forces. What cannot be so readily communicated is the attitudinal changes emerging from these shared dreams of the interbeing of cosmology and community.

Notes

1. Winona LaDuke, "Minobimaatisiiwin: The Good Life," *Cultural Survival Quarterly* 16, no. 4 (winter 1992): 69–71. See also Winona LaDuke, *All Our Relations: Native Struggles for Land and Life* (Cambridge, Mass.: South End Press, 1994), 4 and 132.

2. Roy Rappaport, *Pigs for the Ancestors* (New Haven, Conn.: Yale University Press, 1967).

3. Eduardo Grillo Fernandez, "Development or Decolonization in the Andes?" in *The Spirit of Regeneration: Andean Culture Confronting Western Notions of Development,* ed. Frédérique Apffel-Marglin with PRATEC (London and New York: Zed Books, 1998), 229.

4. Gisday Wa and Delgam Uukw, *The Spirit of the Land: The Opening Statement of the Gitksan and Wets'uwetén Hereditary Chiefs in the Supreme Court of British Columbia* (Gabrola, B.C.: Reflections, 1987), 7, 26, quoted from David Suzuki and Peter Knudtson, *Wisdom of the Elders: Sacred Native Stories of Nature* (New York and Toronto: Bantam Books, 1992), 158.

5. For "interbeing," see Thich Nhat Hanh, *The Heart of Understanding: Commentaries on the Prajnaparamita Heart Sutra,* ed. Peter Levitt (Berkeley: Parallax Press, 1988).

6. "Report of the Sub-Commission on Prevention of Discrimination and Protection of Minorities on its Forty-Sixth Session" Geneva, 1–26 August 1994, *Draft United Nations Declaration on the Rights of Indigenous Peoples.*

7. Richard Peet and Michael Watts, *Liberation Ecologies: Environment, Development, Social Movements* (London and New York: Routledge, 1996), 263.

8. See Lee Irwin, *Dream Seekers: Native American Visionary Traditions of the Great Plains* (Norman: University of Oklahoma Press, 1994).

9. For a vision that initiated the movement of the proto-Crow/Absaroke peoples, see Joseph Medicine Crow, *From the Heart of Crow Country, The Crow Indian's Own Stories* (New York: Orion, 1992); and for Tsistsistas views of their Massaum ceremony, see Karl Schlesier, *The Wolves of Heaven: Cheyenne Shamanism, Ceremonies, and Prehistoric Origins* (Norman: University of Oklahoma, 1987).

10. Tim Johnson, *Miami Herald,* 6 March 1999, quoted in Jeff Wollock, "Eclipse Over Colombia," *Native Americas* 16, no. 2 (summer 1999): 10–31.

11. Kert Lebsock, "She Was So Much: Remembering Ingrid," *Native Americas* 16, no. 2 (summer 1999): 42.

12. Thomas Berry, *The Dream of the Earth* (San Francisco: Sierra Club Books, 1988), 197 and 201.

13. Peet and Watts, *Liberation Ecologies,* 267.

Prologue

RICHARD NELSON

Trekking through the Alaskan forest on a chill September morning, my friend and I were startled by a sudden hiss of wings. Looking up, we saw a raven soaring effortlessly toward us, barely skimming the treetops. As the great bird passed overhead, it tucked a wing, rolled topsy-turvy in the sky, then flipped upright and sailed on, pouring yodeled calls down across the wildland: *"Ggaagga! Ggaagga!"*

My companion, a Koyukon Indian elder named Lavine Williams, watched the bird intently. "When a raven tips over like that," the old hunter explained, "they say he's dropping his packsack full of meat, giving us good luck. And when that raven hollered, he was saying, 'Animal! Animal!' It means he's showing where to look for game— maybe moose or bear."

We stood silently, watching the raven until it vanished over a distant ridge. Lavine, who had taken it upon himself to teach me Koyukon traditions, added something important: "You know, there's way more to it than just seeing what the raven does and hearing what he says. A hunter needs good luck if he's going to find animals. And for that, he's got to treat every animal the right way; otherwise he probably wouldn't get anything. Let's say a hunter killed a moose, but he wasted some of the meat or he didn't take good care of it—then he might lose his luck for getting moose. Afterward, a big moose might be right there in plain sight, but if he didn't have luck he probably wouldn't even see it."

This encounter between man and animal in the subarctic forest opens the door to an entire world: a world overlooked in modern Western culture; a world explicitly denied by contemporary empirical science; a world in which every plant and animal and the earth itself are vibrant with spiritual power; a world bringing all of nature into the sphere of moral and ethical concern; a world that demands humility and respect toward the living community in return for its gifts of sustenance and shelter.

This view of nature—as an assemblage of omniscient, spiritually empowered beings who should be treated with deference and restraint— is expressed in marvelous and almost infinite variety among the earth's traditional peoples. It is an ancient, venerable way of seeing, based on countless generations of intimate experience with the community of life. It is, I believe, the fundamentally *human* way of seeing our universe.

Today, the apparently inexorable trend toward abandonment of this once-universal view ranks among the most profound transformations in all of history—as important as the origin of tools, the invention of agriculture, and the rise of industrial technology. Furthermore, the widespread displacement of traditional worldviews by the Western worldview is probably the most dangerous undertaking humankind has ever attempted.

Indigenous Traditions and Ecology is part of a vital and growing effort to arrest this sweeping pattern of change and loss. It is also a powerful testament to the environmental wisdom braided through traditional cultures on every inhabited continent. The chapters that follow explore a brilliant diversity of cultural lifeways. They reveal the human genius for learning in intricate detail the natural history and ecology of our surrounding world. They describe the myriad forms of spiritual interchange between people and the embracing community of life. And they reveal that, in many cultures, spiritual beliefs are combined with sophisticated ecological knowledge to foster carefully managed, sustainable uses of the environment.

Taken together, these chapters bring to light some of the most significant achievements of the human mind.

But while this book honors traditional cultures, it is a celebration tinged with darkness, detailing cultural loss and environmental degradation on a worldwide scale. This is not, however, a compilation of stories about people watching helplessly as they are overwhelmed by forces beyond their comprehension or control. Far from it. Many of the authors gathered here speak eloquently in defense of their cultural heritage, their beliefs and values, their dignity, and their rights of self-determination. They introduce us to activists working in allegiance to their communities. And, if I understand correctly, they define their communities as including not only the human enclave but also the terrain and waters, the plants and animals—the entire living homeland.

These are informative and intensely moving accounts, bearing the weight of true authority, which is based not only on skillful research but also on prolonged experience with the peoples and places described here. Many of the chapters are written from the "inside," by authors who belong to the communities of which they speak. Other chapters are authored by perceptive "outsiders" who have participated actively in the community, learned the traditions in great depth, and illuminated their work with special gifts of empathy.

The writers of this book combine insightful descriptions of traditional lifeways with passionate defenses of these lifeways. Their work could be viewed as ethnography, in the best sense of that word. But unlike most of mainstream cultural anthropology, these authors are not much inclined to analyze, dissect, or theorize about customs and traditions. Those all-too-familiar academic exercises use other cultures mainly as a stage for intellectual performance. This book sets a higher standard, by taking readers inside cultural communities and valuing those communities purely on their own terms.

It has also been common in anthropology to trivialize cultural traditions by regarding them as mere human inventions, rather than honoring them as sacred truths. The founding principles for these traditions are often contained in bodies of oral literature passed down from ancient times. These stories, usually called "myths," are admired as wonderfully creative fantasies, and they are analyzed as dreamlike fictional tales whose primary function is to undergird systems of belief and values. But this approach, sympathetic though it may be, vastly underestimates the power and significance of traditional stories.

Catherine Attla, a Koyukon elder and teacher, explains that origin stories recounting events from *Kk'adonts'idnee,* the Distant Time, are completely and literally true, not artifacts of the human imagination. "Nobody made these stories up," she states unequivocally. If we respect this viewpoint and aspire toward accuracy, we should speak of "sacred stories," and consign the word "myth" to other uses, such as our children's books of fairy tales.

Catherine Attla—who is both a traditionalist and a Christian—emphasizes that the Distant Time stories for Koyukon people are precisely equal to the biblical stories for orthodox Christians. They are a Koyukon version of Genesis. And rather than seeing the Bible and the Distant Time stories as contradictory, she believes that each reinforces the truth of the other.

"In the *Kk'adonts'idnee* stories that I learned from my grandfather," Catherine recalls, "a big flood covered the world, and the Great Raven put all the animals in pairs on a raft. In the Bible stories that I learned from church, it was God that put all the animals on a boat when the big flood came. Both stories are the same and that shows that both of them are true."

What Koyukon people teach, by their example, is this: every culture is sustained by its own body of knowledge, and there is no hierarchy of value or veracity among different bodies of cultural knowledge. The raven's call that means "Animal!" to a Koyukon hunter could mean something entirely different to a person from another tradition or to a scientist from the Western tradition. Rather than looking for the one version that meets our own test of veracity, we should embrace them all. Every bird, in every place, sings its own perfect truth.

To choose another example: it may be factual—as archaeologists have concluded—that Native Americans first settled the New World fifteen to thirty thousand years ago, migrating via the Bering Strait and possibly navigating across the north Atlantic or even the Pacific. But it may be just as valid that Native American peoples have inhabited their homelands since the world itself was created, since humans and animals spoke the same language and lived together as one society, and since this society was transformed into the community of animals and people inhabiting each place today. Both interpretations are true and wise in their own ways, and both have their own kind of value.

This book brings together an exquisite chorus of truths, wrested from the earth itself over generations beyond reckoning. I have focused on the spiritual truths, but of equal importance are the observable, scientific truths accumulated by traditional peoples, especially the sophisticated ecological knowledge that has allowed these peoples to inhabit a remarkable diversity of environments—from the arctic tundra to the tropical forests, from the arid deserts to the saturated marshlands.

As some of the following chapters demonstrate, this traditional scientific knowledge has led to the development of conservation principles and careful management of harvests based on sustained yield practices. It has become fashionable in recent times, at least among North American critics, to deny the existence of conservation practices among traditional peoples. These critics often focus on the theory—now frequently treated as fact—that "Pleistocene overkill" by Native Americans brought about widespread mammalian extinctions. These assumed paleo-transgressions are invoked not only to prove that ancient Indians had destructive impacts on their environment, but also that their descendants thousands of years later are ignorant of the conservation impulse.

Whenever I encounter those writings, I feel like a returning astronaut who has watched the earth from space, being greeted by an earnest crowd of theorists who have concluded that the earth is flat. During several years of research with the Koyukon Indians in Alaska, I learned about their intricate knowledge of boreal forest ecology, their religiously and empirically based conservation ethic, and their sustained yield practices. Almost every day, I witnessed how people applied these ethics and practices in their hunting, trapping, fishing, and gathering activities. In fact, conservation is a pervasive element in modern Koyukon subsistence life, governing their entire relationship with the natural world.

But we should never forget that the Koyukon Indians and other indigenous peoples are like everybody else: some community members strictly follow the codes for proper behavior, some are less conscientious, and some are habitual violators. Just as individuals vary in their conformity to cultural ideals, entire societies never achieve perfect adherence to their own standards. For example, it would be a serious mistake to conclude that the existence of murder in contemporary American society indicates an absence of social norms, religious canons, or legal strictures regarding homicide.

Overharvest of game, waste of resources, and damage to the environment undoubtedly have happened among indigenous peoples throughout history, and they are certainly happening today. But these occurrences do not mean there are no norms or regulations in these communities to establish responsible harvest levels, discourage waste, or prevent ecological damage. On the contrary, we have a voluminous ethnographic literature filled with carefully detailed examples of conservation practices, land stewardship, and religiously based environmental ethics among traditional peoples all over the world. This book is an important and valuable addition to that literature.

What is beautifully illustrated in *Indigenous Traditions and Ecology* is the need, at long last, for a balanced and reciprocal exchange between the traditional and Western worlds. Over the past few centuries, Westerners have taken it upon themselves to "educate" the people whose homelands they have colonized, ignoring the enormous libraries of tradition that existed before their arrival. And yet, almost miraculously at the beginning of the twenty-first century, there is still time for us to begin learning from each other—time for the teachers and elders, the priests and shamans to travel both ways. Each of the authors in this book stands among those educators and guides. They bring to us a powerful source of hope, by coming together as a community of voices from throughout the world and as a community of voices *for* the world, embracing humanity and nature as one.

It is as if the Raven had flown overhead, tucked a wing, and called out. Leading us all to this place. Showing us how to find each other.

Maps of Indigenous Peoples

The following maps situate selected indigenous peoples mentioned in this volume. The dots indicate the approximate regional locations of most of these peoples.

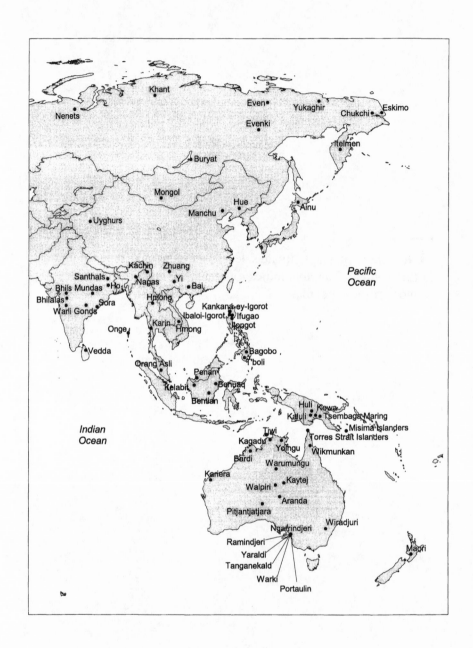

Asia

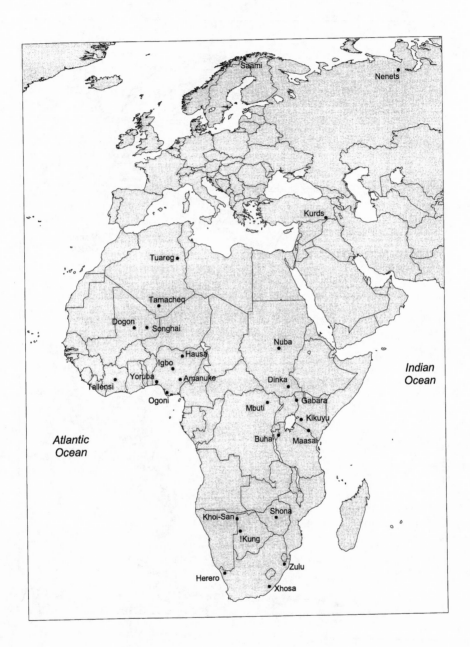

Africa

The Americas

Fragmented Communities

Intellectual Property Rights and the Sacred Balance: Some Spiritual Consequences from the Commercialization of Traditional Resources

DARRELL ADDISON POSEY

The Sacred Balance

Indigenous and traditional peoples have increasingly become the focus for research aimed at the development of new products or the improvement of medicines, agricultural products, body and skin preparations, natural oils, essences, dyes, and insecticides. They have long been targets for expropriation of their music, art, crafts, and images. Trade has removed materials, ideas, expressions of culture—and even human genes—from their social and spiritual contexts to convert them into *objects* for commodification. This shows not only disrespect for other cultures, but also violates basic human rights.

Although conservation and management practices are highly pragmatic, indigenous and traditional peoples generally view this knowledge as emanating from a *spiritual* base. All creation is sacred, and the sacred and secular are inseparable. Spirituality is the highest form of consciousness, and spiritual consciousness is the highest form of awareness. In this sense, a dimension of traditional knowledge is not *local* knowledge, but knowledge of the *universal* as expressed in the local.

In indigenous and local cultures, experts exist who are peculiarly aware of nature's organizing principles, sometimes described as entities, spirits, or natural law. Thus, knowledge of the environment depends not only on the relationship between humans and nature, but also between the visible world and the invisible spirit world. According to Kofi Asare Opoku,[1] the distinctive feature of traditional African religion is that it is: "A way of life, [with] the purpose of . . . order[ing] our relationship with our fellow men and with our environment, both spiritual and physical. At the root of it is a quest for harmony between man, the spirit world, nature, and society." Thus, the unseen is as much a part of reality as that which is seen—the spiritual is as much a part of reality as the material. In fact, there is a complementary relationship between the two, with the spiritual being more powerful than the material. The community is of the dead as well as the living. And in nature, behind visible objects lie essences, or powers, which constitute the true nature of those objects.

Indigenous and traditional peoples frequently view themselves as guardians and stewards of nature. Harmony and equilibrium among components of the cosmos are central concepts in most cosmologies. Agriculture, for example, can provide "balance for well-being" through relationships not only among people, but also nature and deities. In this concept, the blessing of a new field represents not mere spectacle, but an inseparable part of life where the highest value is harmony with the earth. Most traditions recognize linkages between health, diet, properties of different foods and medicinal plants, and horticultural/natural resource management practices—all within a highly articulated cosmological/social context.[2] The plant, animal, or crystal some ethnopharmacologist may want to collect may, in fact, encompass, contain, or be the manifestation of the ancestral spirit— even the healer's grandmother.

Local knowledge embraces information about location, movements, and other factors explaining spatial patterns and timing in the ecosystem, including sequences of events, cycles, and trends. Direct links with the land are fundamental, and obligations to maintain those connections form the core of individual and group identity. Nowhere is that more apparent than with the dreaming places of the Aboriginal peoples of Australia. As James Galarrwuy Yunupingu, chairperson of the Northern Land Council, explains: "My land is mine only because I came in spirit from that land, and so did my ancestors of the same land. My land is my foundation."[3]

As L. A. Whitt[4] explains, the Cherokee see knowledge itself as being an integral part of the earth. Thus, a dam does not just flood the land, but destroys the medicines and the knowledge of the medicines associated with the land. "If we are to make our offerings at a new place, the spiritual beings would not know us. We would not know the mountains or the significance of them. We would not know the land and the land would not know us. We would not know the sacred places. If we were to go on top of an unfamiliar mountain we would not know the life forms that dwell there."

The same is true for the Mazatecs of Southern Mexico, whose shamans and *curandeiros* confer with the plant spirits in order to heal: successful curers must above all else learn to listen to the plants talk. For many groups, these communications come through the transformative powers of altered states or trances. Don Hilde, a Pucallpa healer, explains: "I did not have a teacher to help me learn about plants, but visions have taught me many things. They even instruct me as to which pharmaceutical medicines to use."[5]

These links between life, land, and society are identified by David Suzuki and Peter Knudtson[6] as the "Sacred Balance." Science, with its quantum mechanics methods, they say, can never address the universe as a whole; and it certainly can never adequately describe the holism of indigenous knowledge and belief. In fact, science is far behind in the environmental movement. It still sees nature as objects ("components" of biodiversity is the term used in the Convention on Biological Diversity, or CBD) for human use and exploitation. Technology has used the banner of scientific "objectivity" to mask the moral and ethical issues that emerge from such a functionalist, anthropocentric philosophy. Marilyn Strathern[7] makes this clear when discussing the ethical dilemmas raised (or avoided) when embryos are "decontextualized" as human beings to become "objects" of scientific research.

"Components" of Nature in Extended Society

The many "components" of nature for indigenous peoples become an extension, not just of the geographical world, but of human society. This is fundamentally difficult for Western society to understand, since the extension of "self" is through "hard technology," not nature. For indigenous peoples, "natural models" may even serve as templates for social organization, political thought, and modes of subsistence. This also implies radical differences in concepts of time and space.

"Myths" and "folklore" have been analyzed for their structural, metalinguistic, and symbolic components, and have even been shown to regulate ecological as well as social cycles. They have perhaps been less studied as sounding boards for cultural change. Take, for example, the myth of the Kayapó Indians of Brazil, "The Journey to Become a Shaman."[8] It is exemplary of how oral tradition works to explain ecological-social relationships and changes that occur within them. The myth, dealing with the transformation of the *wayanga* (shaman), goes as such:

Listen!

Those who become sick from strong fevers lie in death's position; they lie as though they are dead. The truly great ones, the truly strong person who is a *wayanga,* shows the sick how to leave their bodies. They leave through their insides. They pass through their insides and come to be in the form of a stone. Their bodies lie as in death, but beyond they are then transformed into an armadillo. As an armadillo, they assume good, strong health and they pass through the other side, over there (pointing to the east).

Then they become a bat and fly—ko, ko, ko, ko, ko . . . (the noise of flying).

Then they go further beyond in the form of a dove. They fly like a dove—ku, ku, ku, ku . . . (the sound of a dove's flight). They join the other *wayangas* and all go together.

"Where will we go? What is the way? Go to the east, way over there." Ku, ku, ku, ku. . . .

And way over there is a spider's web. . . . Some go round and round near the spider's web and they just sit permanently. The true and ancient shamans must teach them how to fly through the web. But those who have not been shown how, try to break through the web and the web grabs their wings thusly (the narrator wraps his arms around his shoulders). They just hang in the web and die. Their bodies are carried by their relatives and are buried without waiting, for the spider's web has entangled them, wrapped up their wings, and they are dead.

Those who have been caused to know themselves, however, go round the spider web. They sit on the mountain seat of the shamans and sing like the dove—tu, tu, tu, tu. . . .

They acquire the knowledge of the ancestors. They speak to the spirits of all the animals and of the ancestors. They know (all). They then return (to their bodies). They return to their homes. They enter and they breathe.

And the others say: "He arrived! He arrived! He arrived! He arrived!" And the women all wail: "ayayikakraykyerekune."

(And the shaman says) "Do not bury me, I am still alive. I am a *wayanga*. I am now one who can cure: I am the one who smokes the powerful pipe. I know how to go through my body and under my head. I am a *wayanga*."

The story is centered around the capability of the *wayanga* to leave his or her body (*ka*) and be transformed into other physical forms. Energy (*karon*) can be stored temporarily in rocks, but inevitably gets transformed into armadillos, doves, or bats. The spider's web represents the barrier between the visible and invisible worlds. Armadillos are persistent animals that know to burrow under the web; doves are powerful flyers and can break right through the barrier; and bats are such skillful fliers that they maneuver through the strands.

The sounds of the dove's and bat's flights represent the different frequencies that their vibrations impart. Frequencies have associated sounds and colors. Just to analyze the variations in frequencies of bee sounds would require discussing the fifty-two different folk species of stingless bees, each of which has a distinctive sound and curative properties.

The most powerful shamans can transform themselves into not just one of the animals, but all of them. And, once on the other side of the spider's web, after they have passed through the endless dark chasm, they enter into the spectral frequencies of different light (or colors). There is a different spectral frequency for each animal (*mry-karon*). The general term for undifferentiated energy is *karon*. Defined energies are given distinctive modifiers (*x-karon*), where x might be *mry* for animals (*mry-karon*), *tep* for fish, or *kwen* for birds.

Some shamans only learn the secrets of a few animals and their energies, while others "know all" (in the words of the myth). They have learned about all of the spectral frequencies and their respective animal energies. Upon return to their bodies, the *wayanga* begin to "work with" (*nhipex*) the animal energies encountered in their transformation.

The basis of the "work" is to maintain a balance between animal energies and human energies. Eating the meat of, coming in contact with, or even dreaming about animals can cause an imbalance in these energies, as can, of course, a well-elaborated list of antisocial actions.

Wayanga use a great variety of techniques for restoring balance (they can also create imbalances—*kane*—that lead to sickness), but plants are the most common "mediators" that manipulate this balance.[9] Plants themselves have energies (*karon*), but do not have distinctive energies or spirits (*x-karon*), per se, except for some of the *mekrakindja* (child-want-thing, or plants that aide in conception). These plants have very powerful spirits and cause the user to dream of a child's conception. Men and women use these dreaming plants, although men are usually the ones who first "conceive," i.e., first "see" (*kra pumunh*) the child in a dream.[10]

Other plants also have spirits (defined energies, or *x-karon*), especially the *metykdja* (the poison plants), the *meudjy* (witchcraft plants), and the most deadly and powerful *pitu* (no direct translation). These plants cause drastic alterations to human beings, such as death, paralysis, blindness, insanity, abortion. Even less powerful plants have qualities that can either harm or help the balance between human and animal energies (*me-karon* and *mry-karon*)—indeed, it appears that all plants have curative values.

In any case, the Kayapó respect both plants and animals, since their energies are keys to the health of their own society. Permission is requested of the *mry-karon* when taking the life of an animal, and songs of appreciation are offered to the spirits of the dead animals. Likewise, annual rituals extol the importance of plants and instill a great sense of respect for their overall role in the socioecological balance. The Kayapó have no question about their existence and future health being dependent upon plants and animals and the forces of nature.

Normally, spirits of the dead pass easily into the other world (*mekaron nhon pyka*) and continue their existence in what is roughly the mirror image of what goes on in this world. "Deceased" (they never really die, for they have already died and just disappear and reappear) *wayanga* live in a special cave in the mountains and, thus, the reference in the myth about their stone seats. Spirits of dead animals also go to "the other world." Devoted pets are sometimes killed and buried with their "owners" at death, so that the human spirit will not be so lonely. (Some Kayapó say that dogs are buried with their owners because the dogs can help the human spirit find its way to the other world.)

Those who attempt a shamanistic transformation and do not succeed, however, have a more tragic end. Their spirits are lost forever in the spider's web. There is disagreement among the Kayapó as to what this really means, but there is no doubt that it is the worst possible fate. There is little wonder that only a small portion of the Kayapó population have ever tried to become a *wayanga*.

Kwyra-ka, another of my shaman-mentors, showed great concern when the first coffin arrived in Gorotire and his nephew was buried in it instead of in the traditional manner. (The Kayapó traditionally bury the body in a crouched position in deep, round pits, covered with logs and soil. Until recently, secondary burial was practiced four days after principal burial. This allowed time for the spirit to return to the body in case the "dead" person was only on a shamanistic journey.) He anguished over the possibility that the soul of the child would not be able to escape from the casket to the other world.

Likewise, Kwyra-ka and Beptopoop, a very powerful shaman and my mentor, have expressed their deep concerns with the plants that were taken during ethnobotanical surveys to be pressed and dried in herbaria. They are concerned with what happens to the plants' energies.

If the plants were kept in such closed, sterile places, would their spirits be trapped, thereby provoking an imbalance and danger to the Kayapó, as well as to those who "kept" them? Like the casket containing the small child, would the energy not become imprisoned, thereby blocking the "natural" cycles?

Even deeper concerns are expressed about the massive quantities of plants that would have to be collected to provide the oils, essences, colorings, and the like for commercialization of plant products. The *wayanga* ask: "Has any one ever consulted the plants?"

Would the dreaming that is necessary for conception of healthy children be jeopardized? Would the plants stop mediating between the human and animal *karons,* thereby leading to loss of ancient cures and provoking new diseases? For Kayapó elders, these are fundamental questions. They were to me, however, unpredictable and non-obvious dilemmas. The central concepts of ecological management are deeply embedded and codified in myth from which environmental and social change can also be measured. However, it is important to realize that the forces or energies exemplified in myths are not historical in the Western sense: time may be cyclical, spiral, or multidimensional. No matter how hard historical ecologists try, the lineality of time and space that pervades our categories of interpretation will never capture the nonlineality of some indigenous ecological concepts.

Recognizing Indigenous and Local Communities

Western science may have invented the words "nature," "biodiversity," and "sustainability," but it certainly did not initiate the concepts. Indigenous, traditional, and local communities have sustainably utilized and conserved a vast diversity of plants, animals, and ecosystems since the dawn of *Homo sapiens*. Furthermore, human beings have molded environments through their conscious and unconscious activities for millennia—to the extent that it is often impossible to separate nature from culture.

Some recently "discovered" cultural landscapes include those of Aboriginal peoples who, one hundred thousand years before the term "sustainable development" was coined, were trading seeds, dividing tubers, and propagating domesticated and nondomesticated plant species. Sacred sites act as conservation areas for vital water sources and individual species by restricting access and behavior. Traditional technologies, including fire use, were part of extremely sophisticated systems that shaped and maintained the balance of vegetation and wildlife. Decline of fire management and loss of sacred sites, when Aboriginal people were centralized into settlements, led to rapid decline of mammals throughout the arid regions.[11]

Another example of cultural landscapes are the "forest islands" (*apete*) of the Kayapó Indians of Brazil.[12] Kayapó practices of planting and transplanting within and between many ecological zones indicate the degree to which indigenous presence has modified Amazonia. Extensive plantations of fruit and nut trees, as well as forest islands (*apete*) created in savanna, force scientists to re-evaluate what have often hastily and erroneously been considered "natural" Amazonian landscapes. The Kayapó techniques of constructing *apete* in savanna show the degree to which this Amazon group can create and manipulate microenvironments within and between ecozones to actually increase biological diversity. Such ecological engineering requires a detailed knowledge of soil fertility, microclimatic properties and plant varietal qualities, as well as interrelationships between components of a human-modified ecological community. Successful *apete* are dependent on knowledge not just of the immediate properties, but also of long-term successional relationships that change as the forest islands mature and grow. Since many plants are specifically grown to attract useful animals, the complexity of the management problem greatly increases: *apete* are managed both as agroforestry units and game reserves. Kayapó knowledge of *apete* formation and succession offers invaluable insights into processes of forestation in savanna and reforestation in denuded areas.

The Kagore Shona people of Zimbabwe have sacred sites, burial grounds, and other sites of special historical significance deeply embedded in the landscape. Outsiders often cannot recognize them during land use planning exercises. Often, so-called wild forests are actually managed landscapes. Forests are more often peoples' back yards, not the "wildernesses" assumed by outsiders.[13] In societies with no written language or edifices, hills, mountains, and valleys become the libraries and cathedrals that reflect cultural achievement. It is often difficult for outsiders to understand that not just parts of mountains—but entire mountains—are sacred to people like the Apache, although it may be certain parts of mountains, such as sacred groves, that are holy for groups like the Khumbu of Nepal.[14] Sacred groves such as the "dragon hills" of Yunan Province, China, are one of the most common types of cultural landscapes and are kept intact because of their sacred nature.[15] Sacred groves in India are extensive and well-known in the literature.[16]

Wells and springs are also frequently considered as holy and the areas around them specially protected from disturbance. Springs, for example, are the "soul of the Hopi people, representing their very identity." Oases, too, can be sacred places for people like the Masai and Fulani pastoralists, whose lives during severe droughts literally depend upon these protected areas.

A failure to recognize anthropogenic (human-modified) landscapes has blinded outsiders to the management practices of indigenous peoples and local communities.[17] Many so-called pristine landscapes are in fact *cultural landscapes,* either created by humans or modified by human activity (such as natural forest management, cultivation, and the use of fire).

This is more than semantics. "Wild" and "wilderness" imply that these landscapes and resources are the result of "nature" and, as such, have no owners—they are the "common heritage of all humankind." This has come to mean that local communities have no tenurial or ownership rights, and, thus, their lands, territories, and resources are "free" to others just for the taking. This is why indigenous peoples have come to oppose the use of "wilderness" and "wild" to refer to the regions in which they now or once lived.

This is poignantly expressed in an Aboriginal Resolution from the 1995 Ecopolitics IX Conference, Darwin, Australia:[18]

The term 'wilderness' as it is popularly used, and related concepts as 'wild resources', "wild foods', etc., [are unacceptable]. These terms have connotations of *terra nullius* [empty or unowned land and resources] and, as such, all concerned people and organizations should look for alternative terminology which does not exclude Indigenous history and meaning.

Cultural landscapes and their links to conservation of biological diversity are now recognized under the 1972 UNESCO Convention Concerning the Protection of the World Cultural and Natural Heritage (The World Heritage Convention). A new category of World Heritage Site, the "Cultural Landscape," recognizes "the complex interrelationships between man and nature in the construction, formation and evolution of landscapes." The first cultural landscape World Heritage Site was Tongariro National Park, a sacred region for the Mäori people of New Zealand that was included in the World Heritage List because of its importance in Mäori beliefs.[19]

The Convention on Biological Diversity (CBD) is one of the major international forces in recognizing the role of indigenous and local communities in *in situ* conservation. The Preamble recognizes:

Close and traditional dependence of many indigenous and local communities embodying traditional lifestyles on biological resources, and the desirability of sharing equitably benefits arising from the use of traditional knowledge, innovations and practices relevant to the conservation of biological diversity and the sustainable use of its components.

Article 8(j) of the Convention on Biological Diversity spells out specific obligations of signatories:

Subject to its national legislation, respect, preserve and maintain knowledge, innovations and practices of indigenous and local communities embodying traditional lifestyles relevant for the conservation and sustainable use of biological diversity and promote the wider application with the approval and involvement of the holders of such knowledge, innovations and practices and encourage the equitable sharing of the benefits arising from the utilization of such knowledge, innovations and practices.

The CBD also enshrines the importance of customary practice in biodiversity conservation and calls for protection of and equitable benefit-sharing from the use and application of "traditional technologies" (articles 10.c and 18.4). W. Pereira and A. K. Gupta claim it is the traditional methods of research and application, not just particular pieces of knowledge that persist in a "tradition of invention and innovation."[20] Technological changes do not simply lead to modernization and loss of traditional practice, but rather provide additional input into vibrant, adaptive and adapting, holistic systems of management and conservation.

"Traditional knowledge, innovations and practices" are often referred to by scientists as Traditional Ecological Knowledge (TEK). TEK is far more than a simple compilation of facts.[21] It is the basis for local-level decision making in areas of contemporary life, including natural resource management, nutrition, food preparation, health, education, and community and social organization.[22] TEK is holistic, inherently dynamic, constantly evolving through experimentation and innovation, fresh insight, and external stimuli.[23] TEK is transmitted in many ways. Most is done through repeated practice—apprenticeship with elders and specialists.

Equity and Rights

Recognition by the CBD of the contributions of indigenous and traditional peoples to maintaining biological diversity may be a major political advance. But there are major dangers. Once TEK or genetic materials leave the societies in which they are embedded, there is little national protection and virtually no international laws to protect community knowledge, innovations, and practices. Many countries do not even recognize the basic right of indigenous peoples to exist— let alone grant them self-determination, land ownership, or control over their traditional resources.

The International Labour Organisation (ILO) Convention 169 is the only legally binding international instrument specifically intended to protect indigenous and tribal peoples. ILO 169 supports community ownership and local control of lands and resources. It does not, however, cover the numerous traditional and peasant groups that are also critical in conservation of the diversity of agricultural, medicinal, and nondomesticated resources. To date, the Convention has only 171 national signatories and provides little more than a baseline for debates on indigenous rights.[24]

The same bleak news comes from an analysis of Intellectual Property Rights (IPRs) laws. IPRs were established to protect individual inventions and inventors, not the collective, ancient folklore and TEK of indigenous and local communities. Even if IPRs were secured for communities, differential access to patents, copyright, know-how, and trade secret laws and lawyers would generally price them out of any effective registry, monitoring, or litigation using such instruments.[25] The following list summarizes how IPRs are considered inadequate and inappropriate for protecting the collective resources of indigenous and traditional peoples:

- recognize individual, not collective rights;
- require a specific act of "invention";
- simplify ownership regimes;
- stimulate commercialization;
- recognize only market values;
- are subject to economic powers and manipulation;
- are difficult to monitor and enforce;
- are expensive, complicated, time-consuming.

The World Trade Organization's General Agreement on Tariff and Trade (WTO/GATT) contains no explicit reference to the knowledge and genetic resources of traditional peoples, although it does provide for states to develop *sui generis* (specially generated) systems for plant protection (Trade-Related Aspects of Intellectual Property Rights article 27.c). Considerable intellectual energy is now being poured by governments and by nongovernment and peoples' organizations into defining what new, alternative models of protection would include.[26] There is skepticism, however, that this *sui generis* option will be adequate to provide any significant alternatives to existing IPRs.

One glimmer of hope comes from the CBD's decision to implement an "intersessional process" to evaluate the inadequacies of IPRs and develop guidelines and principles for governments seeking advice on access and transfer legislation to protect traditional communities.[27]

This provides exciting opportunities for many countries and peoples to engage in a historic debate. Up to now, United Nations agencies have been reluctant to discuss "integrated systems of rights" that link environment, trade, and human rights. However, agreements between the CBD, FAO (Food and Agriculture Organization of the UN), and WTO now guarantee broad consultations on *sui generis* systems and community intellectual property rights (CIPRs) between the World Intellectual Property Organisation (WIPO), United Nations Education and Scientific Organisation (UNESCO), United Nations Environment Programme (UNEP), United Nations Development Programme (UNDP), United Nations Commission on Trade and Development (UNCTAD), International Labour Organisation (ILO), the Geneva Human Rights Centre, and others. It will take the creative and imaginative input of all these groups—and many more—to solve the complicated challenge of devising new systems of national and international laws that support and enhance cultural and biological diversity.

Many of the principles of *sui generis* systems of rights have already been established in international conventions like the CBD and ILO 169, as well as major human rights agreements such as the International Covenant on Civil and Political Rights (ICCPR), the International Covenant on Economic, Social and Cultural Rights (ICESCR), and, of course, the Universal Declaration of Human Rights (UDHR).[28]

For indigenous peoples, the Draft Declaration of Rights of Indigenous Peoples (DDRIP) is the most important statement of basic requirements for adequate rights and protection. DDRIP took nearly two decades to develop by hundreds of indigenous representatives to the UN Working Group on Indigenous Populations of the Geneva Human Rights Centre. It is broad-ranging, thorough, and reflects one of the most transparent and democratic processes yet to be seen in the United Nations. The process itself and many of the principles established will undoubtedly serve as models for traditional societies and local communities seeking greater recognition of rights. Some of the principles affirmed by the DDRIP are as follows:

- Right to self-determination, representation, and full participation.
- Recognition of existing treaty arrangements with indigenous peoples.
- Right to determine own citizenry and obligations of citizenship.

- Right to collective, as well as individual, human rights.
- Right to live in freedom, peace, and security without military intervention or involvement
- Right to religious freedom and protection of sacred sites and objects, including ecosystems, plants, and animals.
- Right to restitution and redress for cultural, intellectual, religious, or spiritual property that is taken or used without authorization.
- Right to free and informed consent (prior informed consent).
- Right to control access and exert ownership over plants, animals, and minerals vital to their cultures.
- Right to own, develop, control, and use the lands and territories, including the total environment of the lands, air, waters, coastal seas, sea ice, flora and fauna, and other resources which they have traditionally owned or otherwise occupied or used.
- Right to special measures to control, develop, and protect their sciences, technologies, and cultural manifestations, including human and other genetic resources, seeds, medicines, knowledge of the properties of fauna and flora, oral traditions, literatures, designs, and visual and performing arts.
- Right to just and fair compensation for any such activities that have adverse environmental, economic, social, cultural, or spiritual impact.

Although international efforts to recognize indigenous, traditional, and local communities are welcome and positive, they are pitted against enormous economic and market forces that propel globalization of trade. Critiques of globalization are numerous[29] and point to at least two major shortcomings: 1) value is imputed to information and resources only when they enter external markets; and 2) expenditures do not reflect actual environmental and social costs. This means that existing values recognized by local communities are ignored, despite knowledge that local biodiversity provides essential elements for survival (food, shelter, medicine, etc.). It also means that the knowledge and managed resources of indigenous and traditional peoples are ascribed no value and assumed to be free for the taking. This has been called "intellectual *terra nullius*" after the concept of empty land that allowed colonial powers to expropriate "discovered" land for their empires. Corporations and states still defend this morally vacuous concept because it facilitates the "biopiracy" of local folk varieties of crops, traditional medicines, and useful species.

Even scientists have been accomplices to such raids by publishing data they know will be catapulted into the public domain and gleaned by "bioprospectors" seeking new products. They have also perpetuated the "intellectual *terra nullius*" concept by declaring useful local plants as "wild" and entire ecosystems as "wildernesses," often despite knowing that these have been molded, managed, and protected by human populations for millennia. It is also common for scientists to declare areas and resources "wild" through ignorance—or negligence—without even basic investigations into archaeological or historical records, or to actual human management practices. The result is to declare the biodiversity of a site as "natural," thereby transferring it to the public domain. Once public, communities are stripped of all rights to their traditional resources.

It is little wonder then, that indigenous groups in the Pacific region have declared a moratorium on all scientific research until protection of traditional knowledge and genetic resources can be guaranteed to local communities by scientists. The moratorium movement began with the 1993 Mataatua Declaration (clause 2.8):

> A moratorium on any further commercialisation of indigenous medicinal plants and human genetic materials must be declared until indigenous communities have developed appropriate protection mechanisms.

The Mataatua Declaration, in turn, influenced the Final Statement of the 1995 Consultation on Indigenous Peoples' Knowledge and Intellectual Property Rights in Suva, Fiji:

> Call for a moratorium on bioprospecting in the Pacific and urge indigenous peoples not to co-operate in bioprospecting activities until appropriate protection mechanisms are in place:
> Bioprospecting as a term needs to be clearly defined to exclude indigenous peoples' customary harvesting practices.
> Assert that in situ conservation by indigenous peoples is the best method to conserve and protect biological diversity and indigenous knowledge, and encourage its implementation by indigenous communities and all relevant bodies.
> Encourage indigenous peoples to maintain and expand our knowledge of local biological resources.

To allay these deep concerns, many scientific and professional organizations are developing their own Codes of Conduct and Standards of Practice to guide research and health, educational, and conservation projects with indigenous and local communities.[30]

One of the most extensive is that of the International Society for Ethnobiology, which undertook a ten-year consultation with indigenous and traditional peoples—as well as its extensive international membership—to establish "principles for equitable partnerships." The main objective of the process was to establish terms under which collaboration and joint research between ethnobiologists and communities could proceed based upon trust, transparency, and mutual concerns, according to these principles:

1. *Principle of Prior Rights.* This principle recognizes that indigenous peoples, traditional societies, and local communities have prior, proprietary rights and interests over all air, land, and waterways, and the natural resources within them that these peoples have traditionally inhabited or used, together with all knowledge and intellectual property and traditional resource rights associated with such resources and their use.

2. *Principle of Self-Determination.* This principle recognizes that indigenous peoples, traditional societies, and local communities have a right to self determination (or local determination for traditional and local communities) and that researchers and associated organizations will acknowledge and respect such rights in their dealings with these peoples and their communities.

3. *Principle of Inalienability.* This principle recognizes the inalienable rights of indigenous peoples, traditional societies, and local communities in relation to their traditional territories and the natural resources within them and associated traditional knowledge. These rights are collective by nature but can include individual rights. It shall be for indigenous peoples, traditional societies and local communities to determine for themselves the nature and scope of their respective resource rights regimes.

4. *Principle of Traditional Guardianship.* This principle recognizes the holistic interconnectedness of humanity with the ecosystems of our Sacred Earth and the obligation and re-

sponsibility of indigenous peoples, traditional societies, and local communities to preserve and maintain their role as traditional guardians of these ecosystems through the maintenance of their cultures, mythologies, spiritual beliefs and customary practices.

5. *Principle of Active Participation.* This principle recognizes the crucial importance of indigenous peoples, traditional societies, and local communities to actively participate in all phases of the project from inception to completion, as well as in application of research results.

6. *Principle of Full Disclosure.* This principle recognizes that indigenous peoples, traditional societies, and local communities are entitled to be fully informed about the nature, scope, and ultimate purpose of the proposed research (including methodology, data collection, and the dissemination and application of results). This information is to be given in a manner that takes into consideration and actively engages with the body of knowledge and cultural preferences of these peoples and communities.

7. *Principle of Prior Informed Consent and Veto.* This principle recognizes that the prior informed consent of all peoples and their communities must be obtained before any research is undertaken. Indigenous peoples, traditional societies, and local communities have the right to veto any program, project, or study that affects them. Providing prior informed consent presumes that all potentially affected communities will be provided complete information regarding the purpose and nature of the research activities and the probable results, including all reasonably foreseeable benefits and risks of harm (be they tangible or intangible) to the affected communities.

8. *Principle of Confidentiality.* This principle recognizes that indigenous peoples, traditional societies, and local communities, at their sole discretion, have the right to exclude from publication and/or to have kept confidential any information concerning their culture, traditions, mythologies, or spiritual beliefs. Furthermore, such confidentiality shall be guaranteed by researchers and other potential users. Indigenous and traditional peoples also have the right to privacy and anonymity.

9. *Principle of Respect.* This principle recognizes the necessity

for researchers to respect the integrity, morality, and spirituality of the culture, traditions and relationships of indigenous peoples, traditional societies, and local communities with their worlds, and to avoid the imposition of external conceptions and standards.

10. *Principle of Active Protection.* This principles recognizes the importance of researchers taking active measures to protect and to enhance the relationships of indigenous peoples, traditional societies, and local communities with their environment and thereby promote the maintenance of cultural and biological diversity.

11. *Principle of Precaution.* This principle acknowledges the complexity of interactions between cultural and biological communities, and thus the inherent uncertainty of effects due to ethnobiological and other research. The Precautionary Principle advocates taking proactive, anticipatory action to identify and to prevent biological or cultural harms resulting from research activities or outcomes, even if cause-and-effect relationships have not yet been scientifically proven. The prediction and assessment of such biological and cultural harms must include local criteria and indicators, thus must fully involve indigenous peoples, traditional societies, and local communities.

12. *Principle of Compensation and Equitable Sharing.* This principle recognizes that indigenous peoples, traditional societies, and local communities must be fairly and adequately compensated for their contribution to ethnobiological research activities and outcomes involving their knowledge.

13. *Principle of Supporting Indigenous Research.* This principle recognizes, supports, and prioritizes the efforts of indigenous peoples, traditional societies, and local communities in undertaking their own research and publications and in utilizing their own collections and data bases.

14. *Principle of the Dynamic Interactive Cycle.* This principle holds that research activities should not be initiated unless there is reasonable assurance that all stages of the project can be completed from (a) preparation and evaluation, to (b) full implementation, to (c) evaluation, dissemination, and return of results to the communities, to (d) training and education as

an integral part of the project, including practical application of results. Thus, all projects must be seen as *cycles of continuous and on-going dialogue.*

15. *Principle of Restitution.* This principle recognizes that every effort will be made to avoid any adverse consequences to indigenous peoples, traditional societies, and local communities from research activities and outcomes and that, should any such adverse consequence occur, appropriate restitution shall be made.

Conclusions

Increases in bioprospecting for new products using traditional knowledge and genetic resources, combined with heightened awareness by indigenous and local communities of how their resources are being exploited, has provoked something of a global ethical crisis. Commodification of what are collective resources—often of a secret or sacred nature—is not only an expression of disrespect for local culture, but a violation of religious principles and human rights. The "decontextualization" of the "components" of biodiversity or culture results in the unauthorized extraction of inalienable information and materials. This ignores the "sacred balance" between all life and violates the kinship relationships that indigenous and traditional peoples maintain with their "extended family" of all living things. Outsiders have also ignored the historical impacts of communities upon ecosystems, forgetting that the "wild" landscapes and resources actually belong to the peoples who have managed and conserved them.

There are some admirable efforts in international processes, such as the implementation of the Convention on Biological Diversity and ILO 169, but there is now general agreement that new and additional instruments will be necessary to adequately protect traditional ecological and medical knowledge systems. It is unclear how these *sui generis* systems will emerge, but concerned scientists and professionals must not await a political solution. Codes of Conduct and Standards of Practice are needed now to counter the growing distrust and animosity that indigenous and local peoples are showing to research and conservation efforts.

Notes

1. See Kofi Asare Opoku, *West African Traditional Religion* (Lagos: FEP International Pvt., K.A., 1978).

2. See Stephen Hugh-Jones, *From the Milk River: Spatial and Temporal Processes in Northwest Amazonia* (Cambridge: Cambridge University Press, 1979).

3. From James Galarrwuy Yunupingu, as quoted from the Australian Catholic Social Justice Council's "Recognition: The Way Forward," in *Native Title Report: January–June 1994* (Aboriginal and Torres Strait Islander Social Justice Commissioner, Canberra, Australian Government Publishing Service, 1995).

4. See L. A. Whitt, "Metaphor and Power in Indigenous and Western Knowledge Systems," in *Cultural and Spiritual Values of Biodiversity,* ed. Darrell Addison Posey (London: UNEP/Intermediate Technology, 2000), 69–72.

5. See Dobkin de Rios, *Visionary Vine: Psychedelic Healing in the Peruvian Amazon* (San Francisco: Chandler Publications for Health Sciences, 1972).

6. Taken from David Suzuki and Peter Knudtson, *Wisdom of the Elders: Honoring Sacred Visions of Nature* (London: Bantam Press, 1992).

7. See Marilyn Strathern, "Potential Property: Intellectual Rights and Property in Persons," *Social Anthropology* 4, no. 1 (1996): 17–32.

8. The complete text and analysis of this myth is found in Darrell Addison Posey, "The Journey of a Kayapó Shaman," *Journal of Latin American Indian Literatures* 6, no. 3 (1982): 13–19.

9. See Darrell Addison Posey and Elaine Elisabetsky, "Conceitos de Animais e seus Espíritos em Relação a Doenças e Curas entre Os Indios Kayapó da Aldeia Gorotire, Pará," *Boletim do Museu Paraense Emílio Goeldi* (Belém, Pará) 7, no. 1 (1991): 21–36.

10. See Elaine Elisabetsky and Darrell Posey, "Use of Contraceptive and Related Plants by the Kayapó Indians (Brazil)," *Journal of Ethnopharmacology* 26 (1989): 299–316.

11. See R. Sultan, D. Craig, and H. Ross, "Aboriginal Joint Management of Australian National Parks: Uluru-kata Tjuta, in Darrell Posey and Graham Dutfield, *Indigenous Peoples and Sustainability: Cases and Actions* (Utrecht: IUCN and International Books, 1997), 326–38.

12. See Darrell Addison Posey, "Indigenous Management of Tropical Forest Ecosystems: The Case of the Kayapó Indians of the Brazilian Amazon," *Agroforestry Systems* 3 (1985): 139–58.

13. See J. Matowanyika, "Resource Management and the Shona People in Rural Zimbabwe," in Posey and Dutfield, *Indigenous Peoples and Sustainability,* 257–66.

14. For details, see S. Laird, "Forests, Culture, and Conservation," in *Cultural and Spiritual Values of Biodiversity,* ed. Posey, 347–58.

15. See Pei Shengji, "Managing for Biological Diversity Conservation in Temple Yards and Holy Hills: The Traditional Practices of the Xishuangbanna Dai Community, Southwest China," in *Ethics, Religion and Biodiversity,* ed. Lawrence S. Hamilton (Cambridge: White Horse Press, 1993).

16. See V. D. Vartak and Madhav Gadgil, "Studies on Sacred Groves along Western Ghats from Maharashtra and Goa: Role of Beliefs and Folklores," in *Glimpses of*

Indian Ethnobiology, ed. S. K. Jain (New Delhi: Oxford University Press and IBH, 1981), 272–78.

17. For example, see W. M. Denevan, "The Pristine Myth: The Landscape of the Americas in 1492," *Annals of the Association of American Geographers* 82 (1992): 369–85; and A. Gomez-Pompa and A. Kaus, "Taming the Wilderness Myth," *Bio-Science* 42, no. 4 (1992): 271–79.

18. See Northern Land Council, *Ecopolitics IX: Perspectives on Indigenous Peoples' Management of Environmental Resources* (Casuarina: NLC, 1996).

19. See M. Rössler, "Tongariro: First Cultural Landscape on the World Heritage List," *World Heritage Newsletter* 4 (1993): 15.

20. See W. Pereira and A. K. Gupta, "A Dialogue on Indigenous Knowledge," *Honey Bee* 4 (1993): 6–10.

21. See M. Gadgil, F. Berkes, and C. Folke, "Indigenous Knowledge for Biodiversity Conservation," *Ambio* 22 (1993): 151–56.

22. See *The Cultural Dimension of Development: Indigenous Knowledge Systems,* ed. D. Michael Warren, L. Jan Slikkerveer, and David Brokensha (London: Intermediate Technology Publications, 1995).

23. From Suzuki and Knudtson, *Wisdom of the Elders.*

24. See R. L. Barsh, "An Advocate's Guide to the Convention on Indigenous and Tribal Peoples," *Oklahoma City University Law Review* 15 (1990): 209–53.

25. For details, see Darrell Addison Posey and Graham Dutfield, *Beyond Intellectual Property: Toward Traditional Resource Rights for Indigenous Peoples and Local Communities* (Ottawa: International Development Research Centre, 1996).

26. See D. Leskien and M. Flitner, "Intellectual Property Rights and Plant Genetic Resources: Options for a *Sui Generis* System," *Issues in Genetic Resources,* no. 6 (Rome: International Plant Genetic Resources Institute [IPGRI], 1997).

27. See UNEP, *The Biodiversity Agenda: Decisions from the Third Meeting of the Conference of the Parties to the Convention on Biological Diversity,* Buenos Aires, Argentina, November 1996 (UNEP/CBD/97/1, 1997).

28. See *Intellectual Property Rights for Indigenous Peoples: A Sourcebook,* ed. Tom Greaves (Oklahoma City: Society for Applied Anthropology, 1994); *Voices of the Earth: Indigenous Peoples, New Partners and the Right to Self-determination in Practice,* ed. Leo van der Vlist (Amsterdam: Netherlands Centre for Indigenous Peoples, 1994); and Posey and Dutfield, *Beyond Intellectual Property.*

29. For example, see David C. Korten, *When Corporations Rule the World* (London: Earthscan, 1995).

30. A summary of some of these can be found in A. B. Cunningham, *Ethics, Ethnobiological Research, and Biodiversity* (Gland, Switzerland: WWF/UNESCO/ Kew People and Plants Initiative, WWF International, 1993); and Posey and Dutfield, *Beyond Intellectual Property.*

Contextualizing the Environmental Struggle

TOM GREAVES

About four centuries ago the peoples of North America were confronted with European intruders who soon initiated an implacable campaign for hegemony over the land and over the lifeway that would be practiced on it. By 1900 the continent's peoples had been reduced to enclaves surrounded by a powerful and controlling Euro-American society, a situation that has become even more true today.

The four-hundred-year conflict between North America's Aboriginal peoples and the newcomers has transited various critical stages, and today the long struggle of the surviving indigenous peoples has reached yet another. Today's vigorous entrepreneurial capitalism does not overlook our surviving indigenous neighbors. Whereas the dominant nineteenth- and twentieth-century practice of Euro-Americans was to treat indigenous groups as nuisances, to push them out into backwater areas where they were expected to whither away, the trend now is to mine the native communities for assets to be commercialized. Whether it is land that can be taken, or water that can be diverted, or mineral resources that can be removed, or timber that can be cut, or religious symbols that can be appropriated, or pharmacological remedies that can be bottled, or treaty rights that can be cheapened, or cell lines that can be patented—wherever indigenous societies have something valued by individuals in the surrounding, dominant society, trenchant struggle is likely to flare.

The papers of this volume explore one of the cultural domains of contemporary native groups—the cosmology of cultural beliefs concerning themselves, ultimate meaning, and the natural world around them. Long dismissing these ideas as primitive, quaint, and wrong, now the dominant society wonders if they contain elements of value. At a time when spiritualist experimentation within the dominant society is strong, do indigenous healers and religions harbor some mystical truth? Do native healers "know" wider realities that the empiricist dominant society has overlooked? Other questions are more pragmatic: do the native societies have techniques the larger society could adopt that would result in less damage to the environment? Does the folk medicine of native societies contain bioactive compounds that might produce new drugs?

The primary intent of this chapter is to place the present dialogue about indigenous spirituality and ecology into its larger context of struggle. Today, indigenous groups in North America are grappling with the powerful societies that surround them, seeking to regain lost territories and rights, to be compensated for illegal deprivations, and to regain some control over their cultural futures. This is the larger arena in which religion and ecology discussions are taking place. In this chapter I will identify and describe five major "theaters of struggle" that help us sense the range of conflicts currently in play. In the process two points should become clear: indigenous societies are mobilized on many different fronts; and the new points of leverage available to indigenous groups have resulted in some astonishing gains. In the interest of coherence, this short chapter will draw examples only from North America, but we need to recognize that the contemporary struggle of indigenous peoples is now actively waged on every continent.

Contemporary indigenous struggle, whether in North America or elsewhere, is framed by certain ruling realities. The indigenous society is numerically small, the surrounding society is numerically large. The indigenous society is politically weak and economically poor, the surrounding society is politically strong and economically wealthy. The indigenous society is a survivor of actual or de facto conquest, the surrounding society produced that conquest. The surrounding society nourishes an underlying view that the indigenous society is intrinsically inferior, a supposition the indigenous society cannot materially change. One might theorize why this set of factors goes together, but my purpose here is not political theory. Instead, it is to observe that, although these factors dictate that their struggle is never over, that indigenous societies can never relax, this reality does *not* mean that their efforts to survive as culturally distinct peoples will end in defeat.

The late twentieth century has witnessed a series of striking indigenous successes, some of them astonishing. There also have been dismal setbacks, of course, and one cannot allow a focus on the recent successes to imply that, globally, indigenous peoples are not under desperate threat. They are. Examining the successes, however, will enable us to see what is working, and why, and to disseminate those findings to those who need them most: other indigenous groups facing similar threats. These pages will attempt to take stock of five major "theaters" of this struggle: 1) recovery of economic rights, 2) sovereignty, 3) management of intellectual and cultural property, 4) sacred and traditional meanings, and 5) efforts to gain control over indigenous cultural futures. Cosmological, spiritual, and ecological dimensions play more important roles in some than in others, but they are present at least to some degree in each. My approach for each theater is to indicate briefly some current North American examples and then to discuss one illustrative case that offers important lessons.

Theater 1: Economic Rights

With only a few exceptions, indigenous societies are poor. By "poor" I mean, of course, lacking money or transferable goods of market value. One could argue that the San, African hunter-gatherers studied by Richard Lee, had leisure time, enough to eat, and enjoyed life, so how could they be poor? Yet, the San themselves are under intense siege by the Botswana government and others,[1] and to fight effectively they need the other kind of wealth. Faxes cost money, telephone calls cost money, travel costs money, building solidarity across camp groups costs money. Although the San may be "wealthy," when it comes to struggle, the kind of wealth that buys leverage in market economies is in short supply.

A number of indigenous groups are starting to control significant amounts of transferable wealth. Certain American Indian groups have cash income from casinos. Brazil's Kayapó have their gold mines.[2] There appears to be a slow, uneven turnaround in the fortunes of the Alaskan Native corporations established under the Alaska Native

Claims Settlement Act of 1971.[3] In Canada and the United States, cash settlements to resolve land claims are up. Of course, all of these new income streams entail costs and disruptive consequences, some of them very high; but where cash is in hand, it is a key weapon of resistance. While most indigenous groups remain dirt poor, largely cashless, and very much in jeopardy, significant monetary resources are coming to some members of the indigenous world and, in terms of their struggle, making a difference.

To cite any one of various instances where a tribal group has come into great wealth would not be difficult. However, the case I would like to discuss here does not involve fabulous income. Instead, it speaks to the ability of a tribal group to entrench its rights more firmly, now and in the future, to particular, usually modest, streams of income. Consider the fifteen tribes of Puget Sound in the state of Washington. In 1974, responding to a determined campaign of Indian civil disobedience and a determination to force the state of Washington and its Euro-American citizenry to recognize their treaty guarantees, a federal judge ruled that the tribes were entitled to 50 percent of the main salmon species in Puget Sound.[4] Known as the Boldt decision, the resulting process of enforcing this entitlement has been very painful, sometimes violent, and never easy. Nonetheless, the treaty tribes have progressively buttressed this economic right, becoming prominent stakeholders who, along with other elements of the fishing industry, are actively intervening to constrain water diversion projects, clearcut timbering, and stream pollution in river headwaters where fish spawn and regenerate. Their struggle following the Boldt decision has been as protracted and difficult as the one that preceded it, but by insisting on their treaty guarantees they have regained a key share of a central economic resource.[5]

1974 is hardly current. What has been happening more recently? In 1994 these tribes succeeded in extending those treaty rights to shellfish (such as clams and crabs) harvested from saltwater beaches and tide flats. This is the Rafeedie decision, the case pitting the tribes against something even more formidable than commercial and sports fishermen: the sanctity of private property. By 1855 incoming whites had so overwhelmed the local tribal groups that the territorial government of Washington was able to impose treaties that forced the Puget Sound tribes onto small reservations and ceded most of the Puget Sound shoreline to the state. Later, the state of Washington issued deeds and sold off the Puget Sound shoreline to private ownership. The state failed to inform new owners that the 1855 treaties guaranteed the tribes' right to collect fish [and, by extension, shellfish] "in usual and accustomed grounds and stations" forever.[6] Though ignored and then forgotten by the state, the right to shellfish collection was never legally terminated. Over the years shore lands were divided, sold, and resold, with the assumption that deeds, including the beaches and all land exposed at low tide, conveyed unencumbered rights of ownership.

The tribes pointed out to the Rafeedie court that their right to collect shellfish had never been ceded or extinguished. Therefore, they argued, the treaty right remains and beachfront property owners cannot claim trespass or prevent members of treaty tribes from entering their beach areas and harvesting clams and crabs. Judge Rafeedie, building on the Boldt decision of twenty years earlier, assigned rights to 50 percent of the annual shellfish harvest to Indians.[7] Like Boldt, the Rafeedie decision generated tensions, denunciations and threats of violence, but the decision is slowly taking hold. The import of Boldt and Rafeedie, and other subsidiary judicial decisions, is that the fifteen Puget Sound tribes have reconsolidated their hold on a significant economic asset by astutely and diligently pursuing long-ignored treaty guarantees in federal court. Recently, hunting rights in publicly owned forests have also been affirmed.[8] Assuring an economic basis with cash income strengthens the tribes' capacity to assert their rights and gives them greater opportunity to pick their battles.

Theater 2: Sovereignty

In 1994 I participated in a seminar in which high government trade officials and economists enthusiastically proclaimed the arrival of the global economy, the maturation of the multinational entities such as the European Union, and the relegation of mere national governments to a residual and marginal status. It struck me forcefully that sovereignty was missing from their calculations. To those international and business economists, sovereignty may seem like a nineteenth-century anachronism, but among large sectors of the world's population, sovereignty is very much a twentieth- and twenty-first-century value. One is reminded of the Panamanian sovereignty demands that led to the handing over of the Panama Canal, of Quebec secessionists threatening to split what remained of Canada into two nonadjacent pieces, and of the resilience of the impassioned political arguments raised against the ratification of the North American Free Trade Agreement (NAFTA). One is also reminded of the hair-trigger sensitivity with which every Latin American country responds to any appearance of intrusion into internal affairs by the "Giant of the North."[9] The consequences of globalization may challenge sentiments of sovereignty and national hubris, but the reverse is at least equally true.

Despite the deprivations and impoverishment that North American indigenous groups face, protecting and enhancing sovereignty is clearly the single greatest priority of American Indian leaders. Their ability to exercise some control over their cultural and economic futures as distinct peoples intimately depends on sovereignty. In the United States Indian reservations are legally known as "Indian Country," a legally defined area within which a distinctive set of federal laws and intergovernmental relationships apply.[10] Since the Marshall Supreme Court decision of 1831, American Indians have been operating on the principle of "dependent sovereignties," a status of limited sovereignty that can be altered by action of the federal government but not by state governments.[11] In the years since 1831, American Indian groups have periodically sought to defend and expand their prerogatives, and their campaign has taken on central importance in the last two decades.[12]

A perennial battlefield for sovereignty is the on-reservation sales of gasoline and tobacco products. The surrounding states cannot impose their excise taxes directly on these sales. To state governments and shop owners near reservations, it seems grossly unfair that on-reservation "smoke shops" sell untaxed products to non-Indian customers without paying the heavy state excise taxes they themselves must pay.[13] In one highly visible instance of this struggle, newly elected New York governor George Pataki undertook a highly publicized campaign in 1997 to force wholesalers to add the retail sales tax to cigarettes before selling them to retailers on Indian reservations. Indian nations vigorously resisted. Once the legal and political complexities began to become evident, Governor Pataki abruptly abandoned the effort.[14] Meanwhile, other U.S. states, and Canada, are waging similar battles.[15]

Other recent examples of the sovereignty issue include struggles over the repatriation of human remains, the blockade by New Mexico and Washington of the delivery of slot machines and other gambling equipment to Indian casinos, the threats and counterthreats over the plan by the Coeur d'Alenes in Idaho to open an internet-based national lottery, the United States Senate battle to impose means-testing on the allocation of federal supports to reservations, and many more.[16] The case I want to look at in more detail, however, is the development, under the 1988 Indian Gaming Regulatory Act (IGRA), of the now extensive Indian casino industry in the United States.

At bottom, the 1988 Indian Gaming Regulatory Act (IGRA) was a legislative effort at damage control. Nine years earlier, the United States Supreme Court decided that the state of Florida did not have the authority to regulate a bingo parlor on the Seminole reservation. Then, in 1987 the United States Supreme Court had affirmed that the State of California could not stop a tiny tribe, the Cabazon Band of Mission Indians, from offering commercial gambling on its reservation, despite the fact that the same games were illegal under California law. With this decision casinos on Indian reservations became legally unstoppable. The United States Congress responded by writing a law that sought to establish a workable framework to deal with a politically explosive situation. With IGRA, Congress established a "compacting process" in which tribes wishing to go into high stakes commercial gambling would have to work together with the *state governor's* representatives to arrive at a compact that would be agreeable to both sides. In the usual case, these agreements covered what games will be allowed, the size of table stakes, the hours and days of operation, payments by the tribe's casino to cover such costs as road improvements, traffic control, auditing, monitoring, background checks for employees, and, in most cases, revenue sharing.

As the 1988 law was being drafted, American Indian leaders were profoundly divided, precisely over the issue of sovereignty. For the first time, the federal law mandated a negotiation process with state governments, giving the state government power over the outcome of a tribal government initiative. Heretofore, most tribes' officers dealt only with the federal government and, although having to accept the fact that the United States federal government had more powerful cards in its hand than the tribe, relations were still cast as "government to government" (nation to nation) relations, as they were when treaties were the vehicles of diplomacy. The 1988 law put tribes in a position where, from their point of view, in order to open casinos they had to deal with state governments. Because states are subsidiary governmental units, the implication was that the tribes' sovereignty was similarly demoted. Further, agreeing to accept the state's coauthority over on-reservation activities in this case would not only bring the state's regulatory apparatus onto the reservation but, they feared, would encourage Congress to make the state a regular player in future tribal affairs.[17] Juxtaposing sovereignty and the lure of casino benefits has been an agonizing choice.[18]

Tribal decisions over whether to proceed with casinos have largely been made in favor of casinos. About one-third of federally recognized tribes in the United States have built casinos, located in about thirty states.[19] The lure of economic benefits in the form of tribal and individual income, jobs and job training, and simply having a reservation business enterprise that Whites envy, has been too great. In several tribes, notably the Mohawk and the Navajo, feelings about the compromises to sovereignty have run very high. The largest Indian-owned newspaper, *Indian Country Today,* has opposed casinos on sovereignty grounds, although its opposition has been more muted in recent years. The struggle to defend and enhance sovereignty is, of course, a perpetual one, figuring in countless decisions and programs on every tribal agenda. For casino tribes, the battle now shifts to insulating the casino industry from further intrusions of state governments into tribal affairs.[20]

Theater 3: Intellectual and Cultural Property

What Darrell Posey and Graham Dutfield have usefully called "traditional resource rights"[21] covers a very large domain of political resistance, the goal being to control the appropriation and uses of cultural information and products of that information. The cultural information at risk includes religious beliefs and practices, ethnobotanical knowledge, knowledge of resources and localities within indigenous lands, traditional designs and symbols, and folklore—in short, all cultural knowledge that has the potential for commercial use. Some of the many examples of its appropriation include the commercialization of traditional crops and botanical wild products, the use of traditional symbols and practices in distasteful commercial ways, and sports mascots using tribal names or referring to Indians in general.[22] The largest factor in stimulating these concerns is what we might call "millennial capitalism," an extreme form of capitalist activity in the late twentieth

century, paired with the view that aggressive and unrestrained entrepreneurial greed is to be admired above practically everything else.[23]
In the global scramble for profit, indigenous societies are attractive
hunting grounds.

When the city of Phoenix wants to build a freeway right through
Petroglyph National Monument in order to serve developers waiting
to build suburbs on the other side, that's millennial capitalism.[24] When
tour groups bring camera-snapping tourists into remote regions, that's
millennial capitalism. When hunting companies helicopter private hunters into remote hunting lands, or simply enable them to shoot from the
air, that's millennial capitalism. When perhaps the most well-known
professional football corporation in America insists on using a team
name based on the skin color of American Indians, that's millennial
capitalism. When a charlatan seeks insight into American Indian religious ceremonies and then, a few weeks later, goes into business offering "authentic" Indian sweat ceremonies for a fee, that's millennial
capitalism. When corporations obtain the blue corn seed developed
and preserved by Pueblo cultivators for centuries, and then establish
large commercial farms to supply blue corn snack chips, that's millennial capitalism.[25] And when a company in Brooklyn names a cheap,
fortified beer after the authentic American Indian hero, Crazy Horse,
whose descendants live today, that's millennial capitalism. In this section
I take up the case of Crazy Horse Malt Liquor.

In 1991 Ferolito, Vultaggio, and Sons of Brooklyn introduced "The
Original Crazy Horse Malt Liquor." Malt liquors are fortified beers, in
this case with an alcohol content of about 6 percent. Crazy Horse Malt
Liquor is sold in large, forty-ounce bottles that, together with several
competing brands, can be purchased for a few dollars at urban convenience stores and bodegas. Crazy Horse Malt Liquor is a commercial success, having reportedly sold one million cases in its first year.
It is now available in about forty states.[26]

The objection to this product is that Crazy Horse (the English-
language name for Tasunke Witko) was a real individual, a member of
a lineage whose third-generation descendants live today on the Pine
Ridge, Cheyenne River, and Rosebud Sioux reservations of South
Dakota. Crazy Horse was an authentic American Indian military hero.
A Teton Oglala Sioux, Crazy Horse attracted a formidable group of
warrior followers in the 1860s and 1870s who recognized his gifts of
military prowess, personal bravery, leadership, and wisdom. The high

point came in the 1876 Battle of Little Big Horn ("Custer's last stand"), the greatest United States military defeat in the western Indian wars. Crazy Horse was one of the three or four principal Indian commanders at the battle. Afterward, Crazy Horse and his followers moved to the north, seeking to evade the vengeful army attacks that were sure to come. That winter his band was located by army troops, routed into the snow, and their horses, supplies, lodges, and food were destroyed behind them. When the winter ended, his band depleted and weakened by frostbite, sickness, and famine, Crazy Horse elected to surrender at Fort Robinson, Nebraska. Four months later he was murdered. Crazy Horse was more than a military figure; he was a sage and a spiritual leader who, ironically, is said to have counseled against alcohol, an evil that would bring the destruction of Indian nations.

The name Crazy Horse has been used by outside commercial interests before. My check of the internet turned up numerous cafés, strip clubs, venders of adult products, shoe and boot venders, and art galleries using his name. The descendants saw the malt liquor, however, to be an affront to the name of a family and cultural hero that was national in scope. Indeed, they argued, the product name could falsely imply that the family or the tribe endorsed the product. Accordingly, they launched a campaign to stop the marketing of Crazy Horse Malt Liquor. They requested the brewers change the name. They challenged the federal alcoholic beverage permit. They got Congress and President Bush to enact a law banning the use of the name on any alcohol-bearing product, a law that was promptly overturned in the courts a year later. They and their allies campaigned in various states to ban its sale, with some success in Nebraska, California, Washington, and Minnesota. The Minnesota law, which banned in-state sales of the brand, was subsequently overturned as unconstitutional infringement on free speech—in this case, commercial free speech. The court ruled that malt liquor called Crazy Horse might be offensive, but that being offensive was not illegal. To date, the campaign to stop the product in the courts of the dominant society has had little success.[27]

The descendants have also pursued another course. They have launched a suit in the Rosebud Sioux tribal courts. This strategy rests on the practice of comity, within which courts of one sovereign entity try to honor the judgments of another in civil matters. United States courts have accorded comity to tribal court decisions on occasion, but the practice remains unpredictable.[28] The malt liquor case's path through the tribal court system has itself been full of complexities, and at this writing remains unresolved.

The lessons of Crazy Horse Malt Liquor are twofold. First, in the era of millennial capitalism, indigenous peoples are ready to oppose the appropriation by outside organizations of certain examples of intellectual and cultural heritages, and to do this tenaciously. Second, the case illustrates the frustrating impediments tribes encounter when they must fight on the institutional home ground of the dominant society: the advantage goes to their opponents.

Theater 4: Sacred and Traditional Meanings

A fourth theater of struggle is the effort by indigenous groups to protect sacred sites and to recoup sacred objects. As will be apparent, an important outcome of these activities is cultural renewal. A very recent example is the hard-won victory of the Makah of Washington State's Pacific shore to renew traditional hunts for gray whales. The Makah, who are experiencing rapid change, see whaling as a lost, core cultural activity that is now needed more than ever if the integrity of Makah culture is to be maintained. The worldwide ban on whaling had put this activity out of reach, but in 1997, with the support of the United States government, the Makahs received permission for up to four whales a year.[29] We see the same drive to renew indigenous cultures elsewhere: the repatriation of archaeological burial remains; the thwarting of the sale of stolen religious art (e.g., the Chilkat Whale House panels and the Zuni's sacred *ayhudas*); the flow of historical and sacred objects returned to tribal groups (e.g., Sitting Bull's necklace, Navajo Yei Jish, wampum belts returned to New York State tribes, the repatriation from London to South Dakota of the remains of Chief Long Wolf, veteran of the battle with Custer); and the proliferation of tribal museums—all show a fierce determination to recover material objects associated with cultural histories. These objects serve to anchor tribal groups' cultural identities even as they accommodate to change.[30]

One of the most engrossing examples is the current struggle between the five Confederated Tribes of the Umatilla Indian Reservation, located in north central Oregon, and various archaeologists for control of "Kennewick Man."[31] Formerly, these groups occupied the mid-Columbia River basin, including the area around the present town of Kennewick, Washington. In the summer of 1996 a college student watching a boat race from the bank of the river literally stumbled on a human skull. The police called the county coroner to ascertain if the Kennewick bones were the remains of a crime victim. The coroner then contacted a local archaeologist serving on an on-call basis in forensics cases. The archaeologist and the coroner then examined the adjacent river bank and recovered almost all of the skeleton. The archaeologist began to suspect that the skull was quite old. He sent samples to a California radiocarbon lab, which judged the age of the skull to be in excess of eight thousand years.[32] Two other features are of note: the pelvis contained an embedded stone lance point, and the skull, curiously, exhibited features that the three archaeologists have thought were more often associated with Europeans ("Caucasians") than with Native North Americans.

Many readers will know that, since 1990, a United States law known as NAGPRA (Native American Grave Protection and Repatriation Act) has required that when prehistoric skeletal material is discovered on federal land (the Columbia River banks are under the jurisdiction of the United States Corps of Engineers), tribal groups are to be notified immediately and all excavation is to be halted until they are called. The tribe must concur with whatever is done next, and it has the prerogative of taking the remains and reburying them elsewhere. In the Kennewick case, whether the tribes were notified promptly has been cause for disputation. Whatever the facts, the tribes' perception is that they were marginalized and ignored, and that the archaeological data gathering went far beyond clarifying the prehistoric age of the find. Indeed, that appears to have been the case since a full modeling of the skull, with flesh, and much other detailed osteological data have appeared, long after the physical remains were placed under lock and key. Much worse, when the very old date was determined (this appears to be the oldest, nearly complete skeletal find in North America and one of just a handful of skeletal finds from that age range), eight professional archaeologists launched a lawsuit to prevent the Corps of Engineers from conveying the bones to the tribes under NAGPRA. The tribal representatives were, and are, incensed.

The grounds of the archaeologists' suit are several: 1) that the bones have to be studied in order to ascertain whether they are Indian; 2) that in the case of rare finds, science is a superior good that overrides the directives of NAGPRA and, in this case, the sensitivities of Indian claimants; 3) that the scientists' personal first amendment right to freedom of expression logically entails a right to gather and receive information, which they are prevented from doing by NAGPRA.[33] The federal judge set up a scientific panel to remeasure the age and to decide if the skeleton is Indian. At this writing, the panel has issued a preliminary finding that physical features of the bones, plus the dating and circumstances of the find, lead them to conclude that the bones are from a native Indian. The tribes have already drawn further conclusions. They have concluded that archaeologists—in fact, most anthropologists in general—are not to be trusted. The struggle over Kennewick shows, they believe, that archaeologists will put their interests first, and see Indians not as owners but as impediments. In the northwest, Kennewick Man has left the fragile relationships between Indians and anthropologists in shambles.

The struggle over the physical benchmarks of cultural heritage is fierce. Repatriation reflects a larger and very long-term need—to strengthen the symbols of cultural ancestry, to wrest control of them from the surrounding, dominant society, and to build thereby a stronger foundation for accommodating the cultural changes that lie ahead.

Theater 5: Cultural Futures

International human rights documents accord to every indigenous society the right to continue the values and meanings it holds dear, while, at the same time, adopting changes that satisfy and improve life. In short, every indigenous society has a right to construct its future. That future may replicate the past, or it may move in new directions, but every society has the right to build or discover its future. That future should include the right to a greater degree of self-rule and a secure economic base. Underlying many conflicts is the commitment of indigenous groups to acquire more control over what their cultural future will be.

The advent of Nunavut, an enormous Canadian arctic territory that is now a fully empowered political unit of Canada, makes news because it was expressly created to allow indigenous people, Inuits, to be the controlling political group.[34] This is the first major political unit to be placed under indigenous control since the European conquest of the Western Hemisphere. A more significant validation of an indigenous cultural future is difficult to imagine. To the south, in the United States, the most apparent struggle to acquire control over a cultural future is casino gambling, the "new buffalo." Although there are many misgivings about casinos among Indian people, it appears that most tribes located where casinos can commercially succeed have established them. Most tribal casinos are small (eight casinos account for 40 percent of the roughly 7 billion dollars taken in by Indian casinos last year), but on impoverished reservations even modest gaming operations make a large difference. For a significant portion of Indian tribes in the United States, a casino offers a chance to take more control of a culture future.[35]

The struggle to assure indigenous futures is being waged on many fronts besides Nunavut and the casinos.[36] The case I examine here deals with a profoundly important ecological issue, the control of fresh water. Residing in the northwest corner of the state of Washington, the Lummi Nation has about thirty-five hundred enrolled members, about half of whom live on a modestly sized reservation located just west of the city of Bellingham. A small river, the Nooksack, supplies fresh water to Bellingham, to the county surrounding it, and to the Lummi's reservation. The Nooksack is a short river, originating only a few tens of miles east of Bellingham in the Cascade Range. Exiting the mountains, the river empties out onto the coastal flood plain, meanders through agricultural lands, then past the city of Bellingham, and, at its lower end, borders the Lummi reservation. Along its length, many farmers tap the river, and the city of Bellingham pipes its water from the river's upper reaches in the Cascades. Smaller users get the water from wells, themselves replenished from groundwater resupplied by rainfall and the river. What has this to do with the Lummi's future?

As the Lummi see it, water is critical to their future. Washington State's water permits have now fully allocated the Nooksack's water —indeed, issued permits may have awarded more water than the river can supply in an average year. Because the water is a finite resource, as the city and county grow (and they are growing rapidly), the share for the Lummi decreases. Realistically, any decrease is probably permanently lost. This alarms the Lummi for at least two reasons. First, much of their ceremonial life revolves around salmon. They have hatcheries that breed and release salmon. Thus salmon, and the Lummi's hatchery program to renew the salmon stocks, depend on Nooksack water. Second, Lummi want to encourage more of their members, not now living on the reservation, to return. That will require housing and jobs, which in turn requires more water than the reservation presently uses. Recognizing that their cultural future depends on preserving, indeed expanding, their share of the Nooksack's water, the Lummi opened a struggle in 1994 to guarantee themselves a percentage of the Nooksack's waters, directly challenging the growth expectations of industry, the agricultural sector, suburban developers, and the city of Bellingham.

The Lummi pressed their campaign by threatening to begin a judicially based process of General Stream Adjudication. An extremely costly process which may take decades to complete, an adjudication results in a court-imposed permanent allotment of water shares among users. In the state of Washington adjudication favors claims in the order in which they were registered as water users, and the Lummi are first on the list. While that may not guarantee a particular percentage of the water, it puts the Lummi in a strong position.

When the Lummi announced their intention, it was immediately seen as a threat to the other users. The claim also triggered a review by Washington State's Department of the Environment, which determined that the river was at least fully allocated. The department began to constrain new water permits. This, in turn, complicated plans for new housing developments in the county and the city and county's efforts to attract new industry to the area. Simultaneously, it threw into confusion the many farmers who had been drawing well and river water without permits. The Lummi succeeded in gaining the full attention of the many elements of valley commerce, politics, finance, and industry that had heretofore given Indians scarcely a thought.

The Lummi have attempted to use the leverage of the threatened adjudication to generate a negotiation process that would be less costly, more quickly resolved, and which would not rely entirely on the decision of a judge. Their move did generate a series of task force and consultative groups, but each bogged down in arguments between entrenched interests. To date, none has produced a politically feasible negotiated agreement. Instead, time passes and the Lummi are no closer to assuring their future water share.

The Lummi's hand has been severely weakened by a simultaneous dispute. Their reservation includes a small peninsula, Sandy Point, on which a group of almost entirely non-Indian homeowners have established vacation homes, buying the land from Indian owners. Though nearly all the lots are owned by non-Indians, the properties lie entirely within the reservation. Sandy Point owners are trenchantly opposed to any control over their affairs by the Lummi. Meanwhile, the Lummi Nation wants to assert some degree of governance over all reservation lands, whether owned by Indians or non-Indians.[37] This has been played out in a contest over the authority to drill new water wells. Their dispute produced a second factor weakening the Lummi's ability to pursue their water strategy, the intervention in support of the Sandy Point homeowners of one of the state's U.S. senators, Slade Gorton, nationally regarded as the foremost opponent of Indian sovereignty in Congress.[38] Gorton's continual attacks, often directed specifically at the Lummi, have left the Lummi with fewer resources to prosecute their water struggle and have suggested to the competing water claimants that a waiting game will succeed. A third factor has further enlarged this effect: the Lummi's small casino has failed, leaving them with fewer financial resources to invest in their struggle. Not surprisingly, their water negotiations have stalled.

Whether the Lummi will succeed or fail remains to be seen. Nonetheless, the Lummi have accomplished something remarkable. The Lummis have perceived that a natural resource lying outside the reservation, fresh water, is essential to their cultural future and that assertive action is required if their future is not to be forfeited. They have taken action and are now enmeshed in a protracted struggle with their opponents.

Conclusions

One thing is certain: indigenous groups are accumulating a huge store of experience. Each struggle reveals more about the nature of the forces arrayed against indigenous groups today. That experience identifies which goals are centrally important and which are peripheral; which are the great prizes and which are the great dangers; which leverage points are strong and which are weak. This is crucial information. Indigenous groups have a great deal to share and an urgent need to share it.

To make sense out of the vast landscape of conflict, I have focused on five theaters of struggle. While leaving much aside, these five at least serve to identify key cultural arenas within which, on a global basis, indigenous groups now contend. What are the lessons that come from them? Here are a few:

1. Where treaties remain unextinguished, the Puget Sound fishing tribes have succeeded in recapturing economic rights that had long been forgotten and appropriated by others. North American treaties conveyed broad, perpetual guarantees to lands, economic rights, cultural persistence, and specific economic assets. The tribes of Puget Sound show what possibilities lie in treaty language.

2. Sovereignty, which in some legal settings can be the foundation of all other rights, is too often defended as an indivisible, archetypal purity. The casino battles in the United States show us, however, that sovereignty is a medley of elements and that the political and negotiational process is one of specific tradeoffs, sacrificing some autonomy here for greater gains there.

3. Intellectual property is a significant arena of battle. The stakes are real and important to cultural survival. The dominant society's caricatures trivialize the symbols on which indigenous cultures are built, and these must be opposed. As the descendants of Crazy Horse can tell us, however, be warned: court fights may not succeed in an age of millennial capitalism.

4. Successful resistance depends on having a secure and solid anchorage for a indigenous culture. This anchorage resides in symbols, ceremonies, language, material items, sacred sites—key parts of which may be in the hands of the dominant society. The tribes along the Columbia River tell us that aggressively repatriating those elements of their cultural anchorage—the bones of ancestors, the sacred objects, the core of oral traditions—must be a priority.

5. Every society must have basic resources: land, healthy air, unpolluted fresh water, and the flora and fauna that undergird its lifeway. For enclaved societies, those resources derive from ecosystems that extend well beyond reservation lands, so that most of the ecosystem is in the hands of the dominant society. The Lummi teach us that when an indigenous group overlooks its larger ecosystem, it does so at its own peril. Even though success may be elusive, their cultural futures depend on aggressively protecting ecosystems outside their own lands.

The above lessons make a further point. The exploration of indigenous insights linking humans, nature, and culture and spiritual values needs to be informed by a keen awareness of the larger struggle in which indigenous peoples are now engaged. Indigenous people across the world have long known that their ancestral cultures, as well as their more recent experiences, contain value and wisdom that can improve the contemporary human predicament. But these peoples are also conscious of their deepening vulnerability as enclaved societies. All of us need to be fully aware of this reality, and also of the energy and excitement spreading among indigenous communities as they exercise their new capabilities and savor recent triumphs in a struggle that is centuries old.

Notes

1. See Megan Biesele, Mathias Guenther, Robert Hitchcock, Richard Lee, and Jan MacGregor, "Hunters, Clients and Squatters: The Contemporary Socioeconomic Status of Botswana Basarwa," *African Study Monographs* 9, no. 3 (1989): 109–51; Robert K. Hitchcock and John D. Holm, "Bureaucratic Domination of Hunter-Gatherer Societies: A Study of the San in Botswana," *Development and Change* 24, no. 2 (1993): 305–38; and Donald G. McNeil, Jr., "In Bushmanland, Hunters' Tradition Turns to Dust," *New York Times,* 13 November 1997, A3.

2. See Terence Turner, "The Role of the Indigenous Peoples in the Environmental Crisis: The Example of the Kayapo of the Brazilian Amazon," *Perspectives in Biology and Medicine,* autumn 1992, 526–45; and "Mineral Extraction by and for Indigenous Amazonian Communities: Gold Mining by the Waiapo and Kayapo" (unpublished paper, Annual Meeting of the American Anthropological Association, Washington, D.C., 19 November 1997).

3. David J. Morrow, "Making Good on the Great Alaskan Windfall," *New York Times,* 15 November 1996, D1.

4. The testimony of Forrest "Dutch" Kinley (Lummi) reflected the tribes' reasoning: "I think that we should be given a chance to build our economic base around our fisheries, and we have never been given this chance in the State of Washington. . . . we need no training to make a livelihood in fishing. Our people, this is their way of life." Quoted in Fay G. Cohen, *Treaties on Trial, the Continuing Controversy over Northwest Indian Fishing Rights* (Seattle: University of Washington Press, 1986), 9.

5. An essential source on the Boldt decision is Cohen, *Treaties on Trial.*

6. Quoted from the Treaty with the Dwamish Suquamish, Etc., 1855, Article 5. The article goes on to state "That they shall not take shell-fish from any beds staked or cultivated by citizens," implying that shellfish rights are provided in other settings.

7. As indicated in the previous note, the calculation does not include "cultivated" shellfish, such as those from oyster farms. In practice, the 50 percent figure could perhaps be applied to the commercial take of Dungeness crabs, but the "catch" of other shellfish is not currently tallied, making their 50 percent share impossible to implement in a quantitative way. Thus, in practical terms the core issue appears to be accessing privately owned beaches in order to gather.

8. A helpful review of the 1996 Washington State ruling and administrative and political responses is found in "Rally, Meeting to Focus on Unregulated Tribal Hunting," *Indian Country Today,* 6–13 April 1998, B1.

9. A political metaphor meaning the United States.

10. In most instances, state laws and jurisdiction have very limited application on federally recognized Indian reservations in the United States.

11. See George S. Esber, Jr., "Shortcomings of the Indian Self-Determination Policy," in *State and Reservation, New Perspectives on Federal Indian Policy,* ed. George Pierre Castile and Robert L. Bee (Tucson: University of Arizona Press, 1992), 213 ff.

12. Indian Country's perennial challenger, Senator Slade Gorton (R-Washington) has introduced measures that would curtail certain judicial aspects of Indian sover-

eignty and treaty rights. Gorton's initiatives have generated vigorous opposition from indigenous leaders as well as strident support from non-Indians. See Timothy Egan, "Debate about Tribal Rights Turns Rancorous," *New York Times,* 8 April 1998, A12.

13. Some reservation governments impose excise taxes of their own, but at lesser rates than those imposed on the same products by the surrounding state.

14. See J. J. Smith, "Pataki Retreats; Stops 'Tax War,'" *Indian Country Today,* 2 June 1997, A1; Raymond Hernandez, "In a Shift, State Won't Try to Tax Sales on Indian Reservations," *New York Times,* 23 May 1997, A27.

15. See also Kallen Martin, "Indians Not Taxed: Will Sovereignty Survive?" *Native Americas* 13, no. 2 (1996): 14–25.

16. Not all of these battles have been won by Indians. Alaskan natives recently lost a major case asserting their right to tax corporations operating on their lands (*Alaska v. Native Village of Venetie* 96-1577); the U.S. Supreme Court ruled that when Alaskan natives accepted the 1971 Alaska Native Claims Settlement Act that those groups had permanently ceded sovereignty rights over their lands (Linda Greenhouse, "Court Denies Indian Authority in Alaska Case," *New York Times,* 26 February 1998, A16.

17. The potential for this is great, given the number of issues where state interests and tribal interests collide. Examples are competitive claims to water and to the preservation of off-reservation sacred sites, competitive claims on fisheries and shellfish, the potential for industrial pollution, the siting of radioactive waste dumps, and so on.

18. A 1996 Supreme Court decision has complicated the matter even further. The 1988 law's mandated compacting process had been resisted by some state governors who stalled or refused to negotiate a compact. Although the law provides that the U.S. Secretary of the Interior can impose a compact in such a situation, in practice that official has been chary of intervening over a governor's opposition. This leaves the Indians with only the recourse of suing the state for failure to negotiate in good faith. The Supreme Court, in a landmark Florida case (*Seminole of Florida v. Florida*), ruled five to four that a federal law could not force a state to be sued in state court against its consent. The effect of the ruling is to set aside that provision of IRGA, providing considerable legal security to the governor who refuses to negotiate. This affects not only new compacts, but also the renewal of existing compacts. See David Melmer, "The Decision: U.S. Supreme Court Rules in Favor of States' Rights," *Indian Country Today,* 4 April 1996, A1.

19. The rate of establishment of new reservation-based casinos appears to be slackening. Among the factors that can account for this are: 1) a softening of the demand for casino-style gambling of the types reservations can offer; 2) a growth of competing non-Indian gambling opportunities; and 3) the remote, economically unattractive locations of many remaining reservations.

20. See Cary Spivak, "Governor Uses High Court Ruling to Put Casinos in Bind," *National Law Journal* 20, no. 21 (1998): A13, for an apt example from Wisconsin.

21. See Darrell Addison Posey and Graham Dutfield, *Beyond Intellectual Property: Toward Traditional Resource Rights for Indigenous Peoples and Local Communities* (Ottawa: International Development Research Centre, 1996), 3.

22. The acute sensitivity of indigenous societies to gene patenting of traditional

crops, gathered products, and human alleles reflects the same concerns, applied to biological substances.

23. The term millennial capitalism seems appropriate not only because of its fluorescence at the change of millennia (according to the Western calendar), but more importantly because capitalism in this period has taken on aspects of a creed or millennial prophesy, that is, as revealed truth.

24. See "Indian Etchings Stand in Way of a New Road," *New York Times,* 5 March 1995, 1, 22:1.

25. Daniela Soleri and David Cleveland, with Donald Eriacho, Fred Bowannie, Jr., Andre Laahty, and Zuni Community Members, "Gifts from the Creator: Intellectual Property Rights and Folk Crop Varieties," in *Intellectual Property Rights for Indigenous Peoples: A Sourcebook,* ed. Tom Greaves (Oklahoma City: Society for Applied Anthropology, 1994), 21–40.

26. Jack Broom, "Indians Fight Crazy Horse Liquor Sales: Spiritual Leader Opposed Drinking, Speakers Say," *Seattle Times,* 26 August 1993, B1.

27. Michael A. Fletcher, "Crazy Horse Again Sounds Battle Cry: Indians Say Namesake Brew Adds to Cultural Insults Everywhere from Sports to Road Maps," *Washington Post,* 18 February 1997, A3.

28. Frank Pommersheim, "The Crucible of Sovereignty: Analyzing Issues of Tribal Jurisdiction," *Arizona Law Review* 31 (1989): 341ff.

29. Doug Mellgren, "Washington State Indian Tribe Gets International Whaling Approval," *Philadelphia Inquirer,* 24 October 1997, A28.

30. Whale House: Marilee Enge, "Battle over a Birthright," *Anchorage Daily News,* in four parts, 4–8 April 1993. Zuni *ayahudas:* "Who Owns Indian Artifacts?" *Christian Science Monitor,* 28 August 1990, 12. Sitting Bull: Avis Little Eagle, "Sitting Bull Necklace to Be Returned," *Indian Country Today,* 21 January 1993, B1. Yei Jish: Valerie Taliman, "Sacred Yei Jish Returned," *Indian Country Today,* 7–14 October 1996. Long Wolf: Kevin Peniska, "Chief Long Wolf Returns Home after a Century," *Indian Country Today,* 6–13 October 1997, 1, 3.

31. I gratefully draw on information provided by various colleagues, including Jeffrey Van Pelt, Robert Winthrop, and Darby Stapp. Misinterpretations of their information and perspectives are, of course, mine alone.

32. A more recent dating (*New York Times,* 14 January 2000) has given an estimated date of 9,320 to 9,510 years old.

33. The grounds of the suit have been variously reported. The above are mainly taken from Alan Schneider, "Why Kennewick Man Is in Court," *Anthropological Newsletter,* February 1997, 18. Schneider is the principal lawyer for the litigating archaeologists.

34. Inuit has replaced the term "Eskimo" in Canada and Greenland, while in Alaska Eskimo continues in use.

35. See Timothy Egan, "Now, a White Backlash against Rich Indians," *New York Times,* 7 September 1997, 3. Casino expansion may be slackening, however, so tribes presently without casinos may not have as much success as those that have them now.

36. This is well documented in Posey and Dutfield, *Beyond Intellectual Property.*

37. About half of the Lummi's reservation land is owned by non-Indians, a pattern common to American Indian reservations due to the Dawes Act of 1887 and subse-

quent federal measures aimed at dissolving Indian governance and political integrity.

38. In the summer of 2000 Senator Gorton surprised many when he objected to a resolution from the Washington State Republican Party opposing Indian sovereignty. Although Senator Gorton offered little explanation, it would appear that his main opposition is to the exercise of Indian Sovereignty where it affects the interests of non-Indians.

In the Eye of the Storm:
Tribal Peoples of India

PRADIP PRABHU

Introduction: Overview of Tribal Status

The tribal people in India today are centered in the eye of a political storm, which threatens their future in the forest where they have lived for centuries. Uncontrolled exploitation of forests began with colonial rule. Viewed as a limitless source of commercial timber and revenue-earning agricultural lands, forests were felled extensively. The earliest British document estimated tree cover around 40 percent in 1854. A century later, it had been reduced by 18 percent. At India's independence in 1947, of a total land mass of 320 million hectares, only 22 percent, or 72 million hectares, controlled by the Forest Department and classified as "forests," had adequate tree cover. The National Forest Policy of 1952, however, stipulated that 33 percent of the country's area should be forested.[1] The policy thus required a 50 percent increase in extant tree cover to ensure the ecological balance. But quite the opposite took place. Rampant deforestation during the next three decades resulted in a loss of 12 percent of the tree cover, a disturbing loss of 0.40 percent per annum. Forest cover plummeted to 10 percent of the land mass, or 34 million hectares.[2] The environment movement brought the deforestation crisis to center stage. Indira Gandhi, then prime minister, appreciated the argument that the nation's forests were the last bulwark against ecological disaster. As a result, wildlife and forest conservation became a major concern for the Indian government, which called for drastic measures. First, the Union government passed a constitutional amendment removing the subject of forests from the profligate state governments and including it in the concurrent list. Second, a Union law, the Conservation of Forests Act 1980, made the forests out-of-bounds for "tree-fellers" and prohibited the conversion of forest land to any other use without the express permission of the Union government. The third measure entailed reestablishing tree cover through a massive program of social forestry and wasteland development. The fourth measure was the conservation option to progressively curb all human interference in the forest by classifying surviving forests as "conservation enclaves." All good forests were to be declared national parks, biological reserves, or game sanctuaries, with minimal or no human interference. While this prevented deforestation by the Forest Department, it also meant that humans living in the "conservation enclaves" were to be "excluded," or "evicted," to allow nature to reestablish itself. This single measure would jeopardize the survival of millions of tribal people.

Ironically, the mandate for environmental conservation was given to a bureaucracy that so far had managed the forest for profit, both public and personal. Forest officials, trained to determine if a tree is ready for felling, were now expected to be competent judges of the ecological "carrying capacity" of the forest, with no evidence of their knowledge, skills, or sympathies to manage the forests for conservation.[3] With the forests still in control of the Forest Department, whose main practice of forest conservation is based on the colonial idea of "exclusion," many ecologists question the possibilities for radical changes. The draft of a new forest law, called the Conservation of Forests and Natural Ecosystems Act, clearly shows that the government wishes to continue a century-old process of discrimination against the rural, and especially the tribal, poor. The fear is that if the present draft act is passed into law, it will represent a victory for the interest groups that plead for strict conservation and strict state control.[4] Though the law stipulates that the requirements of industry are insignificant to those of conservation, history shows that the Forest Department has allowed industrial exploitation.[5]

Exclusion versus Integration: Where Do the Tribals Go?

The political storm assumed threatening proportions. Seventy percent of the tribal people, who had found their ecological niche in these areas for centuries, were threatened. Though only 8 percent of India's overall population, the tribals are concentrated in the forested regions. A good example is the Bastar District of Madhya Pradesh, with a tribal population of 67.79 percent and a forest cover of 55.4 percent. The fact that the population of the towns is omitted from these totals indicates that the forest areas are almost exclusively populated by tribal people. These alarming statistics paints a similar picture of other forest-intensive districts of the country.[6] In the eye of the stormy conservation debate, and reflective of the schizophrenia symptomatic of elitist conservationism, between the "exclusionists" (a large section of environmentalists and foresters) and the "integrationists" (a smaller section of environmentalists and tribal lobbies) are the tribals, mute spectators to their impending ethnocide. The nation's largest landlord, the Forest Department, with the support of influential environmentalists, had won the first round. National parks, biological reserves, game sanctuaries became the sign-posts of conservation. By 1991, 421 sanctuaries, 57 national parks, and 18 tiger reserves were established, and by 2000, the number would increase to 633 sanctuaries and 147 parks. An estimated 5 million tribals were "evicted" between 1951 and 1990,[7] and a million more would face similar consequences in the coming years. History has turned full circle. Notions of progress have translated into other realities. In 1876, while an effort for "scientific management" was made, in actuality the tribals were driven out of their communally held lands while the forests were systematically exploited for commercial use.[8] A century later, instead of witnessing sensitive acts of conservancy, the nation experienced the eviction of a larger number of tribals.

Tribals: Born Ecologists? A Disputed Question

If one section of the environmentalist lobby claims that the continued presence of the tribals in the conservation areas is a major interference in forest ecology and if this section is not averse to relocating them outside the boundaries of the "ecological enclaves," the serious implications of such a step notwithstanding, another section, both inside and outside the government, still insists on the symbiotic relationship of tribals with the forest. An example of such a position is the National Forest Policy of 1988, which affirms the "symbiotic relationship of the tribals and the forest."[9] B. K. Roy Burman, a reputed Indian anthropologist deeply involved in tribal issues, has argued for the rights of tribal peoples to live in the conservation enclaves. He submits that tribal people, who often live in forests close to nature, possess an "indigenous wisdom," having respect for all living creatures—a wisdom that, among other things, offers other communities in India a vision of future survival based on a lifestyle of harmony with nature.[10] He proposes a definition of "the indigenous [read tribal] as those whose livelihoods are tied up with the land in a system of mutual reinforcement—as a moral contract in which social living and negotiation with human and non-human animate beings are basically attuned to the sonic and sensual rhythms of the earth."[11] He elaborates this definition by saying that people are "indigenous" to the extent that they uphold a worldview of oneness with earth and nature, as expressed in thought and action.[12]

However, Roy Burman's definition of indigenous, or tribal, people is of course deeply problematic—as is the notion of "oneness with nature"—and needs to be handled with caution. Beautiful as it may sound, the definition borders more on the ideal and less on the real. It would be difficult to put all tribal people into one "green" category. Levels of ecological consciousness vary with the material conditions, the nature of livelihoods, the level of technological development in which different tribal communities live. While some tribals, like the Madia Gonds of Abujmad or the Onge of the Andaman Islands, still live in the lap of nature and would satisfy Burman's definition nearly perfectly, there are many others who have been pushed out of the security of their "forests" through mining, industrialization, development and conservation projects, and planned migration. They have had to cope with intense pressures placed on their survival resources and severely constricted survival spaces. There are others who are drawn deeply into the process of modernization. A large number of these tribal communities, whatever the nature and content of their "symbiosis with nature," whether real, ritual, or symbolic, are not "green" in the modern sense. Many tribals resist being placed in the romanticized green classification. Most environmentalists, tribals feel, can attain and maintain their levels of ecological consciousness, enjoying as they do the security of survival.

Most tribal peoples face an ongoing threat both to the continuity of their culture and to the security of their sheer physical survival. The character of their green consciousness is, therefore, materially different. If one adheres strictly to Roy Burman's definition, many tribal communities in India would fail to live up to its "green ethos" and thereby not have the right to indigenous status as indigenous peoples. For the right reasons, no doubt, tribal peoples are being made a key metaphor for the human in complete harmony with nature. However, tribal individuals might find it hard to satisfy the romanticized expectations that "greens" bring to the issue. So, the failure to live up to the "indigenous ecological ethos"—be it by forest dwellers who clear land for subsistence agriculture, thus causing deforestation, or pastoralists who keep large herds, causing overgrazing and soil erosion— can be used to abrogate the tribal peoples' rights to continue living in ecologically sensitive areas or to practice traditional forms of subsistence. In other words, by not behaving in an ecologically sound manner according to the "greens," tribal peoples run the risk of losing the moral right to their customary forests, lands, or mountains.

David Hardiman, a scholar who has studied tribal communities in western India, also questions such notions, arguing that studies based on the difference between Indian and Western beliefs lead to what Partha Chatterjee has labeled "reverse Orientalism." With such an "essentialist understanding," one cannot account for such facts as the large-scale deforestation which took place prior to colonial rule.[13] Hardiman finds a fundamental lack of historical understanding in the representation of Indian forest dwellers as born conservationists, seeing this as a sort of ecological functionalism reducing "human behavior to an almost animal-like adjustment to the environment."[14] He refutes this with his own detailed historical account of the forest society of the Dangs in Gujarat, where the tribal Bhil chiefs controlled extraction of timber before the trade was monopolized by the British. The precolonial timber trade did not have any immediate effect on the forest ecology at large, but this was not due to a "conservationist mentality" among the Bhils. For the tribals, the forest was "eternal" and they had "no consciousness" that human beings could ruin it.[15]

Hardiman's critique is indeed important and relevant. But, considering the more widespread notion in India that tribals and forest dwellers are destroying the forests, the shift in focus to indigenous forms of "environmental wisdom" is politically significant. Indigenous peoples themselves today base their political claims on similar notions of having a special lifestyle and culture in harmony with nature. There is a crucial difference between the peoples' representing themselves (self-essentialization) as natural conservationists and outsiders' attempts to represent them as such. Larry Lohman, in an editorial in the *Ecologist,* warns against green environmentalism in which Western environmentalists impose their own "green world view" on indigenous peoples and non-Western societies at large. A more balanced view would be the statement published in *Cultural Survival* that tribal peoples are not "conservationists" in the modern Western sense, though their systems of resource management are often in *"relatively* sustainable balance with nature."[16] Indeed, when tribal peoples' resource use is compared to that of the state or of private firms that have access to the natural resources of a particular area, it is safe to assume that the former will be a more sustainable ecological community.

Even though the situation in India differs from that of the Amazonian Indians in Brazil, for example, it is obvious that these and other tribal struggles for land and forest will be fought in the domain of "ecopolitics," with "sustainability" as the central issue. The present conflict in northwest India between the state and the Van Gujjars, whose traditional grazing grounds were made into a number of sanctuaries and merged into a new and larger national park in the 1980s, is a prime example. Considered by the Forest Department, foreign experts, and the Indian Wildlife Institute as a major threat to the ecosystem of the park, the Van Gujjars were to be evicted. The conflict reached a climax when they were stopped from entering the park with their herds of buffalo. The movement of the Van Gujjars received media attention and was cited as an example of the general conflict between conservation interests and the rights of the local people: were the Van-Gujjars destroying their habitat or, as local forest dwellers living in harmony with the forest, were they the true guardians of their habitat?[17] Roy Burman argued against the conservationists, who blamed the Van Gujjars for ruining the forests, pointing to the necessity of integrating local people into the preservation of wildlife and the forests. The debate turned around, and it was even argued that the Van Gujjars should be made the caretakers of the Rajaji National Park in Uttar Pradesh, making it the first people's national park in India.

Smitu Kothari, an environmentalist, argues that those local communities which give up their traditional way of life experience several consequences. For example, their needs increase and their aspirations change, making them less respectful toward nature and incapable of maintaining a sustainable lifestyle. Some suggest that such modernized tribals should not enjoy "customary rights in natural habitats."[18] But others dealing with forest issues argue that saving the forest can only be realized in collaboration with local communities by finding ways of combining conservation with sustainable uses of the forest by the forest dwellers.[19] Ramachandra Guha and Madhav Gadgil stated it more succinctly, arguing that the core message is the need to blend ecology with equity and to transfer the control over natural resources from "corrupt bureaucracies" to the people who depend on these resources.[20] Unfortunately, this message has not been heard and, thus, the storm rages on.

Among the Santhal of Bihar and Bengal there is a saying that when walking in the forest, if you are confronted by a forester before you and by a tiger behind, you must turn and face the tiger because you have a better chance of survival. The situation hasn't changed much.

The Greening of a People: The Tribal People of India

India is home to the largest concentration of tribal people in the world, their numbers approaching eighty million. Said to be the earliest inhabitants of the country, the tribal people are popularly called *adivasi*s (the first inhabitants, or Aborigines). They were the original natives of the country and had been settled in different parts of India long before the Indo-Aryans entered and settled in the Indus River valley. It is difficult to generalize about India's tribals; they are very diverse in their cultural lifeways, traditions, and practices. They belong to different stocks, such as Kolid, Gondid, Negrito, Mongoloid, Australoid, and Dravidian. Today, they are spread over the nation and reside almost exclusively in the hilly forested tracts of the country. The central region of the country, comprising five states, accounts for 54.7 percent of the total tribal population. The state of Madhya Pradesh has the highest tribal population, or 15.3 million. Lakshadweep, an island in the Indian Ocean has a tribal population of 93.15 percent.[21] The Andaman and Nicobar Islands, the northeastern states, and many other areas of the country have high percentages of tribal populations. The influx of outsiders that accompanied industrialization and urbanization in the mineral-resource-rich tribal tracts has reduced the tribals to a minority. There are over 630 tribal communities, ranging from the Great Andamanese, whose numbers have dwindled to eighteen persons and who face imminent extinction, to the 5.2 million Bhils of Rajasthan, the 4.8 million Gonds of central India, and the 3.6 million Santhals of Bihar and Bengal. The largest number of tribal peoples, numbering 220 tribes, live in the northeastern states. About 94 percent of the tribal population live in the rural areas, and 80 percent still subsist in the traditional economic systems of hunting, food gathering, or subsistence agriculture. Some tribals, like the Onge, Jarawa, and Shompen of the Andamans and the Chenchu and Yennadi of Andhra Pradesh, live solely by hunting and food gathering.

The term "tribe" in India is not merely a sociological term. It has legal and administrative connotations due to the unique history of its usage. Initially, the term tribe was used by the colonial administration to describe communities in the forested areas who resisted colonial intrusion into their homelands. The British first called them "savage tribes," but the pioneering work of anthropologists, who wrote glowingly about their humane societies, and the committed work of Christian missionaries led to a reclassification of these communities as "noble savages." But beyond that, no clear definition was accepted for administrative purposes. As a result, the tribal peoples have been enumerated in different census reports as people having a tribal form of religion (1891), animists (1901), tribal animists or tribal religion (1911), hill and forest tribe (1921), primitive tribe (1931), and tribe (1941).

As these communities were radically different from the rest of caste India, they had to be put in a special category in the Constitution. However, since there was no precise sociological definition of the term "tribe" to guide policymakers, they categorized certain social groups as "Scheduled Tribes" under Article 342 of the Constitution, on the basis of precedents set by the British administrators. Political expediency has also contributed to categorizing some groups as tribes. Consequently, it is a difficult task for social scientists today to define the term "tribe" independently of the administrative legal category.[22] Considering them primitive, backward, economically and socially disadvantaged, the Constitution provides the Scheduled Tribes with reservations, educational institutions, employment, and priority in welfare programs. These special privileges have proved to be a mixed blessing. The policy of reservations has created a "creamy layer" in the tribal communities which garner most of the advantages that the Scheduled Tribe status has to offer. At the same time, a large number of other backward communities demand tribal status. Aware of the ambiguity of the definition of "scheduled tribe," politicians accede to these demands as political patronage. The new tribal elite is distanced and alienated from the core of the tribal ethos, yet members of this new elite remain the tribal spokespersons. The real tribals remain silent and speak a language that the elite often do not hear.

Mainstream India portrays the tribals as communities with rich cultural lives, varieties of colorful attire and ornate costumes, extensive ranges of rhythmic and expressive dances, and varied forms of cultural expression and ritual ceremonies. But this is where the romance with the tribal world ends. The sad part of this portrayal is that it is unrelated to the organic reality of tribal life and values. The commercialization of tribal exotica in the past two decades has only led to the trivialization of their ethos and rich cultural life. The tribals are willing to forgive mainstream India for failing to grasp their inner world. They realize that it is difficult to navigate between two concepts of the world usually presented as mutually exclusive: one that sees nature as an animate counterpart of society, the other that conceives it as a set of phenomena occurring outside the realm of human action. Looking at the wider world with a detachment that has grown with them over centuries of living in and with nature, the tribals accept that the outside world has a worldview totally at variance with their own. Mainstream society cannot understand the tribals' symbiotic relationship between humans and the environment. Dominant Indian societies neither perceive the dynamic interactions between the techniques used in socializing nature, nor understand the symbolic systems that organize them in an organic totality in which the material, cultural, and conceptual aspects are closely interwoven.

Life for tribal peoples is often cruel and hard. Occasions of celebration and joyous festivity only briefly punctuate a life otherwise burdened with exploitation, poverty, and malnourishment. In spite of all the hardships that tribals undergo, life is generally looked upon as an opportunity, and all activity is in thanksgiving for the beauty and sacredness of nature. Many tribal songs have no other purpose except enjoyment. A few have an ostensible social and ritual purpose, but the largest number are concerned with the quest for beauty and holiness, for dreams and fantasies which transform the sordid ordinariness of daily existence into something rich and strange.

Adivasi cultural life is part of a complex communal activity, which includes singing, dancing, and religious celebrations of life. The songs, dances, and religious festivities are intimately and integrally related to finding joy in life as much as they are the means through which the youth are schooled in values of harmony.[23] In the major epic of the Rongmei Nagas of Nagaland, the retriever of cosmic harmony, Gairemnog, through fearless confrontation with the arrogance of power repeatedly exhorts: "know your brothers and sisters [nature] around you in all their forms. The secret of a good life is to live in harmony with them."[24] The root of this harmony, however, lies in the simplicity, contentment, and nonaccumulative and nonsurplus extractive culture of the tribals. Explaining why they have virtually no possessions, the Numad of the northeast repeat that material goods, which we associate with wealth, are a burden they view as "grievously oppressive" and even physically burdensome.[25] For the Onge of the Andaman Islands, the concept of private property does not exist; even food is a common possession, and life always remains corporate and cooperative.[26]

The national commissioner for scheduled tribes, critiquing the thrust of the development process in the tribal areas, reminds the government that the problem is not a matter of securing for the tribals material possessions. Poverty and indigence are both abundant in the tribal areas. There is something in the tribal philosophy which has kept these people free from the unseemly greed for material possessions. Such greed does not fit in with their philosophy. Although tribal societies do not yearn obsessively for improving their standard of living, their approach to the question of need is still normal and rational.[27]

Another social scientist studying the culture of self-governance among tribals notes that it is their view that surplus production depletes nature's abundance, undermines subsistence, and creates a production crisis. A subsistence economy provides the basis for self-rule, and these two practices together constitute a decentralized mode of governance whose knowledge system, technology, and work skills originate in the notion of the commons. Tribal peoples define creativity as a gift of nature. Human skills and human labor, therefore are not directed against nature.[28] Intimate life with nature has strongly imbued most tribal cultures with the values of equality, cooperation, and community life. For centuries, the tribals have lived in various kinds of environments, and they have adjusted their social life accordingly, to the extent that many of their social institutions seem to have arisen from adjustment or adaptation to surrounding ecological conditions. In some cases, cultural traits are conditioned by environmental pressures. At other times, there is simply a fluid adjustment and adaptation. In the case of the Bhil tribes of southern Rajasthan, "certain cultural elements can be explained as having very close association to the imminent environmental conditions."[29] But tribal culture is increasingly coming under attack from the forces of "modernization." Categorized as backward and primitive, assaulted by the market, and facing the loss of the material basis of subsistence, tribal people are rapidly surrendering their rich cultural traditions and expressions.

Tribal communities of India have their own unique religious traditions and practices centered round the forces of nature and the forest. Like many indigenous traditions, their religious practices indicate a belief that the natural universe is continuous with the human world of interactions and sentiments. The human, nature, and the supernatural are all bound in a mutual relationship.[30] A particularly moving example is the prayer of the Bhima Saoras, a people in the states of Orissa, Madhya Pradesh, and Andhra Pradesh. Before beginning their *jhum* (shifting cultivation), the community invokes the spirit of Mother Earth with this prayer:

> O goddess of the great caves, streams and forests, we beg your mercy. As you see we are going to rob the denizens of the wild of their homes. For the sake of ourselves and our children we have to clear the forest lest we go hungry. We now ask the denizens to go away with their children. All creatures big and small must leave. Help us, o goddess, let your mercy be with us. May we eat well this year.

The Bhima Saoras see their clearing of a patch of forest for cultivation as an encroachment on the right to life of the other creatures of the forest. Not wanting to clash with them, they ask the animals to move away with their children. The terms they use, such as "children," reveal their belief that the animals of the forest have the same status as they do. This understanding also acts as a form of self-restraint: their encroachment and, by implication, their forest clearing, must be minimized and pose the least risk to others' survival. The fact that the Bhima Saoras lose hundreds of their own children to starvation every year speaks volumes about their ecological sensibilities.

Similar sentiments are expressed by other tribal communities. The Nicobarese, from the Nicobar Islands in the Bay of Bengal, beg to be excused before plucking a leaf from a plant for medicine, saying: "I pluck you, because we want this for cure and for a good purpose. O dear plant do not be offended, and cure the person to whom the medicine is applied." For the Nicobarese, there is animate life even in plants and trees.[31] The hunting tribes are known to ask pardon of their victim before the arrow leaves the bow. Before striking its target, the arrow is supposed to be a messenger of remorse. The Onge of the Andaman Islands love their dogs so much that they cannot bear to see the dogs starve, even when there is a shortage of food. There are reports that the starving dogs are allowed to eat before the Onges themselves partake of the meal. They also consider the killing of birds, except the pigeon, taboo, because they consider the birds to be the abode of the souls. Regarding them as totemic objects, the Onge associate birds with clan-like groups. This provides another reason for their protection.[32]

There are a variety of tribal perspectives on animals. The assistance of animals in the making of the world is recognized by tribals, as is the fact that animals act as models of instruction, teaching men and women skills in arts and crafts. Though not deifying the forces or phenomena of nature, the tribals regard them as the manifestation or abode of the spirit. The animal world thus finds a prominent place in the myths and folklore of the tribals.[33] Trees are also considered sacred "persons" by most tribes. Among the Mundas, a major tribe of Bihar in central and eastern India, a bride and bridegroom, after being anointed with *haldi* (turmeric) are wedded initially, not to each other, but to two trees, the bride to a *mahua* (*Bassia latifolia*), the groom to a mango, or sometimes both to mango trees.

Among most Indian indigenous people, there is no distinction between the sacred and the profane or even between nature and humans.[34] Believing that the spirits of nature need an abode in nature but close to human habitation, many tribals keep images of their spirits in the sacred groves. The Mundas celebrate at the place for communal worship, or *jahera,* which symbolizes the remnants of the original village forest, the sacred grove. Within the *jahera,* three *sal* trees are dedicated to the three main spirits. The supreme deity, the village deity, and the deity who protects the village from evil spirits are also located in the *jahera.*[35] These groves, which are fragments of the original forest, are trees which have been carefully protected for ages. They have been left standing from the time when the first forest clearance was made, lest the sylvan gods, disturbed at the felling of trees that sheltered them, abandon the locality. The Mundas of Andhra Pradesh and the Oraons, Kols, and Hos of Orissa and Bihar still hold that if a tree in the sacred grove is destroyed, the gods will show their displeasure by withholding seasonal rain. The sacred groves from which nothing could be removed are actually biosphere reserves, a concept recently developed in modern science.[36] For the Bhils, the gods, goddesses, spirits, and ghosts establish a close relationship with the immediate physical environment. The Bhils identify various deities, located on hill tops and in forests, which protect them against natural wrath and wild animals and which also help forests grow and other resources survive. Not only their social and religious perspectives, but also some of the economic relations are ecology based. The Bhils fully realize that they have shaped their relationships as part of this adjustment. This relationship of reciprocity and cooperation is especially evident among the Bhils, who live in the more undulating areas, where the levels of agricultural fields differ sharply.[37]

Tribal myths differ from those of the mainstream world religions on two major counts. First, the realm of the gods is not clearly demarcated from the realm of humans, as there can be no isolated priests whose only occupation is religious ministration. Worship is communal and held on behalf of the community by *bhagat*s, *badwa*s, or *kamadi* (keepers of tradition, keepers of the faith, and traditional healers). The keepers of the faith, however, cannot earn a livelihood from their service to the community or support their own families by their own labor. The sacred and the secular merge in daily life. Second, tribal people do not claim scientific validity for their myths of origin. They merely state that their myths are their reality, and that is all.[38]

Tribal religions are often very ecologically aware and their traditions reflect a deep sensitivity to maintaining nature's balance. Perhaps the most striking example is the Asur legend of the Mundas, Oraons, Birhor (of Orissa), and Hos. The Asur story is unique in that it refers for the first time, and in such a vivid way, to environmental pollution. The Asurs, who manufactured iron, polluted the environment in their eagerness to produce without restraint. Their furnaces belched smoke that endangered all life and life-support systems and tortured the birds. The Asurs earned the wrath of the great sun spirit Sinbonga, who destroyed the Asurs and their furnaces. While this tradition predates the rise of industry, it is still appropriate—and perhaps more appropriate—given modern-day environmental pollution. In the epic the incidence of smoke pollution is magnified in order to dramatize the role of Sinbonga in for destroying the Asurs.[39]

At the center of several tribal pantheons is the mother goddess, or mother earth, or the spirit of nature. The Warlis, Koknas, Katkaris, Thakurs, and Kolis of Thane District, Maharashtra, worship her as Himai; the Gonds as Mari-Ai; the Mauchis and Bhilalas (Dhule and Nandurbar Districts, Maharashtra) call her Dongar Mauli; the Kolis (Nashil and Ahmednagar Districts, Maharashtra) worship Pandhardevi; the Bhils and Barelas of southwestern Madhya Pradesh, Dhartari; and the Jhodias and Pengo Parajas of Orissa worship Bhumi Devta. In most tribal beliefs, the mother goddess is the mother of all creatures, though few myths speak of all creatures being born from her. The tribals often make a distinction between procreation, which they know is a natural process, and nurturing. The mother goddess as earth and nature cares, nurtures, and sustains life. Joining the mother goddess are the forest spirits, the boundary spirits, the village spirits, the spirits of the crop, and so on.

The tribals often fear evil spirits, including those of the dead, whom they call Cheda, Supli, or Hedli. Ancestor worship of the *virs* and *pitars* (ancestors) is central to many tribal belief systems. The ancestors protect the family from harm and guide the elders of the community in managing the village. It is the triad of the mother goddess, the other spirits, and the ancestors which guides the fortunes of nature and man. Most clans are organized around totems, including flora and fauna of the forests. The loss of the forest habitat has left many communities without a tradition in terms of the origin of particular totem names. S. C. Roy, however, mentions that the Oraons have sixteen beast totems, twelve bird totems, fourteen fish and other aquatic animal totems, nineteen vegetable totems, and two mineral totems.[40]

Tribal Ethos under Threat

Subsumed under Modernization

Despite their ecological sensibility and their life-affirming culture, tribal societies currently face a greater threat of extinction than ever before. Their survival, as peoples and cultures, is encountering a two-pronged assault: that of the forces of modernization and that of eviction from their lands and resources. The issue of "primitive lifestyle" came to the fore particularly after India's independence. Until the colonial period, tribal societies existed at the fringes of Indian society. Their isolation guaranteed the survival of their unique cultures. The first real inroads into the homelands began with the colonial regime. The tribals' resistance earned them the ubiquitous name of "savage tribes." Anthropologists, however, freed them from this classification by writing of their arcadian simplicity and humane societies. As long as the British were able to control the forests, they were willing to leave the tribal societies alone. During this period, resistance became a weapon which ensured non-interference in the tribals' life and culture.

After independence, the question of tribal integration into wider Indian society emerged. The challenges were of a totally different order. Their independence could be guaranteed only by a firm commitment of the state to the right to live with dignity and self-respect. In 1950, under the influence of Verrier Elwin, a reputed anthropologist, Jawaharlal Nehru put forward his Panchsheel Policy (Five Principles of Good Governance), which embodied a rational response to the tribal peoples' unspoken demand. The policy affirmed that 1) people should develop along the lines of their own genius and the state should avoid imposition, instead encouraging their own traditional arts and culture; 2) tribal rights in land and forests should be respected; 3) the state should train their own people to do the work of administration and development; 4) the state should not overadminister these areas or overwhelm them with a multiplicity of schemes, but work through and not in rivalry with their own social and cultural institutions; 5) the government should judge results not by statistics or the amount of money spent, but by the quality of human character that evolved.

The policy, however, was forgotten before the ink had dried. The Panchsheel Policy was excluded from the nation-building, which was prepared by national elites. In that agenda, the tribal people, who were categorized as "backward" and "primitive," were to be taken out of their isolation and drawn into the national mainstream through a well-coordinated educational and development policy. The call for a socially homogeneous country, particularly in the unstated Hindi–Hindu–Hindustani paradigm, threatened India's cultural and linguistic diversity, which many believe makes India a unique and vibrant civilization. However, as a result of this homogenization, cultural outlooks such as subsistence, simplicity, and contentment were compromised and ecological concepts of sustainability were undermined.

Victims of Development

The cumulative effect of these policies was manifold. First was the creation of a tribal elite, who cornered the lion's share of the development opportunities, achieved material prosperity, and adjusted well into the mainstream. They became the standard-bearers of tribal development, but they were alienated from their roots. Second was the creation of a large mass of tribals disoriented by the policy and practice of the government and demoralized by what was happening to them and their cultures. When they did rise up in anger, their protests were either co-opted into the political process or suppressed quickly and brutally. Third, a significant number of tribals have joined the ranks of ecological refugees and, as a result, despair and anomie have replaced their political voice and optimism. A greater threat to the survival of the tribals came from the program to build the nation as an economic and industrialized giant. Eighty percent of the nation's mineral wealth and 72 percent of the forests, water, and other natural resources are found in tribal lands. Thus, mines, industrial estates, hydroelectric projects, urban centers, and planned population transfers signaled the internal colonization of tribal homelands. During the colonial period tribal areas were opened up, in the name of "good governance," to contractors, civil and military officials, traders, alcohol vendors, timber merchants, and moneylenders who entered these areas and forced the tribals into indebtedness, alienated lands, polluted environments, and slavery. Forest reservations made tribals intruders in their own home. Sixty years later, the process was repeated in a far more ruthless fashion. The state, the single largest agency of tribal land alienation in the postindependence era, displaced 13.5 million tribals, creating conditions that approximate ethnocide.[41]

Hence, despite resource-rich homelands, tribals remain extremely poor. Eighty-five percent of them live below the poverty line. According to the National Commission for Scheduled Castes and Scheduled Tribes of the Government of India (1986), 83 percent of the total bonded laborers are tribals. Nation-building left the tribes disoriented, demoralized, and defeated people. The process of modernization (read, internal colonization) opened up the hinterland to the new frontiersman. While not all the effects of modernization on India have been detrimental, one cannot deny that it has exposed India's interiors to a sort of new process of colonization and exploitation. In the inaccessible areas, land alienation intensified with the suppression of *jhum,* the traditional shifting agriculture of rural tribes. Disquieted by the progressive pauperization of the tribals, whose conditions were increasingly becoming a national scandal, legislators caused a flurry of land reform legislation to be included in the statute books. But land reform has been a dismal failure, as land laws were rooted in the matrix of colonial land practice, which placed the landless tribal and the landlord on the same legal footing. Legal presumptions and procedures, also of colonial origin, negated the intention of land reforms. Distortions introduced by the colonial government were accepted as important elements of the legal framework in implementing the policies and programs in the tribal areas. Paper laws of colonial dispensation were given pride of place over the laws by which people lived.

An alarming indicator of tribal alienation is the 1971 census data for Maharashtra, a highly industrialized state. The number of tribal cultivators fell by 22.65 percent, from 7.25 lakhs in 1961 to 5.61 lakhs in 1971—precisely when the implementation of land reform was at its peak. While tribals maintained possession of their lands under the law, alienation of lands still continued, either through illegal entries into registers or permission given by collectors for land transfers to nontribals.[42] Today, almost all tribals are small peasants possessing uneconomic holdings or cultivators-cum-tenants-cum-laborers. They practice the most "primitive" yet often the most ecologically friendly technology. They are heavily in debt and are alienated from the lands they have been ploughing for generations. Even when attempts have been made to provide the tribals with land, the land often passes into the hands of nontribals, in spite of legal prohibition against such transfers. The unscrupulous take advantage of the honesty, simplicity, and innocence of the tribals.[43]

Land, the substantial expression of nature, is a central pivot of tribal life. Traditionally, individual rights to land-based resources were embedded in communal systems of access and resource management.[44] Since the concept of private property did not exist, life remained corporate and cooperative.[45] Land circumscribed the individual and the community. Existence was seen as an extension of collective consciousness, incorporating social (belonging to a community), cultural (link to traditions, ethos, and way of life), and political (basis for the power of the elders) significance. Land loss causes alienation, because the individual, or community, is prevented from articulating his consciousness and is progressively pushed into anomie. According to

Burman, the loss of land is related to role dissonance between the economic, sociopolitical, and cultural milieus.[46]

Although modernization has raised health and sanitation standards, introduced an educational system, and emphasized the value of literacy, it has generated, perhaps unintentionally, a host of negative consequences. Tribals constitute the poorest section of society, with an overwhelming majority below the poverty line. Although the enormity of this human catastrophe remains unrecognized, indicators of poverty levels in the community, like high infant mortality, pervasive malnutrition of women and children, and starvation deaths of children, are widespread. The incidence of starvation deaths is no longer confined to the inaccessible and backward areas, but occurs with unfailing regularity even in areas immediately adjacent to the state capitals and financial and industrial centers.

Marginalized in Their Homelands

While the framers of the Indian Constitution debated the character of the nation and decided that India would be a sovereign, socialist, secular democratic republic, little republics were still vibrant in the tribal areas. The tribal communities retained their traditional forms of social and political organization through the entire colonial period. Remoteness and resistance allowed the tribal realms to retain their identity and their existence as realms within realms. This was reflected in the British policy of treating the tribal belts as "excluded" and "partially excluded" for purposes of administration. The Constitution retained this colonial practice in the Fifth and Sixth Schedules. But the principles of the Constitution were subsumed under the agenda of nation-building. Modern governance, for the ruling elites, was the creation of a unified, albeit centralized, polity and the extension of a formal system of governance to the tribal areas. The traditional forms of self-governance came under severe attack, and the forms of governance of independent India replaced the traditional structures. The imposition of this formal system, and of bourgeoisie parliamentary politics in the name of democracy, emasculated the self-governing institutions of the tribals, and with them their internal cohesiveness.

The creation of administrative regions fragmented organic, integral tribal regions and politically marginalized the tribals in most areas.

However, in most communities the two systems run parallel to each other, with their independent realms of authority and control. The traditional *panchayat*s administered by elders, chosen by consensus or with or without a hereditary headman, make decisions in the social, cultural, and religious realms. The state-sponsored *panchayati raj* (village self-governance) institutions broker political and economic privilege that are attractive for the money they bring in the name of village development. The task of nation-building discouraged diversity and stressed homogeneity. The tribals were to be drawn into the national mainstream. Over time, the mainstream began to be defined as Hindu and, by implication, tribals are being called *vanavasi*s (forest dwellers), or traditional Hindu communities that were left behind in the forested tracts. This is an important deviation from the popular nomenclature as *adivasi*s (first inhabitants). As a reaction to Christian missionaries who had entered the tribal areas during the colonial period, Hindu missionaries are aggressively advocating a process of initiation of the tribals into present-day Hinduism. Consequently, various tribal communities are at different stages in the "Hinduization" or "Sanskritization" process. Bowing before waves of Sanskritization and suffering attacks on their traditions as "backward" and "primitive," several tribes, in their search for a "non-backward identity," have begun to call themselves "Hindu." Hindu deities have entered their pantheon, displacing the traditional spirits of nature; however, some may argue that the new deities are unwelcome in their religious traditions.

Conclusion: On the Horns of a Dilemma

The peoples of tribal India are on the horns of a dilemma. In which direction will they go? Their forested homelands have been plundered, their economy disrupted, their ecology ravaged. They are trying to find the tenuous balance between tradition and modernity, which is an uphill task because the ecological values so dear to them appear alien in the race for modernity. Their culture walks the tight rope between assimilation and affirmation. They cling tenuously to a beautiful past in the lap of nature, but they are not sure what awaits them in the future. They have been and remain ecologically sensitive and would opt for a sustainable future in the forest. However, they are being asked to make way for wildlife, with whom they have lived at peace for generations. These dilemmas are real, replete with uncertainties for their sustainable ecological future.

This article is an effort to explore the struggle of the tribals and to look at the past in relationship to their present, with the intention of moving into a better future. Although the past was and the present remains painful, the elders say pain is always present whenever a new life is born. Recently, for the first time in history, tribal communities nationwide came together, under a unified front, to fight to establish authentic self-governance. The struggle continued for five years, from 1992 through 1996, and finally bore fruit. The right of tribal communities to function as autonomous, self-governing societies was recognized by the government. A constitutional amendment was passed on 24 December 1996 (Panchayats [Extension to the Scheduled Arrears] Act 1996). This new law, which is the first departure from colonial governance, grants the village community the right to protect its culture, traditions, common property resources, and customary modes of dispute resolution. The law opens new vistas for tribals, as ecological people, to restore to nature and to humans what has always been theirs: the intrinsic right to live with dignity.

However, the tribals in India face the difficult challenge of translating the law of self-governance into a reality. Their symbiosis with nature—their ecological ethos—has faced enormous threats from the ravages of modernization, particularly of the new generation. Their search for their ecological grounding sways between romanticizing the past and contending with a harsh future. Their struggle for a sustainable ecological existence calls for a dialogue with both the Indian government and the national mainstream. The storm is still raging, and so questions must be asked and possibilities must be considered: Are modernity and development inevitable? If so, can a harmonious relationship between modern modes of development and tribal traditions be reached? Are the ecological traditions of the tribals related to future global environmental problems? Although there are many questions to be answered, one thing is certain: the future is open and the future is ours.

Notes

1. Government of India, *Report of the Committee on Forests and Tribals in India* (New Delhi: Ministry of Environment and Forests, 1952).

2. *The State of India's Environment 1982: A Citizens' Report*, ed. Anil Agarwal et al. (New Delhi: Centre for Science and the Environment, 1982), 33.

3. Amita Baviskar, "Fate of the Forest: Conservation and Tribal Rights," *Economic and Political Weekly* (Mumbai), 17 September 1994, 2499.

4. Ramachandra Guha, "Forestry Debate and Draft Forest Act: Who Gains, Who Loses?" *Economic and Political Weekly* (Mumbai), 20 August 1994, 2196.

5. Ibid., 2193.

6. W. Fernandes, P. Viegas, G. Menon, and K. T. Chandy, "Forest Environment and Forest Dweller Economy in Chattisgarh: A Report on a Study on Deforestation, Marginalization and Search for Alternatives" (New Delhi: Indian Social Institute, 1985, mimeographed), 28–29.

7. *Indigenous Peoples in India*, ed. Sarini, Sarini Occasional Papers, no. 1 (Bhubaneswar: CEDEC, 1977), 33.

8. Government of India, *Report of the Bombay Forest Commission 1887*, vols. 1– 4 (Government Central Press, 1887), 132.

9. Government of India, *The National Forest Policy, 1988* (New Delhi: Government of India, 1988).

10. B. K. Roy Burman, "Homage to Earth," in *Indigenous Vision: People of India, Attitudes to Environment*, ed. Geeti Sen (New Delhi: Sage Publications, 1992), 4.

11. Ibid., 3.

12. B. K. Roy Burman, "Tribal Populations Interface of History, Ecology and Political Economy," in *Continuity and Change in Tribal Society*, ed. M. Miri (Shimla: Indian Institute of Advanced Study, 1993), 32.

13. David Hardiman, *Power in the Forest: The Dangs, 1820–1940*, Subaltern Studies, 7, ed. David Arnold et al. (Delhi: Oxford University Press, 1994), 91.

14. Ibid.

15. Ibid., 105.

16. "Just What Is Conservation?" *Cultural Survival Quarterly* 15, no. 4 (fall 1991): 20.

17. See Pernille Gooch, "Nomadic Van-Gujjars Fight to Maintain Their Life in the Forest," *Indigenous Affairs*, 1994, no. 3, 4–16; and Pernille Gooche, *At the Tail of the Buffalo: Van Gujjar Pastoralists between the Forest and the World Arena* (Lund: Department of Sociology, Lund University, 1998).

18. Smitu Kothari, "Social Movements and the Redefinition of Democracy," *Lokayan Bulletin* (New Delhi), 1996.

19. Baviskar, "Fate of the Forest"; *The Struggle for Land and the Fate of the Forests*, ed. Marcus Colchester and Larry Lohmann (London: Zed Books, 1993); and Madhav Gadgil and Ramachandra Guha, *This Fissured Land: An Ecological History of India* (Berkeley and Los Angeles: University of California Press, 1992).

20. Madhav Gadgil and Ramachandra Guha, *Ecology and Equity: The Use and Abuse of Nature in Contemporary India* (London and New York: Routledge, 1995), 189.

21. Census of India, 1991, New Delhi.

22. Ganshyam Shah, "Tribal Issues: Problems and Perspectives," in *Socio-Economic and Ecological Development,* ed. Buddhadeb Chaudhari (New Delhi: Inter India Publications, 1992), 119.

23. Sitakant Mahapatra, "Invocation: Rites of Propriation in Tribal Society," in *Indigenous Vision: People of India, Attitudes to Environment,* ed. Geeti Sen (New Delhi: Sage Publications, 1992), 4.

24. Roy Burman, "Homage to Earth," 4.

25. Edward Goldsmith, "Gaia Is the Source of All Benefits," in *Indigenous Vision: People of India, Attitudes to Environment,* ed. Geeti Sen (New Delhi: Sage Publications, 1992), 48.

26. R. S. Mann, "Animism, Economy, Ecology and Change among Negrito Hunters and Gatherers," in *Nature-Man-Spirit Complex in Tribal India,* ed. R. S. Mann (New Delhi: Concept Publishing Co., 1981), 202.

27. *Report of the Scheduled Castes and Scheduled Tribes Commission (Debar Commision)* (New Delhi: Government of India, Government Printing Press, 1983).

28. Savyasaachi, *Tribal Forest Dwellers and Self Rule* (New Delhi: Indian Social Institute, 1998), 48.

29. R. S. Mann, "Cultural-Ecological Approach to the Study of the Bhil," in *Nature-Man-Spirit Complex in Tribal India,* ed. R. S. Mann (New Delhi: Concept Publishing Co., 1981), 118.

30. Surajit Chandra Sinha, "Tribal Cultures of Peninsular India," in *Man in India,* vol. 37 (Ranchi, 1957), 46.

31. V. S. Sahay, "The Nicobarese," in *Nature-Man-Spirit Complex in Tribal India,* ed. R. S. Mann (New Delhi: Concept Publishing House, 1981), 227.

32. Mann, "Animism, Economy, Ecology and Change," 201.

33. J. D. Mehra, "A Worldview of Indian Tribes," in *Tribal Heritage of India,* ed. S. C. Dube (New Delhi: Vikas Publishing House, 1977), 82.

34. M. Vanucci, "Tradition and Change," in *Indigenous Vision: People of India, Attitudes to Environment,* ed. Geeti Sen (New Delhi: Sage Publications, 1992), 82.

35. Sitakant Mahapatra, *Unending Rhythms: Oral Poetry of the Indian Tribes* (New Delhi: Inter-India Publications, 1992), 15.

36. M. Vanucci, "Sacred Groves or Holy Forests," in *Concepts of Space, Ancient and Modern,* ed. Kapila Vatsayayan (New Delhi: Indira Gandhi Centre for the Arts, 1991), 324.

37. Mann, "Cultural-Ecological Approach," 123.

38. Suneet Chopra, "Garo Myths," in *Indigenous Vision: Peoples of India, Attitudes to the Environment,* ed. Geeti Sen (New Delhi: Sage Publications, 1992), 92.

39. K. S. Singh, "The Munda Epic," in *Indigenous Vision: Peoples of India, Attitudes to the Environment,* ed. Geeti Sen (New Delhi: Sage Publications, 1992), 88.

40. S. C. Roy, "Oraon Religion and Custom," *Man in India* (Ranchi, 1928), 43.

41. Bhram Dev Sharma, *Twenty-Ninth Report of the Commissioner for Scheduled Castes and Scheduled Tribes* (New Delhi: Office of the Commissioner for Scheduled Castes and Scheduled Tribes, 1986).

42. H. G. Vartak, *Report of Committee to Examine Difficulties Experienced by*

Scheduled Tribe Land Holders/Cultivators in Respect of Their Lands in the Working of Certain Acts (Bombay: Government Press, official, 1972).

43. O. P. Mehra, foreword to *The Tribes in Maharashtra,* by G. M. Gare and M. B. Aphale (Pune: Tribal Research Institute, 1968), 3.

44. Bombay Presidency, *Gazetteer,* vol. 13 (Thane) (Bombay: Central Government Press, 1882).

45. Mann, "Animism, Economy, Ecology and Change," 201–2.

46. B. K. Roy Burman, *Report of the Study Group on Land Holding Systems in Tribal Areas* (New Delhi: Government of India, 1987).

Shoot the Horse to Get the Rider: Religion and Forest Politics in Bentian Borneo

STEPHANIE FRIED

In modern Indonesia, belief in "One, Supreme God" is a require-ment of citizenship. This stems from the Pancasila (Five Principles) laid out by Indonesia's first president, Sukarno, in 1945, in a speech made two months before the Indonesian proclamation of indepen-dence. The official demand for "religions of the book" has often placed practitioners of indigenous religions, which are classified as "beliefs," in uncomfortable, if not untenable, positions. In Indonesia's Outer Islands, many of the followers of indigenous religions also in-habit regions of spectacular wealth in terms of natural resources. This paper explores aspects of the complex interactions between promoters of official religions and practitioners of indigenous religions and the impact of these interactions on cultural and ecological integrity in the Bentian forests of East Kalimantan (Indonesian Borneo).

Introduction

Borneo, the third largest island in the world, lies on the equator be-tween Java, the Philippines, and mainland Southeast Asia. Brunei and the Malaysian states of Sabah and Sarawak occupy the northern third of the island, reflecting former British colonial claims. The Indone-sian provinces of East, Central, South, and West Kalimantan occupy the southern two-thirds of the island, reflecting former Dutch colonial claims.[1] Indonesian Borneo (Kalimantan) contains approximately one-third of the nation's forests, which total just over 120 million hectares. Nearly half of Kalimantan's forests (17 million hectares) are located in the province of East Kalimantan.[2]

The vast tracts of Bornean forest are broken up by river networks radiating from the central highlands.[3] In sharp contrast to the fertile volcanic soils of most of the surrounding islands of the Indonesian archipelago, Bornean soils, although covered with dense vegetation, are for the most part acidic and chemically poor. Often located on moderate to great slopes, these soils are prone to severe erosion if left exposed for extended periods of time.[4] As a result, over the centuries, the indigenous, or *adat,*[5] peoples of Borneo have developed complex and ecologically sound systems of forest management and forest-based agriculture, designed in careful mimicry of and elaboration on natural forest processes and embedded in ecologically oriented cultural practices.

Borneo, like other islands of the "South Seas," has excited the imaginations of foreign visitors for centuries.

[It] entered European thought and writing as a hostile place: inhospitable, dangerous, barbarous and difficult to govern, Pirates, headhunters, primeval jungles were the main elements of European myths and legends.[6]

Adventurers, missionaries, and traders, drawn to Borneo jungles, often recorded detailed impressions of their Dayak[7] hosts, companions, and neighbors. Their descriptions, not surprisingly, revealed almost as much about their own opinions, prejudices, and plans as they did about upriver peoples.

In *The Invention of Africa,* V. Y. Mudimbe, a philosopher, social scientist, and historian of Africa, describes the mutually reinforcing processes of colonial enterprise, written ethnography, and the missionary conversion of "savage" cultures.[8] Although he is primarily concerned with the way in which these processes unfolded in Africa, much of his work and analysis is relevant for an understanding of Borneo. Mudimbe identified three complementary types of "speeches" which contributed to the invention of a primitive Africa: "the exotic text on savages, represented by travelers' reports; the philosophical interpretations about a hierarchy of civilizations and the anthropological search for primitiveness."[9] Noting that the word "colonialism" may be interpreted, in a literal sense, to mean "organization, arrangement," derived as it is from the Latin word *colere* (cultivate or design), Mudimbe identified

> three main keys to account for the modulations and methods representative of colonial organization: the procedures of acquiring, distributing and exploiting lands in colonies; the policies of domesticating natives; and the manner of managing ancient organizations and implementing new modes of production. Thus, three complementary hypotheses and actions emerge: the domination of physical space, the reformation of natives' minds, and the integration of local economic histories into the Western perspective.[10]

Mudimbe's analysis applies quite nicely to the context of Borneo's colonial history as well as to the modernizing Indonesian nation-state. In the case of Kalimantan, the "domination of physical space" has been one of the most important national and nationalizing priorities of the nation-state. In Indonesia's Outer Islands, it is often accomplished by the seizing of traditional *adat* territories and the parceling out of the island to logging, mining, and plantation companies. The "reformation of natives' minds" is accomplished through the inculcation of nationalist, developmentalist, and religious beliefs in a nationalized citizenry. Local economic histories are integrated not simply into "the Western perspective" but into a nationalist, often Java-centric perspective.

Writing with "the passion of the Other, of that being which has been so far a mere object of the discourses of social and human sciences,"[11] Mudimbe identifies the congruence of written accounts of savage civilizations with the "colonizing structure," that which "completely embraces the physical, human, [and] spiritual aspects of the colonizing experience."[12]

> Theories of colonial expansion and discourses on African primitiveness emphasize . . . the promotion of a particular model of history . . . [which focuses on] the discrepancy between "civilization" and "Christianity" on the one hand, "primitiveness" and "paganism" on the other, and the means of "evolution" or "conversion" from the first stage to the second. . . . [This type of] reductionist [discourse] speak[s] about neither Africa nor Africans, but rather justif[ies] the process of inventing and conquering a continent and naming its "primitiveness" or "disorder", as well as the subsequent means of its exploitation. . . .[13]

Returning to the Bornean context, we find the Dutch East Indies colonial apparatus attempting to "civilize" the "wild" populations under its jurisdiction, largely in order to simplify the processes of the extraction of valuable forest goods from the interior of Borneo, the establishment of plantation agriculture, and the opening of mines and oilfields.

By the 1930s, after headhunting had largely been eliminated in East Kalimantan, Christian missionaries made their way upriver and began their inroads into Dayak cosmologies. After the "pacification" of up-river regions, Christian missionaries elaborated upon the colonial process of taming, "rationalizing," and bureaucratizing "savage" lives.[14]

Intentionally framing their religious discourse in terms familiar to former headhunters and practitioners of human and animal sacrifice, their sermons focused on blood sacrifice as well, or "redeeming blood." They sang of the "blood of the Lamb." The figure of Jesus stabbed in the side and nailed to a cross-shaped post resonated with local practice of tying slaves and water buffalo to sacrificial *belontang* poles and stabbing them to death. The difference between the Christian religion and Kaharingan, as some of the Dayak religions came to be called, was that, for Christians, the blood sacrifice had already been made. The sacrifice of Jesus on the cross had been powerful enough for the whole world. With Christianity, the missionaries argued, it was no longer necessary to stab slaves to death or to conduct raids to collect fresh heads. Besides, they continued, if one believed in Jesus Christ and swallowed the proffered white pills, Jesus would take away malaria, worms, and typhoid, proving his magic stronger than that of the shamans and paramount leaders. In addition to medicine, missionaries brought other technological advances of secular science directly into Dayak villages—in the early years, radios and books; later, motor boats and VCRs.

Linn Tjen Yee: Mahakam Missionary

From the sixteenth to the eighteenth century, missionary activity was an intimate part of the political process of expanding European sovereignty over "newly discovered" lands.[15] The basic principles of *terra nullius* (nobody's land) were established by papal decree and denied "nonbelieving" (i.e., non-Christian) natives the right to an autonomous political existence and the right to own or to transfer ownership (of land).[16] Linking Christian religious observance with the seizing of African lands, Mudimbe describes "the mass celebrated on the Guinea Coast in 1481, under a big tree displaying the royal arms of Portugal, symboli[zing] the possession of a new territory."[17]

In a haunting parallel, over five hundred years later, similar scenes would be played out in the forests of Borneo. The actors, however, would be different, reflecting the shift from colonial power to the modern nation-state—no longer the Catholic Church and colonial officials but, instead, evangelical Protestant churches and colonizing timber corporations. Indeed, the concept of *terra nullius* would live on, reformulated in East Kalimantan as recently as 1982 as "terra incognito" by mapping "experts" and advisors to the Indonesian government.[18]

In the case of East Kalimantan, missionary incursions into the Mahakam River basin had been initiated by the 1930s. Missionary Linn Tjen Lee, working for a North American Protestant group and known to English-speakers as Jason Linn, wrote *Pioneering in Dayak Borneo*, which was advertised as "the first Chinese missionary thriller ever to be published in English." In *Pioneering*, Linn reflected on his missionary work in the 1930s among the Bentian and Benoaq of the Middle Mahakam region of East Kalimantan, where he was at times "exalted like a God, at other times despised like dung."

The Bentian and Benuaq, like other indigenous Kalimantan peoples, are swidden agriculturists who practice a form of rotational agriculture well-suited to the poor and easily eroded soils of the region. Clearing patches of old growth secondary forest to plant rice with dibble sticks, Bentian and Benoaq farmers, unlike many other swidden cultivators, also sow large quantities of rattan seeds and seedlings in their fields.[19] These seedlings mature after seven to ten years into productive rattan vines, their weight supported by thick secondary forest regrowth in the fallowed fields. The farmers continue to harvest rattan for up to thirty years or more after planting. Rattan is currently a staple commodity for the local inhabitants of the region, as it has been for well over one hundred years. Forested rattan gardens in the Bentian and Benuaq regions function very much like bank accounts for their owners. When rattan prices are low or when farmers choose not to sell for other reasons, the clumps of constantly growing rattan shoots may be left in the fields, growing longer and more valuable (adding "interest") every day that the farmer does not sell the crop. In the case of a family emergency, a withdrawal may be made from the bank account. Even if rattan prices are still low, the harvest of a ton or two will cover hospitalization costs, school expenses, or other urgent needs. Additionally, small amounts of rattan are harvested every month, regardless of the market price, in order to provide the income necessary for the purchase of goods such as cooking oil, batteries, and soap.

The strategy of a diversified and flexible household economy, which involves rattan production for export markets and fruit, vegetable, and grain production for local consumption, has proven economically successful and environmentally sound for the Bentian and Benoaq peoples of the Middle Mahakam region. Of the Middle Mahakam inhabitants, Reverend Linn stated:

> The Dyaks live a much simplified life, and have they not lived in such fashion all along? They live a far happier life than the cultured man. They live simply whether in food, clothing, housing or travel, as simply as their simple minds think. This simplicity is reflected in any of the things they use. For example, their one-piece wooden bridge, one-piece wooden boat, one-piece wooden ladder, and even one-piece wooden coffin. Yes, they are as simple as infants.[20]

The "simplicity" of constructing a one-piece boat, ladder, or coffin, aside, it was the "simplicity" of the savage mind which was to prove complicated and vexing to outsiders who entered upriver realms as seekers of power, wealth, or the glory of their Christian God.

In a calculated move, Linn took aim at the religious beliefs of the indigenous leaders:

> We discovered in this well-ordered kingdom of nature that the chieftain exercised full authority over his subjects, while the virtue of the people excelled in "obedient following". . . . We took this to be an opening to our mission. As the saying goes, "Shoot the horse to get the rider; catch the robber-chief to catch the thieves."[21]

As Reverend Linn would discover, Dayak rulers were often amenable to conversion to Christianity. This was not necessarily, however, a reflection of the "taming of their savage souls" or their true acceptance of Jesus Christ. In the past, a significant number of Dayak leaders had "converted" to Islam and received, for their religious and political allegiance with the Muslim Malay Sultans, not only new and aristo-cratic titles reflecting their increase in rank, but often the gift of a Malay or Bugis wife. Such "conversions" often had little effect on the religious life of Dayak communities.[22]

Conversion to Christianity, while not associated with the gift of a European wife, was often associated with the high status of white-skinned Europeans and Americans in an increasingly race-conscious colonial context. For pork-loving upriver peoples, Christian religion had the added attraction over Islam of not restricting a favorite dietary item.

Painfully aware of the increasing importance of the politics of identity in the racially stratified colonial regime of the Dutch East Indies, Linn, the Chinese missionary, despaired at Dayak reasons for converting to Christianity:

> [A]t first they thought Christians were Americans and feared to have anything to do with us [Chinese missionaries]. Having joined the Church, their reasonings were clear—they felt a raising of their status, and now they were become "tuan" (masters). In the South Seas, only white men were addressed "tuan". "Tuan" means not only "Sir" but also "Master". We overseas Chinese seem not worthy of this term either. So normally we are called "towkay" or "proprietor" [i.e., shop owner] by the aborigines. . . . They did not know what an evangelist was nor could they differentiate between a minister and a missionary. Nor did they know our names and surnames. They simply called us according to their needs and expectations in us. So they called us "Mr. Salvation" ("Tuan Selamat") or "Mr. Cross" ("Tuan Salib").[23]

The practice of defining the Other by one's own "needs and expec-tations" was not, however, limited to Dayak leaders. The discourse of both colonials and missionaries, privileged as they were by links to vast overseas empires, the written word, firearms, currency, and West-ern medicines, identified upriver Bornean peoples as savages, simple primitives, those in need of being civilized, helped, or saved.

> Pre-figuring the later goals and desires of modernizing nation-states, missionaries, possibly more than members of other branches of the co-lonial establishment, aimed at the radical transformation of indigenous society. . . . They therefore sought, whether consciously or uncon-sciously, the destruction of pre-colonial societies and their replacement by new Christian societies in the image of Europe.[24]

Eboussi-Boulaga labels missionary discourse as "first of all, . . . a language of derision [which] fundamentally ridicules the pagan's Gods."[25] The components of ridicule and refutation, as well as the striving for orthodoxy and conformity, would later be found in the development discourse of the modern nation-state. Linn's writings, as well, evidence a peculiar mix of mockery and envy of the culture and religion of his Dayak "quarry."

> In this Southland of perpetual summer, clothing is not a chief article of use. Whether men or women, old or young, they go about naked except for a rough loin cloth covering. During the Japanese southern invasion they had no more cloth. So they plucked some fibres from the bark of trees and without a weave or spin made them into natural loin cloths. Ah! These well-favoured sons of nature, how they spend their days in unending leisure. You could never find a busy man within their midst. If you come to Dyakland you could immediately spot out under the sun a man lying on the ground pillowed on a girl's thigh while she rivets her two eyes on his shaggy long hair—searching for lice. This interesting picture tells you a story: They are in the process of spending a peaceful, leisurely day. Yes, such is the complacent Dyak life-style of whiling away the time. We know that contentment is the mother of a simple living.[26]

This contrasted sharply with Linn's own experiences in Borneo:

> Living in Dyakland was a laborious life. We traveled either on foot or by canoe. This often took us over hills and through rivers and fords. Mountaineering brought slippery hazards, while on the rivers, dangers of capsizing lurked. Sometimes we spent a night in jungle, sometimes we halted at a sand bank. Sweat, sweat, sweat was the order of the day.[27]

Linn's discussion of Dayak systems of knowledge—including ecological and forest lore—is tinged with both insult and longing:

> Talking about the education of the Dyaks, this may be crisply summed up in a word: they are illiterates. Without any education their knowledge is tightly circumscribed. . . . Since they are illiterate and devoid of any scientific knowledge, they know not how to make aircraft, guns or atom bombs and the whole gamut of weapons of destruction. Nevertheless, they know the art of eking out an existence. They carry on their hip a long *parang* (knife) and in their hands they carry a *sumpitan*

(blowpipe). With these two weapons for eking out an existence they can go anywhere, uphill or down dale. They will not die of hunger with these tools and by their use they can build themselves a home.

They seem to have no difficulty in subduing snakes and wild beasts, for they are not only fully armed but also endowed with agility and cunning. In their village there is hung a brass gong, or else there is a big drum set up before the door. In time of emergency the gong or the drum is sounded to alert one and all to self-defense. Thus they are enabled to live in a tranquil world by themselves.[28]

Linn describes his findings that the blood sacrifice required by Dayak religion yielded a natural entry point for Christian evangelicism:

It is said that some forty years ago a human being bought with money was made a sacrifice in this manner—[tied to a sacrifice pole and stabbed to death—purposely made to suffer pain on behalf of the sins of the whole village]. After he died, his head was chopped off and hung in the centre of the village. As it is said that his soul still lingered over his skull, a fire was lit to smoke it away until the blood was dried. The soul of the victim became the guardian-hero of their houses. This is cruel business and foolish darkness, but the belief in the shedding of blood to atone for sins tallies exactly with the Judeo-Christian truth. How did they get this idea we can hardly know. However, this opens for us an effectual door to lead them out of darkness into the light, to receive the truth of sins forgiven through the Cross.[29]

Linn and his Chinese colleague, Mr. Lenn, formed their plan of conquest:

First, we must abandon that superiority complex of national pride. According to Paul, "I am all things to all men." We would maintain a self-control in our daily life in order that there might be no difference in this respect between us and the Dyaks. Second, we would "enter the tiger's lair" to strike up friendship with them as well as to understand their sentiments, custom and taboos that thereby we might obtain our quarry.[30]

Linn recorded his impressions of the apparently well-rounded indigenous diet:

[T]heir menu consists of wild pigs and deer. But their main dishes display mostly the coarsest of vegetables. Except for several great festivals during the year when oxen and pigs are slaughtered alongside venison to be devoured with gusto, their daily viands comprise only rice, chili salt and all kinds of fruits from their own cultivation or plucked from the wilds. When fruits are in full season they invariably eat of them in lieu of rice. A cornucopia as far as food is concerned, is this tropical South Seas which being favored with balmy winds and gentle rains becomes their storehouse. Here they may eat carefree-rice.[31]

Traveling up remote rivers and hiking through the jungle with a "cumbersome pump organ," Linn baptized almost three thousand Mahakam inhabitants. He detailed his reasons for "backsliding" among the converted, which included the lack of nurturing and follow-through by his mission and attacks by "disciples of a heterogeneous faith" (Muslims) who spread all kinds of weird rumors:

By becoming Christians the [Dayaks] were to be taken to China to be made cannon fodder for the Japanese. By joining the Church they had to drink a cup of medicine from the pastor's hand. Then they would be taken out to sea and have their bellies split for the gold in them."[32]

In earlier centuries, the Muslim Sultans of Kutai, the nominal rulers of the upriver regions traversed by Linn, had issued decrees recognizing the validity of Dayak *adat,* or custom. Dayak communities, likewise, made room for some of the Muslim customs. Missionaries such as Linn, however, were adamant about requiring the "purity" of Christian religion, untainted by *adat* practices. For example, during important Dayak ceremonies, water buffalo are slaughtered. Dayaks of the Kutai region, however, require the killing to be done by a Muslim, rendering the meat *halal* and edible by Muslims attending the ceremony. Linn complained:

It all started with the Christmas celebrations that year. Whenever the Dyaks have any celebrations they love to slaughter a cow. The custom of slaughtering cows is by the hand of a Muslim, without which they cannot eat. Now slaughtering the cow is according to Muslim religious rite. This involves saying a prayer which I regarded as adversely affecting our Christian faith. It was better to lose friends than lose part of our faith.[33]

Linn bemoaned the fact that "Though prostitution is a word not known in their vocabulary, adultery and fornication is a rampant practice. Without instruction and education they regard intercourse between the sexes as a very natural thing."[34]

The first ever mass revival meeting held upriver in Dayak territory during Christmas 1940, attended by "400 believers from 12 or 13 villages exposed the sins of cold-heartedness, backsliding, theft, adultery, concubinage, robbing of another's wife, polyandry, servants, breaking of Church laws, gambling, double dealing."[35] Despite this, Linn felt that:

> One by one things are falling in line, decently and in order, according to the Word—no more that old life of the mountain aborigines. They sought in all things to follow the rules of propriety, etiquette, and culture; whereas adultery and fornication were open secrets, now they were deemed most shameful. They regard mass wedding as the most glorious event in life.[36]

Linn's assessment of his work among the Bentian, however, would prove overly optimistic. Some sixty years later, in the 1990s, many of the Bentian still adhered to the old religion. Certain villages, generally those closest to the more easily reachable confluence of the Pahu and Lawa Rivers, did remain or become Christian, but hostile splits between factions of the church led to the founding of rival congregations, with bad blood between them, in the tiny villages up and down the Lawa River. The two churches were differentiated largely by the fact that one became known locally as the "airplane church"—part of the U.S.-funded missionary network that possessed small aircraft, which flew (apparently illegally) proselytizing American missionaries into Bentian territory. Other less accessible populations, while remaining largely Kaharingan, had integrated Christian ceremonies into certain aspects of their ceremonial life—in ways that did not threaten some of their core beliefs or primary practices (adultery, polyandry, gambling). In one of the more "solidly" Christian communities, for example, the missionaries' insistence on two principles—first, forgiveness for one's sins upon public repentance; second, the idea that premarital sex was a major sin—led to a new ceremony, the *tobat,* or repentance ceremony. Upriver Christian weddings (Linn's "mass weddings") were now routinely preceded, the day before, by a standard *tobat* ceremony, where the prospective bride and groom confess and repent their sins of premarital fornication so that they may perform the Christian wedding ceremony the next day, free of sin.

The Destruction of the Longhouses

Despite their failure at winning over most of the Bentian population, missionaries and their tactics, later combined with Indonesian governmental efforts, did succeed in destroying much of the traditional power structure and disorienting the Bentian community. For years, the church and later the Indonesian government led campaigns against the unwholesome and unsanitary nature of longhouse living.

The Bentian generally have two types of dwelling place in different locations: small and simple field houses (*umeq*), usually with one hearth, designed to house a relatively small family, located in or near current swidden fields, and often a substantial distance from neighbors; and longhouses, often located at a strategic bend in the river, designed to hold many families (i.e., with many hearths—one for each small family group), built for ceremonial and defense purposes. The longhouses are often largely empty during planting and harvest seasons since most families live out in the fields where they keep their livestock. Longhouses, however, formed the nerve centers of communication for the community. In the case of an emergency, a ceremony, a strategy session, or a death, the longhouse gongs would sound, calling the families in from their field houses. The longhouses were generally split in half lengthwise. The front half was a public gathering place where by custom, or *adat,* all who entered were required to describe what they had seen during the day—for example, game and other animals sighted, trees about to fruit, rain, river conditions (especially depth of water), visitors, fires or the potential for fires—as well as the health of family members, disease, potential problems or disputes. In this way, the longhouse served as the nerve center for the community and was a forum for passing on information about environmental and social conditions throughout the region farmed and inhabited by community members.

The back half of the longhouse was divided according to the number of hearths built there—one for each family group, with the *adat* leader occupying the central hearth. In most cases the hearth and sleeping sections of each family group were not separated by physical walls from their neighbors. In the minds of the inhabitants, however, clear separation existed. In contrast to the missionaries' perceptions of unwholesome communal living, where the entire community shared one dwelling, longhouse physical and social structure was more akin to modern condominium living, since each family had clear living quarters and a clear "back yard"—behind their longhouse hearth, planted with the family's fruit trees.

The relentless missionary and governmental campaigns to destroy the longhouses worked, however, and as Bentian families were given or built for themselves small single-family homes to replace their longhouse sections, the longhouse-based environmental and social communications network was destroyed. The new village houses separated the inhabitants from their neighbors, just as Bentian field houses did, but instead of the airy construction typical of Bentian architecture—pole houses, with rattan floors, oriented to the prevailing winds—the new houses were "modern," resembling tightly sealed wooden boxes with—in the 1990s—metal roofs. The fact that the new houses were close to the ground and had individual doors, which Bentian householders preferred to keep closed at most times, lessened the likelihood of casual interactions with neighbors and sharply reduced the flow of information about the surrounding environment and events of the day. Muslim traders eventually set up small shops and coffeehouses, or *warung,* in Bentian villages. Such coffeehouses typically serve Malay society as communication nodes. These were usually frequented by Muslim soldiers and police. Given the long-standing antipathy between indigenous pork eaters and those professing Islam, the Bentian never felt comfortable going to the coffeehouses. As a result, their regional communications system remained in disarray. The only place where large groups of Bentian regularly gathered was now at Sunday church services, which were ceremonial in nature and left little room for communication or exchange among local residents.

The "Prayer Team": Church versus *Belian* in 1992

In March 1992, in a small private prayer meeting, the minister of one of the larger churches founded by Jason Linn in Bentian territory announced that the church had arranged for a prayer team to visit the congregation.[37] The team, like the minister, was from Java and would be performing faith healings for the sick and the infirm of the village. The minister urged the congregation to bring "unbelievers" to the prayer team so that they could "experience the healing power of Jesus Christ."

For the next two weeks, Bentian villagers were approached by church representatives and asked if they had any illnesses, troubles, or disappointments or whether there was anything that they wished for in life. The answers to these questions were written down on three-by-five-inch cards labeled with the names of the villagers. After their questions had been noted, the church asked the villagers if the visiting prayer team could pray for a solution to the person's problems. Most villagers acquiesced.

Two weeks later, the team, accompanied by church dignitaries from other districts and from as far away as Java, arrived in the largest and most prosperous Bentian village. The fifty-year-old battle between the church and the *belian*[38] was about to be played out again. That night, the church was packed to overflowing, as believers and unbelievers alike crowded in. The prayer team had even succeeded in drawing away the crowd of viewers who normally gathered around the public, generator-fueled television set up on a platform outside the government office. The team was introduced to the restless crowd by a regional church official who spoke of the different kinds of beliefs in Java—"the truly biblical, as well as otherwise." He stressed that the work of the team was based on "the word of God, the command of God." He continued, "They have come to rid the region of the remnants of the dark powers [*sisa-sisa kekuatan gelap*] of your ancestors. If you leave these behind, you will be able to enter the Kingdom of Heaven. . . . You must repent and admit your sins. If not, if you still keep magical talismans [*jimat*], you will not be cured."

Pak Sutrisna, the first team member, a thin, nervous, and intense man, stepped forward. "What we do is get rid of ancestral spirits; we [ritually] clean houses, and perform personal services—we help with infertility, finding marriage partners. We're not from Bromo Mountain [a mountain sacred in indigenous Javanese religion] or Lumut Mountain [the sacred mountain considered to be the residence of ancestral spirits in many Kaharingan religions]." He then quoted biblical verses to explain the "laying on of hands" that they were about to perform. "We are anti-*belian*," he shouted, working himself up into a near frenzy. "Bring me your *jimat* and I will destroy them. I am not afraid. Jesus is stronger than the ghosts of your ancestors. I have cured a *belian*. The *gendang,* the waistcloths filled with white buttons and fangs, must be destroyed. Go ahead, test us! See if we're really from God."

The next team member stood up to speak. This was Pak Mardani, a rather heavy-set man with a fiery voice. He told of a Bentian woman in the next village with a crippled child who couldn't walk. When he prayed for the child, he felt the sins of the parents of the child. He asked God what sins the parents were hiding and he saw that when the mother was pregnant, she tried to rid herself of the baby by going to a *belian.* But God did not give permission for the baby to die. So it was born crippled. The result was that everyone suffered—the child because of the parents' sins. His prayer was unsuccessful because the parents did not repent. Such sins can make their way through three or four generations, he noted. Pak Mardani continued: "You must destroy your *jimat.* . . . Lumut Mountain is nonsense. To say 'later we'll meet on Lumut Mountain' is meaningless. People here still believe in spirits. That's why they're all sick, because of sin."[39]

Pak Mardani continued:

> People are childless because of their sins. Whether you are healed or not depends upon your faith. It is useless if you still believe in spirits. You must get rid of the things left to you by your ancestors, the *jimat* that you have inherited. I have healed all types of illness—ovarian cancer, yeast infections, menstrual cramps, impotence. There was a *belian* with a child who was deaf and mute. The *belian* had heart problems, trouble breathing. He had drums, *tiupan,* a waistcloth but he told me that he had already gotten rid of them. This wasn't true. It is useless to pray before Jesus like that if you still have *jimat,* if you still believe in spirits. Do you still have ancient things in your house? wood? bottles [with magical oils], special liquids?

Introducing the last team member, Pak Mardani asked: "Why do we bring a woman with us? All are used by God. Besides, a male healer can't hold women's tits (*tetek*) if they're sick. (Laughter spread throughout the church.) Likewise, a woman healer can't service men who are impotent. You can't just be touching this and that. There is no obscenity here. It must be done respectfully." Pak Mardani then spoke at length about the obscene healers—*dukun cabul*—of Malang, East Java, who had intercourse with their patients in order to heal them. These *dukun,* he elaborated, used *mantra* in order to knock their patients unconscious.[40]

The team announced that one hundred and sixty-nine people had signed up for faith healing. To start the healing, the team called out the names of those who had enumerated their problems to the church workers. Initially, the woman healer, along with hastily chosen female Bentian assistants, healed the women and the male healers, with assistance from hastily chosen male Bentian helpers, healed the men. As the night wore on, however, the gender division of labor disappeared. One by one, in front of the attentive crowd, names were called. Those to be healed approached the stage. The healers put their hands on the sufferer's chest and hissed and shouted between clenched teeth, " In the name of Jesus Christ, release the power!" The afflicted were then told to move their aching parts and, as the crowd watched, were loudly asked if they were healed. The reply was an inevitable "yes," most often said with averted eyes. The plan was to service fifty people the first night, at the rate of one every few minutes. Over in one corner of the church sat a group of frightened-looking elderly grandmothers, in traditional bright red embroidered sarongs, earlobes stretched long from wearing traditional earweights. They had been brought to the service by their young Christian relatives to repent their Kaharingan ways.

Pak Mardani came upon a Muslim name, Djamaluddin, on the list of those to be healed. He could not contain his glee and said to on-lookers, "Look!! A Muslim! Even Muslims need to recognize Jesus Christ!" Pak Mardani, however, was not aware of Bentian naming systems. In recent decades, Bentian children had been given an interesting and unusual range of names, from Moshe Dayan, to Neil Armstrong, Darwin, Aristotle, General Election, Pilatus (wanting a biblical name, the parents had chosen Pilatus, as in Pontius Pilatus), and Djamaluddin. Among the Bentian, a Muslim name was no more likely an indicator of an Islamic heritage than an American name, such as Neil Armstrong, was of U.S. ancestry.

Accompanying the prayer team was Mrs. Eden, as she called herself. A regal-looking sixty-one-year-old Chinese-Indonesian woman with a fresh, strong face, an overpowering character, and Dutch mannerisms, Mrs. Eden ran a beauty salon in East Java before she was "called" into missionary work at age fifty. Married to a wealthy Chinese businessman, who imported Toyotas and owned travel agencies and a corned beef factory, Mrs. Eden made annual journeys to the Bentian region. Her church, the direct descendent of Jason Linn's church, had no access to the missionary aircraft which belonged to the rival church. Thus, Mrs. Eden and her entourage were forced to enter

Bentian territory via river—a challenging proposition since the regional logging companies had, over the years, destroyed more and more of the river system, making boat travel an often arduous undertaking, requiring the substantial portaging of heavy boats. When she was in her twenties, Mrs. Eden had read the original Chinese-language version of Jason Linn's adventures among the Bentian, which had inspired her greatly. The banning of Chinese-language books by the Indonesian government meant the disappearance of Linn's account from church shelves. Leland Wang, a cofounder of the Chinese Missionary Union, which had sent Jason Linn into the Bentian region, was a close friend of Mrs. Eden's mother, herself an evangelist, and spent a good deal of time at Mrs. Eden's childhood home. After the Japanese defeat in the Pacific War, the church founded by Linn split in two. Chang She Ing went to follow in Linn's footsteps and worked and lived among the Bentian and Benuaq for the next forty to fifty years. Finally, when Chang retired and Mrs. Eden took over from him, he gave her his room in the next upriver village. "Of course, I had to renovate it," she said. Her own church, except for the branch founded by Linn, served the Chinese community exclusively.

On the Bentian, she commented, "These people have no sense of sin. They go to church and then go to the *belian* and they don't feel like it's a sin. Sometimes I just want to give up. But then I think of it the same way we have to think of a business—low tide is followed by high tide."

The day after the first night of faith healing, outside the church and near Mrs. Eden's temporary Bentian office, a small crowd was gathered around the thin and nervous Pak Sutrisna who poked at a fire. They were burning *jimat*. Grim Bentian faces stared into the fire which danced over sardine cans, small bottles, and a small book.

The faith healing continued for two additional nights. As anti-*belian* fervor swept through the village, a climate of fear and sadness filled many of the villagers. A Christian Bentian woman, whose mother was a leading *belian,* described the effect:

> I felt terrible when I heard the team saying such bad things about the *belian*. They are so mean and insulting. When church people begin to speak like that, I usually walk out. After all, my own mother is a *belian*. My mother knows her position and never asks me [a Christian] to make the offerings or to help set things up for the *belian* services. Last night, the people living near the church heard terrible screaming and yell-

ing—cries of "Help! Help! I'm dying! Help!" The village guard, wearing his uniform, rushed over to the church and ran inside. There was nothing going on except the team healing in the name of Jesus Christ. All looked calm—no one was in trouble. But outside was a fire and *jimat* were being burned. The screams must have come from the fire as the ghosts of the ancestors were murdered. They were calling for help. It was a terrible thing. I felt so sorry for them. They had helped us for so long and were murdered. I am saddened and very disturbed. A terrible thing it is to burn the ghosts of the ancestors. The wife of the Bentian military chief kept coming to my house, trying to harass and frighten me into going to more of the church services. She said, "You will go to hell if you don't repent and still attend *belian* ceremonies!" I told her, "Let me go straight to hell directly. With all of you around, I'm afraid Heaven will be too crowded!"

After three days, the team was ready to depart. Unbeknownst to them, the evening of the day they left was to mark the first night of the biggest eight-night Kaharingan *belian* ceremony of the year, *petonar,* the rice harvest ceremony. The logging company jeep that was supposed to pick up the team broke down and was almost eight hours late. Bentian church officials expressed relief at the team's eventual departure. As a church leader said:

> Mrs. Eden is very difficult to deal with. She is angry if the food is late. Although the team claims that it does not take donations for its work, they have eaten hundreds of thousands of rupiah worth of our food. "Did you come here to hunt or to serve?" Mrs. Eden yelled at Pak Sutrisna, who went bird-hunting [the Bentian region being known for valuable and endangered species of songbirds]. "Did you come here to gossip or to serve?" she yelled at the female member of the team whom she spotted talking to Bentian women. She is very bad tempered. It is clear that she has not been born again. We must pray for her.

The 1992 *petonar* ceremony went on as usual, despite the all-out assault on Kaharingan beliefs. Initially, the number of participants was lower than in previous years. And the *belian*'s twelve-year-old granddaughter, the only one of her generation trained in *belian* arts and dances, had been made so distraught by the anti-*belian* frenzy enveloping the village that, according to her mother, she was in tears for days, vomited repeatedly, and refused to dance in her grandmother's ceremony. During ceremonies such as this, the *belian,* in trance, voyages back to the ancestral mountain home and invites resident spirits and ancestors to journey back with her to the current Bentian village to share in the new rice of the first harvest. The itinerary of this spirit voyage is a rendering of the actual journeys made from their ancestral home by the particular Bentian group for whom the ceremony is being held, possibly as long as a millennium ago. The *belian* chants often provide the only historical record of the travels, former villages, hardships, and bathing and fishing places of a particular group.

As part of the 1992 ceremony, the house of the *belian,* Grandmother Dinas, was transformed into a fantastic vegetable world. Over the next eight days, as she called visiting spirits down from the heavens, a *balai* was constructed in her main room. The *balai* is a miniature version of a Bentian field house, built of ritually and ecologically important forest and agricultural plants. On the fourth night of the ceremony, the *balai* was transformed from bare bamboo poles into an enchanted plant and cloth-covered structure. Bird carvings topped the house poles and the *balai* was festooned with red *pangir* flowers. Offerings of rattan, ironwood, and *ngangsang* were made. Branches of these and other forest trees are requirements for *balai* construction, as are the aromatic and colorful *telasi, kumpai lati,* and *geronggong* flowers. These flowers are sharply fragrant and appear similar to flowers found elsewhere throughout the tropics and which play a role in reducing insect pests in agricultural fields. They are planted by Bentian farmers.

This year's ceremony differed from the previous year's, in that one family which had gone through the faith healing had secretly saved their heirloom collection of *jimat*—instead of destroying them as instructed by the church—and sent them, sealed in a Chinese urn, to Grandmother Dinas for her ceremony. According to one of the *belian* present at the ceremony, the *antang* [urn] came from a Kaharingan family which had publicly repented but could not bring themselves to burn the contents of the *antang.* The *antang* had been passed on for generations and had not been opened for at least two generatons, perhaps three. Instead of burning it, the family gave it to Grandmother Dinas.

At the end of Grandmother Dinas's ceremony, a group of senior *belian* opened the *antang* and ritually purified, with the blood of a sacrificial pig, the contents—boar tooth necklaces, strangely truncated deer horns, a rhinocerous molar, a crocodile tooth, miniature bronze Dutch canons, and cowrie shells—which were then placed back in the urn before it was sealed again.

Logging the Bentian Territory

The Bentian are world-renowned for their sustainable forestry management system, which preserves forest and river biodiversity while earning valuable foreign exchange through the production of rattan, an export crop. To the untrained eye, Bentian rattan gardens often appear to be "natural" secondary forest filled with looping, spiny rattan vines. To the Bentian eye, however, rattan gardens are easily recognizable and are a sign of human presence and landownership. They are clearly demarcated by borders of fruit trees, small streams, hills, honey trees, and other obvious planted or natural features. Much of the Bentian forest management system, however, remains incomprehensible to and unseen by outsiders. This is often a source of conflict, as outsiders rush in to declare Bentian lands "unoccupied" or "abandoned" without consulting with the Bentian before clear-cutting their forests.

In 1981 the American logging company, Georgia Pacific, built a logging basecamp on traditional Bentian lands near the Anan River and came close to sparking an armed conflict with the Bentian when it resettled villagers and destroyed ancient grave sites during base camp construction. The company built a corridor logging road parallel to the main district river, the Lawa, and, instead of building bridges over the feeder streams to the Lawa, dammed them for over one hundred kilometers, creating malarial swamps along the road. As logging continued, the Lawa, the main transportation and communication artery for the region, filled with eroded soil and became shallow and increasingly difficult to use. In the mid-1980s Georgia Pacific pulled out of Indonesia and its logging concessions were taken over by a wealthy associate of President Suharto, Mohamad "Bob" Hasan, owner of the Kalimanis Group companies.

Since 1986, the Bentian have petitioned the Indonesian government for the issuance of landownership certificates for the traditional territories that they have occupied for hundreds of years and on which they have planted millions of rattan plants and fruit and commercial timber trees. Their attempts to secure a portion of their ancestral lands large enough to ensure their survival had been met for years with official silence. In February 1992, the Ministry of Forestry approved a request by Mohamad Hasan's Kalhold Company to utilize an additional five thousand hectares of Bentian lands for an "industrial forest plantation" (HTI) and a housing site for one thousand impoverished Javanese transmigrants who, in addition to cultivating their own food, were to provide a ready pool of cheap labor for the plantation.

In the spring of 1993, Kalimanis subcontractors sent armed bulldozer and chainsaw crews into Bentian territory to establish a new industrial forest plantation with migrant labor. The bulldozers plowed the first one hundred fifty hectares of Bentian forest and rattan gardens, destroying over ten thousand rattan clumps and two thousand fruit trees. In addition, Bentian grave markers were bulldozed and burned and the bones of Bentian dead were scattered over the charred ground.

In 1993, fearing the total destruction of their livelihoods and territory, the Bentian began to protest, publicly, the destruction of their traditional forest lands. They repeatedly requested a cessation of the violations of human rights and the environmental destruction which accompanied the land clearing carried out by the logging and plantation company. As a result of their protests, they were met with increased repression, threats, and intimidation from Indonesian governmental officials and security forces. Bentian leaders were repeatedly held, interrogated, and threatened with prison.[41]

In East Kalimantan, this was not an unusual event. Transmigrants, sometimes affiliated with plantations run by the Ministry of Forestry or the Estate Crops Division of the Ministry of Agriculture, sometimes not affiliated with any type of plantation, are often placed on the *adat* territories of upriver peoples without their consent. The seizing of *adat* lands without consent by governmental agencies and private sector actors is a common and deeply resented part of rural Kalimantan life. The Bentian case, therefore, is in no way unusual or extraordinary. It is simply a reflection of events that occur on a daily basis throughout Kalimantan and throughout resource-rich regions of the Indonesian archipelago.

"Elections," Loggers, and the Church

By April 1992—a month after the prayer team had left—rumors circulated in Bentian villages near the Kalimanis/Kalhold basecamp that the company would, once again, seize and destroy Bentian *adat* lands.

Fearing the worst, the leaders of the village closest to the rumored
first site of land clearing sent a letter "in the name of people totalling
137 households and 557 individuals" to the director of Kalhold in
Samarinda. Copies of the letter were sent to local- and provincial-
level Kalhold managers, as well as to the heads of the district, the
regency, the Kutai People's Representative Assembly (DPRD II), the
governor of East Kalimantan, and the head of the Provincial Forestry
office. The topic of the letter was: "[M]aintaining/defending [mem-
pertahankan] customary rights to adat lands, rattan gardens, [and] the
agricultural lands of the people of Jelmu Sibak." The authors described
the region that the company planned to clear-cut and bulldoze. They
described the village property as divided into "forest land which is
still . . . intact with potential yield such as timber and other forest
products such as rattan, damar, gaharu wood, and fruit" and "forest
agricultural fields/ rattan gardens." The authors continued, stating that:

> village forests have "already been taken by the company." Because of
> that we here in the name of the people of Sibak Village notify the com-
> pany: We do not permit our agricultural lands and fallowed fields to be
> used in an overlapping manner for the activities of the company even if
> there is compensation or transfer of rights or granting of other lands.
> The positive effect of the above lands is that they are a source of food
> and life for us from former times to the present day. For the activities of
> the company which wishes to develop that Transmigration-Industrial
> Forest Plantation site we invite [you] to seek another location and not
> to disturb the location which we have cultivated since long ago. In the
> places in the middle of the forest where the company is already produc-
> ing [i.e., felling trees], we invite you to continue even though this is
> still on the customary lands of our village.

The authors of the letter identified themselves as *pribumi,* or native
Indonesians.

> In addition to that we also need to notify the company that We as native
> peoples [masyrakat pribumi] have lived in this region since long ago.
> [T]he company has been here for ten years in this region, nonetheless
> we, the people, have never enjoyed sufficient or satisfactory results
> [from the company's use] of our traditional forest territory, whether in
> social, economic development . . . [or] infrastructure. So because of
> that we, the people of Jelmu Sibak Village, firmly reject the activities
> of the company which wants to bring Transmigration Forest Plantation

. . . to . . . the agricultural/garden lands of the people. If this is to be done outside of our agricultural area, we invite you to do so.

As had repeatedly happened in the past with much of Bentian correspondence, this letter, reflecting the wishes and aspirations of the Bentian people of Jelmu Sibak and signed by ten representatives of the people and five government officials from Jelmu Sibak Village (the village head, heads of Lembaga Ketaharan Masyrakat Desa (LKMD) and Lembaga Masyrakat Desa (LMD), and neighborhood heads), received no tangible response. Tensions grew as the company insisted on its right to implement its plans and the local population became both angrier and more fearful.

The climate of fear increased as the nationally orchestrated presidential election drew near and the nation as a whole was plunged into the preemptive state of emergency which has been routinely declared every five years during the months prior to and following a presidential election. In this preemptive period, police and military powers of arrest and detention without trial are greatly expanded, as is the list of "crimes" deemed subversive.

Upriver, preelection rumors of all kinds abounded: Bugis and Javanese logging truck drivers complained of witchcraft attacks by Dayak villagers; strange illnesses, accidents, and deaths occurred. Rumors circulated among the upriver communities that regardless of how secret the secret ballot was, government officials would still know who voted against the ruling Golkar party, and punishment would be sure to follow. Logging companies offered prizes (television satellite dish antennas, loans, and outright "gifts" of cash) to village heads, *adat* leaders, and local police captains if they could ensure a near unanimous victory for the ruling Golkar party and, thus, a glowing endorsement for the continuation of General Suharto's rule, unshakable since 1965.

Daring graffiti began to appear, written on boards tacked to trees along the paths in Bentian villages: "Jangan heran kalau PDI menang!"—Don't be surprised if the [opposition] Indonesian Democratic Party wins!"

As the elections heated up and tensions grew, plans for the Kalhold HTI-Transmigration project on Bentian lands were quietly put on temporary hold. Company officials stated that "the Bentian are not yet ready to receive transmigrants." As the official Golkar election campaign arrived in Bentian villages, tensions increased.

Despite a law banning electioneering on church grounds, the entreprenurial evangelical church which had sponsored the prayer team now offered the use of its facilities to the ruling party, Golkar, during the election campaign. Church officials set up a row of chairs and a podium on a hastily constructed stage on the church lawn for the Golkar dignitaries to use. For their campaign duties, the dignitaries, with two exceptions, wore oversized blazers and baseball caps, sun-yellow in color, the color of the ruling Golkar party. The two who were not wearing yellow blazers were dressed, instead, in military uniforms. It was said that they were high-ranking officers from the urban centers of Balikpapan or Samarinda. The minister of the local church, his Javanese accent matching the accents of the military officers and logging company officials, wore a yellow blazer and called the crowd to order using a microphone powered by the church's diesel generator. Both he and his yellow-jacketed wife offered prayers for the conduct of an equitable and wise election.

The brief public Christian prayer appeared to make the Muslims—that is, most of the dignitaries, police, and military—and the Kaharingans—a fair portion of the audience—somewhat uneasy. The prayer was followed by dignitaries' speeches. The yellow-jacketed district head, a member of Kutai royalty, led off, exhorting full participation in the election. He was followed by the military officers and then by the other more or less portly gentlemen in yellow jackets: managerial staff of the local logging concessions and a Dayak member of the Kutai People's Representative Assembly (DPRD II). Their message was short, simple, and chilling. It was repeated by each speaker: "Development is a government project. Logging concessions carry out development. If you oppose logging concessions, you are opposing the government. This is subversion."

The crowd, which obviously did not need to be reminded of the serious nature of subversion charges, fidgeted uneasily. A voice from the podium led the cheer "Long Live Golkar!" [Hidup Golkar!]. The crowd responded weakly. The military officials glared at the crowd and whispered to each other. "Hidup Golkar!" came the shout from the podium and the speaker raised his fist to the sky as he shouted. The crowd responded, this time more strongly: "Hidup Golkar! Hidup Golkar!" and their fists punctuated the air.

Throughout the rest of the day cries of "Hidup Golkar!" echoed throughout the village, shouted in cynical tones by young village men at the sight of the patrolling yellow-shirted dignitaries and the visiting military officers. The military officers requested the names of the insolent and potentially subversive youths. Their requests were met with silence.

Praying for the Logging Road

Meanwhile, the Roda Mas ("Golden Wheel") logging concession was having difficulties building its road through Bentian forests and fields. Muslim bulldozer drivers reported that part of the area they wanted to put the road through was haunted. They experienced inexplicable illnesses, odd machinery breakdowns, accidents, and saw ghostly apparitions. The road was intended to bisect Bentian territory, ending in the heart of the largest Bentian village, the first major road connection directly from the outside world into the middle of the largest village. The road presaged the company's plans to log all of the Bentian forests along the road, as well. The company posted signs along the roadbed forbidding "illegal farmers" from making agricultural fields along the road. The road, however, actually ran directly through and over Bentian agricultural lands and forests.

Faced with the increasing reluctance of the company's heavy equipment operators to carry out their duties, the manager of the Roda Mas basecamp, a Chinese-Indonesian Christian, approached the leader of the Bentian church. "Would it be possible," he inquired, "to arrange a prayer service and blessing for the haunted parts of the logging road —to drive away the demons and ancestral ghosts?" The church agreed and, over the period of several weeks, succeeded in convincing a number of followers to carry out a prayer and purification service at the site of the road. Some who refused to participate asked if the "demons" to be driven away included living Bentian farmers who were tending their traditional fields, which the road had bisected. Once the ceremony was performed, and the road blessed, the tractor and truck drivers continued their work, no longer harassed by ancestral spirits.

The Roda Mas manager was later to play an interesting role in local religious and forest politics. Seeking to appease the Kaharingan population, which was angry with the forest destruction and land seizures carried out by his company and upset by his favoritism toward the churches—church officials had often praised the company's generous donations—he offered to fund a traditional *nguguh tah'un,* or village purification ceremony, in the largest village, involving the sacrifice of a valuable water buffalo. He did not know that the *nguguh tah'un* had been a target of missionary attacks for the past sixty years or that, in that particular Bentian village, it had been successfully eradicated by the church some two decades before. Singlehandedly, the logging company succeeded in bringing to life a ceremony which reinforced Bentian ethnic identity and bonded the community together with a sense of cultural pride—a pride which later reinforced Bentian struggles against the incursions of Roda Mas and other invading companies.

Conclusion

In this paper, I have outlined the sixty-year history of missionary in-trusion into Bentian cosmology and territory—including the ridicul-ing of and attempts to destroy religious agricultural and forest-based ceremonies, the harassment of practitioners of Kaharingan religion, and the manner by which, through the destruction of longhouses, Bentian environmental and social communications systems were severely disabled. I explored, briefly, the sustainable Bentian forest management system and attempts on the part of state-sanctioned pri-vate sector parties to destroy it—buttressed by the acquiescence of the church. I discussed the efforts of a logging company to secure a Chris-tian blessing for their logging road which was haunted by ancestral demons who were preventing road construction. On the other hand, the same logging company—by sponsoring the first *nguguh ta'un* ceremony in decades—inadvertently undid sixty years of missionary efforts to eradicate this expression of indigenous beliefs.

Throughout the decades, we see a considerable mismatch between the goals and aspirations of the evangelical churches and Bentian attempts to protect their forested territories. We see the consequences of the general congruence of interests between the goals of the church (recall Mudimbe's "domestication of natives," including the eradica-tion of indigenous beliefs and ceremonies which comprised, among other things, systems for the regulation and protection of Bentian forests) and of the state and resource extraction companies ("acquir-ing, distributing, and exploiting lands"). Opposition to Bentian forms of worship moved from the ideological basis of the missionaries to the commercial needs of the logging companies and their desire to manipulate Christian and Kaharingan rituals alike, in order to maximize profits. Most of these attempts, in one way or another, made life more complicated and stressful for the Bentian but—as they continued to battle logging and plantation company encroachment on their forests and continued, more or less, to celebrate the new harvest and hold weekly *belian* healing ceremonies—the strenuous efforts made to influence Bentian cosmology did not necessarily achieve the goals of either church or logging company.

Notes

1. Nancy L. Peluso, "Markets and Merchants: The Forest Products Trade of East Kalimantan in Historical Perspective" (Ph.D. diss., Cornell University, 1983).

2. Victor T. King, *The Peoples of Borneo* (Oxford: Blackwell Publishers, 1993).

3. Jerome Rousseau, *Central Borneo: Ethnic Identity and Social Life in a Stratified Society* (Oxford: Clarendon Press, 1990).

4. Joseph A. Weinstock, "Study on Shifting Cultivation," Phase I and II (Jakarta: FAO, 1989).

5. *Adat*, meaning custom or tradition/traditional, and *hukum adat*, meaning customary law, are terms originally of Arabic origin which have taken on great significance throughout the Indonesian archipelago. The term *adat* is commonly utilized in Indonesia to refer to the customary practices or traditions of the hundreds of cultural groups inhabiting the thousands of islands of the archipelago. *Adat* shapes the marriage ceremonies, birth and death customs, conflict resolution practices, and resource utilization and ownership patterns of the various Indonesian cultural groups.

6. King, *The Peoples of Borneo*, 153.

7. The term Dayak—meaning "upriver" in many Kalimantan languages—at times has had derogatory connotations. Currently, however, members of groups labeled by outsiders as "Dayak," such as the Bentian, the Benuaq, and the Tonyoi, refer to themselves as "Dayak" out of a sense of pride and unity. It is in this spirit that the term is utilized in this paper.

8. V. Y. Mudimbe, *The Invention of Africa: Gnosis, Philosophy, and the Order of Knowledge* (Bloomington: Indiana University Press, 1988).

9. Ibid., 69.

10. Ibid., 2.

11. Ibid., 34.

12. Ibid., 2.

13. Ibid., 20.

14. This was a process which occurred in colonized regions throughout the globe. Again, in his insightful text on the creation of African identities through the writings of outsiders, including colonists and missionaries, Mudimbe discusses the concept of "primitive philosophy" which "was current in the 1920's and 1930's" (ibid., 135). This concept "had been colonizing the continent [of Africa], its inhabitants and its realities. . . . [It posited] a radical difference between the West, characterized by a history of intellectual and spiritual reasoning, and 'primitives,' whose life [and thought] were viewed as having nothing in common with the West." The two types of mentality, rational, logical and pre-logical "dominated by collective representation . . . [, dependent on] the law of mystical participation" were what marked the savage from the civilized. (ibid., 136) This division identified the "primitive mentality as a poor and non-evolved entity." Mudimbe also notes, however (quoting Evans-Pritchard), that peoples as diverse as "the Chinese . . . , Polynesians, Melanesians, Negroes, American Indians, and Australian Blackfellows" were all considered "primitive."

15. Mudimbe, *The Invention of Africa.*

16. Ibid., 45.

17. Ibid.

18. Josia Nasir, "Bertanam Rotan Menerut Tradisi Petani Bentian," *Gaharu Bulletin* (Samarinda: PLASMA), 2 (1991).

19. *Calamus casius,* or sega rattan, is the most commonly cultivated commercial rattan species in the Bentian region. More than thirty other species are also present in the region and are either cultivated, semicultivated, or wild.

20. Jason Linn, *Pioneering in Dyak Borneo* (Singapore: Far Eastern Bible College), 1973.

21. Ibid., 117.

22. Rousseau, *Central Borneo.*

23. Linn, *Pioneering in Dyak Borneo,* 145.

24. Christopher, in Mudimbe, *The Invention of Africa,* 47.

25. Mudimbe, *The Invention of Africa,* 52.

26. Linn, *Pioneering in Dyak Borneo,* 102.

27. Ibid., 145.

28. Ibid., 103, 105.

29. Ibid., 112.

30. Ibid., 96.

31. Ibid., 102.

32. Ibid., 134.

33. Ibid., 137.

34. Ibid., 107.

35. Ibid., 153.

36. Ibid., 152.

37. The events recorded in 1991 and 1992 are based on field notes I took during research sponsored under a Fulbright-Hayes Fellowship.

38. The term *belian* denotes a person steeped in the arts of *adat* religion, including communication with the spirit world, healing practices, childbirth, and death rituals. Bentian *belian* are prominent oral historians. Different *belian* specialize in different areas of expertise and different types of practice. They are respected and often quite feared by the rest of the population.

39. It is unlikely that Pak Mardani knew, however, about the astonishing corruption of the local medical services, where the paramedics stationed in the village had sold most of the antibiotics and other supplies to the nearest logging camp, leaving the village clinic devoid of medicine.

40. *Mantra,* in this context, are incantations, written or spoken, which evoke a spirit for protection, or to assist in a deed.

41. The struggles of the Bentian to protect their forested homelands have been recorded elsewhere in detail (Stephanie Fried, "Writing for Their Lives: Bentian Authors and Indonesian Development Discourse" [Ph.D. diss., Cornell University, 1995]; and Stephanie Fried, "Tropical Forests Forever? A Contextual Ecology of Bentian Rattan Agroforestry Systems," in *People, Plants, and Justice: The Politics of Nature Conservation,* ed. C. Zerner [New York: Columbia University Press, 2000]). It is beyond the scope of this paper to delineate the Bentian forest campaigns and the governmental responses to them.

Complex Cosmologies

Nature and Culture: Problematic Concepts for Native Americans

JACK D. FORBES

Nature and culture are two contrasting concepts, at least as used by some Europeans. Do these concepts have any counterparts in Native American thinking? Are they useful concepts for Native peoples to utilize in their own discourses?

Today, most of us use the terms nature (*la naturaleza*) and culture (*cultura*) in everyday speech, because we have been taught by Europeans to do so. But do we know what we mean? What kind of an ideology are we buying into with the use of these terms, in all of their many forms and nuanced derivatives? Perhaps it is appropriate to begin by looking at the Latino-Italiano roots of these words as well as later modifications in English.

Nature and Bornedness

Nature and nation have the same root, being derived from the Latin verb *nasci,* to be born. From the past participle *natus,* borned, came "nat," which with the suffix "ura" gave *natura,* or nature, a term which can perhaps best be translated as the condition of bornedness. Nation came to mean that fundamental grouping into which one is born. *Natura* came to refer to the in-born and essential qualities of a thing: "the inherent and inseparable combination of properties essentially pertaining to anything and giving it its fundamental character."[1]

Thus we can say that "bornedness" is a key element of the European nature concept, in that "fundamental" or "essential" character is ordinarily that which an entity is "born" with or which develops more or less invariably from potentiality present at birth (or creation). As we shall see, this concept in Middle English came to be applied to living creatures of all kinds, including humans: "the inherent and innate disposition of a person (or animal)."

This idea, that humans and other things have a certain character or "way" of acting, is to be found in many traditions, but the concept of "nature" in English came also to be applied to the universe as a whole, both in the sense of the so-called natural or physical world itself and in the sense of a dynamic process embedded in the life of visible things. (As the dictionary puts it: "The material world or its collective objects or phenomena . . . as contrasted with those of human civilization"; 1662.) And as early as 1477, one can cite such a phrase as "taking place . . . in accordance with the ordinary course of nature." One can also read of "a state of nature without spiritual enlightenment" (1526), a common Christian theological attitude which impacts "natural" religions, as opposed to self-designated "revealed" religions, such as Christianity and Judaism.

Nature, then, by the opening of the modern era, had also come to refer to a condition or state of being which stood in contrast to Christian and, later, scientific-rational states of being. Most importantly, the idea of borned character had come to be taken away from its original locus of meaning and had been transferred to the hugest imaginable realm, that of all things not created by human art and skill, the entire world beyond the human domain of invention, and, as we shall see, virtually the entire world beyond the domain of white, European, and male invention. And this entire realm, which embraces the greater part of all life and phenomena, is seen as being essentially in a "borned" condition, that is, it is predetermined at creation or birth and not subject to self-alteration or learning.

This extension of the concept of borned character to the nonhuman and nonrational (nonmale) world has very profound implications, setting the stage, it can be argued, for the manner in which non-European peoples have been treated, along with women, animals, forests, experimental animals, and other "objects" which came to be linked to the realm of "that which is to be acted upon" as opposed to that which is doing the acting. The white male, whether as seagoing invader, explorer, missionary, theologian, or white-coated scientist, represents "human civilization" in its long-standing effort to alter and "master" the raw, crude (*crudo*), uncooked, wild realm of the undeveloped. That the products of "nature" are often referred to as "raw material," and that humans are also now sometimes so classified (prior to processing), is very telling indeed.

As Western European thought evolved, "nature" came to refer primarily to the physical and biophysical realms, so-called, the realms of matter and of "laws" for the behavior of matter and of organisms. Physics, chemistry, biology, zoology, and (physical) anthropology all developed originally to discover these "laws" of movement or behavior and were part of what was called "natural history" (as opposed to "unnatural" or human history, I suppose).

Outside of "nature" was the "supernatural" realm of deities, spirits, and other entities which do not appear to obey "natural" laws. (On the other hand, it should be noted that one hears scientists today using the term "nature" to replace terms such as "the Creator" or "God," as when they picture "nature" as an active, almost-intelligent process, much as in the quote above from 1477.)

Outside of "nature" also seems to be the physical and mental products of human beings, including changes brought about in the physical-biological world by human actions. (Thus, a paved road in a forest is probably not perceived as being "natural" even though it is comprised entirely of "natural" materials simply rearranged.)

To summarize more recent usage in Englatino (English as creolized by Franco-Latin dominance), we have 1) "nature" as referring to the essential quality of something, as in "it is his nature to do that"; 2) "nature" as a vital force or impulse in humans and other things: "'Twas Nature, sir, whose strong behest Impelled me to the Deed"; 3) the creative and regulative physical power thought to operate in the physical world and "the immediate cause of all its phenomena," something personified as "a female being" (Mother Nature, and perhaps now, for some Caucasians, "the Goddess"; 4) the objects of the material world "as contrasted with those of human civilization"; 5) the moral "state of nature," the state "natural" to humans, including the human "prior to the organization of society" or in "an uncultivated or undomesticated condition."[2]

The idea of "uncultivated" as being applicable to humans who are "natural" is one about which I could write at great length, and I will discuss it further when the term "culture" is taken up. Here it is significant to note that indigenous Americans were frequently referred to by Spanish writers as "naturales," that is, as "naturals," a concept which is in essential agreement with the German depiction of Americans as "wildmen" and with the English, French, and Portuguese use of "savage," "sauvage," and "selvaje," meaning, literally, "forest person" but, according to the *American Heritage Dictionary* (1970), meaning: "1. not domesticated or cultivated; wild. 2. Not civilized; primitive." As a noun, savage refers to a primitive, uncivilized, rude, and even a brutal or ferocious person. Rude, of course, comes from Latin *rudis,* rough or raw, related to *crudus,* bloody and raw.[3]

It is a very popular notion in the modern European-influenced world that "nature" and "culture" are separate and that they are often antagonistic. Nature in this usage is often equated with "wilderness." *Webster's Third New International Dictionary* tells us that "wild" means "living in a state of nature" and "not tame or domesticated," along with other derivative meanings, including "not subjected to restraint or regulation." That a term such as "wild" could ever come to be associated with the realms of animals, plants, trees, mountains, and lands living beyond the control of European-type social structures is very telling, especially when one notes the pre-1492, as well as post-1492, Europeans' ideas about what "wild" men and women looked and acted like. In this connection, it is fascinating to examine the depictions of "savages" and *homo sylvestris* in medieval Europe: hairy people with long uncombed hair, living naked with animals as both food and companions, in a state beyond normal societal controls, or, as a French song of the 1400s expresses: ". . . que ma aprins nature . . . ," that is, "I live according to what nature taught me. . . ."[4]

Even more telling, however, is the fact that the European stereotypes about "wild" people were largely transferred to the Americas after 1492. Americans were designated as raw, uncultivated, wild, and brutish people by European propagandists, that is to say, as "natural" people. The concept of "primitive" (now "primal"), so beloved by generations of European writers, is very close to the idea of "bornedness," since "the first ones" or "the early ones" are seen to be just as they were when born, without cultivation, that is, "natural."

Before proceeding to a discussion of culture, it is worth commenting on the strange fact that a word referring to bornedness, that is, to what something is like at birth or creation, should be applied not only to the long-term character of a person or animal but also to the dynamic life or unfolding of the visible universe and then to the physical-biological world in totality. This is in direct contradiction to what First Americans believe, because they seem to see all of life, which surrounds us, as intelligent, inventive, changing, learning, teaching, evolving, acting, praying, feeling, and responding. The visible universe is indeed dynamic, changing, and often unpredictable, and it certainly bears little or hardly any relationship to how it was at its "birth" or beginning (if it had any beginning). Moreover, it is not a passive, acted upon, place where only "immutable laws" of science operate. Instead, its essence seems to be an ability to modify itself in response to new situations.

An old Lenápe prayer states:

> My relatives, I am thankful now this day that we are thinking how the blessings come when our father Great Spirit remembers us. . . . we are thankful when we see everything coming up and our grandfather trees they send out buds. . . . Also we feel it when our elder brother the sun puts forth heat. He sympathizes with us and besides these our grandfathers the thunders give us plenty of water. All is that created by our father the Creator. Even it is said every *manitu* (spirit-power) prays because sometimes we hear our grandfather trees, that they pray earnestly when the wind goes by. . . .[5]

One can, I think, sense a feeling of the unity of the entire world and, indeed, of the universe in this prayer. This is in contrast to the pervasive dualism of much of European thought, a dualism wherein the "better" or "higher" part of humans (thoughts, inventions, ideas) are separated, along with the Supreme Deity (and lesser deities, such as angels), from such biophysical features as sex, procreation, hunger, defecation, breathing. This is extremely significant since the Roman Catholic Church, along with much of the rest of Christianity, has adopted this dualism. The nonhuman world and the biophysical body become essentially "lower" and designed to serve the "higher" element. Women, who tend to be historically identified with emotions and sex by European and Middle Eastern males, are seen as hysterical and nonreasoning. Indigenous peoples and the "wilderness" together are also seen as dangerous and nonrational, as well as raw, wild, sexual, uncultivated, undomesticated, feral, and ferocious (from *ferro,* wild). Much of the modern romantic interest in indigenous peoples, sadly, often stems from a misguided belief among Europeans that these peoples are indeed wild and emotional, with a "primal" ability to connect with the equally "wild" world of "nature" and prerational "power." New Ageism may be simply a new stage in the defamation of non-European peoples, for example, in seizing upon alleged indigenous "shamanism" while ignoring the numerous Christian faith-healers who behave in precisely "shamanistic" ways, as well as such "shamanistic" ceremonies as the Catholic Mass, exorcism, spirit possession, and so on.

In any case, this dualism triumphed in the Middle East (and elsewhere) as Judaism, Christianity, and Islam replaced older spiritual traditions of African, Semitic, and Mediterranean peoples, doing away with female spirit-powers (except for Mary, who is much reduced from her days as Isis), establishing rigid controls over women, and actively suppressing all forms of "pagan" (rural) religion.

It is well to note that the concepts of cultivation and its near-equivalent, domestication, and their opposition to "nature," arise primarily from a horticultural perspective and also from a human thought process where self-sufficient (free) plants, herbs, fruits are not of great importance, that is, where there is very little gathering or harvesting of free seeds, tubers, and fruits, and also where the skills of helping to care for (cultivate) self-sufficient plants and trees have been lost. (Here I am referring to the ecological management systems practiced by many indigenous groups, such as the Native Americans of California.) In other words, the kind of culture concepts which have come to dominate current Eurocentric thinking are derived from farming or herding peoples who have become cut off from full interaction with the world beyond their village or town area. It is a very narrow perspective, based upon the viewpoint of the "walled village," walled against the "wild" outside.

This perspective also arises out of a fear of the world outside of one's *ham* or *ton* (home village or town). Thus, a knowledge of the rich learning which takes place in the nonhuman environment is lost. The town-dwellers are ignorant, but they interpret their ignorance as knowledge (and even persecute "witches" and others who still gather "wild" herbs or who dare to live in the forest).

Another characteristic consists in the apartness from much of the nonhuman environment as opposed to the togetherness with the whole world, the latter being more characteristic of American indigenous peoples.

The walled-town view of the world may relate to the fears of the outside, which evolved in walled towns and villages which in turn became cities where still greater alienation from the countryside occurred, and especially from the mountains, forests, and "jungles" where "wild" or "unruly" people lived. Coincidentally, depictions of deities made of plaster, stone, or paint and of human form often replaced deities who were conceived of in nonhuman form or actually consisted in the earth, a tree, a river, or a mountain.

Most European intellectuals stemmed from cities, or from walled manor houses, and in their alienation from the world beyond their walls they developed aggressive and exploitative measures directed outward toward their own rural areas and then beyond to other people's territories. The "Away from People" became "the Other" just as did Native Americans, Africans, and other human groups, and all could be exploited because in themselves they were valueless, only acquiring value when commodified by imperialism as "raw materials" (slaves, cheap labor, "raw land," timber, minerals, and so on), or when romanticized and stereotyped and therefore commodified as "wilderness adventure" and "nature."

At this point let us pause to think about other implications of the evolving Euro-Englatino concept of "nature." For one thing, it is in part a negative concept. That is, it is that part of what we know which is nonhuman or, at least, nonrational human (since many see the human body as being part of "nature"). Thus, it is the leftovers, what remains after a decision is made as to what to include in the human realm. Is a formal garden part of "nature"? The answer is determined not by the life of plants but by the focus on human intervention. From the 1870s, we read that "Many fair regions once carefully cultivated . . . were abandoned to nature, and became a scene of desolation. . . ."[6]

The notion that a field which is unploughed for a long time is being "abandoned to nature" reveals that "nature" is a place where plants and animals grow free (relatively, at least) of human control. The "weeds" which take over an old field seemingly follow their own rythym, not that of the farmer. This is also the core of the concepts of "wilderness," where things live which are free and undomesticated, and of "wild people," who supposedly live beyond "civilized" social control.

These are negative ideas, however, and negative concepts, which are also vague and fundamentally misleading, in my opinion—much as the concept of the "unconscious" in psychology (pointing to "that which I am not aware of") is essentially empty of empirical meaning.

"Nature," as that which is nonrational human, or not under human rational control, simply lumps together all of the rest of what we can call in Lenápe *waymee taalee* (*wemi tali*), or "All Where," that is, "Every Where." The Every Where, or All That Is, of course, is a huge category including extremely diverse phenomena ranging from the tiniest known physical particles to massive galaxies and everything in between. To place all of this into a single category, defined by its being not the product of human skill or thought, is absurd, to say the least, and is definitely the result of a homocentric and probably male-centered ideology.

Why, for example, should such social insects as ants, with their remarkable abilities at communication and planning, be grouped together with rocks? I have great respect for the latter, but I would suggest that rocks in their behavior are as different from ants as ants are from humans, and probably more so. Thus, what meaning is there in lumping such disparate entities as deserts, tropical forests, rivers, crabs, and chimpanzees in a catch-all, vague category? The answer is, I would think, that it is the absence of human people, and especially the absence of human beings "who are like us," which is really the crucial factor in all of this.

That is, the modern European, when he wants to get away from people (or at least too many people) and the things made by people, seeks to "go out into nature." Thus, nature is, again, a negative, defined by the absence of humans (or at least by the absence of "modern" types of humans). Of course, there are times when she sees "nature" as being very positive in the sense of having beauty, peacefulness, solitude, clean air, blue skies, and so on, but the defining characteristic is still basically negative, i.e., the absence of too many "non-natural" humans. Going to a well-arranged park, with a great deal of beauty, ponds, and clean air, will not necessarily be experienced as "nature" if there are too many people there or if the evidence of human "domestication" is too apparent, I would think.

For Native Americans, I believe, the Wemi Tali, the All Where, is a single unity of which we, as humans, are just a part, and not the most significant part either. To get away from other people is very important to First Americans, especially in seeking wisdom and spiritual guidance from the All Where and its many powerful sources of enlightenment and assistance. But the "Away from People" (as I shall discuss below) is an active participant with us in the Wemi Tali.

Witapanóxwe, a Lenápe man, told a story from the ancestors about seven men who had great spiritual power, but they disappeared. Then, some pure youths blessed with a vision saw seven stones which were almost exactly alike, stones which spoke to them. Other people went to see the seven, but they disappeared again. Again, after a very long time, they were found once more, this time as seven beautiful pine and cedar trees. These trees were placed together because "both are *mutéinowak* (conjurers)," or, literally, "Heart-Ones."

> Again they notice that those prophet-men had become trees. Again they went away and it was a very long time afterward before they found them again. As soon as they were known here these had formed in a group up above in the middle of the sky as seven stars (the Pleiades) and they are called, when they are seen, as though they were great persons. . . . That is what was said by our ancestors from whom it was rightly known that the cedar was of medicinal purpose.[7]

Here we see the inclusiveness of the Wemi Tali and the presence of wisdom in the nonhuman environment.

It is important to try to discover what American languages reveal about the ideological insights of their speakers, but this is often difficult because so many of the early dictionaries were prepared by European missionaries who may, at the same time, have been trying to match American words with the Christian and Jewish ideas found in English and Latin texts. Bible translators had to find words for ideas such as "desert" and "wilderness," as well as "sinner." With this problem in mind, let us look at a few Algonkian words.

Cree and Ojibwe both seem to have terms which can refer to "nature" as character. For example, *itátisewín* in Cree refers to "conduct, behavior, way, nature," while *itátisew* means "he is naturally so." Ojibwe uses *nind owiiawinodam* (it is natural to me), derived from *owiiaw* (I have a body). *Nind owiitaminodam* means "I have it in my body, it is natural to me, it is incorporated to me." In Lenápe one can use *lauchsin,* meaning "to live, walk, in a certain manner," or *elaosit* (the way he lives), or *wulauchsowagan* (*wilaosowákan*), "for good behavior, good life." The root, to be analyzed later (*-owsi-, awsi-* or *auchsi,* depending on the dialect), is used also to denote one's way of life or culture.

In nineteenth-century Lenápe, *tauwatawik* is translated as "uninhabited place" and *tauwatawique* as "in the wilderness," and both are related to Massachuset (Natick) *touohkomuk* or *touohkomokque,* translated as "wilderness" or "not cultivated." In J. Hammond Trumbull's *Natick Dictionary* we find that *toeu, touweu* is a verb meaning "it is solitary, deserted, unoccupied," while *toueu-appu* signifies "he remains solitary, deserted."[8] John Elliot used this verb and its derivatives in his translation of the Christian Bible to refer to a solitary place, a desert, desolate, wilderness. Roger Williams recorded *towiúwock* for "fatherless children" in Narragansett. However, while the root *towi-* (*touoh*) might seem to mean "solitary" (away from people) in Natick and Narragansett, the same root *tauwa-, tauwi-* in Lenápe points toward a slightly different meaning. Very early *tauwiechen* was recorded as "it (the way) is open," or simply "open." The word *tauwunummen* meant "to open." In Ontario Lenápe today, *tawee-, tawa-* is the root for "to open," "to hang open," "to be blown open," and for "unlocking" and "key." *Táwu-* words in Cree refer to holding one's mouth open, while *tuwá-* and *tuwe-* words refer to a space or opening. For example, *tuwéw* or *towéw* means "he makes room, he gives place."[9] In Ojibwe *tawa* is a verb signifying "there is room," while other *tawa-* words refer to a gap, space, opening, or making room.[10]

I believe that "open" and "solitary" essentially point toward an area which is not occupied or enclosed by people, that is, what we might call "The Open" or the "Away from People."

Perhaps *taw-* words are related to Lenápe *tékene* (*teé-* is drawn out), originally translated as forest (woods) and later as wilderness. Because "wilderness" is a strictly European conception, it is likely that what was meant was deep forest or any other place where humans were not living. (The same root is probably found in Powhatan-Renápe, as in Toe-ink, the name of a swamp in the Chickahominy area). *Kocháming* means "in the outdoors" or "outside" in Lenápe.[11]

Ojibwe and Cree dictionaries also shed some light upon the above idea. In Ojibwe the root *pagwad-* seems to denote places, animals, plants, or trees which are away from humans. *Pagwadadamig* is translated by a missionary as "wilderness, in the desert" and *pagwadakamig* as "desert place, far from human habitation." The root *pagwadj-* seems to be related to *pagidji-* (to be free, loose, released) and perhaps to *pagwa-,* denoting guessing, ignorance, and lack of knowledge, as in *pagwanawisiwin,* translated as "ignorance, wild natural state, savage life." Perhaps the latter is derived from *nin pagwanawiton,* "I don't know how to make it, do it," or *nin pagwanawis,* "I am uneducated, I am ignorant, I am in a wild natural state." Much of this may be the missionaries' interpretation, since the term for "wild" behavior is totally different: *nin wanishkwe* (I am wild).

In any case, *pagwadj-* terms may refer to one being ignorant about a place, tree, or animal, rather than primarily to the lack of habitations per se. It is useful to note that many "wild" animals and trees do not have *pagwadj-* attached to their names. It is primarily creatures such as boars, dogs, goats, horses, snails, trees in general, and turkeys which can be so denominated—that is, things which can be either "domesticated" or nondomesticated. Such things as wildcats, wild cherries, geese, pine trees, and wild rice are not referred to as *pagwadj-*. Interestingly, Bishop Baraga does refer to a "wild man" as *pagwadjinini* and a "wild woman" as *pagwadjikwe*, because, I suppose, humans can be domestic or nondomestic.[12]

The corresponding root in Cree seems to be *pikwu-*. For example, *pikwuche* is said to mean "lonely, wild, desolate" and *pikwúcheuyiséyinew* is "a lonely person, a barbarian, a hermit." But "disorderly" behavior is *kískwawe*. Negative connotations may have been added by the missionaries, but it does seem that *pikwu-* words can refer to things which are common, useless, worthless, and false, as well as to being away from human habitations. *Pikwuchiyek* is defined as "outdoors (nature)," while *pikwuche kakchi* is "wild life (nature)," but the term "nature" seems clearly to be an addition of the dictionary makers.[13]

An Ontario Lenápe dictionary refers to some animals and things as *lawi-*, a term translated as "wild," though this does not mean "running around wild" which is covered by a totally different word. *Lawi-* is prefixed to the names of several animals or foods which have "domestic" counterparts, such as bobcats, pheasants, and food. *Lawi-* is related to words which classify action or which cover a wide range of concepts, from "in the middle" to having no place to live, to looking for something.[14]

It would seem, then, that some American languages did differentiate between their habitation areas, with the associated plants and animals, and things or places far away from habitations. The latter were not seen as behaviorly wild, but negative connotations may have existed. On the other hand, many positive associations also are known to have existed, as, for example, when Lenápe people were required to use only the meat of animals from the *tékene* (*tékenayésa*, or nondomesticated animals) during their ceremonies, because such meat was *pílsit* or clean (pure), from *pílsit a(y)éses* (pure, clean animals).[15]

Culture or Together-Doing

Now let us examine the concepts of cultivation and culture. These terms are said to originate in the Latino-Italiano *colore*, a verb meaning "to till, cultivate, dwell, inhabit, worship," and its past participle *cultus*. The latter is said to refer to "care" as well as to cultivation, adoration, and the like, so perhaps the idea of demonstrating care of something is what tied together such diverse concepts as tillage and worship. In any case, from *cultus* stemmed *cultura, cult,* and *cultivare*.

"Culture" came into English from the French as an equivalent of "cultivation" and, as with the latter, soon came to refer to the cultivation of humans as well as to the cultivation of the soil. The *Oxford Universal Dictionary on Historic Principles* (1933) lists these definitions for "culture": 1) worship (a 1483 example); 2) cultivation as in agriculture (Middle English); 3) cultivation, especially of microscopic organisms and also the product thereof; 4) figuratively, improvement or refinement by education and training (1510); 5) the training and refinement of mind, tastes and manners and the condition of being thus trained, i.e., the intellectual side of civilization. In the late nineteenth century (1870s) we find such expressions as "the culture of corn," the "culture of wheat," and "methods of culture," referring to methods of raising products, as well as "The soil is clay, and difficult of culture"(1806).[16]

The verb "to cultivate," in addition to its obvious agricultural usages, was also applied to human beings, as in "to improve and develop by education and training; to refine" (1681). "Culture" was also used as a verb, but this was rare (1510). Instead, "culture" was usually a noun or an adjective, along with "cultivation" and "cultivated," while "to cultivate" was normally the related verb.

Interestingly, an early work on husbandry was called the *Jewel House of Art and Nature* (1594), thus contrasting these two ideas.[17] Art and arm (weapon) are both derived from Latin *art-* and *ars-*, meaning skill. Thus, skill is juxtaposed to nature in much the same way as culture is set opposite to nature by anthropologists at a much later date. Skill, of course, requires (presumably) learning and practice, things apparently thought to be lacking in "nature."

The *Oxford Universal Dictionary* (1933) did not refer to recent anthropological definitions of "culture," but *Webster's Third New International Dictionary* (1961) lists the older definitions cited above and then goes on to add: 1) "the state of being cultivated" (similar to the older usages); 2) "the total pattern of human behavior and its products embodied in thought, speech, action, and artifacts and dependent upon man's capacity for learning and transmitting knowledge . . . through the use of tools, language, and systems of abstract thought"; 3) "the body of customary beliefs, social forms, and material traits constituting a distinct complex of tradition of a racial, religious, or social group"; and 4) the behavior of a group or class, as in "youth culture."

The modern idea of "culture" has shifted emphasis from the *process of cultivation* to the *results of cultivation,* although these results encompass the "machinery" of cultivation (for example, educational systems as a part of any given "culture"). There has also been a radical shift away from nonhumans. No longer can one refer to "oyster culture" without seeming a bit archaic, although bacteria culture is still permitted. In general, and most significantly, European scholars have tried to teach us that nonhumans do not have cultures. *Webster's Dictionary* does not include chimpanzees or honey bees among those who have "a culture," only humans.

Most modern anthropological definitions of culture seem to emphasize not simply the total way of life of a human group but the way of life as specifically modified by learned behavior or by mental processes. An attempt is made to abstract how one eats, for example, from eating as a so-called biological process. Thus, if I eat with my fork prongs curving upward, with my other hand at rest, while an English person eats with her fork prongs curving downward and with a knife in the other hand, those are "cultural" features, while our salivating, swallowing, chewing, and having the need and desire to put hand to fork are *not* "cultural" but "natural" or biological.

This attempt to separate the cultural (or learned) from the biological (or borned) reminds one of early Greek efforts to separate "form" from "matter." But Aristotle pointed out that these aspects cannot be empirically known and cannot exist apart from each other. Neither absolutely formless matter nor matterless form is ever met in the universe of sense perception: "No form without matter, no matter without form."

In the same way, we can perhaps argue that there can be no cultural act without a corresponding biological act. But, of course, when we consider that neural functions or chemical messengers are all "biological," then we can argue that very little remains which is nonbiological; but this need not cheer up extreme "sociobiologists," since the internal life of biophysical processes is very complex indeed.

From the Native American perspective it seems that everything has always been "bio," including physical and geological processes and all forms of matter. Thus, to say that something is "bio-" is only to assert that it is "alive," from Greek *bios,* life, not that it is genetically predetermined or operating like a "machine."[18]

One problem with the term "culture" is that it is an abstract noun which provides the illusion that there may be something out there in the real world which corresponds with the word. But that cannot be the case, since "culture," as a nonverbal concept, is inherently fixed, static, and separate, while the reality is that what we, as humans, do is always changing (however slowly) and is never separated from other humans or the environment by absolute boundaries.

The way people live, and what they do, how they create, what they make, is always *verbal,* that is, it is dynamic and in motion. Now, it so happens that many Native American languages are essentially verbal (such as Algonkian), so we would be well-advised to abandon Englatino's static abstractions in favor of abstractions which are dynamic verbal words. In this connection, I have been much impressed by the Dutch term *samenleving* (together-living), used as a synonym for the French *société.* It seems that "together-living" expresses in a dynamic way what we want to mean by "society," without being led into the illusion of a fixed, separate, concrete entity, an illusion which has baffled and befuddled so many Eurocentric writers.

In Germanic languages, the "-ing" form is perhaps the best one for expressing intellectual concepts which correspond to anything which is active. Thus, we already speak of running, boxing, skiing, and boating, all of which emphasize the moving, active nature of those activities. But "thought" (instead of "thinking"), "labor" (instead of "working" or "laboring"), and "society" (instead of together-living) all mislead us into an assumption of something static, finished, complete, whole, and separate. (Surely it would be much more accurate to speak of the "Thinking of Plato" than the "Thought of Plato," since Plato, like most of us, must have been thinking at many different times during his life, and perhaps he even changed an idea or two over the years.)

I propose that we use "together-living" (*com-vivir*) in place of "society" (*sociedad*), or at least that we redefine "society" to be a dynamic "ing" concept. Similarly, I propose that we abandon "culture" as an intellectual tool and that, instead, we use *com-hacer* or *com-*

haciendo in Spanish and "together-doing" or "together-making" in Englatino—preferably the former, as "doing" embraces making, creating, thinking, and more. I will also discuss some Algonkian forms for the above, but first let me point out some of the advantages of adopting a dynamic "ing" form.

First, in the face of the "postmodernist" (and other) jargonistic projects seeking to make our academic dialects more elitist, more inaccessible to the nonacademic population, and less comprehensible generally, I suggest that we counterattack by maintaining our Native way of using straightforward concepts which "do the job" in the clearest and simplest manner possible.

Second, the empirical world provides us with behavior which seldom, if ever, stops at interhuman or intergroup boundaries. Thus, the interactions of Navajo people (as an example) with their sacred lands and the animals and plants, and with the Anasazi, Yumans, Uto-Aztecans, other Athapaskans, and Pueblos of many languages, have always been intimate, complex, dynamic, and interpenetrating, at least since about 1000–1200 c.e.[19] The Navajo ways of living (ways of doing things together) have never been static. But when we read of "Navajo Culture," we are faced with a monolithic unity which immediately forces us to erect boundaries—boundaries *against* non-Navajos and boundaries *against* Navajos of earlier eras, and boundaries *against* innovative, nonconformist, or conservative Navajos themselves (since these latter may differ from what has been designated as a singular Navajo culture).

Unfortunately, the culture concept as commonly understood lends itself not merely to a dualistic opposition with "nature" but also to heavy use by extreme nationalists, chauvinists, and state propaganda systems, which can enlist "culture" along with "race," "motherland," "fatherland," and other equally ambiguous (or even nonexistent) entities in order to create a sense of hyperidentity and to exclude all "others." The Nazis made great use of attacks against an alleged "Jewish culture" as well as against a fake Jewish race concept. But now, sadly, extreme religious nationalists in Israel/Palestine use the same process against erstwhile fellow Semites who happen to adhere to a different tradition and who speak Arabic or Hebrew as their first language (although in earlier times, many of their ancient ancestors spoke Canaanite dialects, Aramaic, or Hebrew, or all of these!).

To conceive of ways of living as discrete, bounded, and fixed plays into the hands of those who want to create borders, who want to create "others." The French state, the German state, and many similar governments have tried to create the myth of "a French culture" or "a German culture." We have had enough experience of the results of such experiments, I think.

This is not to say that there are not streams of behavior in the sea of human life which can be given names and studied as specific traditions. There certainly are. But the point is that they are *always moving,* always rubbing off behavioral molecules with neighboring streams, eddies, and surrounding banks and shores. And there will usually be areas where the waters become mixed and very difficult to separate or identify origin.

Let us examine a few examples from several Algonkian languages in order to see if they will help us better to grasp an indigenous approach to the "culture concept."

The Lenápe and Natick (Massachuset) languages share a common root which refers to living, not in the sense of breathing or being alive physically, which is covered by a different root, but in the sense of doing, behaving, or acting. In Lenápe texts this root (*-owsi-* in the Oklahoma dialect, *-awsi-* in Ontario, *-auchsi-* in some early transcriptions; *usse-* and *uhshu-* in Natick; *isse-* or *-ise-* in Cree; *iji-* or *-isi-* in Ojibwe) is used to refer to a way of life, as in *endalausíeng* (how we live), *endalausiengw* (our manner of life), *wáni lenápe endaláusit* (this Delaware way of living), *yúni endalausíengw* (this our way of living), and *wendáusíengw* (our cultural life, beginning of our life). The same root appears in *elaosit* (*ay-láo-seet,* the way he lives), *ay-lao-seet-cheek* (the way they live), *wilaosu* (he lives good), *wilaosowákan* (good, moral life), *welauchsit* (orderly, well-behaved person), *gata lenápe-owsi* (I want to live Indian or Delaware), *wilowsi* (I want to be good), and *taláusi* (you must live there). In some early transcriptions *lauchsin* means "to live, walk morally" and *lauchsowagan* means "life, behavior, conduct."[20]

Thus it is very clear that the Lenápe term for "culture" refers to doing, acting, behaving, or living in a certain way. In Natick *usseáonk* or *usseonk* (a doing, example), *ussenat* (to do, to act, perform), *úshuàonk,* *ushuaonk* (a custom) and *usseu* (he acts, does) are all from the same root as *-owsi-* and point to the same basic meaning of doing.[21] The same root *-owsi-* can be combined with *pom-, pim-, bim-,* or *pamp-* in the Powhatan-Renápe, Lenápe, Cree, Ojibwe, and Narragansett-Natick languages to refer to living in another sense, a more physical sense of walking or going on physically, as in Cree *pimàtisew* (he lives) or *pimátisew máskunow* (life road) and *nin bimadis* (I am alive) and *bimádisiwin* (life) in Ojibwe. A Lenápe form is *pumásuw:* to live, be alive, living.[22]

The concept of "together-doing," or simply "doing," would seem to be what we really want to replace "culture" with. Admittedly, many writers will find it very hard to speak of together-doing instead of culture, and it may be that all of this will fall on deaf ears, since even Native scholars must obtain promotions or appointments within European-focused social science departments. Nonetheless, it is useful, in my opinion, to go back to our indigenous languages for intellectual tools which may allow us to build discourses which are not only authentic but also more empirical and straightforward (*sháxkiw,* be straight, or *shaxkaptonakána,* straight or true words, in Lenápe).

Conclusion

I believe that using "ing" words in Englatino, such as together-doing and together-living, represents a superior approach for us to take than that of using borrowed French nouns, which are often misunderstood and misused, as are "culture" and "society." Of course, "associating" can also be used in place of "society," and I suppose that one could come up with a verb from *cultus,* such as "culturing," or that we could expropriate the cumbersome "enculturating" or "acculturating." However, the most important aspect of all of this is to grasp that ways of life are always dynamic and that teaching, learning, and changing are features not only of the human species but also of other living things.

This is very important, because all too often Native Americans have been led to believe that they are somehow no longer "authentic" or "genuine" unless they can possess a way of life exactly like that of their great-great-grandparents—an impossible task! But the notion of "a culture," which we have been sold, has been very harmful, not only in making Native peoples feel inadequate, but also in exacerbating many fights between different groups within a native nation, groups which may legitimately reflect divergences within the former ways of life, but which fight over who is really "authentic" under the mistaken belief that their nation had a single, monolithic culture.

It is also important that we resist Eurocentric and materialistic-reductionist attempts to deny that the universe is, in fact, a biosphere (a living world), and that *bios,* life, includes everything that acts, moves, combines, splits, sends messages, reacts, and otherwise exhibits the principle of *ollin,* or movement. This may well mean that spiritual forces, which after all must be alive if they exist at all, are also part of the biosphere, the living world.

The long-fought struggle between "biology" (the study of life) and "culture" within anthropology, which parallels the nature-culture split, can be seen as an essentially Eurocentric problem, since *bios* (life) must include all of the material studied by anthropologists, including ideas, thoughts, and the products made from living matter. The issue is really one relating to the locus of decision-making and learning—do decisions and learning occur in the DNA or do decisions and learning occur in the brain or between brains?—a topic which need not concern us here, except as it helps us to understand the unity of living creatures.

It is important also that we deny the homocentric approach to "culture." Together-doing is not limited to humans, even though there are many changes which take place among trees, plants, and other living things that cannot be explained by the ways in which humans and many other animals learn or transmit knowledge. We simply do not know, for example, how a particular tree in Costa Rica "decided" to depend upon a species of ants for protection against predators; nor do we know how it came about that that particular ant nation made the determination to live in that kind of tree only and to protect it from enemies. And how is that symbiotic understanding transmitted to new generations? What is the character of the "schooling" received by trees and by ants which allows their mutual dependency compact to be honored over the generations? It is certain that different nations of ants have determined upon different life-paths, as have different nations of trees. It is also certain that information is transmitted from generation to generation, although room is left for individual adaptation and variation. A Lakota elder, Okute, said many years ago:

> Animals and plants are taught by Wakan tanka [Great Mystery] what they are to do. Wakan tanka teaches the birds to make nests, yet the nests of all birds are not alike. Wakan tanka gives them merely the outline. . . . All birds, even those of the same species, are not alike, and it

is the same with animals and with human beings. The reason Wakan tanka does not make two birds, or animals, or human beings exactly alike is because each is placed here by Wakan tanka to be an independent individuality and to rely on itself.[23]

I am ready to accept that together-doing knowledge (cultural information) can be transmitted in a variety of ways, including, of course, the ones that we humans use or have. But these transmission ways may also include the use of "chemical textbooks" and "biochemical messages," which may indeed represent, in some ways, more sophisticated methods of schooling the young than our often haphazard semichemical methods. What I mean by the latter is that when we influence a child by subtle gestures (or by any other method), we are behaving biochemically and physically ourselves and are stimulating a biochemical and physical response in the child. But between the two partially biochemical processes, there is a break, be it spatial, vocal, textual, or visual. Perhaps many other nations of living things have developed ways of teaching which use synapses instead of what seem to be gaps. Of course, we humans depend upon direct biochemical education (our genetic heritage) as well.

My point is that "culture," when viewed as together-doing and when seen from a multispecies perspective, has no conflict with "nature." There may, however, be conflicts between particular kinds of together-doing and between them and the rest of living things.

Many kinds of human traditions, for example, blend into the world of trees and plants and animals in such a manner that their together-doing is not overly intrusive or destructive. Rather, they live in balance with the world around them. The together-doing of people does not overwhelm the together-doings of animals, plants, and other creatures.

Nonetheless, probably all human beings and animals are aware of the importance of the Away from People, because it is in the latter situation where many kinds of precious herbs, fruits, food for the body, and spiritual knowledge can be obtained. Many kinds of valued friends cannot survive around or in village compounds (or in towns or cities) and must be sought for in the Away from People. And, of course, many types of animals (but not all) also want to be in the Away from People (some snakes and other animals prefer to live with people, in the roofs of their houses, for example).

But the Away from People is not "nature" as such, because there is also "nature" where people are living densely. It is also not "wild" since, as Luther Standing Bear pointed out, the land becomes "wild" only when aggressive types of people are present.[24]

The Wemi Tali (All Where) can be divided into many different categories that have nothing to do with the human/nonhuman split. For example, many animals and even plants can be destructive if they are too numerous. Around a water hole, large hoofed animals may make it impossible for many plants to survive. Too many hoofed animals may cause great damage to the water hole itself, as well as to the immediate surroundings. Some plants, therefore, may need not only to be in the Away from People but also in the "Away from Hoofed Animal Herds," and so on. Thus, the Wemi Tali is infinitely complex, even though we humans, by proliferating and developing aggressive ways of living, have made ourselves extremely significant in ecological terms.

The concept of "nature" is indeed very powerful, and doubtless we will be powerless to combat the continual selling of "nature" by our commercial entrepreneurs. But, perhaps this essay will help us to be a bit more cautious in our use of the term and to try to concentrate on concepts, such as "balanced together-living" and protecting the Away from People, which have concrete meaning.

People can be, and indeed are, part of "nature." The problem is not to drive all of the indigenous peoples out of national parks (as at Death Valley and Yosemite) or out of "game preserves" (as in the Kalahari of Africa) so that tourists generating commercial revenue can be sold "nature" or "wilderness" in what inevitably is an altered environment. The objective is to understand that together-doing of the balanced kind and the Away from People have never been mutually exclusive and that "nature needs people" (just not too many of them!).

Notes

1. *Oxford Universal Dictionary on Historical Principles* (1933).
2. Ibid.; for a discussion of Englatino, see Jack D. Forbes, "English Only," *News From Indian Country* 10, no. 1 (Mid-January 1996): 15A.
3. *American Heritage Dictionary* (1970).
4. *Webster's Third New International Dictionary* (1961); and Roger Bartra, *El Salvaje en el Espejo* (Mexico: Ediciones Era, 1992), 108 and elsewhere.
5. Frank G. Speck, *Oklahoma Delaware Ceremonies, Feasts, and Dances* (Philadelphia: American Philosophical Society, 1937), 77. Also cited in Jack D. Forbes, *Columbus and Other Cannibals* (New York: Autonomedia, 1992), 142–43.
6. John Wilson and W. T. Thornton, "Agriculture," *Werner Encyclopedia* (c. 1875, 1908 printing), 1:261.
7. Witapanóxwe, in *A Study of the Delaware Indian Big House Ceremony,* ed. Frank G. Speck (Harrisburg: Pennsylvania Historical Commission, 1931), 171–73.
8. J. Hammond Trumbull, *Natick Dictionary,* Bureau of American Ethnology, Smithsonian Institution, Bulletin 25 (Washington, D.C.: Government Printing Office, 1903).
9. E. A. Watkins, et al., *A Dictionary of the Cree Language* (Toronto: General Synod of the Church of England in Canada, 1938).
10. Frederic Baraga, *A Dictionary of the Otchipwe Language,* 2 vols. (Montreal: Beauchemin and Valois, 1878).
11. Trumbull, *Natick Dictionary;* Daniel G. Brinton and Albert S. Anthony, *A Lenápe-English Dictionary* (Philadelphia: Historical Society of Pennsylvania, 1888; AMS reprint, 1979); John O'Meara, *Delaware-English/English-Delaware Dictionary* (Toronto: University of Toronto Press, 1996); and my own work with Lucy Blalock and other Delaware elders.
12. Baraga, *Dictionary of the Otchipwe Language.*
13. Watkins, *Dictionary of the Cree Language.*
14. O'Meara, *Delaware-English Dictionary.*
15. Speck, ed., *Delaware Indian Big House Ceremony,* 100, 122, 136.
16. Wilson and Thornton, "Agriculture," 263, 269; *Oxford Universal Dictionary on Historical Principles.*
17. Wilson and Thornton, "Agriculture," 264.
18. See my poem "Kinship Is the Basic Principle of Philosophy," *Gatherings* 4 (fall 1995): 44–50; also see my manuscript "Ancient Instructions" for a discussion of the "nature" versus "nurture" problem. See Aram A. Yengoyan, "Theory in Anthropology: On the Demise of the Concept of Culture,"*Comparative Studies in Society and History* 28, no. 2 (April 1986): 369–74, for an examination of an anthropologist's ideas about culture.
19. See the introduction and text of my *Apache, Navaho and Spaniard,* rev. ed. (Norman: University of Oklahoma Press, 1995), for details.
20. The Delaware words are from William Shawnee and Lucy Blalock in interviews; Witapanóxwe in Speck, ed., *Delaware Indian Big House Ceremony,* and Speck, *Oklahoma Delaware Ceremonies;* Brinton and Anthony, *Dictionary of the Delaware Language;* and O'Meara, *Delaware-English Dictionary.*

21. See Trumbull, *Natick Dictionary.*

22. See Baraga, *Dictionary of the Otchipwe Language,* and O'Meara, *Delaware-English Dictionary.*

23. Okute, in Frances Densmore, *Teton Sioux Music,* Bureau of American Ethnology, Smithsonian Institution, Bulletin 16 (Washington, D.C.: Government Printing Office, 1918).

24. Luther Standing Bear, *Land of the Spotted Eagle* (Lincoln: University of Nebraska Press, 1978), xix.

Local Knowledges, Global Claims:
On the Significance of Indigenous Ecologies
in Sarawak, East Malaysia

J. PETER BROSIUS

To defer to a second language . . . is to reorder what one has in mind.[1]

In a 1994 essay entitled "Earth Honoring: Western Desires and Indigenous Knowledges," Australian geographer Jane Jacobs observed that "Recent developments in environmentalism and feminism have intensified Western desires to affiliate with indigenous people and to call upon their knowledges and experiences."[2] Jacob's observation is echoed in any number of contemporary discussions of indigenous ecologies and the links between environmentalism and indigenous communities, whether from an advocacy perspective or from other sorts of perspectives.[3]

A concept central to contemporary discussions of the significance of indigenous ecologies is that of the "sacred." Whether deployed by indigenous communities in struggles to assert rights to land, by Euro-American environmentalists seeking to articulate a more meaningful relationship with the earth, or by right-wing demagogues capitalizing on the resentments of constituents—Australian Federal Member Pauline Hanson being perhaps the most vivid example at present—the idea of the sacred is today invoked (or rebuked) with remarkable frequency. In the present discussion, I want to focus particularly on the ways in which the idea of the sacred is evoked in indigenous land struggles.

As deployed in such indigenous struggles, the sacred is a concept of enormous emancipatory force. Invocations of the sacred represent an effort to assert forms of connection to the land that are effaced by colonialist and/or statist projects, or deny the alien(-n)ation that underlies the ubiquitous commodification of land. Increasingly, indigenous claims to land based on the recognition of "sacred sites" are being codified by states, provinces, and national governments.

While recognizing the enormous emancipatory force of the idea of the sacred, I want to raise a series of issues that I believe must be addressed if the notion of the sacred is to retain its promise. I want to frame these concerns around the issue of translation, reflecting on a series of recent discussions of the politics of language in colonial and postcolonial contexts.

In his recent study of the bases of New Order cultural discourse in Indonesia, John Pemberton uses both ethnographic and historiographic materials to examine the emergence of a discourse of indigenous culture: a discourse not simply imposed by Dutch colonial authorities, but one in which Javanese themselves participated, and which the contemporary Indonesian government has assimilated into the workings of an oppressive state security apparatus. Much of Pemberton's argument focuses on the role that the concept of "ritual" has played in colonial and postcolonial Indonesia. He notes that

> many analyses of the colonizing mission have produced their insights by working primarily within the language and textual sources of the colonizer. Although these analyses may be referenced with terms from the native vernacular(s) that facilitated such a mission, their focus, quite understandably remains the contradictory ambivalences within the very grammar of conquest.[4]

What I wish to suggest here is that, as with the notion of *ritual* in the context of colonial and postcolonial Indonesian culture and politics, the idea of the *sacred* is also part of the "grammar of conquest" in contemporary indigenous struggles. It bears considering whether deployments of the concept of the sacred may work counter to the interests of those in whose interest it is deployed.

Pemberton's comments about the significance of the concept of ritual in Indonesia resonate with an earlier study by Vince Rafael of the process of conversion to Catholicism in the colonial Philippines.[5] Citing an observation by fifteenth-century Spanish humanist Antonio de Nebrija that "language is the perfect instrument of empire," Rafael frames this discussion with reference to the matter of translation. He notes that

> From the perspective of colonizers imbued with a sense of mission, translation and conversion appeared to be necessarily related, setting and sustaining the conditions for a history of conquest and salvation.[6]

More important for the present discussion however, are the ways in which Rafael describes early Tagalog strategies of "decontextualizing the means by which colonial authority represents itself":[7]

> native converts who failed to anticipate and so to appropriate the terms of Spanish Christianity were unable to convert their desires into a code that could be sent back to the missionary. . . . They found themselves with no position from which to bargain with colonial authority.[8]

In elucidating his argument, Rafael draws upon a study by James Siegel of the relation between translation and social order in Indonesia.[9]

> Siegel claims that translation arises from the need to relate one's interest to that of others and so to encode it appropriately. Translation in this case involves not simply the ability to speak in a language other than one's own but the capacity to reshape one's thoughts and actions in accordance with accepted forms. It thus coincides with the need to submit to the conventions of a given social order. Deferring to conventions of speech and behavior (which, precisely because they are conventions, antedate one's intentions), one in effect acknowledges what appears to be beyond oneself.[10]

What is most significant for the present discussion is the way in which Rafael and Siegel focus our attention on the "politics of translation,"[11] on the idea that there is a relation between translation and domination. In cases such as those provided by these authors, translation becomes an act of deference on the part of subaltern subjects.

Similarly, I would suggest, indigenous rights struggles—a part of which are constituted by the necessity to articulate indigenous ecologies—virtually always involve acts of translation and, therefore, deference to a second language. This is all the more so when those struggles are taken up in broader national and transnational processes of the circulation of images. Nowhere is this more clearly seen than with reference to the idea of the sacred and its predicates. Thus, for instance, Durning states that "Amid the endless variety of indigenous belief, there is striking unity on the sacredness of ecological systems."[12] According to Native American activist Winona LaDuke,

> Traditional ecological knowledge is the culturally and spiritually based way in which indigenous peoples relate to their ecosystems. This knowledge is founded on spiritual-cultural instructions from 'time immemorial' and on generations of careful observation within an ecosystem of continuous residence.[13]

David Suzuki describes "this ancient, culturally diverse aboriginal consensus on the ecological order and the integrity of nature [which] might justifiably be described as a 'sacred ecology'. . . ."[14]

I wish to illustrate my argument with reference to a contemporary site of indigenous dispossession: the East Malaysian state of Sarawak, on the island of Borneo. In the past two decades, timber companies in Sarawak have plunged headlong into the interior in an effort to extract as much of Sarawak's forest wealth as possible, to the detriment of local communities. Since 1987, Sarawak has been at the center of a high profile international environmental and indigenous rights campaign focused on one indigenous group in particular: the hunting and gathering Penan. In the following discussion, I examine the "indigenous ecology" of the Penan with a view toward elucidating the terms by which they establish and assert their relationship to the land.[15]

Situating Penan

The third largest island in the world, Borneo is sparsely populated, particularly in mountainous interior districts. Two central features of the Bornean landscape are worthy of mention. The first are the many large rivers running from the interior to the coast: rivers have been, and remain, the primary route by which access to the interior has been gained. A second important landscape feature are the extensive tropical forests which, until recently, covered most of the island. These forests have persisted, despite centuries of swidden farming along the major rivers by indigenous peoples: for instance, until logging began in the area in the early 1980s, the Belaga District of Sarawak was well over 90 percent forested.

The island of Borneo is also characterized by considerable ethnic diversity: this is particularly evident in interior areas.[16] Malay communities are mostly found near the coast, while urban areas have large concentrations of Chinese. It is primarily as one moves toward the interior that one encounters "indigenous" communities.[17] The most prominent among these in Sarawak are the culturally homogenous Iban and a much more heterogeneous category of communities referred to as *Orang Ulu* ("upriver people"): groups such as Kayan, Kenyah, Kelabit, Berawan, Kajang, and others. Penan are sometimes included in this category, but for present purposes I wish to consider them separately.

On economic/ecological grounds, it is possible to identify two broad classes of interior people: 1) longhouse-dwelling sedentary agriculturalists (Iban and Orang Ulu); and 2) hunting and gathering forest nomads. While most agriculturalists are found along the major rivers, hunting and gathering peoples live in forested headwater areas. While both longhouse peoples and forest nomads derive their subsistence needs from the tropical forest, they do it in very different ways. Agriculturalists, who must clear the forest in order to plant their crops, derive their living by altering the microenvironment of the forest. Though they certainly make use of the forest, and are surrounded by it, in numerous symbolic and cultural ways agriculturalists preserve the border between forest and cleared land. Physically, a buffer zone of some distance between the longhouse and the forest is maintained. Hunter-gatherers such as the Penan derive their livelihoods from the forest as it stands, though they may well affect the population dynamics of particular species by exploiting them, and they may consciously manage such resources.

Though there are several very distinct groups of hunter-gatherers in Borneo, within Sarawak the Penan comprise the largest category. They can, however, be divided into two distinct populations, the Eastern and Western Penan.[18] The Eastern Penan comprise all those groups living to the north and east of the Baram River, along the Tutoh, Patah, Pelutan, Apoh, upper Akah, Selaan, Selungo, and upper Baram Rivers, as well as in the upper Limbang watershed. The Western Penan include all those in the Belaga District, as well as communities in the Silat River watershed and at Leng Beku. Though sharing many characteristics, these two populations display a number of significant differences with respect to subsistence technology, settlement patterns, social organization, and in the tenor of social relationships.[19] Eastern Penan conform much more closely to the pattern that anthropologists take to be typical of band-level societies, while Western Penan depart from this pattern in striking ways. Though these two populations speak mutually intelligible subdialects of the same language and recognize each other as Penan, they nevertheless consider themselves to be of only very distant ancestry. They have little contact with each other and almost no intermarriage occurs. In short, these are two discrete populations, with distinctive adaptations, distinctive histories, and distinctive social norms.

Eastern and Western Penan in Sarawak together number some seven thousand individuals. The Eastern Penan total some forty-five hundred in approximately fifty communities, while Western Penan total some twenty-five hundred in approximately twenty communities. Most Penan are today settled, though they continue to exploit the forest. Among both Eastern and Western Penan the trend toward sedentism has accelerated greatly since about 1960. In 1960 I estimate that 70 to 80 percent of all Eastern and Western Penan were still nomadic. Of seven thousand Eastern and Western Penan today, fewer than four hundred Eastern Penan in the vicinity of the Magoh, Tutoh and upper Limbang River areas remain fully nomadic, approximately 5 percent of the total. The last nomadic Western Penan settled in 1970.

Sago starch from the palm *Eugeissona utilis* has traditionally been the primary source of carbohydrates for Penan. *Eugeissona* grows on ridges and slopes in clumps, reproducing both clonally and by seed. Penan maintain a long-term harvesting strategy by avoiding a foreshortened harvest cycle: when the sago in one area is depleted, it is left to recover for several years.[20] Penan also rely on the hunting of game: bearded pig (*Sus barbatus*), sambar deer (*Cervus unicolor*), barking deer (*Muntiacus muntjac*), and numerous kinds of primates, squirrels, and other small game. As noted, all Western Penan and most Eastern Penan have today adopted swidden agriculture, planting primarily rice and cassava.

Hunter-gatherers such as the Penan have long occupied a specific niche in the economies of central Borneo. They have been a major source of forest products, which are traded to Orang Ulu and thence to the coast for consumption or export.[21] For longhouse communities, the presence of a Penan band in an area meant access to forest products and to the income generated by trade in those products. Longhouse aristocrats were proprietary about "their" Penan, and jealously guarded their prerogatives to trade with certain groups. In short, Penan were regarded by longhouse peoples as a form of wealth.

Among both Eastern and Western Penan, the band or community is the primary unit of social and political identity. However, the way in which bands are constituted and the degree to which they persist is strikingly different.[22] A primary feature of Western Penan communities is their long-term stability: these are enduring social aggregates. Associated with this stability is a very strong sense of community cohesion and solidarity. Eastern Penan bands are much more fluid with respect to composition and much more ephemeral with respect to long-term historical identity. Another point of difference is that Western Penan communities tend to be much larger than those of Eastern Penan, generally with sixty to two hundred members.[23] Eastern Penan communities, by comparison, average only twenty to forty members.

Both Eastern and Western Penan conceive of their territories as a shared corporate estate over which all members of a community have rights. However, there exists one very significant point of difference between Eastern and Western Penan with respect to land tenure. A concept that is of key significance to Western Penan with reference to the management and exploitation of forest resources is *molong*: "to preserve" or "to foster." Implicit in the Western Penan concept is that resources fostered are *claimed,* either by communities or by individuals. A community may *molong* a particular watershed in order that resources there be allowed to grow for future harvest. The term *molong* also applies to the claiming of particular sago clumps or fruit trees by specific individuals. This does not, however, constitute ownership of those resources. Rather, it a slightly proprietary sort of stewardship. Other members of the community may exploit resources which are individually claimed, but they must inform the individual who claimed that resource. The *molong* system provides a way to monitor information on the availability of resources over vast tracts of land and prevents the indiscriminate use of resources which might otherwise be depleted. In a sense, the Western Penan settlement system may be seen as a temporalized manifestation of the *molong* concept. The existence of the *molong* complex is one of the factors associated with the cohesive character of Western Penan communities. Western Penan bands possess a strong sense of belonging to a particular portion of landscape, and this is validated economically and historically by the management of resources in an area. In contrast, Eastern Penan do not *molong* resources to any significant degree, and the concept plays little role in notions of resource management in either its individual or community aspects.

One of the most conspicuous indicators of the nature of Western Penan communities, in contrast to those of Eastern Penan, is group names. When addressed to Eastern Penan, questions concerning the name of a particular group are met with incomprehension. Western Penan, by contrast, unhesitatingly indicate that they are Penan Apau, Penan Seping, Penan Lusong, or the like. Individuals may speak of themselves as belonging to several groups, some of which no longer exist. Such names are used in a segmentary manner, with a historical and genealogical referent. No single name is *the* correct name, but depends on the immediate context of inclusiveness with other Western Penan groups. That is, these names are used to express a shared history, and therefore kinship, however distant. What the Western Penan use of group names points to is the significance of band identity, an identity that persists even after many generations. Eastern Penan contrast markedly in this respect: even extant groups do not designate themselves by the use of group names. The historically situated segmentary group identification of Western Penan is associated with three other aspects of Western Penan society: 1) a historical process of repeated community partition associated with population growth; 2) conceptions of band membership; and 3) genealogical knowledge and claims to aristocratic status. For present purposes, I will discuss only the last of these.

The members of a Western Penan community retain a strong sense of community based on descent from common ancestors. Relative to Eastern Penan, Western Penan have an exceedingly rich orally transmitted genealogical tradition. The fact that Western Penan retain this knowledge to such a remarkable degree, and that communities have narratable histories, says much about the nature of Western Penan society. In the abstract, Western Penan recognize themselves as all related to each other, to varying degrees of distance. Some type of relationship can nearly always be established between two individuals in different communities, however distant. What is remarkable about Western Penan genealogical accounts is not just their depth (five to seven generations), but their breadth as well. Rather than simple vertical recitations of ancestors, these genealogical sequences broaden out to incorporate the ancestors of virtually all Western Penan. Not only are they used to relate individuals from different groups to each other, they are also deployed in asserting claims to leadership and, by extension, to land.

One characteristic of Western Penan society which stands in sharp contrast to that of Eastern Penan is a strong institution of leadership. Though both Eastern and Western Penan bands have headmen, Western Penan are adamant in insisting that their headmen are of aristocratic status. The source of such claims generally lies in reference to the marriage of ancestors with the offspring of Orang Ulu aristocrats many generations before. Such claims not only validate the status of headmen, but also serve to validate the claims of bands to particular watersheds. Western Penan historical narratives are framed in terms of headmen bringing followers to or from certain places, and the contemporary occupation of particular watersheds is validated with reference to ancestral occupation of those areas. When we consider such narratives with reference to the ongoing process of band growth and partition, it is evident that the territories claimed by Western Penan communities have not been occupied by those bands in perpetuity. Communities are enduring social aggregates and strongly corporate with respect to land. But the territories of those communities, viewed over time, float over the landscape. Particular portions of the landscape may be abandoned, only to be reoccupied, perhaps many generations later. Considering that over the course of several decades it is likely that community partition has occurred, it often happens that, on genealogical grounds, several communities can claim an equal right of access to the same watershed. Upon reoccupation, trees *molong* by aristocratic ancestors are seen to verify claims to land. With regard to matters of genealogical knowledge and claims to aristocratic status, Eastern Penan stand in stark contrast to Western Penan. Though they recall certain luminary ancestors, Eastern Penan genealogies lack depth and breadth relative to those of Western Penan. Few people can name ancestors beyond their grandparents. And though every band has a headman, Eastern Penan do not invoke the principle of rank as a qualification for this office.

In the following discussion, I focus in particular on Western Penan conceptions of landscape. Where necessary, however, I also provide comparisons to Eastern Penan.

The Western Penan Landscape

Until just a few years ago, when one flew over the forests of Sarawak, one could see out to the horizon an unbroken expanse of tropical rain forest. If ever there were an untouched wilderness, this was certainly it. Except for small agricultural clearings in the immediate vicinity of Penan settlements, the landscape appeared to be utterly empty and there was little to suggest any human presence.

It is only when one enters the forest that one begins to see, not a wilderness, but something very much like a neighborhood, a landscape imbued with cultural significance, full of places that for one reason or another have meaning to the Penan. Some of these places are physically marked, others are marked only in the domain of memory. Some have direct relevance to subsistence, many others not. Rather than "sacred" in some abstract sense, this significance is often biographical and highly personal: the place where one was nearly bit by a pig, the site where one's great-grandfather was killed in a raid, a former camping site where fruit was plentiful, the marks made on a tree by a now-deceased favorite niece. Everywhere one goes in the forest, one hears stories both personal and fantastic. The biographies of individuals, both living and dead, are written in the landscape. This Penan conception of the forest landscape can be recognized to have three components: one spatial and cognitive, most clearly manifested in place-names, another largely symbolic, and a third relating to the supernatural.

Rivers, Trees, and History: Spatial Aspects of Landscape

As a preface to addressing Penan notions of the physical landscape, it is useful to specify those features which they deem significant. The most important are rivers and streams. These provide the framework around which all other types of information are organized. The Penan are not unique in this: rivers are the common currency for geographical and historical knowledge throughout central Borneo. But the way Penan organize this information is very different from that of longhouse peoples. Penan knowledge of rivers and landforms is based on a dense and detailed sort of supersymmetry: a knowledge of the proximity and contiguity of rivers to each other, as well as to ridges, trails, and numerous particular sites. In Penan usage, rivers are used as the primary idiom for reference to most other aspects of landscape. When Penan speak of where something occurred, where they have been, or where they will go, they inevitably speak of this with reference to a river name, referring to the watershed which is drained by that river. Penan frequently speak of their territories, the watersheds which they exploit, as "the rivers from which we eat."

In an environment where visibility seldom exceeds two hundred feet, rivers and streams form the skeleton around which spatial, ecological, and historical information is organized. The knowledge which Penan have of rivers, and of the landscape in general, is phenomenal. In the course of my research among Western Penan in the Belaga District, I was able to identify some two thousand named rivers and streams, and this did not begin to exhaust the total number. This is not to say that any one individual knows this many rivers. I estimate that, on average, an adult Penan is familiar with some five hundred named rivers and streams.

When traveling in the forest, Penan are always cognizant of their precise location relative to various rivers. As they travel in the forest, they rely on concrete, memory-based knowledge or, if they are in unfamiliar territory where they do not recognize specific places, on a sense of the contiguity of rivers. As one Penan man explained after returning from a long trip to an area he had not previously visited, in order to find his way home he simply "followed his feelings." The keen Penan sense of spatial relationships derives from an awareness of the relative size of rivers, the angle of flow of one river to another, the topography between particular rivers, the proximity of headwaters of different rivers, and other sorts of environmental cues.

To Penan, the landscape is more than simply a vast, complex network of rivers. Above all, it is a reservoir of detailed ecological knowledge and a repository for the memory of past events. A knowledge of rivers is necessary to make sense of Penan historical and genealogical accounts. Rivers are the paradigm around which spatial, historical and genealogical information is organized. It is by means of naming rivers that Penan give meaning to place. The sources of river names are many and varied and a great deal of information is encoded in these names.

Ecological or geographical features are one important source of river names for Penan. A large number of rivers are named for a particular type of tree, fruit, or plant occurring either near the river mouth, or perhaps in some abundance along the course of the river or within the watershed: a certain type of palm perhaps, a plant used to cook fish, or a tree which, when it fruits, provides forage for pigs. A river may be named for a *particular* tree which occurs at the mouth or somewhere along its watercourse: a fruit tree claimed by an ancestor or an *Antiaris* tree which produces particularly strong dart poison. Often a specific name lives on long after a tree itself has fallen and rotted away. River names may also refer to some feature of the landscape: a large rock which is said to look like an elephant, a salt seep where animals come to drink, or a place where a particular type of stone is prevalent.[24] Yet other river names refer to locations where some memorable event occurred: the killing of a rhinoceros, the loss of a favorite dog, or an exceptionally abundant fruit season, a hut burning down, or a person breaking a spear during a hunt. Such river names carry with them stories which serve to keep the memory of events and of long-dead ancestors alive.

Rivers are also named for particular individuals, both living and dead. Often the river name denotes the location where a particular person was born, hunted or built a fish trap, or killed a clouded leopard. These names often recall events involving particular individuals in interesting and unexpected ways. One river is called *Be Mengen Akem Japi* ("the river at which Akem Japi was held"). Many decades ago, in a camp at the headwaters of this stream, the young daughter of a man named Akem Japi died. Akem Japi was off in the forest and, upon his return, people held him as he was told the news of his daughter's death. Another river is named *Be Lake' Kulit Peluβit*. Lake' Kulit was an old man who died in the 1950s. *Peluβit* means to tumble. Shortly before his death, as the Penan Geng Belaga were moving from one camp to another, they stopped to rest on a ridge next to a steep slope. While sitting there this man nodded off and dropped off the side of the ridge, rolling to the bottom.

This relationship between individuals and rivers is reciprocal as well. The Penan have a strong prohibition against mentioning the names of deceased persons, particularly those who have died recently. When individuals die, they are referred to by the name of the river where they died and are buried, prefaced by either *Lake'* (male) or *Redu* (female). In this way the memories of the burial sites of long-dead ancestors are preserved: not the specific grave site but, of more importance to the Penan, the watersheds in which these graves are located are those from which the present generation derive their subsistence. These rivers thus form a sort of charter for each band. The result is that the landscape itself serves as an idiom for the maintenance of historical and genealogical information. This idiom is an important mnemonic device for the maintenance of social relationships. At the same time it serves to establish the rights of Penan communities to exploit the resources of a given area. The rivers in which the ancestors are buried are the source of livelihood for their living descendants.

Reference to the deceased by the names of rivers is an important device for the remembrance of genealogical sequences, anchoring these genealogies in the physical landscape. The result is that among Penan there is a close link between the physical landscape, the memory of historical events, the maintenance of extensive genealogies, and, by extension, knowledge of the nature of kinship relations between more distantly related individuals.

Not only are rivers themselves named, but also various places along them: rapids, deep pools, bends, slow-flowing sections, distinctive rocks, minor river forks, and the like. The most common locational referent is the mouth (*leng*) of a river. There is also a rather extensive vocabulary for speaking of the relative location and/or course of one river to another. For example, rivers which flow parallel to each other are said to be *papan*, while the term *peselep* refers to the contiguity of headwaters of two rivers.[25]

Penan landscape knowledge is far from exhausted by knowledge of rivers, and the cultural density of the landscape is manifested in still other ways. Many types of feature are named: mountain peaks, ridges, low points along ridges, steep portions of trails, resting places along major trails, and rock faces.

Tying this network of rivers and place-names together is a vast network of well-maintained trails. While these trails themselves are not named, numerous way-points along them are. These include cleared resting places (*lasan*) along their course, places where a ridge may dip (*sawak*), particularly steep portions of a trail (*miang*), and passages between rock faces (*ulu*) which may occur along them.

Another class of named sites in the Penan landscape is former (and present) camps (*lamin*). These sites are scattered over the landscape and are the loci and the repositories of innumerable memories, good and bad. When traveling along rivers or in the forest, Penan often point out such sites and speak of events which occurred there. Penan conversation is often filled with references to former *lamin* sites. It is with reference to past *lamin* sites that Penan primarily place events sequentially and map them onto the landscape. *Lamin* sites are almost always named, often with reference to the river where they were located, but often as well with reference to some remarkable event. Thus, for instance, one *lamin* occupied in the 1950s is referred to as Lamin Pagem, "to pull on each other's hair." Two women had an argument here over an accusation of adultery and, in the heat of argument, they grabbed each other's hair, an exceedingly rare thing for Penan and sufficiently so to be retained as a site name.

In speaking of former *lamin* sites, and other places in the forest where past events occurred, Penan speak of *uban*. In its broadest sense, *uban* refers to an empty place left by the withdrawal of an object or being. For instance, pig tracks are referred to as *uban mabui,* young men often speak of former lovers as their *uban,* and the empty place in a hut left by someone who is away or has died is referred to as that person's *uban*. In the latter case, and in reference to former *lamin* sites or other places where past events occurred, *uban* is an evocative and emotionally laden word. In traveling through the forest, Penan often point to such places and recall events that occurred there. Particularly for older people, these recollections are tinged with the bittersweet memories of persons long dead.

In the course of my research, I collected a settlement sequence for one community back to the 1920s. As I spoke to persons of various ages in order to reconstruct this sequence, I began to realize, like Renato Rosaldo, that "Movement was an integral part of . . . biographies" and that Penan, like Ilongot, "care intensely about the relative sequence of a succession of events. . . . these excursions into the past are meticulously mapped onto the landscape, not onto a calendar."[26] For Penan, then, the forest is a place marked not only by biographical events, but a place of remembrance of a series of withdrawals—of self from others and of others from self and from community, through movement or death—that punctuates those events.

In addition to rivers, *lamin,* and other types of sites, the Penan also name particular trees and especially productive stands of sago which have been *molong*. The most important trees, which are almost invariably named, are durian, jackfruit, various members of the mango family, and *tajem* trees (*Antiaris toxicara*), from which blowdart poison is taken. Sago clumps are named because previous yields were consistently good. Such names may refer to the person who first spotted the tree, to a deceased individual buried near it, or to the river near which it occurs.

There is one other aspect of landscape that is important to Penan: the burial sites of ancestors. Along with *molong* trees, it is the locations of burials in particular watersheds which Penan cite as justifying their right to exploit those watersheds. Given the nomadic basis of Penan society, burial sites are scattered widely over the landscape. The degree to which the Penan recall the locations of burials of long-dead ancestors is remarkable. This is in part a result of the fact, noted earlier, that the deceased are for some years referred to with reference to the river near which they died. This provides a mnemonic for the association between individuals and the location of their burial. What is important to Penan is not so much the precise locations of graves, which they generally do not know, but their location within a particular watershed. After some years Penan would be hard pressed to come up with the precise locations of graves, but the memory of watersheds often persists for generations.

Forest and Lamin: *Symbolic Aspects of Landscape*

The Penan view the forest, and their place within it, in a way which is profuse with significance, and this profusion carries over into other domains of Penan existence: a discussion of the symbolic aspects of landscape also touches on issues of gender, the supernatural, and, particularly, on all the implications of the distinction which Penan make between the forest and the domestic domain.

As with the known landscape, Penan view the larger world with respect to rivers. They refer to the outside world as the "realm below" (*daleh ra'*) or the "realm downriver" (*daleh bai*), and they see themselves and the headwaters in which they live as at the center of the habitable world. The "realm below" is seen as a threatening and potentially dangerous place, and Penan have historically been exceedingly reluctant to travel there. They view the most distant areas, the "realm of the rivermouths" (*daleh leng*), as being particularly dangerous—a view reinforced by what they hear today on the radio of wars, famines, and other misfortunes—and believe that there, at the "edge of the sky" (*ujung langit*), people must mix freely with spirits.

The forest, in contrast, Penan find to be a familiar, more comfortable place. A comment often made about the Penan is that they dislike sunlight.[27] Initially, I found this hard to believe, but it is indeed the case. The Penan, particularly those who are still nomadic, find long exposure to sunlight very unpleasant. Even groups which have taken up agriculture complain incessantly about headaches and other maladies when they must spend any length of time in the sun. Penan much prefer to "mix with the trees" (*pekalet ngan kayou*). In contrast to what they disparage as the mud and detritus of longhouse communities and logging camps—with their stands of stagnant green-black water, mosquitos, and unhealthy atmosphere—Penan refer to the forest as "new land" (*tanah mering*): clean, undisturbed, where one is not afraid to drink from any river or stream. Penan compare the forest game they eat to the domestic animals eaten by downriver peoples: while wild game eat only fruits, grubs, and the like, domestic pigs and chickens forage under longhouses for whatever refuse they can find, and Penan find the thought of eating these disgusting.

This is not to say that the Penan view the forest as completely benign. While generally pleasant, it is a place that deserves respect, a place fraught with potential dangers, both physical and supernatural. There are snakes and bears, as well as supernatural dangers, forest spirits who do not like humans intruding on their domain. And there are moments of sheer terror one experiences there, for instance, when the gust of wind preceding a thunderstorm suddenly hits, the trees above ones head swaying wildly, branches falling.

For a people who make their lives within the deep forest, it is perhaps somewhat surprising that the Penan draw a strong distinction between forest and *lamin*. Penan refer to the forest simply as *tanah* ("land"), and a person in the forest is said to be *tong tanah* or *dalem tanah*, at or in the forest/land. Between these two domains—*tanah* and *lamin*—Penan maintain symbolic and ritual boundaries, and certain precautions must be taken when crossing from one to the other. Penan see the camp as warm, whereas the forest is seen to be cool. They speak of returning from the forest as coming *jin genin*—"from the cool."[28] If one crosses from warm to cool, from camp to forest, without observing certain precautions, one is subject to supernatural attack by a class of spirits called Bale' Tingen. *Tingen* is a descriptive term for the state of supernatural attack brought about by this class of spirits. Bale' Tingen do not themselves appear, but rather make themselves known by the actions of certain animals or objects. One might be bitten by a snake, pig, or bear or accidentally be cut by a knife. Thus, before setting off into the forest, Penan are careful to move away from the fire, and to remove from the vicinity of that fire any clothing or tools they intend to bring with them. Likewise, moving from the cool to the warm may present certain dangers. The "cold" of the forest is not intrinsically dangerous. Only when it intrudes too suddenly on the domestic domain when there are persons who are otherwise in a fragile state does it become dangerous.

The distinction between *tanah* and *lamin*, between cold and warm, also appears to be manifested in Penan notions of gender, the forest being seen as the domain of men, the camp as that of women and children. This is indicated as much by the behavior of Penan as by statements they make: among Penan, women almost never go into the forest alone, and only rarely with other women. Even then, they do not travel very far. Women do go into the forest in the process of moves from one camp to another, on the way to sago processing sites, and they occasionally accompany husbands on hunting trips. But never did I witness a woman going into the forest alone, and on only a few occasions did I ever witness women going into the forest with other women. Both men and women say that women are not brave (*makang*) about venturing into the forest. The reasons for this primarily concern perceived supernatural dangers. Women and children are considered to be more subject than men to the attacks of malevolent spirits.[29]

Lest Ungap *Hear: Supernatural Aspects of Landscape*

There is a tendency in descriptions of indigenous religions to focus on those aspects that are either most dramatically performative—rituals and the like—or densely symbolic. If we wish to understand anything about the nature of Penan religion, we must look not to ritual, but to everyday language: language is the primary site for the manifestation of all manner of Penan assumptions concerning the habits and motives of those believed to inhabit the supernatural realm. Penan possess a rich poetic vocabulary used in prayers and in the everyday use of avoidance terms intended to keep malevolent forces at bay.[30] Though Western

Penan recognize the existence of a high god, they are more concerned with the machinations of spirits and souls. They pray to such beings before embarking on trips, during thunderstorms, and in the event of illness. Spirits and souls are interrogated, reasoned with, cajoled, beseeched, addressed with biting sarcasm, and even scolded, in rapidly spoken sequences of rhymed couplets. Western Penan believe in the existence of a range of spirits who can overhear humans and enjoy causing harm. They thus employ an elaborate avoidance terminology to make statements repulsive to spirits or to disguise subsistence activities, movements, groups of people, the presence of infants, and illness.

In the traditional pantheon, Penan recognized a supreme deity called Tenangan or Pesolong Luan. However, most Western Penan are today followers of the Bungan religion, and increasing numbers are converting to Catholicism.[31] Bungan is a syncretic religion which began to spread from the Apo Kayan in the 1940s, at a time when Protestant missionaries were beginning to win large numbers of converts in the Apo Kayan. In a vision which came in the form of a dream to a man named Jok Apui, the Kenyah female deity Bungan Malan told him that the old ritual restrictions, particularly those associated with bird omens, were to be discarded, and that thereafter people should pray to her. Penan and others remark that under the old religion, observing omens was an onerous and irritating task, often causing travelers to cancel their trips. Jok Apui proselytized widely, particularly in Sarawak, and by the early 1950s, much of the upper Balui watershed had been converted to the Bungan religion. This finally reached the Western Penan in the mid-1950s. Thus, today, Bungan Malan has taken a place beside Tenangan.

The Penan recognize one other important deity, Bale' Gau, the god of thunder. Bale' Gau is a male personage living "above" (*bawai*) in the sky, and it is he who controls and dispenses thunder. Penan, it should be noted, fear thunderstorms greatly. It is not so much the thunder and lightning itself as the blasts of wind (*liwen*) which accompany these, creating a real danger to those below the forest canopy. Additionally, Penan fear that more severe thunderstorms, those accompanied by hail, have the potential to turn people, longhouses, or camps to stone (*malui*). The landscape is dotted with rock formations that are regarded as proof of this.

According to Penan, Bale' Gau does not send thunder without

reason. Rather, he does so in response to the mockery of animals or the mixing of certain foods. The archetypal case Penan cite is one of people making fun of dogs, cats, or monkeys by dressing them up and laughing at them. But there are any number of other ways that animals can be mocked or their souls upset. Penan believe that, if offended, the souls of animals report this offense to Bale' Gau, who thereby sends a thunderstorm upon those who are guilty. It is for this reason too that Penan avoid saying the names of animals which have been killed by hunters. For most species of animals, there are alternative names employed once they are brought back to camp, so as to avoid their actual names: for instance, the barking deer, called *telao* in Penan, is referred to as *bale bulun* (red hair). Penan also assume that some animals are intrinsically more dangerous than others: sago grubs, certain kinds of frogs, hairy caterpillars, and animals lacking tails (gibbons, bears) are considered particularly dangerous. One of the greatest dangers is that children, who do not know any better, may through carelessness offend the souls of animals, thus causing *liwen*.[32]

The souls of the dead can also cause thunderstorms, particularly those who have recently died. They do this because they are resentful of the fact that they are dead. This sense of resentment is believed to be increased when the deceased see their surviving kin show insufficient regret at the fact of their passing, perhaps by people playing music or otherwise enjoying themselves too soon after their death. They may also cause thunder simply by their sense of longing, as their surviving relatives do something which they enjoyed or visit a place with which it is assumed they would have some nostalgic feeling.

In addition to Bale' Gau, the spirits Penan are most concerned about are those believed to inhabit the landscape. This is a very broad category indeed, and it is not necessary here to consider every type. Those of greatest concern are of a class called *ungap*. *Ungap* are malevolent spirits, believed to be exceedingly ugly and attracted to graves. Though Penan believe they may harm people, what they most take pleasure in is frustrating the efforts of Penan to find food in the forest. They are said to try to hide pigs from hunters, but may also do such things as deplete starch from unprocessed sago palm trunks. Penan believe that *ungap* may, for example, hear people referring to a hunt, and thus doom that hunt to failure. Should *ungap* become aware of plans to hunt, fish, or make sago, they will hide whatever the object of the search is. They may prevent dogs from catching scent of a pig or, for instance, if in pursuit of a pig, if that pig runs off in one direction, *ungap* will cause the dogs to run off in another direction. It is for this reason that Penan employ a rich vocabulary of avoidance language when speaking of hunting and all other forest-related activities. Among Penan, every effort is made to avoid reference to hunting before or during hunts "lest *ungap* hear." The most common usages with reference to hunting with dogs and spears are "to go look for damar" (*tai pita utip*), to "look for fan palm shoots" (*pita silat*), or "look for luck/fate" (*pita nasip*).

Avoidance terms are also used with reference to other forest-related activities, such as the move from one camp to another. Though they are mostly interested in denying people food, *ungap* are also believed able to harm people, particularly women and children. In the case of a move from one camp to another, the concern is that *ungap* may hear people discuss where they intend to move to and thus cause some harm. Rather than use the conventional word for "move" (*pasu*), Penan speak of "crawling" (*mengamang*). Penan also believe that it is dangerous to have too many people together in a single *lamin*. The noise and crowding is considered likely to attract spirits—both *ungap* and other classes of spirit—who are likely to cause death. Likewise, it is considered dangerous even to refer to the fact that there are many people.[33]

Penan also believe (as do most people in central Borneo) that tigers exist, and these they believe are capable of causing them harm. There are of course no tigers remaining in Borneo today. Nevertheless, myths and stories about tigers abound. Penan say, for instance, that their ancestors used to eat tigers. They believe that though tigers (*saang*) still exist, they have become spirits. They are primarily believed to inhabit steep, rocky areas. Children in particular are believed to be in danger from tigers, who may be attracted by the sound of crying. Penan also believe that fruit or tobacco found in the forest unexplainably has been put there by *saang* and is meant to harm them.

Another important feature of traditional Penan religion (and of most traditional religions in central Borneo) is a concern for omens. Most often, these result from observing certain species of birds in flight: a bird flying from right to left is taken as a bad omen, while one flying from left to right is seen as a good omen. Omens can also be conveyed by certain other species of animal: barking deer, snakes, and so forth. Penan, however, no longer regard such omens, following their conversion to Bungan. Speaking today of the former practice of observing omens, they recall it as a great inconvenience, having constantly led to the abandonment of travel plans,[34] and they describe their conversion to Bungan as having freed them from such an onerous set of observances.

Finally, Penan believe in a series of other categories of malevolent spirits. Two of the most frequently mentioned are *bale' serawah*, which inhabit open spaces, either in the sky or in places such as swidden fields, where the forest has been felled, and *penakoh,* a type of spirit which takes the form of animals that are hunted and may cause harm to hunters if they are shot.

Resistance to Logging

Despite centuries of swidden farming along the major rivers by indigenous peoples, upland forests in the Belaga, Baram, and Limbang Districts of Sarawak remained largely undisturbed until recently. With the advent of large-scale mechanized logging, which accelerated greatly in the 1970s, the areas covered by primary forest have been reduced drastically and deforestation continues at a rapid rate. Sarawak is today a major supplier of tropical hardwood on international markets and is currently experiencing one of the highest rates of deforestation in the world. The speed with which logging has progressed is remarkable. Though timber companies only began to penetrate the interior in the late 1970s, by the 1980s they had moved into areas occupied by Penan, and they have now nearly reached the Indonesian border in several places.

Logging has a dramatic effect on the lives of Penan, both nomadic and settled. The most immediate effect is on the forest resources which they depend upon for subsistence and trade. Among their most frequent complaints is that sago palms (*Eugeissona utilis*) are uprooted by bulldozers, a common occurrence because sago exists in greatest concentration on steep ridges and slopes; precisely those areas where roads are built and where slides from road building occur. Penan also complain that the trees from which they get fruit and blowdart poison are felled, and that as often as not the trunks of those trees are not even taken. Yet another frequent objection to logging is that game disappears because of the noise of logging activities, because the trees which provide forage for pigs and other types of game are felled, and because loggers bring in shotguns in order to hunt. Penan are concerned about river siltation, which kills fish and makes it difficult to find clean water for drinking or for the processing of sago. They are also disturbed by the destruction of rattan, which diminishes their ability to participate in the cash economy. Finally, one of the most common complaints of Penan is that graves are obliterated. While the destruction of graves is a concern of all Penan, it is voiced with particular frequency by nomadic Eastern Penan. These nomadic groups almost always construct their camps on ridges, and bury their dead there as well—precisely where logging roads are constructed. The headman of one nomadic group recounted to me how the graves of thirty-one of his closest kin—a spouse, parents, grandparents, siblings, children, and others—were destroyed by bulldozers.

For Penan—Eastern and Western, nomadic and settled—logging means hunger. But it means more than this. Logging completely alters a landscape with which Penan have a deeply historical relationship. What is of as much concern to the Penan as the privation caused by logging is the way in which logging has altered the landscape in which they live. With logging, the cultural density of the landscape— all those sites with biographical, social, and historical significance— is obliterated. Thus, logging not only undermines the basis of Penan subsistence but also destroys those things that are iconic of their existence as a society.

Whether they are actively engaged in resistance or appear to acquiesce, Eastern and Western Penan everywhere are, with but a few notable exceptions, opposed to logging. The subject of logging is one that is raised constantly in every Penan community. In particular, Penan narratives tell of confrontations between themselves and company representatives or state authorities and recount the arguments which they put forth: why a particular watershed belongs to them, why bulldozers have no place in the forest, why surveyors should not mark trees, why they decided to blockade, why they should not be blamed for those blockades, and who they believe to be responsible for the present unrest. Logging is, for Penan, an all-consuming topic.

When Penan talk about logging, they focus not only on the tangible effects of logging—hunger, river siltation, the destruction of graves, and the obliteration of familiar places—but also on those that are less tangible: the sounds and smells of the forest, coolness and heat, sunlight, vegetation and mud. The words and images they employ are contrastive and tinged with nostalgia: what the forest was like before logging and after. One nomadic Penan said that once their land is finished, theirs will be a life of doing nothing but sitting under *gogong,* a large-leafed tree that grows along logging roads and is associated with bright sunlight, heat, and dust—for Penan, an image of utter desolation.

Among the most poignant expressions of concern about logging are those that refer to sound. Associated with this form of rhetoric is a theme of contrast and separation: that it is appropriate to hear some things in the forest, and appropriate to hear other things downriver. One man stated that in the forest it was good to hear the call of the argus pheasant, but not the crowing of chickens owned by loggers; it was good to hear the creaking of trees, but not the whining of chainsaws. In statements about the appropriateness of separation, Eastern Penan state that they do not interfere in the lives of downriver people and do not bring their sounds to them; likewise it is inappropriate that downriver people should bring *their* sounds to the forest.

Over and above their feelings about deforestation itself, the Penan response to logging is a product of the way they perceive themselves to have been treated by those with an interest in its continuation: camp managers, police, politicians, and others. In short, Penan feelings about logging as a destructive activity must be distinguished from their feelings about those who are carrying it out. Both Eastern and Western Penan feel that they are looked down upon, ignored, and treated unjustly. Consistently, their response has been to try to *familiarize* themselves and their situation, both to those representing timber interests and to environmentalists. Most often, they do so in the form of analogies which they feel will express their feelings in a way intelligible to outsiders, comparing the forest to a warehouse, a shop, or a bank; contrasting their way of life with that of civil servants who must merely go to their offices to make a living; and comparing the act of felling the forest to driving a bulldozer through the middle of someone's house. Penan recognize that their efforts to explain their situation has had little effect, and they find it inconceivable that their concerns are so completely disregarded. I have repeatedly heard statements such as "When they look into our eyes, they see the eyes of a monkey, the eyes of a dog," "They think we have tails," and "They look at us like they look at dog shit."

Notwithstanding the similarity in their perspectives, the ways in which Eastern and Western Penan have responded to logging contrasts markedly. While Western Penan have been largely acquiescent, the Eastern Penan response to logging—beginning in 1987 and continuing sporadically since then—has been to erect blockades.[35] In describing why they have erected blockades, Eastern Penan provide one reason more than any other: they feel that their voices are not being heard.[36] Among the most common refrains among contemporary Eastern Penan is that "The government does not hear what we say."

It was as a result of the 1987 blockades, which brought a great deal of media attention to the Penan, that a concerted international campaign began to be waged. The Malaysian environmental organization *Sahabat Alam Malaysia* (Friends of the Earth, Malaysia) had worked with Penan in the Baram District for several years, and it did a great deal to propel the early campaign. Numerous rain forest groups were also forming in the United States, Europe, the United Kingdom, Australia, and Japan, in response to a growing awareness of the scale of tropical deforestation. The Penan became iconic of forest destruction for many of these organizations, and it was they who worked so hard to give voice to the Penan struggle in the international arena as the Penan articulated their concerns through a series of interlocutors. It is here especially that we see a process of translation occurring, as Penan ideas about rain forest destruction are transformed by both Malaysian and Euro-American environmentalists into a series of globally valorized discourses about indigenous peoples, ecology, and the sacred.[37]

Discussion

For Penan, landscape, history, and kinship—the bonds linking individuals to households to communities to generations past and future —are part of a larger whole. The landscape is more than simply a reservoir of detailed ecological knowledge or a setting in which the people satisfy their caloric and nutritional needs. It is also a repository for the memory of past events, and thus a vast mnemonic representation of social relationships and of society. The Penan landscape, though to all appearances a complete wilderness, is instead one which is imbued with cultural significance. Whether that significance can be described as "sacred," however, is problematic.

From the preceding discussion a number of conclusions can be drawn about the nature of Penan religion and its significance for a Penan "indigenous ecology." The first is that, whatever else one might say about Penan "religion," it has little to do with anything that we might gloss as "reverence," or any sense of the sacred. While there are particular places that have a supernatural significance, to describe these as "sacred" does not really convey what they mean to Penan. For Penan, the supernatural manifests itself in specific incidents that occur in particular places. But such incidents are nearly always negative encounters perceived as targeting particular individuals or communities, either for some kind of transgression or because of a simple failure to disguise intentions. Such encounters do not in any sense consecrate the places in which they occur or imbue them with any sense of the sacred.

There are, to be sure, sites which have a mythological significance or that are believed to be the abode of spirits: proximity to such sites may evoke concern or fear and may result in transactions with supernatural agents believed to exist there. By far the most significant sites to Penan are graves: Penan consider graves to be inviolable, and their destruction is one of the things they decry most forcefully in their complaints about the incursions of logging companies. But it is again worth asking what the consequences might be for describing the significance of graves by the English gloss "sacred."

The issue I am trying to raise here in part hinges on the question of who translates for whom. As I have tried to show, Penan are very articulate about the reasons they oppose the incursions of logging companies onto their lands. Many of the reasons they give are of a practical nature: for instance, the simple difficulty of making a living in a logged-over landscape. Other reasons given are of a more emotional nature: for instance, the pain Penan feel at seeing familiar places destroyed. Yet other reasons are of an aesthetic nature: the heat, dust, and desolation of logging over and against the coolness and cleanliness of the forest, the harsh sound of chainsaws versus the squeaking of trees rubbing in the wind. Whether practical, nostalgic, or aesthetic, such arguments are made in terms of categories and metaphors that are distinctly Penan.

Penan do, however, make a concerted attempt to argue across difference, to frame their arguments in ways that they hope will be recognizable, and therefore self-evident, to external agents. This is precisely what lies behind Penan arguments linking the forest to a supermarket or a bank and linking the act of driving a bulldozer through the forest to driving it through the house of the chief minister. More than anything, such arguments are meant to appeal across difference to a presumed shared sense of justice and respect.

Whether speaking in Penan terms or attempting to speak across difference, notably absent in Penan arguments is any reference to the sacred or ineffable. It is only when Penan arguments are incorporated into a broader circulation of images deployed by external agents—Malaysian and Euro-American activists alike—that we begin to see an appeal to the sacred or ineffable.

What is further striking about Penan commentaries on landscape and forest destruction is the degree to which their arguments are about *locality* and *biography*. Penan do not talk about the need to preserve rain forests, they talk about the need to preserve the Seping River watershed or other "rivers from which we eat": watersheds full of past campsites, trees from which fruit was collected, graves of beloved deceased kin, and the like. It is the very transgression of that densely biographical and genealogical locality that Penan find to be such a great injustice.

Conclusions

My goal in this discussion is to raise questions rather than to provide answers. The real issue here, I believe, is what we make of native ecologies: how we describe them, what we ascribe to them, and why we ascribe those things. What are the implications of globalizing the significance of local ecologies by ascribing to them qualities of sanctity or reverence? Asking this question brings us back to the issues raised at the beginning of this discussion about the relations between translation and domination. The concept of the "sacred" as applied to indigenous ecologies, I have suggested, is part of the "grammar of conquest."

This ubiquitous metacommentary on the quality of sanctity in indigenous ecologies, then, has a number of pernicious effects. The most obvious is that it imposes meanings that may be quite imaginary. In imposing some meanings, it expunges others: for instance, the densely biographical locality just discussed. Penan do indeed have some sense of the ineffable, even when this is not an element in their arguments to preserve the forest, and this is expressed in a range of concepts relating to power, avoidance, respect, and so forth.[38] But it is not the obscurantized sanctity or reverence for "nature" that one sees in so many arguments *about* the Penan.

Second, this metacommentary on the sacred paradoxically genericizes precisely the diversity that it is trying to advance. Whatever else sanctity is, it is not a universal category. In presenting Penan as imbuing landscape with a reverential or sacred quality, one is imposing a falsely universalized quality upon them, thereby effacing or eliding precisely the rich particularity that defines them. The Penan are transformed by the imposition of Euro-American categories into a homogenous "indigenous people" or "forest people."

What is also at issue here is the question of who speaks for whom and who constructs representations of whom: who is the "we" that ascribes certain qualities to indigenous ecologies? In the Penan struggle, as I noted, it has primarily been external agents who have acted as translators of Penan narratives. In other struggles—those of Native Americans, Native Hawaiians, Australian Aboriginals, and the like—it is indigenous actors themselves who are articulating and translating their struggles to a larger audience, whether through the media or in the context of the legal system. It seems to me that in such circumstances it is all the more necessary to consider the implications of using the grammar of conquest. I do not want to argue that we rid ourselves of the idea of the sacred or that there is no place for the sacred in elucidating indigenous ecologies. Rather, I merely want to suggest the need for strategies that more self-consciously interrogate the implications of using such terms. The challenge, then, is to forge a vocabulary of resistance that avoids the genericizing qualities inherent in the idea of the sacred, qualities which, when imposed over indigenous landscapes and ecologies, may in fact distort their significance to indigenous communities. How can we express—and communicate—our respect for other ways of seeing the land, without imposing our own Euro-American categories?

Finally, it is important that we recognize the difference between the deployment of the notion of the sacred in the context of campaigns or media and the way the idea may be deployed in the legal sphere. The idea of "sacred sites" has now been codified into law in the United States and elsewhere. This in itself raises a series of critical questions.

What happens when the sacred is fixed on the Cartesian grid? As legal statutes create the possibility for recognizing specific "sacred sites," how does this in turn foreclose the possibility for challenging broader systems of domination? More fundamental, why does a place have to be declared "sacred" to be inviolable? Shouldn't other kinds of places in the forest—the hole in a tree made by one's father many decades before as he searched for honey, the *uban* of a deceased child—be enough? The more practical question, then, is what strategies can be used to define other kinds of zones of inviolability?

Notes

The research upon which this article is based could never have been undertaken without the support and assistance of a great many people. Foremost I wish to thank En. Lucas Chin and Dr. Peter Kedit, both past directors of the Sarawak Museum, and Dr. Hatta Solhee of the Sarawak State Planning Unit. Many civil servants—residents, district officers, and Sarawak administrative officers—also provided invaluable assistance in Kapit, Belaga, Miri, and Marudi. I am particularly indebted to those Penan in both the Belaga and Baram Districts with whom I resided for most of my time in Sarawak. Without their patience, generosity, and tolerance, this work could not have been undertaken. I have a special debt to Matu Tugang for his constant companionship on our many travels, for the many insights he provided on Penan language and culture, and for his friendship. Special thanks must also go to Jayl Langub whose contribution to my work is incalculable. Finally, I must think my wife Ellen Walker for the many insights she provided on the material presented here and for her superb editing. My research was supported by grants from the Social Science Research Council (which supported both my research in the 1980s and my more recent research), the National Science Foundation (Grant No. BNS-8407062), the U.S. Department of Education (Fulbright-Hays), the L. S. B. Leakey Foundation, and the University of Georgia Research Foundation. Their support is gratefully acknowledged. All responsibility for statements here is expressly mine.

1. Vicente Rafael, *Contracting Colonialism: Translation and Christian Conversion in Tagalog Society under Early Spanish Rule* (Ithaca: Cornell University Press, 1988), 213.

2. Jane Jacobs, "Earth Honoring: Western Desires and Indigenous Knowledges," in *Writing Women and Space: Colonial and Postcolonial Geographies,* ed. Alison Blunt and Gilliam Rose (New York: Guilford, 1994), 169.

3. From an advocacy perspective, see Jose Barreiro, "Indigenous Peoples Are the 'Miner's Canary' of the Human Family," in *Learning to Listen to the Land,* ed. Bill Willers (Washington, D.C.: Island Press, 1991); Julian Burger, *The Gaia Atlas of First Peoples: A Future for the Indigenous World* (New York: Anchor Books, Doubleday, 1990); Alan Durning, *Guardians of the Land: Indigenous Peoples and the Health of the Earth,* Worldwatch Paper 112 (Washington, D.C.: Worldwatch Institute, 1992); Winona LaDuke, "Traditional Ecological Knowledge and Environmental Futures," in *Endangered Peoples: Indigenous Rights and the Environment* (Niwot: University Press of Colorado, 1994); David Suzuki and Peter Knudtson, *Wisdom of the Elders: Sacred Native Stories of Nature* (New York: Bantam Books, 1992); Kenneth I. Taylor, "Why Supernatural Eels Matter," in *Lessons of the Rainforest,* ed. Suzanne Head and Robert Heinzman (San Francisco: Sierra Club Books, 1990). From other perspectives, see A. Booth and H. Jacobs, "Ties That Bind: Native American Beliefs as a Foundation for Environmental Consciousness," *Environmental Ethics* 12 (1990): 27–43; J. Peter Brosius, "Endangered Forest, Endangered People: Environmentalist Representations of Indigenous Knowledge," *Human Ecology* 25, no. 1 (1997): 47–69; J. Baird Callicott, "Traditional American Indian and Traditional Western European Attitudes toward Nature: An Overview," in Robert Elliot and Arran Gare, *Environmental Philosophy: A Collection of Readings* (Milton Keynes: Open University Press, 1983);

154   *Indigenous Traditions and Ecology*

and J. Baird Callicott, "American Indian Land Wisdom? Sorting Out the Issues," in *In Defense of the Land Ethic: Essays in Environmental Philosophy*, ed. Callicott (Albany: State University of New York Press, 1989).

4. John Pemberton, *On the Subject of "Java"* (Ithaca: Cornell University Press, 1994), 21.

5. Rafael, *Contracting Colonialism.*

6. Ibid., 21.

7. Ibid., 3.

8. Ibid., 212.

9. James Siegel, *Solo in the New Order: Language and Hierarchy in an Indonesian City* (Princeton: Princeton University Press, 1986).

10. Rafael, *Contracting Colonialism,* 210.

11. Ibid., 23.

12. Durning, *Guardians of the Land,* 28–29.

13. LaDuke, "Traditional Ecological Knowledge and Environmental Futures," 127.

14. Suzuki and Knudtson, *Wisdom of the Elders,* 18.

15. As a comparison, see Alf Hornborg, "Environmentalism, Ethnicity and Sacred Places: Reflections on Modernity, Discourse and Power," *Canadian Review of Sociology and Anthropology* 31, no. 3 (1994): 245–67, for a discussion of how the notion of the sacred was deployed in the Mi'kmaq struggle against the establishment of a granite quarry on Cape Breton Island, Nova Scotia.

16. Victor King, *The Peoples of Borneo* (Oxford: Blackwell, 1993); and Jérôme Rousseau, *Central Borneo: Ethnic Identity and Social Life in a Stratified Society* (Oxford: Clarendon Press, 1990).

17. I place the term "indigenous" in quotation marks here to underscore the fact that it is a problematic concept in Malaysia (as it is in many other parts of the third world). It would be quite incorrect to regard Malay communities in Sarawak as any less indigenous than communities found in the interior.

18. Rodney Needham, "Punan-Penan," in *Ethnic Groups of Insular Southeast Asia,* vol. 1, *Indonesia, Andaman Islands, and Madagascar*, ed. Frank M. Lebar (New Haven: Human Relations Area Files Press, 1972), 177. For additional background on Penan in Sarawak, see Guy Arnold, "Nomadic Penan of the Upper Rejang (Plieran), Sarawak," *Journal of the Malayan Branch of the Royal Asiatic Society* 31, no. 1 (1958): 181, 40–82; J. Peter Brosius, "River, Forest and Mountain: The Penan Gang Landscape." *Sarawak Museum Journal,* n.s., 36, no. 57 (1986): 173–84, "A Separate Reality: Comments on Hoffman's *The Punan: Hunters and Gatherers of Borneo,*" *Borneo Research Bulletin* 20, no. 2 (1988): 81–106, "Foraging in Tropical Rainforests: The Case of the Penan of Sarawak, East Malaysia (Borneo)," *Human Ecology* 19, no. 2 (1991): 123–50, "Thrice Told Tales: A Review of *The Nightbird Sings: Chants and Songs of Sarawak Dayaks,*" *Borneo Research Bulletin* 22, no. 2 (1991): 241–67, "The Axiological Presence of Death: Penan Geng Death-Names" (Ph.D. diss., University of Michigan, 1992), "Perspectives on Penan Development in Sarawak," *Sarawak Gazette* 119, no. 1519 (1992): 5–22, "Contrasting Subsistence Ecologies of Eastern and Western Penan Foragers (Sarawak, East Malaysia)," in *Tropical Forests, People and Food: Biocultural Interactions and Applications to Development,* ed. C. M. Hladik et al., Man and the Biosphere Series, 13 (Paris: UNESCO, 1993), "Penan of

Sarawak," in *State of the Peoples: A Global Human Rights Report on Societies in Danger,* ed. Marc S. Miller (Boston: Beacon Press, for Cultural Survival, Inc., 1993), "Bornean Forest Trade in Historical and Regional Perspective: The Case of Penan Hunter-Gatherers of Sarawak," in *Society and Non-Timber Products in Tropical Asia,* ed. J. Fox, East-West Center Occasional Papers: Environmental Series, no. 19 (Honolulu: East-West Center, 1995), 13–26, "Signifying Bereavement: Form and Context in the Analysis of Penan Death-Names," *Oceania* 66, no. 2 (1995): 119–46, "Father Dead, Mother Dead: Bereavement and Fictive Death in Penan Geng Society," *Omega: Journal of Death and Dying* 32, no. 3 (1995–96): 197–226, "Endangered Forest, Endangered People," and "Prior Transcripts, Divergent Paths: Resistance and Acquiescence to Logging in Sarawak, East Malaysia," *Comparative Studies in Society and History* 39, no. 3 (1997): 468–510; Tom Harrisson, "Notes on Some Nomadic Punans," *Sarawak Museum Journal,* n.s., 5, no. 1 (1949): 130–46; W. H. Huehne, "A Doctor among 'Nomadic' Punans," *Sarawak Museum Journal,* n.s., 9, no. 13-14 (1959): 195–202; Peter M. Kedit, *Gunong Mulu Report: A Human-Ecological Survey of Nomadic/Settled Penan within the Gunong Mulu National Park Area, Fourth/Fifth Division, Sarawak,* Sarawak Museum Field Report Series, no. 1 (Kuching: Sarawak Museum, 1978), and "An Ecological Survey of the Penan," *Sarawak Museum Journal,* special issue, no. 2, n.s., 30, no. 51 (1982): 225–79; Jayl Langub, "Adaptation to a Settled Life by the Punans of the Belaga Subdistrict," *Sarawak Gazette* 98, no. 1371 (1972): 83–86, "Structure and Progress in the Punan Community of Belaga Subdistrict," *Sarawak Gazette* 98, no. 1378 (1972): 219–21, "Background Report on Potential for Agricultural and Social Extension Service in the Penan Community of Belaga District," *Sarawak Gazette* 100, no. 1395 (1974): 93–96, "Distribution of Penan and Punan in the Belaga District," *Borneo Research Bulletin* 7, no. 2 (1975): 45–48, "Tamu: Barter Trade between Penan and their Neighbors," *Sarawak Gazette* 110, no. 1485 (1984): 11–15, "Some Aspects of Life of the Penan," *Sarawak Museum Journal,* special issue, no. 4, pt. 3, n.s., 40, no. 61 (1989): 169–84, and "A Journey through the Nomadic Penan Country," *Sarawak Gazette* 117, no. 1514 (1990): 5-27; Rodney Needham, "A Penan Mourning Usage," *Bijdragen tot de Taal-, Land- en Volkenkunde* 110 (1954): 263–7, "Penan and Punan," *Journal of the Malayan Branch, Royal Asiatic Society* 27, no. 1 (1954): 73–83, "Reference to the Dead among the Penan," *Man* 54 (1954): 10, "The System of Teknonyms and Death-Names of the Penan," *Southwestern Journal of Anthropology* 10 (1954): 416–31, and "Death-Names and Solidarity in Penan Society," *Bijdragen tot de Taal-, Land- en Volkenkunde* 121 (1965): 58–76; Johannes Nicolaisen, "The Penan of Sarawak: Further Notes on the Neo-Evolutionary Concept of Hunters," *Folk* 18 (1976): 205–36, "The Penan of the Seventh Division of Sarawak: Past, Present and Future," *Sarawak Museum Journal,* n.s., 24, no. 45 (1976): 35–61, and "Penan Death-Names," *Sarawak Museum Journal,* n.s., 26, no. 47 (1978): 29–41; Ian A. N. Urquhart, "Some Notes on Jungle Punans in Kapit District," *Sarawak Museum Journal,* n.s., 5, no. 13 (1951): 495–533, "Some Kenyah/Pennan Relationships," *Sarawak Museum Journal,* n.s., 8, no. 10 (1957): 113–16, and "Nomadic Punans and Pennans," in *The Peoples of Sarawak,* ed. Tom Harrisson (Kuching: Sarawak Museum, 1959).

　　19. See Brosius, "Foraging in Tropical Rainforests," "The Axiological Presence of Death," "Contrasting Subsistence Ecologies of Eastern and Western Penan Foragers,"

and "Prior Transcripts, Divergent Paths"; and Needham, "Punan-Penan."

20. Brosius, "Foraging in Tropical Rainforests."

21. The types of products collected has varied through time. Camphor, *jelutong* (a type of latex), *damar* (a resin), and rhinoceros horn were important trade products at various times in the past. Both in the past and at present, the Penan have been known for the fine woven rattan mats and baskets which they produce. In exchange for these products, Penan have received items such as metal, cloth, salt, and tobacco.

22. Brosius, "Prior Transcripts, Divergent Paths."

23. These figures refer to band size prior to settlement. Both Eastern and Western Penan communities tend to experience growth once they have settled. See Arnold, "Nomadic Penan of the Upper Rejang"; Needham, "Punan-Penan"; and Urquhart, "Some Notes on Jungle Punans in Kapit District."

24. My personal favorite is *Be Ungit Tuen* (White Person's Nose River), named for a sharp ridge between two forks of a river.

25. Penan lack any absolute terms for directionality, i.e., north, south, east, west.

26. Renato Rosaldo, *Ilongot Headhunting, 1883–1974: A Study in Society and History* (Stanford: Stanford University Press, 1980), 42, 48.

27. Harrisson, "Notes on Some Nomadic Punans," 132; Langub, "Background Report on Potential for Agricultural and Social Extension Service," 92; Urquhart, "Nomadic Punans and Pennans," 74.

28. The word *genin* refers both to cool and to loss of potency. Thus, for instance, Penan believe that blowdart poison loses potency with time, becoming *genin*. This can also refer to medicine, batteries, etc. Finally, it is used to refer to the relaxing of ritual prohibitions, such as those which follow a death. One can refer to *genin lumu*, the cooling of mourning prohibitions.

29. However, fear of being accused of adultery also plays a role here.

30. The present discussion is not intended to be a comprehensive description of Penan religious belief or practice and is in fact rather cursory. I discuss only those aspects that are relevant to a discussion of landscape.

31. Eastern Penan, in contrast, have mostly converted to the fundamentalist Christian Sidang Injil Borneo (SIB).

32. On one occasion, camped along the upper Jek River, hunters brought back a pair of flying squirrels (*kubung*) they had shot with blowpipes. Penan children gravitate toward game being butchered, or toward anything unusual they see hunters bring back, and the killing of *kubung* is not a common occurrence. Two young boys took these two *kubung* and were carrying them around, stretching them out to play with the large membrane of skin between the front and back legs. Two days later there was a terrible thunderstorm, and several large branches fell directly adjacent to our huts: one branch came through the palm leaf roof. A woman who was present there began praying fearfully to Bale' Gau—calling this a *liwen kubung*—asking him not to be offended, that no harm was meant, and that children do not know any better. Thus it is that children are considered a primary cause of thunderstorms.

33. Rather than using the word for many, *pine,* they insert the word *tajem,* dart poison, the mention of which is believed to repel spirits because of its bitterness. Thus, rather than say *Purat Penan Plieran tegu ire pine* ("The Penan Plieran split because they were many"), Penan might say *Purat Penan Plieran tegu ire tajem.*

34. Though they no longer regard bird omens, Penan do still express a great deal of concern for omens expressed to them in dreams.

35. Brosius, "Endangered Forest, Endangered People," and "Prior Transcripts, Divergent Paths."

36. Sarawak state law does not recognize Penan principles of land tenure. In contrast to the longhouse communities of Kayan, Kenyah, and other ethnic groups, even settled Penan generally lack the prerequisites for the legal recognition of land claims. According to Sarawak land law, communities can only claim land which they cultivated before 1958. However, the majority of Penan settled after that. Thus, their claims to land are without legal basis. Nomadic groups are in an even more difficult position with respect to land claims. Burials are one basis for the recognition of Native Customary Rights land in longhouse communities. Because Penan graves are scattered and are visible for only a few years, the government does not recognize these as having any legal significance.

37. See J. Peter Brosius, "Green Dots, Pink Hearts: Displacing Politics from the Malaysian Rainforest," *American Anthropologist* 101, no. 1 (1999): 36–57, for a discussion of the history of the campaign against logging in Sarawak.

38. See Brosius "The Axiological Presence of Death," "Signifying Bereavement," and "Father Dead, Mother Dead."

Is Indigenous Spiritual Ecology Just a New Fad? Reflections from the Historical and Spiritual Ecology of Hawai'i

LESLIE E. SPONSEL

Introduction

Four of the more important assumptions about indigenous societies that underlay many of the contributions to this book are that they: 1) have significant *knowledge* about the ecology of the ecosystems in their homelands; 2) practice an economy which uses their land and resources *sustainably;* 3) promote the *conservation* of their natural environment; and 4) are effectively guided in these and other matters by a profound *spirituality* in which the environment is respected and treated as sacred.

If an indigenous society survives for centuries or millennia, then it has been sustainable, and that must be based on acute sensitivity to and intimate knowledge of the local environment. In the process, whether inadvertently or purposefully, the society must also promote environmental conservation to some degree, or at least avoid serious resource depletion and environmental degradation. Behind all of this must be some powerful set of guiding principles that are adaptive, and, in the case of indigenous societies, these are most likely mainly religious. These considerations do not necessarily mean that any society was or is perfectly adapted to its environment in every respect in all areas, times, and manifestations of its existence.

While these four assumptions were commonly accepted by many, if not most, anthropologists and others in the 1960s and 1970s, since the 1980s all four, and especially the second and third ones, have been

challenged by numerous and diverse researchers.[1] Just as a backlash
has developed against environmentalism, it has also arisen against indigenous peoples in some cases, and it is now emerging against spiritual ecology as well.[2] Consequently, it is important to analyze explicitly, systematically, and critically these four and related assumptions,
if the validity and utility of many of the concerns in this book are not
to be summarily dismissed by skeptics, critics, and others. Furthermore, generalizations about these matters are difficult and tenuous. It
is more appropriate to assess, objectively, the specifics of particular
cases bounded in space and time.

This essay is offered as a constructive discussion of some major
points underlying this entire book, and draws from my reflections as a
participant in the original conference and as a specialist on historical,
cultural, and spiritual aspects of human ecology.[3] Hawai'i provides a
convenient example to illustrate some more general points. However,
this chapter is not intended as a thorough case study of the spiritual
ecology of native Hawaiians (Kanaka Maoli).[4] Furthermore, it should
be clear that I am not an expert on Hawai'i; I rely on the publications
of those who are generally recognized as such.

First, a brief overview of island ecology is provided; second, the
environmental impacts of native Hawaiians and subsequent colonizers
are compared, with a focus on introductions of exotic species and extinctions of native species; third, the *potential* importance of spiritual
ecology in guiding human-environment interactions is stressed; and
finally, some general conclusions are drawn. While various studies
have focused on one or another of these themes, this study surveys all
the themes and some of their relationships. In particular, while there
has been much discussion and debate over the environmental impact
of indigenous peoples in many parts of the world, in Polynesia researchers have failed to place this fully within the perspective of historical ecology by comparing the environmental impacts of Polynesians
and subsequent colonizers; neither have they broached the relevance
of spiritual ecology.[5]

Natural History of the Islands

Like many other oceanic islands, the Hawaiian chain is a microcosm
of evolution, ecology, and diversity, both biological and cultural.[6]

Hawai'i, situated in the middle of the Pacific Ocean, is the most isolated island chain in the whole world, with the nearest continental
land mass being about 2,400 miles away. The archipelago is composed of eight major islands and 120 smaller islands, atolls, and reefs
scattered over a distance of 1,500 miles. Most of the larger islands are
mountainous, with wet windward and dry leeward (rain shadow) sides
from the orographic effect on the trade winds. There are more than
150 different kinds of natural plant communities in Hawai'i, as well
as very special ecosystems like bogs, lakes, streams, anchialine pools
(mixture of fresh and salt water), coastal sand dunes, tropical dry and
moist forests, alpine stone deserts, kipukas (forest islands surrounded
by lava flows), and lava tubes.

The lack of whole taxonomic groups, on the one hand, and high
species diversity and endemicity, on the other, reflect the extreme
isolation of the archipelago. In prehuman times there were only two
mammals (hoary bat and monk seal), and no amphibians or reptiles in
Hawai'i. It is estimated that, on average, a new species reached and
established itself on the islands only about once every 100,000 years.
However, through adaptive radiation, founder species proliferated into
many new species. This evolutionary diversification from founder to
descendant species is on the order of from 270 to over 1,000 for
flowering plants, 400 or 500 to some 10,000 for insects, 20–24 to 750
for land snails, and 20 to 100 for land birds. Because of speciation
through adaptive radiation, about half of the native species are endemic (unique) to Hawai'i, and 89 percent of the 1,023 native species
flowering plants are endemic. According to the Hawai'i Biological
Survey there is a total of 22,056 species of plants and animals in the
Hawaiian islands and surrounding waters and, of these, 8,850 are
endemic.[7]

Islands are extremely fragile and vulnerable ecosystems because of
their biogeographic isolation, unique evolutionary history, high endemicity of species, and very restricted space and resources. Furthermore, native species on islands typically have small population sizes,
slow growth rates, restricted genetic diversity, and narrow ranges, and
they lack defenses against new herbivores and carnivores that are
competitors or predators. As a consequence, humans, and the exotic
species they introduce, can be very disruptive to island ecosystems.[8]

The natural environment of Hawai'i has been increasingly influenced
by humans: first, Hawaiians for over 1,500 years, then Europeans,

Americans, and Asians during the last some 220 years, and, most recently, the global system has brought the agribusiness industry, militarization, and tourism.[9] Each culture had previous experiences and conceptions from their ancestral landscape and ecology, and they brought these ideas and associated phenomena (e.g., selected plant and animal species) to Hawai'i, something archaeologist Patrick Kirch refers to as "transported landscapes."[10]

Comparative Historical Ecology

The Hawaiians, like any human society, did have some impact on their environment, and increasingly so. Population size and density are indirect indicators or proxy measures of degrees of environmental impact. The population of native Hawaiians began with a small founder group that probably numbered only in the tens, likely reached 20,000 by 1100 C.E., and then increased exponentially in the centuries just before European contact, to somewhere between 200,000 to 1.5 million, according to estimates.[11] In some regions prehistoric population densities eventually reached about 100 per square mile. (However, today average population densities for major islands range from 19 to 1,513 per square mile, while urban areas may exceed 25,000 per square mile.)[12]

In recent decades archaeologists and others have documented some of the environmental changes precipitated by ancient Hawaiians. Kirch provides a convenient summary:

> There is no doubt that the Hawaiians practiced various kinds of conservation or resource-management (such as *kapu* on certain fish at particular times), or that they valued land highly and strove to make land and sea productive. Nor is there any doubt that the Europeans and the foreign biota they introduced had a profound effect in accelerating the pace of environmental change. But it is increasingly clear that the prehistoric Hawaiians also greatly modified and altered their island world as they went about their efforts to build a new and productive society. As lowlands were cleared for agriculture, valley slopes were terraced, and reef flats were converted to fishponds, forests were exploited for timber, firewood, and medicinal plants, and birds were hunted for food and feathers, the natural ecosystems of Hawai'i were gradually and irreplaceably changed.[13]

Through farming the ancient Hawaiians gradually domesticated and humanized significant portions of the natural landscape, following their own culture. Between 1200 and 1778 C.E., rapid development of large and densely settled populations correlated with the expansion and intensification of both irrigated and dryland farming systems, with resultant deforestation of most of the lowlands.[14] Changes in and decline of wildlife habitat as a result of agricultural expansion and other activities, unsustainable hunting of vulnerable prey, and introduced predators, competitors, and diseases are anthropogenic factors which are hypothesized to have contributed to the extinction of at least 50 species of birds, a figure similar to elsewhere in Polynesia.[15]

Any environmental change, however, needs to be carefully examined in detail, and its significance is best appreciated through comparative historical ecology. For example, consider the contrast between the environmental changes precipitated by ancient Hawaiians and subsequent colonists. (Because of the limited space available for this essay, my comparison will concentrate on the introduction of alien species and the extinction of native species.)

European contact with native Hawaiians started with Captain Cook's landing in 1778. Europeans, Americans, and Asians introduced exotic species of plants and animals to the Hawaiian islands, some intentionally, others unintentionally. These introduced species, predators and competitors of native biota, have played havoc with the fragile island ecosystems. The development of the agribusiness industry, including cattle ranching and monocrop plantations of sugar and pineapple, have also profoundly changed enormous areas of the islands. In recent decades, various sections of native forests have been used for military tests of defoliants like Agent Orange, converted for biomass energy, destroyed to establish plantations of exotic pine, and threatened by geothermal development.[16]

From the above it would appear that the example of Hawai'i, from prehistory to the present, demonstrates that human nature is inevitably antinature; that is, humans naturally degrade and destroy the ecosystems they inhabit. (This idea is called *Homo devastans* by ecological anthropologist William Balee.)[17] However, a closer inspection of the comparative historical ecology of Hawai'i qualifies this picture. Indeed, it reveals that the Hawaiians had far less impact on the environment than subsequent colonists. The difference is large enough arguably to constitute a matter of kind rather than simply degree.[18]

Polynesians introduced some 40 to 50 exotic species of plants and animals to the Hawaiian islands, and they may have caused the extinction of about 60 native species (mostly birds) during a time span of 1,500 years or more prior to European contact. (Among the animals introduced by early Hawaiians were the red junglefowl, dogs, pigs, rats, geckos, and skinks.)

In contrast, subsequent colonizers introduced nearly 16,000 exotic species. More than 13,000 species of plants have been introduced in Hawai'i, over 900 have become established in the wild, and more than 100 of these are serious pests. Twenty-one species of mammals have been introduced by colonists, including feral pigs, goats, sheep, deer, rats, mice, mongoose, and cats. Other introductions of exotic species by colonists in the historic period include some 173 species of exotic birds, 15 species of reptiles, 8 species of frogs and toads, 12 species of freshwater snails, and over 2,500 species of insects.

Furthermore, the rate of introductions during the twentieth century increased exponentially. In recent times, about 25 species of new plants and animals are introduced every year, whereas it is estimated that, prior to human occupation, only about one new species became established every 100,000 years. The current rate of introductions is variously estimated at one to two million times that prior to humans, and 1,000 times that of the Polynesian period.[19] Thus, it is no wonder that species introductions over the last century or so are causing such serious ecological disruptions.

Simultaneously, there has been a quantum increase in the numbers of extinct, endangered, or threatened species. For example, of the 140 original native species of birds, 113 of which were endemic, half are now extinct and half of the remainder are endangered.[20] Since contact, more than 200 endemic species of plants and animals have become extinct, an average of at least one species per year. Hundreds of other native species of animals and plants are listed as threatened or endangered, and the majority are endemic. The Hawai'i Biological Survey characterizes Hawai'i as the endangered species capital of the world, noting that there are more endangered species per square mile on the islands than on any other place on the earth. Biologist George W. Cox asserts that the complete replacement of the native terrestrial biota of the islands is now a possibility.[21]

From all of this there is one especially revealing conclusion: compared with Hawaiians, subsequent colonizers caused at least 260 times as many introductions and three to four or more times as many extinctions, and all of this in a mere one-seventh of the time.

Given the fragility of island ecology and the 1,500 years that Hawaiian communities lived on the island, it is surprising that they did not cause even more environmental change and species extinction than is apparent from available data. Part of the explanation is that their economy was based on subsistence (rather than market, export, and capitalism); their technological capacity to transform the environment was relatively limited and carefully controlled; and their population size and density were lower than subsequent colonists. (The environmental impact of economies focused on food production for local consumption is very different from those focused on production for profit through export.) The ancient Hawaiians reduced competition for resources within a single island through a radial pattern of land use (*ahupua'a*) that allowed communities to use a unit of land extending from the sea inland and up into the mountains, thus dividing the island somewhat like sections of a pie.[22] Also, certain individuals (*konohiki*) served as resource managers to allocate land, irrigation water, and other resources. Through their intimate and constant association with nature—for survival, subsistence, religion, arts, and other purposes— the Hawaiians developed detailed empirical knowledge about island ecology. Among other things, this knowledge must have facilitated the monitoring of natural resource fluctuations and environmental changes, including their own impact on ecosystems.

Spiritual Ecology

Obviously, religion, as the major determinant of worldview, beliefs, attitudes, values, and behavior, has the potential to be a tremendously powerful force in the daily lives of genuine adherents. This is an extremely important part of the significance of spiritual ecology and its explosive growth since the 1980s.[23]

While the great difference between the environmental impact of the Hawaiians and the impact of subsequent colonists may be related to many factors, undoubtedly religion is a very important one, if not the most important.[24] Like most indigenous peoples, Hawaiians traditionally view the natural and supernatural as interwoven and interdependent rather than as completely separate domains. Indeed, virtually every aspect of the daily life, culture, and ecology of traditional Hawaiians is related to their religion. A mystical force (*mana*) permeates everyone and everything, including people, plants, animals, fish, stones, landforms, sea, wind, clouds, and rain. Prayers, chants, dances (*hula*), offerings, and rituals are among the ways of channeling *mana* and communicating with the spirits.

Thousands of diverse spiritual beings exist, many manifest in dozens of different forms, including in nature. For example, among the many gods (*akua*), the god Kane is the provider of sunlight, fresh water, winds, and life force itself. One manifestation of Kane is in clouds. Lono, the god of fertility and agriculture, may appear in the form of clouds, winds, rains, thunder, lightning, and storms. The tides are created as the god of the ocean, Kanaloa, breathes in and out. Sharks are one of many family spirits (*'aumakua*) worshiped by Hawaiians as forms of divine ancestors.

Certain places are especially sacred, such as the Kilauea volcano on the Big Island and the associated goddess Pele. Mauna Kea, the mountain on the Big Island of Hawai'i which is sometimes topped with snow, is the abode of Poliahu, the snow goddess. Other sacred places include certain rivers, waterfalls, coral reefs, trees, forests, and caves. Sites of one or more special stones may be associated with fertility, birthing, or healing rituals. Thus, Scott Cunningham, who studied Hawaiian religion for more than two decades, asserts: "It was this ability to perceive natural phenomena as sentient beings that was at the heart of traditional Hawaiian spirituality."[25]

Native Hawaiian Charles Kekuewa Pe'ape'a Makawalu Burrows identifies six concepts guiding the "conservation values and practices" of traditional Hawaiians. 1) Respect for nature (*mana'o'i'o*) was related to beliefs in spiritual forces (*mana*) in humans and nature. Special rocks, landforms, trees, and other natural features with this spiritual energy were considered sacred. 2) A *kapu,* or sacred prohibition, was placed on natural resources—for example, on certain species of fish during spawning season to save them from over-exploitation. When this prohibition was suspended, the resource became profane (*noa*) and was no longer forbidden. 3) Within Hawaiian society individuals (*kahuna*) with specialized knowledge (*'ike*), such as understanding of medicinal plants, were highly respected, and this knowledge was considered sacred. 4) *'Aina,* the earth, land, or environment, is viewed as a living entity and as nourishing people the way a mother nurses her young. Accordingly, *aloha'aina* means love of the land, comparable to the affection and devotion between mother and children. 5) *Lokahi* refers to the unity, balance, and harmony between people and nature, a relationship the Hawaiians maintained through rituals like chanting, dancing (*hula*), and giving offerings to the spiritual forces of nature. Such religious acts were often performed at shrines and temples (*heiau*). 6) Caring or stewardship (*malama*) for the land included using natural resources wisely without depleting them.[26]

At the same time, it is not clear when each of the various concepts and practices of spiritual ecology and environmental conservation developed: which ones were part of the worldview of the Polynesian ancestors who originally colonized the islands; which were gradually developed in the Hawaiian islands in response to the natural environment and observed anthropogenic changes; or which were relatively rapidly developed in response to environmental problems and crises precipitated by exponential population growth and other factors. In any case, the spiritual ecology of native Hawaiians is surely relevant to their historical ecology.[27]

Christian missionization, beginning in 1820, together with other forces that many view as intrusive and destructive, nearly drove many aspects of Hawaiian culture to extinction. For example, even hula dancing was prohibited by missionaries from 1830 to 1874. Native Hawaiian religion was forced underground to survive, elements being practiced at isolated sacred sites, at night, or in the privacy of the home. For instance, offerings, such as fruit and flowers, often wrapped in *ti* or *ki* leaves, are regularly left for Pele at Halema'uma'u on Kileaua. Such offerings can also be found at temples and shrines of ancient to recent age. As another example, salt water is still sprinkled in public and private rituals to bless construction sites and buildings and to drive away evil. Thus, while many Hawaiians, especially Christians, will not admit to retaining and practicing elements of traditional religion, there are many signs that it is far from extinct. Moreover, since the 1970s, the Hawaiian renaissance has developed with a revival of indigenous Hawaiian interest in their history, language, culture, religion, arts, and so on.[28]

The contrasting attitudes toward and uses of the natural environment by the Hawaiians and subsequent colonists are most strikingly illustrated by the case of the island of Kaho'olawe. From 1941 until 1993 the island of Kaho'olawe was a target for bombing practice by U.S. and allied military. Only in the last few years has this island been demilitarized by the U.S. government and repatriated to native Hawaiians—and this after the long and very difficult political struggle that was part of their quest for the basic cultural right of self-determination. Kanaka Maoli are now recreating Kaho'olawe as a sacred place, and one important aim is to restore the ecology as much as possible.[29] At the same time, it should be noted that it has been hypothesized that around 1550 to 1650 c.e., farming and the environment deteriorated on Kaho'olawe to the point that the island was nearly depopulated.[30] However, the arid island may have been marginal for agriculture to begin with; and natural climatic changes may be another factor in its deterioration.

Another striking and exciting example of the difference in environmental attitudes and practices between Hawaiians and others is the sacred site of Moku'ula in the town of Lahaina on the island of Maui. During the sixteenth to eighteenth centuries Moku'ula was a small island and home of the high chiefs when Lahaina was capital of the Hawaiian Kingdom. Surprisingly and tragically, in historic times land-use changes in the vicinity of this sacred site gradually buried it, and since 1914 it has been under a baseball field in a public park. During the 1990s plans have developed to uncover and restore this sacred site to the Hawaiian people, one manifestation of the Hawaiian renaissance.[31]

If Hawaiian spiritual ecology was important in the past, it may also be in the future, considering trends in the acceleration of environmental changes since World War II. If more non-Hawaiians could avoid their ethnocentrism and racism, and try to understand and appreciate the historical, cultural, and spiritual ecology of indigenous Hawaiians, this might help them to rethink, critically, their own destructive impact on island ecosystems and to develop a more sustainable and greener lifestyle. However, during the 1980s and 1990s, controversy over the construction of the 1.3 billion dollar, sixteen-mile-long, "interstate" highway H3 through Halawa Valley on O'ahu, which degraded and destroyed many sacred and other sites of Hawaiians, shockingly and tragically demonstrated once more just how ignorant and insensitive many non-Hawaiians can still be toward indigenous culture, religion, and ecology.[32]

Discussion

An indigenous culture that has survived for centuries or millennia, as has the Hawaiian, is no recent fad, and neither is spiritual ecology in general or in the particular case of native Hawaiians. What may well prove to be a relatively recent fad is contemporary Western society—with its combination of science, technology, materialism, consumerism, and capitalism in a desacralized and commodified environment. This may be a fad because it may be destined to be relatively short-lived, given its rampant and spiraling resource depletion and environmental degradation and destruction.[33]

Restoring ecosanity to the world seems to be a prerequisite for any viable and desirable future, and indigenous cultures and their spiritual ecology would seem to be indispensable considerations in this effort. However, it is desirable to be cautious and critical and to avoid any simple or automatic acceptance of the four assumptions that were identified in the introduction to this essay. It is also desirable that spiritual ecology be tempered by a realistic, critical, and empirical assessment (as available data allow) of the relationship between ideals and actual behaviors as this plays out in daily life. As the case of Hawai'i suggests, the specifics of each particular case need to be analyzed critically in the context of concrete places and time periods.

Finally, it should be stressed that the issue of whether indigenous societies—prehistoric, historic, and contemporary—were or are conservationists or destroyers of nature is of more than mere academic interest. Those who argue that they are destroyers may be undermining indigenous land and resource rights inadvertently, or, in some instances, even intentionally. For example, in North America, the argument that whites could better use the land than indigenes was repeatedly employed as a rationale for justifying the dispossession of ancestral lands.[34] Western society has always rationalized its practices in relation to indigenous and other non-Western societies, in part by devaluing them in one way or another.[35] Likewise, although the scientific hypothesis that ancient Hawaiians caused the extinction of various bird and other species may simply be the result of the accumulated evidence from palaeontological and archaeological research, it could easily be incorporated into the arguments of the contemporary political opponents of indigenous Hawaiian interests ranging from pig hunting to sovereignty.[36] This is not to suggest that anyone ignore potentially "incriminating" evidence, but to caution that everyone exercise more care in assessing the arguments, assumptions, evidence, and practical implications. As in the case of Hawai'i, comparative historical ecology can be important in placing such matters in perspective.

Conclusion

In the final analysis, however, rather than fixating on the philosophical and political polarization and controversies of such issues, middle-ground and win-win solutions need to be found for the survival and well-being of everyone on the endangered islands of Hawai'i and on island Earth. A necessary ingredient for any solution is an in-depth consideration of the environmental knowledge, sustainable economy, environmental conservation, and spiritual ecology of indigenous traditions. As ecological anthropologist and ethnobotanist Brien Meilleur writes:

> Should Polynesians be blamed for what they did to their Pacific Island forests? Certainly not. Such concepts as biodiversity, endemism, rarity, endangerment, and extinction have only recently been developed and understood on a world scale. To use them retrospectively and judgmentally is contextually inappropriate and unfair. Because forest prehistory in Polynesia is now fairly well understood, we should ask instead whether we have the collective will to apply what we know about these processes and outcomes to our world.[37]

An assertion Charles Burrows has made about Hawai'i applies in the islands and more generally:

> Destruction and change in Hawaii's natural ecosystems have already occurred. Blame should not be placed on any one group, whether it be the prehistoric Hawaiians or the Westerners who followed after the arrival of Captain Cook in 1778. It was largely through ignorance that environmentally degrading practices occurred. However, today we know better. We dare not make the same mistakes. Citizens of Hawai'i, both Hawaiian and non-Hawaiian, must take the best in conservation values and knowledge from both cultures and apply them with diligence.[38]

Notes

1. See Jared M. Diamond, "The Golden Age That Never Was," in his *The Third Chimpanzee: The Evolution and Future of the Human Animal* (New York: Harper-Collins Publishers, 1992), 317–38; Robert B. Edgerton, *Sick Societies: Challenging the Myth of Primitive Harmony* (New York: Free Press, 1992); Tim Flannery, *Future Eaters: An Ecological History of the Australasian Lands and People* (New York: George Braziller, 1995); Thomas N. Headland, "Revisionism in Ecological Anthropology," *Current Anthropology* 38, no. 4 (1997): 605–30; Shepard Krech, *The Ecological Indian: Myth and History* (New York: W. W. Norton, 1999); Charles L. Redman, *Human Impact on Ancient Environments* (Tucson: University of Arizona Press, 1999); and Leslie E. Sponsel, "Human Impact on Biodiversity: Overview," in *Encyclopedia of Biodiversity,* ed. Simon Levin (San Diego: Academic Press, 2000).

Among other sources, exemplary studies dealing with one or more of these four assumptions are found in: William Balee *Footprints of the Forest: Ka'apor Ethnobotany—The Historical Ecology of Plant Utilization by an Amazonian People* (New York: Columbia University Press, 1994); Fikret Berkes, *Sacred Ecology: Traditional Ecological Knowledge and Resource Management* (Philadelphia: Taylor and Francis, 1999); Jason W. Clay, *Indigenous Peoples and Tropical Forests: Models of Land Use and Management from Latin America* (Cambridge, Mass.: Cultural Survival, Inc., 1988); J. Donald Hughes, *American Indian Ecology* (El Paso: Texas Western Press, 1983); International Union for the Conservation of Nature, *Indigenous Peoples and Sustainability: Cases and Actions* (Utrecht: International Books, 1997); R. E. Johannes, *Words of the Lagoon: Fishing and Marine Lore in the Palau District of Micronesia* (Berkeley and Los Angeles: University of California Press, 1981); *World Systems of Traditional Resource Management,* ed. Gary A. Klee (New York: John Wiley and Sons, 1980); Gary Paul Nabhan, *Enduring Seeds: Native American Agriculture and Wild Plant Conservation* (Berkeley: North Point Press, 1996); Richard K. Nelson, *Make Prayers to the Raven: A Koyukon View of the Northern Forest* (Chicago: University of Chicago Press, 1991); *Traditional Peoples and Biodiversity Conservation in Large Tropical Landscapes,* ed. Kent H. Redford and Jane A. Mansour (Arlington, Va.: Nature Conservancy, 1996); Gerardo Reichel-Dolmatoff, *Amazonian Cosmos: The Sexual and Religious Symbolism of the Tukano Indians* (Chicago: University of Chicago Press, 1971); Stan Stevens, *Conservation through Cultural Survival: Indigenous Peoples and Protected Areas* (Washington, D.C.: Island Press, 1997); and Jorge Ventocilla, Heraclio Herrera, and Valerio Nunez, *Plants and Animals in the Life of the Kuna* (Austin: University of Texas Press, 1995).

2. See Stephen Harrod Buhner, *One Spirit, Many Peoples: A Manifesto for Earth Spirituality* (Niwot, Colo.: Roberts Rinehart Publishers, 1997); Andrew Rowell, *Green Backlash: Global Subversion of the Environment Movement* (New York: Routledge, 1996); *Defending Mother Earth: Native American Perspectives on Environmental Justice,* ed. Jace Weaver (Maryknoll, N.Y.: Orbis Books, 1996); and Robert Whelan, Joseph Kirwan, and Paul Haffner, *The Cross and the Rain Forest: A Critique of Radical Green Spirituality* (Grand Rapids: William B. Eerdmans, 1996).

3. For an overview of ecological anthropology, see Leslie E. Sponsel, "Ecological Anthropology," in *Dictionary of Anthropology,* ed. Thomas J. Barfield (Oxford:

Blackwell Publishers, 1997), 137–40. Spiritual ecology may be defined as an arena of diverse activities (intellectual, emotional, spiritual, practical, and sociopolitical), on all levels (individual to global), at the interface between religions and environment (including environmentalism and ecology). The best introduction to spiritual ecology is David Kinsley, *Ecology and Religion: Ecological Spirituality in Cross-Cultural Perspective* (Englewood Cliffs: Prentice-Hall, 1995). Also see the websites <http://www2.soc.hawaii.edu/css/anth/projects/thailand/spiritualecology.htm> and <http://www.religionandnature.com/>.

4. See Jan Becket and Joseph Singer, *Pana Oʻahu: Sacred Stones and Sacred Land* (Honolulu: University of Hawaiʻi Press, 1999); Scott Cunningham, *Hawaiian Religion and Magic* (St. Paul, Minn.: Llewellyn Publications, 1994); Michael Kioni Dudley, "Traditional Native Hawaiian Environmental Philosophy," in *Ethics, Religion, and Biodiversity: Relations between Conservation and Cultural Values,* ed. Lawrence S. Hamilton (Cambridge: White Horse Press, 1993), 176–82; Michael Kioni Dudley and Keoni Kealoha Agard, *Man, Gods, and Nature* (Honolulu: Na Kane o Ka Malo Press, 1990); and *Religion and Culture: An Anthropological Focus,* ed. Raymond Scupin (Upper Saddle River, N.J.: Prentice-Hall, 2000) (pp. 168–75 provide a brief overview of native Hawaiian religion). Also see the video *Listen to the Forest,* by Eddie Kamae and Myrna Kamae (Honolulu: Hawaiian Sons, 1991).

5. Historical ecology refers to the study of the dialectical interaction between culture and environment through time, as they change and, in turn, influence each other. See *Advances in Historical Ecology,* ed. William Balee (New York: Columbia University Press, 1998); *Historical Ecology in the Pacific Islands: Prehistoric Environmental and Landscape Change,* ed. Patrick V. Kirch and Terry L. Hunt (New Haven: Yale University Press, 1997); Brien A. Meilleur, "Forests and Polynesian Adaptations," in *Tropical Deforestation: The Human Dimension,* ed. Leslie E. Sponsel, Thomas N. Headland, and Robert C. Bailey (New York: Columbia University Press, 1996), 76–94; and Frank Thomas, "The Precontact Period," in *The Pacific Islands: Environment and Society,* ed. Moshe Rapaport (Honolulu: Bess Press, 1999), 121–33.

6. See George W. Cox, *Alien Species in North America and Hawaii: Impacts on Natural Ecosystems* (Washington, D.C.: Island Press), especially pp. 173–87, which include numerous citations to the literature; John Culliney, *Islands in a Far Sea: Nature and Man in Hawaii* (San Francisco: Sierra Club Books, 1988); Susan Scott, *Plants and Animals of Hawaiʻi* (Honolulu: Bess Press, 1991); and *Conservation Biology in Hawaiʻi,* ed. Charles P. Stone and Danielle B. Stone (Honolulu: University of Hawaiʻi Cooperative National Park Resources Studies Unit, 1989). The most extensive and current data on alien species and related matters in Hawaiʻi can be found on the website of the Hawaiʻi Biological Survey at the Bishop Museum, Honolulu: <http://www.bishop.hawaii.org/bishop/HBS>. Also see the website <hear.org/AlienSpeciesInHawaii/index.htm;>.

7. Statistics are drawn from Cox, *Alien Species in North America and Hawaii,* and from the Hawaiʻi Biological Survey website.

8. M. L. Gorman, *Island Ecology* (London: Chapman and Hall, 1979).

9. Culliney, *Islands in a Far Sea.*

10. Patrick V. Kirch, "Transported Landscapes," *Natural History* 19, no. 2 (1982): 32–35.

11. David E. Stannard, *Before the Horror: The Population of Hawai'i on the Eve of Western Contact* (Honolulu: University of Hawai'i Social Science Research Institute, 1989).

12. Patrick V. Kirch, *Feathers and Fishhooks: An Introduction to Hawaiian Archaeology and Prehistory* (Honolulu: University of Hawai'i Press, 1985), 287, 302, 304; and *Atlas of Hawai'i,* ed. Sonia P. Juvik and James O. Juvik (Honolulu: University of Hawai'i Press, 1998), 185.

13. Kirch, *Feathers and Fishhooks,* 290.

14. Ibid., 233, 288.

15. For further discussion, see the various chapters by David W. Steadman, Matthew Spriggs, Jane Allen, and J. Stephen Athens, as well as the introductory chapter by Kirch, in *Historical Ecology in the Pacific Islands,* ed. Kirch and Hunt.

16. Culliney, *Islands in a Far Sea.*

17. William Balee, "Historical Ecology: Premises and Postulates," in *Advances in Historical Ecology,* ed. Balee, 13–29.

18. Sponsel, "Human Impact on Biodiversity."

19. F. R. Warshauer, "Alien Species and Threats to Native Species," in *Atlas of Hawai'i,* ed. Juvik and Juvik, 146.

20. Sheila Conant, "Birds," in *Atlas of Hawai'i,* ed. Juvik and Juvik, 130–34.

21. Cox, *Alien Species in North America and Hawaii,* 177.

22. See Kamehameha Schools, *Life in Early Hawai'i: The Ahupua'a* (Honolulu: Kamehameha Press, 1994); and the video *Ahupua'a, Fishponds, and Lo'i* (Na'alehu, Hawaii: Na Maka o ka 'Aina, 1992).

23. See *This Sacred Earth: Religion, Nature, Environment,* ed. Roger S. Gottlieb (New York: Routledge, 1996); Kinsley, *Ecology and Religion;* and James A. Swan, *Sacred Places: How the Living Earth Seeks Our Friendship* (Santa Fe, N. Mex.: Bear and Co., 1990).

24. Peter Coates, *Nature: Western Attitudes since Ancient Times* (Berkeley and Los Angeles: University of California Press, 1998).

25. See Cunningham, *Hawaiian Religion and Magic,* 11. Here, Hawaiian religion is referred to in the present tense rather than the past tense, because, far from extinct, it remains viable for many of the indigenous people of the islands.

26. Charles Kekuewa Pe'ape'a Makawalu Burrows, "Hawaiian Conservation Values and Practices," in *Conservation Biology in Hawai'i,* ed. Charles P. Stone and Danielle B. Stone (Honolulu: University of Hawai'i Cooperative National Park Resources Studies Unit, 1989), 203–13.

27. Some aspects of Hinduism and Buddhism may be a response to ancient environmental problems, according to Madhav Gadgil and Guha Ramachandra, *This Fissured Land: An Ecological History of India* (Berkeley and Los Angeles: University of California Press, 1992), 82, 87–88.

28. Cunningham, *Hawaiian Religion and Magic,* 19–20, 195–98.

29. Kaho'olawe Island Conveyance Commission, *Kaho'olawe Island: Restoring a Cultural Treasure* (Honolulu: Final Report of the Kaho'olawe Island Conveyance Commission to the Congress of the United States, 31 March 1993). Also see Allison Smith, "Reclaiming Spirit and Sanity on Kaho'olawe Island, Hawai'i," in *Sanctuaries of Culture and Nature: Sacred Places and Biodiversity,* ed. Leslie E.

Sponsel (forthcoming). Also see the website: <http://www.hookele.com/kuhikuhi/kahoolawe.html>.

30. Kirch, *Feathers and Fishhooks,* 154.

31. Nancy Becker and Leonard Becker, "Moku'ula," *Site Saver* (Newsletter of Sacred Sites International Foundation) 9, no. 2 (winter 1999): 1, 6–7; Christiaan Klieger, *Muku'ula: Maui's Sacred Island* (Honolulu: Bishop Museum Press, 1998). Also see the website of the Friends of Moku'ula: <http://www.hookele.com/mokuula>.

32. See Paul Christiaan Klieger, *Na Maka o Halawa: A History of Halawa Ahupua'a, Oahu* (Honolulu: Bishop Museum, 1995); and the video *History of the Construction of H3* (Honolulu: Island Issues, 1998).

33. See *The Green Reader,* ed. Andrew Dobson (London: Andre Deutsch, 1991); Jerry Mander, *In the Absence of the Sacred: The Failure of Technology and the Survival of the Indian Nations* (Boston: Shambhala Press, 1991); Clive Ponting, *A Green History of the World: The Environment and the Collapse of Great Civilizations* (New York: Penguin, 1991); Sponsel, "Human Impact on Biodiversity"; and Jack Weatherford, *Savages and Civilization: Who Will Survive?* (New York: Fawcett Columbine, 1994).

34. See John H. Bodley, *Victims of Progress* (Mountain View, Calif.: Mayfield Publishing, 1999); William T. Hagan, "Justifying Dispossession of the Indian: The Land Utilization Argument," in *American Indian Environments: Ecological Issues in Native American History,* ed. Christopher Vecsey and Robert W. Venables (Syracuse: Syracuse University Press, 1980), 65–80; and Hughes, *American Indian Ecology,* 135.

35. See George N. Appell, "The Pernicious Effects of Development," *Fields within Fields* 14 (1975): 1–45; and William Cronon, *Changes in the Land: Indians, Colonists, and the Ecology of New England* (New York: Hill and Wang, 1983).

36. See *Hawai'i: Return to Nationhood,* ed. Ulla Hasager and Jonathan Friedman, Document no. 75 (Copenhagen: International Work Group for Indigenous Affairs, 1994); *Native Hawaiian Rights Handbook,* ed. Melody Kapilialoha MacKenzie (Honolulu: Office of Hawaiian Affairs and Native Hawaiian Legal Corporation, 1991); Matthew Spriggs, "Landscape Catastrophe and Landscape Enhancement: Are Either or Both True in the Pacific?" in *Historical Ecology in the Pacific Islands,* ed. Kirch and Hunt, 101–2; Haunani-Kay Trask, *From a Native Daughter: Colonialism and Sovereignty in Hawai'i* (Honolulu: University of Hawai'i Press, 1999); and the videos *Act of War: The Overthrow of the Hawaiian Nation* (1993) and *The Tribunal* (1994), both from Na Maka o ka 'Aina.

37. Meilleur, "Forests and Polynesian Adaptations," 86.

38. Burrows, "Hawaiian Conservation Values and Practices," 212.

The Road to Heaven:
Jakaltek Maya Beliefs, Religion,
and the Ecology

VICTOR D. MONTEJO

Introduction

For those who are interested in the history of indigenous thought and spirituality, the theories advanced to explain the so-called primitive religions have not been satisfying. The sociological, psychological, and anthropological theories proposed by early scholars explained indigenous religiosity as a product of their magical and mythical thoughts.[1] Most explanations agreed with Edward B. Tylor's argument that indigenous religions were essentially a belief in ghosts and spiritual beings.[2] Others believed that indigenous people's spirituality was the expression of their fear of the unknown, since their minds were continuously oriented toward the supernatural.[3] Another view was that religious practices in general responded to the conformity and willingness of human beings to endure pain and suffering. According to Clifford Geertz: "As a religious problem, the problem of suffering is, paradoxically, not how to avoid suffering but how to suffer, how to make of physical pain, personal loss . . . something bearable, supportable."[4] It is thus evident that Western scholars have tried to explain indigenous religiosity from a Eurocentric point of view. Unfortunately, the belief systems of indigenous people have been seen as outlets for their fear of supernatural beings and the explanations have been centered on the superficial expressions of rituals and ceremonies. Little attention has been given to the idea of how these beliefs work in the daily life of indigenous people.

In the case of the Mayans, the explanations have been based mainly on the hypothetical reconstructions of Mayan religion by early archaeologists and epigraphers.[5] Unfortunately, we do not know much about Maya state religion because there is no surviving "sacred" document (as the Christian Bible) where the doctrine and sacred cannons were codified. Perhaps such a document existed, but it may have been destroyed during the Spanish conquest (note the burning of the Maya texts by Bishop Diego de Landa in Yucatan). What survived as a sacred text among the Mayans is the *Popol Vuh,* which was written after the Spanish invasion of 1524 by a Maya man using Latin characters. Thus, what we are presented with as Mayan religion by today's scholars in fact is their conflicting interpretations of historical accounts and their explanations of archaeological objects and iconography. Very often, these Western scholars confuse figures of rulers depicted in the stelae and murals and elevate them to the status of gods. In other words, we do not know much about Maya religion per se as it was practiced in Classic Maya times. What we know in academic circles is what the interpreters of the iconography have told us about ancient Mayan religion.[6]

Currently, these religious reconstructions by Mayanists have become very important, because they, at least, describe the existence, practice, and continuity of indigenous religious traditions among contemporary Mayans. Similarly, other scholars have shown that modern Mayans practice a syncretic religion, but this, too, is being influenced by the fundamentalist sects that have invaded contemporary Mayan communities.[7] These messianic religions are now sending pastors to the Maya land in an effort to convert and save the soul of the contemporary Mayans before the "end of time," or the closing of the millennium.[8]

Despite current attention to Mayan religion, the indigenous worldview has not been seriously considered in the formulation of theories about indigenous religions and spirituality. Considering these circumstances, I would like to provide an indigenous perspective in the explanation of Mayan spirituality in relation to the natural environment. I argue that the concern for the natural world, and the mutual respect this relationship implies, is constantly reinforced by traditional Mayan ways of knowing and teaching. For indigenous people, the environment and the supernatural realm are interconnected. This holistic perspective of human collective destiny with other living creatures on earth has a religious expression among indigenous people. My intention here is to show how this "interconnectedness" can be understood and explained within a Mayan epistemology. Mayan concerns for nature have different levels of expression and understanding, depending on the age and gender of those engaged in the process of teaching and learning.

Among the Jakaltek Maya, the teachings concerning the relationship with the environment are reinforced at an early age through sacred prayers, myths, fables, and parables. It is interesting to note that contemporary Mayans still teach their children with mythical stories that create a blueprint in their minds and mold their behavior for the future. These sacred stories contain symbolic and ethical messages that are passed from generation to generation in order to ensure respect and compassion for other living beings with whom we share the world. This point of view on religion and the ecology, to be presented here, responds to Clifford Geertz's concern about the empirical need to show how human relationship operates with the cosmic order:

> The notion that religion tunes human actions to an envisaged cosmic order and projects images of cosmic order onto the plane of human experience is hardly novel. But it is hardly investigated either, so that we have very little idea of how, in empirical terms, this miracle is accomplished.[9]

My intention here is to show, from an empirical perspective, how this cosmic order operates. My discussion about the religious approach of humans to nature will be illustrated with the sacred myths from the *Popol Vuh,* also called the Mayan Bible. According to the Mayan genesis, humans were not created first, but plants and animals were the first living beings created, and they later helped in the creation of human beings. According to the *Popol Vuh,* humans were made of corn (plant life), and the animals helped to collect the food which entered into the flesh and blood of the first men and women. This is, then, the starting point of the contribution to life and the collective survival that must exist between humans, plants, and animals. Humans are not separated from plants since, according to Mayan creation myths, corn, the miraculous staple domesticated in the New World, entered into the body and became the flesh of human beings. This, in turn, explains the profound respect, appreciation, and compassion that Mayans feel for the trees and animals for whom they pray during their cyclical ceremonies of the Mayan new year.

There is, then, a three-dimensional relationship—humans, environment, and the supernatural or spiritual world—which comprises Mayan cosmology. In what follows I present a native perspective on spirituality by using a Jakaltek Mayan teaching which I learned as a child. This parable, which I call "The Ocean, Urine, and Heaven," was told to me by my mother as she inculcated in me the appropriate ways to deal with nature.

Interpreting Mayan Religion and Iconography

Before engaging in the explanation of Mayan spirituality, let me briefly refer to the problems in interpreting Mayan religion and iconography. Since the beginning of this century, Mayan religion has been a source of speculation for scholars. The existence of ancient Mayan archaeological sites publicized by travelers and archaeologists at the end of the past century fueled interest in the ancient Mayans, placing them at the center of world attention.[10] The Mayan ruins were, at first, considered to be Mayan palaces (reflecting the existence of kingdoms in Europe), while others considered them to be Mayan temples. Archaeologists and anthropologists constructed their theories explaining the use and function of monumental Mayan architecture as ceremonial centers and temples where the high priests lived a contemplative life and where people came just to worship.[11] Similarly, the idea of the monasteries was used to explain the existence and function of the ancient monuments. According to this interpretation, the archaeological sites were empty centers where priests were dedicated to the arts, science, and the worship of the powers of nature. Later, the archaeological sites were considered full cities where daily life occurred, and the pyramids (temples and palaces) were not quite the isolated centers for contemplative life they were previously believed to have been.[12]

During the Classic Maya times a state religion must have been developed, since highly organized ceremonies are depicted in the ancient codices and murals. Unfortunately, hieroglyphic texts accompanying the figures chiseled in stones cannot be fully understood today. Quite often, archaeologists and epigraphers have provided their own readings of the glyphs in an effort to explain Mayan religion and iconography.[13] Despite some major advances in the decipherment of glyphs,[14] I still believe that a large number of these readings are just speculations which have continued to make Mayan history more confusing and esoteric.

The Mayans have suffered many descriptions, from being depicted as a peaceful and contemplative people who cared for their future and the environment, to being labeled cannibals and abusers of their resources and environment. In this context, the explanations for the religiosity of the Mayan, and the Aztec in particular, have been the result of gross misrepresentations of these ancient civilizations. Anthropologists' insistence on human sacrifice among the Mayans has caused Mayans to be seen as exotic and cruel, further feeding the fantasies of their readers. Without careful research and firsthand documentation, some scholars have insisted on representing ancient and modern Mayan culture as cannibalistic:

> Post conquest records indicate that the Maya of that period were, on occasion, cannibalistic, that they ate their sacrificial victims. Since the victims were considered to have become the flesh and blood of the gods to whom they had been offered, by eating the victims the participants were able to ingest the very substance of the god whom they worshipped.[15]

As I have mentioned above, these scholars write about human sacrifice without providing firsthand references. This quote seems to be an effort to compare the symbolic and "cannibalistic" Christian practice of communion (to eat and drink the body and blood of Christ) to the so-called cannibalistic consumption of the victims presented here. This is the usual process in which strange ideas are presented as fact and then become truth to be quoted by other careless scholars.

Similarly, Mayan iconography is explained totally in Eurocentric religious terms. Thus, it appears that the Mayans were only concerned with representing suffering and pain in their iconography. Even if they were just representing their ideas as art and symbolic representation of ideas, the explanation of the experts will always assure us that they were "facts," activities that definitely took place. Even the representation of numbers and day names in the iconography are immediately called day gods, god numbers, and so on. For these scholars, no figure exists in Mayan art that it is not a god. It is no wonder there is much misconception about the religiosity of contemporary Mayans. They are still accused of being idolaters and devil worshipers when they perform their rituals at their sacred sites.

Fortunately, as a result of the negotiation for peace in Guatemala, one of the agreements in the peace accord refers to Mayan spirituality and sacred sites. It states that Mayans should perform their ceremonies freely and have access to their sacred sites and ceremonial centers.[16] If this accord is fully implemented, Mayans soon will be able to confront the stereotypes and the religious misrepresentations created for them by Mayanists. Recent studies on Mayan spirituality are now developing in a collaborative fashion between Maya priests (*aj k'ij*) and ethnographers, in order to provide a more accurate representation and understanding of Maya spirituality and religion.[17]

I am not saying that the Mayans are good because they were monotheistic, or that it is bad to be polytheistic. Other great civilizations, such as those of the Romans and Greeks, were polytheistic. The issue here is to approach Mayan religion with an open mind and not with the accustomed Eurocentric bias. The *Popol Vuh* talks about the Only-One-God, called both the "Heart of Heaven" and the "Heart of Earth." Among contemporary Mayans, the same god is called *Un-Hab-K'u,* or the Only-One-God. There are, then, references to a supreme deity which has many manifestations on earth. Also, it is true that Mayans practiced self-sacrifice, or "penance," as a way of asking forgiveness for their mistakes and sins. Such a practice continues today among Mayans in the Guatemalan Highlands. Let us not aggrandize this self-sacrifice and penance (like hitting yourself symbolically with a rope, or not taking a bath and putting ashes on your hair) as a form of "human sacrifice and cannibalism." Some would say that, while modern Mayans may not practice human sacrifice now, we have no way of assuring that the ancient Mayans did not practice it either. If Christianity, for example, represented in its art the eating of the body of Christ in communion, it would look terrifying, but it would still be a representation of a symbolic idea and not a real practice or behavior. Perhaps Mayans used symbolic representations and interpretations in their art and iconography.[18]

It is interesting to note the historical development of these Mayan gods and demons through the work and records of missionaries and anthropologists. For example, Bishop Diego de Landa, who burned the books of the Mayans in Yucatan, was the first to list the names of the days and patrons of the months celebrated by the Mayans as

"demons." For example, he called the four year-bearers (Bacab) demons.[19] Now, modern epigraphers and Mayanists have invented many
gods for the Mayans and have called the Bacabs, or year-bearers,
"gods."[20] Mayan religion, then, needs to be carefully documented, and
Mayan people themselves must take part in the process. The religiosity of Mayan people should be seen, not so much as esoteric, but as
a daily practice in which Mayans relate themselves to the natural and
supernatural world with care and respect.

Earth and Heaven: The Generators of Life and Happiness

In the creation stories from the *Popol Vuh,* the lives of humans, plants,
animals, and the supernatural world are interconnected. First, the sky
and the earth are always paired as the source of life and generators of
the seed of creation. Everything that is created is sacred because all
these creatures share the breath of creation. The *Popol Vuh* makes this
connection with a more vivid metaphor: the umbilical cord, which
delimits the sacred geography, is the measuring cord.

> Great were the descriptions and the account of how the sky and earth
> were formed, how it was formed and divided into four parts; how it was
> partitioned, and how the sky was divided; and the measuring cord was
> brought, and it was stretched in the sky and over the earth, on the four
> angles, on the four corners, as was told by the Creator and Maker, the
> Mother and Father of Life, of all created things, he who gives breath
> and thought, she who gives birth to the children, he who watches over
> the happiness of the people, the happiness of the human race, the wise
> man, he who mediates on the goodness of all that exists in the sky, on
> the earth, in the lakes and in the sea.[21]

The above quote reflects clearly the Mayans' concern with and understanding of the workings of the universe. Life on earth is dependent
on the sky forces (sun, wind) and, as the umbilical cord links mother
and unborn child, the measuring cord was brought and stretched from
the sky to the earth. This is the *Kusansum,* or umbilical cord, which
united the sky with the earth according to Yukatek Mayan mythology.
Through this cosmic umbilical cord, the Creator nourished people on
earth and humans maintained communication through prayers. It is
said that the umbilical cord was ruptured as a result of the violence of

the Spanish conquest,[22] and since then we have had to work hard for our collective survival.

In Mayan cosmology the trees, too, are very important, not only as the sustainers of life, but as the supporters of the universe.[23] For example, on each of the four corners and in the center of the earth, it is believed that cosmic trees of different colors grow, sustaining the heavens. Similarly, just as heaven and earth are paired to generate life, the *Popol Vuh* also tells us about the Mother and Father of Life, which is God. Once again, the generating pair are forever present and, in this case, the woman as Mother is given primacy over the Father as the progenitor of life. "She who gives life to the children . . . , he who meditates on the goodness of all that exists in the sky, on earth, in the lakes and in the sea."[24] Finally, the creatures in the sky, on the earth, and in the sea are equally important, and the Creator meditates on their goodness and existence.

In another passage of the *Popol Vuh* we see the images of earth and sky described in metaphorical and poetic terms, picturing the ecology. The Creator is said to be the Lord of the Sky, called the "Blue Bowl" (*Verde Kajete*), and the Lord of the Earth, called the *Verde Jícara,* or "Green Gourd."[25] The term used for the sky shows Mayan understanding of the blue cupula of the sky (the inverted blue bowl), and the roundness of earth, shaped as a gourd (*jícaro*). But the importance of this metaphor is that it relates to the Creator as the one who made life possible on the "Green Gourd" under the "Blue Bowl." This is a very poetic way of viewing the cosmos—living under a blue sky with clear air, while making our living on the "green gourd" of the earth. This is the beauty of the world and of ecology, which our eyes see while we live on earth and under the heavens. Unfortunately, the hole in the ozone layer, the pollution of the air, and the destruction of the forests are changing the beauty and meaning of life on earth, so poetically expressed in the *Popol Vuh* and by other indigenous traditions.

To understand the power of these ecological metaphors, let us focus on creation itself as described in the *Popol Vuh*. The Heart of Heaven and the Heart of Earth and their helpers created first the mountains and the trees. But they were not happy, because there was only silence and calm under the trees. For this reason they decided to create those who would be guardians and inhabitants of the forests. "Then they made the small wild animals, the guardians of the woods, the spirits of the mountains, the deer, the birds, pumas, jaguars, serpents, snakes, vipers, guardians of the thickets."[26] After the animals were created, they were asked to talk and to recognize the name of their creators and give thanks. Unfortunately, the animals could not speak, so they were given a different mission—to become a source of food for human beings. But, even if the animals and the plants serve humans in their survival, the relationship must be one of understanding, respect, and compassion. The fact that the Creator and Shaper provided each animal with its own habitat means that each has the right to a place and the right to live without being exterminated.

> You the deer: sleep along the rivers, in the canyons. Be here in the meadows, in the thickets, in the forests, multiply yourselves. You will stand and walk on all fours. . . . You precious birds: your nests, your houses are in the trees, in the bushes. Multiply there, scatter there, in the branches of trees, the branches of bushes.[27]

This is how animals were given their places to live and multiply. Unfortunately, the attitude of humans toward animals has been one of disrespect and abuse. Too many species have disappeared from the earth because of human carelessness. For example, the buffalo in North America, so sacred and important in all spheres of life for Native Americans, became nearly extinct because of the whites' ideas of freeing the land for colonization. The confinement of Native Americans on reservations was only possible with the elimination of their major source of survival, the buffalo. Also, for many indigenous people today, the poverty in which they live has forced them to take from the few remaining animals to feed themselves. Small animals and birds are not as abundant now because of the human overpopulation on earth and the reduction of forests. The lands of indigenous people all over the world are being encroached upon and their food supply diminished. But, in the *Popol Vuh* we read a warning to humans about abusing and exploiting animals and resources without consciousness of the rights and value of these other beings. Those who abuse and destroy their natural world are like the men made of wood during the second creation. They multiplied on earth, but they did not have minds, souls, or feelings. They did not remember their creator, and they were condemned when a black rain began to fall from the sky, destroying them in a flood. The *Popol Vuh* tells us how the wooden people abused their animals and objects, which finally rose up against them:

Then came the small animals and the large animals, and sticks and
stones struck their faces. And all began to speak: their earthen jars,
their griddles, their plates, their pots, their grinding stones, all rose up
and struck their faces. "You have done us much harm; you hate us, and
now we shall kill you," said their dogs and birds of the barnyard. And
the grinding stones said: "We were tormented by you: every day, every
night, at dawn, all the times our faces went *holi, holi, huki, huki,* because of you. This was the tribute we paid you. But now that you are no
longer men, you shall feel our strength. We shall grind and tear your
flesh to pieces," said their grinding stones. And then their dogs spoke
and said: "Why did you give us nothing to eat? You scarcely looked at
us, but you chased us and threw us out. You always had a stick ready to
strike us while you were eating. Thus it was that you treated us. You did
not speak to us. *Perhaps we should not kill you now; but why did you
not look ahead, why did you not think about yourselves?* Now we shall
destroy you, now you shall feel the teeth of our mouths; we shall devour you," said the dogs and then destroyed their faces.[27]

This quote summarizes the relationship that human beings must develop with other living beings and objects. In this passage we find that
every thing that serves humans—be it an object, an animal, or a tree—
has a sort of spirit, or a condition of being that must be respected. This
is so for the grinding stone, which has been an important tool for
women in Mayan civilization and is used to grind corn for tortillas.
The grinding stone is one of the objects that rose against the wooden
humans. This warning is particularly concerned with women's behavior and attitudes toward their household objects. In Mayan culture,
the woman is the owner of the house (her domain) and the grinding
stone is one of her major tools. With the uprising of the grinding
stones and other household tools, we recognize that everything has its
use and even the objects that help us must not be abused.

Then, we ask ourselves: what does this rebellion of the pots and
grinding stones symbolize? It is true that we can easily discharge
objects as inanimate things, lacking a soul and feeling. But then we
are the ones who must recognize our feelings or attitudes toward the
objects we use. Traditionally, Mayans used earthenware, which was
perishable and recyclable. When the clay pots or jars broke, they
simply turned into dirt. Grinding stones, on the other hand, were not
perishable, so women took special care of them. The grinding stones
were passed as inheritance from mother to daughter and were reused

for generations. There was little waste of the material that made up the tools and wares used in households. Compare that attitude to the present one, which allows for an intense abuse of objects (resources), particularly in industrialized nations. People have two, even three television sets, many radios, and other appliances, and at the slightest sign of a problem with these objects or machines, they are discarded, wasted, without any feeling or concern for the resources that are being thrown in the garbage. The story of the uprising of the pots in the *Popol Vuh* is a lesson to us, that we must care for and not abuse our resources. In modern times, plastic and other nonperishable materials abound, destroying the beauty and the cleanness of the world.

Another important issue humans must consider seriously is their relationship with the animals. The complaint of the dogs in the Popul Vuh is an important issue that concerns humans directly. Dogs are of great service to humans, who do not always treat dogs as kindly as they deserve. The dog is very important in Mayan civilization. In Mayan mythology, dogs are special and are very closely related to the life of humans on earth. This relationship is even extended into the afterlife, according to Mayan mythology. The dog helps the soul to pass across the great river of tears in the underworld only if it is treated kindly on earth by its owner. According to Lacandon mythology,[29] this river is said to be full of big alligators, and it is impossible for the souls to cross without the help of their dogs.

The following story illustrates the encounter of the soul and his dog in the underworld. When a man who abused his dog (by cutting off its tail and its ears) died, his soul could not continue its journey to the land of the spirits. When he reached the river in the underworld, his dog was standing there, but it didn't want to help its master. The dog approached the confused soul who was standing at the edge of the river, and asked:

> "What do you see master?" The soul answered, "Nothing. I cannot cross the water. It is very deep, the current is fast, and there are extraordinary alligators." The dog answered, "I am not sorry for you Master. You cut my ears, you cut my tail, and you did not like to see me. I have no ears. I have no tail [for you to hang on to]. I will not help you pass. You must cross the river alone."[30]

In this myth we see that the relationship between humans and animals transcends human existence on earth and has an importance in the afterlife. The telling of these beliefs about the mysteries of the under-world reinforces the humane treatment of dogs and other animals.

Corn, the Metaphor for Human Life

Another important element from the natural world intimately related to humans is corn. Corn is the crop that helped indigenous peoples of the Americas to build their civilizations. For Mayans, the significance of corn is extraordinary, since the *Popol Vuh* states that the first four men, the first fathers, were created from corn. It is interesting to note that corn, which is native to Mesoamerica, is now providing sustenance in almost all parts of the world. Corn is, then, a miraculous plant that has sustained life on earth, as expressed in the *Popol Vuh*.

Among the Jakaltek Maya, corn is called *komi' ixim* (our mother, corn). In the iconography, corn is represented as a young lady, the *yahaw ixim* or "spirit of corn." For this reason, corn is protected among the Mayans and the kernels are picked up off the ground if they fall because of people's carelessness. Among the Jakaltek it is said that the kernels of corn that are abandoned in the cornfield after harvest, or at the edge of rivers where women wash the corn, cry like an abandoned baby. In some Mayan communities, the relationship between humans and corn is enforced with a ritual during the birth of a male child.

> This ritual consisted in cutting the umbilical cord of the newborn child on an ear of corn. This ear of corn tinted with blood is then placed high above the housefire in order to be smoked, while people sing and pray. Then, during the next planting season, this ear of corn is planted in a selected patch of land called the child's cornfield. Part of this harvest is used to feed the child and the rest is consumed during religious services.[31]

With the above quote, we recognize that corn is represented as a metaphor for human life and, for this reason, corn is sacred to the Mayans.

The role of animals in the creation of humans is also relevant, as it also relates to corn. According to the *Popol Vuh,* these are the names of the animals that brought the food: *yak* (the mountain cat), *itiu* (the coyote), *k'el* (a small parrot), and *hoh* (the crow). "These four animals gave tidings of the yellow ears of corn and the white ears of corn, they told them that they should go to Paxil and they showed them the road to Paxil."[32] When the corn was found, with the help of the animals, it was gathered and ground by the celestial grandmother, Ixmukane. Then, the first fathers and mothers were created. "Of yellow corn and of white corn they made their flesh; of corn meal dough they made the arms and legs of man. Only dough of corn meal went into the flesh of our first fathers, the four men who were created."[33]

Such is the centrality of corn to the life of the Mayans. Corn is respected, for it is *komi' ixim,* our mother corn. Thus, humans are intimately related to the natural world because their bodies are part of nature itself. Humans are not alien to plants, and certainly not alien to animals, since all of them have contributed to the survival of each other. All of these beings live a mutual existence in which they depend on each other for survival. The relationship of humans with their natural environment is one of respect, collaboration, and compassion. If one part of the system does not care for the other, according to this mutual support for life, the abusers may face punishment and destruction, as is the fate of the careless wooden men who abused their objects and the animals. To punish the wooden men, or senseless humans, the objects, plants, animals, and the earth itself rose up against them. From the *Popol Vuh* we have the account of what happened to the abusive wooden men:

> The desperate ones [the men of wood] ran as quickly as they could; they wanted to climb to the top of the houses, and the houses fell down and threw them to the ground; they wanted to climb to the treetops, and the trees cast them far away; they wanted to enter the caverns, and the caverns repelled them. And it is said that their descendants are the monkeys which now live in the forests.[34]

In the case of the monkeys mentioned above, a compassionate relationship of humans toward these animals also exists. In most Mayan cultures the monkey is not killed (except among the Lacandon), since it is considered a distant relative—the descendant of one who abused objects, animals, and the environment. The *Popol Vuh*'s lesson for the future, in the quoted creation/destruction stories, is clearly stated by the dog, who scorned the abusive individuals, questioning their lack of wisdom in ensuring their future. "Perhaps we should not kill you now; but why did you not look ahead, why did you not think about yourselves?" This expresses the Mayan view of the future and their concern for the survival of coming generations.

Contrary to the attitude of the wooden people, the corn people, according to the *Popol Vuh*, were thankful for the gift of life that they received. They were thankful for the gift of their eyes, their mouths, and their language. Language became the vehicle for communication between the supernatural beings and humans. The creators asked humans if they could speak, and they responded promptly: "We really give you thanks, two and three times! We have been created, we have been given a mouth and a face, we speak, we hear, we think, and we walk; we feel perfectly, and we know what is far and what is near."[35] This is the prayer that Mayans still repeat to this day when they reflect on the beauty of the universe created by the Heart of Heaven and the Heart of Earth, God. This understanding of humans' relationship with the earth is essential for the development of a respectful behavior toward nature. In other words, God is not distant and far away in heaven; God is here, too, the Heart of Earth. The earth is sacred because God is the heart of earth itself and of everything that exists: plants, animals, rivers are also important and require respect and compassion. This respect is achieved through learning from rituals and from the experience of the elders in Mayan communities. Mayans are guided by their ritual specialists who know the proper way to give thanks and the appropriate time to act. According to Ruben Reina,

> There is a time to cope with Nature's actions. Modern specialists cannot make rains unless they find the proper atmospheric conditions and the right clouds. Central American Indians have calendrical systems for the right days to act. Men had to prepare themselves for facing those moments. Man had to control their thoughts and needed to tranquilize their hearts. They had to search for peace of mind to feel thankful.[36]

This respectful relationship, initiated in ancient times, continues to be passed on through the oral tradition of the Mayan people. To reiterate these teachings, selected myths are used which are clothed in an aura of mystery or of the incomprehensible. There are myths that emphasize a respectful relationship that must persist between humans and their natural environment. These teachings concerning the supernatural world are intimately related to the ecology and are inculcated in children at an early age, almost unconsciously. Oral tradition plays an important role in this process, because the lessons passed from the elders to the younger generations are told as parables that mold children's behavior. Let me illustrate this religious attitude concerning nature with the following parable, or myth, that my mother told me when I was a boy.

The Ocean, Urine, and Heaven

One afternoon, when I was six or seven years old, I accompanied my mother to the river near our village where she used to wash the clothes. While my mother washed the clothes with other women that afternoon, I played with other children on the sand near her. Since I had taken off my clothes, I decided to enter the water and swim in the shallows, still under the watchful eyes of my mother. While I was standing in the water, which reached to my knees, I began, unconcerned, to urinate. When my mother saw this, she picked me up and put me back on the shore. Then, she scolded me with these words I have never forgotten:

> You should never urinate in the river, because whoever does this, when he dies, he will not be able to go directly to heaven. The soul will be sent to the ocean in search of the urine that he has thrown carelessly into the river, and remove it from the ocean in order to be accepted into heaven (my mother's teaching).

I looked up at her and I was almost paralyzed with fear—fear of the unknown, of the mystery of the immense and incomprehensible infinite. I looked at the river, and it was flowing clear and fast, my urine already mixed with the water, and it was rushing downstream fast, perhaps toward the ocean. This was a powerful teaching that changed my behavior. First, it was clear that it was not acceptable behavior to urinate in the river. I learned this very well, and whenever I saw another boy doing the same, I told him the same story. "You should never urinate in the river, because whoever does this, when he dies, he will not be able to enter into heaven. . . ." The second part of the lesson concerned the concept of death, heaven, and the afterlife. It seems impossible to reach heaven if you have done something wrong to nature. The soul will be sent to the ocean to search for the dirty water (urine) thrown into the river. For a Mayan boy living in the highlands of Guatemala and very far from the ocean, the idea of the ocean itself was a mystery. The statement that the soul will search for the urine and extract it from the ocean seemed an impossible task. The ocean is immense and the little drops of urine in it will be impossible to find and collect. In other words, the soul will be condemned for eternity to keep searching for this urine, kept away from going to rest in peace in heaven as a rightful being. I learned, then, that it was best not to do something that would harm nature.

Why did a mother tell her son a myth or story of this kind? For some people, this may sound like a silly story or a superstition. But for me, as a boy, it was a powerful teaching that has remained with me forever. Considering the Mayan ways of knowing, these teachings reinforced in children the values and knowledge essential for their survival. For me as a boy, the story was clear, and my mother did not have to give a philosophical explanation of it. At the time she told me the story, the Blue River, where the event took place, was clear and drinkable. Along the edges of the river, there were many communities that drank the same water because there was no potable water then.

Through the years, I grew up with the story well ingrained in my mind. These were few words that she spoke, but they were very effective and changed my behavior. So, when I became a school teacher in 1972, I went back to my mother and asked her for the meaning of the story she had told me when I was a boy. She said only that she wanted me to know that it was not good to "pee" in the water, that her mother had also told her this story when she was a girl, and she needed to repeat it to me at an opportune moment.

Her answer made me think about the deeper meanings of the story. Today, the landscape has changed as a result of the strong and irresistible Western ways being introduced to Mayan communities. Some of these changes are beneficial, of course, such as the hospital built in the major town of Jacaltenango by the Maryknoll missionaries during the late 1950s. Unfortunately, the sewage of this hospital was disposed of in a smaller stream that fed into the river at the bottom of the canyon. Then, during the 1980s, a sewage system for the whole town was constructed, and all the black waters are now being emptied into the streams which end up in that same river. As a result, the river is no longer clean, and the people warn themselves about drinking it, or even swimming in it. Now, when we talk about contamination and pollution, I think of the wise message of my mother's story. If children could learn at an early age to respect and protect their natural environment, we would be better off and we would have cleaner air and rivers. Today, most rivers are contaminated. Unfortunately, too, most adults have forgotten these ecologically viable stories and cannot pass them on to their children.

I consider that the road to heaven, presented here as the river metaphor, is a powerful and effective teaching of humans' relationship with the natural world. The halo of mystery with which the story is surrounded provides a powerful and everlasting teaching, fixing important messages in the children's minds. If my mother had just said, "Do not urinate in the water because people down there in other villages will not be able to drink it," it would also have been a teaching, but a less powerful one. I could have obeyed at that moment and then soon forgotten the lesson. But when the story is projected toward the supernatural domain connecting humans, the ocean, and heaven, the message is more powerful and effective. This aura of mystery is, then, what makes the story a powerful lesson and an unforgettable story for children. And, for the adults, the lesson is that whatever you do to other living beings, or nature, can return to affect you. Everything is interconnected, and the imbalance of one part puts the rest in danger. This is not a new idea; it is a common teaching repeated by indigenous people throughout the world.

Conclusion

If we go back to the creation stories in the *Popol Vuh,* we recognize the Creators' insistence that humans continue to give thanks for the gift of life. We must give "double thanks, triple thanks" whenever possible in order to remind ourselves that we have the gift of language and that we live in relation to other creatures on earth. Ecology is not just something to talk about, out of scientific curiosity, but should be seen as a way of life. For us humans, we have our languages to defend our individual or collective rights. But for the animals and the forests we destroy, who speaks for them? The Iroquois elder Oren Lyons presented this plea to the highest office possible. During the indigenous peoples' conference on human rights in Geneva in 1990, Lyons stood and, with the eloquence of the Iroquois orator, he pleaded:

> What of the rights of the natural world? Where is the seat for the Buffalo or the Eagle? Who is representing them here in this forum?

> Who is speaking for the waters of the earth? Who is speaking for the trees and the forests? Who is speaking for the Fish, for the Whales, for the Beavers, for our children?[37]

This is why the attitude of indigenous people toward the environment is religious or quasi-religious,[38] and this is what non-indigenous people must learn from indigenous people: to be more compassionate toward the creatures with whom we share our world, thinking of ourselves and the future of our generations.

For Mayans, this teaching of the rightful use of resources and not abusing nature is emphasized at an early age. Among the K'iche Maya, the teaching begins even when the child is still in his or her mother's womb. Rigoberta Menchu tells us that when a woman is pregnant, she goes to the field and talks to the child in her womb about this, the world with which he will be in contact:

> She talks to the child continuously from the first moment he's in her stomach, telling him how hard his life will be. It's as if the mother were a guide explaining things to a tourist. She'll say, for instance; 'You must never abuse nature and you must live your life as honestly as I do.' As she works in the fields, she tells her child all the little things about her work.[39]

This type of teaching is natural and has worked for indigenous people throughout the centuries. These teachings enhance and promote life through their ecological and spiritual messages. This native form of education continues through adulthood among indigenous people and is reflected in their attitude toward the environment. When a *campesino* (peasant) cuts the trees to plant corn, he asks pardon of the spirit of the forest, the guardian assigned by the Heart of Heaven, the Heart of Earth (God) at creation to protect it. The land is needed for survival, but the relationship must be one of respect. Thus, nature is seen for its beauty and its service in sustaining life and not just as a resource to be exploited and commercialized.

Unfortunately, many of these traditional ways of knowing have been forgotten because they are not considered rightful ways of teaching by the Western educational systems imposed on indigenous people. Mayan children are growing more disrespectful of their natural environment. The teachings from the oral tradition are not practiced as a regular way of passing knowledge from one generation to the next.

Most often, Mayan beliefs are only considered as folklore or superstition, so their deeper meanings are also easily dismissed. Hopefully, with the revitalization of Mayan culture, the elders and the Aj K'ij, or Mayan priests, will, once again, be seen as religious leaders and not as witch doctors. They are the spiritual guides who know and understand the ancient Mayan calendar, a tool that they consult for the appropriate time to petition the supernatural beings for their blessings and to give thanks.

To conclude, I would insist that a respectful attitude toward nature is crucial to the conservation of biodiversity. Some scientists are already focusing on the conscious relationship with nature and have recognized that we must "develop a more humane, more spiritual and sustainable community [by] drawing upon the cultural and spiritual resources of all religions and indigenous traditions."[40] In other words, a change in human attitude toward nature is needed, and indigenous people, with their teachings, can help provide this respectful relationship with the land.

Notes

1. E. E. Evans-Pritchard, *Theories of Primitive Religion* (1965; reprint, Oxford: Oxford University Press, 1987).

2. Edward B. Tylor, *Primitive Culture* (London: John Murray, 1873).

3. Lucien Levy-Bruhl, *Primitive Mentality* (London: George Allen and Unwin; New York: Macmillan, 1923).

4. Clifford Geertz, *The Interpretation of Cultures: Selected Essays* (New York: Basic Books, 1973), 104.

5. Sylvanus G. Morley, *The Ancient Maya* (Stanford, Calif.: Stanford University Press, 1946); J. Eric S. Thompson, *Maya Hieroglyphic Writing: An Introduction* (Norman: University of Oklahoma Press, 1960); J. Eric S. Thompson, *Maya History and Religion* (Norman: University of Oklahoma Press, 1970).

6. Dadi Freidel, Linda Schele, and Joy Parker, *Maya Cosmos: Three Thousand Years on the Shaman's Path* (New York: William Morrow, 1993).

7. Robert S. Carlsen, *The War for the Heart and Soul of a Highland Maya Town* (Austin: University of Texas Press, 1997).

8. David Stoll, "Evangelicals, Guerrilas, and the Army: The Ixil Triangle under Rios Montt," in *Harvest of Violence: The Maya Indians and the Guatemalan Crisis,* ed. Robert M. Carmack (Norman: University of Oklahoma Press, 1988); and David Stoll, *Is Latin America Turning Protestant? The Politics of Evangelical Growth* (Berkeley and Los Angeles: University of California Press, 1990).

9. Geertz, *Interpretation of Cultures,* 90.

10. John L. Stephens, *Incidents of Travel in Central America, Chiapas and Yucatan,* 2 vols. (1841; reprint, New York: Dover Publications, 1969).

11. Thompson, *Maya History and Religion.*

12. J. Eric S. Thompson, *The Rise and Fall of Mayan Civilization* (Norman: University of Oklahoma Press, 1956).

13. Freidel, Schele, and Parker, *Maya Cosmos.*

14. Martha Macri, *The Maya Hieroglyphic Database Project,* Final Performance Report, Department of Native American Studies, University of California, Davis, 1997.

15. M. E. Kampen, *The Religion of the Maya,* Iconography of Religions, sect. 11, Ancient America, fasc. 4 (Leiden: Brill, 1981), 13.

16. Peace Accords: Subscribed between the Guatemalan Government/Army and the Guatemalan National Revolutionary Unity (URNG), sponsored by the United Nations, 1996.

17. Jean Marie Molesky-Poz, "The Public Emergence of Maya Spirituality in Guatemala" (Ph.D. diss., University of California, Berkeley, 1999).

18. Gary H. Gossen, *Telling Maya Tales: Tzotzil Identities in Modern Mexico* (New York: Routledge, 1999).

19. Fray Diego de Landa, *Yucatan before and after the Conquest,* trans. with notes by William Gates (New York: Dover Publications, 1978).

20. Victor D. Montejo, "In the Name of the Pot, the Sun, the Broken Spear, the Rock, the Idol, Ad Infinitum and Ad Nauseum: An Exposé of Anglo Anthropologists' Obsessions with and Invention of Mayan Gods," *Wicazo SA Review* 9, no. 1 (spring 1993).

21. Delia Goetz and Sylvanus G. Morley, *Popol Vuh: The Sacred Book of the Ancient Quiche Maya* (Norman: University of Oklahoma Press, 1983).

22. Nancy M. Farris, *Maya Society under Colonial Rule: The Collective Enterprise of Survival* (Princeton: Princeton University Press, 1984).

23. Davíd Carrasco, *Religions of Mesoamerica: Cosmovision and Ceremonial Centers* (San Francisco: Harper and Row, 1990).

24. Goetz and Morley, *Popol Vuh*, 80.

25. Agustín Estrada Monroy, *Popol Vuh* (Guatemala: Editorial "José de Pineda Ibarra," 1973).

26. Goetz and Morley, *Popol Vuh*, 84.

27. *Popol Vuh: The Definitive Edition of the Mayan Book of the Dawn of Life and the Glories of Gods and Kings,* trans. Dennis Tedlock (New York: A Touchstone Book, Simon and Schuster, 1996), 67.

28. Goetz and Morley, *Popol Vuh*, 90–91; emphasis added.

29. R. Jon McGee, *Life, Ritual, and Religion among the Lacandon Maya* (Belmont, Calif.: Wadsworth Publishing Company, 1990).

30. Ibid., 113.

31. Flavio Rojas Lima, *La Cultura del Maíz en Guatemala* (Guatemala: Ministerio de Cultura y Deportes, 1988), 96.

32. Goetz and Morley, *Popol Vuh*, 166.

33. Ibid., 167.

34. Ibid., 92.

35. Ibid., 168.

36. Ruben E. Reina, *Shadows: A Mayan Way of Knowing* (New York: New Horizon Press, 1984), 90.

37. Oren Lyons, "Land and Environment," in *Words of Power: Voices from Indian America,* ed. Norbert S. Hill (Golden, Colo.: American Indian Science and Engineering Society, Fulcrum Publishing, 1994), 26.

38. David Suzuki and Peter Knudtson, *Wisdom of the Elders: Honoring Sacred Native Visions of Nature* (New York: Bantam Books, 1993).

39. Rigoberta Menchu, *I, Rigoberta Menchu: An Indian Woman in Guatemala,* ed. Elisabeth Burgos-Debray, trans. Ann Wright (London: Verso, 1995), 8.

40. *Ethics, Religion and Biodiversity: Relation between Conservation and Cultural Values,* ed. Lawrence S. Hamilton (Cambridge: White Horse Press, 1993), 14.

Tapu, Mana, Mauri, Hau, Wairua:
A Mäori Philosophy of Vitalism and Cosmos

MANUKA HENARE

Introduction

If I were asked to say in two words how to sum up Mäori philosophy, the answer would be humanism and reciprocity. The theme of this chapter is what vitalism and cosmos mean to Mäori of Aotearoa New Zealand, historically and spiritually with reference to creation, ecology, and the environment. The chapter is an exploration into the cosmic religious worldview and belief system of one group of people of the Pacific Islands. Mäori people have a common culture, a common language with dialects, one kinship system, and a common religious outlook and worldview. The focus is my own tribal region, called Te Tai Tokerau, which is the northernmost part of the main islands, from Auckland to the North Cape.[1] Mäori are the indigenous people of Aotearoa New Zealand, which are islands deep in the South Pacific, Aotearoa being the traditional name for our country. Today, a population of some 800,000 Aotearoa Mäori are found worldwide, with 579,700 living in New Zealand, making up 16 percent of the New Zealand population, with 83 percent of Mäori urban living. Six percent of New Zealand's populations are Pacific Island people, mainly other Polynesians. This means that about 22 percent of New Zealanders are Polynesian.[2]

Oral histories inform us that Mäori are people of the Pacific Ocean, which traditionally is called Te Moana Nui a Kiwa—the Great Ocean of Kiwa. Kiwa is one of the children of Sky Father and Earth Mother and has the domain of the oceans under its care.[3] Pacific Island cultures emerged during thousands of years of constant habitation on small islands, atolls, and reefs that are spread over thousands of kilometers of an oceanic world and its multiplicity of ecosystems and species diversity.[4] In this environment distinctive human cultures developed and are often referred to as Micronesians, Melanesians, and Polynesians. Mäori of Aotearoa are Polynesians.[5]

The cosmic religious worldview of Mäori is as old as the culture itself and constitutes a philosophy, which is a love of wisdom and search for knowledge of things and their causes.[6] In traditional belief creation is described as a dynamic movement, which is expressed in Mäori as "i te kore, ki te pö, ki te ao märama," and rendered as "out of the nothingness, into the night, into the world of light."[7] At the heart of this view of the creation process is an understanding that humanity and all things of the natural world are always emerging, always unfolding.[8] Within this knowledge and enlightenment-seeking framework, Mäori and other peoples of the Pacific have "their own ideas on how relations between people and between people, earth and sea must be conducted." In traditional cosmological chants is found an ordering of the world by "networks of kinship and alliance" and "animated reciprocal exchanges," and the idea that:

> . . . the cosmos began with a surge of primal power. From this, thought emerged, followed by memory, the mind-heart, knowledge, darkness and the *kore* (the nothingness, potential forms of existence). *Tapu,* or cosmic power, was the source of all creation. It brought complementary forms of life together, generating new beings.[9]

Intriguingly, Mäori artists trained in the traditional schools of learning have, in wood and bone carvings, body tattoos, and hand painted scrolls, presented the cosmos process as a double spiral, which swirls into and out of a primal center. The chevrons etched into the spiral represents a key link in the unfolding of the cosmos. The naturalistic images utilized are unfolding fern fronds, the swirling power of a whirlpool, and a whirlwind—all of which depict life as a dynamic force that is sometimes creative and sometimes destructive.[10] Mäori art is vitalistic in its expression of religion and philosophy, particularly where it is the intention of the artist to enhance vital potential. The art is said to be alive.[11] For, as Leonardo da Vinci is reputed to have said about his sculptured monuments, you can compress into an image more than you can ever say.[12]

Pacific languages are languages of metaphor and symbols, where words and phrases often have layers of meaning and context is important. They are also vitalistic languages expressive of life forces, metaphysics, and cosmic energy. Mäori is no exception in such narrative, where primary sources of knowledge and history in oral form have been passed down to the present from ancestors.[13] The oral form of transmitting knowledge is Mäori literature, wrote Sir James Henare, a leading elder, orator of Tai Tokerau, farmer, historian, and sage of the twentieth century, in a booklet of tribal sayings and proverbs. He articulated an indigenous philosophy and a hermeneutics of oral literature when he wrote that such literature was for[14]

> ... centuries preserved only by memory which naturally influenced the development of different forms of literary art, such as proverbs, poetic allusions, metaphor, epics and songs to name but a few. These were handed down from one generation to another in which wise sages embodied the results of their experiences and judicious observations.

These literary art forms, he said, are exemplified in the oral traditions, which are:

> a veritable treasure house of genius, wit, condensed wisdom and silent telepathy in the storied souls of our ancestors calling across the ages to their descendants struggling towards the cultural light.

The foundations of Mäori religion, metaphysics, and philosophy are inextricably linked to those of the material, oral, and psychological aspects of the culture, which all developed over time. There is no known founder prophet like Mohammed, nor is there a sacred written text such as the Christian Bible, but the religion is an observable phenomenon. Mäori religion is a belief in spiritual beings[15] and is both a way of life and a view of life.[16] It is found in rituals, ceremonies, religious objects, sacred places and sites, in art forms and carvings, in songs and dances, proverbs, wise sayings, and riddles, in the naming of people and places, in myths and legends, and in customs, beliefs, and practices.[17] For example, traditional oral sources are replete with detailed accounts of the religious preparations for crossing the Ocean of Kiwa from a mystical homeland of Hawaiki to Te-Ika-a-Maui, the great fish of Maui, which upon first sighting by humans was named Aotearoa—the Land of the Long White Cloud. Fundamental religious and metaphysical concepts, such as *tapu, mana, mauri, hau,* and *wairua,* all life and spiritual forces of the cosmos, did not originate in Aotearoa, having come in the hearts and minds and rituals of the founding ancestral East Polynesian explorers who discovered and settled the islands. This religion of the Pacific, with its philosophy and metaphysics, blossomed in the new complex environment in which the older, narrower worldview was transformed. Traditional indigenous religious beliefs are the core of contemporary worldview.[18]

Ritual of Greeting

Before progressing further in an exploration of Pacific vitalism and cosmos, first let me say that it is customary on occasions in the Pacific Islands to greet, according to ritual, friends and strangers. The following ritual greeting is the type given in hundreds of settings, big and small, each day.[19] So, in traditional Māori language and using the words and thoughts of the elder, Sir James Henare, the following greeting is extended to the reader:[20]

> E mihi ana kia koutou katoa,
> e tangi ana ki te whenua,
> taonga tuku iho a ngä tüpuna,
> ki te whei ao ki te ao märama.
> Tuia te kawe, tairanga te kawe.
> Te kawe oi, te kawe o te haere
> Nau mai, haere mai.
> Tïhei, mauriora.

The elder gave the greeting in 1981 when invited to speak to a local law society on the theme of what land meant to Māori, historically and spiritually, from the time of Kupe, the great Polynesian and Pacific explorer, to 1840. The significance of the year 1840 is that this is when 540 Māori leaders signed a treaty of friendship with the British queen, Victoria, which they believed formalized a close relationship between themselves and the queen. The elder explained what the greeting means:

> Greetings to you all,
> I weep for the land,

handed down by our ancestors,
'tis dawn, it is daylight.
Make the shoulder pack,
take up the shoulder pack, and come.
Welcome. Ah 'tis life.

Worldview and Cosmos

The greeting narrative is an introduction to Mäori worldview. In explicating the deeper meanings of the words of this elder, some insight into Mäori thought is gained. However, no suggestion is being made here that one elder stands for the diversity and richness of Mäori thought. This elder said, "Ki te whei ao ki te ao märama" and explained it as "'tis dawn, it is daylight." The dawn, *whei ao,* refers to the unfolding of the world of light, whereas daylight, *ao märama,* refers to the world of light itself, which is a way of referring to a state of enlightenment. *Whei ao* is a transitional or liminal state between darkness and the world of light and, according to Mäori thought, in every facet of life there exist various conditions of *whei ao.* The first example of it is seen in the creation account of the world. It was during the time of Sky Father and Earth Mother, who were lovers and inseparable in a permanent embrace. The children, through separating the parents in the period known as *te whei ao,* made possible their own escape into the world of light.[21] Creation accounts are the foundations upon which Mäori of the Pacific have built a cosmological, religious philosophy and metaphysics. They are the bases for a Mäori philosophy of vitalism, the idea that in all things in creation, whether material or nonmaterial, there is a life that is independent of the thing itself, and there is an original source of life itself.

Worldview, values, ethics, morals, and associated cultural practices are integral components of Mäori ancestral legacy that preserve both unity and identity with roots in and continuity with the past. They are the signal of where Mäori are in the present. According to two Mäori writers, indigenous worldviews transmit certain crucial features. First, myth and legends are neither fables nor fireside stories; rather, they are deliberate constructs employed by the ancient seers and sages to encapsulate and condense into easily assimilated forms their views of the world, of ultimate reality, and of the relationships between the

Creator, the universe, and humanity. Worldviews, then, are at the heart of Māori culture, touching, interacting with, and strongly influencing every aspect of it.[22]

From the early nineteenth century, with the arrival of European explorers, traders, and Christian missionaries, a religious encounter began and continues today. While Christian dogma, teachings, rituals, and church institutions and denominations became an accepted part of Māori society and culture, Māori Christianity is recognized as distinctive when contrasted with the Christianity of the European settler society. Neither the religious nor the colonial encounter led to the demise of traditional religion, many of its ritual practices and beliefs, and worldview.[23]

Philosophically, Māori people do not see themselves as separate from nature, humanity, and the natural world, being direct descendants of Earth Mother. Thus, the resources of the earth do not belong to humankind; rather, humans belong to the earth. While humans as well as animals, birds, fish, and trees can harvest the bounty of Mother Earth's resources, they do not own them. Instead, humans have "user rights."[24] Māori have recorded their user rights in their cosmic and genealogical relations with the natural world.

The ritual greeting, though brief, is full of the very best of metaphor and symbolism, which alludes to Māori history and fundamentals of cosmological thought. In his address the elder spoke of Māori history, which began in the time before creation progressed to the birth of the mythical and original homeland of Māori called Hawaiki, a place distant in time and space, which is the link with the spirit world. In this sense Hawaiki is a cosmic place. After the birth of Hawaiki, the gods were created. Rangi the Sky Father and Papa-tua-nuku the Earth Mother were lovers locked in an age-long embrace, during which they had many children. The offspring lived between them, becoming the spirit beings of the sea, winds, forests, wild foods, crops, and humanity. In fact, the children are the progenitors of the world and its environment as we know it. The growing children lived in continuous darkness and in the confined space were crushed by their parents. The children decided it was enough and that their circumstances had to change. They separated the parent lovers and created a world of light. One of the children, called Tane, the spirit being of forests, tore Sky Father from Earth Mother and so the New World, called Te Whenua Hawaiki, came into being. The earthly Hawaiki exists. It was light at last.

Like Tane, the other children were allocated domains of the natural world for which they were each responsible, and thus humanity and a diverse natural world was born. In an oratorical way the elder called confidently, triumphantly, "Tīhei mauriora!—Ah t'is life." According to the elder, affection for and attachment to the land and environment historically commenced.

Philosophically and metaphysically, the sundering of the parents and the concomitant burst of light into the cosmos was the spark that started life for plants, fish, birds, and people. Like a wind, says Anne Salmond, it swept through the cosmos bringing freedom and renewal. Once established in the new milieu, the power could be called upon by humans and transmitted through ritual pathways into receptacles such as stones or people. According to Māori thought, the cosmos started with a burst of primal energy.[25]

The narrative of the elder then moved to the time of Maui, a Pacific hero who was half human and half spirit and who, though scorned by his brothers, earned the respect of humanity by taming the sun, capturing fire, and attempting to conquer death. But, above all, said the elder, Maui fished up Te-Ika-a-Maui, the Great Fish of Maui that is the North Island of Aotearoa, using his grandmother's potent jawbone. Much, much later in another time, one of the descendants rediscovered the island of Maui.[26]

Kupe, the Polynesian explorer, and his wife, Kuramarotini, voyaged the eight thousand kilometers from the northeast Pacific, thought to be the direction of the earthly Hawaiki, in their canoe Mata-whaorua. It was Kuramarotini who, upon sighting a long, large white cloud, excitedly pointed to the land, naming it Aotearoa—the Land of the Long White Cloud. On arrival they were confronted with a large, complex ecosystem and environment spanning sixteen hundred kilometers from north to south that was alien to the ecosystem of Hawaiki. Large trees, later identified and named by other generations of Māori, provided the canopy covering the main broad-leafed species. In the coastal areas they would have sighted for the first time the ancestral native trees, particularly the *pohutukawa* (*Metrosideros exceisa*), all much revered today, and, along the muddy margins of the coast, the mangroves.[27]

As they traversed the valleys seeking food and fresh water, they found swamps of flax and bulrushes, orchids, ferns, fungi, mosses, and lichen. Abundant bird life was everywhere and in the undergrowth was to be found astonishing insects and invertebrates unknown to the explorers. While fishing or fetching seafood they would have spotted the endless supply of new fish species living along the larger continental shelf of the islands.[28]

After circumnavigating the islands of Aotearoa, Kupe and family returned to Hawaiki. In time his descendants decided to migrate to the new land, and it was settled according to family groups and tribes. In these early encounters and migrations, the love for the land was consummated, said the elder, and became the foundation upon which the tribes prospered.[29] The historical human link to land and environment was established. Over the centuries there was no buying or selling of land: it was not considered a commodity, a development opportunity, or an article for exchange. It was, according to the elder, his or her very being, as he said, "on and by the land the people lived and died." It became the task of these early communities to begin the identification and naming of the creations of Sky Father and Earth Mother and their children. Names given in the founding times remain important today for local communities who identify themselves with the history of their ancestors.[30]

Mäori Vitalism and the Natural World

After the elder established the historical links, he spoke next of the spirituality of land and its human relations. This spiritual, humanistic value of land and environment makes things vital, holy, and sacred in Mäori understanding. A philosophy of vitalism is expressed in a number of terms in Mäori, namely, *tapu, mana, mauri, hau,* and *wairua.* There are problems associated with translating Mäori terms into English, especially where Mäori terms have multiple meanings. Typically, it is the context in which Mäori terms are used that clarifies the metaphysical and spiritual intentions of terms.

Mäori vitalism can be suggested as the belief in an original singular source of life in which that life continues as a force that imbues and animates all forms and things of the cosmos. Accordingly, life itself cannot be reduced to matter or form, and in Mäori thought life itself is independent from form.[31] In Western theorizing on traditional religions and cultures of indigenous peoples, the religions are often categorized as static[32] and as closed systems not open to quests for new knowledge.[33]

These are provocative judgments and not accurate when applied to the Pacific. Neither do Pacific Islanders share such views about themselves. Anne Salmond has observed that Mäori have their own ideas on how relationships are to be conducted between peoples and between humans and creation. In her studies of the meanings of Mäori cosmological chants, she sees described an ordered world of reciprocity, a "generative relation," that exists between individual human hearts and minds, as well as between human beings and matter.[34]

In his greeting and speech to the lawyers, the elder spoke of weeping for the land handed down from ancestors of the past. Remembrance of the mythic history gone before the people links humanity to the environment. His narrative informs us of the continuing personal relationships of the living with the ancestors and with the land. His words remind us that the land and the resources are a sacred gift passed on to the present generation from the human and spiritual ancestors.

At a deeper affective level, the *tangi,* the weeping, is a declaration about and a reference to the tragedy of land loss and cultural identity. *Tangi* flows from the remnants of land in which resides the wounded soul handed down by ancestors. Such weeping is not just for the immediate material loss, but also for lost potential and the diminution of spiritual and cultural identity. In the Mäori mind there is an ongoing connection between the health of Earth Mother and the well-being of humans in communities with rights and obligations. For generations it has been considered that psychological and social illnesses can be attributed to the mistakes and evils of the past associated with the loss of land and the abuse of Earth Mother. In the context of the elder's narrative to the law society, this is particularly poignant. He reminds all who will listen that Mäori have lost most of the land to others, often for unjust reasons, but also to a lesser degree through ill-informed decisions of Mäori.

The history of Mäori encounters with white settlers, which has significant different interpretations, involves considerations of religion and ecology. The Mäori view of recent history has, following John G. A. Pocock, "shaped assumptions and structures, the ideologies, mentalities and discourses" by which Mäori define themselves, others, and the world.[35] The maintenance of a historical sense and a willingness to learn from experience has ensured the resilience of traditional worldview and religion. And this, despite major changes in elements of Mäori culture, in social organization, in the systematic undermining of kinship groups by the state, in transformations in material culture, and in political and economic activity. Yet, all of these features have abiding elements that remain embedded in traditional Mäori metaphysics and religious outlook.[36] In the twentieth century, traditional Mäori religion has been lived and practiced as an implicit religion, yet in an increasingly Christian or secularist, utilitarian, and positivist society.[37] Mäori worldview values emphasizing the mythico-historical origins of vital life, of the human, and of reciprocity as central to being Mäori were bound to clash with the settlers' Christian or secular utilitarianism and positivism.

The story of the twentieth century is one of Mäori agency initiating a cultural, social, and political renaissance. This rebirth coincides with a dramatic movement away from rural to urban living, where access to improved housing, education, health care, and employment played a major part in survival and development. In this century consistent campaigns were waged for cultural and religious enhancement, kinship group development, land retention and use, language survival, and political and economic rights. Noticeable changes occurred in the 1970s, when the courts and Parliament acknowledged that Mäori rights and duties were of a constitutional order. With the establishment of the Waitangi Tribunal, Mäori rights under the Treaty of 1840 could be given a modicum of effect. The tribunal, a court of enquiry, continues to hear Mäori claims against the Crown government and whether its actions or nonactions are in accordance with the principles of the 1840 *Te Tiriti o Waitangi:* Treaty of Waitangi. Successful claims have led to attempts at social and economic relief. These include the recognition of Mäori language as an official language of New Zealand, some land being restored to the descendants of original owners, and the recognition in law of aspects of Mäori customs and values pertaining to forests, fisheries, broadcasting rights, and resource management.[38]

With the idea of land and environment as gifts, glossed in Mäori as *taonga*, go duties and the responsibility of guardianship. In his speech the elder described why this is so. He said:

> The Mäori word '*whenua*'—land, is the term used for both the land and the placenta or afterbirth, therefore, the land for Mäori people has the same deep significance as the placenta, which surrounds the embryo. Giving it warmth and security, a *mauri*, a life force that relates to and interacts with Mother Earth's forces.[39]

Here, the sage introduces us to one of the essentials of a Mäori philosophy of vitalism. He acquaints us with *mauri,* which he describes as an interactive life force. He states another fundamental Mäori understanding of the purpose and the source of life itself that has metaphysical, psychological, and philosophical implications. He informs us that *mauri,* having been imbued in the embryo at conception, interacts with Mother Earth's forces, the immediate source of life. The land is the nurturing source of human physical existence, just as the placenta is for the newborn child. In Mäori cosmological thought the *mauri,* together with *tapu, mana, hau,* and *wairua,* came from Io, the Supreme Cosmic Being that existed before Sky Father and Earth Mother and from which emanates the cosmos we know and understand. The land as the system of ecological interactions is a placenta that nurtures and sustains humanity. Humans reciprocate in special obligatory roles both to the source of their life and to the "placenta" or ecology that nourishes them.

Since mid-nineteenth-century colonization, Mäori have consistently asserted in New Zealand's political and environmental arenas an understanding of the symbiotic relationships between humanity, the physical world of nature, and the spiritual world.[40] Understanding the contemporary significance of *mauri* requires some familiarity with such associated terms as *tapu, mana, hau,* and *wairua.*

Tapu is a cosmic power imbued in all things at the time of creation and would normally remain for the duration of a thing's existence, its being. In the Sky Father and Earth Mother account, each of the children were conceived with the *tapu* of the parents, and they in turn are the sources of the *tapu* of all the domains and things of creation ascribed to them. Persons, places, or objects are *tapu* and are therefore in a sacred state or condition.[41] Philosophically, *tapu* is linked to the notion of *mana* and is "being with potentiality for power." In its primary meaning, *tapu* expresses the understanding that once a thing is, it has within itself a real potency, *mana.* Each being, material or non-material, from its first moment of existence, has this potentiality and its own power and authority. Coupled with the potential for power is the idea of awe and sacredness, which commands respect and separateness. It is in this sense that *tapu* can mean restrictions and prohibitions.[42] However, *tapu,* a core part of Pacific belief systems, was glossed as taboo by earlier Western observers and recognized largely in terms of restrictions or prohibitions. Unfortunately, it is the limited and negative understanding that is used to explain *tapu,* but this is only one aspect of its meaning.

Mana is religious power, authority, and ancestral efficacy. Together with *tapu* it derives from the creation parents and children, and ultimately from Io. It is humanity's greatest possession. *Tapu* is traditionally applied to many things and there are, therefore, many types of *tapu.* All children are *tapu,* individuals and groups are *tapu.* Houses and gardens are *tapu,* trees and birds are *tapu,* as are rivers, lakes, and oceans. Ecosystems and the environment as a whole are therefore *tapu. Tapu* needs to be treated with respect, awe, and sometimes fear, but it depends on the relationship of one's own *tapu* to the *tapu* belonging to other persons and life systems in the environment. A respectful relationship ensures balance, health, and well-being, but a bad relationship of abuse often leads to disharmony and imbalance. This applies to the *tapu* of distinct features of ecosystems. They need to be protected, strengthened, and constantly confirmed so that balance, harmony, and potentialities can be fulfilled.[43]

Whatever complexities may be involved in understanding *tapu,* it is a significant and distinct concept in Mäori thought. However, *tapu* cannot be separated from *mana.* Below, I discuss *tapu-mana* relations, using the metaphor of a spiral to point toward a core of Mäori ethics that mediates human behavior and the natural world. These are entry points for a broader discussion of Mäori-Polynesian worldview values.

Mauri is variously described as a unique power, a life essence, a life force, and a vital principle. *Mauri* refers to the vital spark, originally possessed by Io, the Primary Life Force and Supreme Cosmic Being. It is a force transmitted by Hauora, one of the children of the creation parents, who is responsible for *hau* and *mauri* and, therefore, life in all creation. It is intimately related to other metaphysical powers—*tapu, mana, hau,* and *wairua*—and all of these forces are essences of forms of life in persons, objects, and nonobjectified beings. They endow a thing with its special character, which must correspond to its nature.[44] *Mauri* is a concentration of life itself, like the center of an energy source and, because of its power and energy, its purpose is to make it "possible for everything to move and live in accordance with the conditions and limits of its existence."[45] Everything has its own *mauri,* its own nature—people, tribe, land, mountains, stones, fish, animals, birds, trees, rivers, lakes, oceans, thoughts, words, houses, factories—that permits these living things to exist within their own realm and sphere.[46]

All *mauri* may be violated, abused, or diminished through neglect or attack. Thus, trees and plants, rivers, lakes, and oceans may not produce in limitless abundance. Fruits would be scarce, there would be fewer birds, animals, or fish.[47] From a Mäori perspective forests, rivers, and oceans can have their *mauri* restored through rituals of conservation accompanied by appropriate ritual prayer forms and ceremonies. The restored *mauri* would ensure that depleted food supplies, such as fish, shell fish, or birds, would be abundant again.

The Mäori explanation of life and growth is illustrated in the poetry and sayings of the ancestors, as well as in the arts and crafts of artists. In both perspectives the seed of life is with the male and the woman represents the sheltering and nurturing receptacle for the seed. Thus, conception and growth are possible where this gender mutuality occurs. The Mäori term *kunenga* denotes the life-forming process of "conception, the assuming of form and the commencement of the acquirement of form." Accordingly, the eyes are said to be the first parts of the embryo to acquire form. The *wairua,* a spirit akin to a soul, is implanted in the embryo when the eyes assume form, but something else is given in the nature of an impetus. With the establishment of the *wairua* also comes the dawn of intelligence.[48]

The implanted spirit, the *wairua,* must remain with the embryo and the developing human body, *tinana,* in order for the body to continue growing. *Wairua* is necessary for the existence of the body. Its conspicuous feature is that it is part of the human being that dreams, and if the person is threatened, it is the *wairua* that experiences the threat. It is the *mauri* that binds the *wairua* and the embryo-body (*tinana*) together, and in this integral entity life exists.

Mauri is life itself. Together, the body, *wairua,* and *mauri* constitute a living being. While the *wairua* is something of a free spirit and can move away from its material resemblance, the body, it must return to it. The *wairua* of humans protects the body by sensing the evil thoughts and presence of others and alerting it to potential danger.[49] However, another force is essential to the totality of life as understood by Mäori. The *hau,* a cosmic power and vital essence, is infused also into the embryo and is another set of specific qualities closely allied to the *mauri,* yet both are decidedly distinct. *Hau* is often referred to as the breath of life or alluded to as the wind, which is sometimes the phenomenon identified as the manifestation of the life force. The *hau* is called up by the priestly leader at birth and bound in humans. With the *hau* is the *tapu* and *mana* of their ancestral spirit being,[50] which are present also at conception and remain with the form in life and in death.

What then is the understanding of death? Mäori thought has it that death occurs when the *mauri* is no longer able to keep body and *wairua* bound together and so guarantee continued life. A separation takes place and, as a consequence, the body is considered dead. The funeral ritual, called a *tangihanga,* is organized and often lasts three or more days when kinfolk and friends gather to pay their respects, which are expressed in speech making, formal prayer, and much discussion about the person. This ritual includes a retelling of the deceased's genealogical and tribal history.

While the social imperatives are important, the primary purpose of the ritual is to ensure that the body is cared for prior to burial and that the *mauri* and the *hau* have departed and returned to their source, Io. And, at the same time, the ritual ought to ensure that the spirit, *wairua,* is freed of earthly attachments so as to return to Hawaiki safely and join the great body of ancestors. It is believed that, should the ritual be held inappropriately, things can go wrong, especially for the *wairua,* which may linger on earth, returning in a malevolent mood or approaching the living to seek ways to return to Hawaiki. Having completed the ritual of burial, those remaining continue their daily lives.

These elements of the life-death process also apply to the natural world—land, mountains, rivers, seas, trees, animals, and insects. According to Mäori, all things in creation have had a *tinana,* a *wairua,* a *mauri,* and a *hau.* This fundamental assembly of life forces gave "form and energy to all matter."[51] For instance, a tree is first formed as a seed resplendent with the *mauri* and *hau* of Tane, the child who separated Earth Mother and Sky Father. The seed now has a being with potential to be a living, creating process that is the *mana* of Tane. In time the form, the seed, is transformed into a trunk, a body, which has a *wairua,* a spirit, and these are bound together by a *mauri,* which, when separated from the tree, causes the tree to die. Thus, in using parts of trees or in cutting down trees, appropriate rituals and customs ought to be followed. If not, there may be malevolent tree spirits in the forest. "All things possess a wairua; otherwise they could not exist.

Matter cannot exist without such a principle," says one Mäori.[52]

Hau, furthermore, is a cosmic power and vital essence embodied in all persons and things and often described as the very essence of vitality. It has an extraordinary range of applications and, when considered in terms of its relationships, it can be seen as "a part of life," which influences the whole.[53] When applied to all aspects and dimensions of the natural world, it is a life force, which is closely linked to the *mauri.* Its purpose is toward goodness. All rivers, lakes, oceans, forests, mountains have this life principle that must be protected by good acts and nurtured because of the association with food and other supplies. The *hau* of tribal land and forests is their vitality and fertility, which are also signs of their *mana,* their honor, prestige, and power. However, if they are not cared for, or are neglected or abused, the land can be rendered infertile and the forests unproductive. The vitality of trees, and this vitality's power, is the agency for attracting birds.[54] It is a gift from Hauora, another of the children of Earth Mother and Sky Father. The significance of the *hau* and its potency is illustrated by the account of the argument of the children over the rights and wrongs of separating of the cosmic parents. At one time, each tried to destroy the *hau* of the others, thus attempting to nullify the power and authority of the others to act.

Religious rituals play an integral role in nurturing and protecting the *hau* of the natural world. One is called "feeding the *hau*" and entails making offerings to the sea, river, lake, or forest. It can be the first catch of fish or birds or the first crop of potatoes that are returned to its source or put aside for ritual use. Like the close association of *tapu-mana,* so is that between *mauri* and *hau,* in which the *hau* is thought to rest in the *mauri.* The *mauri* protects the *hau* in the same way that the *wairua,* spirit, protects its physical basis, the body. In returning the first catch, the fundamentals of reciprocal exchange are identified. By means of these rituals of feeding, *hau* and *mauri* are returned to the original source.[55] Over the millennia *hau* was established as a complex totalizing system of obligatory gift exchange infusing Mäori social, economic, and religious life with profound implications for the management and guardianship of the natural world.[56] Climate change, changing ecosystems, the decline of native forest reserves, declining coastal flora, inshore and deep-sea fisheries, and waterway and land uses will be the central Mäori environmental issues of the twenty-first century. When considered as a unity, *mauri, hau,* and *wairua* appear to protect *tapu* and so maintain the *mana* of the person or group, the tree or forest, the dandelion or flower, the stream or ocean.

Such a holistic approach to environmental and ecological care and management has been impossible during the last 150 years for tribal regions such as Tai Tokerau. Mäori have experienced externally imposed land management policies, which have been motivated by secularist, scientific, Cartesian dualist thinking. Management by quantitative analysis has critically impacted Tai Tokerau spirituality, culture, people, and environment. Alienation and disconnection from land, forest, rivers, streams, tributaries, pools, and seas has distanced people from Earth Mother and nature. Denial of the responsibilities of guardianship over creation, and being unable to nurture and feed both the life forces (*mauri* and *hau*) of the diverse substances and forms of creation, has profound implications both for humans and nature. The obligatory reciprocity between humanity and the natural world has not occurred and the spirit, *wairua,* of the region is sick—an illness which manifests itself in poor production, high unemployment, and other social ills of the century just past.

Mäori Ethics and Ecological and Environmental Sustainability

In recent years there has been a movement toward clarifying the extent to which traditional practices and values can inform the present regarding an ethics relevant to humanity in meaningful relationship with the world. Mäori claimants appearing in courts and other forums have articulated core values parallel to the Waitangi Tribunal. According to the tribunal, a set of criteria underlie Mäori thinking on the resources of the environment and constitute rules that ought to govern human behavior in the environment. They are: a reverence for the total creation as one whole; a sense of kinship with other beings; a sacred regard for the whole of nature and its resources as being gifts from the spiritual powers; a sense of responsibility for these gifts (*taonga*) as the appointed stewards and guardians; a distinctive economic ethic of reciprocity; and a sense of commitment to safeguard natural resources for future generations.[57] These criteria were reiterated in a further development when claimants articulated a set of core values, which the tribunal recognized as conceptual regulators associated with land rights and communal obligations when applied to the environment and land of Tai Tokerau. The values are also part of a general system for regulating human behavior. They are given as:

- kinship (*whanaungatanga*),which stresses the primacy of kinship bonds in determining action and the importance of genealogy in establishing rights and status;
- compassion (*arohatanga*), which is a basis for peaceful coexistence;
- hospitality (*manaakitanga*), which is a desirable character trait of generosity, care-giving, or compassion, and is generally about establishing one's *mana;*
- reciprocity (*utu*), which concerns the maintenance of harmony and balance, and of *mana.*[58]

Finally, our study of Mäori religion, metaphysics, and philosophy of vitalism and cosmos informs us of a spiral of ethics for life. Albert Schweitzer wrote that, in the stillness of the primeval forest in Africa, he realized that worldview is a product of life view, not vice versa. For him, all profound worldview is mysticism, and this is "the germ of all ideas and dispositions which are determinative for the conduct of individuals and society." Following a restoration of a worldview for life he found that "ethics too, are nothing but reverence for life."[59]

Outlined below is what can best be described as a spiral of traditional ethics, which simultaneously presents Mäori worldview and acts as a check on that worldview. This is not a hierarchy of ethics; rather, this begins in the center of the spiral and, together with the above values, constitutes a Pacific Polynesian view of holism and way of linking humanity and environment in a relationship of reciprocity and respect:[60]

- ethic of wholeness, cosmos (*te ao märama*)
- ethic of life essences, vitalism, reverence for life (*mauri*)
- ethic of being and potentiality, the sacred (*tapu*)
- ethic of power, authority, and common good (*mana*)
- ethic of spiritual power of obligatory reciprocity in relationships with nature (*hau*)
- ethic of the spirit and spirituality (*wairuatanga*)
- ethic of the right way, of the quest for justice (*tika*)

- ethic of care and support, reverence for humanity (*manaaki-tanga*)
- ethic of belonging, reverence for the human person (*wha-naungatanga*)
- ethic of change and tradition (*te ao hurihuri*)
- ethic of solidarity (*kotahitanga*)
- ethic of guardianship of creation (*kaitiakitanga*)

I end with the elder's words: "It is a pleasant thing that we meet, because we cannot meet without learning to know and understand one another better. . . . Tīhei mauri ora. Ah t'is life!"

Notes

1. This chapter draws on fieldwork and archival research for interdisciplinary research projects on social, economic, and cultural sustainable development in the Tai Tokerau region. The projects were funded by the New Zealand Foundation for Research, Science and Technology. See Manuka Henare, "The Mana of Whangaroa," in *Sustainable Development in Tai Tokerau. Case Study Three—Whangaroa,* FRST 95 UOA S16 3839 (Auckland: James Henare Mäori Research Centre, The University of Auckland, October 1997), 213–39, and "The Mana of Ngapuhi," in *Sustainable Development in Tai Tokerau. Case Study Four—Ngapuhi,* FRST 96-UOA-13-5556 and 98-UOA-13-6685 (Auckland: James Henare Mäori Research Centre, University of Auckland, 1998), 669–93.

2. A population of 800,000 is my estimate. There is no research on the numbers of Aotearoa Mäori living overseas, but an estimated 100,000 are said to live in Australia. The 1996 New Zealand Population Census records that 579,714 people claim Mäori ancestry, of a total population of 3,618,302. Mäori life expectancy has increased dramatically in the past fifty years. It is currently 73 years of age for women and 68 for men and is expected to reach 75 years and 80 years, respectively, by 2030. The population is young, with 38 percent under the age of 15. Urbanization is another significant factor for Mäori society. Before the 1940s, more than 80 percent lived in rural areas, largely within their own tribal domains, but at the end of the twentieth century, some 83 percent live in urban areas. See the Statistics New Zealand web site, http://www.stats.govt.nz. A majority now live outside their tribal boundaries. Social mobility appears to be an accepted part of Mäori ethos and, together with urban living and easier access to improved housing, education, health care, and employment, has played a major part in Mäori survival and social development.

3. For myths about oceans, see Elsdon Best, *Mäori Religion and Mythology,* vol. 2 (Wellington: Government Printer, 1982), 252.

4. See Roy A. Rappaport, *Ecology, Meaning, and Religion* (Richmond, Calif.: North Atlantic Books, 1979), 4–5; and South Pacific Regional Environment Programme, *The Pacific Way: Pacific Island Developing Countries' Report to the United Nations Conference on Environment and Development* (Noumea, New Caledonia: South Pacific Regional Environment Programme of the South Pacific Commission, 1992), 7, 9.

5. The categories of Polynesian, Melanesian, and Micronesian are not indigenous peoples' classifications.

6. For a discussion of philosophy as a love of wisdom, see Raymond Williams, *Keywords: A Vocabulary of Culture and Society,* rev. and expanded (London: Fontana Paperbacks, 1983), 235. For a discussion on the centrality of cosmology in Mäori culture, see Gregory Schrempp, *Magical Arrows: The Mäori, the Greeks, and the Folklore of the Universe* (Madison: University of Wisconsin Press, 1992).

7. On creation as a dynamic whole, the sources of Mäori knowledge, and the unfolding cosmos, see Michael P. Shirres, *Te Tangata—The Human Person* (Auckland: Accent Publications, 1997), 16, 118–19.

8. For a discussion of the Mäori term *tupu,* glossed as to unfold one's nature and how all things unfold their nature, how they live and have form, see J. Prytz Johansen, *The Mäori and His Religion in Its Non-Ritual Aspects* (Copenhagen: Ejnarn Munksgaard, 1954), 40–47.

9. See Anne Salmond, *Between Worlds: Early Exchanges between Māori and Europeans, 1773–1815* (Auckland: Viking, 1997), 176, 401–2, 509.

10. See ibid., 512; and Anne Salmond, "Māori Epistemologies," in *Reason and Morality,* ed. Joanne Overing (London: Tavistock, 1985), 247.

11. For discussion of the intention of the artists or performer to express vital potential in vitalistic art, see Silvano Arieti, *Creativity: The Magic Synthesis* (New York: Basic Books, 1976), 196–200.

12. Cited by Marina Werner, a guest on the Jeremy Paxton show, *Start of the Week,* BBC Radio 4, London, 24 January 2000, in a discussion on the great monuments of Leonardo da Vinci.

13. Māori history consists of genealogies, kinship systems, poetry, myths, proverbs, songs, and ritual dances, which together constitute a narrative on identity. On the importance of narrative theory and the task of hermeneutics to explicate the world in front of the text, see Paul Ricoeur, "Narrative Identity," in *On Paul Ricoeur: Narrative and Interpretation,* ed. David Wood (London: Routledge, 1991), 188. For Ricoeur, narrative identity is ". . . [the] kind of identity that human beings acquire through the mediation of the narrative function."

14. See Sir James Henare, foreword to *He Pepeha, He Whakatauakï No Te Taitokerau* (Tribal sayings and proverbs of North Auckland), comp. Jane McRae (Whangarei: Department of Māori Affairs, 1987). According to Paul Ricoeur, we can understand human beings and human possibilities through an analysis of symbols and texts, which attest to that existence. He claims that it is only through stories and histories that we gain a catalog of the humanly possible. For a discussion of Ricoeur's ideas, see Kevin Vanhoozer, "Philosophical Antecedents to Ricoeur's Time and Narrative," in *On Paul Ricoeur: Narrative and Interpretation,* ed. David Wood (London: Routledge, 1991), 48. See also Paul Ricoeur, *The Rule of Metaphor: Multi-disciplinary Studies of the Creation of Meaning in Language,* trans. Robert Czerny with Kathleen McLaughlin and John Costello (Toronto: University of Toronto Press, 1993), 69.

15. See Edward B. Tylor, *Primitive Culture: Researches into the Development of Mythology, Philosophy, Religion, Art, and Custom,* 2 vols. (London: J. Murray, 1871).

16. See Robert Schreiter, *Constructing Local Theologies* (Maryknoll, N.Y.: Orbis Books, 1985), 43.

17. For discussion of the phenomenon of traditional religion, see John S. Mbiti, *Introduction to African Religion* (London: Heinemann Educational, 1975).

18. See Manuka Henare and Bernard Kernot, "Māori Religion: The Spiritual Landscape," in *Can Humanity Survive? The World's Religions and the Environment,* ed. James Veitch (Auckland: Awareness Book, 1996), 205.

19. For a discussion of the centrality of religion and ritual in the evolution of life and the making of humanity, particularly Māori religion and ritual, see Shirres, *Te Tangata—The Human Person,* 65–73, 77–90. Shirres studied Māori ritual, particularly ritual prayer form, their structures, and how ritual is a means of being human. In a broader study Roy Rappaport persuasively argues: "first on ritual's internal logic, next on the products (like sanctity) that its logic entails, and on the nature of their truth, and . . . on the place of ritual and its products in humanity's evolution." See Roy Rappaport, *Ritual and Religion in the Making of Humanity* (Cambridge: Cambridge University Press, 1999), 3.

20. Sir James Henare was a leader in Tai Tokerau, Aotearoa New Zealand and Polynesia, and was recognized as an authority on Mäori oral history and Polynesian genealogy. See his "Address to Auckland District Law Society" (4 July 1981, photocopy), 3.

21. See ibid., 6–7; and Cleve Barlow (a Mäori academic and psychologist from Tai Tokerau), *Tikanga Whakaaro: Key Concepts in Mäori Culture* (Auckland: Oxford University Press, 1991), 182–84. Mäori enlightenment is, in the spirit of Kant, liberation from superstition. See Emmanuel Kant, *Critique of Judgement,* trans. W. Pluhar (1790; Cambridge, Mass.: Hackett Publishing, 1987), 161.

22. See Mäori Marsden and Te Aroha Henare, "Kaitiakitanga: A Definitive Introduction to the Holistic World View of the Mäori" (Te Kopuru, November 1992, photocopy), 3. Other indigenous people explain worldview in a similar way: see Alfonso Ortiz, quoted in Peggy V. Beck, Anna Lee Walters, and Nia Francisco, *The Sacred: Ways of Knowledge, Sources of Life* (Tsaile, Ariz.: Navajo Community College Press, and Northland Publishing, 1990), 5–6. According to Ortiz, "The notion 'world view' denotes a distinctive vision of reality which not only interprets and orders the place and events in the experience of a people, but lends form, direction, and continuity to life as well. World view provides people with a distinctive set of values, an identity, a feeling of rootedness, of belonging to a time and place, and a sense of continuity with a tradition which transcends the experience of a single lifetime, a tradition which may be said to transcend even time."

23. See Manuka Henare, "Christianity: Mäori Churches," in *Religions of New Zealanders,* ed. Peter Donovan (Palmerston North: Dunmore Press, 1990), 118–27.

24. See Marsden and Te Aroha Henare, "Kaitiakitanga," 18.

25. See Salmond, "Between Worlds," 401–2.

26. See James Henare, "Address to Auckland District Law Society," 4–9.

27. The trees are the *pohutukawa, totara (Podocarpus totara), kauri (Agathis australis), karaka (Corynocarpus laevigata),* and *kowhai (Sophora tetraptera).* The *pohutukawa* is the national plant of Aotearoa New Zealand and the kiwi is the national bird.

28. For a description of the environment at the time of the beginnings of human habitation, see Department of Conservation [New Zealand], *The Story of the Bay of Islands Maritime and Historic Park* (Russell, New Zealand: Bay of Islands Maritime and Historic Park, 1989), 51, 66–67, 68–69, 70.

29. See James Henare, "Address to Auckland District Law Society," 10–11, 14.

30. See Manuka Henare, "The Mana of Whangaroa," 222–23.

31. For a discussion of Aristotle's and other Western theories on vitalism, see Battista Mondin, *Philosophical Anthropology: Man, An Impossible Project?* trans. Myroslaw A. Cizdyn (Rome: Urbania University Press, 1985), 26–27; Morton Beckner, "Vitalism," in *The Encyclopedia of Philosophy,* ed. Paul Edwards (New York: Macmillan, 1996), 8:253–56; H. E. Wachowski, "Biology, II Current Status—Vitalism," in *New Catholic Encyclopedia* (New York: McGraw-Hill, 1967–), 2:570–73; A. E. Manier, "Vitalism," in *New Catholic Encyclopedia,* 14:724–25. On a comprehensive metaphysics applicable to all phenomena, see Henri Bergson, *Creative Evolution,* trans. Arthur Mitchell (1911; New York: Dover, 1998), 42–43, and *An Introduction to Metaphysics,* trans. T. E. Hulme (London: Macmillan, 1913).

32. For a discussion of Melanesian and Polynesian concepts of *mana,* taboo (*tapu*), and theories on static and dynamic religions, including other indigenous peoples, see Henri Bergson, *The Two Sources of Morality and Religion,* trans. R. Ashley Audra and Cloudesley Brereton (1932; Notre Dame, Ind.: University of Notre Dame Press, 1986), 126–28, 134–35, 165–66, 210–11, 214. For discussion on the problems associated with the comparative studies of religions and cultures and the need for a more holistic approach, see Schreiter, *Constructing Local Theologies,* 43.

33. For discussion of Māori knowledge as an open system capable of a form of systematic enquiry, critiquing and evaluating the world of human beings and spiritual beings, see Salmond, *Between Worlds,* 516–17; and Salmond, "Māori Epistemologies," 240–63.

34. See Salmond, *Between Worlds,* 176.

35. See John G. A. Pocock, "Law, Sovereignty and History in a Divided Culture: The Case of New Zealand and the Treaty of Waitangi," *McGill Law Journal* 43, no. 3 (October 1998): 484, in which, as a New Zealander, he examines the politics in New Zealand arising from the revivification of the Treaty of Waitangi. He considers historiographical consequences that follow the redefinition of a nation's sovereignty, and treaty relations between differing concepts of sovereignty and history.

36. The colonial history and Māori experience of it, and New Zealand society's attempts to deal with its past and make a new present so as to move into the future, represent a new experience. In Māori worldview, the past is like a pathway in front of the present, which leads to the future. The past is never behind but is considered as always being in front of the present. Māori relive the past in the present and, in so doing, find the future. The elder in his ritual greeting to the lawyers referred to past ancestors as if they are standing before the group. He was pointing toward the necessity of the struggle for cultural integrity, including environmental spirituality.

Māori became a minority population in the 1860s and experienced the onslaught of colonization and near extinction. This loss of control over the country and destiny came about despite a Māori Declaration of Independence in 1835, *He Whakaputanga o te Rangatiratanga o Nu Tireni,* and an 1840 treaty of friendship with the British Crown, which Māori considered guaranteed their sovereignty. However, the British Crown and later New Zealand governments considered that sovereignty was ceded forever. The nineteenth century was one of high political and military activity around claims to sovereignty, and the twentieth century one of encounter against assimilation and integration as espoused by the dominant European society. However, minority status was not always the norm. The 1840 population estimates put Māori society at 100,000, constituting the dominant group. It is also the beginning of colonization and European settlement, largely from Great Britain. However, with the first encounter of Māori and European in 1769, the introduction of measles, tuberculosis, typhoid fever, and venereal and other diseases new to Māori became a significant factor in population decrease into the twentieth century. By the end of the nineteenth century, observers considered Māori a dying race, when the population had been reduced to 45,549 people by 1901. The alienation of land to settler ownership was almost complete, with some 66 million acres in 1840 to about 3 million acres in Māori control. See Manuka Henare and Edward Douglas, "Te Reo o Te Tiriti Mai Ra Anō: The Treaty Always Speaks," in *Future Directions, Associated Papers. Report of the*

Royal Commission on Social Policy: The April Report, vol. 3, pt. 1 (Wellington: Royal Commission on Social Policy, 1988), 79–220. See also Claudia Orange, *An Illustrated History of the Treaty of Waitangi* (Wellington: Allen and Unwin, in association with Port Nicholson Press, 1990), 67.

37. Grateful thanks are extended to the Reverend Edward Bailey of the Centre for the Study of Implicit Religion and Contemporary Society, Middlesex University, for a discussion on implicit religions, which are active in societies (conversation with author, February 2000).

38. For a summary of the claims process and its progress, see Claudia Orange, *The Treaty of Waitangi* (Wellington: Allen and Unwin, 1987; reprint, Wellington: Bridget Williams Books, 1997), 97–118 (page citations are to the reprint edition). The chair of the Waitangi Tribunal, Justice Edward T. Durie, has discussed Māori ethics and values in research; see Edward T. Durie, "Ethics and Values," paper presented at Te Oru Rangahau Māori Research and Development Conference, Massey University, 7–9 July 1998. See also Indigenous Peoples and the Law: An Online Institute of Law Affecting Indigenous Peoples, http://www.kennett.co.nz/law/indigenous/1999.

39. See James Henare, "Address to Auckland District Law Society," 18.

40. For instance, a worldview and belief in life forces and their significance in society and nature were highlighted in a 1997 report of a court of enquiry called the Waitangi Tribunal; see Waitangi Tribunal, *Muriwhenua Land Report* (Wellington: GP Publications, 1997), 15. After hearing both oral and written evidence from Muriwhenua people (who live in the northernmost part of Tai Tokerau), anthropologists, and historians, the tribunal summed up the tribal claimant's relationship with the land and seas as follows: "The people's accounts started before time began, at Matangireia, home of the first being, Io-matua-kore, and proceeded from there on a mental and spiritual journey through aeons. It told of an enterprising people, pragmatic but deeply religious, so intimately tied to land, sea, and space that in their cosmos all life forms, and phenomena like the sky, sun, wind and rain, are bound to them by treasured links in ancient genealogy. Māori thus see themselves as descendants of gods, and as partners with them in a physical and spiritual universe." Io-matua-kore, glossed as Io who had no parents, is one of many such attributes used to describe this numinous Supreme Being. Other attributes are Io matua, Io who is the parent of all, and Io wänanga, Io who is knowledge. In the cosmological accounts there are twelve heavens, of which Matangireia is the highest and is the abode of Io. For further discussion on cosmology, see Shirres, *Te Tangata—The Human Person,* 113–18; and Elsdon Best, *Māori Religion and Mythology,* vol. 1 (Wellington: Government Printer, 1976), 72–75, 144–47. Finally, in the two separate reports to the government on claims over sea, coast and fish, and land, the Waitangi Tribunal found in favor of Muriwhenua Claimants; see Waitangi Tribunal, *Muriwhenua Fishing Report* (Wellington: Government Printing Office, 1988). For other reports and summaries of findings, see also the tribunal's web site, http://www.knowledge-basket.co.nz.

41. See Māori Marsden, "God, Man and Universe: A Māori View," in *Te Ao Hurihuri: The World Moves On,* ed. Michael King (Wellington: Hicks Smith, 1975), 197.

42. For a discussion on Māori philosophy, see Shirres, *Te Tangata—The Human Person,* 79.

43. For discussion of *tapu* and religion, see Salmond, *Between Worlds,* 176–77,

510. See also Johansen, *The Mäori and His Religion in Its Non-Ritual Aspects*, 185–213; and Marsden, "God, Man and Universe: A Mäori View," 196–97.

44. For a fuller discussion of *mauri, tapu, mana, hau, wairua,* and their place and applications in an industrial, positivist, utilitarian, and secular society, see Manuka Henare, "Human Labour as a Commodity—A Mäori Ethical Response," in *Labour, Employment and Work in New Zealand, 1994: Proceedings of the Sixth Conference, November 24 and 25, 1994, Victoria University of Wellington*, ed. Philip S. Morrison (Wellington: Department of Geography, Victoria University of Wellington, 1995), 218; Manuka Henare and Kernot, "Mäori Religion: The Spiritual Landscape," 205–15; and Salmond, *Between Worlds*, 176–77. See also Johansen, *The Mäori and His Religion in Its Non-Ritual Aspects*, 118, 237–40; and Marsden, "God, Man and Universe: A Mäori View," 196–97.

45. See Barlow, *Tikanga Whakaaro: Key Concepts in Mäori Culture*, 83.

46. For a discussion of the function of the *mauri*, the life-conservation-death principles, and how *mauri* may be violated and restored, see Barlow, *Tikanga Whakaaro: Key Concepts in Mäori Culture*, 83; and Makereti, *The Old-Time Mäori* (1938; reprint, Auckland: New Women's Press, 1986), 181.

47. Makereti, *The Old-Time Mäori*, 181.

48. For an outline of Mäori customs and belief on birth, see Elsdon Best, *The Whare Kohanga (the "Nest House") and Its Lore* (1929; reprint, Wellington: Government Printer, 1975), 10–12.

49. For an outline of the *wairua*, see Johansen, *The Mäori and His Religion in Its Non-Ritual Aspects*, 26, 254, 257, 259, 260.

50. For a discussion of *hau* and religion, see Salmond, *Between Worlds*, 176–77, 395, 491, 510, 513.

51. Ibid., 510.

52. Cited by Johansen, *The Mäori and His Religion in Its Non-Ritual Aspects*, 261.

53. On *hau* and its several homonyms, see ibid., 117.

54. For a discussion of Mäori lore, including myths, rites, customs connected with flora and fauna, and the writings of Tamati Ranapiri, see Elsdon Best, "Mäori Forest Lore," *Transactions of the New Zealand Institute* 42 (1 June 1909): 433–81; see also Peter Gathercole, "Hau, Mauri and Utu: A Re-examination," *Mankind* 11, no. 3 (1978): 338; and Manuka Henare and Kernot, "Mäori Religion: The Spiritual Landscape," 205–15.

55. See Best, *Mäori Religion and Mythology*, vol. 1, 50–53; and Salmond, *Between Worlds*, 510.

56. For a discussion of *hau*, the spirit of gifts, and Pacific gift exchange theories and practices, see Marcel Mauss, *The Gift: The Form and Reason for Exchange in Archaic Societies*, trans. W. D. Hall (London: Routledge, 1990), 10–18. For further comment on Mauss and *hau* and its wider application, see Maurice Godelier, "The Legacy of Mauss," chap. 1 in *The Enigma of the Gift*, trans. Nora Scott (Chicago: University of Chicago Press, 1999), 10–107; and *The Logic of the Gift: Toward an Ethic of Generosity*, ed. Alan D. Schrift (London: Routledge, 1997).

57. See Waitangi Tribunal, *Muriwhenua Fishing Report*, 179.

58. See Waitangi Tribunal, *Muriwhenua Land Report*, 26–27.

59. See Albert Schweitzer, *Civilization and Ethics: The Dale Memorial Lectures 1922,* vol. 2, trans. C. T. Campion (London: A. and C. Black, 1929), xiii, xiv, xviii.

60. For a discussion of the importance of culture, ethics, and values for sustainable government economic, social, and political policy, see Manuka Henare, "Sustainable Social Policy," in *Redesigning the Welfare State in New Zealand: Problems, Policies, Prospects,* ed. Jonathon Boston, Paul Dalziel, and Susan St. John (Auckland: Oxford University Press, 1999), 39–59.

Embedded Worldviews

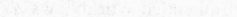

The Sacred Egg:
Worldview, Ecology, and
Development in West Africa

OGBU U. KALU

The Backdrop: Development Failure

In 1996, a state government in southeastern Nigeria sought to combat the devastating collapse of agro-industrial projects in the rural communities. The state acquired some irrigation pumps through the Federal Ministry of Agriculture, aided by a World Bank loan scheme. When workers entered the farmland of a certain community, called Amanuke, to dig trenches, the entire community descended on the workers, wielding machetes, spears, and guns. The hapless workers tried to persuade the irate villagers that the irrigation would enable them to crop year-round. But the villagers complained that the forest adjoining the farmland housed their epical ancestral shrine. Besides, they argued, if the ancestral progenitors had wanted them to harvest crops year-round, they would have caused the springs which coursed underground to burst to the surface. Ancestors are very loving and usually careful about such things.

Obviously, the project officers had ignored the people during the project design and were both insensitive and inattentive to what the people felt and desired socially, economically, and spiritually. They ignored how a people's culture, worldview, and religion affect their perception of development. Currently, much of Africa is plagued by development failure that, in turn, has bred legitimacy crises, economic collapse, environmental degradation, and human rights abuse. It is, therefore, difficult to engage in any meaningful scholarship that does not in some way address these problems. Did the primal worldview of the Amanuke people cause the failure of the agro-industrial project? Can we avoid the romanticization of primal worldviews and still advocate salient traditionalization of agents of change? The perspective here is from a theory of directed culture change that stresses the understanding of how existing indigenous institutions can provide the basis for development models, based on a consideration of the environment, the use of local human and natural resources, and the belief systems.[1] Arturo Escobar notes the current requirement by agencies such as the U.S. Agency for International Development (AID) that project implementation be preceded by a social soundness analysis that assesses the feasibility of development projects and their relevance to the socioeconomic environment.[2] This often does not go far enough.

There has been a tendency to attribute development failure to certain notions about non-Western primal communities. It is assumed that indigenous cultures constrain their own mobility toward economic and technological development; that they slow down agricultural change; and that they contain destructive aspects and retarding features that ought to be eliminated.[3] Some say that their behaviors are not well-thought-out, being guided by complex social and cultural factors. From these shibboleths, advocacy positions have emerged in Western worldviews, replacing both local strategies and the enculturation of non-Western attitude as prerequisites to development and the adaptation of traditional modes to modern technology and systems.[4]

Underlying jaundiced perceptions are clashing worldviews that are informing the definition of development. Western economic perspectives define development in aggregative terms—gross national product, gross domestic product, and the like. Continuing colonial ideals, these perspectives purport to measure socioeconomic progress. Modernization theory has merely articulated more precisely the old idea of progress through successive stages of economic growth. These views separate economic growth from religion. Indeed, it was hoped that religion and ethnicity would disappear.[5] The eradication of religion has not occurred. Rather, there has been a decline in the belief that science and public life are based solely on objective, rational assumptions that have nothing to do with personal or communal beliefs. Questions reassert themselves: Can religious activities be separated from development? Are they compatible? Does the implementation of one enhance or hinder the effectiveness of the other? How do beliefs and ideologies influence resource management?

There has been a paradigm shift toward a holistic concept of development and sustainability, which recognizes the integration of economic, social, and ecological aspects into the process of change. There is a growing recognition of cultural diversity as an ongoing global reality, as opposed to the assumption of increasing homogenization found in modernization theory. For us in Africa, the paradigm shift in theory of knowledge is crucial because of the failure of the agricultural sector on the continent and the horrendous scale of environmental degradation. Worse is the lack of an ecological policy. The paradigm shift should enable us to return to the drawing board to devise a development strategy that is inclusive, more sensitive to the full range of social realities, and conscious of the method, context, and content of change. Tension is inherent in cultural exchanges. Indeed, says David Uru Iyam, "Local circumstances also embody important cultural elements and practices that discourage development initiatives by both external and local agents and constrain the realization of desirable changes in rural communities.[6] Iyam demonstrates this with a fascinating study of the Biase people of the Cross River basin. He neither romanticizes nor trivializes this indigenous culture. Yet, he asks, to what extent are development failures due to the indigenous worldview and the coping mechanism that they legitimate? As Murray Bookchin would argue, to advocate a return to rustic simplicity is unrealistic and naïve.[7] Indeed, urban dwellers often endeavor to coax villagers to preserve primal cultures, while the latter lust after industrial goods. This suggests a search for factors within particular societies that either condone antinature attitudes or promote friendly practices. Many in the West attribute environmental abuse to human arrogance in the exploitation of natural resources. This may be so in some cases, but abuse might also arise from vulnerability and ignorance, as well as from a lack of technological capacity for taming nature. A deeply religious perception of nature may also make a people vulnerable.

Sensitivity to such wider vistas of the problem enables us to see development as liberating efforts to *supplement* indigenous knowledge and institutions. Development involves a modification of both material and nonmaterial factors. It occurs when "a community initiates an adjustment of the ideational and attitudinal components of culture so that enhancing factors are activated for improving an existing state of affairs."[8] It would involve a cognitive disposition by the community to modify their affairs and a mobilization and utilization of their entire populace, men and women.They must be willing to reassess traditional rights and privileges. Here, the gender issue is cogent, because many have connected environmental abuse with the abuse of women and children.[9]

From this perspective, development process runs along a certain groove, utilizing the adaptive nontechnological cultural elements that influence the economic process of communities. The shift from perceiving peasants as tradition-bound to imaging them as rational opens the way to modification of their worldviews in such a manner that closed systems open to the imperatives and possibilities of changes. This is what Robin Horton calls "the open predicament."[10]

The Sacred Egg: Anatomy of Worldview

Indigenous cultures are underpinned by worldviews which serve as reservoirs of knowledge. They are stored in proverbs and folk myths. Myths of origin abound, explaining how the world came into existence. One of these imagines the world as a sacred egg, at once fragile, enfolding, and nurturing. Its sacred origin imbues it with a sacral order which, when understood and followed, would ensure a miracle, namely, that this seemingly fragile frame has the capacity to sustain so many and so much activity. We shall return to this precarious vision later.[11]

From such myths, people begin to construct how and why things are the way they are. Explanation aids prediction of space-time events, and this in turn enables control. Myths of origin are, therefore, the vehicles of worldviews and differ among the ethnic groups who inhabit West Africa. A common structure underlies all of them, and they share a deep-seated meaning. Each is couched in religious, numinous terms: creation was the act of a Supreme Being utilizing the services of subaltern gods. The divine origin confers a sacred shroud on the created beings and the social order.

People, therefore, construct a world order, with a certain rhythm, in order to explain, predict, and control life situations in their ecosystem. This view of the world is a mental construct that empowers peoples' actions and endows both rhythm and meaning to life processes. It is the foundation of customs, social norms, and law. Worldviews are embedded in the people's experience and then expressed or reenacted in their cultures. This can be illustrated with one cultural feature, masquerades. These are very important in the rituals, festivals, aesthetics, and plastic arts. Masqueraders from semi-savannah, grassland communities tend to be clothed in dry grass. Some look like moving bundles of grass. Among the forest-zone dwellers, the masqueraders leap out of the bushes as followers caparison them with leaves and branches. In the Owu Festival of riverine communities of the Niger Delta, the masqueraders arrive in canoes and wear masks depicting various kinds of fishes. The community dances to the waterfront, welcomes them with a chorus into the village, and the celebration begins. At dusk, the masqueraders are led back to the beach; as they paddle off, the people wave and cry for the departing ancestors. That is the crux of the cultural form: the masqueraders are ancestors; they are the gods coming as guests to the human world. With their arrival, the seen and the unseen worlds meet; the living and the living-dead reunite, even if only for a brief period. The Owu cultural form is a celebration of a certain worldview explaining the moral order.

The environment poses a challenge, and the community constructs a worldview which unravels the riddle of the universe. It must address and reflect the specific nature of the challenge by probing its inner experience. People forge culture in the encounter with and effort to tame their environment and harness her resources for the nurture of that community. Worldviews underpin the culture. As culture is the powerful expression of the creativity of the human spirit, the engine that moves civilization and the substance of history, worldview is the hermeneutic, "the cultural lens through which human experience is viewed."[12]

Various anthropologists have sought to capture the nuances of worldview: some call it "mind-world" and explore the differences between Western and non-Western mind-worlds. The ethnologist Edward Sapir termed it "the unconscious patterning of behavior in society . . . the way a people characteristically look outward on the universe." Patterns of thought, attitudes toward life, conceptions of time, a mental picture of what ought to be, a people's understanding of their relationship to unseen things and to the order of things, and their view of self and others—all these, he noted, are included in a people's worldview.[13]

Paul G. Hiebert organizes the content of worldview into three categories: cognitive, affective, and evaluative. These refer to abstract ideas, interpersonal structures, and ethical values.[14] Charles Kraft underscores the place of values in a worldview as "the culturally structured assumptions, values and commitments underlying a people's perception of reality."[15] They are deep-level bases from which people generate surface-level behavior. Therefore, concludes Marguerite Kraft, "worldviews affect how people perceive self, the in-group to which they belong, outsiders, nature around them and [the] non-human world . . . [and] makes it possible for people to feel comfortable in their environment. . . . Worldview is a picture of what is and ought to be, and it provides the motivation for behavior and gives meaning to the environment."[16] It is, indeed, as John Grim puts it, "a story of the world which informs all aspects of life among a people, giving subsistence practices, artistic creation, ritual play and military endeavor a significant content."[17] Like the rest of culture, worldview can be unconsciously learned but deliberately transmitted. It can become enclosed in customs safe in the womb-like warmth of the sacred egg. But, however resistant to the battering waves of change, the enclosure begins to crack as the process of reconfiguration and reconstruction moves forward.

In an effort to demonstrate the relationship between African and Western scientific thought patterns, Robin Horton insisted that worldview is like theory building and is, therefore, a "quest for the unity underlying apparent diversity; for the simplicity underlying apparent complexity and for order underlying disorder; for the regularity underlying apparent anomaly."[18] Worldview goes further: it brings into causal relationship wider vistas of reality and everyday life. Drawing on the Kalabari worldview, Horton demonstrated that the fears and hopes and religious ardor of the Kalabari could easily be understood by looking closely at three basic kinds of forces: ancestors, heroes, and water spirits. Appreciating the idiom of the Kalabari's "mystical" thinking may not only solve the riddle of "primitive mentality" that so bothered Lucien Levy-Bruhl, but may also explain the factors within the mental matrix of the community that help them survive in their ecosystem. The Kalabari can link visible, tangible events as natural effects to their spiritual antecedents as if in the same world of natural causes.

Are worldview constructs simply fantasy? Meyer Fortes, in his study of the theories of the individual and his relationship to society among the Tallensi (Ghana), demurs. He takes the "multiple soul" beliefs of the Tallensi and places them in everyday thought and behavior, as a Westerner would link psychological imperatives and sociological imperatives.[19] The activities of gods and spirits celebrated in rituals and festivals play out, in the social space, much of the concerns of daily living. This is what Peter Berger calls the "cosmization of the social world."[20] He adds that "such a cosmos, as the ultimate ground and validation of human nomoi, need not necessarily be sacred."

Clearly, neither culture nor worldview is static. Indeed, some have surmised the existence of three publics in African social analysis: the primal setting where the gods of our fathers hold sway; the intrusive Western public setting; and the emergent public setting forged in the exegesis of the latter, a public setting that is neither African nor European. Fela Ransome-Kuti, the Afro-jazz maestro, characterizes the emergent public as "shakara." On his album *Authority Stealing,* he explores the moral implications of these cultural shifts, satirizing the nouveaux riches who would steal money from the Western public and dance to the big drum in the indigenous public. The incursion of emergent culture into the primary sector erodes the salient values of the latter without providing an adequate replacement, creating tension and lack of discipline. The people of the emergent culture perceive the Western public environment as other than theirs, and in that environment practice values that cannot be tolerated in the primary public setting. There is a certain sense of moral anomie. The trouble arises when the same people assume leadership roles in their villages. They become bearers of unwholesome values which, like viruses, destroy the traditional value systems. The appeal for American junk culture among youths in the emergent public setting puts an enervating pressure on traditional institutions. The impact of new worldviews within indigenous cultures constitutes one aspect of the task of this paper. The broader goal is, as J. Baird Callicott put it, "The revival and deliberate construction of environmental ethics from the raw materials of indigenous, traditional and contemporary cultures."[21]

Anthill in the Marsh: The African's Precarious Vision of the World

It has been argued that underlying the varieties of cultures in Africa is a core worldview structure (see figure 1). Details may vary, even within an ethnic group. Crucial are the concepts of time and space. Mircea

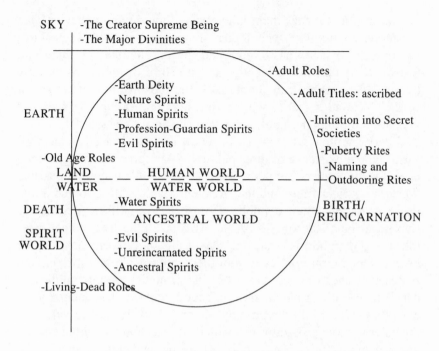

SKY   -The Creator Supreme Being
       -The Major Divinities

EARTH
                    -Earth Deity
                    -Nature Spirits
                    -Human Spirits
                    -Profession-Guardian Spirits
                    -Evil Spirits
       -Old Age Roles
           LAND _ _ _ HUMAN WORLD _ _ _ _ _
           WATER   WATER WORLD
DEATH   -Water Spirits
                    ANCESTRAL WORLD
SPIRIT
WORLD   -Evil Spirits
                    -Unreincarnated Spirits
                    -Ancestral Spirits
       -Living-Dead Roles

-Adult Roles
-Adult Titles: ascribed
-Initiation into Secret Societies
-Puberty Rites
-Naming and Outdooring Rites
BIRTH/ REINCARNATION

Figure 1. African Worldview
*(adapted from Ogbu U. Kalu, "Precarious Vision: The African
Perception of His World," in* African Cultural Development: Readings in
African Humanities, *ed. Ogbu U. Kalu [Enugu, Nigeria: Fourth Dimension
Publishers, 1978])*

Eliade has argued that among traditional societies there is a predominant construction of the concept of time around the movement of the
agricultural season.[22] Time is cyclical, moving from planting to harvest, followed by a repeat of the eternal cycle. The myth of eternal
return is woven within this fabric. Life follows the pattern of nature,
moving from birth, through accession to various stages, rights, and
duties, symbolized by membership in one sodality or another, until
death. Matters do not end there; a new stage of living would begin as
the personality soul of the individual begins a journey through the
spirit world until reincarnation. To fill out the details, rites of passage
celebrate the various stages of life. At birth, the outdooring ceremony
not only provides an opportunity to declare who has returned to the
family, it covenants the individual to the land and the community.

Eight days earlier, the child's umbilical cord would have been put in a calabash and sprinkled with herbs and, after some pronouncements, buried under a tree at the back of the house. The child is rooted to the land with which it shares an everlasting bond. Through open and secret societies, the community would teach the child the salient values and coping mechanisms for deriving nurture from the ecosystem. In the *isi ji* ceremony among the Afikpo-Edda culture complex, adolescent boys are initiated by being sent to the bush to fend for themselves without parental aid for weeks. They live off the resources of the ecosystem, which are regarded as sufficient for all their needs. They are initiated into the secrets of the natural and symbiotic relationship between them and nature.[23] Among the Biase, Ejagham, and Igbo groups on the banks of the Cross River, the *akang* secret societies serve the same function and the initiation ceremony is similar. The *poro* ceremony, which enjoys wide provenance in West Africa, contains elements affirming an identical ecological ideology.

The relationship between the child and the ecosystem is reinforced by the creation myth. The account in the Ifa system appears in most other accounts, with some variation. The Supreme Being delegates gods to create the earth, giving one of them the task of forming the body from clay. But the Supreme Being himself breathes the soul into each human being. Another deity is chosen by the unborn child as the guardian of its destiny. The Igbo call this guardian Chi. The Yoruba call the guardian Ori, as in this Ifa verse:

> *Ori,* I salute you.
> *Ori,* nicknamed *atete niran.*
> He who first blesses a man before any other *orisa*
> No divinity blesses a man without the consent of his *Ori.*
> *Ori,* I salute you.
> You allow children to be born alive.
> A person whose sacrifices are accepted by his *Ori* should rejoice.[24]

At a certain point, the individual accedes to decision-making roles (becoming one of the "judges" of the community and sitting with other elders to make decisions and govern the community—an ascribed authority rather than an achieved one) and when death comes, the unity of the seen and unseen worlds becomes clear in the funerary rites. J. S. Mbiti, in *African Religion and Philosophy,* and Christian Gaba, in his analysis of the sacred songs and prayers of the Anlo

People of Ghana, both emphasized that the human world is a replica of the spirit world.[25] This explains the ritual of burying a slave alive so that he can continue to serve the "achieved person"—one who has achieved the status and life goals of the community, such as wealth, large family, respect of the people—through the journey. People retain the status they held in the human world, and the passage through the spirit world is referred to as a journey. The return is reincarnation, reserved for those who lived honest lives and did not die from inexplicable diseases or from lightning—a punishment from the gods for a secret offence. As an Ifa *odu,* or verse, puts it: "all the good things of life that a man has, if he lacks good character, they belong to someone else." The person will not be able to join his earthly family to enjoy the legacy. Even as the personality soul sojourns in the ancestral world, he remains a part of his family and is endowed with spiritual powers to provide greater aid to his family.

My interest here is not in mining the depths of this worldview, but in focusing on its core structure, with its predominantly religious character. The various names for God reflect his presence in response to the challenges of the ecosystem. Jan Platvoet has argued that major traits of African indigenous religions are embedded in environmental and cultural concerns that "differ markedly after the specific economic use which a society makes of the food resources of its environment for its livelihood."[26] Tumai Nyajeka has argued, from data among the Shona, that the circle, as a shape, can be said to symbolize accurately the nature of the indigenous world, defying the search for a beginning and an end and a hierarchical structure. Life is an organic web. The living and the dead are united. The spiritual and the manifest worlds flow together in a circle.[27]

Although there are three dimensions of space—the sky, the earth (land and water), and the ancestral worlds—they are all united. In 1927 R. S. Rattray described the Ashanti world as "an alive universe."[28] Indeed, the sky was once very near to the earth. When women who were pounding meal constantly hit the sky with their pestles, the Supreme God lifted the sky a little higher out of their way. Etiological myths soon yield to historical consciousness in the pursuit of the unity of the cosmos by imbuing each space with powerful forces. The sky gods, usually male, manifest as Sun, Lightning, Thunder, and the like. Among them is the moon in full beauty, female and inspiring aesthetics and creativity, giving her own light that evokes songs and dances. Otherwise, the sky gods serve as judges, oracles, and arbiters. People swear by them. The sun carries sacrifices above and mediates blessings. The earth consists of land and water. It is said that after the gods finished creation, forming land out of the anthill in the marsh, they stayed, inhabiting various features of the earth—mountains, rocks, rivers, and streams. Land is the heart of the matter. It is under the guardianship of the earth goddess, whose shrine is prominent in many communities. For example, the Mbari Museum in southeastern Nigeria has one of the most elaborate of these shrines in West Africa.

The earth goddess nurtures the communities with her fertility. However, she is more revered in subculture theaters, which suffer acute land shortage or which are endowed with significant land features. G. J. A. Ojo draws attention to the fact that some communities regard hills as their protectors and revere them.[29] People in savannah zones tend to use the hills as shrines for sending messages to God. They name their children after the hills. Land is so sacred that people swear by her, and her powerful allure is the source of "tribalism"in politics.

Trees are often reverenced as being imbued with spirits. Massive trunks and buttresses attract religious ardor—the silk-cotton tree (*Eriodendron orientale*), iroko (*Chlorophora excelsa*), or baobab (*Adansonia digitata*) in deciduous forest areas. It is believed that the *Newboldia Laevis,* or *akoko,* is inhabited by mischievous spirits which come as babies but soon return to the spirit world, breaking the hearts of families. The African satinwood (*Cordia Milleni*) is found to be useful and is inhabited by a munificent spirit. Many believe that, because it is good for making drums, it must be inhabited by a musically inclined spirit. Abnormal trees attract dreadful reverence— for instance, a palm tree with seven trunks or sixteen branches. In Gbarnga, Liberia, a trunk which the community had harvested as firewood suddenly rose again, alive, despite the marks of the axe. The community cordoned it off with palm fronds, marking it as sacred.

Usually, some specific trees on the road to a village are alleged to be protectors standing at the gates of communities. Such trees are linked to trees in the market squares. Shrubs or trees in the market are sacred, and communal sacrifices are made at their feet for the well-being of the entire community and to attract the patronage of neighboring villages to that market. Market days are sacred and on those days farming activities are forbidden. Age grades are assigned to sweep and clean the market square. Taboos define the market square as the abode of benevolent spirits. Fighting and stealing are considered heinous crimes. Production, exchange, and distribution are sacralized. G. H. Jones quipped about the West African that "the towering vegetation silently growing and overwhelming his huts and cultivation, shutting him in, must have filled him with a sense of awe and impotence and fear."[30] Little did Jones realize that indigenous worldviews provided for conservation ethics to ensure the sustenance and protection of land.

Just as the marketplace was sacred, so was the farmland. Contact with farmland was circumscribed by taboos, supervised by various deities under the earth goddess. Such taboos included: 1) Communities must perform fertility rituals before land distribution begins. 2) People must wait for everyone to commence bush clearing before setting fires. 3) Harvesting may not start until the yams at the fertility deity's shrine have been harvested. 4) There is a prohibition against processing certain kinds of food in the village. The processing of cassava must be done outside the village and by the river—possibly for hygienic and health reasons, to remove the cyanide acid properly and protect the goats from ingesting these harmful chemicals. 5) Sexual intercourse in the bush, especially on farmland, is severely prohibited: it may be illicit, and it is an abomination committed on the face of the earth goddess. 6) Fighting, and especially threatening someone with a farm implement, is prohibited. 7) No one may go to the farm to fetch firewood on a market day—thus avoiding the temptation to steal from a farm. 8) The yam god kills those who steal from other people's barns or from agricultural products heaped on the roadside. 9) To harvest another person's hunting trap or fish trap will incur the wrath of the patron deity, who may resort to using thunder or lightning. These taboos and many more ensure the orderly utilization of the resources of nature.The gods control how resources are used. The yam deity, for instance, indicates through a diviner the areas of the farmland to be farmed each year. Crop rotation and preservation of the soil through fallow farming is given sacred sanction.

Many animals are protected in a similar manner. Some communities regard the monkey as the embodiment of the ancestors, others as the embodiment of dead twins. In drier parts of tropical Africa, vultures are reincarnated ancestors. Pythons and many other animals are totem kin and cannot be killed. The Igbo and many other groups recognize that spirits operate in the human world through animals, birds, and fish. In the air, bats, birds, such as owls, crows, and vultures, and insects, such as flies, bees, and soldier ants, may have spiritual importance. On the land, lower animals, such as lizards, tortoises, chameleons, and snakes, may be empowered. Higher animals, such as rats, monkeys, dogs, cats, leopards, lions, tigers, chickens, and humans may also be spirits. Finally, marine animals, such as crocodiles, water snakes, electric fish, and gold fish may be spirits. Michael Jackson discussed attitudes toward elephants among the Kuranko of the Sierra Leone.[31] Some of the Kuranko claim that they can turn into elephants so as to work revenge on their enemies. The interesting point here is that the categories of sacred animals are selected from the three dimensions of air, land, and water, further imbuing the whole universe with sacred quality.

Equally interesting is the attitude toward domestic animals. One is forbidden from killing a pregnant goat or of disturbing a sheep or a goat during parturation. In some villages, such animals are tethered and their droppings used for manure in the garden.

Land is so sacred that it is regarded as the guardian of morality. Interpersonal offences are perceived as polluting her sanctity; secrecy and covenanting bonds are sealed by swearing by her. In decision-making processes, matters are sealed by knocking the staff of authority onto the ground. The earth and the ancestors unite in creating a theory of obligation in communities where there is no secular theory of obligation. Ancestors are buried in the earth's womb, and libations are offered to placate them and to invoke their intervention in human affairs. In certain communities, the chief occasionally performs a ceremony in which he inquires through the priest of the earth deity whether he still enjoys her support. This evaluation exercise keeps the ethics of power from becoming oppressive. Ancestors and the earth deity are crucial to social control, key factors in socialization, restriction, punishment, and reward.[32]

A close taxonomy of deities would show that some communities perceive their water sources as daughters of the earth deity. Spirits inhabit water, and rivers that run long courses have shrines installed at various spots. Ifi Amadiume has provided a rich cameo of this.[33] Marine spirits are female and give wealth, fertility, beauty, and political influence. They inspire musicians and balladiers. Several marine cults figure prominently in ethnographic studies of this region and there is little need for repetition here. Elaborate festivals are held in honor of rivers that are the protectors of communities. Springs are also protected with taboos and sacrifices to ensure that they do not dry up and that drought does not plague the people.[34]

In my research project "Gods of Our Fathers: A Taxonomy of Igbo Deities" I explored a methodology for studying worldviews, focusing on the names, natures, functions, provenance sacrifices, and genders of the priests of each deity. The deities were distributed according to subculture theaters. Using a sample of 615 deities, it was possible to show the organic nature of the worldview and how the emphases in each culture area are related to the predominant ecological challenges. For instance, though the earth deity is said to be so important, she is paid less elaborate attention by riverine communities. The culture areas prioritized seven archetypes according to their needs: oracular, earth, nature, water, guardian/patron, ancestral, and spirit force.[35]

I expect that a similar pattern would be true for the wider West African environment. Some communities have engaged in long-distance trade and therefore have risked their worldview to wider perspectives. In others, secret societies have predominated as the guardians of indigenous knowledge. Some developed pictographic writing, but the severe ambits of secrecy prevented the skill from developing.[36] In all West African communities there is an emphasis on tapping spiritual forces to augment coping abilities. This is because existence is precarious.

In one liturgy, the votary gives oblation to both the munificent and the malevolent gods, saying that he came to the world and found them at loggerheads. He is ignorant of the cause for their disagreement and would rather be left out of the controversy. This is easier said than done. According to Ifa texts, the Yoruba believe that there are two pantheons of gods who compete for the domination of the universe. There are four hundred benevolent gods and two hundred hostile ones. Between them and the Supreme Being is Eshu, a capricious deity who can bring aid or cause harm depending on the sacrifice given. In this cosmology the good gods want to bless, while the evil ones would thwart personal and societal goals. This precarious vision induces an ethic of stewardship, care, and attention to the unity of all creation. The world is a sacred egg in which humans weave covenants with the good gods so as to ward off the machinations of the evil gods. A covenantal understanding of this worldview is crucial. Festivals are sacred moments for reenergizing and renewing covenants with the gods of the sky, land, water, and ancestral world. Jacob Olupona has examined the political implications in the use of festivals to legitimate the sacralized political order.[37] Taboos delineate the bounds of behavior, while the boundary between the sacred and the profane collapses.

"The sacred," according to Peter Berger, is

> a quality of mysterious and awesome power, other than man and yet related to him, which is believed to reside in certain objects of experience. This quality may be attributed to natural or artificial objects, to animals or to men. . . . The sacred cosmos is confronted by man as an immensely powerful reality other than himself. Yet this reality addresses itself to him and locates his life in an ultimately meaningful order.[38]

Since this order was created from the anthill in the marsh, darkness ever threatens. Nature is at once a nurturer and mysterious, wild, uncontrollable, and unpredictable. Human beings are hardly the masters.[39]

This order requires salient moral values for it to be maintained. The Ifa system of proverbs for divination is found in many parts of West Africa, including Nigeria, Benin, and Togo and especially among the Yoruba, Fon, Igbo, Edo, and Ewe. It teaches a number of normative values, including hardwork, self-help, good character, and maintenance of nature through sacrifice. "Sacrifice is the weapon that brings about resolution and tranquility in a universe in which conflict is the order of the day."[40] Ifa divination teaches deep reverence for nature. Thus, libations, spells, incantations, and chants are used as modes of communication. When a herbalist sets out for the forest, he pours libation to the patron deity and, inside the forest, he uses chants and incantation to arouse the healing herbs to draw attention to themselves. He calls them by their secret names and they respond. Pharmaceutical efficacy is achieved through ritual. The patron deities are addressed as human beings. For instance, according to Abimbola, the mountain is addressed as "The old immortal man on top of a locust bean tree: if the locust bean tree does not fall down, the fat old man will not descend therefrom. Good health and immortality are the attributes of the mountain."[41] Nyajeka concludes that among the Shona of Zimbabwe cosmology is non-anthropocentric, "but at the same time celebrates as unique the experience of being human in the universe."[42]

In West Africa, much of the religious ardor is spent on environmental matters. As Sara Mvududu shows with data from Zimbabwe, environmental changes tend to have severe effects on families. Deforestation vitiates the energy supply, drought and soil degradation ruin the food sources, and there are no synthetic alternatives as there are in the West.[43] Patterns of spirituality preserve fragile and vulnerable elements in human-nature relationship. As the old priestess said, the world is like an egg that can easily break; and, if it does, we are ruined. Therefore, we regularly give eggs to the gods in sacrifice so that they may remember and gently preserve us.

The Open Predicament: Primal Knowledge and Development

In spite of the sacralization of the environment, the question still remains whether primal cultures of West Africa promoted healthy ecological ethics. How do beliefs and ideology influence resource management? David Iyam underscores this point when he points to three contemporary trends: 1) the capacity of indigenous practices to manage rural social organization has been overwhelmed by the demands of new cultural elements generated from within and outside the society; 2) the resulting reconfiguration of indigenous institutions renders them less effective for communal management; and 3) consequently, a weakened array of cultural conventions and institutions have become minimally able to influence rural socioeconomic relations and have created disadvantageous conditions for economic growth.[44]

The internal source of the weakening process could be related to the fact that primal cultures responded to the challenges of nature in a vulnerable manner. Vulnerability is the inability to control one's response to challenges. Does veneration constitute stewardship? Veneration as a coping mechanism was a vulnerable response that was not supplemented with resource management. There was little of the ethic of replenishment. The tendency was to tap the resources of nature but leave it to the gods to replenish the earth. For instance, if one wanted to use satinwood, one would go to the tree with a pot of palm oil and entice the spirit inhabiting the tree to come down for a meal. During the interval, the man tricking the spirit would fell the tree. There was, however, no cult of tree planting. Population pressure and intensified land use led to abandonment and resettlement. Thus, new settlements grew up in farmlands, usually identifiable by their names which would indicate that they were new outgrowths of old settlements. Glenn Davis Stone has contrasted the "yeoman" and the "entrepreneurial" attitudes.[45] Indigenous ethics were at heart environmentally friendly, but lacked a sustainability suited to modern pressures. This raises the question about how that ethic can be utilized in a more entrepeneurial manner.

An analysis of features of indigenous worldviews as obstacles to ecological development would include seven crucial areas. 1) Environmental changes are sometimes due to natural sources, but intensified and insensitve land use—such as unplanned habitat structure, road-building, procuring laterite for house construction, and other practices which intensify soil leeching—explains much. Moreover, pollution of rivers often caused the silting of waterways without the benefit of dredging technology. 2) Sociocultural factors, such as kinship lineage and landholding patterns, may affect the availability of arable land for the community. When authority structures were strong, the elders, with their wisdom, could obviate obstructionist tendencies. 3) Agricultural practices, such as bush burning, removes nutrients from the top soil and affects the quality of the yield. Lack of facilities for storage of surplus and a poor distribution network because of fixed market days combine to keep production at a subsistence level. 4) Poor infrastructural facilities, and resulting inaccessibility, compound difficulties for many communities.Lack of adequate health care delivery, water supply, and education vitiate new opportunities and encourage urban migration, which spirals into the mobilization of a new power node and purveyors of a new worldview. 5) Cultural factors—a gender ideology—prevent women, the primary entrepreneurs, from maximizing market opportunities. Patriarchy diminishes the role of men in production and reproduction and, thus, the full labor force is not mobilized. At the same time, men lose respect and authority in their families and that affects the capacity of the political system to mobilize the entire populace toward an identifiable social goal. 6) The breakdown of social control models due to emergent values, or the growing challenge to traditional beliefs and practices, says Iyam, has resulted in a loss of awe in and reverence for traditional belief systems.[46] The absence of any visible supernatural retribution as a punishment for violating proscriptive rules has demystified the deities, and elders and many community members have become unwilling to cooperate on locally initiated projects. The power that moves the living universe is weakening. 7) Certain festivals, especially those related to communal ancestral rites that tend to last for months or even a year, are wasteful of time and material goods because they obstruct capital accumulation.

These obstacles are not barriers. Rather, they merely raise what Robin Horton has called "open predicament," models for configuring closed systems into open ones. It is clear that the so-called closed systems are not closed inflexibly. On the contrary, as indigenous societies changed, so did the highly dynamic and adaptable religions, which were unencumbered by fixed canonical scriptures. There was a built-in adaptability resulting in part from loose articulation of beliefs and in part from the fact that certain cults were attached to institutions and sets of social relations and were liable to change. Some years ago, the Association of African Earthkeeping Churches was formed in Zimbabwe with a commitment to healing a severely degraded environment after the recent civil war. Interestingly, such an association has emerged among the indigenous Shona peoples as well, called the Independent African Christian Churches. Both of these incorporate ingredients of traditional African culture in reconstructing and directing their faith toward tree-planting projects.[47] They engage in the conservation of wildlife, water purification, and reforestation by establishing environmental hospitals dispensaries. Most importantly, they have developed inter-religious rituals called tree-planting eucharists. The rituals tap salient aspects of indigenous knowledge and ritual life, but also add a missing element—conscious, proactive conservation. They translate and adapt indigenous knowledge for a modern need.

For development ethics, they suggest listening, learning, and translation. Projects should be fitted into the worldview of the community, empowering it to move to a new level of human development with as little disruption as possible. To end with the case that I mentioned at the outset, the West African Amanuke community claimed that its forefathers moved across the Niger and Anambra Rivers and settled on a certain spot. The ancestral shrine was built on the southern edge of a large tract of land. By balancing the types of crops and through rotation and the preservation of a large tract of virgin forest, the community has managed, for over a century, to keep its members well fed. Inaccessibility protected them. Then the government came with an irrigation project designed to enrich arable land for many communities. One possible outcome was that as soon as the pumps began operating, the state could invoke the land-use decree to declare the entire tract government property. The government would then parcel out portions to the Amanuke farmers, who would become tenants on their own land. Diminished control subverted Amanuke indigenous life, and the loss of emotional attachment to the ancestral shrine was acute.

The community's greatest need was not irrigation. The people were not resistant to change. Indeed, they had built a secondary school at their own expense. The proposed project merely divided the community and left it vulnerable to outside agents of change. The Amanuke sense of indigenous development was more holistic than the outside state development model. The Amanuke recognized the implications of change for all areas of their life. Amanuke life was rooted in their primal beliefs, and in their own experiences of the ecosystem. The tensions resulting from recent technological development betrayed the gap between the urban elite and rural decision makers. An eloquent leader reminded the community of its glorious past and of the threats that modern development held for the future. The recitation was electrifying as some of the pro-government councillors were declared to be saboteurs.

Rural communities possess instruments of change that can be used for environmental healing and development. Beyond the web of kinship, there are age-grade societies, women's societies, and other secret societies. These evoke loyalties that are powerful. When traditional loyalties collapse under the anvil of modernity, these bastions of rural worldview could still be employed. People dread the loss of face that is the penalty for failing to fulfill obligations to one's age-grade society. Joking relationships are also a powerful instrument for shaming renegades who sell out to outsider influences.

The urban elite cannot be easily ignored, and their influence extends into the countryside. Village "improvement unions," for example, become powerful modern pressure groups for change and adaptation to modernity. They serve as the bridge or, to change the imagery, as priests guiding the emergent culture in becoming interpreters of modernity to their root cultures. This is reflected in Wole Soyinka's novel *The Interpreters,* in which he explores this dilemma of development for indigenous peoples.

Conclusion: The Future through the Rearview Mirror

My contention is that, although change brings tensions as the traditional worldview is besieged, by listening carefully to the calabash of wisdom, the path through the seven obstacles becomes apparent. Our folktales contain precedents describing how our ancestors went through seven forests to establish thriving communities. There is a call for deeper renewal in the midst of a culture of deconstruction, for directed change and worldview transformation that does not damage the community. Northrop Frye, the Canadian literary critic, wrote that the only guide to the future was through a rearview mirror. The challenge for our times is to address the problem of development failure in a new way, by reaching back to our oldest values of community and responsibility, by inspiring a greater respect for the land and its resources as something sacred. Each assault against African indigenous peoples is different and requires unique strategies.

The Amanuke case underscores certain principles for building an alternative development paradigm: 1) self-determination—the shaping of development strategies from the inside rather than from outside the region; 2) participation—the broad-based involvement of people in the definition and implementation of alternative strategies; 3) self-reliance—building upon local structures and capabilities in order to enable the region to redress its dependence on goods, resources, and assistance from outside the region; 4) equity—the fair distribution of the assets, resources, and other benefits of development among the various social groups, genders, and generations; 5) sustainability—the grounding of alternative strategies of development in a sound and secure environment and in local human capacity; 6) holism—the promotion of policies which give as much priority to social policy as to economic and which pay attention to the cultural and political needs of people, as well as to the economic and social. Before Christianity came, West African societies believed that in the beginning, God made the whole inhabited earth, and that his spirit brooded over it as the hen would brood over her egg. The Christian implications embedded in these indigenous metaphors point toward the realities of syncretism and mixing that has occurred between these religious traditions.

There are enormous resources within the Christian tradition for developing an environmentally friendly ethic. The structure and promises of the covenant are embedded in sacral understanding of nature.

When misused, the earth will cry out and groan for liberation. Ecological disasters become an aspect of social sin, and social injustices have catastrophic consequences on the ecological sphere, affecting animals and plants. Poverty has ecological roots. A sensitive approach to environment, in spite of the misused dominion passage in Genesis, is by divine directive.[48] This has immense implications for Africa because of the effects of the decline of the agricultural sector of the economy and the decline in health issues. The World Bank Report of 1992 estimates that tropical deforestation occurred at the rate of 0.1 percent annually during the 1980s in Sub-Saharan Africa.[49] There has been a loss of watershed protection, local climatic changes, and lost coastal protection and fishing grounds. Ironically, there is an inverse relationship between environmental protection and reduction of poverty; yet poverty is both a cause and effect of environmental problems. For instance, debt burden, the Structural Adjustment Program (imposed by the World Bank/IMF agencies), and the collapse of the economy have made it impossible for African countries to spend on environmental preservation. The population is exposed to diseases. The growth strategies have caused pollution of the air, water, and land. Population growth has intensified land use and destroyed the quality of soil and forest. There is, therefore, an acute need to address the dire relationship between poverty and environmental degradation; the possibility of achieving development through environmentally friendly strategies; and the imperative for indigenous peoples and Christian churches to approach these matters together.

Notes

1. David Uru Iyam, *The Broken Hoe: Cultural Reconfiguration in Biase, Southeast Nigeria* (Chicago: University of Chicago Press, 1995), 205.

2. Arturo Escobar, "Anthropology and the Development Encounter," *American Ethnologist* 18, no. 4 (1991): 658–82.

3. Carlos Ramirez-Faria, *Origins of Economic Inequality between Nations: A Critique on Western Theories of Development and Underdevelopment* (London and Boston: Unwin Hyman, 1991).

4. E. L. Shiawoya, "Small-scale Farmers, Local Goverments and Traditional Rulers in Agricultural Production," in *The Role of Traditional Rulers and Local Governments in Nigerian Agriculture*, ed. Adefolu Akinbode, Bryan Stoten, and Rex Ugorji (Ilorin, Nigeria: Agriculture and Rural Management Training Institute, 1986); Escobar, "Anthropology and the Development Encounter."

5. W. van Geest, "Development and Other Religious Activities," *Together: A Jounal of World Vision International* 55 (July–Sept. 1997): 1–8.

6. Iyam, *The Broken Hoe*, 7.

7. David R. Kinsley, *Ecology and Religion: Ecological Spirituality in Cross-cultural Perspective* (Englewood Cliffs, N.J.: Prentice Hall, 1995), 212.

8. Iyam, *The Broken Hoe*, 1.

9. Eleanor Rae, *Women, the Earth, the Divine* (Maryknoll, N.Y.: Orbis Books, 1994); *Women Healing Earth: Third World Women on Ecology, Feminism, and Religion*, ed. Rosemary Radford Ruether (Maryknoll, N.Y.: Orbis Books, 1996).

10. Robin Horton, *The Patterns of Thought in Africa and the West: Essays on Magic, Religion, and Science* (Cambridge: Cambridge University Press, 1993).

11. Ogbu U. Kalu, "Precarious Vision: The African Perception of His World," in *African Cultural Development: Readings in African Humanities*, ed. Ogbu U. Kalu (Enugu, Nigeria: Fourth Dimension Publishers, 1978).

12. Marguerite G. Kraft, *Worldview and the Communication of the Gospel* (Pasadena, Calif.: William Carey Library, 1995), 20.

13. Cited in *Selected Writings of Edward Sapir in Language, Culture and Personality*, ed. D. G. Mandelbaum (Berkeley: University of California Press, 1958), 548.

14. Paul H. Hiebert, *Anthropological Insights for Missionaries* (Grand Rapids, Mich.: Baker Book House, 1985).

15. Charles H. Kraft, *Christianity with Power: Your Worldview and Your Experience of the Supernatural* (Ann Arbor, Mich.: Vine Press, 1989), 182.

16. Marguerite Kraft, *Worldview and the Communication of the Gospel*, 21.

17. *Worldviews and Ecology*, ed. Mary Evelyn Tucker and John Grim (Lewisburg, Pa.: Bucknell University Press, 1993), 42.

18. Horton, *The Patterns of Thought in Africa and the West*.

19. Meyer Fortes, *The Web of Kinship among the Tallensi: The Second Part of an Analysis of the Social Structure of a Trans-Volta Tribe* (London and New York: Published for International African Institute by Oxford University Press, 1949), and *Oedipus and Job in West African Religion* (Cambridge: Cambridge University Press, 1959).

20. Peter L. Berger, *Sacred Canopy: Elements of a Sociological Theory of Religion* (Garden City, N.Y.: Doubleday, 1967).

21. J. Baird Callicott, in *Worldviews and Ecology,* ed. Tucker and Grim, 32.

22. Mircea Eliade, *The Sacred and the Profane: The Nature of Religion,* trans. Willard R. Trask (New York: Harcourt, Brace, 1959).

23. S. Ottenberg, *Leadership and Authority in an African Society* (Seattle: University of Washington Press, 1971).

24. W. Abimbola, "Ifa: A West African Cosmological System," in *Religion in Africa: Experience and Expression,* ed. Thomas D. Blakeley, Walter E. A. van Beek, and Dennis L. Thomson (London: James Currey; Portsmouth, N.H.: Heinemann, 1994), 112.

25. John S. Mbiti, *African Religions and Philosophy* (Nairobi: Ibadan; London: Heinemann, 1969); *The Scriptures of an African People: Ritual Utterances of the Anlo,* trans., ed., and with an introduction by Christian R. Gaba (New York: NOK Publishers, 1973).

26. Jan Platvoet, "Religions of Africa in Their Historical Order," in *The Study of Religions in Africa: Past, Present, and Prospects,* ed. Jan Platvoet, James Cox, and Jacob Olupona (Cambridge: Roots and Branches; Stockholm: Almqvist and Wiksell, 1996), 52.

27. Tumai Nyajeka, "Shona Women and the Mutupo Principle," in *Women Healing Earth,* ed. Ruether, 135–42.

28. Robert Sutherland Rattray, *Religion and Art in Ashanti* (Oxford: Clarendon Press, 1927).

29. G. J. Afolabi Ojo, *Yoruba Culture: A Geographical Analysis* (London: University of London Press, 1966), 150.

30. G. H. Jones, *The Earth Goddess: A Study of Native Farming on the West African Coast* (London: Royal Empire Society, 1936), 193.

31. Michael Jackson, *Barawa and the Way Birds Fly in the Sky* (Washington, D.C.: Smithsonian Institution Press, 1986).

32. Ogbu U. Kalu, "Gods as Policemen: Religion and Social Control in Igboland," in *Religious Plurality in Africa: Essays in Honour of John S. Mbiti,* ed. Jacob K. Olupona and Sulayman S. Nyang (Berlin: Mouton de Gruyter, 1993), 109–31.

33. Ifi Amadiume, *Male Daughters, Female Husbands: Gender and Sex in an African Society* (London: Zed Press, 1987).

34. Ogbu U. Kalu, "Gods in Retreat: A Taxonomy of Igbo Deities" (Igbo Worldvew Seminar, Institute of African Studies, University of Nigeria, 1991).

35. Ogbu U. Kalu, *Embattled Gods: Christianization of Igboland, 1841–1991* (Lagos, Nigeria: Minaj Publishers, 1996), chap. 2.

36. Ogbu U. Kalu, "Nsibidi: Pictographic Communication in Pre-Colonial Cross River Basin Societies," *Cahier Etudes des Religions Africaines* 12, no. 23-24 (1978): 97–116.

37. Jacob K. Olupona, *Kingship, Religion, and Rituals in a Nigerian Community: A Phenomenological Study of Ondo Yoruba Festivals* (Stockholm: Almqvist and Wiksell International, 1991).

38. Berger, *Sacred Canopy,* 24.

39. Eleanor Rae pursues the implications of this for gender ideology in *Women, the Earth, the Divine*.

40. Abimbola, "Ifa: A West African Cosmological System," 106.

41. Ibid., 115.

42. Nyajeka, "Shona Women and the Mutupo Principle," 138.

43. Sara C. Mvududu, "Revisiting Traditional Management of Indigenous Woodlands," in *Women Healing Earth*, ed. Ruether, 143–60.

44. Iyam, *The Broken Hoe*, 2.

45. Glenn Davis Stone, *Settlement Ecology: The Social and Spatial Organization of Kofyar Agriculture* (Tucson: University of Arizona Press, 1996).

46. Iyam, *The Broken Hoe*, 209.

47. Marthinus L. Daneel, "African Independent Churches Face Challenge of Environmental Ethics," *Missionalia* 21, no. 3 (1993): 31–32, and "Earthkeeping Churches at the African Grass Roots," in *Christianity and Ecology: Seeking the Well-Being of Earth and Humans*, ed. Dieter T. Hessel and Rosemary Radford Ruether (Cambridge, Mass.: Harvard University Center for the Study of World Religions, 2000), 531–52.

48. *Ecology and Poverty: Cry of the Earth, Cry of the Poor*, ed. Leonardo Boff and Virgil Elizondo (London: SCM Press; Maryknoll, N.Y.: Orbis Books, 1995).

Melanesian Religion, Ecology, and Modernization in Papua New Guinea

SIMEON B. NAMUNU

Introduction

The purpose of this paper is to examine the relationship between Melanesian religious worldview and ecology.[1] My contention is that spirits and ecology are part of a single, complex Melanesian vision of life. Today, Melanesians themselves try to adapt their concept of life to a foreign model of life, namely, modernization.[2]

The process of modernization, which began with the colonial administration, is a process changing the Melanesian way of life. From the administration's point of view the Melanesians did not change in expected ways. The administration saw obstacles to change that had to be overcome. These obstacles were deemed to be magico-religious ones, mixed with socioeconomic complexities of relationships, values, and meanings held by Melanesians.

At that time Melanesia had been generally called an uncivilized region and its people thought not to be religious. Colonialists saw only heathenism and fear of evil spirits, intensely obvious at grave and burial sites.[3] This attitude persisted until the 1960s and gave Christian missionaries reason to pacify, permeate, and influence the passive Melanesian worldview through the aggressiveness of Western Christianity. What was not envisioned is that the traditional knowledge of places and peoples and the core values have much to contribute to happiness, security, peace, and other elements of power enshrined in the environment. Consequently, there has been some reaction by interest groups, such as cargo cults movements on Misima Island, the Paliau movement on Manus Island, the Mataungan movement on the Gazelle Peninsular, and others. I will contend that these cases all fall under the "give-and-take" paradigm of traditional religious worldview, which involves the Melanesian peoples and their traditional knowledge of places, how the people work to develop relationships with those places, and how places can contribute toward sustainable development of the environment.

To speak of "Melanesia" is too general; I will try to limit myself to the specific case of Misima Island, especially under the section "Spirits and Ecology," to demonstrate how Misiman cosmology plays out in terms of ecological concerns. But first, I will make some general statements about Melanesian worldview.

Melanesian Worldview

The general Melanesian worldview forms the fundamental base for stability in Melanesian societies. Bernard Narokobi describes the worldview:

> Melanesians certainly do not hold the secular belief that man exists of his own power and for his own ends. Man is born according to most ancient legends either of himself, or birds and animals or other entities. Upon his birth or creation the Melanesian man is endowed with a sense of history, purpose, a set of values, and a vision of the cosmos by which his life is guided. He is given a culture and autonomy within a defined community territorially and in terms of human relationships. Thus, he is born into a spiritual and a religious order. Much of his life is devoted towards the maintenance and promotion of that given order. For example, the Melanesian is born to the knowledge that he lives and works within a spirit world. His actions and his omissions are always being watched by the spirit world. Departure from that given or received spiritual order can only lead to immediate physical and temporal punishment.[4]

Here, Narokobi outlines a common holistic view of Melanesian religious values central to the practice of their cultures. Central values are "culturally structured to include assumptions, meanings, commitments and allegiances underlying people's perception of reality and their responses to those perceptions."[5] I call this "worldview."[6] A sense of the environment[7] is an important part of worldview. The environment is a place where humans, plants, animals, and various spirits play an important role in providing for the good life. The exchange of power links humans to spirits and to other living and nonliving organisms. The environment is filled with life, and that life is a gift from the spiritual order. People spend much time maintaining that spiritual order through friendly relationships with the environment in the form of reciprocal exchanges of giving (working, planting, sowing, relating, and sharing) and taking (reaping the benefits). Hence, the ecosystem is not merely a system of natural phenomena within the environment, but includes spiritual phenomena. The concern here is not scientific: rather, "the heart-beat . . . is a religious heart-beat."[8]

In this sense the environment is a place of worship, where the ancestors and other classes of spirit-gods are venerated. Spirits serve a function, toward a desired end of communal happiness. Life is a gift for service. It is the beginning of an end. Happiness is achieved as a final goal. Viewed in this sense, "life" is not limited by material things nor by earthly existence, but is preeminently pneumatic and numinous, as portrayed in Narokobi's prose.

This traditional knowledge leads to certain environmental practices. Intrinsic to this view is the belief in personal spirits. This worldview of spirits structures special relationships linking the natural resources and environment to the human dimension of life.

Today, Melanesian religions are recognized to be compatible in their ability to coexist with Christianity, either side-by-side or through contextual assimilation. At the same time, we note here the fact that Christianity, by and large, has secularized traditional knowledge and religious beliefs and is often a strong advocate of modernization in Melanesia.[9]

For this reason it is important now for us to return to our native places where our earthly community—our kinship relatives, friends, and spirit-gods—is at home in the natural and physical environment. These are places where everyone finds meaning and reason to be happy. Life, before the Europeans came, was surrounded with creative energies flowing through trees, grasses, streams and rivers, mountains, sea, sky and all the galaxies, animals, birds, and humans. The forests were untouched by logging, mining, and petroleum entrepreneurs. The ecosystem was viewed with awe. This is an ideal Melanesian vision of the beautiful earthly order, before the doctrine of progress and its negative deleterious energies were put into force.[10] To achieve this ideal vision, Melanesians have developed their socioreligious cultures, though imperfect, in order to maintain this ecologically harmonious relationship.

Myths, Rituals, and Ecology

Having stated the Melanesian worldview, I would like to go on to the next point: in Melanesian belief, unlike in Western thinking, ecology is holy. Ecology is a vehicle that encapsulates myths and rituals. And, "Every myth possesses as its kernel or ultimate reality some natural phenomenon or other, elaborately woven into a tale to an extent which sometimes almost masks and obliterates it."[11] What Malinowski calls "other," I interpret to mean cosmic organisms, such as flora and fauna of the ecosystem. I understand that what people recognize as life and well-being, they show interest in and verbalize their interest through poetic symbolism. Myth is a poetic form of symbolism in which people have artistically and scientifically described, in their traditional ways, their interest in nature. Ideas are incorporated into symbolic tales, making myth a "living imagination of cultural ideals with religious dynamism."[12]

The land and the sky are places of everyday events in life. Landscapes describe the events of myths and tell the story of the cosmology of the past events as symbols of life.[13] One story tells of the habitation of the spirits in caves, rocks, trees, mountains, rivers, valleys.[14] By and large, to the Melanesians, spirits are good to think about and good to live with each day.[15] Belief in, or knowledge of, spirits dwelling in the natural environment surrounding their village communities gives people a sense of security and meaning and responds to a deeper human longing for a happy life.

According to Melanesian experience, life is based on bio-cosmic relationships.[16] The Melanesian worldview is a primal conception of truth and reality emanating from the empirical observation of cosmic energies. When power and dynamism are demonstrated, the physical materials cannot resist these forces. A mark left on the material things signified the awesome presence of power. The Melanesians dignified the power of such an event with reverent mythical stories. The spirits, as the essence of creative power, are concerned with redeeming the community life from competing power structures. That is the primary concern of the Melanesian religious community. The creative energy is the spirits themselves; this is the source of physical and mental motivation toward the development of rituals, wherein work, place, and relationships are regarded as rituals expressing ultimate meaning and fulfilling religious life.

The Kewa people's ritualistic relationship with the bird of paradise in the Southern Highlands is one example. They have a myth about one species of bird of paradise. They believe that it has significant creative and regenerative power. The sound it makes and its colorful feathers carry creative energy for fertility and successful gaming activities whenever the Kewa people use them. The ritual, which functions as a redeeming activity within Kewa communal life, involves human participation in the movement of the bird. It sustains and renews the community and ensures the fertility of gardens, animals, and humans. The ritual seeks to reform and renew the community and to restore the environment. In these ways the ecosystem provides resources for the human community, which benefits from the economic value of wood, fish, water, land, birds, fresh air, food, and so on. For this reason Melanesians protect and preserve ecology while at work around their homes, gardens, graves, and places where awesome power is encountered.[17] Such places are places of respect to honor the spirits which guard the community. Can you imagine what could happen to life if such places are destroyed by a logging operation, a dam, or a mining operation? The whole cycle of life of the local inhabitants, both humans and the ecosystem, would be seriously jeopardized. Indigenous people are conscious of the relationship with their environment because it is the place where spirits live—spirits whose presence provides hope for the security, peace, and happiness they share together.

Let me illustrate this with an experience I had recently. My wife and I had decided to build a house in her village. The bush and forest trees on the land where the house now stands were clear-cut, allowed to dry, and then burned. The house was built, and in the fifteen-meter radius around the house I decided to leave the trees and forest undergrowth intact because I love its beauty. My wife's aunt, who lives in the house and looks after it, has a different reason for leaving the trees and undergrowth undisturbed.

As a village woman, she and her husband viewed the forest environment from their traditional knowledge of the place. She believes that the forest trees and their undergrowth are the spirits' abode. In

February 1998 my wife's brother cut trees within the ten-meter area outside of the fifteen-meter radius limit already cleared. I had agreed with my brother-in-law that the forest canopy within that ten meters limit should be cut because mosquitoes infest the area.

One evening, after the trees were cut down, my wife was on the lawn using a bucket of water to wash. It was dark and the fireflies started to come out. She noticed one firefly, which appeared to be blinking directly at her. Her hair stood on end, and she assumed this to indicate the presence of power. This happened several times, repeatedly, and made her wonder what it meant. She shared her experience with her aunt and received an astounding response. Her aunt said: "Ben should not have cut the trees down. Do you not know that these forest trees are the homes of our friends? Ben disturbed them [our friends] when he cut the trees and the vines and the undergrowth environment." By friends she meant the spirits of the forest whose watchful eyes and presence protect and enrich the village livelihood—gardens, domestic animals, fishing trips, trading ventures. The spirit friends were grieved by this act of disrespect because neither Ben nor my wife nor I performed or uttered any word of ritual apology or appeasement.[18]

Spirits and Ecology

This story directs our attention to a relationship Melanesians know to exist between spirits and ecology. Land is the home of the spirits. Land contains rivers, mountains, rocks, minerals, and habitation for humans. Land also grows trees and other flora species and provides homes for many species of fauna. So, when clearing land for gardening, there must be rituals symbolic of reciprocal relationships. For instance, a spirit locally known as *tokwa tokwa* in Dobu language, or *totowoho* in Misima language, is assumed to be the guardian of a village and the area within its boundary. If a foreigner, not known and not introduced to that guardian spirit, happens to be in the area, either the locals or the foreigner could get sick, an expression of the displeasure the spirit feels for not being consulted about who is in the area and for what purpose.

Let me illustrate this point in the following story an informant told me. A community decided to build a school. An area of land was selected and on a given day the whole village gathered to clear the school ground. In that place there also stood a big tree known to the locals as the home of a *totowoho*. In spite of what they knew of that tree, the villagers cut it down. My informant's uncle, who at that time was a small boy and, like all children, ignorant of the tree as a home to the spirit, decided to climb onto the stump of that tree and sit on it. The boy sat, singing joyfully, and nobody, even his father, bothered to stop him. Nothing happened to him at the end of the day and everyone went home after work.

That night as the family slept, the boy had an experience during his sleep. He dreamt that he saw the figure of a fearful-looking human person appear on the tree stump on which he had sat, singing. From there, this figure followed the same path the boy had taken until he came to him in the house where he slept. The boy was so fearful of this human figure that he cried out and, at the same time, opened his eyes and saw a real human person squatting beside his bed. The person immediately disappeared. The boy's crying brought his father, who asked about his experience. The boy retold what he saw in his dream, right up to the appearance of the human person beside his bed. The following day the boy's body was swollen all over. The father concluded that the spirit of that tree was responsible for his son's ailment. The father led his son back, retracing the same path the son had taken the previous day, until they came to that tree stump. The father apologized to the spirit of the tree by speaking to the tree: "We know this is your home and we did not respect you when we cut this tree and destroyed your home. Take away from my son this swelling. And, can you leave this place and find a new home elsewhere in some other big trees? This place is for our children and for the whole community. Help us prepare this place for this use. We need your help."

After that, the father and his son went away respectfully. The boy recovered from his ailment the following day.[19]

My people on Panaeati Island were traditional canoe builders before the coming of the Methodist mission in August 1891. These oceangoing canoes were called *waga gowa* (pandanus canoe) and had sails made from pandanus leaves. The leaves were sewn together in an oval shape with string made from the special bark of a tree called *holvag*. These canoes linked the people on Panaeati with people on Misima, with those on the Calvados, and with those of the Sudest and Rossel Islands to the east, and with the people of the Engineering Group and D'Entrecasteaux Islands to the west. The present Panaeati canoes are called *saelau*. The canoes are made from a special tree called *malawi* (*Callophylum inophylum*). The traditional belief says that the *malawi* tree is a person (*gamagal*) and that it is possible for it to move about. If a person wants to build a canoe, he must refrain himself having sex with his wife during the time he plans to work on the canoe.

Stuart Berde writes that "The traditional Panaeati sailing canoe had elaborate carvings, lashed side strakes and braces, and a pandano oval-shaped sail. To build a canoe called *waga hot* ("true canoe") or *gowa* ("pandanus") it was necessary to incorporate sixteen varieties of woods, creepers, and roots."[20] Canoe making takes place during the food months, June to December. By October, people start replanting the yam seeds and live on hoards of yams stored in a *gonu* (yam house), usually built in the gardens or in another suitable location. Hosting a canoe building requires much pork eating, and the hoarding of yams allows work on the canoe to continue during the lean (*huwalu*) period. The same applies for the hosting of memorial feasts. The traditional ecology places these concerns and others in the life of Panaeati people.

Every step of canoe building symbolizes, through rites, the possibilities of undertaking successful goals, such as *usu* (preparatory trade for the hosting of feasts), the smooth flowing speed of the canoe on the sea, the fertility of the regrowth of the *malawi* and other trees, and the appeasement of the spirit person of the *malawi* tree to ensure all these possibilities. Berde interpreted the food eaten by the laboring builders as "investment."[21] The Panaeati metaphor of eating consumable goods during the canoe building signifies the maximum capacity load the canoe will carry after its completion. Panaeati mentality does not perceive investment in the sense that Berde uses it: that the eating is done on behalf of the canoe, or "waga iyan nabi" (canoe eat a lot).[22] What Panaeati people mean by this metaphor is that it is a ritual which will affect the "success" or "failure" of the canoe. The outcome depends on whether the canoe builder provided the laborers with sufficient or insufficient amounts of food and consumables. This is tested after the canoe is completed to see whether the canoe can travel fast or carry lots of cargo or is successful in bringing home lots of food, pigs, and *bagi* (threaded round shell beads as valuables for exchange) on trading trips.

The *malawi* tree provides a prestigious wood for the economic livelihood of Panaeati people. Therefore, before chopping down a huge *malawi* tree, the canoe builder must carefully and respectfully assess and approach the forest, speaking kind words of acknowledgment to the trees as he searches for the right *malawi*. When he finds one that he likes, he clears the base of the tree and prepares the tree for cutting. In doing this, he must be careful not to disturb other vegetation surrounding the *malawi* tree. He always addresses the tree as though it is a person. If he fails to do all these things, the *malawi* tree will move itself to a new location or disguise itself from the prospective canoe builder, so that he will not find it when he comes to chop it down. It is assumed that through these symbolic acts the spirit person will be satisfied and will give by ensuring success. Any failure to perform these ritual acts correctly may grieve the spirit person (*gamagal*) of the tree, and the spirit will withdraw its support. The understanding is that, if the tree is going to give its wood away to be used for the service of its owner and his party, in return the spirit wants the respect it deserves. With the spirit's support, "possession of a sailing canoe meant that the owner and his party could gain access to resources beyond the Deboyne Lagoon."[23]

The very name, *waga hot,* given to sailing canoes is significant to Panaeati people, for it reinforces their identity as canoe builders. *Waga* means canoe and *hot* means "very real," "honest," or "true." Thus, *waga hot* means "true canoe" or "real canoe." This says something about Panaeati people's attitude toward themselves, toward spirits, and toward other people in the ecological relationships surrounding their own canoe production. The canoe is "*waga hot*" because of these relationships.

Separate from canoe ecology, but associated to it, is the memorial feasting ecology. This involves selecting places for gardens, clearing the land, tilling it, planting, and then harvesting the crops. All these stages involve a commitment to maintaining friendly relationships with the environment, remaining consciously alert to avoid disturbing the spirits of the area and jeopardizing their support in gardening. Only certain places are open to garden activities. When gardening, or creating new gardens, no turtle meat is allowed to be eaten in the garden area. If turtle meat is eaten, garden spirits will destroy the yam crops and the gardens will not produce yams for domestic consumption, for the hosting of memorial feasting, or for canoe building and other ritual work. If one has consumed turtle meat, then one should keep away from the garden for a period of up to one month. For these reasons,

Panaeati people do not eat turtle meat. Panaeati people are very proud of themselves and of their relationships with the spirits. Their friendship with the spirits has enabled them to achieve their goals and to retain their identity through the cycle of feasting and canoe ecology. Considering the resources of the environment as gifts from the spirits has led to a rich and sustainable economy. The sailing canoe ecology helps them to have further access to outside resources and to secure further possibilities of success and social progress. To elaborate further on the spirit-ecology relationship, I would like to provide one other example of Panaeati social ecology.

There is a kind of wild yam called *mwau* the Panaeati people have never domesticated. It grows and propagates itself in the forest. This yam is very delicious. The belief about this yam—*mwau,* like *malawi* —is that *mwau* is a person with a significant personality. *Mwau* assumes spirit-power characteristics. To harvest *mwau,* women go into the forest either in groups or alone. A woman preparing to harvest *mwau* is not permitted to talk to any family or community members. To avoid this, she gets up very early in the morning, while everyone is still asleep, gets her basket, a digging stick, a knife, a coconut, some cooked food, and water and goes into the forest. She will spend the whole day in the forest. While searching for *mwau* she is not allowed to say the names of the implements she brought with her. Instead, she uses a metaphor, *bilibili* (soil), to name all these implements. For instance, if she mentions the knife (*kaini*) by name, the place where *mwau* is located will be covered with rocks and unreachable. Her success depends on careful observance of this rite. A woman is not supposed to talk to her friends during her search. If she must request any of the implements to be brought to her, she must do so in metaphoric terms: *bilibili u pem* (give me the soil). The other person responds according to the action of the one making a request.

Mwau grows year round under the thick forest canopy. It belongs to a family of yams that is grown domestically, and the vines die at the same time as the domestic yams are being harvested. But by the time the women go to harvest *mwau* during the lean (*huwalu*) period, the vines have started to decompose, making it very difficult to locate the roots. The women have developed skills to trace the vines to the roots. This process requires perseverance and the patience to maneuver through the undergrowth in silence. The rule says that *mwau* can only be harvested during the lean period. As the yams from the old gardens (*sigaba*) are ready to be harvested, women stop harvesting *mwau* until the next year. Panaeati society ridicules a woman who breaks this rule by gossiping about her, saying she is too lazy to support her family. Such gossip brings great shame.

The land also provides places for the spirits of the dead, who, in Misiman, are called *tubulau sevasevaniliau* (ancestors' spirits). Ancestors are the living dead; their spirits are still members of the earthly community. Such places as forests, caves, mountains, and islands are like chapels where people go with reverence toward a higher life. For example, Misimans believe that at a certain place called Panaesuna, located at the very eastern tip of the island of Misima,[24] there is a cave which is the entrance to Tuma, the residential home of the spirits of the dead.[25] The cave is sealed by a flat circular rock. Whenever there is a death, the rock opens and allows the spirit to enter the cave after a ritual bath in a stream of fresh water called Dumwaga. The spirit world is believed to be the exact, but supernatural, replica of the earthly world. From that supernatural habitation, the spirits of the dead come to help the living relatives.[26] The very place where the cave is, its flora and fauna, is looked upon with awe and, therefore, left untouched.

The spirits of the natural environment, referred to above, are spirits that live on certain areas of land as well as in other elements that are part of the land, such as rocks, trees, rivers, forest areas, sea, islands, reefs, and even the sky. These spirits connect humans with all living creatures. They also ensure security from malicious and unexpected dangers and meet other human needs, such as ensuring the fertility of garden crops.

Spirits give power and charisma to clan leaders, sorcerers, or war leaders.[27] These individuals warn of or correct mistakes by urging other people to learn and keep traditional knowledge about how to relate to land and other people and when to hold feast and initiation ceremonies. These traditions must be adhered to diligently, for they lay the foundation for the survival of communal life. When the head person announces, "*vevegali*," everyone stops their activities and listen to the wise advice.

The *vevegali* about life, psychologically and empirically, is experienced and is realized in the rituals for forgiveness, reconciliation, and healing. People's religious knowledge allows them to identify and use the leaves, bark, or roots of certain plants and herbs for healing, either through dreams or cosmic intuition. These are collected and chewed, boiled, or squeezed to extract the juices given to the sick person.

One example of the relationship between the environment and traditional knowledge is provided by the many uses of *ome*. A Sudest word, *ome* was borrowed by Misima people through the intercultural exchange of the *kula* trade.[28]

Literally, *ome* refers to a particular tree and its bark found only on Rossel Island. There are two other trees which, like *ome,* are worth noting. These are *kelala* and *pepelo,* trees whose bark is used in a similar way. My informants told me that *kelala* and *pepelo* were found only on Duau, at the eastern end of Normandy Island. They then spread into the Louisiade Archipelago, again along the *kula* trade route. Two other root plants native to Misima Island, used for the same purposes, are *seiala* and *banaha.*

Ome is often used as a perfume, which is made by cooking it in coconut oil. It has a strong soothing odor and is often used as a medicine in massage. It can be chewed with betel nut to freshen bad breath and to strengthen the body against sickness and cold.

Ome, like *kelala* and *pepelo,* is also used as a magical omen. Those who practice sorcery, both for good and with malicious intent, use the tree, with the help of the spirits. The power of the bark comes from the spirits of those trees, who are invoked through rituals and incantations. The bark is most often used for healing by means of rituals. When used with malign intent, especially by witches, the evil spirit known as Tamudulele is invoked to harm and kill.

During the pre-missionary period, people did not regard *ome* as a religious institution. Rather, it was a practical matter. What is religious about it is the ritual incantation. *Ome* by itself does not instill awe requiring communal worship. It is the incantation itself which gives *ome* the power to activate the spirits, which demonstrate power.

Certain animals, birds, reptiles, fish, and insects are also not to be touched or harmed, because they represent totemic spirits who are the custodial agents. To this end, peace, forgiveness, healing, and harmonious relationships are maintained between the humans and the ecosystem. These beliefs and practices point to "life" (*gut pela sindaun*).[29] To achieve forgiveness, for instance, one's approach is to use both words and actions in the form of ritual ceremonies. Life is something to be celebrated because it is an integral part of the spiritual realm— more so than of the physical cosmos. So, words alone are not sufficient to induce spirits to offer blessings. Actions are necessary to achieve a blessing of permanent forgiveness and peace.

Lasting peace in Misima can only be achieved through memorial feasting, a time of celebrations when wealth from the land is shared as part of the inner concern for communal well-being. Feasting is social but, more significantly, is religious, because during feasts people call on the spirits to heal their lives. Thus, ritual festivities, when spirits are regarded as the connection between people's basic needs and the earth, help affirm people's identity as part of the cosmic community.[30] Pigs are slaughtered and shared, together with other food and shell wealth, with the other humans and spirits within the community. During such ritual ceremonies, humans demonstrate their wealth by decorating their bodies as a way of expressing thanks and appreciation to the spirits of the environment and the ancestors. It is through the power of the spirits that they acquire ecological wealth. Humans make the spirits happy through this collaboration.

Melanesian Work Ethics

For Melanesians, good and healthy relationships with the cosmic realities are a paramount concern. Broken relationships invite catastrophe. Ritual as work is a process of symbolic activities, combining actions and words, to placate or even manipulate spiritual power. In my Misiman culture, we use the same word, *tuwalali,* for both labor and ritual activities.[31]

Work provides for and preserves life. Our good work contributes to the well-being of the community. Whether we are clearing a forest for new gardens, preparing for a feast, raising pigs, digging the soil and planting crops and caring for them, fishing, or sailing across oceans for trade, we are working. In all such activities Misimans apply their religious emotions and moods, so work involves religious rites which must be closely supervised by the elders of the community. Consequently, we could say that work is motivated by religious moods and emotions. Work always involves collaborating with the spirits.

There are traditional proverbs which stress how important work is for Melanesians. One traditional proverb in Misima goes like this: "Bela mola bela aupe, bela koli bela sisinali" (fire cook, fire give food; fire uncook, fire farce). This proverb teaches that if one just sits and stares at uncooked yams, one will go hungry. But if one is wise and works, the yams will be cooked and one can eat. Sitting and doing nothing for a long time will not help improve life or life's situations.

Likewise, the environment is full of many things which, through work, can contribute to well-being. If they are abused, however, no one will benefit from them in the future. Sifting cultivation, for example, had been practiced for thousands of years before outsiders came to Papua New Guinea. Our beliefs helped to control overuse of land. Cutting down vegetation without good reason is farcical, and the person who does this and shows no care has no credibility in the community.

In Papua New Guinea, there are varieties of vegetation which can subsume and take over other forms of vegetation. One such variety is a type of swordgrass (*Miscanthus floridulus*) found in the highlands but not in lowland areas. According to its history, this grass is frequently associated with the woody regrowth of small trees and shrubs.[32] Some scholars, such as Ron Crocombe and R. G. Robbins, say that the grasslands are the result of slash-and-burn agriculture: hence, in the highlands of Papua New Guinea, traditional ecological knowledge does not seem to have prevented ecological destruction.[33] I agree with Crocombe and Robbins to a certain degree. We do have grasslands in many parts of Papua New Guinea. We have them in the Central, Sepik, Morobe, and Milne Bay provinces and in the island provinces. On Misima, there are types of savanna grassland that seem to have no direct relation to traditional slash-and-burn gardening principles, for there are other factors causing the spread of grasslands. Most of the vegetation changes have been caused by the introduction of steel cutting edges. David Lea suggests that "Subsistence gardening has shown little apparent modification from the pre-contact situation compared with social, demographic, and political changes."[34] If that is the case, then steel tools and their effect on indigenous people have led to general cultural and ecological decline. Culturally, the numbers of men in large labor groups decrease, the number of man-hours plummets, and there are more men underemployed.[35] Consequently, the environment becomes vulnerable to modern equipment and modernization models of development.

Coupled with this are climatic changes, which cause variations in ecological status and species composition at different levels of elevation, ranging in Papua New Guinea from the lowlands to the mountain ranges at ten thousand feet. For instance, E. Reiner and R. G. Robbins recognized that Sepik grasslands, covering six hundred square miles, "may well constitute natural grassland."[36] They have noted that the area consists of infertile clay soil that is constantly waterlogged from the streams flowing across the plains to the Sepik River during the wet season and is drought-cracked, with restrict tree growth, during the dry season.[37] The savannas along the Central Province coast, composed of scattered eucalyptus species mixed with kangaroo and other short grasses, and the swamps of the Western, Gulf, and Sepik Provinces have at least shown that the traditional customs of the people have had very minimal impact on natural vegetation.[38] On the contrary, traditional indigenous religious knowledge has helped to preserve or otherwise accommodate the conditions of the environment created by climatic changes by respecting the land as a religious place and honoring certain areas as the home of the ancestral spirits.

This work ethic understanding, in my opinion, inserts sustainable subsistence into the indigenous Melanesian world. Damage to the environment was kept to a minimum because land was held by clans or lineages. Whatever grows on the land is cared for so that future generations of children can also benefit from it. The methods used in land cultivation and the harvesting of its vegetation (cutting trees for a canoe, or logs for a house) are intrinsically ritualistic. These methods relate to ancestral and other spirit gods, although modern industrialized societies have moved in and influenced indigenous people to change their habits of farming, harvesting of forest and marine resources, and, in more recent times, mineral and petroleum extractions. In the precolonial era in Papua New Guinea, traditional core values were the foundation of people's social and religious thinking about their relationships to the ecosystem.

Work empowered people to exploit their relationships with the environment to create new inventions and make discoveries which served their communities. This led to specialized skills, such as the carvings on masks, canoes, story boards, houses, and spears, to new methods of preparing gardens, and to how festivals were organized and celebrated. These skills were the consequence of linking the spirit world to the material world through the medium of human activities.

Ritual still represents not only the carver's skill but the spirit. The object of the carving is the spirit. The carver's personal reflections and experiences of the material world are denied in order for the work of art to conceptualize the object into spiritual symbol. A. L. Crawford supports this view by suggesting that the Olokolo patterns and motifs of designs on carvings represent various clan groups, imitating people's totems, which metaphorically impute supernatural meaning in various local flora and fauna. Although he was not clear himself how these ritual devices were used, he sensed that

> it is almost certain that they were the media through which the powerful forces of the spirit world were controlled. The fact that these masks and boards were greatly venerated possibly indicates that like other religious objects created in other parts of the world, they possessed a supernatural spirit/ancestor connotation. In function they probably provided, through the symbolic representation of the totem, an access to important spiritual powers. Certainly there was, according to religious belief, an alliance between the members of a social group and the supernatural as depicted in artistic creations.[39]

Carvers in Sepik, Trobriand, and South Irian Jaya have similar socioreligious concerns.[40] Looking at the Gogodala people, we see that their social structure consists of two moieties. Each is comprised of four clan groups, called *udaga,* and each clan is identified by a particular mythological canoe. At the same time, the canoe is symbolically and synonymously a primary totem: "so we can say that there exists a strong identification between the social group and the canoe belonging to it, probably brought about by the fact that the life of the Gogodala, by reason of their environment, is spent perhaps more on the water in a canoe than on the land."[41] Just as the environment influences the correct way of behavior, belief in the spirits of the environment influences traditional modeling patterns, so that relationships between the spirits, the environment, and the people are not violated, as they all coexist harmoniously.

The give-and-take relationship is proof of the interconnectedness people feel toward each other and the environment. This relationship is communally inward looking.[42] Community is composed not only of human beings but of spirits and the ecosystem. Such a holistic view of communalism has no boundaries in its attitude toward environmental protection. This traditional belief system has been, for thousands of years, a mechanism of controlling, intentionally or unintentionally, environmental degradation. For the Melanesians, the environment cradles life and the community, in turn, vows to protect it.

Here is a schematic representation of the Melanesian cradle of life.

The basis for making ethical decisions rests on these principles.[43]

Life	The fullness of life as a value means to enjoy security, peace, happiness, justice, and good health, which one finds in the community here on earth as humans relate to spirits and the environment (trees, rivers, land, rocks, and others). The environment gives to and receives from humans the benefit of "life" as well.
Community	is made up of the living, the spirits of the dead, the spirit-gods, ecology, and the land. Community is the protector and provider of life known to people. It offers life to its members. As a basic social unit, community symbolizes life in society. Other social units count, so long as they help one's community and offer the benefits of peaceful relationships.
Relationship	is symbolized by basic socioeconomic and religious bonds sealed by exchange relationships between the ancestors, the spirits, the living kin members, other communities, and ecosystems.
Exchange	is symbolized by the give-and-take concept of sharing wealth to seal relationships. This is where the process of life begins. Exchange brings into the community life and its benefit of wealth for all to share and enjoy. It symbolizes economic sharing to enhance friendly relationships and paying back a death when one is given through sorcery or war. The execution of give-and-take is expressed through such representations as sharing bride price (dowry), compensation, land, shell money, feathers, pigs, beads, food, and others. Exchange of high-valued wealth builds and expresses lasting relationships which bring the fullness of life known to people.

These principles are deeply embedded in the psychology of the Melanesian people. These principles make up a single process by which the community acts ethically to achieve life, reaching its climax in exchange. Exchange is the foundation of the upward-moving process toward the ultimate goal—life. Exchange is carried out through such observances as bride price, compensation, and ritual, all working as a single process to achieve fullness of life. People feel very strongly about how they carry out their exchanges. Exchange must be done properly, or one loses the vital support that one's basic social unit offers. Individuals want the support of the community, which they need in order to survive and enjoy life on the land.

Wealth from the land heals broken relationships and restores life for kin and those clans with common bonds. Every member of the clan is obliged to observe good relationships in order not to harm relationships within the basic social unit. Community as the progenitor of life stands for life. Hence the ethical principle:

> What is good for the community is ethically good.
> What is bad for the community is ethically bad.
> What is indifferent for the community is ethically indifferent.[44]

This view of life can open up other wider possibilities for progress as well as improve ethical responsibility for the protection of human and ecological life. Melanesians know that the human community is made up of complex relationships expressed toward the spirits, ancestors, plants, land, animals, rivers, mountains, sea, sky. Therefore, "fullness of life" can be a possible opening to a wider Melanesia, rather than simply to the local group. This ethical principle might also enrich global community, so that life is respected and all peoples' traditional cultures are put into the right perspective in matters of development.

Westerners see in Melanesian spirituality a degree of ambivalence in the way people think, talk, and behave. Consequently, Westerners think that people of Papua New Guinea seem uncertain about behaving toward and respecting ecology in terms of its sacredness (for example, the habit of burning grassland). Logically, the two realities, respecting and altering the ecology of a place, do not seem to be linked. Why slash-and-burn the trees and grass of a given area, if it is the sacred residence of spirit divinities? All that Westerners see is the destructive side of agriculture. They overlook the indigenous perspectives and they fail to see the cultural system which distinguishes between gifts and places for venerating the divinities. Spirits give gifts and empowerment for subsistence food production, which can be received from places set aside for that purpose through such activities as hunting and gardening. What is found in those areas are gifts to sustain life in the community. Places considered to be the abode of the spirits are not to be tampered with because of the devastating effect on individuals and community life. In both types of places, people acknowledge religious experiences as they connect with the spiritual power to move beyond their human limits.

Here, we derive a principle of interdependence for life, between humans and the ecosystem and between humans and spirits. This principle concerns the recreation, revitalization, and giving of new hope for life in the world in order to save it. It is based on creation, recreation, and natural evolution of the life-support systems rooted in every human culture. Melanesians realize this through the teachings of their cultures.

Modernization and Ecology

To develop means to unfold gradually, like a flower unfolds its petals to expose the beauty of its creation. Development is also a word used to describe the policies of governmental and nongovernmental organizations. People mean different things when they speak of development: development projects, development of resources, development of people, development of land, underdevelopment, and development assistance.

The perception of some is this: When people are in the way of extracting wealth, like gold, copper, oil, timber logs, roads, they are seen as obstructing development. They have to be moved away from their sacred sites, land, and gardens to give way to development. People are rated as objects and not as the subject of development.

It seems to me that when we speak of development in this way, we are equating development only with modernization and economic growth: the more growth there is, the more development we will have. We often think of Papua New Guinea as an underdeveloped nation. According to many Western perspectives, happiness for all means more economic growth to overcome underdevelopment. This ideology of development is quite materialistic. Thus, if our nation is to grow, we must achieve a higher gross income; we must look to outside investors to come and develop our resources. Often, we remain passive, the result of paternalistic attitudes already embedded in our systems of governance.

Fast-changing attitudes of the relationship of religious knowledge to traditional life and of personal relationships with environments return to this concept of development. "In the end it is people who generate change and meet challenges and we believe they are our greatest asset"[45] is a statement in an advertisement that indicates a new understanding of the economic value placed on people. People are the agents of the changes they bring about through the energies they possess, and thus the equation "people and time equal money." Such change generates challenges that continue to meet and revolutionize traditional worldviews. The new energy, for example, gained from the knowledge of modern scientific education and farming technology has influenced traditional knowledge of subsistence gardening and animal husbandry. This new knowledge has also changed the family and communal sense of traditional values.

Modern developmental principles have caused the pace of change to outdistance people's readiness to accept change. People need time to educate their minds to understand complex modern worldview values that differ so much from traditional values. Westerners, reflecting upon Melanesian worldviews and their consequent practices, fail to recognize the destructive impact of modern commercial farming, logging, mining, and accompanying technologies on the ecosystem.

The Western view of development has been espoused by an elite group of Papua New Guinea leaders who have aligned themselves to foreign industrial domineering societies. Such an alliance denies the desires and values of the rural majority of indigenous people, and in so doing, the core values of the rural traditions are suppressed. The rural majority do not recognize as valid the actions taken by the elite, which do not contribute culturally to the benefit of their community. When the ecosystem is disturbed by modern developmental technologies because a member of their own blood has signed a piece of paper to allow foreign activities in their area, their indigenous sense of worth is degraded. Consequently this situation could lead to compensation claims. But could money ever buy back lost values? Places where spirit divinities are venerated cannot be replaced once their original values are destroyed.[46] People have to adopt a new set of values to accommodate the change. This is not easy, because people fear the unknown future. In fact, the knowledge of things which hold the balance in traditional societies, such as social relationships, knowing geographical places, climatic changes, and flora and fauna, contributes to security, good relationships, and happiness. Such knowledge also helps explain ideas pertaining to inspirations emanating from the spirit divinities.

Consider the relationship between the wind and rain, thunder and lightning, forest, birds, and spirits. While there seems no connection between all of these, according to logic and reason, the Melanesian people see concrete reality in two ways: events manifest the reality of truths implied; and events represent a symbol for life. These representations in literal events are not easily seen by one who is trying to learn another culture.

It is easier for the foreigner to deny the authentic indigenous core elements of traditional culture and impose his or her own cultural values. If one pursues this approach, the indigenous symbols pertaining to the spirits would have to be replaced with foreign cultural symbols representing new images of life and power that could devastate and degrade the indigenous values. This could then lead to a loss of security for indigenous peoples. If money becomes a new symbol for security, power, and value, then the whole ecological cycle might suffer from the pressure for new economic development and its accompanying symbols of material wealth, investment, politics, employment, and so on.

Within traditional understanding, the sense of values pertaining to empirical realities finds meaning in beings and energies. These beings and energies are symbolized in spirit divinities. The spirits, according to people's beliefs, are classified according to the function they attribute to them. This is what Melanesians see as a personal life force, a creative and awesome reality that transforms attitudes and psychic expressions in their relationships to natural environments. Western scientific investigators are in danger of undermining Melanesian religious psychology and transformative knowledge, and thus denying the power of primal cultural values. The recognition of the eternal sources of power symbolized in the belief in spirits is purposely serving human need for redemptive healing, forgiveness, and reconciliation toward a just society. Thomas Berry argues:

> Just now one of the significant historical roles of the primal people of the world is not simply to sustain their own traditions, but to call the entire civilized world to a more authentic mode of being. Our only hope is a renewal of those primordial experiences out of which the shaping of our more sublime human qualities could take place.[47]

In the Melanesian tradition it is essential for cosmic unity to coexist with other forms of life. The sense of right and wrong, success and failure, depends on the coexisting pattern of cosmic community. The empirical energies ensure life, harmony, and a balanced relationship between human and environment. The primal worldview, therefore, constructs varieties of Melanesian societies, and the role of each inherent culture is to sustain the environment and the belief system for social security.

The environment is the symbol of power and reality of the living, all-pervasive, numinous world of nature. In Berry's words:

in our early tribal period we lived in a world dominated by psychic power symbols whereby life is guided toward communion with our total human and transhuman environment. We felt ourselves sustained by "a cosmic presence that went beyond the surface reality of the surrounding natural world."[48]

Melanesians understand that human consciousness of the earliest sense of ordered life takes its form in the realm of the spirits. For example, consider the metaphors of flora and fauna, land and sea in the myths of origins.[49]

Knowledge of these spiritual origins has given order and meaning to social and artistic moral responsibility. The spiritual order provides energy for life, equipping people to feel their moral obligations, to care for and protect selected environmental areas. The same spiritual order animates the ecosystem of places. Thus, the ecosystem is endowed with beings seen to be preternatural symbols of power, and people enter into the ecosystem with "remarkable affinity with the environment." The "important component in this environmental consciousness" is the way Melanesians express their sense of fear, accompanied "with experiences and common sense" in order to find security, safety, peace, happiness and to ensure their well-being.[50]

Transnationalization of capital manipulates our environment to the advantage of distant peoples. Consequent to this approach, the West has viewed our world as an object of measurement. This view teaches us to see our world as distinct from ourselves. But our Melanesian traditional religious knowledge provided supernatural explanations for the vast areas of natural resources in our environment. Some Western scientists have developed quantifiable and technological knowledge that, along with commercial institutions, has fragmented this traditional knowledge through exploitative consumerism and manipulative scientific ideology. Such a millennial type of vision has demeaned our mystical, bio-cosmic relationships with reality. The interdependence with living and nonliving organisms in the environment that has sustained human survival for thousands of years is diminishing. In reference to Western modernization, Berry is correct when he writes:

> Human effort, not divine grace, was the instrument for this paradisal realization. The scientists and inventors, the bankers and commercial magnates, were now the saints who would reign. This, then, was the drive in the technological age. It was an energy revolution not only in

terms of the physical energies now available to us, but also in terms of the psychic energies. Never before had we experienced such a turbulent period, such a movement to alter the world, to bring about an earthly redeemed state, and, finally, to attain such power as was formerly attributed only to the natural or to the divine.

This achievement was associated with a sense of political and social transformation that would release us from age-old tyrannies. The very structure of existence was being altered.[51]

This emphasis on human over supernatural instrumentality has changed the direction of Papua New Guinea since its independence on 16 September 1975. There is no respect shown the environment by the Western governments, and commercial entrepreneurial companies engage in mining, logging, petroleum, fishing, and cash crops like palm oil, coconut, coffee, and cocoa. Large areas of land and vegetation have been cleared for these commercial purposes.[52] Consequently, some indigenous peoples have become careless because of the love of money. On the whole, the money economy has improved, to some degree, indigenous living standards. Yet, love of it has made people forget their mystical vision of power and reality. They have enslaved themselves within a system of competitive living based on Western standards. The government is now caught in the globalization paradigm of capitalist economy and democratic political systems. The traditional concept of interdependence is replaced with individualism, which is now undermining communal living and the process of give-and-take. This process is no longer concerned with people, their work for environmental protection, or the just distribution of goods and services. The protection of every living species of life in the natural and supernatural realm is now the struggle of traditional indigenous peoples. As one of the modern Papua New Guinean poets, Billy Oa Ume, referring to the abundance of land destroyed by a logging company in pursuit of lumber, has written:

> Lavongai of our forefathers
>   Was a rich land
>   Abundant in life and gifts
> From the forest-clad mountains
>   And jungles of the mainland
>   Full of birds and beasts
>   to the reefs of the islands

Bringing everything in plenty
    To animals and man alike
    A land respected in plenty
And cherished for thousands of years
    Till our fathers were taught
    To think otherwise

    The Lavongai we inherit
Is but a shadow of the treasure
    That was taken from us
        Yet all is not lost . . .
    So we come together
        To take a last stand

A last stand to make people realize . . .
    To give the children of tomorrow
    A chance to know
    The flight of the butterfly,
        The song of birds . . .
        The rich variety of life[53]

The poet has suggested that Melanesian indigenous people need the support of interest groups within the global community to fight together the kinds of ideologies that destroy our environment and our bio-cosmic relationship to the earth.

Conclusion

It is too simplistic to say modernization, as a model for improving living standards and the environment, is a terrible model. The concept offers an alternative worldview of globalization on our planet earth. The implications of the global movement for the secularization of human civilization does threaten our very human existence. For example, the domination of one society over another and the emissions from factories, aircraft, and fossil and nuclear wastes have all contributed toward our environmental and human degradation. It appears that human beings have lost their spiritual vision and, for that reason, are responsible for such a catastrophic situation.

We cannot stop "progress" and the negative destructive power advocated by industrial and dominant societies threatening our traditional living conditions and worldview. We can, however, consciously maneuver our progress in ways that benefit and conserve our local habitat. We must acknowledge that all cultures have their own limitations. The worldviews of the dominant societies should be controlled so they do not jeopardize indigenous knowledge and traditions. Today we live in a global community, and Melanesia no longer exists independently. The industrial West and North and the rest of the regions like Melanesia are limited in their understanding of ecosystems. We all need to bridge our worldviews if we are to come to a new understanding of how awesome life is. By sharing our traditional knowledge of energy events, we can contact the mysteries implicit in our cosmologies and ecologies.[54]

Cultural holism is characteristic of all Melanesia. In our investigations we find that Melanesian religious culture does not discriminate between the religious, economic, political, social, and other aspects of life. Its primary concern is to nurture people and their lives. The fullness of life is ensured by the community within which every individual is cared for and protected from physical, spiritual, and social harm. Of course, individuals still express their desires as freely as they can, but there are certain limits set by the community. Life is guided by the community through the sacred stories presenting the laws of the ancestors and the supernatural spirit beings. Melanesians do not blindly follow their instincts, but have, through their culture, a system of self-preservation. By submitting to the religious rules which guide their human instincts, individuals follow the religious principles that transmit strength and wisdom to develop communal and individual responsibility for the well-being of everyone.

Having recognized this traditional knowledge, we have to admit that modernization and traditional knowledge have different relationships to ecology and culture. Melanesians emphasize both the religious and the aesthetic aspects of culture. Modernization seems to stress the aesthetic and to respond to it in different ways, such as creating botanical gardens and beautifying homes. The fact that aesthetics and spirits combine to produce life is the crucial point of contemporary Melanesian religious culture. Realizing this, the founding fathers of Papua New Guinea's constitution acknowledge "the worthy customs and traditional wisdoms of our people."[55] This cluster of constitutional ideals is undergoing a process which has not yet been fully realized in the present phase of modernization. We have abandoned the Melanesian spirit that was protected by the ancestral laws narrated in the sacred stories of our ancestors and revealed in the spirit beings of the environment.[56]

If indigenous traditional values have anything to teach us today, it is that the Melanesian people, too, need to rethink their own destiny. Will we uphold the spirit of the constitution, the noble tradition, or allow Western forms of modernization to replace our worthy ancestral values?[57] Foreign agents of change will also have to remodel and re-evaluate their aggressive attitudes toward the development of indigenous people and toward the ecosystem. If they do not, they will end up destroying themselves and the Melanesian people in the process. By reconsidering their goals and rethinking their methods, they would show the international community that they do care about and respect indigenous peoples and their traditions.

Notes

1. In my use of the term "worldview," I take the position defined by Charles H. Kraft. He defines worldview as "the culturally structured assumptions, values, and commitments/allegiances underlying a people's perception of reality and their responses to those perceptions"; Charles H. Kraft, *Christianity with Power* (Ann Arbor, Mich.: Servant, 1989), 20. Another way of expressing this notion is to say that culture is structured by worldview. Just as culture exists in the heads of a people, so does their worldview. The ideas of how people should behave are formulated by their assumptions and values and the level of their commitment to those same ideas. And, as Kraft further pointed out, the "power of the worldview lies in the habits of people. People are the ones who do things"; Charles H. Kraft, *Anthropology for Christian Witness* (Maryknoll, N.Y.: Orbis Books, 1996), 52.

Worldview is the product of human creation because humans are culture-producing creatures. The assumptions, values, and allegiances they produce form their structure of reality. In the case of Melanesians, their perceptions of reality and their habits of responding to this reality form their holistic view of culture. Security, peace, happiness, and anything else pertaining to achieving fullness of life is taken care of by their culture. I will from time to time use "worldview" interchangeably or synonymously with "core values."

2. By modernization I mean "the complex series of changes in economic, social and cultural life by which less developed societies acquire characteristics common to more developed societies. Among these characteristics are industrialisation; self-sustaining economic growth; enhanced social mobility; the spread of literacy, education, and communication; national unification; and the expansion of popular participation in the political process"; *The HarperCollins Dictionary of Religion* (San Francisco: HarperSanFrancisco, 1995), 725.

In my use of modernization I do not intend to view religion as a negative factor in development, as many social scholars have tended to do, from Karl Marx to post–World War II writers in America who saw religion as an obstacle to modernization. In Papua New Guinea the contrary is true: Christianity, as a religion, is seen to be an advocator of modernization—hence, the secularization of Melanesian religions in Papua New Guinea and the Pacific region. See G. W. Trompf, *Melanesian Religion* (Cambridge: Cambridge University Press, 1991), 241–59. People question development, because the development agencies do not always respect their religious places, noble cultural habits, relationships to the land, and the cultural values from which they draw their sense of security, identity, and livelihood. If any negotiation takes place, the deal is suspect, with negotiators taking advantage of people's ignorance of the complex series of changes that will affect them and their ways of life.

3. Simeon Namunu, "Ancestors and the Holy Spirit" (thesis, Rarongo Theological College, Rabaul, 1983), 65.

4. Bernard Narokobi, "What Is Religious Experience for a Melanesian?" in *Christ in Melanesia: Exploring Theological Issues*, Point Series (Goroka, Papua New Guinea: Melanesian Institute, 1977), 8f.

5. Kraft, *Anthropology for Christian Witness*, 52.

6. On my use of "worldview," see n. 1 above.

7. Environment comprises the mountains, trees, rocks, rivers, ponds, sea, swampland, mangroves, forest, beaches, riverbanks, sky, sun, moon, caves, fish, grass, and the like.

8. Trompf, *Melanesian Religion,* 252.

9. Ibid., 246–48.

10. See Thomas Berry, *The Dream of the Earth* (San Francisco: Sierra Club Books, 1988), xiff.

11. Bronislaw Malinowski, "Myth in Primitive Psychology," in *Malinowski and the Work of Myth,* selected and introduced by Ivan Strenski (Princeton: Princeton University Press, 1992), 79.

12. Simeon Namunu, "Symbols of Life in Melanesia" (thesis, University of Papua New Guinea, 1995), 57.

13. I use the term "symbol" from a cosmic dimension, to mean the power and dynamism that enlightens understanding and drives people's meaning, emotion, and direction and uniformly functions to motivate them to positive and dignified actions. The cosmic dimension of symbols demonstrates life as personified in many different forms, changing to suit mood and circumstance. For example, a spirit of vegetation appears from time to time in a mythical creation, lives, becomes widespread, and finally vanishes. What remains, what is basic and lasting, is the "power" of vegetation, which can be felt and manipulated into a mythological figure. See ibid., 47f.

14. Spirits in Melanesian religion are symbols of life, reality, truth, personal being, power, energy. The giving of life is built on relationships between people and the spirits. See Mary MacDonald, "Symbolism and Myth," in *An Introduction to Melanesian Religions: A Handbook for Church Workers,* ed. Ennio Mantovani, 2d ed., Point Series, no. 6 (Goroka, Papua New Guinea: Melanesian Institute, 1995), 124f.

15. Ibid., 125–35.

16. See *An Introduction to Melanesian Religions: A Handbook for Church Workers,* ed. Ennio Mantovani, 2d ed., Point Series, no. 6 (Goroka, Papua New Guinea: Melanesian Institute, 1995), 31–39, for a detailed explanation of bio-cosmic relationships. Mantovani's treatment of the bio-cosmic concept as the experience of Melanesians is one of seeing from the point of view of life in natural phenomena, of the environment being animated with life by the spirits.

17. A foreigner, visiting or new to the situation in Papua New Guinea today, would be confronted with some paradoxes—paradoxes that would seem to contradict traditional Melanesian understanding of their worldview. These paradoxes have resulted from the changes brought about by modernization processes, which give a misleading impression of models of relationships that are unfriendly toward ecology. Life is composed of fragmented complex rituals, realized in memorial feasting. Yet, it may seem that children or adults are unfriendly toward the birds, trees, animals, or reptiles, and so on. The effects on nature of commercial development—as in the extraction of natural resources like fish, minerals, petroleum, forestry products and the like—is devastating. In order to exploit these resources, the developers often do not respect indigenous knowledge about holy places or the awesome relationships people have toward the ecosystem. Such behavior or actions by developers leads to misconceptions about the integrity of indigenous peoples' relationship with nature which, for the people, has been the cradle of their religious knowledge and thinking.

18. Oral testimony of Judith Namunu, February 1998.

19. Oral testimony of Benjamin Sopilagai, retold to me by S. John Namunu, 10 November 1998, in Goroka.

20. Stuart James Berde, "Melanesians as Methodists: Economy and Marriage on a Papua New Guinea Island" (Ph.D. diss., University of Pennsylvania, 1974), 41.

21. Ibid., 241.

22. Ibid.

23. Ibid., 45.

24. I come from Misima. The first chapter of my thesis "Ancestors and the Holy Spirit" discusses the Misiman spirit worldview. Since 1988, a gold-mining company owned by Placer Pacific, Ltd., has been extracting gold through opencast excavation. In the process of constructing the mine infrastructure, the operations have disrupted the people's environment and their belief in spirits. The environment the company has destroyed has been important as a place of spirits. One consequence of this development is that younger people no longer respect the beliefs—having experienced the lack of respect to the place—which has led to the disruption of the socioreligious structure and control mechanisms of the society.

25. Tuma is an underworld of the spirits of the dead. It is located at the eastern tip of Misima Island. Kila Matthew told me the following story of what Tuma is like, which I will recount here as best as my memory allows. During the construction of the mine processing plant, Kila and other Misiman employees were on a night shift working with a white Australian supervisor. The supervisor had worked elsewhere in Papua New Guinea and had heard stories about beliefs in spirits. That night, the men he was supervising, most of whom were Misimans, were talking about human skulls and jaws said to be found in one of the caves located at Hinaota village. The supervisor heard them talking and became interested and wanted to know more about their story. He listened to the men's story and became curious to see the place where the cave was. He decided to go and see for himself and prove what the men had said. Without telling any of the men of his intention, he handpicked four men, one from Hinaota village, Kila, and two other men from Gulewa village. He told them to get in a vehicle, asking the Hinaota man to sit with him in the driver's cabin, and he drove off.

It was about twelve o'clock midnight. When they got to Hinaota, he drove off the main road. The supervisor parked the vehicle and he and the four men, each with head and hand torches, followed a path, with the man from Hinaota leading the way. After perhaps twenty to thirty minutes, they came upon a round and flat rock. The local man said, "This is it." All five of them, using all their strength, lifted the rock. As soon as there was a large enough opening, the white supervisor crept through. Immediately, the rock became free of what seemed to be a power holding it and moved by itself. The four men outside the cave, looking in, could see layers, like shelves, along the walls of the cave. On these shelves were laid many skulls and jaws. They were placed in rows as though someone laid them there. The men could clearly see human skulls and jaws, all carefully placed in rows, from what looked to be old ones to new or very recent-looking ones. And on separate rows of shelves, they saw what seemed to be children's skulls and jaws. The cave dropped down for about ten meters. They could see nothing but skulls and jaws on these layers of shelves, all of them intact. The white man reappeared ten to fifteen minutes later, with three skulls wrapped in white cloth. As soon as he came out of the cave, the men replaced the rock over the entrance to the cave without much problem. They walked back to the vehicle and drove back to the mine camp at Lagua. The white man went to his room, where he left the skulls, and then he drove back to work. The other men were very frightened. They thought the spirits would harm them, according to the Misiman belief. Somehow, that did not happen, and the white man left the country the following day, taking the skulls back to Cairns, Australia.

I believe the skulls of the dead people are symbolic of the spirits of the dead in Tuma. This story fits in well with the myth that a certain woman, the custodian of the entrance to Tuma, is responsible for the ritual washing of the spirits to rid them of earthly dirt before they enter the spirit world. From Tuma, the spirits of ancestors come to visit their people in this life to help in times of trouble and difficulties. In my opinion, this white man had committed an act of injustice toward the people of Misima by doing something that, traditionally, people would never have done. It is taboo to enter a place such as this cave, and to do what he did is to belittle a place of awe. His action demonstrates, for me, the careless attitude Westerners and those from industrialized nations hold toward traditional beliefs and knowledge of indigenous people. Volumes such as this need to help educate others to be conscious of ecology and of indigenous traditions.

26. See Namunu, "Ancestors and the Holy Spirit," 10–11, for a description of Tuma according to Misiman worldview. Cf. Jutta Malnic with John Kasaipwalova, *Kula: Myth and Magic in the Trobriand Islands* (Wahroonga, NSW: Cowrie Books, 1998), 195–200.

27. See Trompf, *Melanesian Religion,* 12–19. Trompf discusses the varieties of "spirit-beings" and points out that there is no uniform pattern of belief system about deities and spirits in relation to the Melanesian cosmologies and mythologies. Rather, Melanesian traditional cosmologies are viewed in relation to, on the one hand, the natural environment with its economic resources and the human beings, and on the other hand, the non-empirical realm of spirit beings and impersonal occult forces.

28. *Kula* is a system of trade common in Milne Bay Province. The guiding principle of *kula* is give-and-take with a correct attitude and good manner. See Strenski, *Malinowski and the Work of Myth,* 3–39.

29. "Life," as used in this paper to translate the Pidgin *gut pela sindaun* means peace, happiness, well-being, and harmonious living relationships with one another within one's community.

30. See Donald E. McGregor, *The Fish and the Cross,* 2d ed., Point Series, no. 1 (Goroka, Papua New Guinea: Melanesian Institute, 1982), 82f.

31. When a Misiman traditional healer performs his healing rites on a sick person, he is regarded as doing his work, for which he would be compensated by the sick person's relatives. Work is considered a service to the community.

32. R. G. Robbins, "Vegetation and Man in the South-West Pacific and New Guinea," in *Man in the Pacific Islands: Essays on Geographical Change in the Pacific Islands,* ed. R. Gerard Ward (Oxford: Clarendon Press, 1972).

33. Ron Crocombe, "Overview," in *Customary Land Tenure and Sustainable Development: Complementarity or Conflict?* (Noumea, New Caledonia: South Pacific

Commission; Suva, Fiji: Institute of Pacific Studies, University of the South Pacific, 1995), 5f.; and Robbins, "Vegetation and Man in the South-West Pacific and New Guinea," 74–90.

34. David A. M. Lea, "Indigenous Horticulture in Melanesia," in *Man in the Pacific Islands: Essays on Geographical Change in the Pacific Islands,* ed. R. Gerard Ward (Oxford: Clarendon Press, 1972), 254.

35. Ibid.

36. Robbins, "Vegetation and Man in the South-West Pacific and New Guinea," 86. See also E. Reiner and J. A. Mabbutt, "Geomorphology of the Wewak-Lower Sepik Area," in *Lands of the Wewak-Lower Sepik Area, Territory of Papua and New Guinea,* comp. H. A. Haantjens et al., published as *Land Research Series,* no. 22 (1968).

37. Ibid.

38. Ibid., 87.

39. A. L. Crawford, *AIDA: Life and Ceremony of the Gogodala* (Port Moresby and Bathurst: National Cultural Council of Papua New Guinea, 1981), 187f.

40. See Giancarlo M. G. Scoditti, *Kitawa: A Linguistic and Aesthetic Analysis of Visual Art in Melanesia* (Berlin and New York: Mouton de Gruyter, 1990), 26–27, for a discussion of the *kula* canoe and its carvers. See Crawford, *AIDA: Life and Ceremony of the Gogodala,* 183–243. Crawford writes: "In some areas of Papua New Guinea, the people hoped to invoke the spirit by providing a variety of carved and pigmented devices of certain traditional design that were symbols belonging solely to a particular ancestor. Used ceremonially, they showed that the ritual was being symbolically directed to the spirits, and on many occasions special 'cathedral-like' constructions were provided for such rites" (185). The basic characteristics of this type of carving may be found among the Kiwais and extend into the Asmat group of the South Irian Jaya coast.

41. Crawford, *AIDA: Life and Ceremony of the Gogodala,* 246.

42. By "inward looking," I mean that, because the Melanesian philosophy of life says that life belongs to the community, every member has, as a priority, the right to protect the community's integrity and security as far as possible within his or her means. Thus, if community is the source of life, it is logical that it must be defended at all costs. When dealing with people from outside the community, each member of the community has a responsibility to see that community interest is safe, because that community is the individual's social unit, which cares for his or her security, happiness, and belonging.

43. My outline of Melanesian values and ethics is inspired by Ennio Mantovani's studies. For details, see Mantovani, *An Introduction to Melanesian Religions,* 195–212.

44. Mantovani, *An Introduction to Melanesian Religions,* 206.

45. This statement is taken from an advertisement in *Air Niugini's Paradise Magazine* 127 (May-June 1998), 7.

46. For more details, see *Development and Environment in Papua New Guinea: An Overview,* ed. Hans-Martin Schoell, Point Series, no. 18 (Goroka, Papua New Guinea: Melanesian Institute, 1994). See also *The Ok Tedi Settlement: Issues, Outcomes, and Implications,* ed. Glenn Banks and Chris Ballard, Joint Publication of the

National Centre for Development Studies and Resource Management in Asia-Pacific (Canberra: National Centre for Development Studies, Research School of Pacific Studies, Australian National University, 1997).

47. Berry, *The Dream of the Earth,* 4.

48. Ibid., 39.

49. Malinowski, "Myth in Primitive Psychology," 89–100.

50. Trompf, *Melanesian Religion,* 18f.

51. Berry, *The Dream of the Earth,* 40.

52. See M. R. Chammbers, "Development and Environment in PNG," *Catalyst* (Goroka, Papua New Guinea), 15, no. 2 (1985): 120–28 ; and, in the same volume, Friedhelm Goeltenboth, "Clear-Felling: A Case Study," 129–36.

53. The poem by Billy Oa Ume, of New Ireland Local Environment Foundation, Lavongai, was published in *NSV Newsletter: A Publication for National Volunteers* 11 (January-February 1998): 7. Lavongai is the local name for New Hanover Island in New Ireland Province, where a logging company is operating. The logging operation has destroyed much of the flora and fauna of the area's land and river system.

54. Berry, *The Dream of the Earth,* xiiff.

55. Preamble, *The Constitution of the Independent State of Papua New Guinea* (Port Moresby: Government Printer, 1975).

56. In an effort to highlight some of the damage done to the sacred places and natural environment, the Melanesian Institute published an issue in its Point Series to document the injustices and unequal distribution of the benefits to the people of the affected area and to Papua New Guinea at large by both developers (companies) and the government. This publication includes a follow-up of the earlier publication of the results of the research done by an independent nongovernmental institute, the Starnberg Institute of Germany, on the operations of the Ok Tedi Mining Limited: see the Melanesian Institute's journal *Catalyst* 21, no. 3 (1991). See also *Development and the Environment in PNG,* ed. Schoell, which incorporates this concern and other development-related issues.

57. If there are such things as noble traditions in Melanesia, then we have to look for them within the culture of the Melanesian people. The indigenous Melanesians are the ones who must search out and preserve their worthy traditions and tell others to respect them as the source of true life for Papua New Guinea. Indigenous Melanesians will need to dig deeply into their culture and be able to distinguish between the noble and the ignoble aspects of their traditional customs. Discard the ignoble ones and hold on to the noble ones to pass on to our children.

Interface between Traditional Religion and Ecology among the Igorots

VICTORIA TAULI-CORPUZ

Introduction

As a growing child in my hometown, Besao, Mountain Province, one of the most important lessons I learned concerned the concept of *innáyan*. This is a Kankana-ey Igorot word which can be literally translated in many ways, such as "exercise caution," "don't do it," or "have limits." Still, these translations cannot capture fully what the word means. It encompasses a value system and a principle which guides one's behavior and one's relationships with other human beings, other creations (animal, plant, microorganisms), the spirit world, and nature in general.

A closely related concept is *lawá,* which means taboo, forbidden, holy, or sacred. *Lawá nán mangpukan is ado-ado ay ka-iw isnan pagpag* (It is forbidden to cut trees indiscriminately in the forest). *Lawá* and *innáyan* contain in their meanings some of the fundamental principles which underpin the traditional religion of the Igorots and by which every Igorot should live. Our adherence to the customary laws revolving around what is *lawá* and *innáyan* is crucial for our continuing existence as a people. We have a whole set of values deemed good (*gawis*), such as respect for the ancestors, nature, and elders and honesty, community solidarity, and collectivity. It is *lawá* and *innáyan* to go against these.

Igorot is a generic term for the more than one million indigenous people who live in the Cordillera region in northern Philippines. It is an indigenous term which means "people of the mountains." The main ethnolinguistic groups which compose the Igorots are the Ibaloi, Kankana-ey, Ifugao, Kalinga, Bontok, Isneg, Tingguian, Kalanguya, and Balangao. I am a Kankana-ey Igorot who was brought up as a Christian, my parents being among the first generation of Igorots educated by the American missionaries. My father became an Anglican priest and my mother a nurse. Fortunately, I had the privilege of growing up in my parents' village, and my community organizing work in the late 1970s was in neighboring traditional villages. Thus, my experience and knowledge of the traditional religion and spirituality of my people is mainly informed by this background.

This paper will discuss the interface between the traditional religion (*sináng-adum ay pammáti*)[1] and ecology as manifested in the worldviews, belief systems, and practices of the Igorots. It will highlight a few cases which will demonstrate this nexus. As Igorots are composed of different ethnolinguistic groups or tribes, the cases presented cannot be representative for all. There are many similarities among us, though, especially in the area of culture and religion, which will be dealt with in this paper. The last part will present some challenges, not only to the government and churches, but to the indigenous peoples.

Colonization Experience

The Spanish colonizers, who occupied the Philippines for more than three centuries, were not successful in Christianizing the Igorots. William Henry Scott, a historian who has written extensively on Igorots, says that ". . . Spanish records make it clear that they (Igorots) fought for their independence with every means at their disposal for three centuries, and that this resistance to invasion was deliberate, self-conscious, and continuous."[2]

Thus, the heavy influence of Spanish Catholicism seen among the colonized lowlanders can hardly be found among the Igorots. The Spanish colonizers considered the Igorots heathens, savages, and infidels. This discriminatory attitude was also internalized by members of the dominant population, who think of themselves as more civilized and superior to the Igorots.

The American colonizers, with their extensive experience in subjugating the American Indians and their highly sophisticated weaponry, were more successful in subjugating the Igorots. American missionaries, both Protestant and Catholic, and the public school system played key roles in the pacification and colonization of the Igorots. In spite of aggressive Christianization efforts, a significant number of Igorots, up to now, would be characterized as nominal Christians. Ancestral and nature spirits are still revered, respected, and feared.[3] Igorots practice a unique kind of Christianity, mixed with traditional religion, or, more accurately perhaps, *sináng-adum ay pámmati* sprinkled with Christianity.

Sináng-Adum Ay Pámmati and Ecology

The persistence and conservation of the *sináng-adum ay pámmati,* or of some of its aspects, can be credited to the indigenous peoples' resistance to colonization and discrimination by the West and the dominant population. The assertiveness of the Igorot traditional religion is exemplified by an account of a Spanish friar, Fray Vivar, who said that a friar was told by an Igorot priestess, "If you're the priest of the Christians, so am I of the Igorots!"[4] It could also be partly explained by the fact that traditional economic activities, such as subsistence agriculture, are still practiced by most Igorots. Swidden and wet rice production for domestic consumption are still the main activities of the majority of Igorots who live in the traditional villages. This environment in which we have developed as peoples conditions our biological and mental being as well as the quality of life we have.

As for our political institutions, we still have elders (*amám-a, lállakay,* or *papangat*) who make decisions and arbitrate. Among us northern Kankana-eys, we have the *dap-áy* (tribunal or ward center) where the *amam-á* make decisions. The *ili* (village), the largest political unit, is composed of several *dap-áy*s. The Bontocs and Kalingas have their *pechen* or *bodong* (peace-pact agreements), the institutions which establish the *bugis,* or territorial boundaries, and resolve intertribal conflicts. Customary laws still operate even if they are not formally codified. It must be admitted, though, that the influence of these laws are diminishing in some communities.

My early memories as a child were of the fights my father had with his siblings and relatives from the villages. These fights revolved around his vehement protests against those who still believed in spirits (*aníto*) and performed traditional rituals. I did not understand why he considered their beliefs inferior to Christianity. I only knew that our relatives from the villages were hardworking, good people. In fact, I thought they had better relations with each other and had greater concern for the community than the educated Christians. Besides, I enjoyed taking part in the village religious rites much more than going to church.

It was only later that I understood that categorizing religions in a hierarchy is a tool used to discriminate against religions or belief systems which do not fit within Western standards or norms. My father, who no doubt sincerely believed and was passionate about his mission, became an instrument in promoting the superiority of mainstream religions. Fortunately, he mellowed with age, and later on in his vocation as a priest, he accepted that our indigenous religion is not the work of the devil. For me, asserting the validity of indigenous ancient religions is a way of reclaiming what has been denigrated or consciously eroded by the colonizers and the postcolonial governments.[5]

What are the basic features of *sináng-adum ay pámmati* for us Igorots, and what are the links with ecology? What are the concepts associated with this traditional religious worldview? What are the links between the mythical ancestors, human ancestral spirits, and the "deities" and land and nature? What are our concepts of land use, land ownership, and resource management and how are these related to our traditional beliefs and customary practices?

Traditional Igorot religion is characterized by ancestor worship and nature worship. The key elements of this religion are as follows.[6]

a. Living things are attributed with souls or spirits. When a person dies, her or his soul will become a spirit (*aníto*), which will reside nearby.
b. A major religious concern is the placation of spirits of the dead (*aníto*) through animal sacrifices in communal ceremonies.
c. Spirits are invoked to partake of the sacrificial meat or wine and are requested to bring good fortune, bountiful harvests, and good health.
d. Spirits make their presence and wishes known through female shamans or priestesses (*mensíp-ok, mandàdawak*) and male priests (*mombaki*).
e. Land formations, water bodies, rocks, etc., are believed to host spirits who protect them from pollution or destruction.

   f. Deities have particular roles to play. For instance, the Ifugao
have Bulol (Rice God or Goddess). The Ibalois have Balitok
(God of Gold).

   g. There is a belief in the Creator, or the Supreme Being, who is
called Kabónyan.[7] Prayers of intercession to Kabónyan are
done through the ancestral spirits.

   h. There are specific religious rituals for each of the seasons in
the agricultural cycle in which specific roles are played by
male elders, older women, and young boys and girls.

The Igorot believe that land is a gift from Kabónyan. Land is
synonymous with life. It is the source of identity and it provides the
material and spiritual link between the past, present, and future
generations. We do not consider ourselves the owners of the ancestral
territory and resources found therein. We are but the stewards,
trustees, or custodians. The beings in the spirit-world and the deities
are the real owners of the land. Thus, it is imperative to consult these
spirits and deities when land is used, converted, or transferred and
when resources are harvested, planted, or hunted. The forms of consultation range from a simple petition, prayer, or chant to elaborate
rituals in which every village member participates.

Igorot prayers are mainly different prayers of petition. The most
common plea is for fertility—fertility of domestic animals, of growing crops, fertility for the married couple or the tribe in general. There
are also prayers to thank and praise the spirits for an abundant harvest,
for striking gold in the mines, and for other such instances of good
fortune. These are offered to acknowledge the proprietary rights of the
spirits to the land, resources, and material blessings bestowed upon a
family or clan.[8]

In their prayers the people ask the spirits, the plants, animals, and
insects to do something beneficial for the individual, the clan, or the
ili (village). The need to sustain good relationships between human
beings, between humans and the rest of creation, and between humans
and the spirits and deities is always reiterated in Igorot prayers and
chants. If there is a break in these relations, the Igorot believe that
harm or bad fortune will befall them.

Rituals are for the propitiation and appeasement of the *anitos*, because when they are displeased, disease or an accident can happen. If
a hunter catches wild game beyond what he needs, a resident spirit in
the forest might get angry and make the hunter sick. For the hunter to

get well, special offerings and prayers should be offered to the nature spirit who has caused him to get sick. The ancestral spirits are regarded as guardians of both the people and the environment. They discipline those who don't behave properly. These spirits can also be invoked by the oppressed to seek justice and to ask for the punishment of the oppressors.

The belief that every living thing has a soul (*ab-abí-ik*) is a central feature of Igorot traditional religion. The living can communicate with the spirits of dead people, plants, and animals through mediums. Traditional shamans, priestesses and priests, or healers (*mensíp-ok, mandàdawak, mombaki*) are the usual mediums. The presence and wishes of the spirits are made known through them. They mediate between the ordinary world and the spiritual and supernatural world. The gift or skill—or curse—of being a *mensíp-ok* is usually inherited. If a woman is a *mensíp-ok,* chances are at least one of her daughters will become one. The *mensíp-ok* and *mandàdawak* are almost always women.[9]

Not only ancestors, plants, and animals (that is, living things) are endowed with spiritual powers; places, symbols, sounds, and moments also have special powers attributed to them. Some land formations, water bodies (especially springs and rivers), and rocks are considered sacred due to the power of spirits residing in them. It is *lawá* (forbidden) to disturb these sacred places by constructing residences, roads, dams, and the like on or near them. This is especially so for water sources, because the belief is that any disturbance or pollution will anger or disturb the spirits protecting the place. And, if the spirits leave, the water will disappear.

The spiritual powers attributed to a place can be enhanced or strengthened by significant events taking place there. Each village has *patpatáyan*s (sacred groves), where rituals are observed. No one is allowed to cut the trees in this sacred site, since these trees are also the residences of nature spirits. The *pináding* is a nature spirit who inhabits the *patpatáyan*. The Madukayan *pináding*s are described as "invisible creatures who can be heard on various occasions and whom we think of as neighbours."[10]

The *dap-áy* is another ritual place complementing the *patpatáyan*. This place, which is paved with stones and has a hut, has multiple functions, serving as the social and religious center. The hut is both a dormitory and a learning center for young boys. Village and inter-village rituals are held here. The *dap-áy* also marks the political divisions of the village. For instance, the *dap-áy* of my paternal grandparents in our village, Payeo, is called *Pap-ayangan* and around seven to ten families belong to this *dap-áy*. Disputes are settled in the *dap-áy*, and thus it is also a tribunal center. During the days of headhunting and tribal warfare, this was where strategies were planned and victories celebrated.

The Ibaloi Igorot's traditional concept of land is that it is a resource that should be shared reciprocally with the gods and goddesses, ancestors, kin, and future descendants. The beings in the spirit world are responsible for protecting the natural world from human greed.[11]

Land is inextricably linked with our identity and survival as distinct peoples. It is precious not only because it is the abode of our deities and of the nature spirits; it is doubly precious because these deities and spirits were nourished and defended by our ancestors with their sweat and blood. The intricate web of relationships between human beings and nonhumans and the ways human beings adapt to their physical environment are regulated by taboos (*lawá*) and customs.

The tales of the Ibaloi Igorots on how their territory and resources are protected depict the roles played by ordinary mortals, animals, supernatural beings. They have Balitok (God of Gold), from whom people should ask permission to mine; *mamantala* (witches) who protect the wild animals; and wild pigs who lure hunters away from trails leading to the forests.[12] Elaborate rituals and animal sacrifices are offered to the gods and goddesses, deities, spirits, and ancestors before productive activities—hunting, tilling the soil, planting, harvesting, or mining—commence.

Igorots respect usufructuary rights to land, especially in relation to swiddens. If you don't till the land, you don't have any rights to it. The systems of land classification among the various groups have many commonalities. The Bontocs and the northern Kankana-ey Igorots have similar systems of land classification. Tribal territory is first established, which includes the forests, farms, bodies of water, rice fields, and the *ili* (village). Next are areas considered communal property, which are available for use by any member of the *ili*. These are pasture lands, rivers and lakes for fishing, and the forest. The Bontocs call this type of land *lamoram*. The *tayan* are lands considered the corporate property of a certain clan or bilateral descent group. These also consist of pasture lands, *umá* (swidden), fishing areas, and forests.

Figure 1. The dap-áy *in Payeo, Besao, Mountain Province.*
(Photograph Victoria Tauli-Corpuz)

Finally, there are lands owned by individual families, such as the *ba-ángan* (house lot) or the *payew* (rice field). Prior use or constant use of the land gives one greater rights over the land. For example, my parents have their own house lots and rice fields which they inherited from my grandparents. By tradition, these lands should be inherited by their children. Since no one of us siblings now resides in the *ili*, these lands are being used by our relatives and they are not obliged to share the harvests with us. They have more rights to the resources of the land because they are the ones using the land. However, if any of us decide to stay in the village and work on these lots, the right to the land's produce returns to us.

Indigenous Rice Cultivation

Rice cultivation is a common activity among Igorots. So central is it that other agricultural activities revolve around it. While religious rituals are conducted in relation to the life cycle of birth, sickness, and death, a whole set of rituals is also held during the different phases of the agricultural cycle of rice cultivation. William Henry Scott describes these rites:[13]

> Formal religious rites accompany every phase of the Igorot agricultural year, from preparation of the seedbeds through the sowing of the seeds, the transplanting of seedlings, and danger from worms and drought, to the harvesting and actual storing in the granary, to say nothing of periodic sacrifices for flourishing growth meanwhile. Indeed, such rites even precede the preparation of the seedbeds, for a day when the Igorots' ancestors knew no irrigated rice is reflected in the ritual planting of taro roots before the year's cycle of farming is even begun. All the seasonal festivities are atuned to this agricultural calendar, and the proper time for weddings, weeding, house repairs, pig-pen cleaning and gardening are all accompanied by religious ceremonies by which a variety of deities are worshipped, some privately and some publicly, some on behalf of an individual and his immediate family and some on behalf of the whole town or some section of town.

The main religious rituals among us, the Kankana-ey Igorots, are linked with birth, marriage, death, and the agricultural cycle. Most of these are held at the *dap-áy* and the *patpatáyan*. In my village, Payeo, the agricultural calendar starts the first of August with a ritual called *lakat.* An old woman or man is designated by the *amám-a* to plant *lakat* (taro, or *gabi,* tubers) in a rice field. A three-day religious holiday called *obáya* is declared. During this time, an old man called the *mamacdé* goes to the *patpatáyan* along with young boys and a young pig.

The sacrifice of the *pacdé,* the sacrifice of a pig, is performed and a prayer said, which goes, "may the *lakat* have a good harvest and may our pigs and chickens multiply and not be attacked by pests and may our crops be bountiful."[14] The old man and young boys return to the village and the pig meat is distributed to the *dap-áy*s, which in turn will share the meat among the individual houses in each *dap-áy.* After the *obáya,* anybody is allowed to plant taro or sweet potato (*camote*).

The next ritual, called *binitoto,* takes place around September. A small amount of *palay,* or rice seeds, is sown in a stone basin containing mud and water to test the germination capacity of the seeds. By October, before the sowing of rice seedlings (*padog*) in the prepared seedbeds is done, another ritual takes place. An old woman is again designated to *menpadog,* or sow seed, in her seedbed. After this, a five-day *obáya* is again declared, with the *pacdé* performed daily. This time, the prayer asks for the protection of the seedlings from pests so they can mature for planting.

Tóned, or planting rice, follows. Again *obáya* is declared, and only after this is over will everybody proceed to plant. *Ug-ugbo,* or mutual labor exchange, is practiced widely during this season. A big group will plant in one field and then proceed to do the other fields of the members of the *ugbo.* At the *pacdé* during the *obáya,* the prayer asks that the crops be protected from pests, the harvest be good, and erosion of the fields not happen.

Finally, when harvesttime arrives, a series of rituals again takes place, starting with *pus-ok,* the thanksgiving ritual before the actual harvest. After the harvest, another ritual, called *a-aw,* is observed where each family offers chicken or pig sacrifices in the *agamang* (rice granary) or in the *payew* (rice field). A *bégnas* is then declared. The *bégnas* (community feast) is where the sacrifices and prayers are offered to the ancestral and nature spirits. Pigs and chickens contributed by the villagers are slaughtered and offered to the spirits and eaten by the people afterwards. Gongs are beaten and people dance until sundown.

A prayer called *siksíka* is said by the first woman who will step onto the field to be harvested. The prayer (*sápu*) goes:

Sumika ka ay pagey. Pagey ay kintoman, menkatogawan di litaguan, pagey ay labbasi, mapno mapno'y gimata di lalalaki ya luwan di babbabai. Makileg ka ay gawis ta siay amay. As gumtekan di onga sia am-amed. Nan payew dampay, kukumneg. Dey, no waday maitapi as omali ay maki-ani, epdas nakwani. Maseg-ang ka ay adi kaila ta olay no kungaw dampay waday suntena. Sumika sika ka tay naay da ay nabka nan sinin-a ay mang ani ken sik-a.

Oh unseen Creator, multiply the grains of rice! *Kintoman*[15] grains which give life to the tribe. Fill up the baskets of the men and women. Watch over the fields so they will never erode. Should more people come to help us harvest, the prayers are already said. Grant us a bountiful harvest! Increase the harvest manyfold so that it will be enough for everyone.

A five-day *obáya* is declared in which no one is allowed to leave the village and no one is allowed to come in. Signs in the form of twisted reeds (*sagangsang* or *pudong*) are put at the entrances to the

Figure 2. Cordillera Day Celebrations, 1994. Second from right: Victoria Tauli-Corpuz, then chairperson of the Cordillera Peoples' Alliance (Photograph Catalino Corpuz, Jr.)

village to indicate that no one may enter or leave the village. Those who violate this restriction, and those who do not take part in the festivities, will be fined (*mamulta*). The *bégnas* occurs several times within the agricultural cycle—before planting, after harvest, or even to call on the rains to come.

The religious or ritual holidays (*obáya, té-er, téngao, tungo*) last from one to five days. During this period, aside from the ban on entering or leaving the village, no one is allowed to work in the rice terraces. There are various reasons for this. First is the need to synchronize agricultural activities. This is very important for rice planting because it is a sure way of deterring the proliferation of field rats and mice, which are major pests. When there is an attack by these pests, the whole community can be mobilized to deal with it. Those who don't synchronize their planting will find pests concentrated in their fields. Second, synchronized planting is also important for water distribution. The water supply needed to irrigate a rice field depends on what phase the rice plants are in. If there is no synchronization, then there will be chaos and fighting because the demands for water will vary from one field to another. Third, with synchronization the practice of mutual labor exchanges (*ug-ugbo*) can be better organized. During planting and harvesting seasons the need to concentrate people in work groups is greater. If the work force is inadequate during the labor-intensive periods, production will be adversely affected. If the rice is not harvested at the proper time, the rice will become *nakset* (burned) by the sun and the grains will be destroyed. Finally, unity-building among the village members is heightened with cooperative planning. Social cohesion is one of the main objectives of community rituals. Another purpose is to enhance the harmonious relationship between the villagers and nature. When rituals are held, one component of the prayers offered to the spirits is for them to help strengthen community solidarity.[16]

Seed selection, storage, and processing (removal of grain from the stem) and the sowing itself are all done by the women. There is a special way of casting the seeds, for which some women develop an expertise. The reputation of these women extends far and wide, and they are asked to render their services free to those who request them.

Sowing the seedbeds (*menpadog*), transplanting the rice (*tóned*), and putting scarecrows in the fields containing rice almost ready for harvesting are all started by a "priest" or "priestess" who has also gained a reputation by having worked in fields which had a good harvest, little or no pest infestation, or no adverse weather conditions to threaten the crop.

The Kalingas, who produce rice in both swiddens and wet terraces, have a belief in a female divinity of the rice which is different from the beliefs of the Bontoks and Kankana-eys. The harvesting of rice in the swidden begins with a prayer by an old woman. She addresses the petition for greater harvest to a female goddess of rice, Cabunian—who should not be confused with the male Kabónyan, who plays the role of a creator god. When the rice is stored in the granary, another prayer is said to ask that no harm befall it and that it not be consumed easily. Unlike the Bontoks, Ifugaos, and Kankana-eys who use chicken and pork, the Kalingas prepare sticky rice (*inarkay*) for the ritual feast during the harvest.

June Prill-Brett, an Igorot anthropologist, has described the role of rituals in agriculture:

> Rituals have played an important role in the Bontok farmer's adaptation to ecological constraints which they have faced for many generations. For instance, religious beliefs and other symbolic systems may be seen to have directly adoptive functions for these beliefs result in behaviors which have ecological consequences. Ritual performances give farmers confidence and some feeling of control over their daily encounters with unpredictable phenomena or with uncertainty caused by environmental perturbations. These rituals emphasize the relationships between farmers, the biophysical world, the social world, and the supernatural world. Moreover, rituals enable farmers to adopt to continue to survive in their particular environment. Rituals allow the cooperation of neighbours and co-villagers, and reinforce group solidarity in relation to common crises and benefits.[17]

Whereas the Kankana-eys perform many of their rituals in the *dapáy*, the Ifugaos, who do not have such an institution, conduct many of their rituals in or under the house or rice granary. Among the Igorots, it is the Ifugaos who have the most gods and goddesses, deities, and ancestral spirits. Roy Barton, one of the first anthropologists who studied the Ifugaos, has listed around fifteen hundred deities ranging from gods and goddesses to imps, demons, spirits living in trees, stones, mountains, and rivers, and the omnipresent ancestor spirits.[18]

Some deities have specific assignments or roles. For instance, there are twenty-three deities charged with overseeing the art of weaving:

Manlotlot is the winder of the thread and the spindle and Mamiyo stretches the skeins. For pest control there are eleven deities: Bumigi looks after the worms and Lumadab takes charge of drying the rice leaves. Among the major gods, Ampaul is the one who gave animals and plants to the people and is in charge of rice transplanting. Wigan is the God of Harvests and Bulol is the Rice God or Goddess.

Pest Control, Forest Management, and Ifugao Deities

Some key resource management practices of the Ifugaos need to be mentioned because these again show the clear interface between their religion and ecology. One practice concerns the use of *holok,* which is a mixture of at least ten plants gathered from the forests to control rice pests. This is described by Elizabeth Omengan, an Igorot botanist.[19] The ritual takes place when the rice crop is about one meter high, which is usually the time the rice pests appear. The people gather at least ten kinds of plants from the forest in quantities enough to fill many large sacks. One chicken is collected from each of the involved households and brought to the granary. The *mombaki* (native priest) butchers each chicken and reads the bile. He invokes the name of a *maknongan* (a mythical ancestor) who has to be appeased. Many other names of other gods and goddesses are invoked while the bile from the chickens is read. After this, the collected plants are chopped and pounded.

A ritual performer takes the pestle and places it in the mortar while the *mombaki* stands. With one stroke of the pestle, the *mombaki* falls to the ground and then those gathered around shout, "the pests have died. They went downstream and drowned." The *mombaki* stands and the people start pounding the plants. After the *holok* is pounded, it is placed in two winnowers and a series of prayers is said from midday until dawn. The prayers end when the cock crows, and the *holok* is distributed and placed strategically in a paddy determined by the *mombaki* as the favorable site. The smell of the pesticide spreads to the surrounding paddies and slopes. Within three days, rice bugs, rice leaf folders, stem borers, even rats and rice birds are found dead around the paddies. This usually takes three days. No one is allowed to go into the area so the effect of the ritual is not diminished.

An analysis of the plants used indicates that these do indeed contain pesticidal properties. These plants include *balballatong; bulwang*

(*Marattia sp.* Swartz), *hanakta* (*Budleja asiatica* Lour), *huh-ig* (*Justica gendarussa* Burm), *ludon agohep* (*Ampelopsis heterophylla* Planch), *page-page:paktiw* (*Capsicum frutescens* L.), and *wakal* (*Uncaria sp.* Shreber).

Of the various land forms described in the Ifugao agricultural system, the *pinugo* (microforest) and *muyong* (private woodlot) are the most interesting. Not only are they the centers of biodiversity, they also serve as the watersheds. Nature spirits are believed to live in these forests, in the trees and stones. Thus, several rituals have to be observed before any activity is undertaken in the *muyong*. Harold Conklin estimated that there are around two hundred plant varieties found in these areas.[20] Several customary laws govern the use and management of the *muyong* and *pinugo*. Robert Ngidio, an Ifugao forester, has this to say of the *muyong*:[21]

> The Ifugaos for many years have been managing biodiversity quite successfully without professional intervention. As an Ifugao myself, I have firsthand knowledge on how the Ifugao forefathers handle muyong resources with utmost care. Year round activities are concentrated on thinning, cleaning and salvage cutting. Harvesting of crops are [sic] highly selective in nature. Selection cutting is hinged on Ifugao farmers' good knowledge of classifying in detail which tree is suited for firewood, timber and other purposes. Seasonal cutting of trees is a highly beneficial silvicultural practice, allowing the forest to recover from disturbance before another cutting is made. In the previous years tribal elders or the mumbaki (native priest) decide on matters such as when to extract resources and settling disputes related to resource use.

To be sure, the traditional beliefs, taboos, and practices related to resource use and management have proven to be effective deterrents in preventing the clear-cutting of the trees in the *muyong,* even for those Ifugaos for whom wood carving has become a profitable commercial activity.

Conclusion

The cases I have described indicate the interface between religion, culture, and ecology. This interface is better appreciated in pre-industrial societies like the Igorot villages, where people still believe that living things have souls or spirits. Those who still know what *innáyan* and *lawá* mean are more likely to be better nurturers of the earth, of other human beings, and of the rest of creation. What had been maligned by our colonizers and even by the postcolonial governments as primitive and heathen practices and beliefs is now being seen in a different light.

It is important to note the seamless web of activities surrounding a particular productive activity, where the divisions between agriculture, forestry, rituals, and ecology become blurred. For researchers and academics it might be useful to deconstruct and label each activity and put them in separate boxes. For the average Igorot, however, this way of doing things is hard to understand. To them, these are all related activities, and separating one from the other effectively destroys the integrity of indigenous systems.

The struggles which our ancestors waged against the Spanish colonizers to ensure their independence were struggles to maintain their ways of life and ways of relating to each other and to the earth. They have paid a price for this in terms of not being able to have access to more modern technology and to what is known as development. They have been subjected to the worst forms of discrimination and oppression, not only by the colonizers but also by postcolonial governments. Their customary laws and indigenous sociopolitical institutions have not been recognized and, instead, national laws and policies that are contradictory and inappropriate have been imposed. Land laws which negated indigenous land concepts and use have been legislated. The imposition of Christianity has further exacerbated the marginalization of traditional religion and belief systems.

In spite of all this, however, many Igorots tenaciously hold on to some of their traditional beliefs and practices, especially those which reinforce the harmonious relationship between themselves and nature. The fights they have waged and are still waging against destructive "development" projects (dams, mines) are still very much influenced by their traditional concepts of land and land use. They cannot allow these lands, which are the abodes of their ancestral and nature spirits and their gods and goddesses, to be destroyed or appropriated. These lands, which are the sources of their identity and which have nurtured generations of Igorots, cannot be given up so easily.

During the struggles against the Chico River Dam Project, a project funded by the World Bank in the early 1970s, the Bontocs and Kalingas, who were directly affected, put up a formidable fight against the dam.

At that time I was already doing organizing work in the villages and I had the opportunity to visit and live with the people in some of these areas. The main reason the people cited for their opposition to the dam project was not that the environment would be destroyed. There is no local language for environment. They opposed the dam because their rice fields would be drowned, their ancestral burial grounds would be destroyed, the nature spirits who live in the river and the stones in the river would lose their abodes. Then, if the *ili* were to disappear, so too would their identities and belief systems.

It was the same story when the northern villages of Sagada, the villages where I was primarily based, were included in the Cellophil Resources Corporation logging concession. This was a three-hundred-thousand-hectares concession given to a crony of Marcos. I took part in the meetings where the multilateral peace-pact agreements were forged between the Kankana-eys of Sagada and Besao, the Tingguians of Abra, and some Kalinga tribes. The same reasons for opposing the project were cited.

These experiences reinforced further my belief that indigenous worldviews or cosmologies, belief systems, and economic, cultural,

Figure 3. View of the traditional terraced rice fields in Banga-an, Sagada, Mountain Province (Photograph Victoria Tauli-Corpuz)

and political institutions should not be allowed to disappear just for the sake of so-called progress or development. Indigenous peoples were able to preserve their environment and maintain a balanced ecology precisely because of their beliefs. The claim that indigenous peoples are the real stewards or custodians of the environment is not sheer romanticism. This claim has behind it a whole history of life-and-death struggles, which has resulted in the deaths of many indigenous peoples, from the past up to the present.

It has been acknowledged that belief systems are very much inter-twined with the level of economic development reached. With the increasing incursion of modernity in the Cordillera, traditional beliefs and practices are threatened with extinction. However, the fact that they still exist, in spite of the incursion of Western-style education, Christian churches, and cash-cropping, says something. Undoubtedly, the continuing struggles of the Igorots to assert their right to self-determination, their rights over their ancestral territories, and their right to their own culture and knowledge have helped in the continuing existence of such belief systems and practices. It should also be acknowledged, however, that the continuing beliefs and practices of the *sinang-adum ay pámmati* (traditional religion) have strengthened the resistance offered by the Igorots against modernization projects that are anti-environment.

The strength gained by the indigenous peoples' movement in the Cordillera has also influenced the churches to become more sensitive to the indigenous peoples' cosmologies and practices. Now, some churches have started to indigenize their liturgies and others have gone even further to make their teachings more socially relevant. Labeling as pagan or heathen traditional practices related to the agricultural cycle and life cycles of birth, marriage and death is no longer blatantly done, especially by the mainstream churches. The new fundamentalist churches, however, are taking over the role played by mainstream churches during colonization and the recent past and are even more vicious in denouncing Igorot traditions as works of the devil.

The Philippine government passed the Indigenous Peoples' Rights Act in 1998. Although there are many problems with the Act, it opens up some possibilities for indigenous peoples to continue their fight for their rights to be recognized. With the ecological and social crisis faced by the country, the government should seriously look at how the Igorots have managed to maintain some degree of ecological balance, especially compared to the rest of the country. However, the government should not make the mistake of looking only at indigenous resource management systems and indigenous technologies without taking into account the social-cultural-religious context.

Academics who are researching indigenous knowledge systems and indigenous resource management systems should be more active in influencing government policy. They should contribute to maintaining the integrity of indigenous systems instead of fragmenting them and taking only those which will fit into their own framework or agenda. Together with the communities they are researching, they should explore further what needs to be done so that the sustainable resource management practices which are undergirded by distinct belief systems will be allowed to flourish.

Finally, we ourselves, the Igorots, should continue reexamining what within our own traditions should be enriched further and what should be allowed to wither. The odds we face are tremendous because of the globalization efforts of international bodies like the World Trade Organization, the World Bank, and the International Monetary Fund. What is worse is the complicity of our government in supporting the agenda of these global bodies. The liberalization of investments has led to aggressive measures to force us to have our territories mined by big foreign mining corporations. The liberalization of trade is pushing us to convert our lands to produce cash crops considered globally competitive.

The harmonization of intellectual property laws to fit into the Western mold of intellectual property protection means appropriation of our indigenous knowledge and biogenetic resources by agricultural, biotechnological, and pharmaceutical companies. It also means the patenting of plants, animals, microorganisms, and even human beings. The collection of the genetic materials of indigenous peoples under the Human Genome Diversity Project is still continuing, and several of the Igorot tribes have been chosen as targets. While we assert our rights to our culture, religion, indigenous knowledge, and resources, we should not lose sight of these global threats.

Other indigenous peoples from other parts of the world are also active in asserting their rights, and it is imperative that we join hands with them because we all have a message to tell the world.

Indigenous peoples' traditional religions and beliefs have been suppressed and made invisible by colonizers and by the colonized dominant populations. The homogenizing process of globalization which we are presently witnessing poses even greater threats to these cultures and religions. I hope that more indigenous peoples will be encouraged to write of their own experiences and perspectives. This is one way of reclaiming what has been appropriated, denigrated, and misrepresented.

Notes

1. In an earlier draft of this article I used animism as the term and concept for the Igorot traditional religion. I justified the use of this as a way of reasserting the validity of our traditional religion, which attributes souls or spirits to nature. Our belief system has been denigrated and consciously eroded by colonizers and the postcolonial governments, and it was placed on the lowest rung of the hierarchy of religions. However, a reader of that early draft commented that the concept of animism is "still a substitute theoretical construct" and suggested that I use Igorot native terminology instead. Thus, I am now using our native terminology, which is *sináng-adum ay pammáti,* literally translated as "ancient or traditional religion." I think that animism might still be used to describe our traditional religion since it is defined as a belief that spirits dwell in nature and parts of nature. However, because I am not familiar with how the term "animism" has evolved or with the debates surrounding its use, I will use our native terminology.

2. William Henry Scott, *Of Igorots and Independence* (Baguio City: ERA, 1994), 20.

3. Victoria Tauli-Corpuz, "Reclaiming Earth-based Spirituality: Indigenous Women in the Cordillera," in *Women Healing Earth: Third World Women on Ecology, Feminism, and Religion,* ed. Rosemary Radford Ruether (Maryknoll, N.Y.: Orbis Books, 1996), 100.

4. William Henry Scott, *The Discovery of the Igorots: Spanish Contacts with the Pagans of Northern Luzon* (Quezon City: New Day Publishers, 1974), 194.

5. The historian of science Carolyn Merchant, in her book *The Death of Nature: Women, Ecology, and the Scientific Revolution* (San Francisco: Harper and Row, 1980), 121, says: "The animistic concept of nature as a divine, self-active organism came to be associated with atheistical and radical libertarian ideas. Social chaos, peasant uprisings and rebellions could be fed by the assumption individuals could understand the nature of the world for themselves and could manipulate its spirits by magic. A widespread use of popular magic to control these spirits existed at all levels of society, but particularly among the lower classes."

6. One of the earliest recorded descriptions of Igorot religious worldview and practices was done by Fray Francisco Antolin in his writings of 1789, cited by William Henry Scott in *The Discovery of the Igorots.* Some of the elements cited came from his descriptions. However, I have added to the list what I have observed to be key elements.

7. Kabónyan is regarded differently by various Igorot ethnolinguistic groups. For the Kankana-ey he is the Creator God or the God of Nature. For the Ifugao he is a miracle-working demigod. The Kalinga consider him the greatest god. See William Henry Scott, *On The Cordillera: A Look at the Peoples and Cultures of the Mountain Province* (Manila: MCS Enterprises, 1969), 147.

8. Kate C. Botengan, "Bontoc Concepts on Sickness and Death," in *Filipino Tribal Religious Experience,* ed. Henry W. Kiley (Quezon City: Giraffe Books, 1994), 39.

9. Cordillera Research Briefs, *Three Generations: Indigenous Health Knowledges and Practices of Women in Barlig Central* (Baguio City: Cordillera Studies Center at the University of the Philippines, 1998). This study contains stories of relatives of

some *mensíp-ok,* or shamans, who claim that the restrictions attendant to being a shaman are strict, such as abstention from eating some meats, salt, and even from sex during the period of being a healer. Thus, it is when the *mensíp-ok* becomes meno-pausal that she will resume her healing vocation.

I spoke with several *mensíp-ok* and most of them said that they inherited their skills, or gift of healing, from their mothers and grandmothers. Urbana Aquintey of Besao, for instance, said that both her mother and grandmother are *mensíp-ok* and she inherited this gift, or curse. The gift can also be a curse, she said, because one has to cope with the demands expected by both the spirits and the living. Her mother must sacrifice a chicken each time she heals somebody who has gone through a compli-cated disease. This is done to protect herself or for cleansing purposes. Furthermore, she cannot charge her clients as this could lead to the loss of her healing powers. Urbana said she did not go through any training with her mother. After she herself had become sick and gotten well, she discovered that she could diagnose what is wrong with those who come to her for advice, and she can also heal. She is the only one of four sisters who has this skill.

10. Scott, *On The Cordillera,* 112.

11. *Contemporary Life and Issues: Igorot, A People Who Daily Touch the Earth and the Sky,* ed. Angelo J. de los Reyes and Aloma M. de los Reyes (Baguio City: Cordillera Schools Group, 1987), 115.

12. Anavic Bagamaspad and Zenaida Hamada-Pawid, *A People's History of Benguet Province* ([Benguet Province, Philippines: Benguet Province], 1985).

13. Scott, *On The Cordillera,* 145.

14. The various rituals held in my village, Payeo, have been described by my uncle, Simon Aquino, in his 1954 article, "Life in Payeo, Bontok, Mt. Province," *University of Manila East Asiatic Studies* 111, no. 4 (1954). Many of these rituals are still performed in this village.

15. *Kintoman* is a specific species of upland rice, which is colored red or brown and is one of the best-tasting types of rice cultivated and nurtured by the Kankana-ey Igorot.

16. Tauli-Corpuz, "Reclaiming Earth-based Spirituality," 103.

17. June Prill-Brett, *Coping Strategies in the Bontok Highland Agroecosystem: The Role of Ritual* (Baguio City: Cordillera Studies Center, 1997), 14.

18. Mariano A. Dumia, *The Ifugao World,* ed. Jean Edades (Quezon City: New Day Publishers, 1979), 22.

19. Elizabeth Omengan and F. Dumondon, "Holok: Forest Plants, Rice Pests and Ifugao Gods," *Montanosa Research and Development Center Occasional Papers* (Sagada), July 1989, 25.

20. Harold C. Conklin, *Ethnographic Atlas of Ifugao: A Study of Environment, Culture, and Society in Northern Luzon* (New Haven: Yale University Press, 1980), 9.

21. Robert Ngidio, "Conserving Biodiversity: The Case of the Ifugao Farming System," in *People, Earth and Culture* (Los Banos: Philippine Council for Agri-culture, Forestry and Natural Resources Research and Development, and National Commission for Arts and Culture, 1998), 25–26.

Religion, Ritual, and Agriculture among the Present-Day Nahua of Mesoamerica

JAVIER GALICIA SILVA

Introduction

According to Guillermo Bonfil Batalla,[1] there are two civilizations coexisting in contemporary Mexico as a result of an encounter between two worlds. On the one hand, the wisdom of the Mesoamerican civilization has maintained a cultural continuity among indigenous communities throughout the territory. This continuity is evidenced by enduring nomenclatures, languages, toponyms, social life, rituals, myths, customs, the distribution of space, as well as the identification and use of plants, foods, cultigens, and environments.

On the other hand, the "project" of Western civilization, imposed on indigenous communities at the time of the conquest of the sixteenth century, continues to be imposed even after the war of independence. For over five centuries this project has been used as a model of acculturation to supplant that which has survived for millennia, namely, those worldview values in which our people find motivation to go on each night after a tiring day in the fields. Yet, Western civilization simply refuses to recognize our indigenous culture.

This essay can only suggest the rural, ritual agricultural life of contemporary indigenous communities that has been active for millennia in the mountains of Mesoamerica. Its purpose is to reaffirm existential ties between humans, seeds, natural settings, and the gods through communications with the Cemanahuac, "that which surrounds us." Through this ritual process, indigenous peoples constantly create and recreate their culture in order to adjust to the pressures of change, reinforce their true and private environments, incorporate and modify foreign cultural elements to make them theirs, and cyclically repeat collective dramatizations as a way of expressing and renewing their identity. All of these strategies are designed to promote and ensure the survival of their cultures.

The existence of indigenous people is based on interwoven cycles of long and short duration. Each cycle implies a distinct ritual life. In other words, the distinct feasts and rites are the crystallization of diverse juxtaposed cycles. We simultaneously participate in an agricultural cycle and an indigenous-Christian ritual cycle, both of which are interlaced with social rituals that are family and community oriented.

The Mythical Character of Maize as Our Sustenance

In the *Florentine Codex,* a mythical origin of maize as the food for humanity is described:

> Listen: *Tonacayotl* [maize], Our Sustenance, is for us, all-deserving. Who was it who called maize our flesh and our bones? For it is Our Sustenance, our life, and our being.
>
> It is to walk, move, enjoy and rejoice. Because Our Sustenance is truly alive, it is correctly said that it is he who rules, governs and conquers. . . .
>
> Only for our sustenance, *Tonacayotl,* the maize, does our soil subsist, does the world live, and do we populate the world. The maize, Tonacayotl, is the true value of our existence.[2]

In part dedicated to the legends of the suns, the *Chimalpopoca Codex*[3] describes the obstacles overcome by the wise god Quetzalcóatl in finding maize. He fooled the red ant in order to discover the location of Tonacatépetl, "the mountain of our food" where the maize was hidden. This manuscript narrates how this maize was put to the lips of the first human couple. Below is a section of the myth that narrates how "our sustenance," Tonacayotl, was obtained:

> And so they [the gods] spoke once more:
> What oh gods shall they eat (the humans)?
> may our sustenance the maize descend!

But then the ant will gather
the maize from within the mountain of our sustenance.
Quetzalcóatl encounters the ant.
He asks him:
Tell me, where did you go to find the maize?
But the ant did not want to tell him.
Quetzalcóatl questions him insistently.
Finally the ant responded: "Over there."
He leads *Quetzalcóatl*.
This one immediately transforms into the black ant.
The red ant guides him.
He shows him the Mountain of our sustenance.
Then they both gather and gather the maize.
And the red ant guided *Quetzalcóatl*
To the edge of the field,
Where they were storing the husked corn.
Later, *Quetzalcóatl* carried it to *Tamoanchan*
There the gods ate profusely and
afterwards, on our lips *Quetzalcóatl* placed the maize
which made us strong.
And later the gods spoke:
What shall we do with the Mountain of our sustenance?
Moreover, the Mountain wants to remain there.
Quetzalcóatl tries to lift it, but could not move it.
Soon *Oxomoco* tried his luck,
and *Cipactónal* also tried hers,
the wife of *Oxomoco,* because she was a woman, *Cipactónal.*
Later *Oxomoco* and *Cipactónal* spoke:
"If only *Nanáhuatle* would strike it with lightning,
then would the Mountain of our sustenance be opened.
So the Tlaloque (gods of rain) descended
The blue Tlaloque
The white Tlaloque
The yellow Tlaloque
The red Tlaloque
Nanáhuatle immediately shot [a bolt of] lightning
Then the robbery occurred,
of the maize, our sustenance, by the Tlaloque.
The white maize, the dark, the yellow,
The red maize, the beans,
The sage, the wild amaranth, and the *bledos de pez*
Our sustenance, was robbed for us.[4]

Historian Miguel-León Portilla commented upon this myth in the following manner:

> The *Manuscript of 1558* describes a type of aboriginal genesis. It describes the myth of the cosmic ages to the creation of the fifth sun in which we live today. According to the legend this event took place in *Teotihuacán*. After mentioning the new creation of Man by *Quetzalcóatl,* the origin of maize myth, that I transcribed, tells how the gods were concerned over what humans should eat. They said: What will humans eat? May the maize, our sustenance, descend![5]

This narration demonstrates that an understanding of maize as our sole food has an ancient, mythic character. It is not merely a ballast of custom, because it lets us see what we were, what we are, and how we will be in the future. Here, Quetzalcóatl symbolizes wisdom, the black and red ant who stole the maize from the Mountain of Our Sustenance and put it to the mouths of the first humans, Oxomoco and Cipactónal, so that they "become strong."

The gods realized that a few grains of maize would not assure humanity's long-term survival. It was necessary for them to possess it all in order to cultivate the grain. The myth describes the intervention of the *tlalohqueh,* the gods of rain, who live in the mountains and come from the four corners of the universe to offer their assistance. However, the help of Nanáhuatle was required to open the Mountain of Sustenance with his lightning that liberated, once and for all, the diverse types and colors of maize.

By bestowing maize as our sustenance, the gods did more than grant a simple grain. They created a form of life and subsistence based on *tonacayotl,* "our food and our flesh." The people use an endearing diminutive term, "maicito" [little maize], to express their reverence and affection for maize. Below, I will demonstrate that this concept is still alive in the daily lives of the Nahua of Santa Ana Tlacotenco, located near Mexico City.[6]

Agriculture in Nahuatl Cosmovision

Daily life in the Nahua community is portentous. A bridge maintained between the night and day also links the past and the present. At night the ancient gods roam the ravines, caves, mountains, and village streets. During the day these beings wander the countryside, the forests, the gardens near the ravines, and among the holm oaks on the mountain tops. Their sacred space contracts during the day and expands during the night. The Nahua know of these deities whom they fear and venerate. They are beings of whom one asks for favors and protection, especially when evil befalls one's family. They are temporarily disavowed when other sacred beings approach, namely, that of the Virgin Mother, Mary, Santa Ana and the other saints of the Catholic Church. However, the former deities are not rejected. Rather, they form complementary images in local religious thought, where each has its space. While the domain of the virgin is the village during the day, the domain of the other, more numerous beings, is in the ravines, mountains, caves, and rocks, from where they govern during the day and the night. With them, one must also live in peace.

The ancient gods are more human than the Christian deities because they eat what we eat. Consequently, when we give thanks for our food, *tonacayotl,* we share with them so that they do not become angered and cease to share with us of the bread that sprouts from our mother earth.

For us, the narratives of the supernatural (*in Tetzahuitl*) symbolize all that which escapes Western reason, but which in our world possesses a deep and substantial meaning. The narratives are about a mythical and almost miraculous existence. There is an intimate connection between the myths, the sacred stories of the indigenous people, their villages, rituals, moral behavior, social organization, and daily activities.[7] Myth is neither a dark fantasy nor a senseless infusion of vain dreams; rather, it represents a laborious and important cultural force.

As one anthropologist suggests, "myth is not a narration that is simply told, but a reality that is lived"[8] where fiction has no place. It is a live reality believed to have occurred in remote times and which influences daily life and human destiny. For indigenous people, myth is alive in ritual and moral decision making. The *zazanille*[9] (narrations) and the *tetzahuitl* (the portentous) are present in the spaces and activities of daily life. They govern faith and control behavior toward other humans and toward the environment.

For the Nahuatl, *tetzahuitl* (the portentous) is not simply a symbolic expression but a direct experience of that spiritual being from which it flows. *Tetzahuitl* functions throughout the entire culture but is not derived from social forces. It expresses, illuminates, and codifies the creed, protects and reinforces morality, responds through the efficacy of the ritual, and contains the practical rules with which to guide humans. As such it is portentous, an indispensable element of human civilization that is neither a narrative nor a story, neither an intellectual explanation nor an artistic work. It is an active, working force, a practice of faith and of the moral wisdom of Nahua culture and people. This concept of reality lives in human consciousness and behavior. In other words, it is found in the oral tradition of the communities and not confined to the written word.

In Tlacotenco, some pre-Hispanic religious rites have adopted several Christian images, such as the cross and the saints. The people venerate their ancient gods, which are today represented by Christian figures utilizing the ancestral ritual forms described by the informants of Fray Bernardino de Sahagún and other friars and chroniclers of the sixteenth century.[10] But, what is the sacred universe of the contemporary rural Nahua living to the southeast of the urban Federal District?[11]

In the sacred world of Tlacotenc, the "portentous" traverse space to dominate humans and objects. Each object touched by these beings acquires a little of the divinity. One could say that the significance of many of these practices and concepts has varied over the past five centuries. But, as the Nahuatl continue to whisper their narratives in their own language, they also continue reproducing these religious concepts and adapting them to the new era. Here are a few examples.

The Mechanics of Agriculture

Around 1620, Father Hernando Ruiz de Alarcón described in his treatise *Tratado de las Supersticiones y Costumbres Gentilicias* "the superstitions of farmers and their magic" among the Nahua people living in the present state of Guerrero. He wrote the following:

> Arriving at the field of the maize . . . the conjurer enters in conversation with the *tarequa* spirits saying: "Listen you spirits whose words are in the rains. Do your task now that the spirit-gods in the clouds have come. Now I leave the spirit-maize who is princely among the others such as seven snakes. . . .[12]

Today, the central Nahua approach Tlatamachiuhque, "he who controls" or "he who knows about good weather," to ask him about the coming agricultural year as the clouds and whirlwinds that will send the rains approach. The agricultural cycle begins in the last days of December and continues through the month of January. The first agricultural rite consists in preparing Totlaltonantzin, "our mother earth," or *Totlaltzin*, "our earth," to be impregnated by the seed.[13] The sacred seed is conceived of as an infant that we must offer to nature. The maize is our brother, because he is our flesh, *"in Tonacayotl,"* and because we humans have fed from this divine substance since primordial times.

The first task of the peasant-farmers is to prepare the ground. They soften the soil and remove any remnants from the prior harvest. The areas around the field are also cleaned to avoid problems with rodents and insects. Finally, an organic material is added that will function as a fertilizer for the maize.

The purpose of turning the soil is to maintain the necessary humidity needed for the planting in the weeks following the beginning of February. The field is then raked with branches from bushes to level the surface area and to break up any remaining clods of dirt. This guarantees that the sun's rays do not reach holes in the soil and evaporate the vital humidity.

Before planting, the seeds are taken to the church to be blessed. The grains of maize selected for seed are taken to the churches on the second day of February, the celebration of Candlemas, to be blessed by the priests of the parish. Young animals (chickens, hens, pigs, mules, and goats) are also brought so that they may grow to be healthy and productive when they reach maturity. This activity is all tied to a fertility ritual in which the grain, especially, represents a being in a different phase of human growth.

Once the mass has been celebrated and the grains and animals are blessed, the peasants leave the church satisfied that they have completed their religious obligation. There is a sense of having brought to the house of God the future bread of the home. Now the only thing left to do is to ask Totlaltonantzin, "our mother earth," to begin her generative labors and protect our seeds in her bosom.

On the dawn of the planting, the people exclaim, *"Omoquixte totahtzin dios"* (God our Father has risen). By "God" they are referring to the sun. They may also say, "Hopefully, we will have a good working day." Having said this, they believe that they will have a productive day of labor in the fields. Sahagún made similar observations in his *Historia General de las Cosas de la Nueva Espana,* where he summarizes the ritual that our forefathers conducted at sunrise:

> . . . and when the morning came, they said: "The sun has begun his work. What will be? What will happen today?" At sunset they would say: "His work is finished" or "the Sun has finished his work."[14]

The comments provided by Sahagún's informants in the *Primeros Memoriales* are more illustrative:

> *Oquizaco in Tonatiuh, in totonametl, xiuhpiltontli, yn quauhtleuanitl auh ¿quen onotlatocaz, quen cemilhuitiz? ¿cuix itla ipan mochihuaz yn ycuitlapil yn iatlapal? Conilhuiaya:*
> *—Ma ximotequitilli, ma ximotlacotilli, totecuioe, Auh ynin momoztlae yn iquac ualquizaya Tonatiuh. . . .*

> The sun has risen, he who produces heat, the precious child, ascending eagle. What will be of his journey? How will be his day? Will something happen in us, his tail, his wing [the people]? They told him: "Do your task and complete your mission, our Lord." This was said every day at sunrise.[15]

The peasants, bent over the field in order to plant the maize, made a point always to be facing and following the sun. As they did so, they would recite the following:

> *Inon ce tacatl tlin qui tocaz, mo teochihua ica occequi tucaque ihuan tlapehque, quitlamach ihtoa chohue ica tlin itocatzin Toteotl ma ce cualli cemilhuitl inin ce tacatl ihuan occequi tacame ipan cuentin itic milli ma Toteotl qui mocahuile tlaihquion mochihuazto tlamachpaquiliz-mochuihuaz ihquiu yez.*

> Let us plant the first maize in the name of God that it be a good day. And that it be fruitful for all of us and also the plants of maize and fields that we will plant. So be it.[16]

The people of the Elutia and Cuatzintla regions ask of their gardens, and of the larger earth, that these deities begin their generative labors with the rainy season and the approaching clouds.[17] Now, the maize is left in the ground on the slopes of these higher elevations.

The local population refers to the second phase in the field as the replanting and weeding. It is the stage where the sun and the first rains have created a beautiful green carpet covering the ground of the maize fields. It is now time to replant the infant plants that the worms, the dryness of the earth, the moles, or *xalpitz* (a small species of mole), and the squirrels (*techelumeh*) have left.

In the fields one hears the voices of the children who, obeying their parents, sing a song of hope intended to ward off the predators of their crops, namely, the maize, *habas* (large beans), and the common bean (*frijol*). These children sing:

> *Techelotl, techelotl,*
> *ahmo xoconcua notlatlaol,*
> *onca hualaz tlamotlanqui,*
> *mitzontlatlacueponiliz,*
> *mitzonnanacatamaloz*

> Squirrel, squirrel
> do not eat my maize,
> because the hunter will come,
> to shoot you and eat you with *tamales.*

To control the rodent population further, tin cans are tied to blankets (*mantas*) and set up in the fields. The noise produced by these cans, aided by the wind or a farmer throwing a stone against them, will frighten away the animals. The farmers also put up scarecrows and wood traps to protect the crops and give them the necessary time to mature, with only minimal damage from pests.

As I mentioned, the farmer approaches his garden in constant dialogue with nature. This dialogue takes many forms. He listens to the birds, especially Mezutechitl, Cenzontle, and Huerecoch, understanding that their song announces the arrival of the first rains. The Nahua know how to interpret nature's messages announcing the arrival of the new season: humid soils in the gardens, the smell of moisture in the air, and the splendor of the leaves on the holm oaks and buddle trees. They also look for snake tracks on the paths to the gardens and, along the borders of the gardens, the paths exposed by moles. These are all ways of conversing with nature that reveal the time of the next morning or afternoon rain. They say that in spring, the whirlwinds cause the water to fall from the clouds. In autumn the whirlwinds cause the same clouds to return. These winds are the sounds of the ancient god Ehecatl, who sends us the rains.

With the arrival of June and July, the rains become more intense and the weeds have proliferated throughout the gardens. This is the time when the plants will be fed for the last time, using the *montón*. *Montón* is a term describing the process of forming small mounds of earth around the bases of the maize stalks. *Montón* has two functions: first, to discourage the reemergence of weeds that have germinated since the last weeding; and second, to protect the frail and easily broken plant stems from the winds of September and October. The weeding process is selective. A number of edible wild plants, such as *quelite* and *quiltoniles* (amaranth), *chivitos,* and *jaltomatoes,* medicinal plants used to cure *tenamitiliztli* (bad air), and plants used as animal fodder are allowed to grow among the corn.

Once the selective weeding is accomplished, the farmers urge the plants to grow, mature, and be fruitful. The maize is then allowed to thicken and mature. Four additional months must pass before the maize can be harvested. During this time the peasant-farmers dedicate themselves to other subsistence activities.

It is now summer, a time in which nature is also providing other products. The wild edible plants have matured, and one must go to the forest to gather them. During this period the people ascend into the level of the forest to obtain firewood from fallen trees. From the wood of the *oyametl* (pine wood) tree, they produce charcoal and shingles for roofing, which function much like clay tiles. Because the *oyametl* tree is the brother of Cemanahuac, "that which surrounds us," the people ask permission before using its wood so that the substance that lives within the tree and in the larger forest will not harm them. They also collect resin, edible fungi, rasp agave fruit, and produce *metzal* (a product extracted from the agave) which is used as pig feed.

Certain activities produce a necessary income to sustain the family during the period when there are no cereal crops, products, or money. Nowadays, the growing of nopal is a steady source of income that diminishes somewhat only during the colder months. Nevertheless, it produces enough income to feed one's family on a daily basis. Although nopal generates a larger income than maize, it is not the predominant cultigen, because of our pre-Hispanic understanding of maize as our primordial food, given to us by the gods. An example of the priority given maize is illustrated by Señor Margarito, a farmer whose children urged him to dedicate all of his lands to the cultivation of nopal. They urged him to cease planting corn because there was no profit in it, to which he responded: "If we do not plant *maícito,* what shall we eat?"

Even some Nahua interpret Señor Margarito's decision not to change crops as clinging to an ancient and obsolete tradition. However, at the foundation of this traditional attitude is the belief, inherited from the ancestors, that maize is "our food" given to us by the gods. The planting of maize, therefore, is much more than an activity of production. Our agriculture connects human lives with larger forces of meaning, knowing, and obligation. For example, one ritual prohibition for peasant-farmers is not to allow any of the maize leaves to be covered by the soil and remain covered. Indeed, farmers will scold those who permit this to happen. Maize is treated with compassion, and it is said that "if we do not care for the plant, then what shall we eat next year?" Similarily, if a woman comes across grains of maize lying in the street, she has no qualms about picking them up, because maize is our sustenance. We reverence the maize grains and stop, stoop, and take them in our hands.

In Book 5 of his *Historia General de las Cosas de la Nueva Espana*, Sahagún describes ancient Mexican beliefs concerning maize:

> it was also said that when maize spilled onto the ground, that he who saw it felt obliged to pick it up, and he who did not do so, committed an offense towards the maize, and the maize would report him to the gods saying: "Lord, punish this one who saw me spilled upon the ground and did not pick me up, or let him go hungry for not appreciating me."[18]

This quotation demonstrates that the understanding of maize as "our unique food" has a mythical and pragmatic character. It is not the baggage of ancient custom, but a way of seeing what we were, what we are, and how we are going to be in the future.

The Role of Mountains in Nahua Agriculture

A common ritual among many of the indigenous communities of Mesoamerica, including the Nahua, is the concept that the mountains cause good and bad weather, rains, hail, and frost. In the sixteenth century, Sahagún's informants said the following:

> When the feast of the *Tlaloque* was celebrated, all debts were paid on the summits of the mountains [and] all of the men *macehuales* . . . participated in the procession. They went, carrying on their shoulders

their *tetehuitl* . . . . They climbed there to the summits of the mountains to pay their debts—the *macehuales.*[19]

Once on the mountains, they implored the gods to send rain:

> We call to you, we invoke you, that which is green, providers from the four corners. You, lords of the forests, lords of the caves. Return here and comfort the *macehual*. Pour your waters over the earth, the animals, the plants, and the reeds. All await. Come quickly gods, our lords.[20]

The modern-day Nahua still believe that the mountains, ravines, streams, pools, and caves are inhabited by gods who, depending on their disposition, can be either malevolent or benevolent beings. These beings are called by different names, ranging from *Ahmo cualli Tlacatl, Nahuatoton* (the bad, the evil), *pingo* (devil), to *compadre* (godfather).

These figures, which are so often spoken of in evening conversations, inhabit the places mentioned earlier. When people eat, or drink *pulque,*[21] near a ravine, mountain, boulder, cave, or in the garden, they toss some of the food or drink to the being who inhabits that particular place (the *nahuatzitzin*). They believe that if they do not observe this custom, they run the risk of encountering "bad air" (*tenamitiliztli*) which manifests itself in the forms of nightmares, canker sores, or, in severe cases, insanity.

In *Primeros Memoriales,* some informants of Sahagún commented on the custom of *tlatlazaliztli,* "the throwing of food":

> *icoac intlein qualoz, yn aiamo quallo, azo tlacualli, achtopa achiton tepiton mocotonaia tlecuilixcoac unmotlazaia. Yn untlatlatlazaloc niman ic peoa ynic tlacualoz.* . . .

> At the point of eating something, before anything was consumed, such as food, first a small portion was cut and thrown into the fire. And when this portion was thrown, then one could eat. . . .[22]

In daily life, the first glass of *pulque* is usually dedicated to the earth or to the places mentioned above. In the home, a little was thrown into the ashes of the *tlecuil.*[23] Sahagún's informants commented on this custom as follows:

> *icoac in tlauanaloya, azo utiziecoloya, icoac in aca iacuican quitlaliaya uctli, unicuac oquitlapiuiyyoc ic tenotzaya, yoan tetlauan caxtepiton.*

Auh yn icuac ie tetlauantiz, conxopiloa tetlauantica yn uctli, niman yc contoyaua in tlecuilizquac. . . .

When they drank fermented liquor, or brought out the first batch of *pulque,* or when someone had acquired a new batch of *pulque,* when his strength was increased, he would call the people and the *pulque* was served in mugs or in small leaf cups in front of the fire. When they are ready to drink, he would serve the *pulque* in the cup and immediately spill some before the fire. . . .[24]

To get rid of bad air—*tenamitiliztli* or "malaire"—sent by the *nahuatzitzin* for not throwing or sharing food, tortilla or *pulque,* the affected person would be cleaned with herbs, including *estafiate* (*iztahiatl*), rue, *jarilla* (*achayatl*), *pirú* leaves (*tecapuleuahuitl*), or eggs. The person who performs the cleansing is called Tlamaqueh. If the patient is a man, a woman must perform the cleansing, and if the patient is a woman, it must be a man who cleanses her. The dual masculine-feminine meaning is believed to be complementary. Contamination by *tenamitiliztli* (bad air) or *tlailehuiliztli* (evil eye), which is transmitted in the streets, is attributed to either cold or hot qualities, and the herbs used to treat the illness are also of either a cold or hot quality, depending on the situation or location where the victim contracted the condition.

Because the mountains cause good and bad weather, rain, and hail during the month of April, it is the custom to climb the Metlaxinca and Ehcatépetl mountains (located approximately eight and fifteen kilometers, respectively, to the south of Tlacotenco) and request that they do not allow the hail to reach the lands of Santa Ana. These mountains are believed to be the home of Nahuatototzin who, depending on his disposition, can either protect or send evil upon the population. On the peak of the mountain there is a cross where people pray, offer flowers and incense, and ignite sky-rockets. This mountain, according to anthropological theory, plays the role of a totem, the protective substance of a group. In this case, however, this being is more than a collective protector for humans. The ritual is also performed for the defense and protection from "sudden attacks by other mountains (Ayoquemetl and Texicalo) who wish to dominate the region of Tlacotenco." Those charged with protecting the people from water spouts (*yecacoatl*), whirlwinds (*yecamalacatl*), frost (*cetl*), and hail (*tezahuitl*) are the Tlamatques ("those who know"). It is they who direct the ritual and climb the mountains to request good weather for the region.

The people believe that these two mountains (Metlaxinca and Ehcatépetl) are in constant combat to protect their respective populations. When an inhabitant dies after being struck by lightning, it is believed that the being from the "other" mountain has taken him to watch over his cattle (hail), and it is he who will watch that the hail does not destroy the terrain belonging to Tlacotenco. When it does hail on the fields while the maize is in flower, the people go out and spread ashes or salt on their patios in the form of a cross. Some launch sky-rockets because they believe that the noise will ward off the hail. The informants of Sahagún said this about hail:

> When very white clouds were seen above the mountains, they say that it was a signal of hail (*tlaloques*), which had come to destroy the crops and therefore there was much fear . . . and to protect the corn fields from being damaged, shamans, called *teciuhtlazques* (hail obstructers) would come forth. It is said that they knew a particular art or enchantment to get rid of the hail . . . to send it to the deserted areas where there were no crops. . . . It is said that when one had a field planted with maize, chili, chía or beans, and it started to hail, he would "plant" ashes in the patio of his home.[25]

There are narratives that describe the protection of maize from hail, the solicitation of rain from the mountains, and protection from a particular mountain called Ehcatépetl believed capable of generating great winds that could destroy crops. In this fashion the mountains are imagined as beings who can protect or destroy depending on the population of whom they are guardians.

The Harvest

Once the corn has been harvested from the last furrow, the workers kneel down and sing a song of thanks to "our fathers and mothers," the beings of nature who allowed the harvest of our food for this year.

In the home, the harvest ritual begins in a site selected for the granary, or *zincolote*.[26] The site of the granary is fumigated, and thanks are given to the gods for "bestowing" us with *tonacayotl*, "our food." The fumigation, or smudging, is directed to the four corners of the universe to form a cross. During this ritual the gods are asked that the corn suffice for the needs of the people and that worms and grubs not invade the maize. The base of the granary is formed with four pieces of wood over which additional boards are placed. In the center of the *zincolote,* corncobs are used to form a cross. The owner of the house blesses each of the boards of the base through fumigation. The people greet the arrival of the first baskets of corn with copal incense and with signs of the cross, exclaiming, *"axan yumaxitico tonacayoltzintle,"* "our sacred food has arrived."

Today, most of the peasants do not recognize the cosmological and traditional religious significance of the cross. They do not know if the fumigation is directed toward the four corners of the universe or if it is the sign of the Holy Cross. They do, however, pray to "Our Father."

After emptying the baskets of maize into the granary, the sign of the cross is made once more, using copal. The censer is placed in the center of the granary, below the boards, as the one holding the ritual says, *"Icayehuatzin ticnotzintilia, matichaxele tonacayotl"* (with this offering we make your base, that our food may endure). The people hope, by doing this, that there will be enough food for the entire year. In the ritual of receiving the maize, which is conceived of as a human being who is to be respected, the Almighty is thanked for having allowed the harvest. The granary is designed with air filters through slits in the sides of the walls to dry the corn, so that it can be husked four to five months later.

On the day of the harvest, a typical meal (*ahuaxmolli*) is prepared. The owner asks the help of all, regardless of age, to harvest the corn from the field. Among the population there exists a well-known narrative about maize and poverty. The story explains the attitude of the people who go to the trouble of picking up even a single kernel of corn that may have fallen on the ground:

> There once was a very rich man who had extensive lands and always harvested much. One day he told his workers, "Select only the corn which is good, and that which is *apoxcahuada* (humid, contaminated, or beginning to rot) is to be gathered and left in the field." The workers did so and only brought the good maize. Another man passed close by this field and heard someone crying. As it was very late in the day, he approached to see who might be crying. He saw that it was a boy who lay on the ground, crying. He asked the boy, "Why do you cry?" The boy said, "They do not want me because I am small and ugly. That is why they left me here. I have been abandoned."

The man responded, "Do not worry, I will take you to my home. Don't cry anymore." "Are you really going to take me to your home?" the boy asked. The man wrapped the boy under his cloak (*manta*) and carried him on his back. Upon arriving at his house, which was constructed of *tejamanil* (the man was poor), his wife asked what he had brought. The man answered that he had brought an abandoned boy.

His wife said, "Take him to the living room so that I may see him." The man lowered the boy and sat him on a sleeping mat only to see that the boy had turned into maize. Since then, this man always had a harvest, his fields always produced, while the lands of the rich man who wasted the small and rotten corn never produced another harvest.

The lesson of this narrative—as well as that of all of the ideas presented here which speak of this evil called "traditional mentality"— has a millennial origin. Sahagún, in Book 5 of his *Historia General,* describes the concept of maize held by the ancient Mexicans, saying:

> They also said that when maize spilled onto the ground, he who saw it was obliged to pick it up. He who did not do so insulted the maize and the maize would complain about this individual to the Gods saying, "Lord, punish this individual who saw me on the ground and did not pick me up, send him hunger because he did not appreciate me."[27]

The Garden and the Environment

The indigenous Nahua farmer is in dialogue throughout the agricultural cycle with the living beings[28] of Cemanahuac, "that which surrounds us." He seeks to hear the communications of the birds, the insects, and other animals and to learn of their knowledge regarding the approach of good and bad weather. He converses with the beings that inhabit the forest to request rain, wood, and other foods that they provide.

The garden is the place where various types of knowledge come together. The interpretation of weather, the words of the animals, the knowledge of soils, the coexistence with other animals all converge in the relationship with seeds, with whom the gardener pleads, "Give us our flesh and food" (*tonacayotl*). The Nahua speak with the gods in their gardens. This is where rites and songs acquire significance.

The Ecological Significance of Cemanahuac, "That Which Surrounds Us"

The modern Nahua have a ritual that manifests their sense of kinship with the beings that inhabit the Cemanahuac. The umbilical cords of newborn children are taken to the forest, where one goes in search of food. One practitioner, Francisca Romero, observed, "When the umbilical cord falls from the infant, the father carries it to the forest and places it in the bark of a tree. With time, it becomes a pine. This is done with all infants so that when they are big, they do not fear the night." The umbilical cords of girls are also taken to the forest so that they do not fear the night. The chroniclers of the sixteenth century wrote that the umbilical cords were placed in proximity to enemy villages to make them passive and so that the children whose umbilical cords these were would not fear war.

The Cemanahuac is where we live. It is our home. Because the tree is the brother of Cemanahuac, one must ask permission before using its wood. If this is not done, the substance that lives within the tree and in the forest can do harm to the peasant or his family by causing disease and even death. If the gifts of the forest are overexploited, there will come a time when the forest will cease to produce, because all living things become tired. Even the earth must be given time to rest so that it might produce better crops in the following year. Everything that exists in nature has its limits, can be exhausted, and is invaluable. We must take care not to misuse nature's resources so that we do not suffer one day.

By conceiving Cemanahuac, "that which surrounds us," to be our home, all of its members, including animals and plants, become mutually important for the existence of any one being. This is why the hunting of animals that prey on crops is limited to controlling their presence and not to eliminating them. We consider that these animals, when mature, will also benefit us by becoming our food.

Earlier, I said that, by conversing with animals, farmers perceive the arrival of the rains, storms, and the changing seasons. Other types of knowledge are also learned from animals. One also learns of bad omens from animals. The *comadreja* is a small animal that comes into the villages to prey on chickens. The people believe that when one of these animals is seen in the house, this is a forewarning of someone's death.[29] When the pinacate bug (Nahuatl, *pinacatl*)—a black beetle of ill repute because of the aroma it sprays when attacked—is found within a house, it is believed to be an omen that someone will fall ill. It is also a bad omen if an individual encounters a snake on the path: illness or death will come to him or to someone in his family. It is also thought that a large, dog-like animal blocking the path of an individual or group of individuals will cause people to return from whence they came, because the presence of the animal is believed to be a warning of something dangerous lurking in the field. Sahagún's informants observed:

> it was said that *Tezcatlipoca* often transformed into a wolf-like animal called *cóyotl*. And in this form he would block the path of an individual as if to close the road so that they would not continue. The individual would realize that danger lay ahead.[30]

Last to consider is Tecolote, the owl, the most efficient messenger of Mictlantecutli, "the Lord of the region of the Dead." The myth describes him as a bird, one of the animals elected by the Lord of the Underworld to advise people of their deaths. The informants of Sahagún interpreted the myth in this way:

> When someone hears above his house the call of the owl, he takes it as a bad omen. He would suspect that someone of his household was going to die or fall ill; especially if he heard the call two or three times over his house. They said that he was a messenger of the god *Mictlantecutli* who came and went to hell . . . who went around calling those who had sent him.[31]

Indigenous people also believe that there should be food for both animals and humans. For this reason, a diverse number of plants should be grown in the fields. Above, I noted that weeding within the agricultural cycle is selective. Left to grow between the furrows of maize are other legumes, such as the pumpkin, beans, *chilacayote,* chili, and chícharos. Edible wild plants, including quelite and quiltoniles (amaranth), chivitos, and jaltomatoes, as well as medicinal plants used to remove *tenamitiliztli* (bad air), are also permitted growing space. Farmers also allow plants to grow between the rows that are used as fodder for their beasts of burden. Finally, as Stefano Varese has observed, the Indians try to copy the natural habitat of plants in their fields:

From an agro-ecological perspective the garden and the strategies of multiple usage of natural resources from econiches and ecosystems represent two complementary aspects of a unique system of production whose principle consists in reproducing, within the cultivated parcel (and other areas of agroecological activities), the same order of diversity—various species in a reduced space—found in a natural state of non-cultivated environments.[32]

Conclusion

With this small sample of active rituals, myths, and beliefs concerning agriculture among the villagers of Tlacotenco, there is the feeling of a magical reality. Some of the rituals have been reactivated and accommodated to more modern perspectives. However, the astonishing fact is that there does still exist Nahua mythic criteria that motivate agricultural practices. In many ways, these traditional practices continue to respond to the real necessities of daily life. As a myth ceases to be functional or credible, it becomes disarticulated and seemingly lost; yet this fragmentation may be only surface deep in the realm of the mythic dimension. The Nahua mind absorbs all foreign myths and places them into a specific endemic space of beliefs. The ancestral, that which is "pagan," is recreated in the countryside, on the mountains, in the ravines, and, during the night, in the streets of the village. That which is Christian is generated during the day, only in the streets of the village, and is open to religious acts and pilgrimages, rosaries, and masses, where the power of the Christian pantheon predominates over that of the lords that inhabit the caves, mountains, fields, and ravines. These ancient lords of the night, however, maintain their reputations, qualities, exploits, and names in the native language. In Nahuatl, these lords acquire importance and power different from, yet related to, simply intellectual meaning. The mythical power of the language enters into pragmatic life among the Nahua by locating the people in an indigenous agricultural symbology. For the Indian, then, these are the intersecting and interpretive faces of this mythic reality, namely, the cosmic faces of local nature and the faces of the crops, the animals, and the people all gathered among the faces of time.

Notes

1. Guillermo Bonfil Batalla, *México Profundo: Una civilización negada* (Mexico: Cien de México, 1988).

2. *Códice Florentino: Book VI y X de la Colección Palatina de la Biblioteca Medicea Laurenziana,* 3 vols. (Mexico: Secretaria de Gobernación, Archivo general de la Nación, 1979).

3. *Códice Chimalpopoca: Anales de Cuauhtitlan y leyenda de los soles* (Mexico: Universidad Nacional Autónoma de México, Instituto de Investigaciones Historicas, 1975).

4. "El descubrimiento del maíz," extracted from the *Chimalpopoca Codex,* cited and translated by Miguel León-Portilla, *Toltecayotl: Aspectos de la cultura náhuatl* (Mexico: Fondo de Cultura Económica, 1983).

5. León-Portilla, *Toltecayotl,* 169.

6. Santa Ana Tlacotenco is of Nahuatl origin and is located in the Federal District in the Delegation of Milpa Alta, Mexico.

7. Bronislaw Malinowski, *Magic, Science, and Religion,* ed. Robert Redfield (Boston: Beacon Press, 1948).

8. The historian Alfredo López Austin considers that "the myth is a historical fact of social thought immersed in long-term discourse. It is a complex fact and its elements gather and cohere primarily around two nuclei that are reciprocally dependent, namely: a) a casual and taxonomic conception of holistic concepts that attribute the origins and nature of individual beings, the classes and the processes to particular conjugations of personified forces; a concept that resides in the actions and thoughts of humans about themselves and their environments. It becomes manifest in expressions, behavior and heterogeneous works, and dispersed in the diverse areas of social action; b) a construction of narratives that refer to the conjunction of personified forces under the pattern of events of the social type, which is expressed in narrative discourse, principally in the form of oral literature." See Alfredo López Austin, "Una definición de un mito" (manuscript, 1991), 2.

9. Sociolinguistically, the term *zazanille* is only used in the Tlacotenco community. That population systematically replaces the vowels "u" with "o" and "i" with "e." A similar pattern occurs among the Nahuatl of Texcoco.

10. See the *Florentine Codex,* the *Matriteuse Codices,* and the *Primeros Memoriales* in Bernardino de Sahagún, *Historia general de las cosas de la Nueva España,* ed. Ángel María Garibay (Mexico: Editorial Porrúa, 1985). And of other chroniclers, Fernando Alva Ixtilxóchitl, Domingo Francisco de San Antón Muñoz Chimalpahin Cuauhtlehuanitzin, Fernando Alvarado Tezozómoc, Gerónimo de Mendieta, Diego Durán, and Toribio de Benavente Motolinía.

11. López Austin says this concerning the sacred universe of the ancient Mexicans: "The Mesoamerican world was replete with gods and invisible beings; their presence reverberated throughout the countryside, in the springs, the homes, and in the fields. The stars traversed the skies, and in them bustled the small carrier of water, winds, lightning and hail. From the mountains, housing the water, the protector gods of the people warded off disease. The powers of the forefathers guarded the family honor . . . as the nights filled with spirits. The evil penetrated in the bodies and took

over the centers of power." Alfredo López Austin, *Los mitos del Tlacuache* (Mexico: Ed. Alianza, 1990), 147.

12. Hernando Ruiz de Alarcón, *Tratado de las supersticiones y costumbres gentílicas que hoy viven entre los indios naturales desta Nueva España* (1629; Mexico: Ed. SEP. Colección; Cien de México, 1988), 131.

13. In other communities, this preparation consists of a dance. The Talcolero, dancing in pairs, lift one foot and hop on the other. They imitate the preparation of the planting field on the slopes of the mountains. They clear it of bushes and burn the weeds in order to scare off the rodents (represented by a dehydrated opossum). The thunder produced by their whips imitates the lightning, representing the dynamics witnessed in nature when various physical elements come together.

14. Sahagún, *Historia general*, 478.

15. Bernardino de Sahagún, *Ritos, sacerdotes y atavios de los dioses*. Introducción, paleografía, versión y notas de Miguel León-Portilla, 2d ed. (Mexico: Universidad Nacional Autónoma de México, 1992), 72–73.

16. Information obtained from Carlos López Avila. The Nahuatl also give this information. See Joaquin Galarza and Carloz López Avila, *Tlacotenco Tonantzin Santa Ana: Tradiciones: Toponimías, técnicas, fiestas, anciones, versos y danzas* (Mexico: Centro de Investigaciones y Estudios en Antropología Social, 1980).

17. In the region of Cuetzalan, the people invoke the following: "But you, put your sacred flesh, Jesus Christ, into this seed that you have given us. And you, put your blood here in this garden, it is this corn cob, so that in the earth may achieve a beautiful planting." Enzo Segre, *Las máscaras de lo sagrado* (Mexico: Instituto Nacional de Antropología e Historia, 1987), 60.

18. Sahagún, *Historia general*, 298.

19. *Primeros Memoriales* (Nahuatl texts from the indigenous informants of Sahagún), ed. Francisco del Paso y Troncoso, 6 (Madrid, 1905, Photocopy of Hauser Menet).

20. Códice Florentino, Book 6, 78.

21. *Pulque* is an alcoholic drink made from agave. It is also known for its high nutritional value.

22. Sahagún, *Ritos, sacerdotes y atavios de los dioses*, 50.51.

23. Tlecuil is the home fire where food is prepared.

24. Sahagún, *Historia general*, 50–51.

25. Ibid., 302.

26. The *zincolote* is constructed of *oyametl*, or pine wood.

27. Sahagún, *Historia general*, 298.

28. Western biological criteria do not coincide with that of the indigenous cosmovision because, for the Nahua, stones, mountains, and stars are living beings that harbor the vital substance of Nemitiliztli, which allows life. Therefore, these beings must be respected and cared for.

29. Sahagún, *Historia general*, 291.

30. Ibid., 291.

31. Ibid.

32. Stefano Varese, "Caracterización de la población Indígena," in Alain de Janvry et al., *Reformas del sector agrícola y el campesinado en México*, Serie FIDA/IICA, no. 4 (San José, Costa Rica: Fondo Internacional de Desarrollo Agricola, 1995), 65.

The Life and Bounty of the Mesoamerican Sacred Mountain

MARÍA ELENA BERNAL-GARCÍA

In Mesoamerica, cosmogonic myths tell not about the creation of the universe at large but about a universe narrowed to a specific land-scape, town, or city where indigenous peoples live.[1] In fact, and in contrast with other cultural traditions, in Mesoamerica (most of Mexico, Guatemala, and parts of El Salvador and Honduras) city and nature were designed by the deities at the same time. Hence, one cannot exist without the other.[2] Within this conceptual framework the world of nature and the human world become tightly interwoven in their daily functions. For the indigenous peoples that inhabit Mesoamerica, the relationship with a particular territory becomes exceptionally intense because the place is considered sacred. Be it city, town, village, ham-let, or plot of land, all places on Earth are where deities and humans interact every day, and collective life develops within a sacred space.[3]

This paper's purpose is to share with the public one of Mesoamerica's fundamental myths, that of the creation of Earth. The myth explains to dominant national cultures the need for not relating to nature by im-posing radical transformations on it for the purpose of satisfying their own logic of production. The myth explains why Mesoamerican in-digenous societies adapt to the Earth rather than impose disturbing techniques of exploitation upon her. Nonetheless, since 1521, the year the Spaniards conquered the Aztec-Mexica city of Mexico-Tenochtitlan (today's Mexico City), the dominant culture, be it colonial or national, has continuously lost precious ecosystems and great extensions of land to human devastation. As recently as 30 January 2000, urban sociologist

José Luis Lezama directly linked the tremendous poverty afflicting a large percentage of Mexico's population to the presence of critical environmental problems.[4] Lezama affirms that these issues generate, reproduce, and generalize poverty, since the "loss of our biodiversity cancels the poorest's possibilities at providing for themselves the food they need to live." Paradoxically and in spite of the myth about to be told, Mesoamerican indigenous peoples are among the most affected by ecological deterioration, and this generates economic, political, and social problems not only for them, but also for the national culture.[5] Getting to know the Miraculous Mountain of Mesoamerican myth will help us all to understand why indigenous people may die of "sadness" or acute depression when, for whatever reason, they are compelled to leave their homelands.[6] And, because in Mexico we share in the Mesoamerican tradition, it will benefit us all to internalize the indigenous way of perceiving the universe in order that we may work in tune with it.

In Mesoamerican religions, one of the most influential icons is the Sacred Mountain in its various manifestations. In its physical form, it may be spotted all over the geographical area between the north of Mexico and the Central American countries of Honduras and El Salvador. Often, a particularly hallowed hill in the landscape may be adorned with one cross, or with several crosses of different sizes, and revered by the peoples living under its protective presence. Almost every indigenous and non-indigenous town and city in Mesoamerica is proud to be contained within the boundaries created by a particular set of mounds, where at least one is considered holy. These sets of hills usually function to mark the four cardinal or intercardinal directions, as well as a center which provides stability to the physically and ritually kept environment. Today's ever-present pilgrimages and offerings to venerated mountains are rooted in pre-Hispanic beliefs that may go as far back as 2,000 B.C.E., if not further.[7] Through this constant and intimate bond, each town or city is wholly familiar with its own natural and/or supernatural mountains. Concerning the latter, there is a wealth of documentation in the geographical *Relaciones* gathered under the rulership of King Philip II and in the *Land Titles* granted by the Spanish Crown during the colonial occupation of Mesoamerica.[8] Some of the same and other sacred mountains were also registered in pre-Hispanic and early colonial indigenous codexes that integrate mythical and historical events. I believe these codexes functioned additionally as "land titles" within the indigenous socio-cultural systems.

Compared with the profusion of holy mountains and hills throughout the landscapes of Mesoamerica, only a few mythical and legendary hills are dealt with in the academic literature. Best-known are "At the Hill of Those Who Have Ancestors-At Seven Caves" and the "Mountain of Our Sustenance," known in Náhuatl as Colhuacatepec-Chicomoztoc and Tonacatepetl, respectively.[9] The latter has also been recognized in the Maya K'iche' myth, recorded in the *Popol Vuh* under the name "At the Broken Place-At the Bitter Water Place," or Pan Paxil-Pan Kayala.[10] At the seventh-century Maya site of Palenque, this same mound appears to have been called Yax Hal Witznal, or "Place of the First True Mountain."[11]

In recent papers, I have tried to demonstrate that these two, apparently distinct entities (Colhuacatepec-Chicomoztoc and Tonacatepetl) belong to different phases in the life of the Mesoamerican Holy Earth.[12] Following the path suggested by specialists in the history, art, and anthropology of religions,[13] I went searching for the fundamental relevant sequence and structure in several myths and histories recorded in the sixteenth century. In this essay, I will deal mainly with the *Historia de los Mexicanos por sus Pinturas* and the *Popol Vuh,* the former belonging to the Central Mexican tradition and the latter to that of the Maya K'iche' peoples of Guatemala.[14] Basically, the stories may be divided into five parts: 1) A long and dark primordial period of time where only deities act, organizing and creating the universe in three parts, the Night Sky, the Ocean, and the Earth. This ancient universe would develop and mature through three or four Eras, Suns, or Dawns. 2) A time of myth and legend linked to the light of dawn and before sunrise. 3) A time of transition from legend to history, associated with the first appearance of the sun and morning light. At this moment, the first true people on Earth are created. 4) A time of legend and history characterized by limited human participation and the preponderance of mythical events. 5) The time of history proper (see my appendix).[15]

At the beginning of primordial time, the universe was composed of two bodies of matter—the waters of the Ocean and the winds of the Sky. Their union was almost imperceptibly separated by the line created between two shades of darkness at the horizon. Only the light of the stars lit this universe, which remained for a long time in a silence made audible solely by the soft winds brushing against the sparkling waves of the water. According to the *Popol Vuh*, at this point in time "the face of the Earth was not yet clear":

> Now it still ripples, now it still murmurs, it still sighs, still hums, and it is empty under the Sky. Here follow the first words, the first eloquence: there is not yet one person, one animal, bird, fish, crab, tree, rock, hollow, canyon, meadow, forest. Only the Sky alone is there; the face of the Earth is not clear. Only the Sea alone is pooled under all the Sky; there is nothing whatever gathered together. It is at rest, not a single thing stirs. It is held back, kept at rest under the Sky. Whatever there is that might be is simply not there: only the pooled water, only the calm Sea, only it alone is pooled. Whatever might be is simply not there: only murmurs, ripples, in the dark, in the night.[16]

A rather quiet universe enveloped in a soft veil of darkness was also the subject of Central Mexican stories: "In the beginning, before the light and the sun were created, this Earth was in darkness and in shadow and empty of all thing created."[17]

The first element that the deities created and placed in this primordial universe was the Earth, which appears in different forms in different narratives. In the *Historia de los Mexicanos por sus Pinturas*, two of the four sons of the Primordial Couple gently introduced the terrestrial plaque in the form of its best known zoomorphic metaphor, a fantastic animal called Cipactli in Náhuatl (fig. 1).[18] This dragon had

Figure 1. Cipactli. Codex Zouche-Nuttall, *p. 75, detail. Mixteca, west of Oaxaca, post-Classic. Screen-folded manuscript, animal skin, ca. 19 x 25.5 cm. British Museum. (From Zelia Nuttall,* The Codex Nuttall: A Picture Manuscript from Ancient Mexico *[New York: Dover Publications, 1975], 75)*

the head and long body of a crocodile and the tail of an enormous fish, probably a shark, swordfish, or whale. Sometimes the body is that of a snake and the tail that of a crab. It was always represented in profile and lacking a lower jaw. In contrast, the upper jaw showed a menacing row of large, sharp, spiky teeth. Its back was covered with scaly and/ or spiny skin. On the other hand, its paws could take on a variety of forms coming from either saurians, chelonians, or the largest Mesoamerican cat, the jaguar. In the Puebla-Mixtec, pre-Hispanic *Codex Borgia,* the dragon has the ears of a deer.

In the Maya area of Yukatan, and in the times prior to the Conquest, the terrestrial dragon's description emphasized its fish-like qualities: the body was that of a whale or shark, with saurian extremities. It was known as *Itzam Kab Ain,* or "Crocodile and Shaman of the Earth," a fantastic being living amongst primordial waterlilies.[19] The Classic Maya (200–900 C.E.) dragon had the body and snout of a crocodilian, a net or waterlily leaf over its head, half-closed eyelids with long eyelashes—sometimes marked with the sign for Venus as a star—ears and/or hooves of a deer, and an abstract shape known as "aquatic volute" in the extremities' junctures (fig. 2).[20] Since the Classic Maya saurian carried a star glyph for Venus on its head and hauled a bowl marked with the glyph for the sun in his tail, it was rightly believed to represent the path of Venus and the Sun across the heavens.[21] Further studies identify the sun-bowl with the sacrificial offering plate believed to represent the Heart of Heaven. The bowl generally contained a stingray spine or shark's tooth flanked by a pectoral medallion

Figure 2. Maya Saurian Dragon. Altar 41 *(drawing by Linda Schele). Maya, Copán, Honduras, 600–800 B.C.E. Horizontal slab, sandstone, measurements unavailable. Copán's Museum. (From Linda Schele and Mary Ellen Miller,* The Blood of Kings: Dynasty and Ritual in Maya Art, *photographs by Justin Kerr [Fort Worth: Kimbell Art Museum, 1986], fig. 22)*

marked with crossbands and a shell.²² The assemblage may represent
the three elements of the universe in their primordial form: the Earth
in between the Sky and the Ocean.²³ Adding to these complementary
interpretations, in this paper I put forward the hypothesis that the sacrificial bowl represents the Earth holding the Sun inside her, showing
the three main elements of the grown-up universe in embryonic form.
It is likely that the stone knife carried in the tail by the Central Mexican Cipactli corresponds to the stingray spine of Maya iconography,
functioning also as a symbol for One Stoneknife, the date when the
Four Eras began in Central Mexico.²⁴ The sacrificial objects, stingray,
and obsidian knife would generate the cosmic trees, as well as the
flowers and maize.²⁵

   The primordial Earth was also conceptualized, by both K'iche' and
Nahua peoples, as a flat disk,²⁶ the "Earth's own plate and platform"
according to the *Popol Vuh*.²⁷ But, whether plate or saurian, its distinguishing traits remained basically the same. Sixteenth-century informants to chronicler Fray Diego Durán emphasized the Earth's primordial characteristics as "all flat, with no hill and no cracks, and all
surrounded with water . . . without trees and empty of all created
things."²⁸ A Chortí Maya legend agrees by stating that "there were no
mountains on the Earth . . . because it extended itself over the waters."²⁹
Similarly, the Mixtec universe ". . . in the years and days of darkness
. . . [was] covered with water and only lime and moss grew over the
face of the Earth."³⁰ These statements bring forth an image of a crust
of soil so thin and smooth that only the simplest of aquatic plants grew
on its surface.

   The primordial Earth's flat condition drastically changed at the
time the Cosmic Eras began. In the *Historia de los Mexicanos por sus
Pinturas,* the four sons of the Primordial Couple get together to
transform the saurian into an amphibian dragon, now known as
Tlaltecuhtli, or Lord of the Earth (fig. 3). Tlaltecuhtli keeps Cipactli's
saurian head, now depicted frontally with a wide-open upper jaw.
Additionally, his body turns into that of a toad, depicted splayed in a
female's birthing position. Skulls, or "Tlaloc heads," mark his joints
and extremities (fig. 3).³¹ I believe the "Tlaloc heads" represent the
main primordial mounds dotting the Earth and that Tlaltecuhtli was
made from parts of a dismembered Cipactli. My proposition is based
on the *Historia de los Mexicanos por sus Pinturas*'s affirmation that
"Tlaltecuhtli is painted like an Earth Lord lying over a fish because it was

made from it."[32] Returning to the description of the primordial land-scape in the *Popol Vuh*, the birth of the Earth from the Ocean parallels the Nahua transformation of Cipactli into Tlaltecuhtli:

> And then the Earth arose because of them [the deities], it was simply their word that brought it forth. For the forming of the Earth they said "Earth." It arose suddenly, just like a cloud, like a mist, now forming, unfolding. Then the mountains were separated from the water, all at once the great mountains came forth. By their genius alone, by their cutting edge alone they carried out the conception of the mountain-

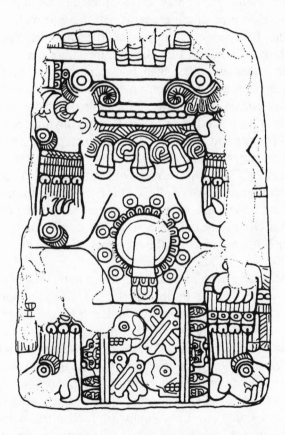

Figure 3. Tlaltecuhtli. Drawing of a low-relief carved plaque. Nahua, Mexico-Tenochtitlán, fifteenth century. Greenstone, 86 x 57 cm. Mexico City, Museo Nacional de Antropología e Historia. (From Esther Pasztory, Aztec Art [New York: Harry N. Abrams, 1983], plate 98)

plain, whose face grew instant groves of cypress and pine. . . . And the Earth was formed first, the mountain-plain. The channels oäVwater were separated; their branches wound their ways among the mountains. The waters were divided when the great mountains appeared. . . . The Sky was set apart, and the Earth was set apart in the midst of the waters.[33]

At that moment in her development, the Earth was conceived as a malleable crust, unfolding and stretching to create mountains and gorges. This continuity of form may be the reason why most Mesoamerican words for Earth are composed of a complementary metonym, "valley-mountain" or, as the *Popol Vuh* says, "mountain-plain."[34] As some specialists have pointed out, metonyms like these provide one of the basic elements for the formation of spatial metaphors. Specialist in Andean literature Claudette Kemper Columbus prefers the idea of a space rich in metaphor rather than one rich in metonyms, because "[w]here mythology and geography meet, space is immanent, inter-connected, full-bodied, and kinetic."[35] The difference between the meto-nymic and metaphoric landscape is that "[a] metonymic [relationship] suggests a container and a contained. [But a metaphoric relationship] suggests the container as itself contained . . . pot within pot within pot."[36] Although Kemper Columbus works with Andean myths and geog-raphy through literary analysis, her ideas correspond to those of the aforementioned description of the birth of the Earth in the *Popol Vuh:* the Primordial Ocean not only contained the saurian/platform of the Earth, but the Earth also formed the receptacle holding the Primordial Ocean.

The two Mesoamerican sources considered in this paper thus coin-cide in the change that the Earth experienced, from flat and level to creased and rolling. Simultaneously, the Earth grew forests of trees: hence, trees and mountains became her most conspicuous links with the Sky;[37] and ravines, gorges, and caves to the Ocean or Underworld. After this metamorphosis, the Cosmic Eras ensue. In other papers, and based on studies by Brandt Gardner, I have proposed that the Cosmic Eras describe the slow development of this young Earth and its original and crude dwellers—humans, foodstuffs, animals, and even culture—into the elaborate forms of complex ecosystems and societies.[38]

At the end of the Fourth Cosmic Era in the Central Mexican myth, and of the Third in the K'iche', the Sky falls upon the creased Earth, producing a great flood. In the Central Mexican myths, the waters drown Tlaltecuhtli, returning the fantastic animal to a state similar to that of its birth, before the Cosmic Eras began. In this latter part of the narrative, the violent intervention of the four Nahua male deities opposes the gentleness by which they first sat Cipactli among the waves of the primeval waters. Nonetheless, the action also evokes Cipactli's mildly violent transformation into Tlaltecuhtli. Similarly, the birth of the Earth in the *Popol Vuh* is made possible through an act of sacrifice, perhaps by heart extraction.[39]

With the purpose of restoring the Earth's reproductive functions, the Central Mexican gods insert themselves into Tlaltecuhtli's body. Although at the beginning of this paper I spoke of Tlaltecuhtli as Lord of the Earth, the dragon's sexual attributes seem to change according to his/her position in the myth. In this section of the story it is clearly female. The *Historia de los Mexicanos* tells how the male deities introduced themselves through Tlaltecuhtli's navel and mouth and then met at her heart, or center, in order to create four roads.[40] Instead, the *Historia de los Mexicanos por sus Pinturas* says that the deities ordered four roads to be created from the center of the dragon in order to enter and depart from it.[41] Regardless of these nuances in meaning, when the four gods leave the Earth, they most likely do so through the dragon's extremities. Once outside, they turn themselves into trees to support the four corners of the Sky so as to prevent it from falling over the Earth again. In still another version of the story (contained as well in the *Historia de los Mexicanos*), the male deities become serpents who constrict the middle of Tlaltecuhtli's body, her back becoming the Earth's platform and her chest the Sky's dome. Miraculously and paradoxically, Tlaltecuhtli is revived but finds herself cut in half, according to some texts, or dismembered into four sections, according to others. Observing Tlaltecuhtli's great suffering, caused by their very own sons, the Primordial Couple compensates the Earth by decreeing her regeneration, broadening and perfecting her body's forms and functions. From her hairs grow trees, flowers, and grasses; from her skin fine herbs and little flowers; from her eyes come wells, fountains, and small caves; from her mouth, rivers and caverns; from her nose, valleys and mountains.[42] The dramatic aftermath delivers a full-flowering Earth that will propitiate the development of urbanism and complex human societies.[43]

In a similar fashion, the *Popol Vuh* prepares the Earth for today's humans during the Third Era.[44] In that Era all mythical events happen over the face of the Earth, contrasting with those of the first two where an exchange of actions takes place between the Earth and the Ocean (Underworld). Of all the personages included in this episode, a pair of twins represents the Earth. One is Sipakna, a cognate of Cipactli, who, as a typical crocodile, bathes at the shores of the primeval Ocean, resting and eating during the day and lifting mountains throughout the night.[45] The myth actually states that Sipakna is the one actor responsible for the existence of the six primordial mountains—Fire Mouth, Hunahpu, Cave by the Water, Xcanul, Macamob, and Huliznab—that appeared "in a single night," at the time the Earth was born from the Sea.[46] So strong was Sipakna that he also could easily lift lintels and posts for a house being built over the Earth at that time. Once, he even entered the ground headfirst to become a post himself, although immediately thereafter he was replaced by a real one.[47] After so much work, including the killing of four hundred boys, who become the Pleiades, the saurian becomes so hungry that he desperately begins to look for his daily ration of fish and crabs.

Unfortunately for him, Sipakna then meets the Hero Twins in the myth, Hunahpu and Xbalanke, who are themselves slaying all the supernatural personages inhabiting the Earth of the Third Era. As a lure, Hunahpu and Xbalanke build a crab with a red flagstone for the shell and bromeliads for the forearms and claws. The Hero Twins then place the artificial crab inside a tight hole at the foot of a mountain named Meuan, which was situated toward the west. Sipakna falls for the trap and tries to eat the false crab twice, failing as many times. During the first attempt, when he enters the cave right side up, the crab ends up on top of his back, preventing him from turning his head back to grab her. To solve his problem, Sipakna exits the cave and reenters it on his back, but again he cannot move because, in this awkward position, the crab and the mountain end up upon his chest. Deprived of movement, Sipakna dies and turns into stone. Subtly told in the story, the saurian becomes the base for the Earth's platform in the form of the red flagstone. Thus, the false crab and the western mountain lie on Sipakna just as Tlaltecuhtli laid on Cipactli's back.[48]

Another connecting point between the Central Mexican and Maya myths is that the Earth's death involves a previous act of sexual intercourse. Sipakna's attempt at eating the false crab is a parody of coitus,[49] as is the act of the sons of the Mexica primordial couple who "enter" Tlaltecuhtli's body. One difference is that in the *Popol Vuh,* the crocodilian twins represent the telluric energies in an actual landscape, while in the Central Mexican stories the fantastic animals are metaphors for the landscape itself.

Contrary to Sipakna's constructive role, his twin brother Kabrakan, or Earthquake, destroyed and scattered mountains all through the day—most likely the ones his older brother built the night before.[50] To kill Kabrakan and stop these constant and much too frequent cycles of construction and destruction, the Hero Twins trick Kabrakan by telling him of a great, tall mountain to the east, one he has missed altogether and surely would love to destroy. Kabrakan is then lured into accompanying the Hero Twins to the east with the promise of being fed a tasty, roasted bird on the way. When Kabrakan stops to eat the bird, he dies (apparently of indigestion) because he simultaneously ate the clay in which the bird was cooked.[51] Because of Kabrakan's death, the great mountain of the east still remains intact.

Besides the fertile Tlaltecuhtli, another zoomorphic metaphor for the bountiful Earth in Classic and post-Classic Maya iconography is the turtle. From its cracked carapace, the Maize God is resuscitated at the end of the Third Era.[52] Less conspicuously, the turtle also appears as a metaphor for the Earth in documents from Central Mexico, also corresponding to the Earth's latter stages of development; however, its specific role has not yet been examined.[53] What does seem clear is that the hard shell of either crab or turtle is the prime animal metaphor for today's Earth's plate and platform.

The Mythical Earth's Sacred Mountains

Of the mountains that appeared with the primordial Earth, whether they be those associated with Tlaltecuhtli or the six hills listed in the *Popol Vuh,* Mesoamericans appear to have chosen a single icon to represent "divine mountainhood." Both Nahua and Mixtec peoples name and illustrate it as their mythical place of origin, but now it is known solely by its Nahua appelatives, Colhuacatepec-Chicomoztoc, or "At the Hill of Those Who Have Ancestors-At Seven Caves." The place called Tullan-Zuyua–Wukub Pek-Wukub Ziuan, or "Place of Reeds-Zuyua–Seven Caves-Seven Canyons," in the K'iche' story corresponds to Colhuacatepec-Chicomoztoc. Suggestively, this mountain is not named in the mythical sections of the two stories I follow in this paper. It appears only in the latter ones, those dealing with the time of legend and history (see the appendix).

Up to this point I have translated "At the Hill of Those Who Have Ancestors" from the Nahua toponym Colhuacatepec, provided by the *Historia Tolteca-Chichimeca.* I choose to do so because the hill, in the *Historia de los Mexicanos por sus Pinturas* and other Central Mexican chronicles, is named Colhuacan, or "At the Place of Those Who Have Ancestors," obviating the toponym *tepec,* or "at the mountain." Nonetheless, even as just "place," Colhuacan is represented by a hill in most, if not all, pictorial manuscripts (fig. 4). One of this hill's outstanding and distinctive features is the large, elegant volute crowning its top. Here, I will address only basic aspects of the mound's body and volute and their rich iconography.

Colhuacan, or Colhuacatepec, translates as "At the Place of Those Who Have Ancestors."[54] However, due to its formal qualities and the sixteenth-century interpretation contributed by a Nahua informant to Durán, the mountain is known under several synonyms for "Bent Hill." In the *Historia Tolteca-Chichimeca,* one of this place's apellatives is "Coliuhquitepetl," from *coliuhqui,* "something bent or re-

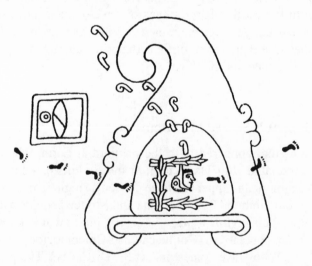

Figure 4. Colhuacatepec. Codex Boturini, *detail. Nahua, sixteenth century. Manuscript in rolled bark paper, 19.8 549 cm. Mexico City, Museo Nacional de Antropología e Historia. (From Esther Pasztory,* Aztec Art *[New York: Harry N. Abrams, 1983], plate 148)*

clined," and *tepetl,* "hill."[55] A similar concept alluding to the form of the volute is *uicoltic,* an adjective meaning "bent thing, like a jar's handle, or a lean and dry person."[56] *Uahcaliuhqui,* comparably, is the adjectival form of *uahcaliui,* the present tense of the verb "to cripple, shrink, or bend."[57] Therefore, the adjectives appear to qualify oldness, whether a person's or a plant's. Fray Bernardino de Sahagún, another sixteenth-century chronicler, provides a Nahua riddle to support this contention: "What is it, in the whole wide world that above us bends? It is the crest of the maize cane when it goes about drying and bending."[58] Likewise, Colhuacatepec was considered a hill arching over, under the weight of time.

In spite of its old age, the essence of youth was inherent to Colhuacatepec. Durán's same informant, the also aged Cuauhcoatl, describes the hill as "bending toward the floor" and tells the following story. An old man with a youth's energy resided at the foot of Colhuacan while the goddess Coatlicue lived at its summit. The man was Coatlicue's messenger, and thus he often climbed and descended the mountain with no effort whatsoever because he became younger or older depending on the distance he traveled up and down. Extraordinarily, the same happened to all those who lived around the magic hill. The higher they got, the younger they became, and thus, despite the passing of time, they never died.[59]

It appears, then, that from the point of view of the Present Era, the mountain was very, very old. However, from the standpoint of mythical times, it is barely being born, and so, conceptually, it remains fresh to this very day. This is the reason why, when the Aztec-Mexica priests visited the mountain in the sixteenth century, when they departed and looked back, the paradisiacal place

> turned dry, covering itself with thickets of rockgardens, thorny and dense, greatly rugged terrains, all covered with sandhills and lagoons, all blanketed with lush canes and reeds . . . and once they left the place, everything turned into thorns and thistle; the stones became sharp as to hurt [anyone], grasses stung and trees became thorny. . . .[60]

This legendary place and city was known as Aztlan and Tollan by Nahua peoples and as Tollan-Zuyua by the K'iche' Maya.

As seen above, the magic hill had two names. From the outside, it was known as "At the Hill of Those Who Have Ancestors," and from within it was known as "At Seven-Caves." Some authors, since the end of the nineteenth century, have understood the interdependence of the two sites, but recently a clear semantic difference has been recognized through the study of the *Historia Tolteca Chichimeca*.[61] As explained elsewhere, the combination of attributes in the visual representations of this icon—including conflation—contributes to the researcher's confusion when trying to specify its functions.[62] Nonetheless, at its most basic level, the sequence of mythological and legendary events introduces, first, the role played by the mountain's crust, and then that of the caves.[63] Colhuacatepec addresses the masculine roles of pro-creation, and Chicomoztoc emphasizes the feminine ones. The consecutiveness may be detected, particularly, in the *Historia Tolteca Chichimeca,* a manuscript of post-Conquest date (ca. 1544), and in the *Codex Borgia,* a pre-Conquest book and probable prototype for the *Historia Tolteca-Chichimeca.* Colhuacatepec, the hill, may be represented as mountain or tree, whereas Chicomoztoc is generally shown as an elongated, rounded, or flower-like cave within the mountain.

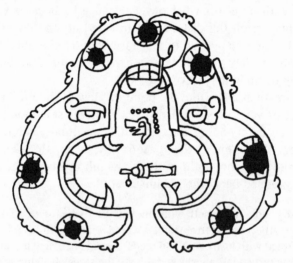

Figure 5. Chicomoztoc. Lienzo Antonio de León o Tlalpiltepec I, *detail. Mixteca, west of Oaxaca, sixteenth century. Cloth, 432 x 165 cm. Toronto, Royal Ontario Museum. (From Doris Heyden, "Caves, Gods and Myths: World-View and Planning in Teotihuacan,"* in Mesoamerican Sites and World-Views: A Conference at Dumbarton Oaks, October 16th and 17th, 1976, *ed. Elizabeth P. Benson [Washington, D.C.: Dumbarton Oaks Research Library and Collection, 1981], fig. 18)*

Of all pictorial representations of Chicomoztoc, the best known is the frontal depiction of the open-mouthed saurian's head (fig. 5). It is easily recognizable in Nahua and Mixtec books and other art monuments. Recently, I found it adorning Maya temples of the Late Classic period at Palenque and Toniná, and on Early Classic artificial mountains at Tikal.[64] The crucial difference between the hill's exterior and interior is that the former alludes to the Earth's emptiness of "all things created," and the latter to an Earth filled with life. In the *Popol Vuh,* the hill's crust may be represented through the nance tree, where the false-sun Seven Macaw feeds himself each day, while Meuan's hole may stand for the seventh primordial mountain and/or cave, counting the first six named in the manuscript.

Having followed the development of hill and cave in several myths, "The Hill of Our Sustenance" appears to coincide with the stage immediately after "At the Hill of Those Who Have Ancestors-At the Seven Caves" breaks open to deliver its bounty.[65] To distinguish one mountain from the other in the artistic record, one must return to the loop at the top. If it is split in two, it shows the "Mountain of Our Sustenance." Sometimes a plant—maize or a tree—grows from the break (fig. 6). The mountain may also appear cracked at its base, allowing the spring inside her to deliver two rivers. Often, either from its top or its bottom, human beings emerge together with maize, and less often with other plants. In Mesoamerican myths the fully developed human beings of the Present Era were made of the maize kept by this hill, just as it is told in the *Popol Vuh:*

> [Just before dawn, the deities] . . . sought and discovered what was needed for human flesh. . . . Broken Place, Bitter Water Place is the name: the yellow corn, the white corn came from there. . . . They [the animals] showed the way to the break. . . . And this was when they found the staple foods. And these were the ingredients for the flesh of the human work, the human design, and the water was for the blood. . . . And so they were happy over the provisions of the good mountain, filled with sweet things, thick with yellow corn, white corn, and thick with pataxte and cacao, countless zapotes, anonas, jocotes, nances, matasanos, sweets—the rich foods filling up the citadel named Broken Place, Bitter Water Place. All the edible fruits were there: small staples, great staples, small plants, great plants.[66]

To this section of the *Popol Vuh*'s narrative corresponds the Central

Mexican legend of Quetzalcoatl, who either breaks the Tonacatepetl
or becomes a black ant in order to steal the corn from inside the magic
mountain. The corn was needed to make the human beings of the
Present Era,[67] but other edible and non-edible treasures came from it:
cotton, amaranth, as well as white, black,[68] yellow, and red corn,
beans, greens, sage, and sweet potatoes.[69] It is highly probable that the
great Maya mountain to the east, which Kabrakan could not destroy,
corresponds to "At the Broken Place-At the Bitter Water Place" or to
the "Mountain of Our Sustenance."[70] With this hill, I believe, the
K'iche' book counts eight mountains, and a play between the numbers
seven and eight is a characteristic of its delivery of goods in other
documents.[71]

Besides the natural sequence of the dragon's transformations in the
narratives analyzed, the metamorphosis synchronizes itself to the
260-day Nahua calendar. On One Cipactli, the first day of this chart,
the conception of Cipactli occurs; on One Tecpatl, the 118th day, the
creation of Tlaltecuhtli with Colhuacatepec-Chicomoztoc takes place;

*Figure 6. Tonacatepetl. Tripod vase, detail of drawing. Mixtec,
Nochiztlan, 1000–1521 c.e. Polychrome ceramics, 15 cm high. México
City, Museo Nacional de Antropología e Historia. (From Karl A. Taube,
"The Teotihuacan Cave of Origin: The Iconography and Architecture of
Emergence Mythology in Mesoamerica and the American Southwest,"
RES: Anthropology and Aesthetics 12 [1986]: fig. 12)*

and on One Tochtli, or the 248th day, the dismemberment of Tlaltecuhtli and/or Tonacatepetl's split occurs.[72] According to the calendar, then, the three stages presented here correspond to the beginning, middle, and near end of the mythical day count (see table 1).[73]

Table 1. Vital Cycles of the Nahua Terrestrial Dragons

Dragons	Forms	Vital Cycles	Dates
Cipactli	Amorphous or flat Earth	Gestation in primordial times	1 Cipactli (day 1)
Tlaltecuhtli	Earth with valleys and mountains and/or Colhuacatepec-Chicomoztoc	Birth and development (Cosmic Eras)	1 Tecpatl (day 118)
Dismembered Tlaltecuhtli	Full-flowering Earth or Tonacatepetl	Delivery and death	1 Tochtli (day 248)

Thus, for Mesoamericans then and today, the bountiful Earth of the Present Era is the result of a complex transformation attributed to three different but complementary processes. First is its inherent value as a living body whose life-cycle—gestation, birth, maturation, reproduction, old age, and death—is comparable to that of humans, animals, and vegetals. In fact, in K'iche', the word for Earth, *uleu*, also means "flesh,"[74] and the metonym for Earth, mountain-plain, is the main metaphor for the human body.[75] López-Austin has studied the close association between the Earth and the human body.[76]

The second process entails a number of complex mythological, zoomorphic metamorphoses that extend through great periods of time. These changes appear to have had as a model those experienced by reptiles and amphibians, from eggs to fish-like tadpoles, and then to batrachians and chelonians, who are all able to live outside the water even though they were engendered within it.

The third and most perplexing change of all is when the flesh of the last mythical dragon (still swimming in the waters of the Sea) becomes the stone and dirt of the Earth as we know it today. López-Austin has proposed, for example, that the world of the supernatural is wet and cold while that of humans is hot and dry.[77] Conjugating death and birth,[78] the procedure entails the immolation of supernatural beings in order that their remains may become the substance from which life springs on our own land. Tlaltecuhtli and the Maya Earth die by fragmentation because in Mesoamerican thought, birth and multiplication include the concept of smashing, cutting, or sectioning a ripe fruit in order for it to scatter its life-giving seeds.[79] When the great "Mountain of Our Sustenance" breaks, it produces the many mountains of today's geography, especially the eight mountains corresponding to the cardinal and intercardinal directions.[80] We, in Mesoamerica, are sustained by the bowl which they encircle in the landscape and by the bowl of riches each one of them contains.

Appendix: Basic Structure of the Universe and the Earth's Development in Mesoamerican Myths and Stories

I. Primordial Times. In darkness.
   A. Creation of the three levels of the universe in the following order:
      1. Night Sky. The Night-Sky is lit by fire and a half-sun.
      2. Ocean or Underworld. Cipactli is set in the primordial waters, or an amorphous Earth exists under the Ocean.
      3. Earth. The four directions and Tlaltecuhtli/the Earth emerge from the Ocean, the latter showing its primordial mountains.
   B. Cosmic Eras: Evolution of the Universe. Stars provide light to these Eras.
II. A time of myth and legend linked to the appearance of dawn's clear light. Actors are deities who begin acting upon the Earth.
   A. Mature and full-flowering Earth appears.
   B. Mature maize and other foodstuffs appear.
   C. Real human beings made of maize dough are created.
III. Transition from legend to history associated with the appearance of the sun. People's first generation.
   A. The sun and the moon are created.
   B. Legendary heroes and cities appear: Tula and Quetzalcoatl in *Historia de los Mexicanos por sus Pinturas;* remembrances of Tullan-Zuyua, Seven Caves-Seven Canyons in the *Popol Vuh.*
IV. A time of legend and history still heavily related to mythical events. Transition from general legends to each group's own stories. Re-creation of all previous stages, including this one.
   A. Exit from the place of origins. Aztlan or Colhuacatepec-Chicomoztoc in the *Historia de los Mexicanos por sus Pinturas;* frustrated trip to Tullan-Zuyua, Seven Caves-Seven Canyons in the *Popol Vuh,* followed by a trip to visit a magnificent Lord Nacxit (a cognate of Quetzalcoatl) and its city.
   B. Migrations to a promised land.
   C. Arrival at a particular area for settlement.
   D. City foundations.
V. The time of history proper. Royal genealogies and historical events of all kinds, nonetheless, still attached to myths and legends through religious practices.

344   *Indigenous Traditions and Ecology*

Notes

1. Miguel Alberto Bartolomé, "Presas y Relocalizaciones de Indígenas en América Latina," *Anales de Antropología* 30 (1993): 127; María Elena Bernal-García, "Carving Mountains in a Blue/Green Bowl: Mythological Urban Planning in Mesoamerica" (Ph.D. diss., University of Texas at Austin, 1993).

2. Bernal-García, "Carving Mountains," chap. 3.

3. Bartolomé, "Presas y Relocalizaciones," 127; Bernal-García, "Carving Mountains," chap. 1.

4. José Luis Lezama, "Amnesia ambiental electoral," *Reforma,* 30 January 2000, 24A.

5. Bartolomé, "Presas y Relocalizaciones," 121, 133–34.

6. Ibid., 129.

7. There is a copious ethnohistoric and ethnographic literature on the matter. I refer the reader to the sixteenth-century chroniclers and to the contemporary work of Carlos Martínez Marín, "Santuarios y Peregrinaciones en el México Prehispánico," in *Religión en Mesoamérica, XII Mesa Redonda,* ed. Jaime Litvak King and Noemí Castillo Tejero (México: Sociedad Mexicana de Antropología, 1972), 161–78; Johanna Broda, "Templo Mayor as Ritual Space," in *Great Temple of Tenochtitlán: Center and Periphery in the Aztec World,* ed. Johanna Broda, Davíd Carrasco, and Eduardo Matos Moctezuma (Los Angeles: University of Los Angeles Press, 1987), 119, n. 144.

8. Angel J. García-Zambrano, "El Poblamiento de México en la época del contacto, 1520–1540," *Mesoamérica* 13, no. 24 (1992): 239–96.

9. Coatepec, or "At the Hill of the Serpent," is another, but it will not be addressed here because it falls beyond the scope of this paper.

10. Dennis Tedlock, trans., *Popol Vuh: The Mayan Book of the Dawn of Life* (New York: Simon and Schuster, 1985), 328. I am using the new orthography introduced by Mayan speakers; see David A. Freidel, Linda Schele, and Joy Parker, *Maya Cosmos: Three Thousand Years on the Shaman's Path* (New York: William Morrow, 1993), 17–19.

11. Freidel, Schele, and Parker, *Maya Cosmos,* 111.

12. Bernal-García, "Carving Mountains," chap. 2; María Elena Bernal-García, "From Mountain to Toponym in the *Historia Tolteca-Chichimeca,*" in *Messages and Meanings: Papers from the Twelfth Annual Symposium, Latin American Indian Literatures Association,* ed. Mary H. Preuss (Lancaster, Calif.: Labyrinthos Press, 1997); Bernal-García, "Carving Mountains," 413–31; María Elena Bernal-García, "La Montaña Sagrada Mesoamericana: Iconografía," unpublished article in possession of the author.

13. Mircea Eliade, Edmund Leach, and, particularly for Mesoamerican religions, Linda Schele, Alfredo López-Austin, and Davíd Carrasco.

14. In a parallel study, two fairly well-studied pre-Hispanic books, the *Codex Vienna* and the *Codex Borgia,* were used to compare post-Conquest data: Bernal-García, "Carving Mountains," 413–33; Bernal-García, "From Mountain to Toponym," 85–102.

15. I will use capital letters for Sky, Ocean, and Earth, not only because they are sacred places in Mesoamerican religions, but to facilitate the reading of this paper.

Alternate divisions for the text of the *Popol Vuh* may be found in Tedlock, *Popol Vuh,* and, from a structuralist point of view, in Carol Hendrickson, "Twin Gods and Quiché Rulers: The Relationship between Divine Power and Lordly Rule in the Popol Vuh," in *Word and Image in Maya Culture: Explorations in Language, Writing, and Representation,* ed. William F. Hanks and Don S. Rice (Salt Lake City: University of Utah Press, 1989).

16. Tedlock, *Popol Vuh,* 72. For this paper I will be using only Tedlock's translation.

17. Fray Diego Durán, *Historia de las Indias de Nueva España e Islas de Tierra Firme,* paleographic ed. of the Madrid manuscript, 1570–1579, with introduction, notes, and vocabulary by Angel María Garibay K., 2 vols. (México: Editorial Porrúa, 1967), 2:17.

18. I am summarizing from *Historia de los Mexicanos por sus Pinturas,* in *Anales del Museo Nacional de México,* transcription from the original manuscript, 1547 or 1533, vol. 2 (México: Imprenta de Ignacio Escalante, 1882), 85–106; Fray Bernardino de Sahagún, *Historia general de las cosas de Nueva España,* sixteenth-century manuscript, ed. and notes by Angel María Garibay K., 4 vols. (México: Editorial Porrúa, S.A., 1956), 1:317; *Historia de los Mexicanos,* in Angel María Garibay K., *Teogonía e Historia de los Mexicanos: Tres Opúsculos del Siglo XVI* (México: Editorial Porrúa, 1965), 111; Eduard Seler, *Comentarios al Códice Borgia,* trans. from the German by Mariana Frenk, 3 vols. (México: Fondo de Cultura Económica, 1988), 63; Henry B. Nicholson, "Religion in Pre-Hispanic Central Mexico," in *Archaeology of Northern Mesoamerica,* vol. 1, ed. Gordon F. Ekholm and Ignacio Bernal, vol. 10 of *Handbook of Middle American Indians,* ed. Robert Wauchope (Austin: University of Texas Press, 1971), 395–446; Cecelia F. Klein, *The Face of the Earth: Frontality in Two-Dimensional Mesoamerican Art* (New York: Garland Publications, 1976), 54.

19. The last translation of *itzam* is "shaman," or "One Who Does/Handles Cosmic Saps," in Freidel, Schele, and Parker, *Maya Cosmos,* 51, 410–12. The summary is from *Chilam Balam of Chumayel,* in Juan Martínez Hernández, "La creación del mundo según los Mayas: páginas inéditas del manuscrito Chumayel," in *Proceedings of the Eighteenth International Congress of Americanists* (London: Harrison and Sons, 1913), 165–66, cited in Karl A. Taube, *Itzam Cab Ain: Caimans, Cosmology, and Calendrics in Postclassic Yucatán,* Research Reports on Ancient Maya Writing, 26-27 (Washington, D.C.: Center for Maya Research, 1989): 2–3; Alfredo Barrera Vásquez, "La Ceiba-Cocodrilo," *Anales del Instituto Nacional de Antropologia e Historia,* época 7a., vol. 4 (1974); J. Eric S. Thompson, *Historia y Religión de los Mayas,* trans. from the English by Félix Blanco and Arturo Gómez (México: Siglo XXI Editores, 1975), 259–76; John B. Carlson and Linda C. Landis, "Bands, Bicephalic Dragons, and Other Beasts: The Skyband in Maya Art and Iconography," in *Fourth Palenque Round Table, 1980,* ed. Elizabeth P. Benson, vol. 6 of the Palenque Round Table Series, gen. ed. Merle Greene Robertson (San Francisco: Pre-Columbian Art Research Institute, 1985); Andrea Stone, "Variety and Transformation in the Cosmic Monster Theme at Quirigua, Guatemala," in *Fifth Palenque Round Table, 1983,* ed. Virginia M. Fields, vol. 6 of the Palenque Round Table Series, gen. ed. Merle Greene Robertson (San Francisco: Pre-Columbian Art Research Institute, 1985), 39–48; Linda Schele and Mary Ellen Miller, *The Blood of Kings: Dynasty and*

Ritual in Maya Art, photographs by Justin Kerr (Fort Worth: Kimbell Art Museum, 1986), 45; Tedlock, *Popol Vuh,* 372.

20. Stone, "Variety and Transformation," 39–40.

21. Carlson and Landis, "Bands, Bicephalic Dragons and Other Beasts"; Stone, "Variety and Transformation," 39–40; Schele and Miller, *The Blood of Kings,* 45; Linda Schele and David Freidel, *A Forest of Kings: The Untold Story of the Ancient Maya,* color photographs by Justin Kerr (New York: William Morrow and Company, 1990), 408, 415.

22. Freidel, Schele, and Parker, *Maya Cosmos,* 217.

23. Schele and Freidel, *A Forest of Kings,* 415.

24. Bernal-García, "Carving Mountains," 167.

25. Freidel, Schele, and Parker, *Maya Cosmos,* 244 and fig. 4:29; Bernal-García, "La Montaña Sagrada."

26. Esther Pasztory, *Aztec Art* (New York: Harry N. Abrams, 1983), 59.

27. *Popol Vuh,* in Tedlock, *Popol Vuh,* 71 and 73.

28. Durán, *Historia de las Indias,* 2:17.

29. Cecelia F. Klein, "Woven Heaven, Tangled Earth: A Weaver's Paradigm of the Mesoamerican Cosmos," in *Ethnoastronomy and Ethnoarchaeology in the American Tropics,* ed. Anthony F. Aveni and Gary Urton, Annals of the New York Academy of Sciences, vol. 385 (New York: New York Academy of Sciences, 1982), 11.

30. Fray Gregorio García, *Origen de los Indios del Nuevo Mundo, 1607–1729,* preliminary study by Franklin Pease G.Y. (México: Fondo de Cultura Económica, 1981), 327–28.

31. This summary is from Francisco del Paso y Troncoso, *Descripción, historia y exposición del códice [Borbónico] pictórico de los antiguos Nauas que se conserva en la Biblioteca de la Cámara de Diputados de París (antiguo Palais Bourbon)* (Florence: Tip. de Salvador Landi, 1898); Eduard Seler, *Gesammelte Abhandlungen zur Amerikanischen Sprach- und Altertumskunde,* 5 vols. (1902–1923; reprint, Graz: Akademische Druck-u. Verlagsanstalt, 1960–1961), 11–13, cited in Klein *The Face of the Earth,* 55; Pasztory, *Aztec Art,* 82; Henry B. Nicholson, "A Fragment of an Aztec Relief Carving of the Earth Monster," *Journal de la Société des Américanistes* 56, no. 1 (1967): 81–94.

32. *Historia de los Mexicanos por sus Pinturas,* 87. Instead of a zoomorphic dragon, an image in the Templo Mayor of Mexico-Tenochtitlan—"half-man and half-lizard, encrusted with precious stones . . . the body of this creature contained all the seeds that there are in the world, and they said he was the god of all the fields and fruits"—was most likely that of Tlaltecuhtli, as suggested by J. M. Cohen in Bernal Díaz del Castillo, *La Conquista de la Nueva España,* ca. 1581, trans. J. M. Cohen (Harmondsworth: Penguin Books, 1963), 237; Eduardo Matos Moctezuma, "The Templo Mayor of Tenochtitlan: Economics and Ideology," in *Ritual Human Sacrifice in Mesoamerica: A Conference at Dumbarton Oaks, October 13th and 14th, 1979,* organizer Elizabeth P. Benson, ed. Elizabeth H. Boone (Washington, D.C.: Dumbarton Oaks Research Library and Collection, 1984), 139.

33. *Popol Vuh* in Tedlock, *Popol Vuh,* 73–75.

34. Tedlock (*Popol Vuh,* 351) specified the metonymic relationship of the K'iche' concept, but others had already seen its two parts in other languages: see, for

example, Zelia Nuttall, *The Fundamental Principles of Old and New World Civilizations: A Comparative Research Based on a Study of the Ancient Mexican Religious, Sociological and Calendrical Systems,* Archaeological and Ethnological Papers of the Peabody Museum, Harvard University, vol. 2 (1900; reprint, New York: Kraus Reprint Co., 1970), 46; Mary Elizabeth Smith, "The Mixtec Writing System," in *The Cloud People: Divergent Evolution of the Zapotec and Mixtec Civilizations,* ed. Kent V. Flannery and Joyce Marcus (New York: Academic Press, 1983), 241; Bernal-García, "Carving Mountains," 194, nn. 117 and 146.

35. Claudette Kemper Columbus, "Where Map and Metaphor Meet: Andean Deities in the Plains of Nazca and the Mountains of Huarochiri," unpublished manuscript in possession of the author, 27. In his studies on Andean iconography, Jeffrey Quilter also points out the similarity between some episodes in Andean myths and in the *Popol Vuh;* see his "Continuity and Disjunction in Pre-Columbian Art and Culture," *RES: Anthropology and Aesthetics* 29-30 (spring/autumn 1996): 303–18.

36. Kemper Columbus, "Where Map and Metaphor Meet," 68.

37. The association of tree and mountain is so close that sometimes, in certain iconographies, their shapes are interchanged or their images are conflated. See, for example, Doris Heyden, "What Is the Significance of the Mexica Pyramid?" in *Atti del XL Congresso Internazionale degli Americanisti,* vol. 1 (Genoa: Tilgher, 1973), 109–15; Robert Carlsen and Martin Prechtel, "The Flowering of the Dead: An Interpretation of Highland Maya Culture," *Man* 26 (1991): 23–42; Alfredo López-Austin, "La cosmovisión mesoamericana," in *Temas Mesoamericanos,* ed. Sonia Lombardo and Enrique Nalda (México: Instituto Nacional de Antropología e Historia and Dirección General de Publicaciones del Consejo Nacional para la Cultura y las Artes, 1996), 486–93.

38. Brant Gardner, "Reconstructing the Ethnohistory of Myth: A Structural Study of the Aztec 'Legend of the Suns,'" in *Symbol and Meaning beyond the Closed Community: Essays in Mesoamerican Ideas,* ed. Gary H. Gossen, Studies on Culture and Society, vol. 1 (New York: Institute for Mesoamerican Studies, University at Albany and State University of New York, 1986), 19–34; Bernal-García, "La Montaña Sagrada."

39. Tedlock, *Popol Vuh,* 253.

40. *Historia de los Mexicanos,* 105; Nicholson, "Religion," 400.

41. *Historia de los Mexicanos por sus Pinturas,* 88–89.

42. *Historia de los Mexicanos,* 108; Nicholson, "Religion," 400.

43. Bernal-García, "Carving Mountains," chap. 6; Alfredo López-Austin, *Tamoanchan y Tlalocan* (México: Fondo de Cultura Económica, 1994), 162.

44. Tedlock, *Popol Vuh,* 35; Dennis Tedlock, "La siembra y el amanecer de todo el Cielo-Tierra: Astronomía en el Popol Vuh," in *Arqueoastronomía y Etnoastronomía en Mesoamérica,* ed. Johanna Broda, Stanislaw Iwaniszewski, and Lucrecia Maupomé (México: Universidad Nacional Autónoma de México, 1991), 164; Freidel, Schele, and Parker, *Maya Cosmos,* 109.

45. Tedlock, *Popol Vuh,* 372; Tedlock, "La siembra y el amanecer," 169–71.

46. *Popol Vuh* in Tedlock, *Popol Vuh,* 89.

47. This is, most likely, the vertical and upside-down saurian that becomes a tree in Mesoamerican art.

48. These subtleties in personages and narrative organization are what give identity to each culture and its stories.

49. Tedlock, *Popol Vuh*, 37.

50. *Popol Vuh*, in Tedlock, *Popol Vuh*, 99.

51. Ibid., 99–101. Tedlock, on page 37, suggests that Kabrakan died because he fell under a spell: "just as [the bird] was cooked inside a coating of earth, so he will end up covered by earth." Carol Hendrickson treats this passage in much the same metaphorical terms, proposing that Kabrakan died because he ate the same earth that would receive him in a short while; "Twin Gods and Quiché Rulers," 133. López-Austin would explain it in terms of a supernatural being able to eat only light, raw matter; *Tamoanchan y Tlalocan*, 23–43. Thus, when Kabrakan eats the cooked and thus heavy Earth, he introduces into his body an alien substance and dies. However, there is still a practical reason for Kabrakan's death by swallowing a roasted bird covered with clay, and this became clear to me not long ago. A pre-Hispanic recipe for clay duck, by Susana Pérez, appeared in a recent issue of *Artes de México: Los espacios de la cocina mexicana* 16 (1997): 14. The bird must first be cleaned of its entrails and its blood drained. Then, it is stuffed with prickly pears and spices, and with its feathers unplucked, it is covered with clay. When done, the hardened ball of clay must be hit to expose the meat and stuffing, with the feathers adhering completely to the clay. Kabrakan was so voracious, and ignorant of human ways, that he apparently ate the bird, still with its feathers and enclosed in the clay.

52. Karl A. Taube, "A Prehispanic Maya Katun Wheel," *Journal of Anthropological Research* 44, no. 2 (1988): 183–203; Taube, *Itzam Cab Ain*, 1; Karl A. Taube, "The Teotihuacan Cave of Origin: The Iconography and Architecture of Emergence Mythology in Mesoamerica and the American Southwest," *RES: Anthropology and Aesthetics* 12 (1986): 57–58, fig. 4; Freidel, Schele, and Parker, *Maya Cosmos*, 281, fig. 6:20.

53. Bernal-García, "La Montaña Sagrada."

54. Thelma Sullivan, personal communication in Doris Heyden, "Caves, Gods and Myths: World-View and Planning in Teotihuacan," in *Mesoamerican Sites and World-Views: A Conference at Dumbarton Oaks, October 16th and 17th, 1976*, ed. Elizabeth P. Benson (Washington, D.C.: Dumbarton Oaks Research Library and Collection, 1981), 15; John Sullivan, personal communication, October 1997.

55. Fray Alonso de Molina, *Vocabulario en Lengua Castellana y Mexicana y Mexicana y Castellana*, facsimile edition of the 1555–1571 manuscript, with a preliminary study by Miguel León-Portilla (México: Editorial Porrúa, S.A., 1977), 24r.

56. Molina, *Vocabulario*, 157r.

57. John Sullivan, personal communication, October 1997; Molina, *Vocabulario*, 154r.

58. Sahagún, *Historia general*, 2:234. Angel García-Zambrano made the original observation on the similarity between the drawing, in pre-Hispanic books, of the maize's round pinnacle and Colhuacatepec's curved and bent summit.

59. Durán, *Historia de las Indias*, 2:218, 222–23.

60. Ibid., 216. My translation.

61. The close association between these places has made impossible the study of one without the other, since the beginning of the century until this decade: Eduard

Seler, "Dónde se encontraba Aztlán, la patria [original] de los Aztecas?" in *Mesoamérica y el centro de México: Una antología,* trans. from the German by Jesús Monjarás-Ruiz (1893; reprint, México: Colección Biblioteca del Instituto Nacional de Antropología e Historia, 1985), 309–30; López-Austin, *Tamoanchan y Tlalocan,* 214–17. However, Dana Leibsohn does recognize the non-absolute interchangeability of the terms: Dana Leibsohn, *The "Historia Tolteca-Chichimeca": Recollecting Identity in a Nahua Manuscript* (Ann Arbor, Mich.: University Microfilms, 1993), 102, 136, n. 27. And, in a previous paper, I differentiated their consecutive roles in the process of creation: Bernal-García, "From Mountain to Toponym."

62. Bernal-García, "La Montaña Sagrada."

63. Bernal-García, "From Mountain to Toponym."

64. Bernal-García, "Carving Mountains," 142.

65. Bernal-García, "La Montaña Sagrada."

66. *Popol Vuh* in Tedlock, *Popol Vuh,* 163.

67. "Leyenda de los Soles," in *Códice Chimalpopoca: Anales de Cuauhtitlán y Leyenda de los Soles,* translation from the Náhuatl, 1558 and 1570, ed. and notes by Primo Feliciano Velázquez (México: Universidad Nacional Autónoma de México, 1992), 120.

68. This is most likely the dark blue corn still considered a delicacy in Mexico and the southwestern United States.

69. "Leyenda de los Soles," 121; *Historia de los Mexicanos,* 110.

70. Alfredo López-Austin also states that the "great hill" belongs to the east: *Tamoanchan y Tlalocan,* 162.

71. Bernal-García, "La Montaña Sagrada."

72. The *Leyenda de los Soles* (p. 120) may have the cracking happening on 1 Tochtli and the flowering the following day, 2 Acatl.

73. Days may actually represent years when addressing mythical events. See Freidel, Schele, and Parker, *Maya Cosmos,* 63–64; Bernal-García, "From Mountain to Toponym," 95 and n. 16.

74. Hendrickson, "Twin Gods," 133.

75. Tedlock, *Popol Vuh,* 253.

76. Alfredo López-Austin, *Cuerpo Humano e Ideología: Las Concepciones de los Antiguos Nahuas,* 2 vols. (1980; reprint, México: Instituto de Investigaciones Antropológicas, Universidad Nacional Autónoma de México, 1989).

77. López-Austin, *Tamoanchan y Tlalocan,* 161.

78. Ibid., 162. López-Austin believes that the interconnection between death and reproduction links the new generations with the ancestors' bones. On the same idea in Maya religion, see Carlsen and Prechtel, "The Flowering of the Dead," 23–42.

79. Bernal-García, "Carving Mountains," 386, n. 121; Bernal-García, "La Montaña Sagrada."

80. Freidel, Schele, and Parker, *Maya Cosmos,* 113; Bernal-García, "From Mountain to Toponym," 98.

Calabash Trees and Cacti in the Indigenous Ritual Selection of Environments for Settlement in Colonial Mesoamerica

ANGEL JULIÁN GARCÍA ZAMBRANO

Under the label of "government projects for collective well-being," indiscriminate intervention into specific ecosystems occupied by indigenous communities from time immemorial, in Mexico and other Latin American countries, has produced severe alterations of those systems and traumatic changes in traditional ways of life. According to Miguel Alberto Bartolomé, the implementation of such projects since the colonial period proves that the phenomenon is a structural one in the politics of dominant groups, rather than a circumstantially isolated problem. In Bartolomé's opinion, when an official commitment qualified as a "national endeavor" is espoused by the government, nothing appears to prevent the relocation of an Indian society living in harmony with a particular environment.[1] Since most of this compulsory moving of peoples affects ecological niches where natives relate specific plants to land features and religious beliefs, I consider it pertinent to relate this paper's argument to two early colonial episodes which have recurred throughout history, with some variation. In 1584, the Royal Audience of New Spain (Mexico) confronted the problem of sentencing in regard to a legal plea introduced by a Spanish settler from the town of Santa Maria Tepexi who firmly believed the indigenous "barren territory"—dotted with cacti and maguey plants—ought to be cleared away so that pasture could be cultivated and used to raise sheep. However, in the natives' perception no other kind of land economics could act as a substitute for their traditional cultivation of cacti, calabash, corn, and beans. Dramatically responding to the Royal Court of Appeals, the Indians described the situation as they saw it: "If the claim were to favor Alonza de Sande, the decision would entail the town's destruction, for the Indians would be driven out due to the fencing of the land, in a way resembling a corral, a situation not permitted by divine or human law."[2] In another example of this misperception of ecosystems permeated with metaphorical meanings, Bishop Pedro Cortés y Larraz reported in a *Relación Geográfica* dated around the end of the eighteenth century that:

> Many Indians nowadays still refer to this city as Panchoy, meaning 'lagoon's belly', in the belief that the said Valley, where Guatemala is located, was indeed a lagoon; but I understand that such etymologies and derivations are quite arbitrary, and thus I began to consider it soon after I first set foot in America, when I barely found a thing with an etymology derived from its own; because at every step I heard 'this hill is named so, for it has much stone or many trees'; and this other town is thus called since it is founded between two hills, or above much water; but if this were really so, barbarian languages would then be more eloquent and telling than Latin and even Greek, for under quite simple conditions they explain the whole concept perfectly, to the point that I content myself by saying that this city is named Goathemala, and if at another time it was called Quauhtemallan, it has lost this [original] name just because the pronunciation of the former is much softer.[3]

As may be surmised, the Bishop's words demonstrate his own difficulty in perceiving the relationship the Indians had with their living environment and his disregard for their acute conceptualization of the landscape as expressed by their language.

These two examples should suffice to illustrate the type of non-Indian reasoning which continues to prevent government agencies from allowing indigenous peoples to remain in their own lands, even though these lands are full of spiritual and practical characteristics. Thus, this paper seeks to call attention to some of the sacred metaphors embedded in the indigenous landscape in order to discourage actions that indiscriminately destroy these sacred realms.

The process by which specific flora conditioned the ritual selection of sites for settlement in colonial Mesoamerica implies metaphorical ties between natural environment and myth which need to be understood. For this study, the tubular or spherical shape and storage capacity of several types of calabash gourds, as well as a variety of barrel cacti, known in Mexico as *biznagas de agua,* or "cactus filled with water," must be considered.[4] Familiarity with these plants' features led indigenous peoples to look for a valley or cove that replicated the attributes of these two vegetables that made it possible for them to hold water. Geographically speaking, the ideal environment for settlement consisted of a basin confined by hills or mountains, which contained springs, cesspools, rivers, and/or lakes. Under these ecological conditions, an abundance of plants and animals in the locale was ensured, and with them human life flourished.

Beginning with the correlation envisioned by the Indians between calabash gourds and the most desirable physiography of a cove, there is plenty of colonial data demonstrating the natives' tendency to select settlement sites based on this formal and functional relationship. Place-names or toponyms found in the *Relaciones Geográficas* (1579–1585) attest to the natives' proclivity to inhabit valleys or other confined spaces with permanent water sources, since they physically and metaphorically replicated the characteristics of gourds. Although many of the surveyed place-names encompass other elements of flora and fauna that may have accounted for the choice of the site—such as reeds, mesquite trees, waterfowl, turtles, snails, and serpents—these elements exist concurrently with a lacustrine environment confined by mountain ranges. In previous papers I have suggested that in colonial Mesoamerica such an environment corresponds to the modern notion of a gorge, cove, horseshoe valley, or box canyon, known in Spanish geographical terms as a *rinconada.*[5]

On a mythical level, the interdependence between a habitat permeated with primordial vegetable referents and its human occupants is evoked by the natives when bringing about episodes of generative character that occurred at the core of a calabash gourd. In *Codex Vaticanus 3738,* or *Códice Ríos* (c. 1580), for example, a calabash tree of life shows infants approaching the ripe gourds in order to suck their milky content (fig. 1). Glosses supporting the painted scene indicate that this is the Chichiualquauitl, or "milky tree that rejuvenates infants who died before reaching the age of consciousness."[6] An image of the god Tezcatlipoca and an explanatory text on this same page of the illuminated manuscript relate tree and divinity to an aspect of the "Mountain of Sustenance," one that persists among contemporary Nahuas when they evoke "the milky little calabash growing on one side of the white mountain."[7] This calabash fruit is known in Meso-america as *jícara, tecomate,* or *guaje.*

At the root of these Mexican terms, or "aztequismos," lie Nahua words specifically used to designate calabash gourds. *Xicalli,* for example, corresponds to *jícara, tecomatl* to *tecomate,* and *huaxin* to *guaje.*[8] *Xicalli,* in turn, comes from the Nahua nouns *xictli,* or navel, and *calli,* or house; thus, a "house with a navel." Certainly, a navel is left on a *jícara* when the peduncle is pulled away from it. In another metaphor, the calabash's "navel" becomes a nipple, known as "pezón de la jícara" in Spanish.[9] Such an association is visually implied in the Chichiualquauitl, or "Tree of Milk," depicted in *Codex Vaticanus*

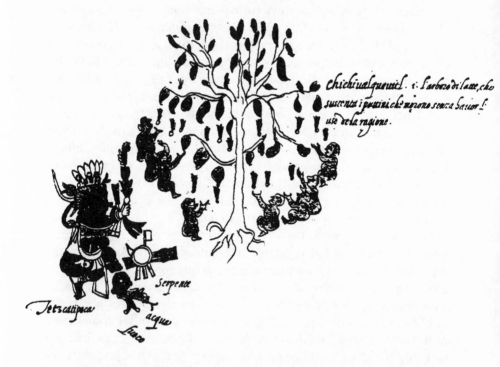

Fig. 1. Chichiualquauitl, or "Tree of Milk." Codex Vaticanus 3738, fol. 3v. Illuminated manuscript, European paper, original panel measuring 46.5 x 29.5 cm. Central Mexico, ca. 1570–1589. (Author: Fr. Pedro de los Ríos, Vatican Library, Rome, vol. 65. Facsimile published by Akademische Druck-u. Verlagsanstalt, Graz, Austria, 1979)

3738. Because *calli,* or house, also means storage box or receptacle,[10] Fray Alonso de Molina, the sixteenth-century colonial philologist, records a composite noun, *xicaltecomatl,* to describe clay bowls, implying the equivalence of form and function that vases or bowls had, whether they were made out of calabash gourds or of clay.[11] The third word, *huaxin,* is the Nahua name for the tree whose fruit, similar to the *algarrobo,* is edible, and is the root for the Spanish word *guaje.*[12] This latter Mexican word is used to describe a receptacle obtained after the longitudinal sectioning of a gourd.[13] In all cases, the pulp and the abundant seeds are extracted from the calabash, permitting the cortex to dry and harden to the point at which a container for storing water is created.[14] Other domestic and ritual uses included the storage of corn tortillas, cacao, chocolate, maize, achiote (*Bixa orellana*), and many kinds of seeds.[15]

In Mexico, the calabash tree (and its gourds) lent its name to a number of places: Jicaltepec, or "Hill of the Gourd"; Xicalhuacal, or "The Gourd's Box"; Tepehuaxtitlan, or "Site among Mountain Calabashes"; and Huaxtla, or "Place of Abundant Gourds."[16] Such designations were conceived to evoke either cucurbits or calabash gourds readily available in the nearby environment or the likeness between physiography and vegetable. For example, Tecomatlan or Cuauhtecomatlan, "Place of the Gourd Vessels," and Cuauhtecomatzinco, "[Subsidiary] Place of the Gourd's Tree Vessels," are toponyms that contain logograms alluding to the "place of calabash trees," for they illustrate the importance of the vegetable in the founding of these towns (fig. 2).[17]

Further inquiries about the proposed relationship between calabash gourds and physiography in the *Relaciones Geográficas* (1579–1585) often point to the natural environment of a cove, or *rinconada.* According to René Acuña,[18] Tecomahuaca, for example, refers etymologically to the "place where *tecomates* or calabash gourds drained," a condition stressed by the indigenous informants who described the site as a plain traversed by a river and surrounded by mountains.[19] This overlapping is substantiated by John Sullivan Hendricks (personal communication), who translates the term as "Place of the Gourd Owners." A similar riverine and geographically confined environment chosen for settlement was Tecomaxtlahuaca, or "Place of the Plain of Abundant Gourds." According to the etymology of the town's placename, the site is a "plain with *tecomates* or gourds," a circumstance complemented by the colonial indigenous population's "use of gourds as vases."[20]

Similarly, Ayusuchiquizala is a basin or "vase . . . within a rough terrain and . . . a stream that goes by the town."[21] One of the components of the Nahua place-name for Ayusuchizala is another word for gourd, *ayotl,* followed by the plant's flower, *xuchitl,* and the locative *-tzalan* in between.[22] Thus, the toponym designates a site "among gourd flowers." Other cases where mountains confining coves, or *rinconadas,* were particularly known for their abundance of calabash trees, or for the likeness between fruit and physiography, are recorded in three documentary geographical reports from Oaxaca (1579–1581). Guaxilotitlan, for example, "was thus named from ancient times because the settlement was located on a plain where many trees, known in the Nahua tongue as Quauhxilotl, were found. The said fruit has the form of cucumbers . . . and it is eaten either raw or cooked, and it is sweet to eat."[23] A subsidiary *sujeto* town attached to this greater settlement, or *cabecera,* of Quauhxilotl was located within the same cove, but it was given the place-name of Apazco. Apazco comes from the Nahuatl *apaztli,* a large bowl, plate, or vase.[24] Although no trace of

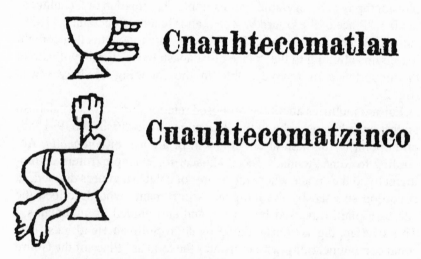

Fig. 2. Logograms for Cuauhtecomatlan and Cuauhtecomatzinco. (From Antonio Peñafiel, Nombres Geográficos de México *[México: Oficina Tipográfica de la Secretaría de Fomento, 1885], p. 94, figs. 42.23 and 42.8)*

toponymy seems to refer to gourds in this case, the indigenous inhabitants envisioned, by extension, the properties of the plant in the naturally irrigated basin located nearby.[25]

In the Oaxacan region of Peñoles, or Rocky Hills, one of the visible orographic protuberances gave its name to the town of Quauhxiloticpac. Here, the rocky hills were likened to the gourds produced by two genres of calabash trees commonly known in Mexico as *quauhxilotl*. According to the indigenous informants documenting the town's *Relaciones Geográficas*, the globular aspect of the said geographic accident was reminiscent of "some kind of fruit above a hill. This fruit is called in [the] Mexican tongue Quauhxilotl . . . [because] it looks like an elongated cucumber, has good odor and it is sweet to the taste."[26] The same tubular-shaped gourds inspired the town's name of Piaztla, a description based on the toponymy, and meaning "place where tubular gourds are abundant."[27] Besides being a part of a larger district known as Corregimiento de Papaloticpac, this locale is an area distinguished by the presence of sites literally regarded as "crooked, bent, twisted, or overturned," apparently in view of the correspondence between the irregular shape of some gourds and the rugged terrain containing coves, or *rinconadas,* where the natives preferred to live.

Complementary to the aforementioned environmental and floral interdependence is the metaphorical function that marine fauna, such as turtles, had in a town's foundation, given the likeness of the animal's rounded shell to the shape and hardness of calabash gourds. Such was the case of Ayutla, Oaxaca, whose linguistic meaning derives from *ayotli,* calabash gourd, and *ayotl* or *ayutl,* turtle.[28] This interrelationship was further underscored by an allusion to a turtle, regarded as the cornerstone for the town's foundation and as one of the metaphors for the Primordial Earth.[29] Indeed, in the corresponding colonial *Relaciones Geográficas,* the natives record that "this town always stood on a plain . . . by a sizeable river . . . [and] the site was known since ancient times as Ayutla . . . for there is a stone resembling a turtle which in the Mexican tongue means Ayutla or turtle, and it has been more than a thousand years that our ancestors from time immemorial retold the history of this town's foundation."[30]

Although not all place-names explicitly describe the physiography of the ecosystem chosen for settlement, there are colonial sources to corroborate the relationship between calabash gourds and the geography of a given site. For instance, in the Oaxacan *Relaciones*

Geográficas of Teutitlan, the town's toponym literally means "Place of God" or "Sacred Place," a designation enhanced in the document by two idols revered in two temple-pyramids. But, according to the native informants, the foundation took place "among bushy hills of mesquite, calabash gourds, and other fruit trees."[31] A further example derives from indigenous consciousness and practical use of the gourds' floating properties. In one case from Cuseo in Michoacan, the mass cultivation of large gourds led the population to develop the craft of boat making to cross rivers or lakes. As might be anticipated, this kind of trade was vital to the colonial indigenous preservation of this site's place-name, Cuseo, described in the *Relaciones Geográficas* as a "town where gourds are grown." Excerpts from the document confirm the assertion:

> Cuseo is given that name for it is a town where a great quantity of round calabashes were planted and harvested from time immemorial . . . and thus the town is named so, as if we could label it 'the town where calabashes are grown' . . . because, with the said gourds, rafters used as boats were made to cross the rivers as they were used in Mexico [Tenochtitlan] and elsewhere.[32]

Cuseo also has linguistic associations with *cuiseo,* a Tarascan derivative of *kusi,* the earthenware jars equivalent to the large Castillian vase called the *tinaja.*[33] Thus, Cuiseo describes both a lacustrine cove and a place where bowls are made. This relationship is further emphasized by the composite place-name Cuiseo de la Laguna, or Cuiseo of the Lake, and by the historical description recorded in the sixteenth-century *Relaciones Geográficas* stating that the site is "located in a cove adopting the shape of a horseshoe [and] its name means in Castillian 'place where earthen-ware jars are made'."[34]

Since colonial records show the interchangeability of gourds and ceramic vases to describe a given environment, a brief digression is needed to explain the circumstantial transformation of the organic recipients into the clay ones.[35] Indeed, as early as 4,000 b.c.e. there is material evidence of the lending of the gourd's shape and function to Mesoamerican early ceramics. Obviously, the eventually perishable condition of the gourds may have led to the invention of clay vessels.[36] Throughout the Formative and Classic periods of Mesoamerica, this substitution materialized in fine vases modeled after *jícara* and *tecomate* gourds. Ceramics found at Chiapa del Corzo, Holmul, and Ocós, the phase Tepeu III at Uaxactún, and especially the Barra ceramics from Mazatan, Chiapas,[37] and Salina La Blanca in western Guatemala[38] confirm the functional replacement. About 90 percent of the shards found in the Barra ceramics assemblage show a variety of forms exclusively modeled after *tecomates*.[39] So pervasive was the influence of this kind of cucurbit (*Lagenaria siceraria*) in the trade that Donald Lathrap has encompassed these types of vessels under the generic name of "pumpkin tecomates."[40] A fine archaeological example of such formal and functional continuity is Alfonso Caso's discovery of a gilded *yetecomatl* in Tomb 7 at Monte Albán (fig. 3).[41] A *yetecomatl* is a vase made of a calabash gourd to keep tobacco ritually, for shamanistic purposes. This term is a composite noun derived from the Nahua *yetl,* tobacco, and *tecomatl,* a gourd container.[42] In the Monte Albán sample, the gold leaf retained the form of the disintegrated organic receptacle. Perforations in the gourd for the hide strings used to hang the ceremonial container may be seen both in the gold remains, and in the *jícaras* carried around the necks of the male and a female

Fig. 3. Drawing of a Yetecomatl rendered in gold leaf. Artifact found by Alfonso Caso in 1931 at Tomb 7 in Monte Alban, Oaxaca, Zapotec, Phase III: 600–800 c.e. (From Alfonso Caso, Interpretación del Códice Selden, *3135 A-2 [México: Sociedad Mexicana de Antropología, 1964], p. 26, fig. 3)*

deities, Oxomoco and Cipactonal, depicted in the *Codex Borbonicus* in their roles as primeval shamans (fig. 4).[43]

The abundance of archaeological remains attesting to the role of gourds in the ritual and daily life of Mesoamericans, including the indigenous proclivity to visualize their shapes in coves or valleys chosen for settlement, is corroborated by modern toponyms originating in indigenous place-names that survived throughout the colonial period. This custom is best preserved in Guatemala, where the ancient tradition continues well into the present in a total of forty-one *caseríos*, or hamlets, that retain the Nahua place-names of El Jícaro or El

Fig. 4. Oxomoco and Cipactonal as patrons of sustenance and origin in Codex Borbonicus, *p. 21 (portion). Screenfold manuscript, panel 339 x 39.5 cm., México City. Pre-Conquest or Early Colonial. Bibliothèque Nationale, Paris. (From Esther Pasztory,* Aztec Art *[New York: Harry N. Abrams, Inc., 1983], p. 195, plate 147. Courtesy Esther Pasztory)*

Jicaral (*Crescentia cujete*), emphasizing the perceived likeness of the calabash fruit and the inhabited environment. Since this toponym is frequently shared by the locally contiguous hamlets (*caseríos*) and villages (*aldeas*), and at times sustained in the larger hierarchy and geography of the district municipalities, it is possible to follow up the recurrence of the said referent. So clear is the proposed concordance between the abundant fruit and a specific ecosystem that it is consecutively repeated in ten of the forty-one place-names recorded in Guatemala at the various levels of sociopolitical occupation, from hamlet, to village, to municipality.[44]

The lower the spatial scale shared by hamlets and villages, in view of their physical proximity, the greater the propensity to retain the same floral and geographical allusions. Of the forty-one hamlets, twenty-two communities at the village level continue the use of the place-name El Jícaro or El Jicaral. However, with the broadening of the civil hierarchy, the increase in size of the physical territory of the municipalities, and the complexity of historical events, the settlement units at the higher levels tend to lose consistency in retaining the common toponymy. Therefore, only four complex sites named El Jícaro preserved their original designations from the level of hamlet, to that of village, and then to the district level of municipality. Various economic activities intensively practiced since the colonial period, namely, mining and the feudally derived *encomienda,* promoted the adoption of historically concurrent place-names, such as Concepción Las Minas or Asunción Mita, in at least five municipalities in Guatemala. Additionally, seven others were renamed on account of Christian advocacies, while the cases of Cabañas and Quezada exemplify a more pervasive substitution of Hispanic patronymics.

The remaining municipal and departmental denominations tend to mask the metaphorical perception of the landscape, originally based on the calabash fruit, by using toponyms which appear, superficially, to depart from vegetable motifs. To clarify, the original sequence, whereby the hamlets are consistently called El Jícaro, or "The Calabash Tree-Gourd," begins to be altered at the village level by using terms denoting concomitant geographical features, such as Lagunilla ("little lake"). In the two instances of municipal and departmental hierarchy, the initial meaning of the calabash fruit, mirrored in the lake environment, is enhanced even further by bringing into the toponymy allusions about riverine fauna, metaphorically endowed with all the previous phyto and physiographic characteristics. Such an interesting polysemic perception occurs when the sequence of place-names shows the unusually recurrent term of Jutiapa. Since Lagunilla, or "little lake," may be regarded as an allegoric transposition of the gourds' capacity for holding water, a conclusion confirmed by the vicinity of the hamlet El Jícaro, Jutiapa has, correspondingly, a riverine fauna equivalent. Indeed, Jutiapa derives from El Jute, a river snail that often lends its name, in Central America, to places where streams and larger rivers form, either from a single spring or from a group of springs.[45] Archaeological ceramic vessels, found on the shores of underground rivers located in caves in Belize and Guatemala, and accompanied by offerings containing large quantities of river snails, seem to corroborate the proposed correspondence.[46] In this causal context, I believe it is safe to suggest that the river snail, a hydrographic basin, and the calabash gourd are metaphorically equivalent. No wonder, then, that in the larger territorial and administrative entities known in Guatemala as *departamentos,* Jutiapa is a place-name designation found fifteen times in twelve of these jurisdictions. Again, this may well be attributed to the sequence of the metaphorical transposition of the gourd, El Jícaro (or its alternate fruit-derived name from gourd vessels known as Tecomates), into the river snail, El Jute, as well as to the varied terminology listed in the official records for a basin.

In El Salvador, similar samplings illustrate the proposed correlations, again amplifying the symbolic meanings suggested. In two cases, the alternate term for the calabash gourd, *jícara,* given to hamlets at El Tecomatal and Los Tecomates, is derived from the predominantly rugged terrain at El Cerro, or "The Hill," the substitute name adopted for the two lesser districts, or *cantones.* However, a subtle but pertinent transmutation occurs at the higher level of the municipality, where a deeper figurative meaning is bestowed by designating both of these districts Apastepeque, "Hill of the Apaztli," a large bowl or vesse. In another example, the calabash's substitute hamlet place-name of El Morro is identified with the appellative for a cave at the nearby village, while the entire municipality identifies itself with the metaphor for Tonacatepeque, "The Mountain of Sustenance."

In order to understand the metaphorical underpinnings controlling the inextricable relationships between the environment selected for settlement and the properties of calabash gourds as they were envisioned by Mesoamerican natives, it is necessary to consider some of the main passages of creation myths. In the Maya area, the *Popol Vuh* focuses on the triad of the gourd, the flesh head, and the skull.[47] The father of the Hero Twins, Hun Hunahpu, returns to life as a skull in the form of a gourd and finds refuge and anonymity in the plant's potential to reproduce itself without cultivation. Under the dual concept of seminal life, a gourd and a skull coexist within a context of existential dynamics by which all fecundity comes from ancestors, be they divinities or human beings. Given this cycle of life out of death, Robert Carlsen and Martin Prechtel found among contemporary Maya Atitecos an explanation of this ancient belief.[48] At the altar of the Church of Santiago, located on the shores of Lake Atitlan—which, incidentally, displays the physiographic profile of a curved calabash gourd—a stump of an old "Tree of Life" represents the bone matrix capable of generating new offspring in the form of bountiful gourds. During the transitional days between the autumn and spring equinoxes, the sacred tree is referred to as "Gourd-Head" or Tzimai Awa, and at this crucial moment it is represented as a skull.[49] With the arrival of spring, the world takes on a metaphorical aspect as "Tree of Life" or "Flowering Mountain Earth," when it is virtually inseminated. It is in this instant that the stump of the ancestral calabash tree, represented also in the gourd, fully blossoms, promoting the simultaneous birth of the sun, maize, and the regeneration of time itself.[50]

Colonial documentary data for Central Mexico has also revealed that the natural profile of coves or gorges suggested to indigenous minds correlates to the large bowl where humanity was created.[51] Such an allegorical transposition is rooted in the instant when Quetzalcoatl descended to Earth in the form of an *apaztle,* a large receptacle or bowl, to promote the rebirth of humankind.[52] Ashes from disintegrated bones belonging to ancestors were gathered by the hero, and with the collaboration of deities who dropped seminal fluids into the maize flour contained in the bowl, contributed to the creation of humankind. Likewise, a miraculous rebirth is the core of an illustrated migration story depicted in the *Lienzo de Jucutácato* (fig. 5).

Pertinent to the present argument are the glosses which provide a metaphorical toponym for the legendary place of origin: Chalchiuitlapazco. In this composite noun, *chalchiuitl* means "precious green stone,"[53] most likely turquoise or jade, and is used in a symbolic fashion to describe a large aquatic realm.[54] The second part of the compound, *apazco*, derives from *apaztli*, and translates as "in the large water bowl," according to A. M. Garibay.[55] Initial studies of the *Lienzo* done by Bishop Plancarte and Eduard Seler have already identified the associations between the clay bowl, *apaztle*, and the origin of humanity.[56] According to Remi Siméon,[57] *apazco* derives from *apatzquitl*, a Nahua word for "spring," "fountain," and "water that runs." Supplementary to this set of meanings, the main gloss complements the iconographic meaning of the painted image of a crumpled vessel that allows human beings to exit from its interior. This primordial container, and additional glosses relating the scene to an emergence "from the squeezed or milked vessel [and] from the precious green water [from which] came those formed from ashes . . . ,"[58] may very well fit into the proposition heretofore advanced regarding the nourishing milk tree/gourd vessel/water receptacle replicated in the physiography of a gorge or cove (*rinconada*).

Together with this physiography, cucurbits and calabash trees of various genres are part of a predominant xerophytic flora enhancing

Fig. 5. Chalchiuitlapazco in Lienzo de Jucutácato, *detail. Jicalan-Uruapan, Michoacan, Mexico. Early Colonial, cotton canvas, 2.60 x 2.00 m. (From Eduard Seler,* Comentarios al Códice Borgia, *vol. 2 [México: Fondo de Cultura Económica, 1988], p. 219, fig. 273. Courtesy Fondo de Cultura Económica)*

the Mesoamerican landscape. Spiny vegetation of various kinds, such as mesquite trees, magueys, barrel cacti, or *biznagas,* and xerophilous plants (*tuna* and *nopal*), grow next to each other in the same eco-systems. Indigenous peoples in northern Mexico thought of barrel cacti as being endowed with generative and environmental attributes

Fig. 6. Barrel cacti (biznagas) *and allegoric Chicomoztoc.* Codex Azcatitlan, *plate 5, detail. Painted manuscript, European paper, 21 x 28 cm. Valley of Mexico: Cuauhtitlan-Xaltocan-Tlatelolco, ca. 1572. Collection Aubin-Goupil, Bibliothèque Nationale, Paris. (From Doris Heyden,* The Eagle, the Cactus, the Rock: The Roots of Mexico-Tenochtitlan's Foundation Myth and Symbol, *BAR International Series, 484 [Oxford: B.A.R., 1989], p. 107, fig. 8. Courtesy Doris Heyden)*

similar to those of the calabash gourds because both could store water
and had spherical or tubular shapes. *Teocomitl*, or "Holy Vessel," from
teotl, divine or sacred, and *comitl*, clay vessel, is the name of both the
plant and the sacred landscape embraced by the metaphorical
relationship implied in the word. For example, in Michoacán, Mexico,
a mountain range confining the northwestern flank of a ravine where
the Indian towns of Alimanzi, Cuzcacuauhtla, and Epatlan were
founded, was named Teocomitl, or "Sacred Pot."[59] Although the corresponding *Relaciones Geográficas* stresses the sacredness of the site,
due to its specific name, no further references are made to a pri-

Fig. 7. Sacred mountain and barrel cacti Teocomitl. Codex Azcatitlan,
*plate 2, detail. Painted manuscript, European paper, 21 x 28 cm. Valley of
Mexico: Cuauhtitlan-Xaltocan-Tlatelolco, ca. 1572. Collection Aubin-
Goupil, Bibliothèque Nationale, Paris. (From Doris Heyden,* The Eagle,
the Cactus, the Rock: The Roots of Mexico-Tenochtitlan's Foundation
Myth and Symbol, *BAR International Series, 484 [Oxford: B.A.R., 1989],
p. 105, fig. 3. Courtesy Doris Heyden)*

mordial cactus tree. Inferences can be drawn from the analysis of various early colonial chronicles and codices. Beginning with the *Anales de Cuauhtitlan, biznagas,* or barrel cacti, played a fundamental role in penitential rites performed in preparation for the quest of land for permanent settlement. Right from the start, *biznagas* were ceremonially killed and burned to provide ashes kept in a bundle, which was considered the holy receptacle for the guiding patron deity.[60] In the *Codex Boturini,* or *Tira de la Peregrinación,* the first time the deity revealed itself to indicate the route to the sought-after land, a sacrifice was performed over a *biznaga* cactus flanked by mesquite trees.[61]

The *Anales de Cuauhtitlan* and the *Codex Azcatitlan* provide an additional legendary and historical framework for this type of migrant story. In the *Anales,* Chichimecs often found refuge inside these cacti when threatened by extinction in desert lands, reemerging from them in more propitious times. In addition to barrel cacti, a logographic mountain enhanced by the seven caves profile of the mythical place of origin, Chicomoztoc, is shown in the *Codex Azcatitlan* as the key nurturing environment of the Nahua (fig. 6). Additional literary images recall the temporary stay of the Mexica at places named Apazco, or "In the Water Vessel," and Contitlan, or "Place Near *Ollas,* or Pots."[62] Allegorically, the wandering migrants, on occasion, either departed from or entered sacred mountains enhanced by the presence of the barrel cactus, Teocomitl, to save their lives (fig. 7). Such reiteration of the support offered by nature, which nurtures, is commemorated by the indigenous peoples of Mexico in two dramatic scenes depicted in the early colonial codices. In *The Selden Roll,* arrival at the ideal cove, or *rinconada,* is symbolically recorded by two complementary icons placed opposite each other and flanking the allegoric image of the ideal site for settlement (fig. 8). On the left side of this foundation emblem, the *biznaga* cactus constitutes a reminder of the deceased ancestors whose memory and actions were invoked along the migrants' route. Upon reaching the mountain, cave, or riverine ecological niche at the promised land, the revived head of the ancestor's offspring, shown on the right hand side, comes out of a clay *olla,* or pot, modeled after the symbolic *tecomate* gourd vessel.[63] The long speech scroll in serpentine form becomes the loud call of a ritual convocation to start the ceremonial circumambulation of the new lands to be occupied.[64]

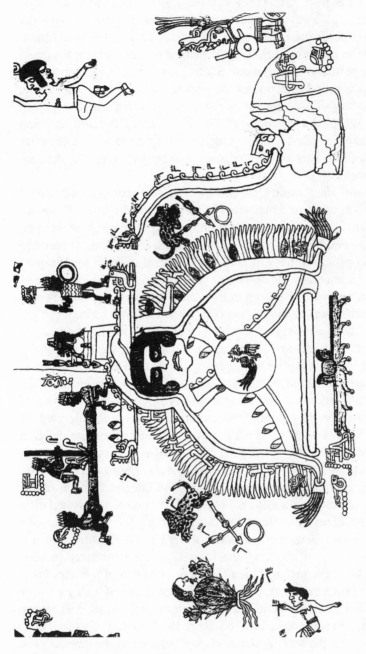

Fig. 8. Foundation emblem. The Selden Roll, detail. Painted manuscript, ficus paper; 38 x 350 cm. Mixtec, Western Oaxaca. (Courtesy of the Bodleian Library, Oxford University; MS. Arch. Selden. A. 72 (3), fols. 7–8. Reprinted from Cottie A. Burland, The Selden Roll. An Ancient Mexican Picture Manuscript in the Bodleian Library at Oxford, Monumenta Americana, 2 [Berlin: G. Mann, 1955].)

Similarly, the *Codex Azcatitlan* depicts two key scenes describing a Nahua group stopping during the long search for the ideal environment (figs. 9–10). The first scene is the arrival in Mexico-Tenochtitlan, and the second, in this illuminated manuscript, is what looks like the foundation ceremony of Azcatitlan. At Mexico-Tenochtitlan, the guiding deity, Huitzilopochtli, takes the place of a thick cactus leaf where prickly pears grow, while still maintaining his hummingbird aspect.

Fig. 9. Mexico-Tenochtitlan's arrival scene. Codex Azcatitlan, *detail, plate 12. Painted manuscript, European paper, 21 x 28 cm. Valley of Mexico: Cuauhtitlan-Xaltocan-Tlatelolco, ca. 1572. Collection Aubin-Goupil, Bibliothèque Nationale, Paris. (From Robert H. Barlow, "El Códice Azcatitlan," in* Fuentes y estudios sobre el México indígena, *ed. J. Monjaráz Ruiz et al. [México: Instituto Nacional de Antropología e Historia and Universidad de Las Américas, 1994]. Courtesy I.N.A.H)*

In a detail of the second scene, a half-fleshed head of the group's ancestor occupies the bottom section of a tree, along with fruits in the shape of the common *guaje,* or gourd. It is probably in this context that the heads of ancestors were called *tzontecomates* or *"tecomates* [with hair, from "tzontli"] in the form of a head," a noun that also appears as a toponym and as another name related to calabash, or

Fig. 10 Ancestor's head as Tzontecomate. Codex Azcatitlan, *detail, plate 22. Painted manuscript, European paper, 21 x 28 cm. Valley of Mexico: Cuauhtitlan-Xaltocan-Tlatelolco, ca. 1572. Collection Aubin-Goupil, Bibliothèque Nationale, Paris. (From Robert H. Barlow, "El Códice Azcatitlan," in* Fuentes y estudios sobre el México indígena, *ed. J. Monjaráz Ruiz et al. [México: Instituto Nacional de Antropología e Historia and Universidad de Las Américas, 1994]. Courtesy I.N.A.H.)*

jícaras.[65] Similarly, in the *Lienzo de Jucutacato* a human being is shown as one of the multiple tubular fruits springing from a plant that resembles the calabash tree of the most common variety, known in Mexico as *quauhxilotl* (see fig. 5). Finally, in a Maya vase in the Museo Popol Vuh's collection in Guatemala, the head of Hun Hunahpu hangs hidden down below and among numerous gourds from a calabash Tree of Life (fig. 11).

Fig. 11 Maya vase showing Hun Hunahpu's rebirth from a calabash "Tree of Life." Late Classic ceramic, Guatemala; Private Collection, Museum Popol Vuh, catalog no. 0093. (Courtesy Universidad Francisco Marroquín, Guatemala City)

Notes

1. Miguel Alberto Bartolomé, "Presas y Relocalizaciones de Indígenas en América Latina," *Anales de Antropología* 30 (1993): 119, 121.
2. In the original Spanish: ". . . y si se diese lugar la dicha merced seria causa de destruirlos y echarlos de sus tierras y natural . . . [pues] los vendrían a cercar y a cerrar a manera de corral lo qual no es permitido en ley divina ni humana"; in Autos del Pueblo de Santa María Tepexi, Land Suit Against Alonsa de Sande, 08/07/1584, University of Texas at Austin, Nettie Lee Benson Latin American Collection, Genaro García Manuscript Collection (G-61), folios 1v, 27r, 34v, 42r.
3. Pedro Cortés y Larraz, *Descripción Geográfico-Moral de la Diócesis de Goathemala,* vol. 1 (Guatemala, Sociedad de Geografía e Historia de Guatemala, 1958), 21.
4. Endemism of *Lagenaria* and *Crescentia* in Thomas W. Whitaker, "Endemism and Pre-Columbian Migration of the Bottle Gourd, Lagenaria siceraria (Mol.) Standl," in *Man across the Sea: Problems in Pre-Columbian Contacts,* ed. Carroll L. Riley, J. Charles Kelley, et al. (Austin: University of Texas Press, 1977), 321–25. Helia Bravo, *Las Cactáceas de México* (México: Universidad Nacional de México, 1937), 374, 450–51, discusses the barrel cacti available in Mexico.
5. Angel Julián García-Zambrano, "El poblamiento de México en la época de contacto, 1520–1540," *Mesoamerica: Plumsock Mesoamerican Studies* 24 (1992): 274–75; and "Early Colonial Evidence of Pre-Columbian Rituals of Foundation," in *Seventh Palenque Round Table,* ed. Virginia M. Fields, vol. 9 of the Palenque Round Table Series, gen. ed. Merle Greene Robertson (San Francisco: Pre-Columbian Art Research Institute, 1994), 218.
6. *Codice Ríos, Codex Vaticanus 3738, Códice Vaticanus,* Biblioteca Apostólica Vaticana, Códices Selecti, vol. 65 (Graz: Akademische Druck-u Verlagsanst., 1979), fol. 3v.
7. Luis Reyes García and Dieter Christensen, *El anillo de Tlalocan: Mitos, oraciones, cantos y cuentos de los Nawas actuales de los Estados de Veracruz y Puebla, México,* Zur Alten Geschichte Amerikas, Band 12 (Berlin: G. Mann, 1976), 77.
8. Lawrence B. Kiddle, *The Spanish Word Jícara. A Word History,* Philological and Documentary Studies, vol. 1, no. 4 (New Orleans: Middle American Research Institute, Tulane University of Louisiana, 1944), 123–24.
9. Cecilio A. Robelo, *Diccionario de Aztequismos* (México: Ediciones Fuente Cultural, n.d.), 414–15, in Luis Luján Muñoz and Ricardo Toledo Palomo, *Jícaras y guacales en la cultura Mesoamericana* (Guatemala: Sub-Centro Regional de Artesanías y Artes Populares, 1986), 17.
10. Remi Siméon, *Diccionario de la lengua Nahuatl o Mexicana* (México: Siglo Veintiuno, 1977), 61.
11. Fray Alonso de Molina, *Vocabulario en lengua castellana y mexicana y mexicana y castellana,* 2d ed. (Facsimile of the original, dated 1555–1571; preliminary study by Miguel León-Portilla; México: Editorial Porrúa, 1977), 93v, 159v.
12. Siméon, *Diccionario de la lengua Nahuatl o Mexicana,* 745.
13. Cecilio A. Robelo, *Diccionario de Aztequismos o sea catálogo de las palabras del idioma Nahuatl, Azteca o Mexicano, introducidas al idioma castellano bajo*

diversas formas (México: Imprenta del Museo Nacional de Arqueología, Historía y Etnología, 1912), 145–46.

14. Thomas W. Whitaker and Hugh C. Cutler, "Cucurbits from the Tehuacan Caves" in *The Prehistory of the Tehuacan Valley*, vol. 1, *Environment and Subsistence*, ed. Douglas J. Byers (Austin: University of Texas Press, 1967), 217.

15. Luján Muñoz and Toledo Palomo, *Jícaras y guacales*, 2. Carl V. Hartman, *Kalebassträdet i Tropiska Amerika: Etno-botaniskt Bidrag* (Uppsala: Almqvist and Wiksells Boktryckeri A.-b., 1911), 266.

16. Cecilio A. Robelo, *Nombres geográficos indígenas del Estado de México* (Cuernavaca, México: Luis G. Miranda, 1900), 124, 175.

17. Siméon, *Diccionario de la lengua Nahuatl o Mexicana*, 449. Antonio Peñafiel, *Nombres geográficos de México. Catálogo alfabético de los nombres de lugar pertenecientes al idioma Nahuatl. Estudio jeroglífico de la Matrícula de Tributos del Códice Mendocino*, 2 vols. (México: Oficina Tipográfica de la Secretaría de Fomento, 1885), 94.

18. *Relaciones Geográficas del Siglo XVI*, vol. 2, *Antequera I*, ed. René Acuña (México: Universidad Nacional Autónoma de México, Instituto de Investigaciones Antropológicas, 1984), 238, n. 18.

19. Ibid., 238–39.

20. Ibid., 284, n. 3. R. *Diccionario de la lengua Nahuatl o Mexicana*, 449.

21. *Antequera I*, ed. Acuña, 300, n. 30.

22. Siméon, *Diccionario de la lengua Nahuatl o Mexicana*, 19, 727.

23. *Antequera I*, ed. Acuña, 214.

24. Siméon, *Diccionario de la lengua Nahuatl o Mexicana*, 33.

25. *Antequera I*, ed. Acuña, 218.

26. *Relaciones Geográficas del Siglo XVI*, vol. 3, *Antequera II*, ed. René Acuña (México: Universidad Nacional Autónoma de México, Instituto de Investigaciones Antropológicas, 1984), 47.

27. Ibid., 35.

28. Siméon, *Diccionario de la lengua Nahuatl o Mexicana*, 19.

29. Karl A. Taube, "A Prehispanic Maya Katun Wheel," *Journal of Anthropological Research* 44, no. 2 (1998): 183–203.

30. "Relación Geográfica de Xalapa, Cintla y Acatlan," in *Antequera II*, ed. Acuña, 286.

31. *Antequera II*, ed. Acuña, 41.

32. *Relaciones Geográficas del Siglo XVI*, vol. 9, *Michoacán*, ed. René Acuña (México: Universidad Nacional Autónoma de México, Instituto de Investigaciones Antropológicas, 1987), 268.

33. René Acuña in ibid., 268, n. 19.

34. *Michoacán*, ed. Acuña, 77–78.

35. Thomas W. Whitaker, "Lagenaria: A Pre-Columbian Cultivated Plant in the Americas," *Southwestern Journal of Anthropology* 4, no. 1 (1948): 53, 59.

36. Joyce Marcus and Kent V. Flannery, *Zapotec Civilization: How Urban Society Evolved in Mexico's Oaxaca Valley* (London: Thames and Hudson, 1996), 75.

37. John E. Clark and Dennis Gosser, "Reinventing Mesoamerica's First Pottery," in *The Emergence of Pottery: Technology and Innovation in Ancient Societies*, ed.

William K. Barnett and John W. Hoopes (Washington: Smithsonian Institution Press, 1995), 212–13.

38. Michael D. Coe and Kent V. Flannery, *Early Cultures and Human Ecology in South Coastal Guatemala* (Washington, D.C.: Smithsonian Press, 1967), 22, 29.

39. John E. Clark and Michael Blake, "The Power of Prestige: Competitive Generosity and the Emergence of Rank Societies in Lowland MesoAmerica," in *Factional Competition and Political Development in the New World,* ed. Elizabeth M. Brumfield and John W. Fox (Cambridge: Cambridge University Press, 1994), 25–26, fig. 2.5.

40. Donald W. Lathrap, "Our Father the Cayman, Our Mother the Gourd: Spinden Revisited, or a Unitary Model for the Emergence of Agriculture in the New World," in *Origins of Agriculture,* ed. Charles A. Reed (The Hague: Mouton Publishers, 1977), 722, plate 4.

41. Alfonso Caso, *Interpretación del Códice Selden (3135 A-2)* (México: Sociedad Mexicana de Antropología, 1964), 26.

42. Siméon, *Diccionario de la lengua Nahuatl o Mexicana,* 449.

43. *Codice Borbonicus: Oxomoco and Cipactonal as Patrons of Sustenance and Origins,* p. 21, in Esther Pasztory, *Aztec Art* (New York: Harry N. Abrams, 1983), 195, plate 147.

44. See tables on pages 21–28 in Luján Muñoz and Toledo Palomo, *Jícaras y guacales.* Further inferences on the persistence of cucurbit-inspired toponyms within larger civil hierarchies and territorial municipalities are from tables shown on pages 26–28.

45. Jutiapa; from *jute,* a river snail; *atl,* water; and *-pan,* a locative; in Alberto Membreño, *Toponimias Indígenas de Centroamérica* (Honduras: Editorial Guaymuras, 1994), 139.

46. Gregory Mason, *Pottery and Other Artifacts from Caves in British Honduras and Guatemala,* Indian Notes and Monographs, no. 47 (New York: Museum of the American Indian, Heye Foundation, 1928), 40.

47. *Popol Vuh: The Mayan Book of the Dawn of Life,* trans. Dennis Tedlock (New York: Simon and Schuster, 1985), 113.

48. Robert S. V. Carlsen and Martin Prechtel, "The Flowering of the Dead: An Interpretation of Highland Maya Culture," *Man: The Journal of the Royal Anthropological Institute,* n.s., 26, no. 1 (1991): 23–42.

49. Ibid., 30.

50. Ibid.

51. García-Zambrano, "El poblamiento de México en la época de contacto," 273, 275. María Elena Bernal-García, "Carving Mountains in a Blue/Green Bowl: Mythological Urban Planing in Mesoamerica" (Ph.D. diss., University of Texas at Austin, 1993), 194–95.

52. "Historia de los Mexicanos," in *Teogonía e Historia de los Mexicanos,* ed. Angel María Garibay K. (México: Editorial Porrúa, 1965), 106.

53. Siméon, *Diccionario de la lengua Nahuatl o Mexicana,* 91.

54. Bernal-García, "Carving Mountains," 128, nn. 113 and 114.

55. A. M. Garibay, in Fray Bernardino de Sahagún, *Historia General de las Cosas de Nueva España,* ed. Angel María Garibay K., 4 vols. (México: Editorial Porrúa, 1956), 4:321.

56. In *Lienzo de Jucutácato,* ed. José Corona Nuñez (México: Vargas Rea, 1951), 15–17.

57. Siméon, *Diccionario de la lengua Nahuatl o Mexicana,* 33.

58. Translated from the Nahuatl by Bishop Plancarte, in *Lienzo de Jucutácato,* ed. Corona Nuñez, 16.

59. *Michoacán,* ed. Acuña, 144–45.

60. *Anales de Cuauhtitlan,* ed. Primo Feliciano Velázquez (México: Universidad Nacional Autónoma de México, Instituto de Investigaciones Históricas, 1945), 13.

61. For an illustration, see *Tira de la Peregrinación Mexica: Bibliografía, Descripción, Interpretación,* ed. Salvador Mateos (México: Librería Anticuaria G. M. Echaniz, 1944), 13, fig. 17.4.

62. Robert H. Barlow, "El Códice Azcatitlan," *Journal de la Société des Américanistes* 38 (1949): 107, 114.

63. In vertical fashion, *Lienzo Tlapiltepec,* or *Antonio de León,* shows the opposition of an emblematic *biznaga* cactus and the primeval pot, a kind that Lathrap ("Our Father the Cayman, Our Mother the Gourd," 722, plate 4) designates as "neckless olla" in view of its derivation from calabash gourds. Alfonso Caso ought to be credited with the first inferences about the symbolism of pots in Mixtec codices and *lienzos.* His association of the loud speech scroll with what he called "La olla que habla o grita" (Alfonso Caso, "Comentario al Códice Baranda," in *Miscellanea Paul Rivet, Octogenario Dicata* [México: Universidad Nacional Autonoma de México, 1958], 379–83; and Alfonso Caso, "Los Lienzos Mixtecos de Ihuitlán y Antonio de León," in *Homenaje a Pablo Martínez del Río en el XXV Aniversario de la Edición de los Orígenes Americanos* [México: Instituto Nacional de Antropología, 1961], 257), or "The Pot's Crying Call," however, remained unexplained until my own current studies and those of M. E. Bernal-García.

64. García-Zambrano, "El poblamiento de México en la época de contacto," 249–57.

65. Membreño, *Toponimias Indígenas de Centroamérica,* 271.

Warao Spiritual Ecology

WERNER WILBERT

Introduction

Warao Indians have inhabited the wetlands of the Orinoco Delta since prehistoric times. Native anthropogenic impact on their environment, however, appears to have been limited to abandoned village sites, where the temporary substitution of one endemic species (*Rhizophora mangle*) by another (*Mauritia flexuosa*) is the only noticeable modification.[1] Reflecting on Western society's penchant for environmental domination and the critical conditions this leaning has precipitated, one wonders whether the integrity of the deltaic biome has persisted until recent times due to ecologically sound "hunter-gatherer" precepts and practices or whether the Warao population was too small and native technology too rudimentary to have effected quantifiable change. As detailed below, Warao traditional society conforms to a philosophy of systems ecology. It promotes sustainable-subsistence and resource-management strategies designed to maintain a world order in which environment, society, and culture are entwined in a latticework of interdependent constituents. The proven efficacy of this philosophy as a template for propitious and enduring environmental management evidences the inherent interactive properties of systems ecology that encourages personal responsibility and mediation while dispensing with institutionalized agencies of environmental control.

To demonstrate the strength of this design, I characterize the taxonomies and ecological concepts the Warao employ to classify and interpret their environment. I describe the manner in which individual and society become integrated into the native world order and point out specific resource-management strategies deemed appropriate or inappropriate by the Indians. Form and function of internalized control mechanisms are identified that assure survival through compliance with the world order and prevent transgression by instilling fear of sickness, famine, and extinction.

While going beyond ethnosemantics and as the ontology of the Orinoco Delta begins to unfold, it becomes apparent that, according to the Warao, maintenance of ecological equilibrium depends on constant vigilance, precise interpretation, and strategic adjustments. This process is not devoid of mental and biological affliction, however, as checks and balances inherent to any ecosystem do not invariably favor the human species. Thus, while ecological equilibrium tends to guarantee long-term survival, it does not eliminate the stark reality of periodic hunger, disease, and untimely death for every member of a species.

Environment

The Warao consider their homeland to encompass the entire basin of the Orinoco Delta, parts of littoral Guyana, and a major portion of Trinidad.[2] The vast majority of the population lives in the delta proper, however, located in northeastern Venezuela between 8°30' and 10°00 N lat. and 59°45' and 62°40' W long (figure 1). Oriented in a general northeasterly direction, the territory is flanked by the foothills of the Cordillera de la Costa to the west and the Sierra de Imataca to the south. The Gulf of Paria and the Island of Trinidad to the north protect the region from unfavorable oceanic conditions.[3]

The delta proper constitutes an alluvial flood plain of 22,500 km². It was created and is maintained and constantly modified by the sediment-laden waters of the Orinoco River as well as by the northwesterly Atlantic longshore current. With its apex barely 10 m above sea level and a shoreline of under one meter above sea level, the predominant overall slope of the delta is less than 0.07 percent.[4]

The deltaic flood plain is traversed by nine major distributaries[5] spread fanlike across the territory. At the apex, near the Criollo river town of Barrancas, the white waters of the Orinoco's main stem are initially diverted by the Río Grande and Manamo distributaries. Channeling about 84 percent of the Orinoco River waters eastward to

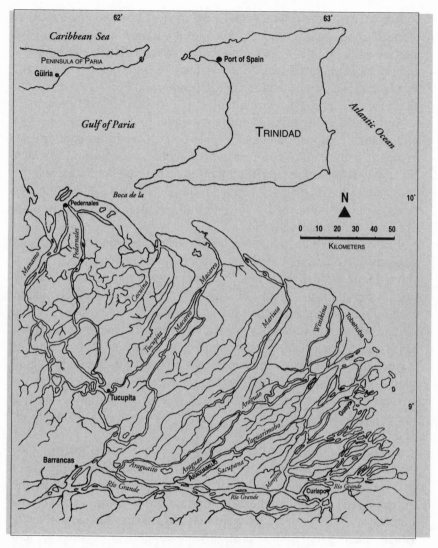

Figure 1. Orinoco Delta

the Atlantic Ocean, the Río Grande demarcates the southern boundary
of the delta. Along its 200 km trajectory, it feeds the Araguaito,
Araguao, Sacupana, and Merejina distributaries, whose northeasterly
flow irrigates the fluvial labyrinth of the southern delta. Dating back
to the Quaternary period, this subregion is the oldest formation of the
flood plain.

The Manamo distributary marks the western boundary of the delta. Formed about one thousand years ago, it channels the remaining 16 percent of the Orinoco waters northward, over a distance of approximately 190 km, to the Gulf of Paria. These waters supply such north-bound distributaries as the Macareo, Cocuina, and Pedernales that drain the relatively large land formations of the western delta (figure 1).[6]

Warao ethnogeography identifies two additional divisions based on soil texture: an upper delta and a lower delta. This differentiation corresponds to the classification system of geologists according to which the upper delta is characterized by the distribution of entisols[7] and the lower delta by its primary composition of histosols.[8] The boundary lines in both the native (figure 2) and the Western scientific systems are almost identically placed.[9]

Levee and chenier formations are among the prominent topographic features of the region. Levees are most frequent and best defined near the apex of the delta. Created by precipitation of sediments during annual flood stages of the Orinoco River, they form well-contoured banks along the headwaters of major distributaries and extend into the deltaic heartland, where they gradually give way to featureless marsh-lands and estuaries along the coast. Levees create islands of undulating profiles whose banks are considerably higher relative to the inland plains of the islands they define. From the banks of the fluvial artery to their summits, levees are composed of fine sands. Further inland, these sediments grade into sandy loam, silty loam, clay, peaty clays, and peat.

Cheniers are found on the seaward side of the western delta. They constitute elongated sand dunes of low profile parallel and subparallel to the coast. The sands of these formations were transported by the northwesterly Atlantic longshore current from as far away as the mouths of the Essequibo River in Guyana and the Amazon River in Brazil. Their geographical positions are suggestive of three ancient coastlines, or "delta fronts," symptomatic of an ever-expanding deltaic flood plain.[10]

The hydrodynamics of the delta is affected by the discharge of the Orinoco main stem, tidal fluctuations, and local rainfall. The most dramatic hydraulic episodes occur during the months of June and July when the Orinoco may rise as much as nine vertical meters at the delta's apex. As a result, the upper delta may experience complete inundation for weeks at a time.

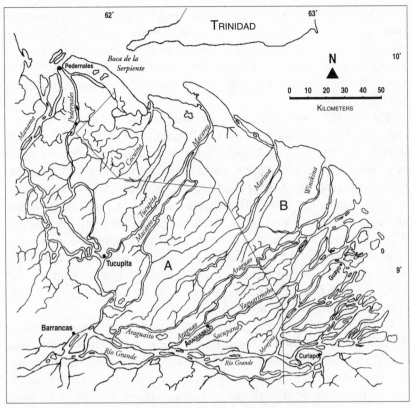

Figure 2. Subdivision of the Orinoco Delta According to
Geological and Warao Ethnogeographical Criteria.
A=Upper Delta; B=Lower Delta

As the fluvial waters enter the lower delta, the diversionary effect
of the distributaries, coupled with the elaborate network of secondary
channels generally, tends to retain the fast-flowing waters within their
causeways. However, the overall surge of freshwater discharge into
the ocean displaces the marine waters far enough seaward to permit
freshwater fish to move freely along the deltaic coast.

The tidal pulses are relatively constant. High/low fluctuations measure 160 cm at the mouth of the Río Grande, 130 cm at the mouth of
the Manamo distributary, and 60 cm at the apex.[11] Although their effects appear relatively benign in comparison to those of the Orinoco
flood waters, their principal influence is over the littoral estuaries,

completely irrigating them for approximately half of every twenty-four-hour period. During the dry season, however, with the force of the Orinoco greatly diminished, the effect of the incoming tides is so strong that they actually reverse the direction of flow of the fluvial waters in the lower delta, halting the down-coming Orinoco waters of the upper delta.

The salinity associated with incoming tides variously affects the estuaries and riparian flora over a distance of approximately 60 km inland from the coast. Although sensitive instruments discern traces of salinity at the delta's apex, these usually go unnoticed by the human population for most of the year except in critical dry seasons.

Rains also play a significant role on a local level. The deltaic climate is tropical monsoonal. Annual precipitation ranges between 2,000 mm near the apical region to 3,253 mm along the coast. The relative humidity fluctuates between 60 and 80 percent, and the trade winds keep the mean annual ambient temperature around 26°C.[12] Most precipitation occurs from May to October, leaving a relatively dry season from November to April.

During the dry season, masses of decomposing faunal and floral detritus accumulate on the forest floors. But with the onset of the rains, the forests and savannas tend to flood, and a single night of precipitation may raise the generally stagnant waters in large riverine islands by 30 cm. Since most of the deltaic savannas are bordered by levees, the elimination of rain water is achieved through percolation under the levees into the main channels and by evaporation. The pluvial waters that flood the levees, however, are channeled through drainage canals either into savannas or into swamp streams that connect with major distributaries. Owing to the high content of tannic acid (pH 4.6–5), these waters are usually transparent and black. The volume of the runoff is often sufficient to transform entire distributaries into black-water causeways, provoking severe anoxic conditions that force many aquatic species into neighboring white-water channels.

The botanical configuration of the delta is complex. Complete communities may occupy only a few hectares. But generally speaking, the coastal communities are dominated by mangrove forests (*Rhizophora mangle*). Their tolerance of saline conditions allows this and other mangrove species to extend inland along the banks of the fluvial arteries for 60 km. Behind these forests are levees and savannas. Levees support gallery forests comprised of seven to eight species of palm and between 150 and 200 species of softwood and hardwood trees. Savanna vegetation is lacking in trees and limited to tall reeds, woody brush, and extensive groves of sago palm (*Mauritia flexuosa*). The gallery-forest and savanna communities extend into the upper delta, where palm species other than *Mauritia* drop out of the botanical communities.

Society and Culture

Relatively little is known about the prehistoric Warao. Their biodegradable material culture and their marshland habitat are not conducive to archaeological exploration. Nevertheless, archaeologists identify the Warao as prototypical Meso-Indians[13] whose littoral lifestyle developed along the Caribbean coast and in the West Indies as of approximately 7,000 years ago.[14] The tribal ethnonym (from *wa*, "canoe," *arao*, "people"; canoe people) as well as their coastal lifestyle, emphasis on fishing and shellfish gathering, and overall marine orientation—including open-sea and star navigation—support the supposition that the Warao are survivors of the ancient South American Littoral Tradition.[15] Linguistically, Waraoan has variously been classified as independent or as of Macro-Chibchan stock.[16]

Tribal lore also places the ancestral Warao in or near the Orinoco Delta during the early Holocene. It speaks of times when one could walk dry-shod from Trinidad to Venezuela and when the Serpents' Mouth and the Gulf of Paria became flooded by the rising sea.[17] Oral literature even makes an astonishing allusion to what seems to have been *Macrauchenia*, a Pleistocene mammal.[18] Referring to it as *mosomo*, contemporary Warao describe it as a very large herbivorous quadruped with an elongated neck, living on the savannas of the delta, foraging from the lower branches of trees in savanna/forest transition zones.

Warao culture probably evolved in this relatively isolated coastal region over thousands of years prior to the arrival of Arawak (ca. 2,800 B.P.), Carib (ca. 750 B.P.), and European (500 B.P.) invaders. Lacking the technology and strategic knowledge necessary for survival on the lower floodplain, however, the newcomers did not settle permanently in the delta but established outposts along its principal distributaries, using them as thoroughfares of communication with the West Indies and the Orinoco River basin.[19] As a consequence of their seclusion, the Warao were largely spared the scourges of inter-tribal conflict, warfare, Old World pestilence, ethnocide, and slavery that ravaged the surrounding lands.[20] To this day, they have remained the only true inhabitants of the lower Orinoco Delta.

The Warao are an acephalic egalitarian society of foragers and fishermen, whose population of roughly 28,000 individuals occupies approximately 250 villages, mostly in the lower delta.[21] Typically consisting of one or more extended families spanning up to four generations, mature and successful settlements comprise between 50 and 250 individuals, half of whom are children. Four to six of such settlements, cohering as a local group or subtribe, represent the largest sociopolitical unit to which an individual feels attached. Though emotionally related to all who speak their language, the Warao lack paramount chiefs and do not conceive of themselves as a tribe or nation. There are no full-time professionals. Instead, individuals distinguish themselves as expert canoe makers (men), hammock and basket weavers (women and men), herbal curers (women), or as shamans of different callings (mostly men).[22] Practicing village exogamy, local groups are predominantly endogamous and furnish the human resources required for occasional team work and rituals.

Daily routines are assigned on the basis of age and sex. Whereas boys enjoy a relatively carefree childhood, girls of tender age are called upon to help their mothers care for younger siblings, prepare herbal remedies, or harvest and prepare food.[23]

Living in a gender-symmetrical society, Warao women exercise much power within their social ambit.[24] The principal woman[25] is the "owner of the house." Together with a core group of matrikin, she makes decisions that affect the daily and seasonal routines of all villagers. Her power is bolstered by uxorilocality, village exogamy, and local-group endogamy. According to these rules of residence and marriage, the women of a settlement form a consanguineal matripotestal unit. In contrast, men, upon marriage, leave the village of their family of orientation to reside among the kinfolk of their spouses. There they join a loosely bonded group of sons-in-law and classificatory brothers under the authority of their mothers-in-law.

Villages tend to be situated along secluded secondary channels rather than on more exposed principal distributaries. Compensating for the low topographical relief and surging tidal waters, villages are constructed on pilings made from trunks of mangrove trees.

Houses average 60 m². They are fitted with gable roofs and side screens of temiche-palm fronds (*Manicaria saccifera*) to protect their occupants from streaming windblown rains. The downwind side of a typical home is usually left open to allow light to enter and air to circulate. Constructed with whole stems of manaca palm (*Euterpe oleraceae*), floors provide a clean and easily maintained surface on which domestic activities are conducted. At night netted palm-fiber hammocks are slung from the crossbeams of the house. On the floor between each pair of hammocks is a hearth of clay or of a section of hollowed-out moriche-palm stem on which smoldering fires are kept burning to provide heat and ward off nocturnal blood-sucking arthropods. A larger cooking hearth is constructed either in a far corner of the home or in a small adjacent structure that simultaneously serves as a kitchen and a work place for the manufacture of hammocks, baskets, and other articles.

Individual homes are often interconnected by a "boardwalk" of manaca-palm stems laid side by side over an infrastructure of mangrove pilings. The walkway provides ample space for children to gather safely and to play. Each home has a dock, using the same structural technique, extending ten to twelve meters beyond the boardwalk in a perpendicular direction. It facilitates access to the river for laundering, bathing, and water fetching. Canoes are moored here at a distance from the riverbank to prevent the crafts from beaching at low tide and becoming damaged.

The beauty of Warao technology lies in its effective simplicity. With an assemblage of native implements (hammock, basket, dugout, sago hoe, bow and arrow, harpoon, spear, fishing tackle) and imported tools (knife, machete, axe, adze, metal hooks, and nylon line), the Indians are capable of exploiting sizable nutritional resources from a variety of microhabitats, including riparian, flood forest, open forest, savanna, and maritime environments. In this connection it is important to realize that not all Warao lead the same kind of life. In general terms, they certainly are a seminomadic people who roam within subregional territories of their own definition. Among themselves, however, they distinguish between the swamp foragers, or *hobajiarao*,[26] associated with savannas of the western delta; the river people, or *warao*, who live on or in proximity of the fluvial arteries of the lower delta; and the uplanders, or *hotarao*,[27] who frequent the upper delta. Obviously, these distinctions reflect a difference in regional resource exploitation.

The Warao staple consists of fish and palm products. Especially morocoto fish, *osibu,*[28] together with the sago, fruit, and palm-borer larvae[29] of moriche, *ohidu,*[30] are appreciated by the Indians as their predilect "true food." However, sago availability is limited to the dry season, and to extend their access to this staple, subtribal groups store up to 1,000 pounds in a large barrel-like container protected from the elements in a structure that doubles as a sanctuary. Toward the end of the rainy season, when food is scarce, the Warao celebrate their *nahanamu* festival, in the course of which the sago store is ritually offered to the supernaturals in exchange for health and fertility. The sago is subsequently rationed out among the villagers. So vital was the Warao's access to moriche-palm forests that local groups engaged in internecine conflict to maintain control over their food supply.[31]

Even during the dry season sago production can be severely curtailed by an unexpected local rainstorm. Short and unusual as such episodes may be, they trigger the flowering phase of the palm for which the plant draws on its sago reserves for energy, provoking spells of hunger and of famine for affected local Warao groups.[32] To buffer the severity of food shortages, the Warao turn to another, less productive sago palm, called temiche, *yaha (Manicaria saccifera).* Rather than its limited supply of low-quality sago, they esteem the clusters of golf ball-sized fruit the palm produces in great abundance on a year-round basis and consume both its fleshy endocarp and its "milk." This food source was so important as a stop-gap measure that the geographical distribution of the temiche palm greatly influenced, if not actually determined, site selection and distribution of Warao settlements in the Orinoco Delta.[33]

As with moriche sago, Warao fishing strategies concentrate on a single species, the morocoto, as a major source of food. However, this predilection does not prevent them from also exploiting thirty-eight other species of habitat-specific fish.[34] Being of wide distribution, the morocoto does not provoke the same access rivalries as the regionally more confined sago palms.

Hunting is of lesser importance to Warao economy. Occasionally the diet is supplemented by turkey, agouti, paca, and capybara meat. Marine and land turtles, iguanas, iguana eggs, crabs, fruit, palm hearts, and honey are important lesser foods.[35] Larger pieces of game like deer, tapir, peccary, and giant fish otter were traditionally not taken.

Of twenty-seven food-producing botanical species identified, five palms are considered of prime importance to the Warao's food economy. Fruiting trees and vines, though sought after, produce relatively little food and do not call for organized or ritual harvest activities. Rather, their products are usually consumed as snacks en route to or from the village.

Evolution of a Biome

The world of the Warao owes its existence to a series of primordial events that established the ecological parameters of the delta biome. These etiological incidents depict the creation of a disk-like earth, the origins of meteorological phenomena, and the appearance of life-forms—plants, animals, and humans.

Most natural events are embodied or affected by mythological protagonists whose etiologies provide a quasidiachronic order to Warao cosmogony. While some of these actors originated sui generis and/or in situ, others eventuated by voluntary or involuntary metamorphoses or by sudden arrival from other lands. Certain trees, for example, were created by the giant Sea Turtle, while others appeared in the delta from Trinidad. Animals, on the other hand, originated in a western world region, and humans descended from the sky.

Land and Flora

First to emerge in the primordium of deltaic existence was Hobaji Arani, the Wetland Mother.

> In the beginning the earth was an aquatic realm, totally lacking in land, forest, and terrestrial animals. Then Hobaji Arani gave birth to male quintuplets. She lost much blood delivering. As her blood mingled with the world ocean, it turned into clumps of dark soil, creating the first land on earth. From its dark blood-soils trees emerged, shrubs and vines. The red blood of Hobaji Arani courses through them. And that is how Hobaji Arani became the mother of the land and the trees of the wetlands.[36]

Accordingly, Warao genesis knows of a Great Mother who conceived of and gave birth to the male gender, establishing the condition of sexual reproduction. Omnipresent and seemingly permeating the world ocean, her body and those of her offspring were ethereal and of undisclosed appearance. Mingling with the ocean's fertile water, the Creator's fecund blood coagulated to give origin to an earthly womb, the peat bog of the wetland with its dark productive forest environment.[37] From it rose all those trees and plants that are nurtured by the Mother's blood (red sap). They are united by a bond of blood relationships, centered in the Wetland Mother.

The environment resulting from this process of creation initiated the final construction phase of the Warao's three-tiered universe, consisting of netherworld, earth, and sky. Enclosed in a celestial vault, each level is disk-shaped and a mirror image of the other two. As the inhabitants of the netherworld gaze upward, the clouds and sky they see are islands and rivers of the terrestrial world. Similarly, the clouds and blue sky earthlings behold from their intermediate level are islands and waterways in heaven. The earth is kept afloat on the horns of a four-headed serpent, each head pointing in a cardinal direction.[38]

More land was added to the incipient earth-disk by a giant sea turtle. She created the coastal edge that separates the land from the sea. Digging in the sand, Turtle scooped up sticks of driftwood, which she planted on the spot. Sea Turtle allowed each sapling to choose a name that would determine its ultimate form and identity. She then ordered the trees to disperse and occupy her land in places of their choosing. The mangroves settled the coastal belt and the edges of the islands in the lower delta. Several others species colonized the levees behind the mangrove belt and parts of the tidal zone.[39]

The earth's tidal zone was fully settled by Baabe, the white cedar. She was ordered by Bisi, the red cedar, her elder sister, to take her family (Yaha, Ohoru, Eburu, Wasimoru, Mutumutu, Winamoru, Anare) and reconnoiter this new land (Orinoco Delta) across the channel from Trinidad.[40] When she did not return to report as instructed, Bisi gathered her people, packed provisions of *wasimoru* and *horoene* fish,[41] as well as a supply of special soil, and went after her sister.

Reaching the other shore, she found the low-lying tidal zone in what is now the lower delta populated by Baabe's people. She became enraged, whipped her little sister, and left to live elsewhere. As she walked she threw handfuls of soil before her to the ground, creating the levee system of the new earth. She came to a place that suited one of her people, Ohidu. But she went on to complete the creation of the earth by adding the upland in what is now the upper delta. Had everything gone according to plan, Bisi would have stayed in the lower delta and the earth would now be thicker and higher than it is today.

What becomes apparent from these stories is the Warao's preoccupation with land and vegetation. Yet, how could it be otherwise in a land where daily tidal surges, bimonthly spring-tides, and annual riverine and maritime inundations, as well as long-range catastrophic flood cycles, serve as constant reminders of the precariousness of soil and vegetation? In addition to their preoccupation with size and distribution of the land, however, the Warao are concerned about its depth and layered sedimentary composition that determines land quality. Not surprisingly, native ecological knowledge in this regard is detailed and significantly more sophisticated than mythic descriptions of soil deposition suggest. To be precise, within the sedimentary gradient of Turtle's sand and Wetland Mother's peat bog, the Warao differentiate an organic surface layer and fourteen types of sediments according to texture, odor, color, and structure, assigning them to the three basic categories of sand, silt, and clay (table 1). Exact sedimentological

Table 1. Sedimentary Differentiation

Sands (0.083–0.130 mm):	
Waha	True sand
Waha hoko	White sand
Waha simo	Orangelike sand
Waha ana	Black sand
Waha ana sabuka	Semi-black sand
Silts (0.041–0.083 mm):	
Hobahi taera	Silt (firm)
Hobahi taera sabuka	Silt (semi-firm)
Hobahi simo	Silt (orangelike)
Hobotoboto	Silt (water-saturated)
Hoboto taera sabuka	Semi-firm silt (water-saturated)
Hoboto ana	Black silt (water-saturated)
Clays (0.00024–0.041 mm):	
Hokoroko	White clay
Hokoroko ana	Black clay
Hokoroko sabuka	Semi-clay

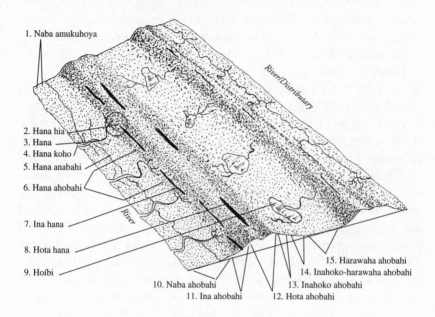

Figure 3. Schematic Representation of a
Deltaic Island and its Ethnogeographic Units.
(1) Riparian zone; (2) Swamp stream headwaters; (3) Swamp stream;
(4) Confluence of swamp stream with major river; (5) Swamp stream
tributaries; (6) Swamp stream "mini" basin; (7) Flood forest trough-like
channel; (8) Levee sumit trough-like channel; (9) Pond; (10) Floodplain;
(11) External levee slope; (12) Levee summit; (13) Open forest on internal
levee slope; (14) Levee/savanna transition zone; (15) Savanna.

knowledge is common among the men of Warao society and means
more to them than idle erudition in matters of adaptation. As the presence, absence, or combination of certain sediments determines the
topographical relief and geobotanical quality of deltaic life-zones, intensive environmental wisdom of the habitat has proven to be an asset
to human survival in the Orinoco Delta (figure 3).

As to the life-zones that evolved on the land Sea Turtle, Wetland
Mother, and Red Cedar created, there are coastal\riparian floodplains,
levees, and savannas (table 2).

Table 2. Geobotanical Life-Zones

Arauna:	FLORA
Naba amukohoya arauna	Riparian flora
Nabarauna	Floodplain flora
Inarauna	Flora of outside levee slope
Hotarauna	Flora of levee summit
Inahokorauna	Flora of inside levee slope
Inahoko harawaharauna	Flora of levee/savanna transition zone
Harawaharauna	Flora of the savanna
Ohidunarauna	*M. flexuosa* groves in the savanna

Sea Turtle's floodplain (*naba ajobahi*), occupied by her own and by White Cedar's people, is generally composed of firm silts and clays, traversed by swamp streams that form "minibasins" and whose principal function it is to drain the levees (figure 3). The headwater regions and tributaries of these basins tend to consist of permanently water-saturated silts, *hoboto,* conforming a surface too soft to support trees and generally devoid of vegetation. Floodplain and riparian forests are characterized by dense growths of tall buttressed trees with a very sparse understory flora.

The levees originated as Bisi's raised pathways through peat bogs of the Wetland Mother. This domain starts at the fluvial high-water line at the foot of the levees (figure 3). As noted, levees consist principally of sands over a clay substratum. Topographically varying levee environments include: the outer slope (*ina ahobahi*) rising up from the floodplain; the summit, or "upland proper" (*hota*); and the inner slope which inclines toward the savanna (*inahoko ahobahi*). The transition zone between the slope and the inland plain is known as *inahoko-harawaha ahobahi.*

The topographically featureless summits of the levees where Bisi walked usually remain dry owing to effective drainage into the savanna and the floodplain. In contrast, the slopes of the levees are characterized by a gentle parallel undulating topography with subtle trough-like formations.[42] Filled with organic detritus, these troughs are Wetland Mother's peat bogs of various textures. The flooding of the surrounding forests is entirely due to precipitation, and the difference between the two levee slopes lies in their capacity to drain this pluvial excess. The outer slope is usually steeper and more effective in this regard than the inner slope (figure 3). This creates relatively dry conditions propitious to the maintenance of dense forests. The waters accumulating in the troughs of the inward slope stagnate to form a soft and highly acidic muck of reduced biodiversity and forest density.[43]

Crossing the transition zone between the foot of the inner slope of the levee and the savanna, Bisi traversed an area whose sedimental strata are also composed of various types of sand, supporting a savanna reed-like vegetation some two meters high. Arboreal flora is sparse here, extremely stunted and parched. The Warao explain this phenomenon by referring to poor water quality (which has been tested to be pH 4.5–5.5).

Beyond the transition zone lies the savanna, which native taxonomists divide into savanna proper and extensive low-profile mounds. Savanna consists primarily of two layers of sand, one white, forming the top soil, and one black, furnishing a substratum.[44] Savannas are usually covered with water whose depth varies from several centimeters to one meter according to the season. The water is characteristically black, with a pH of 4.5 to 5.0. As noted, the dominant vegetation of the savanna proper is comprised of woody reeds. Due to the prevailing anaerobic conditions, the reeds are often found growing on top of several meters of fallen vegetation of the same kind, whose rate of decay is so slow that its morphology remains recognizable for many years.[45]

Significantly, the barely distinguishable hummocks of the savanna are covered and maintained by dense groves of sago palm (*Mauritia flexuosa*). The soils of the mounds are composed of slowly decaying organic matter of fallen palms. They are usually black, extremely sticky, and up to one meter thick. This higher ground is the place where Bisi, the Tree Mother, left the moriche palm, her companion, behind in an otherwise treeless environment, while she herself proceeded to colonize the uplands of the delta. Just as the senior daughter of the ranking family in a Warao village may become the principal woman of her community, so did Bisi, the Tree Woman, upon completion of the earth, assume leadership over the forest people in all parts of the delta's geobotanical realm. Although her closest ties remained with her consanguineal kin of origin (red cedars), she became the matriarch of the entire tree-people society. As Forest Mother, she resides along the path of the winter sun, where she functions as the only female member in the Warao pantheon (*kanobotuma*) residing at the cardinal and intercardinal points of the cosmos, looking after her people and governing the interactions between forest people and humans.[46]

Fauna

Following the completion of the land, its newly created life-zones were populated by faunalogical communities, each governed by guardians of their constituent species. In these early times of earth's existence, the trees stood motionless in silence and sweltering heat; there was no wind.[47] Among the first to arrive were the animals. Their master was Oka, the giant armadillo,[48] who led the boisterous intruders. He engaged Huru, the earthquake, in combat[49] to determine who should govern the land. The contest ended in a draw. Oka descended into the river to become master of the water people (*nabarao*). Huru decended into the center of the earth, which still trembles with his every move. The panting and shoving to-and-fro of the contestants, however, gave origin to the alternating land-and-sea-breeze regime. Its periodicity initiated the seasonality of reproduction through wind pollination, putting an end to the primordium.[50]

Next to arrive were the Warao. They originated on the uppermost level of the universe, from where a part of their community descended on a rope. They were led by a hunter whose falling arrow had accidentally pierced the sky-disk. The hole was obstructed by a pregnant woman, preventing the rest from descending. Infuriated, they changed into spirits and sorcerers, inflicting great harm upon their kinfolk below. Dreadful curses befell humankind: painful birth, disease, and mortality. Since then, babies have been born too weak to walk, hammocks must be laboriously made, and food procured on a daily basis.[51]

The Warao began identifying all animals (including themselves) by the root form *arao,* meaning "life." They added qualifiers to differentiate among the various forms and communities of beings (table 3). Rather than ranking them hierarchically, however, they grouped beings according to econiches they occupy in the water, on land, in trees, or in the air.[52] The criterion by which species were assigned their natural places was the location they occupied when asleep. Correlating the strata of the forest profile with environmental categories, animals were arranged in a vertical, multitiered system (table 4, figure 4).[53] With this, the ethnoecological system of the Orinoco Delta biome was complete. Still missing was the fundamental modality that activated the design and made it work on a daily basis.

Table 3. Biological Communities

Araotuma	*arao,*	"life,"	*tuma,*	"plural";	life-forms
Honaiarao	*honia,*	"in water,"	*arao,*	"life";	aquatic life
Wakaiarao	*wakaia,*	"on ground,"	*arao,*	"life";	terrestrial life
Daukuarikarao	*daukuarika,*	"above trees,"	*arao,*	"life";	aerial life

Table 4. Vertical Classification Faunal Communities

Honaiarao:	AQUATIC COMMUNITIES
Nabarao	Species that sleep in distributaries
Hanarao	Species that sleep in swamp streams
Naba/Hanarao	Species that sleep in distributaries and swamp streams
Ina ahomakabarao	Species that sleep in flood-forest pools and channels
Wakaiarao:	TERRESTRIAL COMMUNITIES
Hobahi ekuya	Species that sleep in the ground
Hobahi araia	Species that sleep on the ground
Dahuarao:	ARBOREAL COMMUNITIES
Dau ekuya	Species that sleep in tree trunks
Dauna aukua tanaia	Species that sleep in the overstory
Dauna akuawaha	Species that sleep in desiccated crowns
Dau autuya	Species that sleep in the main canopy
Dau araia	Species that sleep in the crowns of emergent trees
Daukuarikarao:	AERIAL COMMUNITY
Daukuarika	Species that sleep above the trees

Balanced Complementary Diversity

The arrival on earth of plants, animals, and humans precipitated chaotic turmoil, conducive to promoting perpetual contention. It was imperative, therefore, for all species to find their niches of existence in the new land. Since hierarchical station and inborn advantage were to play no role in this endeavor, merit for all was vested in balanced complementary diversity, whose inherent dynamics of reciprocity came to provide the fundamental agency of the Warao's ecological

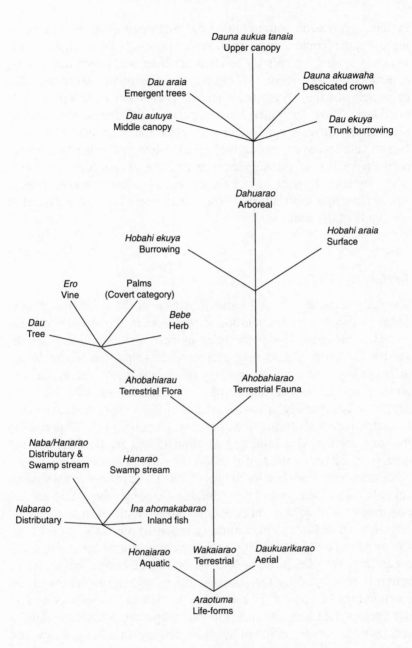

Figure 4. Biotaxonomy of the Warao:
Ecological Communities

system. Aggression among biological communities of the same eco-logical plane (aquatic, terrestrial, arboreal, aerial) were ruled out, and violence against species on levels other than one's own was strictly controlled by *lex talionis*. Of course, the dilemma of postprimordial existence was the interdependence of species as part of the worldly condition. Thus, tolerance among coequal life-forms enforced by retributive justice is what maintains the Warao's ecological system. Negotiated exchange among biological communities accommodates both the reality of interdependence and the necessity of predation while keeping the system in balance. Preservation of the ecological equilibrium and arbitration of interspecific relations were placed in the hands of the shaman.

To Hunt and Be Hunted

The daily necessity of food acquisition (one of the evils visited upon earthly existence by the marooned sorcerers in the sky) encumbers primarily the men. Under the rules of balanced complementary di-versity, human predators may pursue species that live arboreally on different levels of the forest canopy (birds, mangrove snails, larvae), underground in hideouts and burrows (iguanas, turtles, armadillos, ro-dents), or subaquaticly in various bodies of water (fish, crab, manatee). But large mammals (tapir, deer, peccary, giant river otter)[54] pertain to the same terrestrial community as humans and are traditionally not hunted or are only reluctantly killed for such purposes as making a ritual drumhead from howler monkey skin. There are some ambiguous animals, like monkeys and river dolphins, among others, that are not consumed out of behavioral concerns characteristic of their species.[55]

To guarantee biological continuity and avert reprisals against him-self and his family, the hunter must be cognizant of these rules and exceptions. Whether he be hunting or fishing, he knows that his every action is monitored by the spirit guardians and the members of the communities he targets. To minimize the damage he inflicts on any one species, he hunts and fishes in various places. Should he abuse a species by overexploitation or by allowing a creature to die a slow and painful death, the spirit(s) of the victimized may target him and his kinfolk for mental (*sinaka*) or physical retribution.[56] The worst imaginable scenario ensues when a guardian spirit, disgruntled over immoderation, gathers his or her community and moves away to another region, leaving the people of the abuser without food. Conversely, given the same rules of balanced complementary diversity, a man pursuing food species from planes other than his own expects to be hunted by members of aerial, arboreal, or aquatic communities himself. A great number of magical chants are dedicated to the curing of human victims suffering from such attacks.[57]

Although the natural and supernatural hunters of any community are considered powerful, they are not perfect. Much of their success depends on surprise and good luck.[58] Nor are hunters invariably lethal. Sometimes they spare, ignore, or even help a potential victim in the spirit of moderate exploitation. Nevertheless, a potential victim's best defense is avoidance of dangerous situations. Enculturation plays a major role in imparting an attitude of perpetual vigilance. Lullabies warn children not to cry when the jaguar is on the prowl in the forest or when the king vulture circles overhead on the savanna.[59] From childhood on, people are taught to avoid the stingray that attacks them in swamp streams and the electric eel that ambushes them in fishing ponds or under docks. They learn how to evade the attack of the venomous snake, the scorpion, and the spider that lurk under the litter of the forest floor. Menstruating women are warned to beware of certain eels and fish (piranha family) when bathing.[60] All adults are wary of spirit hunters and try to learn their stalking patterns, how to avoid meeting them, and how to escape the clutches of these shapeshifting predators.[61]

Trading with Floral Communities

The Warao are traditionally entirely dependent upon the forest for food, medicine, and raw materials. The various species of the forest constitute populations comparable to human local communities, each with its particular place, history, and manner.

Under the law of balanced complementary diversity, the Warao treat the forest as a coequal population from a common ontological plane. A tacit agreement between the two populations allows humans to harvest forest products in exchange for protection of the floral world from wanton injury and death. The removal of floral products is permitted as long as it proceeds in a circumspect manner and without extinguishing life. The felling of trees is considered a capital offense perpetrated among members of the same (terrestrial) community.

Accordingly, the harvesting of arboreal fruit is done either by climbing the tree or by waiting for the fruit to fall. Fruit-bearing vines are not "tree people" and can be dealt with as one pleases. Belonging to the understory, they originated as a tactical ploy to protect the culture hero (Haburi) from a pursuing jaguar.[62] Of a total of twenty-seven species producing edible products, the Palmae are the primary supporters of human life in the Orinoco Delta. The edible parts of only five palms produce the traditional mainstay of the Warao diet; two produce sago, palm-heart, and fruit, two fruit and palm-heart, and one only fruit. Although palms are not considered trees "because their stems contain no wood,"[63] the felling of *Mauritia* is highly ritualized. Ancestral gods depend on the palm's sago for rejuvenation and pledge to keep epidemics and famines away from their human suppliers. Profanation of sago would be cataclysmic: it would provoke the death of the gods and destroy humankind as a consequence of mystic retribution.

Herbal medicine is governed by the same modality of reciprocity. From relatively small amounts of root, bark, leaves, flowers, fruit, and seeds, female phytotherapists produce 259 remedies to treat 45 locally recognized illnesses.[64] The women approach the forest, not as an inert resource of *materia medica,* but as a community disposed to trade their therapeutic products for protection from humans. Herbal curers are closely monitored by the Forest Mother and her people. Curers exercise great care in selecting the appropriate ingredients at the right time and place. They prepare and administer the remedies according to a protocol handed down by generations of practitioners. A phytotherapist would never consider preparing a remedy for frivolous purposes (as, for instance, merely to show a researcher how to do it). She would never fell a mature medicinal tree if a young specimen could be found whose leaves, flowers, fruit, or seeds were within her reach. Abuse is punished by the Forest Mother, who neutralizes the therapeutic properties of her charges. Her retaliation would take a great toll among the young and the elderly of the abuser's community.

With the exception of a few objects made of bone or shell, the material culture of the Warao is made entirely of floral materials, mostly taken from palms.

One of the most essential elements of Warao material culture is the dugout canoe. Because it requires the felling of a large tree (preferably a red cedar [Bisi] of the Forest Mother's kind), its fabrication stands in stark violation of native ecological precepts. Before beginning his task, the canoe maker must seek permission from the Forest Mother, via the shaman. The permission may or may not be granted, depending on the craftsman's renown as a boatbuilder and his reputation as a responsible member of society.

The permit to make a dugout canoe amounts to a marriage license that establishes a nuptial relationship between the canoe maker and the red cedar, perceived of as a maiden daughter of the Forest Mother. The process of opening the hull symbolizes the defloration of the tree maiden. Under these circumstances, the felling of the tree signifies not the end but the beginning of life. The tree-maiden becomes the spiritual wife of the craftsman and is given the respect all women receive in Warao society. Respect for a large canoe is expressed in a code of ethics that governs the uses to which the craft can be put, burdening the artisan with an onerous responsibility for the lifetime of the vessel.[65]

Warao society places a premium on excellence in craftsmanship. As in the areas of food and resource procurement, the key to success lies in the ability of artisans to muster respect for the animal and plant beings they deal with and to treat them as their equals. The desire to excel is inculcated through enculturation. It equips the individual with the necessary technical and mental skills and motivates the artisan by bestowing socioeconomic stability, personal recognition, and supernatural patronage.[66]

Concluding Remarks

Readers of ethnoecological studies tend to admire the depth of native environmental wisdom, as it compares favorably with the models of Western ecologists. This is particularly true in instances of comparing physical aspects of traditional and scientific ecological systems. When it comes to explicating the spiritual dimensions of native ecologies, however, and to expounding their organismic nature, Western readers become easily bewildered, failing to appreciate the pragmatic value of such schemes. Within the context of Judeo-Christian culture they are more familiar with the opposition of science and religion and/or the disarticulation of culture by science and technology. In the modern self-centered world, spirituality has widely been replaced by unrestrained materialism attended by economic growth as its overriding creed. Ecological concerns of preservation are often trivialized as emotional fixations, inimical to technological, economic, and social progress. Religion and spirituality are confined to the privacy of the home to prevent moral principles espoused within the family from clashing with diverging values upheld in public life.

Needless to say, this worldview is profoundly at odds with Warao ethnoecology which, based on the theory of balanced complementary diversity through proactive reciprocity, integrates nature, society, and culture into an organismic whole. The world of the Warao is a manifestation of the supernatural, experienced through life not understood through scientific thought.[67] The product of longitudinal empirical observation and interpretation, it enfolds human society in a mythologized landscape of primordial origin. Rather than self-centered atomistic individualism, it promotes a moral bond of society, restrained by principles of pluralistic coexistence. Principles of restraint are encoded in the world order by holistic design and perpetuated through enculturative learning both private and public.

Instead of unrestrained self-interest, the native world order has built-in checks and balances applying equally to all life-forms. Biological communities are aligned with protector spirits, whose sole common purpose is to maintain the equilibrium of the biome. Master spirits punish interference by members of their own community as well as by members of others. Whether intentional or unintentional, violations of moral values and principles are subject to retaliation equivalent to the offense committed, always insuring the restoration of the natural balance they disturbed. Moral culture disallows victimization of life-forms considered congenerous by virtue of inhabiting a common existential plane.

Enculturation teaches the individual how to accommodate this principle to the basic condition of interdependence of all elements of the natural world. There are acceptable and unacceptable ways of mutual exploitation; either option depends less on personal aspiration, however, than on the degree of danger it poses to the continued well-being of a biological community. Always aware of their roles in this struggle between personal gain and the common good, men and women rely on precise ecological knowledge to determine their options and thus avoid retribution. Usufruct of environmental components from ontological planes other than one's own is subject to the rule of measured mutual dependence to avoid overexploitation. Major infringements dictated by the human condition and requiring the destruction by humankind of "cospecific" life-forms like large mammals and trees are arbitrated by shamans and subject to sanction by pertaining powers in the Warao universe.

The ethnoecological system of the Orinoco Delta is not impervious to untoward change. Since the mid-twentieth century, the Indians have become gradually involved in commercial lumbering, fishing, and hunting. Many have replaced their traditional palm-sago economy with swidden agriculture, requiring the clearing of large plots of forest, trees and all. The Warao have watched Criollo entrepreneurs enriching themselves by overexploiting natural resources. Although the foreigners become ill just as the natives do, they always seem to escape divine retribution by curing themselves with powerful medicines, not from the Forest Mother, but from the outside world. Irrespective of the severity of their offenses they never starve, never are without homes, and always seem protected by a godhead more powerful than the ancestral gods and species masters.

Unbridled exploitation has since taken a heavy toll on the deltaic environment. Even after lying fallow for twenty-five years, fields fail to recover. Stretches of forest stand deprived of their most valuable trees. The rivers yield smaller fish than before. Although native systems-ecology has always recognized degradation and extinction of the environment as looming possibilities, it is the present generation of Warao that, after 7,000 years of effective environmental management, actually experiences these effects.

Some local communities have begun responding to this hazard by refusing to participate in the wholesale destruction of their land. True to the ecological precepts and practices of their forebears, they continue living in the delta. Other groups, however, opted to adopt the modern ways, choosing either to live in the Creolized mission environments of Pedernales, Araguaimuju, Curiapo, and Guayo or to leave the delta altogether and settle in the nearby Criollo towns of Tucupita and Barrancas. A very serious new threat endangering Warao culture is posed by the petroleum industry currently in the process of installing itself in parts of the delta. This new invasion is likely to destroy the native ecological system in the affected regions and extinguish its age-old environmental wisdom.

Like many Warao, so too are persons and institutions in the Western world increasingly questioning their attitudes toward an ever-deteriorating environment. Ecological strategies establish "acceptable levels of contamination" for expanding industrialized populations, protect singled-out species on the edge of extinction, and create natural reserves partially or totally out of bounds to humans. But until industrialized society finds its place within the holistic actuality of nature, spiritual ecology remains a folkloristic topic and ecology will exhaust itself in academic and political polemics.

Notes

The author gratefully acknowledges the financial and logistical support of the La Salle Foundation of Natural Sciences, Caracas, the Edward John Noble Foundation, and the Institute of Economic Botany of the New York Botanical Garden.

1. The Warao harvest large quantities of *M. flexuosa*-palm fruit that they bring to the settlement for consumption. The seeds of the fruit are discarded in the village clearing, where some germinate and grow to maturity. For more detailed information, see H. D. Heinen, José J. San José, Hortensia Caballero Arias, and Rubén Montes, "Subsistence Activities of the Warao Indians and Anthropogenic Changes in the Orinoco Delta Vegetation," *Scientia Guaianae* 5 (1995): 312–34.

2. See Michele Goldwasser, "Rememberances of the Warao: The Miraculous Statue of Siparia, Trinidad," *Antropológica* 84 (1994-1996): 3–72; and Johannes Wilbert, *Mystic Endowment: Religious Ethnography of the Warao Indians* (Cambridge, Mass.: Harvard University Center for the Study of World Religions, 1993).

3. Space does not permit a comprehensive discussion of the geomorphology and ecology of the delta. I merely summarize the more significant topographical, hydrological, and climatological phenomena that influence biodiversity, species distribution, and, ultimately, the make-up of the biological communities of which Warao society forms a part.

4. See Enrique Vásquez and Werner Wilbert, "The Orinoco: Physical, Biological and Cultural Diversity of a Major Tropical Alluvial River," in *The Rivers Handbook: Hydrological and Ecological Principles,* ed. Peter Calow and Geoffrey E. Pitts (Oxford: Blackwell Scientific Publications 1992), 1: 448–71.

5. Distributaries function to divert waters away from "a trunk stream, which they may or may not rejoin." See Michael Allaby, *The Concise Oxford Dictionary of Ecology* (Oxford: Oxford University Press, 1994), 122.

6. The Warao identify the Araguao distributary as the boundary between the western and eastern delta, a criterion largely based on land size. Whereas the western delta features relatively large land formations, some extending over 100 km, the fluvial labyrinth of the eastern delta is comprised of a multitude of much smaller islands.

7. Entisols are embyronic mineral (sand/clay) soils that lack distinct horizons and represent the beginning phases of soil-profile development. As such they are characteristic of recently formed flood-plains such as those of the Upper Orinoco Delta. See Allaby, *The Concise Oxford Dictionary of Ecology,* 138.

8. Histosols are soils composed of organic materials. See Allaby, *The Concise Oxford Dictionary of Ecology,* 194.

9. See Werner Wilbert, *"Manicaria saccifera* and the Warao in the Orinoco Delta: A Biogeography," *Antropológica* 81 (1994-1996): 51–66; J. Comerma, "Suelos: ordenes y subordenes," in *Atlas de Venezuela* (Caracas: Ministerio del Ambiente y de los Recursos Naturales Renovables y No Renovables, 1979), 182–83; and Tj. van Andel, "The Orinoco Delta," *Journal of Sedimentary Petrology* 37, no. 2 (1967): 297–310.

10. Van Andel, "The Orinoco Delta," 300–304.

11. Ibid., 298.

12. Vásquez and Wilbert, "The Orinoco: Physical, Biological and Cultural Diversity of a Major Tropical Alluvial River."

404   *Indigenous Traditions and Ecology*

13. The Meso-Indian epoch began just before the extinction of the Pleistocene megafauna. It is characterized by a riverine/sea-oriented littoral tradition based on fishing, large-scale shellfish exploitation, and foraging.

14. Irving Rouse and José M. Cruxent, *Venezuelan Archaeology* (New Haven: Yale University Press, 1963), 38, 53, 111; Mario Sanoja, *Los hombres de la yuca y el maíz* (Caracas: Monte Avila Editores 1981), 25; Mario Sanoja, "El poblamiento inicial de San Rafael de Barrancas (Estado Monagas) 900 a.C.–1500 d.C.," in *Barrancas del Orinoco: el pueblo más antiguo de Venezuela,* ed. Tulio López Ramirea, Pablo Ojer and Mario Sanoja (Caracas: Imprenta del Ministerio de Educación 1990), 23.

15. Gordon, R.Willey, *An Introduction to American Archaeology,* vol. 2, *South America* (Englewood Cliffs, N.J.: Prentice-Hall, 1971), 261–77.

16. Cestmír Loukotka, *Classification of South American Indian Languages,* Latin American Center, Reference Series 7 (Los Angeles: University of California, 1968); Joseph H. Greenberg, *Language in the Americas* (Stanford: Stanford University Press, 1987).

17. The oceanographic literature places this era into the third transgression period of the Holocene (8,400–9,000 B.P.), when the sea level dropped approximately 37 meters, leaving a major portion of the Gulf of Paria and the Boca de la Serpiente exposed. (For detailed bathymetric data, see the following authors: Hno. Ginés, *Carta pesquera de Venezuela,* Fundación La Salle de Ciencias Naturales, Monografía 16 (Madrid: M.E.L.S.A., 1972), map G-2; J. Butenhko and J. P. Barbot, "Características geotécnicas de los sedimentos marinos costafuera del Delta del Orinoco," *Fourth Latin American Geological Congress Trinidad and Tobago* 1 (1979): 144–54, figs. 1 and 2; Tj. H. van Andel and H. Postma, "Recent Sediments of the Gulf of Paria: Reports of the Orinoco Shelf Expedition," in *Verhandelingen der Köninklijke Nederlandse Akademie van Wetenschappen, Afdeling Naturkunde* (Amsterdam), 20, no. 5 (1954). See also Johannes Wilbert, "El violín en la cultura Warao: un préstamo cultural complementario," *Montalban* 4 (1975): 189–215.

18. There is no fossil evidence for *Macrauchenia* in the delta. Warao lore recalls its existence in a myth of territorial exploration.

19. The Arawak (Lokono) were farmers of the Orinoco floodplain. The Carib expansion was spurred by commercial interests rather than by the desire for colonization. Carib dominance over the major deltaic arteries is reflected in such non-Waraoan river names as Merejina, Sacupana, Araguao, and Macareo. For a more detailed discussion of these events, see H. Dieter Heinen, "The Early Colonization of the Lower Orinoco and Its Impact on Present-day Indigenous Peoples," *Antropológica* 78 (1992): 51–86.

20. The Warao did have peaceful as well as hostile contacts with other Indian groups and with Europeans. During the colonial era, Caribs periodically raided the delta, seeking to capture slaves for their European allies. During the rubber boom of the late nineteenth and early twentieth centuries, the Warao of the western delta were forced into hard labor by Criollos until Capuchin missionaries put an end to this practice. The missionaries, in turn, disrupted indigenous family life by forcing parents to send their children to the mission boarding schools where many became thoroughly acculturated.

21. H. Dieter Heinen, "Los Warao," in *Los Aborígenes de Venezuela,* ed. Walter

Coppens and Bernarda Escalante, vol. 3, *Etnografía Contemporania*, part 2, *Etnología contemporania*, ed. Jacques Lizot, Fundación La Salle de Ciencias Naturales, Instituto Caribe de Antropología y Sociología, Monograph 35 (Caracas: Monte Avila Editores, 1988), 594; Werner Wilbert, *"Manicaria saccifera* and the Warao in the Orinoco Delta: A Biogeography," 54.

22. "Upon the death of an individual his or her life essence is believed to return to a maternal womb. Within that womb the masters are reunited according to their area of specialty"; H. Dieter Heinen, "Warao," in *Encyclopedia of World Cultures,* ed. David Levinson, vol. 7, *South America,* ed. Johannes Wilbert (Boston: G. K. Hall and Co., 1994), 359.

23. According to ongoing field research by Cecilia Ayala Lafée (pers. comm.), girls have already mastered the basics of hammock weaving by the age of eight.

24. Claudia Kalka, *Eine Tochter ist ein Haus, ein Boot und ein Garten: Frauen und Geschlechtersymmetrie bei den Warao-Indianern Venezuelas* (Münster: Lit Verlag, 1994).

25. The "principal woman" and her spouse are the founder couple of a given village; theirs is a position demanding great knowledge and diplomatic skill.

26. *Hobajiarao: hobaji,* "swamp," *arao,* "people"; swamp people. These groups were capable of spending years on the savannas and did not require the resources of the major distributaries.

27. *Hotarao: hota,* "upland," *arao,* "people"; uplanders.

28. *Piaractus brachypomus, morocoto,* a Carib term. A species most often associated with main channels, island affluents, and aquatic macrophytic environments.

29. *Rhynchophorus palmetum,* the palm-borer beetle.

30. *Mauritia flexuosa,* the *moriche* palm (from the Carib term *mürüjshü*). On the savannas of the western delta, between the Araguao and the Macareo distributaries, moriche grows from near the coast to the apex of the delta. Also see map 2 on page 8 of H. Dieter Heinen, "El abandono de un ecosistema: el caso de los morichales del Delta del Orinoco," *Antropológica* 81 (1994-1996): 3–36.

31. For a detailed discussion of ritual sago production, see: Johannes Wilbert, *"Manicaria saccifera* and Its Cultural Significance among the Warao Indians of Venezuela," *Botanical Museum Leaflets* 24 (1976): 275–335; and Johannes Wilbert, *Mindful of Famine: Religious Climatology of the Warao Indians* (Cambridge, Mass.: Harvard University Center for the Study of World Religions, 1996), 137–60.

32. Johannes Wilbert, *Mindful of Famine.*

33. Werner Wilbert, *"Manicaria saccifera* and the Warao in the Orinoco Delta: A Biogeography," 51–66.

34. See Verónica J. Ponte, "El arte de pescar: un debate entre el conocimiento, la destreza y la suerte según los Warao del Delta del Río Orinoco," *Antropológica* 81 (1994-1996): 37–50; and Verónica J. Ponte, "Contributions of the Warao Indians to the Ichthyology of the Orinoco Delta," *Scientia Guainae* 5 (1995): 371–92.

35. Werner Wilbert, Wade Davis, and Cecilia Ayala Lafée, "Economic Botany of the Warao Indians of the Orinoco Delta" (unpublished ms.).

36. The story was told by Pedro Rivero, an elderly Warao man from the Winikina River.

37. Modeled after the native theory of conception according to which semen,

awata ho, lit., "penis water," mixes with the woman's blood and coagulates *in utero,* creating the fetus.

38. Johannes Wilbert, *Mystic Endowment,* 9.

39. Werner Wilbert, *Fitoterapia Warao: una teoría pneumica de la salud, la enfermedad y la terapia,* Fundación La Salle de Ciencias Naturales, Monograph 41 (Caracas: Editorial COQUI, 1996).

40. Bisi and Baabe are two species of tree belonging to *Calophyllum.* In the literature, the tree *bisi* is also referred to as "red cedar" and *baabe* as "white cedar." In Venezuela they are known as *cachicamo rojo (bisi)* and *cachicamo blanco (baabe).*

41. Horojene (*jorojene, jorowene*) is an armored catfish, *Hoplosternum littorale.*

42. These formations vary in depth but were not observed to exceed 60 cm. Their length, however, may exceed several hundred meters.

43. The term *inahoko ahobahi* translates as "land of the open forest." The Warao point out that this is the only forested region where the distance between trees is great enough for sunlight to fall directly onto the ground.

44. Soil sampling tests were not made beyond the 1.5 m mark, due to the high water table. Native assistants insisted that if one kept digging, the clay layer would be reached.

45. So great is the accumulated floral biomass that recent savanna fire, covering approximately 300 hectares, burned for almost two months.

46. Johannes Wilbert, *Mindful of Famine,* 192–95.

47. The Warao maintain that plant reproduction depends on wind for pollination (ibid., 130).

48. Oka, the mythical armadillo, is modelled on the nine-banded armadillo (*Dasypus novemcinctus*) that frequents the levees in the upper delta. See ibid., 131. Given the long-range traditional history of the Warao, Oka may also recall the existence of glyptodonts in the area during the Pleistocene era, measuring over 2.5 m in length. See also Cecilia Ayala Lafée, "La etnohistoria prehispánica Guaiquerí," *Antropológica* 82 (1994-1996): 9; and José Royo y Gómez, "Características paleontológicas y geológicas del yacimiento de vertebrados de Muaco, Estado Falcón, con industria lítica humana," Memoria del Tercer Congreso Geológico Venezolano, vol. 2, *Boletín de Geología,* special publication, 3 (1960): 501.

49. Ritual combat between two adversaries takes place on a court. Each contender uses a shield to push his opponent out of bounds.

50. Lawrence E. Sullivan, *Icanchu's Drum: Orientation to Meaning in South American Religions* (New York: Macmillan, 1988), 170; Johannes Wilbert, *Mindful of Famine,* 130–34.

51. Johannes Wilbert, *Textos Folklóricos de los Indios Warao,* UCLA Latin American Studies Center Publications, 12 (Los Angeles, University of California, 1969), 35.

52. Ethnoecological research in economics, medical botany, biogeography, and ichthyology has revealed the Warao's comprehensive anatomical knowledge of plants and animals. It has also become clear that the Warao perceive species to be personified actors on a world stage, each having its own name. This makes a taxonomic key in the Western sense unnecessary. In the most confounding situations, as, for instance, in determining the taxonomic status of a given plant, they use odor to make

the final decision. The primary taxonomic method is identifying the species that make up biological communities. Critical to this key is the concept of *araotuma,* which serves as a cover term denoting "all life-forms."

53. Werner Wilbert, "Bush-spirit Encounters in Warao Life and Lore," *Antropológica* 77 (1992): 71

54. Although the giant river otter (*Pteronura brasiliensis*), *hoetobu,* spends much of its time in the water, it sleeps in dens on the ground.

55. Because of their form and behavior, monkeys, especially howler monkeys, are believed to be the humanoid residents of the underworld with a life-style similar to that of humans. Dolphins are primordial Warao women who went to live in the water. Like male shamans on the terrestrial level, they possess shamanic attributes that enable them to transcend cosmic levels: "sleeping" on the aquatic level, while breathing on the terrestrial level.

56. Werner Wilbert, "Bush-spirit Encounters in Warao Life and Lore," 71.

57. Basilio M. de Barral, *Los indios Guaraúnos y su cancionero: historia, religión y alma lírica. Biblioteca Missionalia Hispánica,"* vol 15 (Madrid: Concejo Superior de Investigaciones Científicas, Departamento de Misionología Española, 1964); Dale A. Olsen, *Music of the Warao of Venezuela: Song People of the Rain Forest* (Gainsville: University Press of Florida, 1996).

58. Johannes Wilbert, *Folk Literature of the Warao Indians: Narrative Material and Motif Content,* UCLA Latin American Studies Center Publications, 15 (Los Angeles: University of California, 1970); Ponte, "El arte de pescar: un debate entre el conocimiento, la destreza y la suerte según los Warao del Delta del Río Orinoco"; and Ponte, "Contributions of the Warao Indians to the Ichthyology of the Orinoco Delta."

59. Owing to its size and strength, the king vulture is reputed to be capable of carrying off babies; the bird is said to "appear with the sound of a shotgun."

60. Many species of fish in the Orinoco Delta use their olfactory sense to hunt. They have been known to attack menstruating women while bathing. To the Warao, this constitutes an act of expected aggression by hunters from a nonterrestrial plane of existence.

61. Vásquez and Wilbert, "The Orinoco: Physical, Biological and Cultural Diversity of a Major Tropical Alluvial River."

62. Werner Wilbert, *Fitoterapia Warao: una teoría pneumica de la salud, la enfermedad y la terapia.*

63. Western taxonomists also classify palms as plants rather than trees.

64. Werner Wilbert, *Fitoterapia Warao: una teoría pneumica de la salud, la enfermedad y la terapia.*

65. Johannes Wilbert, *Mystic Endowment,* 61–86.

66. Ibid., 220.

67. Åke Hultkrantz, "Ecology," in *The Encyclopedia of Religion,* ed. Mircea Eliade (New York: Macmillan, 1987), 4:581–85.

Resistance and Regeneration

Hunting, Nature, and Metaphor: Political and Discursive Strategies in James Bay Cree Resistance and Autonomy

HARVEY A. FEIT

James Bay Cree representations of their hunting society, which were developed during the debates over the James Bay hydroelectric projects in northern Quebec, were shaped both by Cree cultural meanings and by the cultural patterns of non-Native North Americans. Cree elders and younger spokespersons sought effective means of communicating to non-Natives a sense of Cree relationships with the lands on which they live and with the animals they hunt. These intercultural discourses took place in the context of developing international alliances between Cree and environmentalists, as well as in the historical context of fur trade relations and of Christian missionization. The metaphors that were used by Cree and non-Natives to enrich these dialogues were exchanged back and forth, carrying earlier meanings as they took on new nuances. They were also vital to discourses building unity among Cree of different generations and of different "lifestyles." In this paper I will explore the development and importance of several features of these political and discursive strategies for indigenous resistance and autonomy. At the center of these communications are dialogues on nature, production, spirituality, moral standing, and political action.

The Problematic of Discourse and Power

The Cree people's opposition to development of their lands without their consent acknowledges fundamental and enduring conflicts of interest and control with non-Native polities and economies, and it involves them in diverse forms of political action and complex forms of communication with sectors of non-Native North American society.[1] Current strategies of the Cree leadership depend on their already having developed a substantial political organization and regional government, on their having some monetary resources under their own control, and also on having developed rich understandings of the linkages and differences between Cree and non-Native North American cultural meanings and practices. The first two of these conditions are more frequently emphasized than the last.

Their representational strategies depend, in part, on their presenting Cree positions with frameworks and terms drawn from the encapsulating societies. One challenge the Cree leadership faces is to resist fighting the battles in forms the state or market institutions proscribe and, instead, to find ways to communicate and reassert Cree cultural meanings without extensively or simply remaking them in the image of the dominant cultures of North American institutions.

Social analysts have differed about whether the use by partly subordinated groups of the concepts, metaphors, and rhetorical strategies of dominant institutions and cultures entails an incorporation of dominant forms of knowing, representing, talking, valuing, acting, and self-restraint into their societies. Do such uses entail increased subordination or limitations on forms of resistance to dominant institutions?

One of the most original features of James C. Scott's seminal analyses of resistance was his emphasis on how everyday forms of resistance depend on the very categories and claims of dominant groups within a society.[2] By claiming to serve society-wide interests and not just class or group interests, ideologies of dominant groups create the conditions on which they can be challenged and critiqued. Resistance thus draws on dominant ideologies; it takes up their affirmation of values of common good and collective interest and reaffirms and reproduces those values as it critiques performances that do not achieve them. Resistance does so, even as those values are under erosion by dominant groups, and even though those values are being simultaneously promoted and denied in the practices and legitimation strategies of dominant groups.

Many critics, however, have seen this as also limiting and subordinating resistance, and as channelling it into acceptable forms. This may be enhanced where the political action is not between village classes in daily face-to-face interaction, as in the case analysed by Scott, but between social groups or encapsulated societies and nation-states. Here, claims of serving the common good are distanced and may be more totally dependent on imagined commonalities and claims.[3] In these cases many of the categories and values drawn from dominant discourses in the course of political action are not values of a daily shared community, but values of nation-building and economic institutions—including national histories, property and labor laws, public education, institutionalized technology and science, systems of public order, mass media news and entertainment, gender and ethnic differentiation, and consumerism. Critics are a lot less sanguine about what is gained and lost when political action takes up these dominant categories and values. Yet, Scott's emphasis on the particular role of tropes that reference past social relations is important, especially where those relations are still claimed as present and future possibilities.

In *Custom and Confrontation,* Roger Keesing examined the sphere of local autonomy within a colonial, and then developing, state and challenged too limited a reading of the possibilities for resistance.[4] He argued that even where resistance to the state uses the categories, terminology, organizational structures, and semiotic patterns of colonial and neo-colonial authorities, this can lead to more effective resistance rather than increased subordination, as it did in the case of the Kwaio people in the Solomon Islands whose century-long struggles of resistance he recounts. Keesing argued that even though the Kwaio adopted discourses and practices from the state institutions asserting domination, this did not enhance domination because they used these practices oppositionally. Keesing's exploration of the Kwaio's sustained colonial resistance is, like Scott's, sensitive to the constraints on and limits of resistance.

Both these accounts of resistance leave open possibilities that need to be explored in other contexts, such as political action by indigenous peoples encapsulated in modern neoliberal states, where the oppositions as well as linkages richly connect the local-, regional-, and national-level practices. These linkages make assessing "fourth world," or indigenous, political action particularly complicated. For example, in *Labors Lot,* Elizabeth Povinelli, looking at indigenous resistance within Australia, noted how legal dominance was asserted without erasing indigenous discourses of resistance and autonomy, and also how these latter discourses were themselves used by and benefited the state.[5] On the one hand, Aboriginal discourses and practices were richly reproduced, locally and regionally, as they were being re-shaped in changing contexts. But Aboriginal customary practices, on the other hand, she argued, also contribute to state projects—political, economic, and cultural—as in Australia's tourist promotion and film and media industries and in legitimating both national identity and its asserted achievement of social progress. In each instance, she argues the state offers limited land-rights and self-determination in exchange for a form of Aboriginality useful to it. However, while Australian practices thereby shape the local, she also shows that Aboriginal political action and their relations with the land intrude in unanticipated ways on Australian understandings of self, knowledge, property, and nation through legal cases and daily practices of land use. Here, political action is both subordinated and sustained.[6]

In this paper I want to explore and elaborate on some elements of each of these analyses, by considering indigenous political action under conditions where the local group interacts beyond the state itself in international political, media, and market arenas, and where indigenous communities use strategies that seek alliances with other communities and organizations of opposition within the wider polities. I will argue that in these cases, and especially where indigenous political strategies do not depend solely or primarily on the central arenas for state control of diversity—including legal claims and the assertion of indigenous rights, political lobbying, or idealized ethnic traditionalism—political action need not necessarily lead to enhanced domination even though the resistance uses discursive resources of the dominant society. Furthermore, state uses of indigenousness may also be thwarted, and indigenous resistance may limit the means of control at the disposal of state and market institutions, although without undermining these capacities in themselves.

The case of the James Bay Cree opposition to hydroelectric projects serves this purpose well, because here, indigenous groups move directly into the public spheres, engage internationally with markets and media, and actively seek to remake the image not only of themselves as indigenes, but of the state as well. I draw on each of the contributions cited above in order to explore contemporary conditions for indigenous Cree political action. I do so more or less in the reverse order to that which I have just set out:

- First I explore some of the ways James Bay Cree challenge neoliberal state and market institutions, and in the process significantly limit the utility of their own indigenousness to those who would govern them and develop their lands.
- Then I explore how this depends, in part, on a several-decades-long process of developing intercultural discursive strategies essential both to building alliances and to shaping media and wider public opinion.
- Last I explore how the potentially subordinating outcomes of using these political and discursive borrowings were limited by the capacity to sustain an indigenous dialogue among elder Cree, Cree spokespersons, and school-educated Cree youth about what it is to be and to remain Cree.

I will thus move from the story of political events, to cultural and intercultural practices, to the history of colonial relationships, and on to intergenerational discourses. In addition, I highlight three features of the semiotic practices the Cree develop that play key roles in their strategies:

- Cree sought concepts, terms, and metaphors from among the elements of an encapsulating culture which were not primarily used to legitimate and naturalize state power or economic interests, but which were commonly associated with social relations of domestic arenas, self-sufficient production, and collective moral responsibility.
- Thus, when these metaphors are taken up and used both by Cree and by non-Native institutions, they convey meanings that refer beyond central institutions and legitimations of state and market power to alternative social relations: in Cree usage conveying across cultures a sense of the Cree social universe to non-Native North Americans; and in state usage unwittingly reducing the state claims that opposition be restricted to acceptable forms.

- Cree elders use these same metaphors and discursive practices to build images among Cree of different generations of
their relations to historical and contemporary "others," both
emphasizing spiritual and civilizational commonalities with
non-Natives and highlighting cultural and social differences.

Background to the Cree Struggles and the Problem of Explaining Public Support

The approximately twelve thousand James Bay Cree Indians are a
subarctic people living in nine separate communities east of James
Bay in northern Quebec and Canada. Since the 1970s they have had
modern housing, and they live in villages with schools and health services when they are not out hunting. A compromise agreement on the
land claims of the James Bay Cree and the Inuit of Quebec,[7] which
resulted from the opposition to the first phase of the hydroelectric
project, was signed in 1975. In the agreement the Cree were unable to
prevent the completion of the first of three massive phases of hydroelectric development and the opening of the region to expanded resource developments, including forestry and mining. The agreement
negotiations accelerated the development of a Cree regional society
and political institutions; they formalized Cree regional and local
governments, and recognized the distinctiveness of Cree society.[8]
From the point of view of Quebec and Canadian officials, the agreement clarified and formalized the place of the Cree as a collectivity
within the Quebec and Canadian states, administratively and legally.[9]
Nevertheless, Cree political and self-government organizations now
have over C$200 million of investments and manage over C$75 million
per year of government funds for schools, health care, social benefits,
community administration, and income support payments for full-
time hunters. Their cultural, organizational, and financial resources
provide a capacity for relatively autonomous political actions.

Today, about one-quarter of the adult population hunts full-time,
spending an average of seven months of the year in small camps of
one to five families located at sites in the "bush." It is not widely
recognized that the number of "full-time" hunters is as high as it has
ever been, although it is a declining proportion of the growing Cree
population. About one-third of the population have steady jobs, mostly in

the Cree governmental organizations which service the communities. The balance are underemployed and generally young. Hunting is highly valued and actively participated in on a part-time basis by nearly all workers and unemployed, who themselves spend an average of approximately two months a year hunting. Hunting therefore continues to be a key to Cree identities and extended domestic relations, and it provides a significant input to family and community diets, health, and well-being.

The Hudson's Bay Company (H.B.C.) established its first fur trade post on James Bay in 1668, although French trade goods and traders had been in the region earlier than that. The early traders were dependent on Cree for food as well as furs, and both Cree stories of encounters with "whitemen," the common term in Cree English for non-Natives, and European records suggest that the relationships between the isolated traders and Cree hunters involved slowly changing dependencies and opportunities for actualizing significant profits by traders and that Cree autonomy continued, waned, and was renewed.[10]

The Cree people were missionized initially in the seventeenth and eighteenth centuries, and more effectively and continuously since the middle of the nineteenth century. Most Cree were Christians by the mid-twentieth century, although some have maintained or returned to solely traditional spirituality. Earlier in the twentieth century, nearly all Cree were Anglicans, with a few Roman Catholic converts, but many have become adherents of Pentecostal denominations in the last four decades. Most of the Christian James Bay Cree hunters, whichever denomination they belong to, have incorporated Jesus at the head of a hierarchy of spirit beings and animal masters, all of whom have become his helpers. Adult Cree hunters still dream of animal spirits to learn where to look for the animals they will catch, and they often say that both dreams and Jesus are sources of their knowledge and power.

The cultural meanings and practices of the James Bay Cree people have thus gone through continuing changes and transformations, but they remain distinct from the surrounding cultures and societies by choice. There are, however, diverse Cree meanings and practices today.

The James Bay Cree have been involved for nearly three decades in a series of struggles against the massive hydroelectric and forestry developments being conducted on their lands. The challenges to date have been fought in large part by a formally educated Cree leadership working closely with traditional leaders and hunting territory "owners." The leadership has taken their message to centers of political and economic power in Canada, the United States, and Europe. They have had support from a variety of journalists, filmmakers, indigenous rights supporters and environmental organizations, lawyers and social scientists.

In 1989 when Hydro-Québec announced that it would start seeking approvals to build the second phase of the hydroelectric projects, there were diverse Cree views. Some Cree thought it was a chance to strengthen the 1975 agreement and get the additional funds needed to improve social and economic conditions in the villages. But when the community at the mouth of the main river to be developed, Whapmagoostui on the Great Whale River, said the hydroelectric project had to be stopped, other communities and leaders united behind them. The immediate goal was to prevent the start of construction, so that the Cree would not have to fight while the project was being built, as had been the case in the 1970s.

Cree leaders realized that Hydro-Québec was dependent on international capital markets to sell its bonds to investors in order to raise part of the C\$6 billion of funds it needed to continue building. To convince potential investors that this was a safe and profitable place for their capital, it sought an assured market for the sale of its electricity, partly by negotiating for large export contracts with Maine, Vermont, and New York State electric power utility companies in the northeast United States. The Cree leaders realized that if they could block these contracts, they would make it considerably harder for Hydro-Québec to borrow the capital it needed to go ahead at attractive rates.

Such a challenge did not just involve direct lobbying of decision-makers and investors in the United States and Europe; it involved mobilizing active sectors of the U.S. public whose opinions could not be as easily ignored by U.S. authorities and politicians, as could the Cree themselves. The Cree mounted a campaign based on contesting the economic and ecological arguments used to legitimate the proposed project and the contracts and also based on explaining to the public how their lives and the lands they hunted would be damaged by the project. The Cree argued that hydroelectric projects were not a "clean" source of power, as was being claimed: they flooded massive land areas, destroyed wildlife and habitats, threatened Cree society, and ignored Cree rights. The Cree hired experts who showed that energy conservation could save more energy than the new project would produce, at less cost and with more employment benefits. These arguments showed that the "rationality" of the project could be questioned and that there were plausible alternatives. These arguments were used to stimulate political commentaries and expert opinion pieces in the media and in formal or legislative reviews of the contracts.

But, to mobilize a wider public opinion, the Cree had to convey a sense of how the Cree ties to the land could be damaged. A group of Cree, mainly from Whapmagoostui, paddled a unique combination canoe and kayak from James Bay through Vermont to New York City in 1990, stopping at small and large communities along the way to meet environmentalists and media and to ask for public support. A variety of environmental organizations helped the Cree at each daily stop during their travels.[11] In Vermont and upper New York State they met many small townspeople and people from farmsteads, with strong farming and rural traditions, who valued individual responsibility and direct involvement with the environment. This trip personalized the Cree to many local activists and to an interested public who saw the numerous local media pieces done about these unusual visitors.

But, in New York City and other urban areas they had to present themselves as a people tied to the land to audiences far removed from land-based livelihoods or lives, and in much less personalized contexts. For example, at a massive Earth Day rally in lower Manhattan, they were one of dozens of speakers and groups seeking support and media coverage.

The decisive political victory was won in New York State, where public opinion swung against the electricity supply contracts just as the campaign for election of a governor was underway. Cree leaders sensed they were having an impact as one U.S. environmental organization reported gaining five thousand new members from its James Bay campaign, and the offices of public officials were reportedly flooded with public expressions of concern. The Cree then commissioned a public opinion poll which showed politicians and their strategists that there was declining public support for the contracts. Just as some economists began to question the terms of the contracts because energy prices were declining, political support for the New York contract eroded, and the incumbent governor up for re-election refused to endorse it. It was cancelled by the state power utility in 1992.

A short time later, the premier of Quebec announced that the development of the second phase of the James Bay project was stopped and would be delayed indefinitely. This was nationally significant because Hydro-Québec was the foremost state and economic institution controlled by Quebecers, both in the views of Quebec officials and the Quebec public, and it was also prominent in the international reputation of Quebec. The victory by the Cree and their allies therefore deeply marked the international face, the self-image, and the assumed sense of secure development of the Quebec state administration, and to some degree the Canadian state as well, and it changed Cree relations to both.[12]

The Cree were successful in this challenge to development by combining diverse skills: a complex political strategy that identified economic and political structural weaknesses as it used opportune moments; a sophisticated use of economic and engineering analyses and media and polling techniques to influence opinion makers and strategists; and several rich discursive strategies for presenting Cree hunting as both a productive and protective activity, worthy of public concern and support. It is the last of these types of strategies that is not examined in many accounts of these events and that is the focus of this paper. How the Cree were able to generate broad public support for their cause needs analysis because it is not obvious that hunters and hunting, even indigenous hunters, would be supported by either environmental movement supporters or the general public. The link the Cree built here between indigenous hunters' struggles and environmental concerns was not the first time such a link had been made—it had been made before in the Amazon, for example—but this was the most elaborate linkage developed to date, and the most important for the future of both social movements. To see how it was achieved, it is necessary to look at Cree cultural symbols and at two decades of developing representational strategies that preceded these events.

Cree Symbols of Nature, Culture, and Sociality

Cree spokespersons often find it difficult to get more than a very simple image of themselves and their relationships to land and wildlife across to their non-Native audiences. This is an enduring problem, which governments and developers have exploited in responding to the Cree campaigns and which Cree spokespersons and elders have sought to address by creating intercultural metaphors of land and hunting.

For Cree hunters, the concepts of "human" and "animal" are distinguished, but there is no radical division of nature from culture or society. The animal world is a part of the same kind of social world that humans inhabit, and in much conversation a social metaphor serves to talk about the whole world. Many phenomena we would call natural, such as clouds or snow, are also considered to embody person-like qualities or capabilities of action.[13] Cree hunters say that many kinds of animals have distinct families, such as beaver colonies and geese mates, and are capable of willful action and responsibility for the things they do. This, the Cree say, is evidenced in the everyday experience of a hunter, who finds that many of the actions of animals are intelligible and predictable. The whole world is therefore a socially informed world, in which habit and learning rather than natural law explain the actions of animals and other nonhuman persons. As a result, communication between all beings is possible, and animals can in their turn interpret and understand the actions and needs of humans.

This is a world in which there is a unified, but not rigid, hierarchy of beings descending from God to spirit beings to humans to animals. The metaphor and value of social reciprocity, and the moral responsibility that it highlights in social relations, permeate this social universe. When asking why an animal went in a trap, or allowed itself to be caught, the Cree answer with similar kinds of reasons to those they would offer for why a human gives food away to another person. That is, because it appreciates the need of the other. The implication is that it is a responsible thing to do as a moral social being. The separation between humans and animals is thus one of degree, and continuities of humans and animals, culture and nature are therefore assumed in the Cree symbolic universe.

A critical feature of human-animal relations for the Cree is that animals are symbolically associated with non-kin. Cree hunters not only say animals are persons, they say they love the animals they hunt. This is expressed in the ways hunting is linked to sexual love, and Cree words for hunting often have dual meanings associated with sexual relations and pursuits. Colin Scott gives several examples of how hunting and sexuality share a common vocabulary: *mitwaaschaau* can refer to both "he shoots" and "he ejaculates"; *paaschikan* can refer to both "shotgun" and "penis"; and *spichinaakin* to both "gun case" and "condom."[14] Recurrent themes in jokes and stories associate hunting with sexual pursuit.[15]

The Cree linking of love for animals and the hunting of animals can appear self-serving to an outsider, but in Cree cultural structures there is no radical separation of home and family from work or production groups. Therefore, love can and does permeate the Cree world in a way that on the surface seems false or impractical to non-Natives. This loving care is expressed in an elaborate ritualization of everyday hunting practices, from seeing signs of animal presence to hunting, retrieving, transporting, butchering, distributing, consuming, and disposing of the remains of animals.[16]

That animals love humans is implicit in the commonplace Cree statements that when a Cree hunter kills an animal properly and treats its body respectfully, its surviving soul will want to be reborn again. Thus, when hunters only take animals that are given, animals are reborn. Hunters note that if they do not take animals that are given, the health and survival of the animals clearly deteriorate, and the con-

Figure 1. A beaver dam, partly broken so that when beaver come to repair the dam overnight, one may be caught in a trap set nearby.
(Photograph Harvey Feit)

tinuing birth and survival of those animals are endangered. There is clear evidence that these understandings, in conjunction with the practices of the Cree hunting territory "owners," do conserve and manage key game populations.[17]

Having constituted animals as part of a social world, it is the social collectivity that can survive the death of individual animals. This is manifest both in the survival of the souls of animals and in the survival of their offspring in whom those souls may be reborn. The idea for both humans and animals is to prepare for death when it comes and, in death, to bestow blessings on the living, so as to play a role in the continuity of family and community. When humans live in balanced reciprocity with animals, each creates the continued conditions for the survival of the other as members of a society.

Rhetorical Choices

A central problem for Cree hunters and spokespersons is how to convey these understandings of their own lives and of hunting to Quebecers, Canadians, and Americans in the context of the Cree struggles over what happens on their lands. It is a problem because none of the common Cree metaphors of hunting and of relations to the land—social reciprocity between humans and the animals they hunt, or conjugal partnerships that extend from death to the rebirth of hunted animals— facilitate easy comprehension across cultural differences.

One metaphor used by Cree leaders to mobilize public support for a changed and more respectful relationship between governments and the Cree has been the popular North American cultural image of the "Indians" as a noble and victimized people. These images have been critical in mobilizing significant support against hydroelectric developments, and they have played important roles in Cree campaigns. But they also have had definite practical and semiotic limits.

The image of the noble indigene is widely circulated among a broad public and it conveys sympathetic concerns, but at the same time it is also associated with a negative and disempowering set of images. "Indians" are alternatively a people who are noble, but who are also naïve and unchanging, or devastated by modernity, or inevitably becoming like "us." These images of Indians are Euro-American creations, clustering positive with negative views, and long manipulated to explain and justify claims of Euro-American and Canadian dominance.[18] The Indian is either tied to the past, or caught in associations with the disappearing Indian who cannot be really traditional while obviously modern and changing.

Cree uses of the image of the Indian are powerful, but they also inevitably highlight supposed contradictions between the image of the Cree people as traditional hunting people and the complex technologies they use in contemporary hunting and in their sophisticated international political and public relations campaigns. Cree leaders and spokespersons have been challenged with these "contradictions" by politicians and corporate leaders eager to imply that the Cree are no longer tied to the land, but rather that they manipulate the image of tradition in the cause of enhancing wealth and power. For example, when Armand Couture, then vice president of Hydro-Québec and a negotiator to the Cree, says that the real issue in conflicts with the Cree is the "ownership of resources," and that claims for territorial control and self-government are the strategy, he asserts that the Cree are just like other Quebecers and North Americans.[19]

The images of the Indian have been partly effective for the Cree, because even modern audiences are used to disjunctures in experience and between domains of knowledge. However, the images are also limited by the public's susceptibility to perceiving disjuncture as inconsistency, and as a possible indication that images are being manipulated by those whose moral causes the public, politicians, investors, jurists, and environmentalists are being asked to support. The uses by the Cree of the images of the Indian have thus brought both support and subordination.

Claims based on distinctive indigenous legal rights, important as they are, are fraught with the same contradictions and weaknesses. They are necessary, but limited and limiting, strategies.

Gardens and Gardeners

In contrast to these widely used discourses, one of the most frequently cited of the rhetorical strategies that the Cree hunters themselves developed to communicate their relationship to the land has been the metaphor that hunting is like gardening and their hunting lands are like a garden.[20] It conveys complex meanings to non-Native North

Americans and additional signification to Cree. Cree hunters want to draw both similarities and difference between the whiteman's concept of ownership and their own, as well as to claim ownership of land.[21]

This metaphor was the product of a complex Cree collective process, and many Cree elders used the metaphor of a garden to express this dual claim. When initial Cree mobilization developed against the hydroelectric project in 1971 and 1972, there were extensive discussions among elder and younger Cree leaders about how to respond, and they shared insights and phrasings.[22] The pattern developed further in late 1972 and 1973 when communities sent people to testify in a Cree-initiated court case against the project that was heard in Montreal. Both what might be said to the judge in the court and what was said when one was in court were extensively discussed back in the communities. Cree elders often informally encouraged one another to take the role of spokesperson and speak to outsiders. Cree elders and spokespersons used the garden metaphor on many occasions throughout these encounters.

For example, Job Bearskin, from the community at the mouth of the main river dammed by the first phase of hydroelectric development, Fort George, later relocated to Chisasibi, used the metaphor in 1972 with journalist and filmmaker Boyce Richardson, who quoted him in his books and first film.[23] At key meetings in 1974 in the village at Fort George, where the possibility of negotiating an agreement between Cree and Hydro-Québec about the ongoing hydroelectric project construction was discussed, the garden metaphor was heard repeatedly as community members tried to explain to Quebec and Hydro-Québec negotiators why they opposed the project. An unidentified Cree speaker said:

> Land is like a garden to the Indians, everything grows, life [is] sustained from the garden. Dam the river, and land is destroyed. No one has right to destroy land except the Creator.[24]

Another said:

> The river is our road, [he] does not want to see dams on it. Our people have lived from the river. Like a garden, we do not want our land destroyed. Want our demands met.[25]

At a follow-up meeting two months later, Harry Matthew said:

> We lived off the land since the beginning of time. Land is a garden
> to us, we want to keep it that way like our forefathers have done.[26]

Elder Daniel Rupert explained:

> My father was a tallyman [a hunting territory "owner," often called
> a "trapline boss"]. We put in beavers [that is, they relocated live beavers
> to their hunting territory from other areas] so they would reproduce.
> When he did not hunt anymore I became tallyman. He gave extensive
> care to the trapline, which is what I want to do too. When he made me
> tallyman, his last words were to look after what it would produce, like
> a garden, for all the children that would come. That's why I want it to
> be productive. . . . What you own as an individual, its only natural that
> you fight [for] it. What you have you want to retain, it is like a white-
> man's garden.[27]

In these statements the garden metaphor refers to land ownership,
to the productiveness of land, to Cree inheritance of land, and to the
care that goes into using and protecting the land. The statements both
call up common knowledge to help outsiders understand the Cree
relationship to the land and extend that knowledge into unexpected
areas. For example, recalling the relocation of beaver to areas where
they had declined, sometimes called "replanting beaver," is a claim
that, for the Cree, hunting, like gardening, not only cares for but
restores the land and renews its productivity. Cree elders knew that
non-Native North Americans have gardens throughout Canada and
the United States, and they were calling on the proprietorship and the
personal caring and nurturing that Quebecers, Canadians, and Americans give to garden plots, and their sense that gardens can be used in
perpetuity, to express the Cree relationship to the land as hunters. The
rich metaphoric significance of the trope became clearer as it was
picked up by some of those non-Natives who themselves actively
sought richer dialogue with Cree elders.

Spreading the Word

The gardening metaphor played an important role in mobilizing support for the Cree opposition to hydroelectric development among the
general public and especially those concerned about indigenous peoples.

It initially became known outside Cree communities as "Job's garden," an intercultural social creation. Boyce Richardson used "Job's Garden" as both the name of a documentary film[28] and the title of a chapter in his second book on the Cree struggles against hydroelectric development.[29] "Job's garden" was a partly fortuitous coincidence of a rhetorical strategy which had long roots in Cree discourse, the political context of the Cree opposition to hydroelectric development, the name of a Cree man with a gift for respected oratory, and the presence of a committed documentary journalist with a sense of the biblical proportions the Cree saw in their struggles.[30] But Job Bearskin himself noted that "I have heard many people call this land our garden."[31]

In Boyce Richardson's second book and first film on James Bay, Job Bearskin spoke of the Cree hunters' relationship with the land while standing near the LaGrande River on his hunting lands in the summer of 1972. Gilbert Herodier, a young Cree filmmaker who worked with Boyce Richardson, translated for Job:

> "It is really beautiful what he has been saying. He said this whole place is like a garden, because many things grow here, and the Indians are one of the things that grow here. He says that animals were given to the Indians so they could feed their children and old people, and everyone has always shared the food from this garden. He says everyone here will always share. It's always been like that."[32]

Here, the use of the metaphor not only asserts a caring relationship, it also counters the view, often presented by the media and by Hydro-Québec and government spokespersons, that northern Quebec was an area of wilderness, unproductive and virtually uninhabited. The metaphor gains part of its significance from its opposition to images widely circulated in state ideologies and by mass media.

The metaphor responds directly to the public legitimation of the development by Quebec and by Robert Bourassa, the premier of Quebec who initiated the project. They used the discourses of nationalism, wilderness, and the histories of European occupation to claim legitimacy when they announced the project in 1971. In his 1973 book, Bourassa cited the lack of Quebecers' control of their economy, and the resulting poverty and underdevelopment,[33] and his desire to modernize Quebec through hydroelectric energy development under Quebec control. He said the challenge was "the conquest of northern

Indigenous Traditions and Ecology

Quebec. . . ."[34] Reporting on his visit to the James Bay construction sites, he wrote that when he looked at the young workers, "I cannot help but think of the first settlers of our land," and he also wrote about "what a strange contrast it is to see modern machinery and equipment lined up in the wilderness and solitude of the north."[35]

The metaphor of the garden is a fundamental alternative to these linked metaphors of wilderness, European settlement, and nation. Gardening analogies deny that this is a wilderness, and, instead, assert that it is a place that sustains humans. The productivity of the land is highlighted, and it is made a place where people survived and belonged, not a barren land but a home to the Cree.

The garden also calls up images of divine creation, not nation. In Cree elders' usage, the metaphor makes clear that the animals are given by God so the Cree may survive; the Cree are not masters of the game. In this view, the Cree themselves are "one of the things that grow here." Thus, it is not just contemporary gardens they speak of; there are implicit references to the biblical Garden of Eden. It is divine creation, and there are sacred rights and obligations that also concern the Cree.

References to sharing thus refer both to Cree traditional values and practices of reciprocity and to the biblical commands to care for God's creation and look after one another. In the garden metaphor, caring also extends beyond any boundaries between people and animals and beyond divisions between humans from different societies and nations, for all are God's creatures. The elders thus seek to express from within Cree knowledge a common sacredness with the land, which they know can be shared by many non-Cree listeners. Here, the metaphor draws on Christian values that today are no longer uniquely dominant values in North American societies, albeit that these are still values often used to support dominant institutions and ideologies as well as alternative traditions and organizations.[36]

Many non-Natives heard these discourses, and they helped to build public support for the Cree opposition to hydroelectric development. An early example of taking up and using the metaphor was the "Public Hearing on the James Bay Project," organized by citizens groups in Montreal in April 1973, that united scientists, social and environmental activists, politicians, representatives of the labor movement, lawyers, and educators who opposed the project. The published proceedings of the forum included a section of papers on the Cree, titled

"Native Peoples" and a section of papers on the James Bay territory, called the "Garden of the Cree."[37]

Nearly two decades later, journalist Roy MacGregor's account of the Cree struggle against the hydroelectric project and the negotiation of the James Bay and Northern Quebec Agreement included an appreciation of the power of Cree metaphors. His 1989 book refers to the 1973 court ruling by Justice Albert Malouf in favor of the Cree, which forced the province of Quebec to negotiate with them, in these words:

> This land, Malouf believed, had the status the old trappers had claimed it had: it was their garden, which had provided them with their livelihood for longer than history could record. That they pursued a traditional way of life on this land was, he believed, beyond dispute.[38]

Note here the addition of a prehistory, and of a claim to traditional lives.

Metaphors and Alliances

In 1989, when the new and multistranded alliance of Cree with environmental movement organizations in Canada, the United States, and Europe was formed to fight against the new plans for hydroelectric development, the Cree gave the lead article in the tabloid they issued a banner headline, "Our land is like a garden to us," quoting the author of the lead essay, Brian Georgekish, a sixth grade student from the community of Wemindji:[39]

> We don't want our land to be flooded. You've killed a lot of animals and contaminated our fish and drinking water. Our land is just like a garden to us. We survive from it. Just like the people who grow vegetables, they survive from it selling their vegetables. We love our land and way of life. When I grow up, I would like to go hunting and trapping where my grandfather, great-grandfather and father hunted and trapped for years. . . . But now after the dams have been built there are not as many animals as there were before you built the dams and flooded our land. Stop destroying our land and our future, and our way of life."[40]

This statement echoes and amplifies elders' usage, picking up issues of contamination that come from wider environment movement campaigns and issues of the transmission of culture, as well as of the selling of the produce of hunting, that come from younger generations' concerns. The same theme was echoed by a new generation of Cree leaders, such as Robbie Dick, the middle-aged chief of Whapmagoostui, the Cree community on the Great Whale River: "Now they want to build the dam and to destroy that land. That's somebody's back yard. That's somebody's garden."[41]

In this new context, many environmentalists picked up and elaborated on the garden metaphor and gave it new emphases. In 1993 the Parisian quarterly newsletter *Message Amérindien International* reprinted three pieces on the Cree of James Bay, including a background paper by Farley Mowat, probably Canada's most prolific environmental essayist and author, and environmental lawyer and activist Elisabeth May,[42] which began:

> Depuis 1971, les étendues sauvages du Nord du Québec sont destinées à devenir le site de la plus grande entreprise hydro-électrique de la terre. Depuis de nombreuses générations, cette région est appelée le "Jardin" (*Kistikani*), par ses habitants: le peuple Cri.[43]

In the United States, a thirty-two-page tabloid-format pamphlet published in 1991 by the Northeast Alliance to Protect James Bay in Cambridge, Massachusetts, highlighted the passage by Roy MacGregor cited above.[44] The Northeast Alliance was a major grouping of organizations opposing the Great Whale River developments and supporting the Cree. In Canada, the tabloid pamphlet of Earthroots, a leading Ontario environmental organization, headlined a report on the Cree in its spring 1991 issue "Aboriginal Genocide: Drowning of the Cree Garden." A series of new videos appeared, most of which contained statements by Cree using the garden metaphor, including one entitled "Flooding Job's Garden" by Boyce Richardson.[45]

The frequent use of the garden metaphor in speeches, publications, and videos, and especially its use in the titles and headlines of major campaign communications, indicates the prominent place of the garden metaphor and signals the effective role it was sensed to be playing by Cree spokespersons and their supporters in mobilizing public understanding and support.[46] Its headline and title use also suggests that it was, or was becoming, a covering metaphor which itself referred to the other rhetorical strategies and tropes. To understand these processes it is necessary to look more carefully at the complexities of this representation.

Transforming Metaphors across Cultures

Environmentalist uses of the garden metaphor do not just convey the Cree usage, they also sometimes allude romantically to the connections of present Cree to ancient patterns and to the wisdom of time and of the elders. Here, "old trappers" pursue "traditions" maintained over "générations" in order to survive. Thus, the power and productivity of the garden metaphor used across cultures is broadened in ways that transform Cree elders' emphasis, although some of these themes are found in Cree usage as well.

For example, none of the new texts are fully spiritual, although allusions remain. Whether in Paris, Boston, or Toronto, the garden reference is to a largely secularized world in which the garden ideal is not quite Eden. Thus, Mowat and May can accuse Quebec of "sacrifier les territoires sauvages du Nord pour des dollars américains."[47] The reference to "territoires sauvages" contrasts sharply with Cree elders' typical socialization and domestication of land.

Mowat and May's usage, however, signals the importance of several other metaphorical meanings which come into prominence when the garden metaphor is used by contemporary environmentalists. Mowat has been a vocal defender of environments, animals, and indigenous peoples. He has described, for example, the ecstatic experiences with animals he witnessed while living with Inuit hunters and their enduring impact on him.[48] But, in another voice, he is also passionate to decry the "hideous results of five centuries of death-dealing [sport hunting] on the continent" that followed European settlement[49] and to share the experiences of his youth that convinced him never to hunt for sport again.[50]

Mowat resolves the tensions between his commitments to indigenous hunters and those against hunting and for animals, not by learning the specifics of Inuit or Cree views, but by separating traditional indigenous people from modern societies and the latter's relations to animals. He creates a space for indigenous hunting by romanticizing

Cree and others, setting them apart from the brutality he associates with moderns by ignoring their modernity. Cree are given a place, by being tied to past generations and living in an unchanging traditional way. His usage is unlike the Cree, for it supports the view of the Cree as a people of the past, as noble indigenes.

Mowat is not alone in this conundrum. Many who supported the Cree in their struggle against the Great Whale project did so as urban environmentalists, wanting both to protect land and wildlife of northern Quebec and to support the Cree who hunt and use those very animals in ways that urbanites find uncomfortable, that they do not understand, and that they could easily oppose. They do not have the commitment to indigenous hunters that Mowat draws from experiences on the land. The garden metaphor came to play a special role in mediating this disjuncture during the 1990s campaigns, for it could open up possibilities for understanding Cree as hunters.

Plural Garden Images and Intercultural Dialogues

The metaphor of the Cree world as garden, in the environmentalist citations above, conveys images of gardens as both wilderness and as nurtured terrain. It is this plurality of meanings and ambiguities that make the Cree garden metaphor more effective than might have been anticipated. The metaphor opens rich possibilities for intercultural understandings partly because of the way it unites opposites among European and North American cultural symbols.

Historians Keith Thomas, Carolyn Merchant, and Leo Marx have indicated in their respective histories of changing attitudes to the "natural world" in sixteenth- to nineteenth-century England and America that the idea of gardens has gone through numerous variations during these centuries.[51] Leo Marx, for example, notes in *The Machine in the Garden* that the idea of the garden appears both as "nature's garden" and as "garden-in-fact."[52] Commenting on Robert Beverley's *History and the Present State of Virginia* (1705) he notes:

> When Beverley calls Virginia one of the "Gardens of the World," . . . the garden stands for the original unity, the all-sufficing beauty and abundance of the creation. Virginia is an Edenic land of primitive splendor inhabited by noble savages. . . . But when Beverley says that

there are too few gardens in Virginia, he is speaking about actual, man-made, cultivated pieces of ground. This image also is an emblem of abundance, but it refers to abundance produced by work or, in Beverley's idiom, improvement. The contradiction between the two meanings of "garden" is a perfect index of the larger difference between the primitive and the pastoral ideals.[53]

The dual image of the garden as natural, sufficing abundance and as a product of civilizing labor cuts across major oppositions in North American thought. Gardens reunite nature and culture.[54] They bring together natural substance and reproductive potential with social labor and production. In the Cree world, where humans, animals, and God live in a spiritually and socially unified world, separations are not so radical and do not need to be so complexly bridged. For Quebecers, Canadians, and Americans the image of the garden offers the possibility of bridging the oppositions, and as such it does convey a sense of the Cree world, a world in which people are part of the landscape, a spiritual land that one can both work and love, and yet never fully possess. These ambiguities were significant for the rich usage the Cree developed.

Gardening and Environmentalists

For example, the image of the garden also has an ambiguity with respect to gender—an ambiguity that hunting does not. Gardening, depending on the variety and the time period, has associations with both genders. From decade to decade the loci can shift but, throughout much of the last century in Europe and America, there have often been gardening roles available to and associated with both women and men. The Cree world of work is clearly gendered, although either gender can easily take on almost all of the productive roles associated with the other. To render hunting as gardening is to take a predominantly male-associated image of hunting, in North American symbols as well as Cree meanings, and associate it with a more gender-neutral context. This opens up the possibility of non-Natives unlinking hunting from male sport and aggressivity. It thus obscures the male dominance in Cree society as in Cree hunting.

But it also echoes the subsistence, reproductive, and procreative aspects of Cree hunting. It "fits" the structure of Cree subsistence activity insofar as Cree production depends on the mutuality of gendered tasks of predominantly male hunting with women's butchering, distributing, and preparing foods in Cree hunting camp life.

Garden images also unite the domestic and the wider work worlds, for there are flower gardens and home vegetable gardens and market gardens. Gardens thus offer the possibility of combining the aesthetic and nurturing needs with the goals of provisioning and earning cash. In the Cree world aesthetic and loving values, nurturing and work are united across the range of spaces, activities, and time. Again, the image of the garden gives non-Natives the opportunity to appreciate a world in which people can be seeking to produce for exchange and reproduce themselves and their world in unison through work at home and in a homeland.

At a more specific level, the metaphor transforms the killing associated with hunting into a harvest that is closer to urban environmental sentiments. This association with harvesting also happens to echo the Cree world, where animals give themselves to needy and respectful hunters. The linkage of hunting to harvesting also emphasizes the renewal of the "crop" and that the harvest does not need to be a "depletion," which is part of Cree images and practices.[55]

Such refocusing is, I suspect, very important in building broad support within environmental movements, where support of Cree as hunters is often uncomfortable, but where protecting Cree productive and domestic life is a potentially strong motivation. The fact that women are often a majority of the membership in environmental organizations is a part of this response.

In these senses, then, the metaphors of gardening facilitate understanding and support of Cree concerns among non-Native North Americans. This occurs both by moderating the oppositions and contradictions of North America's environmental concerns and by enriching the possibilities of new understandings that accord in part with Cree meanings and social relations. These meanings go beyond those that need to have been fully anticipated by Cree elders or by those non-Natives who have recontextualized the Cree elders' messages, although the potentialities may have been sensed.

Yet, some of the richness of the metaphor and of the unanticipated semiotic parallels could have been anticipated, because the metaphor is itself the product of the long contact the Cree have had with both

Christian discourses and the civilizing mission of fur-trade and church institutions. This plurality of meanings not only makes gardens a useful metaphor for alliances of resistance but also for nation-states and economic institutions.

Gardens and States

Gardens can serve very diverse state interests as royal gardens, public gardens, botanical gardens, urban green belts, or national parks. Each expresses specific state ideologies, power, and identities. These developments were repeated in the contemporary period, during the LaGrande project at James Bay, where Hydro-Québec set up nurseries and where it has planted tens of thousands of shrubs and trees at the portals of the most accessible public sites and along public highways. Its dams are major Quebec tourist sites, and guides point out the landscaping to tourists and, where possible, take them to see the nurseries and biological research centers. These horticultural and landscaping activities are part of its public relations claim that hydroelectric projects are not destroying the land, and that they are even "improving" on the northern environment, not least by making it more productive.

But these gardening and horticultural claims are constrained by productive circumstances, for the main project is still industrial. Alongside the thousands of plantings, the tourist guides and brochures also recount the millions of tons of earth moved, the miles of dykes built, and the cubic miles of water impounded. These glorifications of industrial accomplishments serve to support the technological and nationalist legitimations of the project and the state, but they also serve as a limit on the credible uses of the garden metaphor by the state.

On a more distant economic frontier, Jean and John Comaroff have linked the exemplary gardens of nineteenth-century southern African church missionaries to their anticipated role in transforming Tswana society and economy in the direction of English yeomanry and an idealized peasant life.[56] They have also linked these gardens back to England, where gardening was promoted in the nineteenth century among the emerging working classes. Here, it was the loss of rural and feudal societies—as the growth of markets, industrialization, and urbanization transformed social conditions for workers—which some churches sought to moderate as they evangelized.[57] Gardens and gardening were practices and metaphors mobilized in response to, or in the hope of, economic and social transformations. But, again, gardening was used by dominant institutions not simply or continuously as an expression of economic motors of change. Gardening was either to repair the ills of economic change, as in England, or to create a change different from that which could be expected as a result principally of economic forces, as in southern Africa.

Thus, gardening, even as mobilized by states and market institutions and for economic ends, carried a complex set of social meanings and evaluations that did not facilitate restricting its service to the narrower interests of those dominant institutions. It carried with it references to alternative pasts or to other possible futures, which supported forms of resistance not intentionally encouraged by the state. Christian missions and fur trade posts in the James Bay region echoed this pattern.

Colonial Gardens at James Bay

The image of the garden in the Cree world speaks directly to the relations between Cree and whitemen and to the problems arising in those relationships. Gardens and the garden metaphor raise questions about whitemen's claims to land ownership and their exclusionary claims to being civilized. In the James Bay Cree communities, garden metaphors recall specific experiences of colonial relations, where the H.B.C. and the Anglican and Roman Catholic Churches all staked out and worked garden plots.

The mission and H.B.C. plots were mainly to produce vegetables, and especially potatoes that could serve the traders' households and the mission houses through the long winters in the settlement. The gardens required a lot of care to produce a worthwhile crop in these northern locations, and they were the focus of considerable attention in the small enclave of Euro-Canadians. Gardens were a symbol of difference, but Cree who worked closely with the church missions or the H.B.C. had plots of their own.[58]

Gardens in the north often involved a rather particular transformation of foods, because many of the gardens were fertilized with locally caught fish. The transformation of good fish into potatoes signalled the superiority given to gardening and its harvests by Euro-Canadians, in comparison with how Euro-Canadians valued Cree hunting and fishing products and bush foods.[59]

How gardens symbolized civility for Europeans is indicated in the first widely circulated popular book on the James Bay region in the twentieth century, W. Tees Curran and H. A. Calkins' *In Canada's Wonderful Northland: A Story of Eight Months of Travel by Canoe, Motorboat, and Dog-Team on the Northern Rivers and along the New Quebec Coast of Hudson Bay* (1917).[60] Their account also suggests how they judged fellow Euro-Canadians, and how Cree had some access to colonial discourses as household servants.

Their account of each fur trade post visited on James Bay begins with a description of its gardens and includes photographs.[61] The local and colonial meanings attached to the gardens as symbols for, and general means of, occupying northern lands and civilizing indigenous peoples was clear in their description of arriving at Fort George:

> As soon as we could get the camp in order and don our town clothes, we repaired to the [H.B.C.] Factory to partake of a sumptuous repast in real civilized fashion, the first in nearly a month. What a pleasant experience it was to sit on a chair and eat appetizing food from china dishes, with silver cutlery, on a real table covered with snow-white linen.
>
> . . . [Mr. Griffith, the H.B.C. Manager] did not fare so badly, having a number of servants to attend to his needs. He was particularly fortunate in having a good Indian cook, who had been practicing the art under the direction of Mrs. Griffith.
>
> On entering the house, we were strongly reminded of our former visit. Mr. Gillies was the Factor [Managing Partner] at the time, and during the intervening five years we had never thought of Fort George without having recollections of him and his fine vegetable garden. It had been a great surprise to find so large a collection of vegetables in such a well kept garden. . . .[62]

Curran and Calkins went on to visit the famous Anglican missionary W. G. Walton, whose work and influence they praised. They then turned their attention to the future of the region, noting that:

> As has ever been the case where Indian people have encountered the advances of the white man's civilization, the result has been either an-

nihilation or their assimilation. If the former is not to be the case, . . .
preventive measures should be taken.

    Firstly educative: . . . for as the white man crowds the Indian from
his natural means of livelihood, it certainly becomes the white man's
duty to educate and fit him for the farm and workshop. . . .[63]

As it turns out, agriculture proved to be an illusion for regions this
far north, and white men "crowded" the Indian from his lands only
later, as industrial resource developments became attractive. But colonial visions of civilizing influences and change were points of contention and dialogue between Euro-Canadians and an often hidden
indigenous discourse.

    The civilizing and educational value of gardening for Euro-Canadians
was expressed in the protection they gave to garden plots, by putting
up fences and by making clear that the harvests belonged to those who
claimed the gardens. It was these features, among others, that were
part of the historical roots of Cree elders' usage of the garden metaphor to convey specific meanings about the land to other Cree.

Critiques of Neo-Colonial Relations

By contrast to the published Canadian visitors' accounts, Cree elders'
stories and messages about gardens convey partial disapproval. Some
widely told stories in Cree villages recount instances of whitemen
lecturing and punishing Cree children and adults who took crops from
fenced garden plots. Others tell of incidents when some church representatives were not as generous with their crops as Cree thought that
they should have been, especially when Cree who were in need came
for help. These stories assert a Cree value of reciprocity with land and
food in the face of whitemen's ideas of how the land and harvests
should be owned and used.

    Cree elders use stories of gardens to draw both analogies to white-
men and distinctions, for Cree hunters also insist that the way they
share the land contrasts with some whitemen's gardens and land uses.
This is explicit in the stories above as well as in another statement by
Job Bearskin. While standing on a hill on the hunting lands he was
steward of, and pointing out all the places he could see for miles
around which were good for animals, he said to the filmmakers and to
the young Cree translator:

That is why we call the whole place our garden. . . . Around here you do not see any fences preventing people from trespassing. We let others help themselves. I am happy when other Indians kill something because it helps me. And that is why we care for this place. This is the place where the animals and the plants reproduce every year. The whole place is a garden, and they have done well this year.[64]

Here, the garden is not a private plot, but the whole land, which is used by those in need and cared for and shared by those who use it regularly. A critique of missionary resource use in very similar terms was debated in the community in the years immediately preceding Job's comments.[65] Thus, Job's and other elders' comments on Cree reciprocity can be set in the context not only of hydroelectric development, but of both the current general relations between Cree and whitemen, and of the longer term, critical Cree discourses—public and hidden—on colonial relations.[66]

Job's emphasis on the reciprocity of Cree land use asserts and re-asserts Cree understandings as the correct ones, as opposed to white-men's views and practices. Here, the metaphor of the garden is also an example of Cree resistance to values of dominant social institutions. It distinguishes Cree culture from non-Native values, understandings, and practices. It is a representation intended to mobilize and empower, by affirming the civilized nature, the ultimate morality, and the value of Cree understandings and practices. It questions the inevitability of the demise of hunting, and of its subordination, and shares that vision with other Cree. It affirms Cree values partly as a means to limiting the spread among Cree of values from non-Native society.

Intergenerational Alliance and Consensus

When Cree elders spoke out about the dangers of adopting whiteman values within Cree society, they often addressed Cree youth. When Job spoke to Boyce Richardson on film, he spoke to and through Gilbert Herodier, the young Cree filmmaker recently returned from schooling and from living outside the village, who was impressed by the beauty of Job's speech. Job and other elders were generally concerned about the youth. During his preparation for appearing in the Cree court case in 1972–1973, Job said:

> Since education started for our children, our children are not the same. Our children and grandchildren do not think of the future like we old people think of the future. . . . The white school teaches you not to think like an Indian but only like a whiteman. Children are no longer Indian minded today . . . .
>
> . . . The people are not the same since the whiteman came, everyone is becoming strangers. The whiteman is trying to throw their culture, if they have any, on us. They are trying to make us become like the white-man. Our children are affected and their future is uncertain.[67]

Many of the statements of Cree elders were addressed to Cree youth, and the message of Cree hunting as gardening has circulated throughout the Cree communities over the last three decades, both as oral history and in diverse contemporary media. It has served Cree of several generations who have found it a felicitous way to express their concerns to each other.

For example, elder John Petagumscum from Whapmagoostui used the metaphor to address Cree and non-Cree audiences. Petagumscum's comments in 1990 were quoted in the Annual Report of the Grand Council of the Crees, a document circulated mainly among young and middle-aged Cree in administrative and political positions within Cree organizations: "The land and the rivers where the people hunt and fish are a garden, a gift from the Creator. It has to be treated with love and respect to ensure that its spirit lives forever."[68]

An extended and personal use of the metaphor by a middle-aged adult is exemplified in Chisasibi resident Margaret Sam-Cromarty's poems in her volume *James Bay Memoirs*. Her poem "Garden" speaks of the garden "hidden from many men," which nurtured Cree youth. "Seven Steps" recalls hunters' own understandings of land as gardens in the midst of destructive transformations of the land, such as the massive stepped overflow sluice at the LG-2 dam:

> . . .
> The trappers watch
> the massive hydro dam
> Out of rock, seven steps.
> In their tongue they spoke of the cunning of the white man.
>
> No one hears
> the lowly trappers'
> whisper there was a garden.

The big corporations
said Indian land was worthless.
. . .
The trappers seldom spoke.
To learn the other man's ways
would not be wise.
They move on
with their beaver traps.
(1988)[69]

A felicitous and playfully familiar use of the metaphor was the naming of the new hockey arena for Chisasibi youth, many of which are ardent hockey players and followers of professional hockey on television, as Job's Memorial Gardens.[70]

These uses help to educate and mobilize Cree of different generations and lifestyles about how to see relations with whitemen and how to support the hunters to resist transformations of the land. They have played a role in the political mobilization among Cree and in the building of critical alliances in villages between Cree elders, hunters, administrators, political leaders, and youth. Those alliances are foundations of the broad consensus that the Cree "garden," and the hunters' "way of life" should be defended by Cree leaders and organizations for the benefit of all generations of Cree.

A recent usage that makes these connections comes from a middle-aged hunter and leader who offered support and encouragement to fellow Cree to continue hunting and trapping the land. He started by talking of the loss of elders and the need to learn from them while they were alive, and he went on to talk about the threats to the Cree hunters from animal rights activists whose efforts to ban fur pelt sales were negatively affecting the ability of Cree to continue to hunt. In between he said:

> Next thing I would like to say, to all of you who are still hunting and living off the land: it's very important that you carry on this tradition. . . . I truly believe what it says in the book of Genesis 11: 7-8. In verse 7 it says that God gave people different languages. . . . In verse 8, it says "He scattered them." He gave them different languages and made them different nations, and that's you and me. We might ask two things, where were our ancestors placed and why were they placed there? He placed our ancestors in a middle of a garden from where they could benefit from the land. Land and nature we call it. This is where

*Figure 2. Three seated Cree youth (l. to r.: Flora [Saganash] Gilpin,
William Saganash, Jr., and Jacob Otter) displaying ducks shot by Paul
Ottereyes, standing in the background. Display composed by Cree elders
for Harvey Feit to photograph as a sign of respect for the animals.*

you trappers who are still hunting to survive from the land are right now. A place that was given to us to benefit from in the beginning of creation. Why did He place the Crees amongst the beauty of his creation when He scattered the nations of the world. This is why we should benefit from this garden, just like Adam and Eve when God placed them in the Garden of Eden, but our garden is the land and nature. He put berries in Adam and Eve's garden and He also put berries in our garden but not the same kind. The fruits in our garden are the animals, all kinds of animals, birds, fish and also different kinds of fruits, from which we can benefit and make our living. These are the fruits He created for us in the garden that He placed us to live in. I'm sure that all of you are getting anxious now, that September is getting near, and preparing to go to your traplines. I'm like that too, I'm anxious that I'll be able go to my trapline for three weeks next month, and to find out what blessings God has in store for me.[71]

Jean-Elizabeth Meskino, a secondary student from Nemaska, echoed many of these themes, as well as themes from environmentalist interpretations of hunting, in her 1991 essay for the Cree School Board's James Bay Day publication:

> Many young children, such as young boys that are 7–12 years old, enjoy hunting with their fathers and grandfathers. The children believe in what they fight for. They tell their parents 'Once I am old enough to go do things on my own, I want to be a hunter or a fisherman and share or sell an animal I killed!' But phase II and Hydro Quebec will destroy what they believe.
>
> Many elders stand up against Hydro Quebec. . . .
>
> Many young native girls enjoy sewing. They make moccasins, mittens, gloves, lampshades and other things out of caribou or moose hide. If phase II does happen there will be less moose and caribou to eat and use the hide for sewing with. I don't know many cultural traditions, but I still care for them. . . .
>
> Once hydro finishes planning phase II and tells . . . what they are going to do, then they will tell the Crees. Now the Crees are fighting for the land. But so far the Crees are not winning yet. If the young natives want phase II stopped, they too have to stand up against Hydro Quebec. They can't just complain to their peers. Once all the phases are done with, where will the Crees live? Where will our sons and grandsons hunt?
>
> What do you think would happen if you were in Ottawa and saw a garden with a lot of roses and other flowers and you started to pick

them? Or if you walked on someone's lawn? You'd get a fine of course, maybe we should give Hydro Quebec a fine too. They've destroyed a lot of trees and land.

I enjoy going to old Nemiscau with my family, it is very peaceful. There are no loud machines. People could go hunting and fishing anywhere they wanted to.[72]

Conclusions

Cree use of the garden metaphor not only instructs Cree youth, it invites Quebecers, Canadians, and Americans to understand the Cree, to see them as civilized and moral. It is intended to encourage whitemen to learn from the Cree about proper relations. The colonial and local cultural context for understanding some of the meanings that are conveyed in these discourses are not available to many Quebecers, Canadians, and Americans. Yet, the basic call to generosity and respect is conveyed in the domestic, Christian, and moral references, if not by the colonial contexts. These communications depend both on coincidental parallels and on quiet echoes of historical relations and discourses from the partially shared histories of missionization and trade which leave traces of connections in some of the mutualities between Cree and Quebecer, Canadian and American understandings.

The metaphor of the garden is an example of Cree cultural production, which uses symbols from an encapsulating culture, in combination with Cree discourses, to communicate with and oppose white man development. It is also a means to enrich Cree resistance and autonomy by conveying Cree understandings that limit the spread of the values of the encapsulating society among Cree themselves. The Cree are able to direct their political actions toward both these goals in complex ways.

They use metaphors derived not only from the institutions that assert dominance over them and their lands, but from historical and ongoing experiences of relations and communications between Cree and nondominant non-Native institutions. They use these discursive strategies not only to oppose dominant institutions but to build understandings and international alliances with groups opposing those institutions within non-Native societies, as well as to mobilize public opinion in jurisdictions where decisions are taken that affect

Cree lands and lives. They use complex and ambiguous metaphors in ways that highlight the values of sociality, productiveness, and morality in non-Native society, emphasizing, for example, the domestic and self-sufficient aspects of their lives as well as those spiritual aspects that they share or that echo with wider Christian understandings. These rhetorical strategies help us to understand how broad public support for Cree, and against the impacts of development, can be mobilized in urban centers at considerable physical and interpretive distance from the Cree and their lands.

Cree spokespersons build these understandings with non-Natives without sole reliance on more conventional strategies of claiming an idealized traditionality or religiosity, or solely on indigenous legal rights, or solely on political lobbying as citizens or ethnic groups. They thus limit the marginalization, subordination, and constraint that are inherent in focusing solely on being Indian, or on legal rights, or in accepting the political system as it is.

While specific metaphors are used to highlight commonalities, these same metaphors have a long colonial history of oppositional use within Cree society, where they highlight differences between Cree and non-Native values and practices for new generations of Cree.

Gardening draws on, reproduces, and modifies Cree symbols of land, sociality, autonomy, reciprocity, and spirituality. By joining meanings from both cultures, Cree elders show that we can understand representations of environment most effectively at the intersection of cultures, but that we have to attend to the histories and uses of political and discursive strategies. The partially successful campaign by Cree against the second phase of hydroelectric development exemplifies these complex practices, linking Cree and non-Cree supporters in dialogues which build bridges while strengthening commitments to differences and enhancing long-term autonomy.

Notes

A version of this paper was delivered as the Harry Hawthorn Lecture at the Canadian Anthropology Society annual meetings, May 2000. In the course of developing this paper, I have drawn insights from discussions with many people, and at the risk of omitting some, let me thank: Philip Awashish, Mario Blaser, James Bobbish, Brian Craik, Rick Cuciurean, Paul Dixon, Christian Feest, Jasmin Habib, Glenn McRae, Marie Mauzé, Toby Morantz, Douglas Nakashima, Bill Namagoose, Alan Penn, Richard Preston, Boyce Richardson, Marie Roué, Wendy Russell, Diom Saganash, Cory Silverstein, Colin Scott, Bill Simeone, Chris Trott, and Jeremy Webber. The research on which this paper is based was funded through grants from the Social Sciences and Humanities Research Council of Canada (SSHRC Grants 410-99-1208, 410-96-0946, 410-93-0505, 410-90-0802, and 803-91-0035), and from the Arts Research Board of McMaster University.

1. I will refer to non-Native North American societies also as Quebecers, Canadians, or Americans, or occasionally as Euro-Canadians or Euro-Americans, depending on the context.

2. James C. Scott, *Weapons of the Weak: Everyday Forms of Peasant Resistance* (New Haven: Yale University Press, 1985).

3. Benedict Anderson, *Imagined Communities: Reflections on the Origin and Spread of Nationalism,* 2d ed. (New York: Verso, 1991).

4. Roger M. Keesing, *Custom and Confrontation: The Kwaio Struggle for Cultural Autonomy* (Chicago: University of Chicago Press, 1992).

5. Elizabeth A. Povinelli, *Labor's Lot: The Power, History, and Culture of Aboriginal Action* (Chicago: University of Chicago Press, 1993), 242.

6. Barri Cohen makes a partly similar argument for Canada, and especially for James Bay, although I only read his piece after I had finished this article ("Technological Colonialism and the Politics of Water," *Cultural Studies* 8, no. 1 [1994]: 32–55). While Cohen notes how indigenousness is constructed by and to serve nation-states, he also stresses that it has unintended effects and becomes a tool in oppositional politics (p. 38). His argument complements some of the analysis of the Cree presented in this paper, albeit with different materials. I am indebted to Suzie O'Brien for pointing his work out to me.

7. The Inuit of Canada were formerly called Eskimos by Euro-Americans.

8. See Richard F. Salisbury, *A Homeland for the Cree* (Montreal: McGill-Queen's Press, 1986).

9. Cohen ("Technological Colonialism") makes a similar point, but he implies that the state sought this construction of Cree collectivities. In the initial years of the Cree opposition to the James Bay projects, from 1971 until the court ruling at the end of 1973, recognizing that the Cree had rights, it was the Cree who claimed indigenous legal rights and political status and it was state officials that denied any role for the Cree other than as citizens or townships. The court recognition of the rights claimed by the Cree forced other state institutions to use a strategy founded in part on the distinct indigenousness of the Cree.

10. I will use the term "whitemen" to refer to Cree ideas of non-Natives, as distinct from how non-Natives see themselves. On fur trade history, see: Daniel Francis and Toby Morantz, *Partners in Furs: A History of the Fur Trade in Eastern James Bay,*

1600–1870 (Montreal: McGill-Queen's University Press, 1983); also Harvey A. Feit, "The Enduring Pursuit: Land, Time and Social Relationships in Anthropological Models of Hunter-Gatherers and in Hunters' Images," in *Key Issues in Hunter-Gatherer Research,* ed. E. S. Burch, Jr., and L. J. Ellanna (Oxford: Berg Publishers, 1991), 421–39.

11. For accounts of these trips and of the campaign, see Michael Posluns, *Voices from the* Odeyak (Toronto: NC Press, 1993); Michael Posluns, "The James Bay Story So Far," electronic text circulated through web.native, 3 March 1993; and Sean McCutcheon, *Electric Rivers: The Story of the James Bay Project* (Montreal: Black Rose, 1991).

12. The clearest evidence of these impacts has been the alienation of the Cree within Quebec political life, a shift that was articulated by the minister of energy at the time, and that has cost the Cree much in workable relations since. At the time the minister said:

> Yes, I blame them [the Cree] for what they've been doing. I blame them for discrediting Quebec all over the world. Do you think a Quebecer can accept that? I don't think so.
>
> Are they Quebecers or not? They live in our territory. They live with us, they work with us and they're penalizing Quebecers. That's what I cannot accept and I will never accept. (*The Gazette,* Montreal, 4/1/92. The minister's statement also appears, in part, in the documentary film *Power,* directed by Magnus Isacsson, Cineflix Productions in association with the National Film Board of Canada [distributor] and TVOntario, 1996).

The minister's anger reveals the inutility of the Cree to the state at this moment. Subsequent confrontations between Cree and later separatist Quebec governments have entrenched this division, although the issue remains complex. In the case of Quebec separation, the Cree claim a right to decide which state they would ally with, and they assert that their lands would go with them (ca. 140,000 sq. mi.). This has become a major problem for Quebec's assertion of a right to separate from Canada, because the integrity of its boundaries would enhance chances of international legitimation and recognition. But it has also made the Cree useful to the Canadian state in its fights against Quebec separation, and therefore also made it easy for separatists to portray Cree in Quebec as tools of the Canadian state.

13. See A. Irving Hallowell, for his pioneering work on the related views of the Ojibwa, *Culture and Experience* (Philadelphia: University of Pennsylvania Press, 1955), and *Contributions to Anthropology: Selected Papers of A. Irving Hallowell* (Chicago: University of Chicago Press, 1976).

14. Colin H. Scott, "Science for the West, Myth for the Rest? The Case of James Bay Cree Knowledge Construction," in *Naked Science: Anthropological Inquiry into Boundaries, Power, and Knowledge,* ed. Laura Nader (New York: Routledge, 1996), 75.

15. Richard J. Preston, *Cree Narrative: Expressing the Personal Meanings of Events,* Canadian Ethnology Service, no. 30 (Ottawa: National Museums of Canada, 1975); and Scott, "Science."

16. See, for example, Adrian Tanner, *Bringing Home Animals: Religious Ideology and Mode of Production of the Mistassini Cree* (London: Hurst), 1979.

17. Harvey A. Feit, "Hunting and the Quest for Power: The James Bay Cree and Whitemen in the Twentieth Century," in *Native Peoples: The Canadian Experience,* ed. R. B. Morrison and C. R. Wilson, 2d ed. (Toronto: McClelland and Stewart, 1995), 181–223.

18. See Robert F. Berkhofer, *The White Man's Indian: Images of the Indian from Columbus to the Present* (New York: Vintage Books, 1979).

19. Couture's statement appears on film in *Power,* directed by Magnus Isacsson. Also see other statements in that film by Couture and by Hydro-Québec President Richard Drouin, as well as statements by Hydro-Québec spokespersons in the documentary *Power of the North,* directed by Catherine Bainbridge and Anna Vander Wee (Wild Heart Productions in association with MTV, CityTV, MuchMusic [Canadian distribution by Kaleidoscope Entertainment], 1994).

20. For discussions of other discursive strategies, see Donna Patrick, "Language, Power and Resistance: Discourses on Hydroelectric Development in Great Whale River, Quebec" (unpublished manuscript, University of Toronto, OISE, [1992]); and Cohen, "Technological Colonialism."

21. See Colin H. Scott, "Property, Practice and Aboriginal Rights among Quebec Hunters," in *Hunters and Gatherers,* vol. 2, ed. Tim Ingold, David Riches, and James Woodburn (New York: Berg, 1988), 35–51.

22. See Harvey A. Feit, "Legitimation and Autonomy in James Bay Cree Responses to Hydro-Electric Development," in *Indigenous Peoples and the Nation-State,* ed. Noel Dyck (St. John's: Institute of Social and Economic Research, Memorial University of Newfoundland, 1985), 27–66.

23. Boyce Richardson, *James Bay: The Plot to Drown the North Woods* (San Francisco: Sierra Club; and Toronto: Clarke, Irwin and Company, 1972), 184; Richardson, *Strangers Devour the Land* (New York: Alfred Knopf; Toronto: Macmillan, 1975; reprint, Toronto: Douglas and McIntyre, 1991); and, Richardson, *Job's Garden* (Toronto: Tamarack Productions, 1974), film.

24. Fieldnotes, Fort George, 9 April 1974, translated from the Cree at the meeting.

25. Ibid.

26. Fieldnotes, Fort George, 19 June 1974, translated from the Cree at the meeting.

27. Ibid.

28. Richardson, *Job's Garden.*

29. Richardson, *Strangers.*

30. Richardson has written about how he met Job Bearskin in 1971 on a trip to write some freelance pieces on James Bay:

On that trip, I met a number of people in Fort George, including a man called Job Bearskin who was one of the many hunters brought to my hotel to discuss with me what they thought about the hydro-electric development. I was very impressed by the dignity of this man—he's a wonderful, tall, proud man (Boyce Richardson, "A Return to Job's Garden," in *On the Land: Confronting the Challenges to Aboriginal Self-Determination in Northern Quebec and*

Labrador, ed. Bruce W. Hodgins and Kerry A. Cannon [Toronto: Betelgeuse Books, 1995], 150).

31. Richardson, *James Bay: The Plot,* 184. A parallel usage that was widespread in an earlier period in the regions to the south of the James Bay Cree area was the related metaphor of indigenous hunting territories practices as farming. Its use was common among indigenous spokespersons for communities whose lands were experiencing expanded colonization by non-Natives early in this century, as well as among anthropologists who discussed the Algonquian family hunting territory system with them. See Harvey A. Feit, "The Construction of Algonquian Hunting Territories: Private Property as Moral Lesson, Policy Advocacy and Ethnographic Error," in *Colonial Situations: Essays in the Contextualization of Ethnographic Knowledge,* ed. George Stocking, Jr., History of Anthropology Series, vol. 7 (Madison: University of Wisconsin Press, 1991), 120–21.

32. Recorded on film, Richardson, *Job's Garden,* and in print, Richardson, *Strangers,* 151.

33. Robert Bourassa, *James Bay* (Montreal: Harvest House), 7–8.

34. Ibid., 10.

35. Ibid., 117 and 120.

36. Job and other elders were active Christians, and Job had served for many years as an active lay reader at St. Philip's Anglican Church (Nellie Pashagumiskum, "In Memory of Joab Bearskin," *Northland* 46 [winter, 1989–90]: 7), which often lacked a resident minister. The Cree elders were well familiar with biblical texts and references, and their speeches frequently refer to the sacredness of the land. One anonymous reviewer of an earlier version of this paper noted that there was no direct evidence and only an inference that Job Bearskin was influenced by Judeo-Christian ideas of "Eden," ideas which the reader pointed out do not correspond to Cree usage, for example, with respect to whether animals are subjected to human authority. I have inferred that Cree elders' use of the garden metaphor referred in part to ideas of Eden and biblical references based on the way Christian ideas and ideals informed the lives and speech of so many of that generation of Cree elders. In conversations at this time, there was also frequent reference by Job and others elders not only to gardens but to the flooding the project would cause. I should, however, also be clear that I am not saying that Cree are referring to authoritative Judeo-Christian ideas of "Eden." I think they are referring to Cree-Judeo-Christian ideas that emphasize the harmonious relations between all divinely created creatures in the garden. (See below for other instances of Cree perceptions of differences as well as similarities between Cree and some non-Native Christians' ideas of Christianity.)

37. *James Bay Forum: Public Hearings on the James Bay Project Held in Montreal, April, 1973,* ed. Fikret Berkes (Montreal: James Bay Committee, 1973), 83, 65.

38. Roy MacGregor, *Chief: The Fearless Vision of Billy Diamond* (Markham: Viking Penguin, 1989), 104.

39. Wemindji, directly south of Chisasibi, had significant flooding of its lands during the first phase of the project. This statement was also published, along with texts from many other Cree youth opposing the hydroelectric developments, in *James*

Bay Day (Mistassini: Cree School Board, 1991). Brian Georgekish's text is on page 5.

40. Grand Council of the Crees (of Quebec), *Fighting for Our Future* (pamphlet, "Supplement to the Hill Times, August 1, 1991"), 1.

41. Posluns, *Voices from the* Odeyak, 74. For parallel uses at this period, see Sanders Wiestchie's talk at the Northeast Regional James Bay Action Conference at Cornell University, quoted in Glen Cooper et al., "Cree Stories," *Northeast Indian Quarterly* 8 (winter 1991): 31; and, Charles Cheezo's statement to Hydro-Québec, quoted in Laurent Lepage and François Blanchard, "Analyse de contenu des audiences publiques 'Grande-Baleine': étude exploratoire," ([Montreal]: unpublished report presented to the V.P. Communication et Relations publiques, Hydro-Québec, 1992), 90.

42. Elisabeth May had been the director of Indigenous Survival Canada. She had worked with the Sierra Club Canada and with the Grand Council of the Crees (of Quebec) on its campaign against the Great Whale River hydroelectric development.

43. Farley Mowat and Elisabeth May, "James Bay: le plus grand projet hydro-électrique d'Amérique du Nord," *Message Amérindien International* 1 (spring 1993): 22. First published in *Wild Earth,* 1991.

44. Jamie Sayen and Michael Posluns, *A History of James Bay Development* (pamphlet; Cambridge, Mass.: Northeast Alliance to Protest James Bay, 1991), 5.

45. Boyce Richardson, *Flooding Job's Garden* (Toronto: Canadian Broadcasting Company and the National Film Board of Canada, 1991). Also see Isacsson, *Power;* and Bainbridge and Vander Wee, *Power of the North.*

46. Despite the widespread use of the garden metaphor by Cree and activists, there is little independent evidence of public responses to it, especially in the larger urban centers where its impact would be expected to be most significant. However, for an important analysis of other specific forms of rhetorical, experiential, and organizational connections that did develop between Cree and environmental supporters in Vermont, see Glenn McRae, "Fighting the Distant Battle: Multi-faceted Mirrors of Vermont Solidarity with James Bay Cree" (Ph.D. diss., The Union Institute, Cincinatti, Ohio, forthcoming).

47. Mowat and May, "James Bay," 22.

48. "During the rest of that Arctic sojourn I abandoned the blinkers of scientific attitudes and struggled instead to fathom the nature of the inter-species empathy and understanding which existed between the Inuit and other creatures of the Barren-lands." Farley Mowat, *Rescue the Earth! Conversations with the Green Crusaders* (Toronto: McClelland and Stewart, 1990), 17.

49. Mowat, *Rescue,* 25.

50. Ibid., 15.

51. Keith Thomas, *Man and the Natural World: Changing Attitudes in England, 1500–1800* (Harmondsworth: Penguin, 1984); Carolyn Merchant, *The Death of Nature: Women, Ecology, and the Scientific Revolution* (San Francisco: Harper and Row, 1989); Leo Marx, *The Machine in the Garden: Technology and the Pastoral Ideal in America* (London: Oxford University Press, 1964).

52. Marx, *Machine,* 84.

53. Ibid., 85.

54. On this cultural duality, see David M. Schneider, *American Kinship: A Cultural Account,* 2d ed. (Chicago: University of Chicago Press, 1980).

55. Some animal rights activists have attacked the rhetoric of calling hunted animals "harvests" on precisely these grounds: it confuses and obscures that hunting is killing. See John Livingston, symposium presentation in *A Question of Rights: Northern Wildlife Management and the Anti-Harvest Movement—National Symposium on the North,* ed. Robert F. Keith and Alan Saunders (Ottawa: Canadian Arctic Resources Committee, 1989), 118.

56. John L. Comaroff and Jean Comaroff, *Of Revelation and Revolution: The Dialectics of Modernity on a South African Frontier,* vol. 2 (Chicago: University of Chicago Press, 1997), 121.

57. Jean Comaroff, *Body of Power, Spirit of Resistance: The Culture and History of a South African People* (Chicago: University of Chicago Press, 1985); Jean Comaroff and John Comaroff, *Of Revelation and Revolution: Christianity, Colonialism, and Consciousness in South Africa,* vol. 1 (Chicago: University of Chicago Press, 1991); John Comaroff and Jean Comaroff, *Ethnography and the Colonial Imagination* (Boulder, Colo.: Westview Press, 1992).

58. Cree were also sometimes employed to do work in the gardens of fur traders and missionaries.

59. I am indebted to Ignatius LaRusic, who pointed this out to me.

60. W. Tees Curran and H. A. Calkins, *In Canada's Wonderful Northland: A Story of Eight Months of Travel by Canoe, Motorboat, and Dog-Team on the Northern Rivers and along the New Quebec Coast of Hudson Bay* (New York: G. P. Putnam's, 1917).

61. The trip was motivated by the building of the new transcontinental railway, some 150 miles south of the foot of James Bay, and the conviction that new transportation routes and agricultural settlement would follow around the Bay gave gardening a particular role in their accounts of the future potential of the region (Curran and Calkins, *In Canada's Wonderful Northland,* vi and 120).

62. Ibid., 115–16. Note their opposition of "Indian" and "white man."

63. Ibid., 120.

64. Richardson, *Strangers,* 167.

65. The specific point of conflict in 1969 was over reciprocity. The new Anglican missionary had tried to make the parish self-supporting, in keeping with an Anglican Church vision statement that parishes be localized. To do so, he had shifted the focus from the church as giver and had dramatically increased demands for collections and for volunteer labor to create parish self-sufficiency. Jacqueline Hyman, a McGill graduate student in anthropology, did fieldwork at Fort George in the summer of 1969, focusing on the conflict between the minister and the Cree parishioners. The minister told her that the church should be run like a business, and indeed he was a retired businessman. He offended Cree with regular and direct demands, which Cree said implied that they never give enough, and he failed to meet Cree standards of generosity himself, paying wages to volunteer labor from the south but not compensating or reciprocating local parishioners for their work. Jacqueline Hyman, "Conflicting Perceptions of Exchange in Indian-Missionary Contact" (master's thesis, McGill University, 1971).

66. For a fuller analysis of the elders' views at this period, see Feit, "Legitimation and Autonomy."

67. Job Bearskin, "Dialogue with Job Bearskin" (legal briefing notes, copy in the possession of the author, two pages typescript, [1972 or 1973]).

68. John Petagumscum, quoted in the Grand Council of the Crees (of Quebec), *Annual Report,* 1989/90, 23.

69. Margaret Sam-Cromarty, *James Bay Memoirs: A Cree Woman's Ode to Her Homeland* (Lakefield, Ont.: Waapoone Publishing, 1992). I am indebted to Margaret Sam-Cromarty and her publisher for permission to quote from her poem. I am indebted to Cory Silverstein for bringing these poems to my attention.

70. I am indebted to Marie Roué and Douglas Nakashima for this example.

71. Transcript of a presentation by Thomas Coon of the Cree Trappers Association (C.T.A.) to the C.T.A. Waswanipi Assembly, 25 August 1998.

72. Cree School Board, *James Bay Day,* 11. See also the quotes from Cree of several generations in Cooper et al., "Cree Stories."

Sovereignty and Swaraj: Adivasi Encounters with Modernity and Majority

SMITU KOTHARI

> The whole universe is one single nest. Let there be peace with all the five elements, viz., earth, water, fire, air and ether. Let there be peace with herbs. Let there be peace with all living-beings. —*Rgveda*

> Throughout the *gayana,* the Bhilalas invoke the themes and symbols that are central to their universe—the teak tree, juvar,[1] the stars, the animals, the basis of social differentiation. Throughout the gayana flows the Narmada river, bestowing life-giving gifts to all whom she meets, naming and making sacred the geography of the land along her banks.[2]

The *gayana* is the myth of creation of the Bhilalas.[3] An epic poem celebrating the earth's gifts and giving thanks for fertility and plenitude, it is sung on the occasion of an annual festival. It celebrates the sharing of the prosperity of the family with the community. The creation and nurturing of life takes place in a complex process of negotiation and collaboration between humans and their gods. As part of this process, Beelubai, one of the first people, makes clay animals, breathes life into them, but then must engage in a long and tedious dialogue with the gods to ask them to give blood to the animals, which they do in the form of seeds, flowers, and trees. Each source of blood—*juvar,* grass, flowers, trees—becomes central to sustaining the web of life whose defense is a natural extension of their creation. The *gayana* is at once a creation myth, an extensive storehouse of knowledge and memory, and a cultural expression that nurtures identity.

Creation myths and sacred ways that celebrate life are intrinsic to the vast majority of India's adivasis. Today, they number about seventy-five million—roughly 7.5 percent of the country's population and 23 percent of the world's population of indigenous and tribal peoples. They are spread among 635 communities comprising 414 main tribes and other subtribes listed as Scheduled Tribes.[4] Speaking over one hundred languages, this remarkable diversity of cultural identities is geographically spread throughout the country, though the main areas of concentration are in the northeast, the east, and the entire central zone of India.

While any generalization is disrespectful of the vast diversity of traditions that has evolved in geographically diverse areas, there are clearly four elements that define the core of tribal traditions, their ecological practices, and their assertion of identity.

1. The centrality of forests, land, and place to their life sphere. An overwhelming majority still live in forest areas, and the forest has historically been the primary source of their physical and cultural life, the host of their gods and goddesses and of the spirits of their ancestors. Dispersed throughout adivasi areas are numerous sacred groves, encompassing a relatively undisturbed space of pristine biodiversity, numerous spirits, and gods and goddesses.

The forest has also been the center of private and state accumulation as colonial and post-independence governments have appropriated—legally and militaristically—most rights over the forests. In the past two centuries, an overwhelming majority of popular struggles and rebellions in adivasi areas have centered on the defense of place, where they, their histories, their ancestors, and their traditions reside. The forest is therefore also the space that encompasses the continuity of their collective resistance.

A series of comprehensive studies on the extent of alienation from land and forests was commissioned by the Department of Rural Development in the Ministry of Rural Areas and Employment of the Government of India. The reports paint a grim and disturbing picture and confirm that massive alienation of tribal lands continues in tribal regions in all parts of the country. Tribal land alienation is the most important manifestation of the pauperization as well as the growing insecurity and cultural erosion of tribal people. Their economic situation, which is vulnerable even at the best of times, has become even more precarious. The access of tribals to forests for their livelihood has shrunk, both because forests themselves have shrunk and because the regulatory regime continues to restrict tribals from collecting and processing nontimber forest produce for their livelihood. Shifting cultivation has also been severely restricted. The most important livelihood option of the tribal today is agriculture. However, as tribals are systematically deprived of their cultivable holdings and access to commons by nontribals and even by the government itself, they are reduced to assetless destitution. Starvation and large-scale migration are the end result, and it is this bleak scenario that recurs in all tribal regions throughout the country.

What has been witnessed in the valleys of the Narmada River, and in valleys and lands of the adivasis across the country, is not just administrative and bureaucratic negligence but an active process of engineering that subjects the adivasis to continuous interference and oppression. It is common that senior officials of the government rarely meet adivasi communities in their own villages; yet, they have accumulated a body of legislation that gives them the power to dominate almost every aspect of the adivasis' productive life. Often, officials visit communities only to bring the news that the people are to be displaced for a development project. In the case of the Narmada dams, for instance, these visits are all that communities, who will lose everything, get. For the Bhilalas and Bhils who reside in the area, the river is their mother, and the river, the valley, and the sphere of "life in place" are all an integral part of their identity. There are, for most of them, no boundaries between the cultural, the ecological, and the spiritual. To be compelled to leave, often with only a few weeks' notice, is tantamount to social and cultural violence. Several scholars have documented the enormous physiological and psychological pain that communities are subjected to when displaced from their sources of subsistence and meaning. The degree of attitudinal insensitivity to the importance of place, of spaces imbued with value, with spirit, and with livelihood, of the connection of place and the cosmos, raises critical questions for those concerned about the value of cultural pluralism in our world today. The inevitable justification, that "you are sacrificing for the larger good," or "for progress," or "in the national interest," has raised additional issues regarding who speaks on behalf of whom, who speaks for the nation—indeed, who comprises the nation? The dominant attitude is most sharply expressed in what a politician in the state of Gujarat said about tribals who were to be displaced by the reservoir of a proposed dam and who were resisting or seeking just and comprehensive resettlement: "they are rats who will be flushed out of their rat-holes when the waters rise."

In a recent article in one of India's leading newspapers, the *Hindustan Times*, Sumir Lal expresses this set of concerns quite succinctly:

> What a movement like the one in the Narmada Valley does is carry the voice of the people, the ones most directly affected by development policies, into the realm of public debate and policy making. It ensures that policy is negotiated in an informed manner by those formulating it and those affected by it.
>
> The people of the Narmada Valley have intense grievances; they are being destroyed in a manner that should send a chill down every citizen's spine. Yet, through their peaceful, mass, 15-year struggle, they have shown maturity, patience, understanding of the nation's imperatives, and democratic spirit. The nation should cherish and respect such citizens. To crush them, and to dismiss those willing to hear them as publicity-seekers or eccentrics or romantics, is to insult the very building blocks of our yet-evolving democracy.[5]

2. The primacy of community and the collective. The numerous creation myths and daily practices of the adivasis, such as the *gayana* of the Bhilalas, exhort the community to respect and nurture all life, communally. In the years after India became independent, Prime Minister Jawaharlal Nehru drafted a "policy," the *Panchsheel,* which pledged that the country would respect adivasis and allow them to nurture their own ways of being and come to terms with the "mainstream" in their own ways.

It is not a coincidence that even when the state spoke a language of non-interference, it systematically sought to undermine and subvert the customary rights and the collective stewardship of the forests that adivasi communities enjoyed, that is, by the creation of individual (predominantly male-centered) titles to land. Additionally, the power of eminent domain[6] and the concept of *res nullius* legalized the state's superiority. Consequently, a new basis for conflict was generated in an "independent" country whose administrative machinery became increasingly intrusive and interventionist in enforcing its dominion.[7] In the process, the developmentalist state, while mandated to mediate on behalf of the less privileged and the discriminated against, contributed to a process of alienating millions, appropriating or threatening their sovereignty. This contestation between the sovereignty of the nation and the sovereignty of peoples within the nation remains one of the most difficult cultural and political processes in post-independent India. The peoples' struggles reflect the need to limit the excesses in the use of state power. There is an urgent need to strengthen peoples' sovereignty, not only by recognizing the potential of communities to govern themselves and to control the natural resource systems that are at the center of their economies and identities, but also thereby to create conditions where the rights and powers of the state are limited and redefined. It is this critical process—of asserting the importance of place, of seeking greater control over one's life and life sphere, of redefining what independence and freedom mean, of strengthening self-governance, of reclaiming the sovereignty that has been systematically taken away, and, therefore, of seeking to democratize the state and other economic and cultural processes—that is currently at a nascent stage not only in India but all over the world.

3. The defense and regeneration of language. Every adivasi community's creation myths or epic verses and songs have been narrated and sung in their own language. They weave together an elaborate fabric of responsibilities within the natural world, often elaborately defining practices which regenerate life. The post-independence state organized and internally divided the country around dominant languages. All adivasi languages were neglected or consciously devalued. Additionally, the imposition of "national" or regional languages through the formal education system, including the privileging of English, has played havoc with most adivasi languages, many of which have become extinct in the last few decades. This process has contributed to the social and cultural fragmentation and the loss of self-confidence.

Language is a critical element in what constitutes tribal and indigenous heritage. While there is growing acknowledgment and mobilization around how their knowledge systems will be protected in a "hegemonizing" intellectual property rights regime,[8] addressing the conditions needed to nurture and strengthen language as a fulcrum of identity—when even the best schooling privileges dominant languages rather than a pluralism of languages, of which the tribal is a dignified, integral part—remains a neglected element of the struggle for sovereignty.

4. The struggle for political and economic autonomy. In the recent past, the sacred and natural worlds of the adivasis have been under an unprecedented threat, both from a developmentalist state that privileges national and transnational capital over its duties to nurture greater justice and equity and from a reductionist, distorted ideology of Hindutva[9] that is far removed from the essentially plural and tolerant Hindu ethos. A decline in, or retreat of, plural religious sensibilities, coupled with the degeneration of public morality, has fueled an aggressive, violent, and fascistic ideology that is attempting to reconfigure India into a Hindu "kingdom." Supported by a diaspora predominantly in North America and Britain that feeds on this illusion of a faith, the purveyors of this ideology seem comfortable with a marriage of convenience with the forces of economic globalization. This marriage has brought a new onslaught on adivasi areas and, as a related development, greater unrest and agitation among adivasi communities who are witnessing, like never before, the adverse impacts of economic development and the desacralized, aggressive, and instrumental use of religion. This growth in cultural and economic insecurity is a direct consequence of a process

> introduced into South Asian public life by a clutch of social reformers, intellectuals and public figures—seduced or brainwashed by the ethnocidal, colonial theories of social evolution and history—to subvert and discredit the traditional concepts of interreligious understanding and tolerance that had allowed thousands—yes, literally thousands—of communities living in the subcontinent to cosurvive in reasonable neighbourliness.[10]

The ecological essence of the Hindu ethos reflected in the extract of the *Rgveda* at the beginning of this essay has similarly been violated and forgotten.

National economic and cultural mainstreaming is now being globalized both by the diaspora of the forces of Hindutva and by the slow process of relinquishing economic control to transnational capital—

both in alliance with and autonomous from national capital. The national project of integration and absorption into the post-independence building of a new nation and the consequent loss of community sovereignty is being reinforced in the current phase of economic globalization—a phase that is also compounding the loss of political control in community affairs.

Despite these relentless processes, from within the margins and spaces of exclusion, facing overt and covert efforts to subjugate and co-opt them, adivasis have crafted remarkable initiatives of resistance. Based on a profoundly simple demand—that their lives and life systems could only be nurtured in a legally sanctioned framework of self-rule, or swaraj, they have launched local and nationwide agitation, mobilizing in the process support from a diverse range of social and political forces. Self-rule is seen as an essential ingredient of sovereignty.

Toward Swaraj

In 1994, the Indian government was compelled to form a parliamentary committee, headed by an adivasi member of parliament, to define the content and terms of self-rule. Following the committee's report, nationwide mobilization successfully pressured the government into legalizing the adivasis' right to govern themselves. On 24 December 1996, the Indian parliament passed legislation—Provisions of the Panchayats (Extension to the Scheduled Areas) Act, 1996 (hereafter referred to as PESA)—that called for the amendment of the Indian Constitution. Granting the right to self-rule in adivasi areas, the historic step marked, in Pradip Prabhu's words, "the first serious nail in the coffin of colonialism."[11] PESA is historic because it legally recognizes the capacity of adivasi communities to strengthen their own systems of self-governance or to create new legal spaces and institutions that not only can reverse centuries of external cultural and political onslaught, but can create the opportunities to control their own destinies.

The Gram Sabha of the village, comprising all adult men and women, would be the focal institution, which now has been endowed with significant powers. For instance, under section 4(d) of PESA: "every Gram Sabha shall be competent to safeguard and preserve the traditions and customs of the people, their cultural identity, community resources and the customary mode of dispute resolution."

Not only has the adivasi Gram Sabha been recognized as the institution that will be at the center of the process of restoring adivasi rights over their natural systems, but the adivasis have secured the right to adjudicate collectively all "external" development projects and programs. Finally, a framework for self-rule is in place.

There is some concern in this age of commodification and commercialization that, if given rights over resources, adivasis will themselves become predators. Communities (like the Warlis who are part of the Thane district–based Kashtakari Sangathna in the state of Maharashtra) which have begun to realize the potential of PESA argue that while these dangers do exist, this should not be used as an excuse to delay the implementation of PESA. In fact, they argue, efforts should be made to discuss how the whole gamut of democratic institutions needs to be rethought to strengthen local autonomy and provide checks to its misuse. The reality at the moment is that as communities assert greater control, they encounter apathy, even hostility, from local administrators who are under pressure from external and internal interests wishing to retain their exploitative hold over adivasi India.

The reluctance of those who have historically enjoyed power to accept its devolution and eventual loss is understandable. Some of this reluctance can even take vicious form, as those in power try to subvert local unity. It is time to realize that the growing aspirations of historically discriminated against and exploited peoples are not going away. Across the country, there is growing demand for greater transparency of government functioning and greater participation in defining what the content of development should be. Additionally, there are steadily growing instances of innovative efforts to redefine the structure and content of democratic institutions so that power is closer to the people. This has brought into sharp focus the severe limitations of representative democracy and the need to recognize and strengthen structures of direct democracy, particularly where communities depend on natural resources for sustaining their livelihoods and their identities.

Adivasi activists recognize the gravity of what lies ahead, particularly in a country that has had a formal representative democratic process and where they have been forced to reconfigure their collectivities to align themselves along political party lines. And, there are other challenges.

Having been targets of colonial and postcolonial "social engineering," the adivasis' main experience has been assimilationist policies, exploitation, repression, exclusion, and displacement.[12] Ironically, as a consequence of administrative inefficiency and graft, the extent of "mainstreaming" that would have further eroded their cultural worlds was limited.

Given the scale of their victimization, even the resurgence of human rights activism after Indira Gandhi's state of emergency in 1975 neglected their plight, except when there were major acts of social or state repression. Political parties rarely addressed the structural context of their repression and exclusion, despite the fact that adivasis have had the longest history of resistance when compared to other cultural groups. They were among the first to oppose British colonization. From the capture of the British fort at Panamaram, in Kerala, in the nineteenth century, to the Kol (1830), Santhal (1855), and Munda (1895) rebellions, militant sustained resistance has been part of their history of defending the sources of their identity and culture.

Sustained resistance in the past two decades and the growing demands for political and cultural autonomy—among the Gonds of central India, the Nagas, Mizos, and Bodos of the northeast, and others—have brought their issues to the center of political concern. The task of boundary making that was done in the first two decades after independence was a process primarily based on dominant linguistic lines. That whole process has been unraveling as identities and culturally more coherent entities have succeeded in compelling the state to redraw these boundaries. New states have been carved out of Uttar Pradesh (Uttaranchal), Madhya Pradesh (Chattisgarh), and Bihar (Jharkhand). Other movements will almost certainly lead to new states: Telengana in Andhra Pradesh and Vidharbha in Maharashtra are next in line.

But these developments have come at a cost. Politicians, administrators, external donors, and nongovernmental organizations have become increasingly intrusive and competitive in wanting to "deliver development" to and "represent" these communities. To what extent will a more caring and nurturing wisdom and vision survive this onslaught? How much political space can be extracted from this renewed interest without being swamped by or co-opted into it? How "peacefully" will those who have established their hegemonical political, economic, and cultural ways step aside?

The radical self-rule law has, since its passage, mostly remained forgotten in the corridors of power and has not become part of the mainstream political debate and action. Many state governments have passed laws that are not in full conformity with the central law. Academics, administrators, policy makers, and even parliamentarians remain largely unaware of it. Tribal communities, who were informed about the provisions of the law, greeted it with enthusiasm, but found themselves progressively handicapped by the lack of competence and capability to negotiate development and democratization as the law envisaged.[13]

The law also presumed the survival of "homogenous," "egalitarian," and "altruistic" tribal communities, not fully recognizing or acknowledging that adivasi societies have undergone vast changes. Transformations in their cultures have followed the drastic mutation of their material conditions. The relatively egalitarian internal organization of their societies was also distorted, including the roles and position of women. Alcoholism and other social symptoms of the degradation and exploitation of tribal societies have resulted in the tribal women bearing nearly all the burdens of household economic processes. In many areas, the breakdown of traditional control over consumption of alcohol has increased male irresponsibility, drained domestic resources, and encouraged greater domestic violence. Ironically, women have often become partners in their own oppression, since it is primarily women who manufacture illicit liquor. Although rape is still uncommon in tribal societies, domestic violence is rampant, and the community has ceased to intervene, regarding this as a "personal matter." And, instead of rape, some women are terrorized by witch hunting, which legitimizes their being stoned to death. Women have virtually no right to property. Women are excluded from any traditional modes of conflict resolution, even when women are parties to the dispute. Tribal societies have also begun to practice untouchability and to oppress weaker tribal groups.

Dialogues among the Ho and Warli communities in southeastern and western India, respectively, reveal an increasingly clear strategy to couple the building of "village republics" with a way of life that respects justice and natural cycles of regeneration. They recognize that they will have to join together or forge unities beyond the local.[14] This unity—between nonparty political and cultural formations and a vision for a just and ecologically sane lifestyle—is the essence of the new adivasi assertion. There is a powerful recognition that the struggle against a repressive state machinery and entrenched *diku*s (outsider traders, moneylenders, and the like) has to be waged simultaneously with the struggle against unaccountable economic globalization and Hindu nationalism. There are crucial discussions on how to reconfigure the relationship between community and the state and, where communities have been individualized and divided by party affiliation, between the individual, community, political party, and the state. (This is particularly crucial in the context of a devaluing of the centrality of communal stewardship of resources in a sea of private and state property.) Far-reaching changes have taken place in the fabric of traditional communities. Everywhere, however, there are signs of determination to pick up the challenge of renewing and rebuilding a collective ethos. Even though the task seems enormously difficult, a growing number of adivasis realize that these challenges have to be faced. Only then can the wellsprings of their wisdom and the collective commitment to their *gayana*s (and other sources of cultural and historical definition) find the cultural and political space to stand as a beacon for others. For many in the Ho communities and elsewhere, even among non-adivasi movements, there is a realization that there is no alternative to a second freedom struggle—supported by the manifold ways of passive and active resistance and of the determined unfolding of a commitment to the regeneration of life.

Adivasi self-awakening is no longer an abstract goal. The possibilities opened up by the formal recognition of their right to self-rule have created a firm basis for a confident expression within the modern world and the modern epoch. Evolving a strong fabric that ensures that adivasis do not feel compelled or tempted to indulge in demeaning imitations of the modern world, or to suffer the humiliation of seeing their ways and their seeking despised, will be one of the greatest challenges in the coming decades.

Notes

1. *Juvar* is a hardy, protein-rich grain.
2. "Creation Myth of the Bhilalas," trans. Amita Baviskar, *Lokayan Bulletin* 9, no. 3/4 (1991).
3. The Bhilalas are an adivasi community predominantly scattered in villages located in three states of western and central India: Rajasthan, Gujarat, and Madhya Pradesh.
4. Adivasis are classified as Scheduled Tribes because of the special "protection" defined for them in separate schedules of the Indian Constitution.
5. Sumir Lal, "Don't Shoot the Messenger," *Hindustan Times*, 17 August 1999.
6. Eminent domain is a legal power that is based on the premise that the state acts in the public interest and can therefore claim its dominion over all citizens who, therefore, by definition, must accept this authority. A crucial manifestation of this is the Land Acquisition Act, drafted by the British for reasons of empire and adopted almost unchanged and systematically used by post-independence Indian governments to acquire land "in the public interest." It has been grossly misused and is facing a significant challenge from increasingly aware tribal and rural populations.
7. For instances from other continents, see *Cultures of Politics, Politics of Cultures: Re-visioning Latin American Social Movements,* ed. Sonia E. Alvarez, Evelina Dagnino, and Arturo Escobar (Boulder, Colo.: Westview Press, 1998).
8. Among the best recent documents on these issues are: Tony Simpson (on behalf of the Forest Peoples Programme), *Indigenous Heritage and Self-Determination: The Cultural and Intellectual Property Rights of Indigenous Peoples* (Copenhagen: International Workgroup for Indigenous Affairs, 1997); and *Valuing Local Knowledge: Indigenous People and Intellectual Property Rights,* ed. Stephen Brush and Doreen Stabinsky (Washington, D.C.: Island Press, 1996).
9. Propagated by a powerful coalition of fascistic Hindu nationalists, the ideology of Hindutva is a primarily upper-caste, middle-class, urban response, mobilizing a growing Hindu minority that has grown increasingly insecure as a consequence of economic and cultural uprooting.
10. Ashis Nandy, "The Twilight of Certitudes: Secularism, Hindu Nationalism, and Other Masks of Deculturation," *Alternatives* 22 (1997): 162.
11. Personal communication, January 1997.
12. Smitu Kothari, "Whose Nation? The Displaced as Victims of Development," *Economic and Political Weekly,* 26 June 1996.
13. Smitu Kothari, "To Be Governed or to Self-Govern," *Folio (The Hindu),* July 2000.
14. The National Forum for Tribal Self-Rule, the South India Adivasi Forum, and other coalitions of indigenous and tribal peoples are some instances of these alliances.

Respecting the Land: Religion, Reconciliation, and Romance— An Australian Story

DIANE BELL

Here is the dilemma. Those of us who have had the privilege of working with indigenous peoples, who have developed deep respect for their relationships to places and have engaged in various struggles around issues of religious freedoms, have all too often despaired of ever moving beyond the rhetoric of respect for difference and the romanticization of the exotic "other," to a place of mutual respect and real redistribution of the resources in favor of the original inhabitants of relatively rich nations such as Australia, the United States, Canada, New Zealand. Working with indigenous peoples as an anthropologist is a fraught enterprise. Critiques, challenges, personal and professional assaults come from within the discipline and from those on whom the work impinges. Who needs an anthropologist anyway? Cannot people speak for themselves? Is this not just an extension of the colonial frontier, when members of the dominant society grow rich peddling the knowledge of those who live on the margins? Cultural critics declare the "culture concept" moribund, wallow in their crises of representation, and fret that applied anthropology tarnishes the fundamental research conducted by scholars in universities. Development lobbies and conservative governments delight in these internal disputes and mount public campaigns which cite "experts" who reframe the disciplinary debates regarding the "invention of tradition" as cases of fabrication and authenticity. The media, always ready to report conflict as news, is quick to jump on these.

Religion

Let me begin with a personal narrative that is, I think, instructive. Just over twenty-five years ago I undertook my first in-depth fieldwork in Australia. I lived in a desert community in Central Australia, with my two children, then aged nine and seven, for eighteen months.[1] Although I had read a great deal about "Aboriginal Religion," kinship systems, myth and ritual, I was barely prepared for the learning that was ahead. I remember the first time I drove through the barren, arid stretch of land and into the settlement (reservation) which was to be my home. I thought it was the most boring stretch of land I'd encountered. A year later I couldn't walk, let alone drive for any distance, without stopping to reflect on the country. Here was the remains of a small fire. Who had cooked here? What had they been hunting? Over there was evidence of a bigger fire. Who had lit that fire and when? I did not walk alone. I needed to be in the company of other women, my sisters, sister-in-laws, aunties, grandmothers, and mothers. Kin and country: the twin pillars of Aboriginal society.

And what do fires, families, and food have to do with religion? Everything. You need the permission of the "traditional owners" to light fires that flush out the game and allow regeneration of the landscape. Light them at the wrong time and you burn off the larger trees. Light them just before the rains and you create a veritable wonderland of plant foods. Here is a small fire: a family fire perhaps? Careful inspection can reveal who camped there, when, with whom, and for what purpose. Maybe a woman, her sisters, husband, their unmarried children camped there. The hearth, a little away from that of the couple, may be the hearth of the woman's mother. Or a hearth may indicate a group of women out for the day, looking for small game, fruit, berries. In the cool months a brush shade would shelter the hearth fires from the winds but remain open to the sky to catch whatever warmth the sun might offer. In the warm months the shade would be open on all sides with a roof as protection from the sun. All this can be read from the remains of old camp sites. But there is much more that can be read. Country is a complex text: a delicate weave of people, places, and beliefs about their interrelations. Under the gentle but purposeful tutelage of older women, I learned to read the country at a pragmatic level of daily survival but also as a religious text of mystery, wonder, order, and the law.

In the creative era, known as the Dreaming or Dreamtime, when the land was a shapeless mass, creative heroes traveled through the country.[2] They named places of significance. In the *jukurrpa,* as this period is called in Warlpiri, the *altjirra* in Aranda (and by other terms in the some two hundred odd languages—depending on definition—that were spoken across the continent), the creative beings met and through their interactions established the law: the moral code which permeates all aspects of life. They established the rules for marriage and performed the first initiations and the first mortuary rites. At places where they rested, celebrated, fought, ate, and engaged in all manner of interactions, their power entered the land. Today the body of the ancestors is visible in the land itself. Anomalous formations are explained, as are regularities in this spiritually charged landscape. The deep red streaks on a cliff face recall the place where the ancestral dingo (wild dog) fought; the low ridge the sleeping form of the emu; the regular sand ridges the tracks left by the dancing feet of the ancestral women in their long journey from one water hole to the next. Fire burns, but it also has a spiritual identity.

Everything has a Dreaming. All the animals, natural phenomenon, wind, rain, fire, the heavenly bodies. This is an integrated world. There is no one, all-powerful being. There are no hereditary chiefs. One is born into certain rights and responsibilities in land and into a web of relationships to specific places. How these relations are configured varies across the continent. In the central desert one has rights and responsibilities through certain lines of descent: through father's father, mother's mother, and mother's father; through place of birth, place of residence, the country of one's spouse.[3] And there are sentimental attachments that cut across and complement these structural considerations. Here, I focus on the desert regions. Tom Trevorrow (in this volume) explains that, by way of contrast, in the well-watered southeast, people lived in more tightly defined clan groups, and his people, the Ngarrindjeri, had developed a governmental system known as the *tendi.* This council of elders heard disputes and adjudicated on a range of matters, including sorcery, clan territories, marriage, and inheritance.

Across Australia, to persons schooled in the law of the ancestors falls the responsibility of passing knowledge to the next generation. Through ceremonial reenactments of the travels of the ancestors, the past is made concurrent with the present. Through singing, the putting on of body paint, preparation of sacred objects, and dancing, the power of the ancestors is evoked. At such times one is in direct contact with the Dreamings. Their power is called forth and pervades the ritual space. The places being celebrated by the performers are represented by various designs, ritual objects, and songs. These are like the title deeds for land, and the inner meanings of the designs, songs, steps, and stories are known only to ritual experts. These are also one's relatives. Not surprisingly, such ceremonies carry enormous significance for the participants. Not surprisingly, not all details are shared with the casual visitor.

When I first began work in the desert in 1976, I was assured by senior colleagues I would soon be back, because my project, the religious life of Aboriginal women, was not one that would yield much data. Everyone knew that women did not have sacred sites or secret ceremonies, and even if they did have "women-only" ceremonies in some remote parts of the country, the ceremonies were about babies, reproduction, and the like. They were just "women's business"—a term that came to trivialize the ritual work of women and their contribution to the well-being of the whole society. Women did not address the major themes of societal and religious renewal as celebrated in men's ceremonies.

That prophecy proved false. Women, I soon learned, had a separate sacred ritual life which was at times pursued independently of the men and at others intertwined with men's ceremonies. It took the ritual labor of both sexes to sustain and nurture the world of the ancestors and that of the living. Access to this world took time. I needed to build trust, to demonstrate I didn't talk out of turn. I was watched. I was tested. I was only taken deeper into ceremonial meanings as it became obvious I had understood what I had already been taught.[4]

In this period of participant observation fieldwork in the 1970s, I was working with so-called traditional peoples. I explain this because often it appears that the people of the desert regions, people for whom contact with outsiders is within living memory, are the only "real indigenous people," and that the people of the more densely settled regions of Australia, the people hardest hit by disease, dislocation, and massacre, are somehow "inauthentic." The argument goes that they cannot have any "traditional" knowledge and therefore they must be politically motivated in their attempts to protect their sacred places. Tom and Ellen Trevorrow explain, in this volume, some of their history as Ngarrindjeri people and the need to overcome such stereotypes and prejudices. Here, as context for consideration of matters of "tradition," I offer a summary of select politico-legislative moves and countermoves of the last several decades and note key moments in race relations in Australia over two centuries (see table 1).

Table 1.

60,000 B.P.	Skeletal remains
1770	Captain Cook surveys the east coast of the continent
1778	British Penal Settlement, Sydney Cove
1901	States federate to form the Commonwealth of Australia. Constitution explicitly excludes Aborigines from the national census and Aboriginal affairs remain a state matter.
1967	Constitutional referendum carried. Aborigines to be counted in the national census and the federal government to have concurrent rights with the states to legislate for Aborigines.
1976	*Aboriginal Land Rights (Northern Territory) Act*
1984	National Land Rights legislation derailed
1984	*Aboriginal and Torres Strait Islander Heritage Act*
1988	Australian bicentennial and promise of a treaty
1992	Mabo decision, High Court (Native title is part of the common law of the land)
1993	*Native Title Act*
1995	South Australian Royal Commission re Hindmarsh Island
1996	Wik decision, High Court (Native title and pastoral lease holders rights co-exist)
1997	*Hindmarsh Island Bridge Act* amends Heritage Act of 1984. Move to amend *Native Title Act*
1998	*Native Title Act* amended

Reconciliation

In the early 1990s, the Reconciliation Movement promised to bring Aboriginal people into dialogue with non-indigenous Australians in ways which would acknowledge the fundamental rights and responsibilities the original inhabitants have to the land and its resources. Launched with great gusto and until 1997 supported, albeit with reservations by many indigenous leaders, the Reconciliation Movement is now floundering. Under the conservative government of Prime Minister John Howard, there has been a move to limit the scope of Aboriginal rights and to weaken existing heritage legislation. When added to the refusal of the government to apologize for the damage done to Aboriginal families and individuals by the forced removal of children, so graphically documented in *Bringing them Home,* the report of the Human Rights Commission,[5] the claims and aims of the Reconciliation Council ring hollow. In 1997, key members of the council resigned and any lingering legitimacy that body may have had evaporated. The advances in understanding and changes in law which, over the last several decades, had reworked the relationship between the settler and indigenous populations were under challenge.

When the Council for Reconciliation first met in 1992, it was a bipartisan group of twenty-five individuals—twelve of whom were indigenous and eleven were from the wider community. The council was working toward a better understanding between Aborigines and Torres Strait Islanders and the wider community. Key issues identified by the council were: 1) "Understanding Country," wherein the importance of land and sea for indigenous peoples is stressed; 2) "Improving Relationships," which includes paying attention to the fracturing of families through government assimilation policies;[6] 3) "Valuing Cultures," which recognizes that cultures are diverse, that they change, adapt, and thereby survive and grow; 4) "Sharing History," which includes listening to indigenous voices and revisiting colonial history (Australia was not discovered in 1770 by Captain Cook. It was home to between 500,000 and 2 million peoples, depending on one's choice of source); 5) "Addressing Disadvantage," which focuses on health, housing, employment, and education; 6) "Custody Levels," wherein the finding of the Royal Commission into Deaths in Custody is noted;[7] 7) "Destiny," whereby people would have greater opportunities to control their own destiny and could culminate in, perhaps; 8) the formulation of an agreement (treaty, compact, constitutional preamble) regarding the position of indigenous peoples within Australian society. These are laudable goals and if honored would go a long way toward building a mature and diverse nation. If honored, the content of "tradition" would be the right and responsibility of Aboriginal people to decide. Of course, this is not entirely unproblematic. Within communities, and even within families, there are different views. But if the framing of matters of tradition was governed by Aboriginal sensibilities, "tradition" would not be subject to disputation according to the rules of evidence of an Anglo court.

Why a reconciliation movement? Unlike the treaty-making with Native peoples in the United States, in Australia there were no sovereign-to-sovereign-nation negotiations to form a framework for "Native policy." When the British flag was raised at Botany Bay in 1788, the colonial understanding was that the land was *terra nullius,* a land belonging to no one. Obviously there were people there. Artists sketched their quaint appearance. Learned gentlemen pondered their modes of communication. The instructions to the first governor were to live in peace and amity with them, but these natives of New Holland did not till the soil. They built no permanent houses. In the view of the early administrators they were "nomadic." Through the era of transportation, through the gold rushes of the 1850s, to the federation of the states to form the Commonwealth of Australia in 1901, Aboriginal people made their presence known. They kept up spirited resistance in some parts of the country and held back settlement in others. They were massacred. They died of small pox, influenza, and venereal diseases. They were herded onto reserves for their own protection and taught the "benefits" of civilization. They were missionized. Their traditional ceremonies were banned and their sacred objects burned and confiscated. Some were put in museums. Aborigines and Torres Strait Islanders were not part of the nation that was born in 1901. The Constitution explicitly excluded them. They were not to be counted in the compulsory national census and the new Commonwealth government had no legislative power to enact laws for Aborigines: that was a matter for the states.

Relations to Land

In 1967, when 90 percent of the voting public endorsed a constitutional referendum to give the Commonwealth government concurrent rights with the states to make laws for the benefit of Aborigines and to have the indigenous peoples counted in the national census, the script changed. Not much was forthcoming until 1976 when, following the Woodward Commission in 1974, the *Aboriginal Land Rights (N.T.) Act* was passed. It applied only to the Northern Territory and only to those stretches of land that had not been taken up for some other use (thus, it was mostly waste lands and reservations). Only those people who could prove that they were "traditional owners" could become claimants. What it was to be traditional was defined in the act in terms of membership of a local descent group, attachment to the land, exercise of primary responsibility for the sites and common spiritual affiliation to the land and its sites. This was a period in which there were no unemployed anthropologists and many lawyers made names for themselves as crusaders in the Aboriginal rights field. There can be no doubting that the land rights act was a critically important recognition by the state of Aboriginal rights, but it also helped entrench what I will call the "tyranny of tradition." It was ceremony, language, and unbroken clan genealogies that were being recognized, not the survival of knowledge in the face of disruption, dislocation, and depopulation. Claims on the basis of need, as recommended by the Woodward Commission,[8] out of which the legislation had grown, were shuffled off the legislative agenda.

Some 42 percent of land in the Northern Territory is now under Aboriginal control. This has raised the specter of an Aboriginal state with resources—the Northern Territory is resource rich. In such a state, indigenous title holders would be people with whom one would need to reckon, not just recognize. However, the transfer of title and power has not been so dramatic. There are regional councils which represent traditional owners; various local enterprises that allow places to be protected have been developed; and, most important of all, the traditional owners have the right of veto over outside development. Although rarely exercised, it is the measure which brings parties to the negotiating table and it is the provision that has been most hard fought by development lobbies. Then there are joint ventures with the state and with developers. Two of the most successful arrangements which allow multiple use of Aboriginal land are the Uluru Kata Tjuta National Park in Central Australia (Ayers Rock) and Kakadu National Park in Arnhem Land. In both cases there are Joint Management Plans where Aboriginal people set policy, educate visitors, manage the lands, and are able to protect their places. At Uluru the tourist accommodation was moved back from the rock, and the local rangers have almost taught people not to climb on this most sacred site. In Arnhem Land the locals have began to control the destructive water buffalo introduced to this fragile landscape and have been part of the monitoring of uranium mining that occurs on a lease within the park.

During the 1967–1992 period, individual states accommodated the cry for land rights in various ways—grants, deeds in trust, reserves, planning authorities, and so on—and legislation to protect sacred sites was enacted. At the federal level the *Aboriginal and Torres Strait Islander Heritage Act* of 1984, designed to come into play when all other avenues had been exhausted, was passed. Aboriginal "tradition" is defined in section 3.1 as "the body of traditions, observances, customs and beliefs of Aboriginals generally or of a particular community or group of Aboriginals, and includes any such traditions, observances, customs or beliefs relating to particular persons, areas, objects or relationships." In its thirteen years of operation the Heritage Act has proved to be a failure and a source of frustration for many parties. Justice Elizabeth Evatt records that of the ninety-nine applications for protection brought under the legislation, only four resulted in declarations for protection of places.[9] Two of these were overturned in court appeals, and one was revoked. The remaining protected site, in Alice Springs, is, interestingly, a woman's site and is in relatively "traditional country."

The Heritage Act is one of the few pieces of legislation passed in exercise of the 1967 constitutional referendum. All attempts to generate more meaningful and far-reaching national legislation for land rights have been thwarted by campaigns of the development lobby, pastoralists, farmers, and conservative politicians who, with a little help from a muddle-headed media, have recycled emotional appeals in each successive campaign. *"Aborigines enjoy rights no one else does. They are impeding development by locking up the resources of the land. Whenever we find something they declare it is a sacred site."* In its extreme form, Aborigines are said to be a threat to national security and to pose a risk to the unity of the nation. Places like Uluru belong to everyone, goes the argument, and its return to the traditional owner in the 1980s was accompanied by appeals to the notion of "One Australia."

The next watershed is 1992 when, after ten years of the case bouncing back and forth between various jurisdictions, the High Court ruled that the native title of Eddie Mabo and his people of the Torres Strait Islands had not been extinguished. Their rights in their land continued to this day. In this case Mabo established the principle of "native title" as part of the common law of the land. The High Court found the doctrine of *terra nullius* to be a flawed and convenient historical fiction. Unless there had been explicit repeal by a legitimate exercise of state power, native title continued, the court ruled. The people who had brought this case were in an unusual position in that they had excellent documentary proof of their continuing exercise of native title. Other peoples in Australia would not be so fortunate. But, *"Chaos,"* cried the developers. *"Nothing is secure. Anyone can bring a Mabo-like claim." "Justice,"* cried the Aboriginal leaders and their lawyers. *"Legislate, exercise those powers of 1967, recognize native title. Make reconciliation real."*

The *Native Title Act* 1993 attempts to address all of the above. It sets up a tribunal to hear cases. So far, no land has been transferred but millions of dollars have been spent and the development lobby and the pastoralists haven't changed their tune. An Indigenous Land Fund was established to buy land for those whose land was permanently alienated and thereby address their needs. The Mabo decision and the *Native Title Act* have generated considerable controversy: on the one hand, developers seek amendments, on the other, indigenous peoples are seeking clarification. In 1996 the Wik people of northern Queensland asked if pastoral leases alienated their lands. Some 40 percent of Australia is held under some form of leasehold by a few thousand persons who, for the most part, pay a nominal rent. The persons who concerned the Wik were those who held leases for the purpose of running cattle. Did the granting of a pastoral lease constitute an interest in land that extinguished their native title? The High Court ruled native title was not extinguished but, rather, that it coexisted with the rights of the leaseholder. Should there be conflict, the rights of pastoralists would prevail. *"Chaos,"* cried the development lobby again. *"You mean we have to negotiate on a case-by-case basis? Amend the legislation. It is unworkable. Australia is being held to ransom by a tiny percent of the population. This is undemocratic." "Native title is now the law of the land,"* argued indigenous peoples. *"Negotiate with us."* And indeed, there are many examples of successful negotiations, one of which was happening in Wik lands.

In March 1996 the Labor government which had supported Native Title lost to the Liberal Party (the conservatives in Australia) and the new prime minister began to pay heed to the cries for amendment of the act. Soon there was a ten-point plan to amend Native Title, to create security, to make it fair for all, for that "One Nation." The wordplay necessary to argue that the proposed amendments are consistent with the High Court decision in Mabo are predictably problematic. Of course we support native title, say the miners, pastoralists, and conservatives alike. *"It is the law of the land, but within reason, without prejudicing the well-being of other interests, we need to be practical. The greatest needs for Aborigines are for education, health, work, not native title."*

Along with the change of government came a shift in public discourse. There was an outpouring of mean-spirited anti-Aboriginal and anti-Asia rhetoric. It was a replay of the mid-1980s when National Land Rights was on the legislative agenda. Then, Professor Geoffrey Blainey, a historian who saw Aborigines and multiculturalism as a threat to national security, and Hugh Morgan, who spoke for mining concerns, were the storm troopers. In 1997, Pauline Hanson, an independent from Queensland, burst on the scene with her "One Nation" party. What had been unsayable under the Labor government was now commonplace, and it was all in the name of "free speech."

Meanwhile, on the international stage Australia's posture is one of deep commitment to its indigenous peoples. When the report of the generations of Aboriginal children, who were taken away from their parents and raised in foster homes and institutions, appeared in 1997, there was an outpouring of emotion for people whose families had been destroyed. Some one in three to one in ten children were removed. Commissioner Ronald Wilson wrote: "The devastation cannot be addressed unless the whole community listens with an open heart and mind to the stories of what happened and, having listened and understood, commits itself to reconciliation."[10] Here was a chance to make reconciliation real.

While the big constitutional question of native title was hanging in the balance, the Heritage Act was also being assaulted. As I have noted, this legislation is the fallback position for people whose sacred places are not protected in any other way. It is the legislation of last recourse. Where there are land rights, there is hope of protection of sacred places under the provisions of that legislation. But most people in the southeast have not enjoyed the benefits of the Land Rights Act and have been looking hopefully to the possibilities of lodging Native Title claims and to acquiring land through the Land Fund. Native Title claims in the southeast of Australia require massive research and face resistance from a number of quarters. This is the area of Australia which was first colonized and which was heavily missionized. It is where people were punished for speaking their own language, where ceremonies were banned, where assimilation policies and removal of children hit hardest. It is a cruel irony that the people who most need the recognition offered by Native Title are in the worst position possible to argue for it. Most of the land is alienated and therefore beyond claim. What is claimable remains highly contested. Mounting successful land claims like those in the Northern Territory is a risky and sensitive enterprise. Families have been broken up, and doing genealogical research is an invasion of privacy for many families. Asking why ceremonies are no longer being performed is a gross insult. And when people turn to the written record, they do not find accounts of their religion, which in the nineteenth century was not recognized as such. Rather, they find accounts of superstition and sorcery. They find detailed accounts of kinship and disagreements in the literature about land tenure, the clan system, the location and naming of sites, the stories of the creative heroes. Instead of contextualization, conflicting sources are used to counter current claims of continuing links to land and lore. If an anthropologist, missionary, or learned gentleman did not record it (site, ceremony, relationship), to those contesting Aboriginal claims it doesn't exist.

Those sensitive to context point out that Aboriginal religion was not recognized as such until recently. Those concerned with women's lives point out that the worthy recorders were all men. There is virtually nothing in the record about women, unless one knows how to read the silences. By the mid-twentieth century there were women in the field but, for the most part, they were not undertaking work with women as women who may well have known things that were not to be shared. When I first raised this issue of women's restricted sacred knowledge in the 1970s in Central Australia, it was a popular put-down to say that I was projecting my feminist politics onto another culture and that this attention to women was divisive. Through a number of land claims and sacred site registrations in the desert regions, it has become perfectly plain that unless women are part of the research and consultative structures, binding decisions will not be made. It behooves developers to ask the women. And it is not the business of Aboriginal men to speak for their women.

At various times I have worked for Aboriginal Land Councils, the Aboriginal Land Commissioner, the Australian law Reform Commission, the Aboriginal Sacred Sites Protection Authority, and the Aboriginal Legal Aid Services on land claims, registration of sacred sites, and court cases where Aboriginal customary law came into conflict with Anglo law. Always there was a question of tradition. *"My father and grandfather before him told this story. I learnt it from the 'old people.' I am still doing that business for those places. I visit them all the time."* This, an Aboriginal witness tells a court. Hearsay evidence? Indeed it is, but this is an oral culture. This is how knowledge is transmitted. *"This is my aunty's song,"* an elderly woman flanked by her sisters, father's sisters, and daughters explains to the judge. The painted designs of her body tell in cryptic code of the travels of the ancestors through her aunt's country and of her relationship to that person, one of ritual reciprocity. All these people need to be present when she testifies. They are her witnesses that she has not strayed into the country of another.

Group evidence plays havoc with the court transcript. Who has said what to whom and in answer to what question? Then, in answer to the question "Who are the traditional owners for the land?" the men decide to show the judge sacred objects. These are their title deeds to land. All women are excluded from the session. In such situations the court manages to function. But the women have sacred objects also. They too have stories and sites that are for women only, and not just any women. Some knowledge can only be imparted to older women, some only to women who have children, or only to women of certain kin groups. In this situation the court flounders. The judge is male and, apart from the transcript person, everyone else is male. Male lawyers, male field officers, male anthropologists.

Real Life: Enter the Ngarrindjeri

We have, I think, made some progress over the past twenty years. Group evidence is admissible. Gender-restricted knowledge has been held in confidence in land claims, though the solutions have been far from perfect. The temptation is to say a claim can be won without having to take evidence from the women. Thus, a body of expertise is built that is male-oriented. However, there are cases where women's evidence is crucial, and it always requires taking special measures. I first began this work in 1976. Now fast forward to 1996 when I was asked to act as consultant to a group of Ngarrindjeri women who were fighting to protect their sacred places in the southeast of Australia. They were attempting to use the Heritage Legislation. They had been at logger heads with the state government in South Australia and with developers who wanted to build a bridge to service a marina on a small inland in the mouth of the Murray River, which drains the southeast of Australia (see map 1). This fight had been going on for some four years. The state legislation, which was supposed to protect their places, had failed miserably. These people do not have land rights. Their lands were colonized in the early nineteenth century. Their food sources were damaged by extensive farming, irrigation, and drainage systems. But there are still people who know their sacred places. They feel the connection. They are still living on or near their places. The Ngarrindjeri women have a story to tell, but they cannot tell it to a man, be he Ngarrindjeri, a "whitefellar" lawyer, bureaucrat, or politician. This would be a violation of their law.

However, some Ngarrindjeri women insist that they were not told these stories. A Ngarrindjeri man appears on television and states it

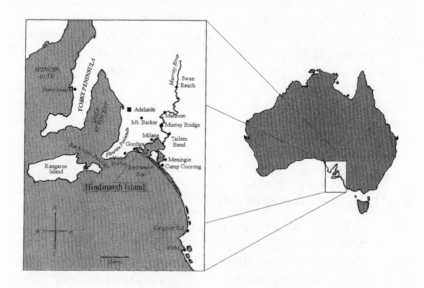

Map 1. Southeast of Australia
(Map: Stephen Shaheen, reproduced with permission from Ngarrindjeri
Wurruwarrin: A World That Is, Was, and Will Be *by Diane Bell, published
by Spinifex Press, Melbourne, 1998, p. xvi)*

was he who suggested the land resembled a woman's "private parts." He later withdraws this statement, but accusations that it was all made up with the express purpose of frustrating development take root in the popular imagination. "Where is the proof in the written sources?" developers, the state, and media demand. The community is divided on the issue. Anthropologists are divided. There is a Royal Commission to determine whether there has been a deliberate fabrication.[11] The Ngarrindjeri women believers refuse to accept the jurisdiction of the Royal Commission, and in their absence they are found to be fabricators. For technical reasons two applications for protection under the federal Heritage Act fail. To forestall further litigation and to achieve that security so desired by the settler population, the parliament moves to amend the legislation so that this site is excluded from the reach of the Heritage Act.

There are competing accounts of the politico-legal maneuvers around the politics of the moves to protect or develop this site and the trail left by the case as it has bounced around the Federal Court and been up and down to the High Court.[12] It is more of the same. It is not about reconciliation, or respect for religious beliefs, or understanding the past. In February 1998, the High Court heard an appeal against the legislation which had been enacted for the sole purpose of permitting the bridge to be built. The case turns on a constitutional question which will be critical to the preservation of Native Title. Does the Commonwealth have the power to pass laws *for the benefit of* Aborigines, or simply *with respect to* Aborigines? Could the Commonwealth pass laws that are to the detriment of indigenous peoples? Could such laws limit their rights? The 1967 referendum gave the Commonwealth the power to legislate *for* Aborigines, but what does that "for" mean? The High Court denies the appeal. It appears "for" simply means "with respect to." All domestic remedies are exhausted. There is nothing in the law to prevent the site from being desecrated. December 1999, construction begins on the bridge.

Although I have written at length about law and indigenous peoples, I am not a lawyer. I am an anthropologist who has seen people betrayed by the law and courts too many times to believe that justice and law are synonymous. I know there is another story to be told about the Ngarrindjeri, not the one about the contesting of their religious beliefs in the public forum, but about the daily lives of the people who, in the face of such opposition and assault on their beliefs, have continued to provide for their families, to maintain their humor and dignity. I decide a contemporary ethnography which engages with the written sources is warranted.[13] The book, written in a whirlwind of travel and research, is unlike anything I have ever written before. Working with people who are literate in English, who know the sources, who read what I have written, who have opinions on anthropological theory and a sophisticated understanding of Australian law, but who privilege the spoken word, has been exhilarating. That is the up side. The down side is that much of the work has felt like a replay of the 1970s. Women are not believed when they say, "We have sacred places and the knowledge is restricted to certain peoples." The Heritage Act offers no confidentiality. This act was reviewed in 1996 by Justice Evatt. Problems were identified and remedies suggested, but the report languishes. In the meantime the rush to amend the *Native Title Act* 1993 to create security of title for developers and the rush to amend the Heritage Act to clarify and expedite continue apace. The Aboriginal concerns with confidentiality and gender-restricted knowledge have been set against those of natural justice, which requires that all parties have the right to test the evidence. If people want to use the Heritage Act to protect the sacred places, they must violate their sacred law by allowing restricted knowledge to be written down and read by men. The constitutional guarantee of freedom of religion rings hollow in such a situation. Reconciliation is revealed as rhetorical posturing.

Romance

And the romance? It exists at a number of levels. It exists in many of the portraits of indigenous persons who are cast as intuitively and mystically related to land, living in a world filled with song and ceremony. It is too difficult to understand the specificities of relations to land; the intricacies of colonial history; the different beliefs of peoples in the central desert from those in the temperate south. The religion was certainly holistic and it certainly was one of reverence for land, but it was also a set of practices for survival. It was not a wilderness philosophy. The land was used. The land was respected. The land was burnt. Animals were hunted, killed, and eaten. Their fur was used for clothing and bedding. The original peoples were not mild-mannered vegetarians singing and dancing the whole day long.

They left a mark on the land, but they marked it with respect. They do not now want to lock the land away, and where negotiations have been pursued with respect and in good faith, a great deal has been achieved.

The romance exists in many advertising campaigns which appropriate images of indigenous peoples. They are nearly always dressed in traditional garb, poised on one foot, and holding a spear in one hand, gazing across sixty thousand years of Dreaming. Rarely do they look at the camera. The image is not of the hard-working citizens who worry about the education of their children, constantly tinker with their cars to keep them on the road, attend to their health, pay taxes, and fret about all the things other citizens fret about. These are not the people for whom legislation was intended. Their deep concerns with when they can next visit their special places, meet with family, collect rushes for weaving, and so on are invisible to a population fed a diet of "tradition" in remote areas, expensive art work, and the occasional tug at the heart strings with the story of a child taken away from his or her family or of a death in police custody.

The romance exists in the popular books that become best sellers and are devoured by well-meaning but naïve readers. Marlo Morgan's account of her bare-footed fourteen-hundred mile trek across the burning deserts of Australia appeared first in 1992 and then was picked up by HarperCollins, who made it into a runaway best seller.[14] They knew it wasn't true and to cover themselves have "fiction" in fine print on the back cover. The author, however, lectures about her trip as a real experience. She calls the Aborigines who abducted her the "Real People," people who were untouched by white civilization and hence were authentic. I don't think a week goes by that I do not hear from someone about this wonderful uplifting book they have read about Aborigines, and it is *Mutant Message Down Under.* I even hear of it from colleagues. But no one could walk that far without having to negotiate permission to enter the territory of another, I point out over and over again. "How could I know that?" asks the gullible reader. How so?

I think anthropologists need to take some responsibility here. We have not always written to educate the general public. There are no "untouched natives" from the "stone age" waiting to be contacted by a New Age visitor, I explain. But what a convenient fiction. Should there be such people with a message for the developed world, it would be untouched and untainted by colonialism. No wonder these books are so popular. No need to struggle with the messy realities of the lives of people who have been in contact for centuries. Just declare them to be not authentic and simultaneously appropriate their beliefs. And, on the way, get rid of any reference to place, to kinship, and to language. Such matters are too complicated. The single figure poised on one foot is silent and may only speak when contacted by a Marlo Morgan. The rest cannot be believed. Of course, I have much more to say about the New Age and its appropriation of indigenous spirituality.[15] Here, I am simply flagging that whatever we say about the wisdom of indigenous peoples needs to be grounded in the specificities of peoples and place, not homogenized and romanticized as an exotic, simple, unchanging "tradition."

On what basis do we assume that indigenous peoples hold some mystical secret waiting to be plumbed, that they exist to save Western society and the planet with their knowledge? Where we might begin is to ask: "How have they survived?" Where we might honor indigenous knowledge is to stand with people in their struggles, and not only in faraway romantic locations, but right at home, right where it bites, right where it may mean going without something, or making radical changes in our lives. Where we might do better for our children and with our peers is to become critical consumers of popular media. A Disney Pocahontas is not fun. It does real harm. A homogenized indigenous spirituality portrayed in New Age texts, and also popular with some scholars of comparative religion, disenfranchises the people who most need our critical rethinking of notions of "tradition."

People like Tom and Ellen Trevorrow (this volume) have been shuffled around by government policies, but they have never abandoned their beliefs in the power of their places and stories. They and many of their Ngarrindjeri kin have always lived on their land. Here is a lesson in the tradition of spiritual connection from which we might all learn. It is a story of spiritual and physical survival. It is a real story of real people who have worked hard at various enterprises that keep them in touch with the land while educating other Australians about their shared heritage.

Notes

I am grateful to the organizers of the indigenous traditions and ecology conference, particularly Mary Evelyn Tucker and John Grim, who assembled a remarkable group of scholars, activists, and resources persons (not mutually exclusive categories) at the Center for the Study of Religions, where we spent four days in November 1997 locked in intense debate, being fed splendid food and weathered the first, and surprise, snowstorm of the season. In the session on Australia, I was joined by my friends and colleagues from Australia, Tom and Ellen Trevorrow from Camp Coorong, a cross-cultural race relations educational center they run on Ngarrindjeri lands in southeast Australia.

1. Diane Bell, *Daughters of the Dreaming*, 2d ed. (Minneapolis: University of Minnesota Press, 1993).

2. Ibid.; W. E. H. Stanner, *On Aboriginal Religion*, Oceania Monographs, 11 (Sydney: University of Sydney, 1963); and T. G. H. Strehlow, *Songs of Central Australia* (Sydney: Angus and Robertson, 1971).

3. Bell, *Daughters of the Dreaming*.

4. Ibid.

5. Ronald Wilson, *Bringing Them Home: Report of the National Inquiry into the Separation of Aboriginal and Torres Strait Islander Children from Their Families* (Sydney: Human Rights and Equal Opportunity Commission, 1997).

6. Ibid.

7. Elliott Johnston, *Royal Commission into Aboriginal Deaths in Custody. National Report: Overview and Recommendations* (Canberra: Australian Government Pub. Service, 1991).

8. A. E. Woodward, *Aboriginal Land Rights Commission*, Second Report (Canberra: Australian Government Pub. Service, 1974).

9. Elizabeth Evatt, *Review of the Aboriginal and Torres Strait Islander Heritage Protection Act 1984* (Canberra: Australian Government Pub. Service, 1996).

10. Wilson, *Bringing Them Home*, 3.

11. Iris E. Stevens, *Report of the Hindmarsh Island Royal Commission* (Adelaide: The Royal Commission, 1995).

12. Chris Kenny, *It Would Be Nice If There Was Some Women's Business* (Potts Point: Duffy and Snellgrove, 1996); Marion Maddox, "Sticks and Stones: Religious Freedom, State Neutrality and Indigenous Heritage Protection," in *Proceedings of the 1997 Australasian Political Studies Association Conference, 29 September–1 October 1997*, ed. George Crowder et al. (Adelaide: Department of Politics, Flinders University of South Australia, 1997); Greg Mead, *A Royal Omission: A Critical Summary of the Evidence Given to the Hindmarsh Island Royal Commission with an Alternative Report* (Adelaide: Greg Mead, 1995); Lyndall Ryan, ed., "Secret Women's Business: Hindmarsh Island Affair," *Journal of Australian Studies* 48 (1996); and Diane Bell, *Ngarrindjeri Wurruwarrin: A World That Is, Was, and Will Be* (North Melbourne: Spinifex Press, 1998).

13. Bell, *Ngarrindjeri Wurruwarrin: A World That Is, Was, and Will Be*.

14. Marlo Morgan, *Mutant Message Down Under* (New York: HarperCollins, 1994).

15. Diane Bell, "Desperately Seeking Redemption," *Natural History* 106, no. 2 (1997).

Kumarangk:
The Survival of a Battered People

TOM TREVORROW and ELLEN TREVORROW

Tom Trevorrow

It is an honor to speak at this conference of my people, known today as the Ngarrindjeri. I want to speak of our land, of our cultural heritage and spiritual beliefs relating to our land, and of what is happening to us today. The destruction and subversion of Ngarrindjeri peoples' cultural and spiritual beliefs, especially as they relate to their land, continue from the early invasions into modern developments. In 1995 the government of South Australia held an inquiry into the culture and beliefs of Ngarrindjeri people, called the Hindmarsh Island Royal Commission. This paper will provide a background to this issue and a discussion of its implications for the future.

My wife and I, along with a few other Ngarrindjeri people, manage and operate a small Race Relations Cultural Education and Recreation Centre, which is called Camp Coorong. At Camp Coorong we have accommodation facilities where groups can come and stay and learn such things as our Ngarrindjeri cultural history, environmental history, and Australian history. Our main user groups are primary and secondary schools, universities, colleges, and church groups and various other groups of people.

The idea of the development of Camp Coorong was a vision that we, the Ngarrindjeri people, had back in 1985. We believed that we must have a place where people can come to learn about our heritage and culture. We also believed that this would lead to non-Aboriginal people developing a better understanding of our Ngarrindjeri traditions and our relationships to the land, waters, trees, plants, and animals.

Up to today, Camp Coorong has been operating very successfully, and the Ngarrindjeri people as a whole are very proud of its success. At Camp Coorong, to develop better understandings, we tell of our traditions and our way of life before the European invasion of our lands. We teach the ways that my ancestors lived.

We look upon the land with respect because we see and feel it as our own body. We take groups out on field trips upon the land, talking about places that are very important to us.

We teach our Ngarrindjeri basket-weaving techniques. We tell of our stories relating to the land, waters, trees, plants, birds, and animals—people call them dreaming stories.

We do all these things, sharing our culture to develop better understanding, to help overcome false interpretations and racism toward Ngarrindjeri people, and to help correct stereotyped history about the European settlement of the land.

The Ngarrindjeri Nation

The Ngarrindjeri Nation was made up of several large clan groups. These clan groups were broken up into smaller clan groups. For example, the larger clan groups to the southeast of my land, along the Coorong, are called the Tangenakald, to the west we are called the Ramindjeri, to the northwest we are called the Permangk, to the northeast we are called the Yaraldi, and so on.

The majority of the clan groups lived along the waters of the River Murray, the fresh water lakes, the islands within the lakes, the Southern Ocean and the Coorong, and the islands within the Coorong. This is where our heritage and our cultural and spiritual beliefs still remain a strong significant part of our lives today, even though we do not live upon the land in a traditional way.

To the Land

One of the most important things about the land that was taught to all the clan groups is that the land is like our bodies. It is alive and must be respected. That is why parts of the land are named after our own bodies. For example, the Coorong is supposed to be called Kurangk, meaning long neck—*kurri,* meaning neck, *angk,* meaning place of. Another example is Hindmarsh Island. It is supposed to be called Kumarangk—*kumuri,* meaning pregnant women, *angk,* meaning place of—or place of women's business. We were also taught to respect the land as our mother, because she is the one who feeds you when you are hungry, gives you a drink when you are thirsty, keeps you warm when you are cold, and keeps you cool when you are hot.

The land provides everything that we need to survive, such as the air that we breathe, the water that we drink, the foods that we eat, the trees and grasses for our basket weaving and weaponry for hunting, and all our needs.

We, as Ngarrindjeri people, were a rich race of people. We have lost so much through the destruction of our land. Even though the white man says he owns our land by means of a piece of paper, in our heritage, our cultural and spiritual beliefs, it will always be our land, and we must protect it.

Ngarrindjeri Sixth Sense

The majority of Ngarrindjeri people today believe we have a sixth sense, which we call Miwi. We believe it is in our stomach and enters the body through the navel or umbilical cord at birth. Our Miwi tells us what is right and what is wrong, where we should walk and where we should not walk. It tells us when someone is following us or watching us. It tells us if a person is good or bad.

One example that I use to try and explain this to people is when you are getting ready for a race and you want to win. You feel the pressure in your heart or in your stomach. Some call it butterflys in the stomach. I say, you have not got butterflys in your stomach, it is your Miwi speaking to you. Another example is when a woman is walking along and she is being followed by a person with wrong ideas. She will sense this and know before she sees or hears that person. Miwi is a power that can be used outside of the body without speaking or hearing.

Ngaitje

Each clan group of the Ngarrindjeri has a Ngatji, and the Ngatji is what clan group you identify yourself with. The most important thing about the Ngatijis is that they are your closest friends. They give you signs and messages of good news or bad news through their actions. Because of the close relationship with your Ngatiji, you have to show great respect to it. It is bad if you kill it. You will bring a curse upon yourself or a member of your family.

A Ngatji is animal, fish, or bird. For example, my Ngatji on my father's side is the pelican, on my mother's side, it is the blue crane. Today, I still respect and read my Ngatijis' messages and do my utmost to protect them and their home. The land and waters belong to our Ngatjis. To destroy the land and pollute the waters is to further destroy our cultural beliefs.

White Settlement on Ngarrindjeri Land

From oral history we know that around 1820 whalers and sealers were the first white people to invade our lands. When my ancestors first saw white people, they called them Krinkaris, which means ghost spirits from the dead come back to life.

They soon learned that they were not ghosts by the terrible things that they did to my people. They shot my people and kidnapped young men and young women, taking them to places like Kangaroo Island for slavery and sexual purposes.

Later on, as history shows, about 1830, Captain Charles Sturt traveled down the Murray River and discovered the Ngarrindjeri people and our land. When Sturt traveled down the River Murray, the small pox disease had killed many of my people. According to oral history, my people were in a state of shock and confusion because so many people were dying and there was no cure for this strange sickness.

Later on, the land was being taken over by settlers who were developing farms. Once again, terrible things happened to my people. They were shot, poison flour was left for them to eat, and once again Ngarrindjeri women were used for sexual purposes.

Then came the missionaries, with good intentions of protecting my people. They established missions and encouraged my people through the word of God, food, and clothing rations to come and live in the missions. Then they said, "You must stop speaking your language and learn to speak English so that the Lord can understand you. You must stop your Corroborees and come to church, you must stop your initiations, you must stop your types of marriages. If you don't, the Great Spirit God will send down fire and brimstone upon you. He will punish you." At that time my people thought that the Ngarrindjeri Creator had sent these men to teach a new way of life and that the punishment that had already happened would stop.

You see, my people thought that way because our name for God, or the Creator, is Ngangai Winamulde, Creator of all things, who lives in the Spirit World, who gave powers to our ancestors, Ngurunderi, Wyangare, Nepelle, and others.

To teach the Ngarrindjeri people the law, sharing, taking of food, hunting of food, and ceremonies, the ancestors carried out their duties before leaving earth to live in the Spirit World. There is a similiar connection to the Ngarrindjeri spiritual beliefs and beliefs within the Bible. That is why the missionaries were able to change a lot of Ngarrindjeri people's ways of traditional living, but not their cultural and spiritual beliefs relating to the land.

Not all Ngarrindjeri people would live on a mission. Families like my ancestors and my wife's ancestors stayed and moved around, squatting on vacant crown land and living off the land. This went on until approximately 1967, when houses were made available in the town for us to live in. If we didn't move to the towns, the welfare department more or less stated that they would take all the children away.

Living in the camps and the fringe-dwelling camps was a good life. We were still living in a semi-traditional way, we were still being taught our cultural heritage and the laws of respect toward the land and each other, and the hunting and taking of food.

Much has changed since traditional times. Ngarrindjeri have been forced off their land, forced to live in missions and fringe-dwelling camps, and then forced to live in town. The treatment of the Ngarrindjeri people over the years has not changed our inner feelings and beliefs for our heritage, culture, and the land. With the missionaries, you could say that one religion was used by people in the wrong way to destroy another religion.

Over the years we have been given some rights within our own country. I remember the 1967 referendum which gave Aboriginal people the right to vote and be counted in the census, the 1975 Racial Discrimination Act, which helped to overcome open racism, the 1984 Federal Aboriginal Heritage Act, and the 1988 South Australian Heritage Act.

These heritage acts were put in place for Aboriginal people to protect our heritage, our cultural beliefs, our sacred sites, our burial grounds, our land, and the trees, plants, animals, and birds upon it. These heritage acts have not been working fully to the benefit of the Aboriginal people. Where there have been disputes from mining companies, developers, or roadways, the minister for Aboriginal affairs has the power to override the rights of Aboriginal peoples.

The Hindmarsh Island Royal Commission

The example that I want to talk about to show what is still going on is our island Kumarangk, at the Murray mouth. What happened in the beginning is that there was a development company which built a small marina on Kumarangk. In 1988, when the South Australian Aboriginal Heritage Act was passed, I, together with other Ngarrindjeri people, formed the Lower Murray Heritage Committee to consult with development, mining, roadways, farmers, and other groups about our sites of importance.

In 1990 the marina development company sent an anthropologist to meet with us and discuss the further extensions to the marina. At this meeting, we stated there should be no more interference with the island until all Ngarrindjeri people had been properly consulted. The marina development company took this meeting as consultation and moved ahead with development and the proposal to build a bridge from the mainland to the island to service the marina. The building of the bridge was not mentioned to us by the anthropologist and was not part of his brief for the consultations.

We believed that our sites, which were already registered, would be protected under the South Australian Heritage Act. But the South Australian minister used his powers to allow the site to be desecrated so that the building of the bridge could go ahead. We then had no choice but to go to the federal minister and ask for protection under the 1984

Heritage Act. Robert Tickner, the federal minister for Aboriginal affairs, sent a woman law professor, Cheryl Saunders, to study our heritage and to talk to our women about their sacred beliefs about Kumarangk and the surrounding waters. She then made a report and the minister agreed there was sufficient reason to issue a twenty-five-year ban on development. Attached to her report were two sealed envelopes containing the women's personal knowledge. This was never to be shared with a man.

While this was happening, there were a few women who said they knew nothing of the women's business associated with the island and waters. They became known as the "dissident women." The media and liberal politicians (that's our conservatives) were pursuing the story. Then, the sealed envelopes turned up in parliament in the hands of the male minister who had been consulting with the dissident women. We were shocked and disgusted. One woman said that the Ngarrindjeri men had fabricated the women's business. Next, a Channel Ten reporter and friends of the developers took a Ngarrindjeri man to a pub for the evening and interviewed him while he was intoxicated. The next day they broadcast an edited version of the interview, where he said he had fabricated the "women's business." Later, when sober, he retracted this statement and apologized to his people for being influenced into making that statement.

At this point, the South Australian government called for a royal commission to establish if the "women's business" had been fabricated for the purposes of stopping the development. One month into the process, they had to suspend the hearings and go out and consult with Ngarrindjeri people, because they had given a wrong order under a section of the Aboriginal Heritage Act. When they had these consultations, the majority of Ngarrindjeri people told them, "leave it alone." However, they took this as adequate consultation and went ahead with the royal commission anyway.

After six months of further hearings from many "experts" of Ngarrindjeri culture, the commissioner found the beliefs were a fabrication. This came as a shock to us, to have a government hold a royal commission into our cultural and spiritual beliefs relating to our land. The majority of Ngarrindjeri people decided that this was a racist commission, that the system was totally against us, and that they would not give evidence to the commission, especially about the women's sacred beliefs. Only the dissident women gave evidence. From our perspective, this royal commission was a legal and political picnic held at our expense.

So once again we had to go back to the federal minister and the Commonwealth Heritage Act. This time we had a woman judge, a woman lawyer, and a woman anthropologist and hoped we could tell our story. The Ngarrindjeri saw this as a more culturally appropriate setting because it was heard out on the land. We then had another series of disasters. The federal government changed halfway through the process, and the new minister refused to appoint a woman to receive the report. The dissident women challenged the appointment of the judge in the High Court and we had another breach of confidentiality. The story just keeps on getting more and more complicated and any hope of justice gets further and further away. Where we are now is that we have tried to challenge the royal commission and failed. The government has amended the Heritage Act by passing the Hindmarsh Island Bill to allow for the development. Through two of our elders, we are challenging that bill in the High Court because the bill will have a rippling effect on all other Aboriginal groups in Australia. The High Court should hear the matter in February 1998.

I came over here to speak to this conference about my culture, about my beliefs, about my land, and to share with you what developers and governments are doing to us at present. I would appreciate any type of support that participants at this conference could offer us. We are not giving up.

Ellen Trevorrow

Basket Weaving

I'm Ellen Trevorrow and I'm a traditional cultural basket weaver. I was taught by an elder, Aunty Dorrie, about sixteen years ago. Basket weaving was around me as a child, but my grandmother and mother did not teach it to me. They said I needed to have an education, a white education. The welfare department would take children away if they didn't go to school. So I missed out on a lot as a child, but now my mother is starting to pass on important cultural information to me because we are running the Race Relations Cultural Education and Recreation Centre.

I would also like to mention a basket-weaving conference that was held at Camp Coorong in November 1997. We had a large number of indigenous people that came, including some Native American women, and we shared our basket-weaving skills and shared stories about our weaving. We spoke a lot about the problems we face today in collecting our weaving materials—problems like pollution of the land caused by the spraying of pesticides, water drainage of the land, and private property disputes with parks and wildlife administrations. It was a very successful basket-weaving conference. In June 1998 there was a basket-weaving conference in Los Angeles and Tom and I and about sixteen other Ngarrindjeri women were able to come over and share our weaving skills and stories once again.

This is one part of our culture that the land provides for us. Take away our land, destroy our land, and it will destroy our freshwater rushes for our cultural weaving. The land is already salting up, and pesticides are ruining the rushes. We have to travel a long way today to collect our freshwater rushes for weaving.

Miwi

I'd like to make a comment on what Tom said about Miwi. When I went across to Kumarangk for the first time, I was with my elders and I felt it in my tummy, all stirred up, and I cried. And that's when I believed what my elders were saying about the island being sacred women's business. When I went home that night and told Tom, he said that was my Miwi speaking to me, so it's true.

Contemporary Native American Responses to Environmental Threats in Indian Country

TIRSO A. GONZALES and
MELISSA K. NELSON

Our Native American culture has been strip-mined by the European's Judeo-Christian ethic. It is clear to indigenous peoples that we are dealing with a desperate society trapped inside a crumbling mythology. . . . Indians know how to play games with nature. Europeans—Whites—have been at odds with nature for many centuries. The Man vs. Nature argument is a contrived dichotomy with ancient roots in Christianity, Descartes and Francis Bacon. What you end up with is a race of people trapped by myth, striving to claw its way back to Eden against ever-growing odds. The project of nature is ongoing, we are part of it, yet the European continues to set himself outside of it. . . . Non-Indians will never have Western eyes so long as they cling to the Man versus Nature dichotomy.[1]

Introduction

This paper examines two case studies as part of a set of environmentally damaging economic development projects on Native American lands in North America and outlines a spectrum of tribal responses, from tribal council endorsements to grassroots protest and initiatives.

Underlying this discussion will be our fundamental understanding that, ultimately, there is no separation between environmental protection and cultural survival. To have a sustainable culture means having healthy land—one nurtures the other, physically and spiritually.

Due to decades of imposed governmental control of tribal resources, many tribes often feel backed into a corner and are coerced into exploiting their lands with the false hope that development will increase economic benefit to the community. The capitalistic assumption that economic profit will necessarily increase tribal well-being, despite damaging natural resources, is and has been a dangerous delusion in the minds of global developers and tribal members who adopt this assumption. Native scholar Jack Forbes calls this colonial impulse to access, commodify, control, and monopolize global resources a type of "mental illness." Those who express this impulse are psychologically infected by greed and blatantly consume other life-forms "for one's own private purpose or profit," which Forbes calls a form of cannibalism.[2] We will, throughout this paper, refer to the commodification and consumption of Mother Earth (i.e., "global resources") by industrial "cannibals" as the basic underlying urge behind most environmentally damaging projects on reservation lands.

In this chapter, we take a holistic approach to studying "Native Americans and the environment." That is, we are really talking about "Native Americans *in* the environment," or, as Corbin Harney, spiritual leader for the Western Shoshone, has stated, "Native Americans *are* the environment—the environment is us![3] We are operating from an indigenous model of wholeness, where people and place, matter and spirit, nature and culture are interrelated in a dynamic process. Consequently, we will limit our use of conventional academic labels that tend to fragment reality into artificial divisions. Instead we will use open-ended, dialogical terms that invite deeper inquiry into eco-cultural wholeness. This perception of the interconnected wholeness of nature and culture is one of the fundamental underlying insights of indigenous spiritual traditions.

It is no accident that the title of this volume is "indigenous traditions," as opposed to "indigenous religions." As has been stated numerous times, many indigenous languages have no word for religion because, for indigenous peoples who still value and practice the old ways, "religion is what we are, what we do."[4] The quality of our being and the actions we take in our daily lives shape our spirituality. To "walk in the beauty way" or follow "the good red road" requires that we look into ourselves: Are we participating in creation in a harmonious way? Are we honoring our ancestors for giving us life? Are we nourishing our Mother Earth as she has nourished us, so that she will continue to nourish future generations? Or, as the Peacemaker from the Iroquois Confederacy has said, "think of those faces coming from beneath the ground."[5] Indigenous spiritual traditions recognize the sacred in the immanent as well as the transcendent because they do not see a division between spirit and nature. Creation is a holy process that is ongoing and, as human beings, we have the responsibility to participate in this creation, to co-create, in a balanced blending, like the confluence of two rivers.

> Unlike the Torah, or the Bible, or the Koran, creation did not end on the sixth or seventh day and god rested on the seventh day. It is a commitment and obligation of all human beings, in fact, all life, to participate over and over again, as we did with our salmon ceremonies, in the renewal of the Earth. In this sense, creation never ends. It is an eternal task and occupation by human beings as set forth in the original instructions. All humans have an obligation to perform this responsibility and if we do not, the Earth suffers. Then the plants begin to go away and the animals begin to go away. And have we not seen this in recent decades. . . .[6]

To realize that, with each breath, thought, and action, we are at the threshold of creation is an enormous responsibility. Indigenous peoples have traditionally taken on this responsibility by following the natural laws of their creation stories and by performing ceremonies to renew the earth and maintain balance between people, place, and spirits. Many of these ceremonies continue today, yet tribal leaders are often prohibited from conducting their earth-based ceremonies because their sacred places are on private or governmental property, or worse yet, they are being degraded or destroyed by economic development projects. For Native spiritual leaders to exercise their religious freedom and maintain balance in the world, they must have access to their sacred sites where indigenous ceremonies have taken place "since time immemorial."

Although there is not *one* indigenous voice, but a diversity of native perspectives on the "environment," most traditional Native peoples agree that the "environment" is Mother Earth—our Mother and the giver and sustainer of life. We come from her, so we are part of her and she is part of us. If she is sick, I am sick, and vice versa. This reciprocal relationship goes back to the creation myths of many Native nations. This exchange is not just one of give-and-take but, as Kashaya Pomo elder and archaeologist Otis Parrish has stated, "it is give and be given." So *giving* is always the focus, not the taking. This philosophy and practice of reciprocity is prevalent among most indigenous peoples worldwide and certainly among the traditional ceremonial leaders of Turtle Island, the common Native name for North America based on several Northeast nation's creation stories.

It is important to note at the beginning that although we strongly believe in the ecological wisdom and practices of many Native nations, we do not subscribe to the belief in the "ecologically noble savage."[7] Indian people are just like any other group of people—we have values, ethics, and ways of doing things, but we also make mistakes and wrong decisions. Hopefully, we all learn from them. In fact, some scholars have noted that Native nations have specific codes and instructions for taking care of the earth precisely because they *did* make ecologically harmful decisions in the past and consequently created specific stories and rules to learn from those experiences. According to the cosmology of the Hopi nation, for example, we are nearing the end of the fourth world—three others have been "purified" through destruction because humans separated themselves from the other animals, forgot to sing to and give thanks to the Creator, and became greedy.[8] As ecopsychologist Alan Kanner has put it, "indigenous cultures, like all cultures, are imperfect, yet urban-industrial societies can still learn from them about sustainable living."[9] The issue of romanticism is an important one, and we acknowledge that in the past some things were better and some were worse. We know that we cannot, nor would we want to, "go back" to some romantic ideal. But we want to preserve, strengthen, and regenerate the traditional ethics, beliefs, and values that understood the subtle yet tangible language of harmony between humans and the dynamic processes of the earth. Restoring the spirit and structure of this harmony is humanity's modern challenge—indeed, the lives of our children depend on it.

In a contemporary context, this chapter addresses the complexity of protecting place-based tribal cultural practices in an era of economic globalization. It challenges the romantic idea of Native Americans as essential environmentalists, yet cites examples of traditional Native peoples who have retained and continue their land-based spiritual and economic practices.

Land Is Everything

Land is everything to Native American peoples for several reasons. First of all, indigenous land-based spiritual practices are rooted in an understanding of culturally and ecologically specific creation stories and oral histories.[10] These stories serve many purposes: education about tribal history, ethics, and spiritual values; oral maps of sacred homelands and information about the extended kin of plants and animals; entertaining community exchange; and the continuance of the intergenerational collective imagination of a nation. These stories, as examples of cultural diversity, differ from nation to nation because the traditional territories, the "biodiversity," of each nation is different. These geophysical changes in the land give rise to different cultural expressions because, for place-based oral cultures, "the visual counterpart to the spoken word is the land."[11] For example, in the Pacific Northwest, Raven has a special role because he is the omnipresent trickster power-bird of the temperate rainforest region. In the Southwest, in desert habitat, coyote is the main trickster character of creation stories and tribal myths. This ecological-cultural continuum is so ingrained in Native cultures that it is difficult for Native peoples to understand the Euro-American concept of wilderness as "pristine" nature absent of humans.[12] "The idea that human use *ensures* an abundance of plant and animal life appears to have been an ancient one in the minds of native people."[13] The land cannot be separated from people for a second obvious reason, that is, the very bones of our ancestors are present in the earth and help make the soil that grows our food. Our indigenous ancestors gave us life, we are part of them, and their bodies have become part of the earth, therefore we are part of the earth. Thirdly, there are certain places, such as Mount Shasta and Medicine Lake in northeastern California, that are considered the sources of life and sacred power for surrounding tribes. These sacred sites are unique places where people trained in the medicine way communicate with the Creator and gain healing powers. Sacred sites are the holy lands and special places of worship for indigenous traditions. One's spiritual connection to the Creator or Great Mystery happens in this life, in this place, in this moment. Again, we are reminded that creation is an ongoing responsibility and the sacred is as much an experience of immanence—being embodied—as it is of transcendence—being otherworldy. And last, land is everything because without it, we simply

Figure 1. Mount Shasta, California, sacred site to Wintu and other local tribes. (Photograph Claire Cummings)

Figure 2. Panther Meadows, Mount Shasta, California, sacred site to Wintu and other local tribes. (Photograph Toby McCloud)

cannot survive. Our very survival as a species and as individual humans depends on the health of Mother Earth. From an indigenous perspective, survival is not just a matter of "managing environmental resources," but of living in balance by actively participating in creation through reciprocity and world renewal ceremonies. As Vine Deloria, Jr., has so eloquently stated, "The underlying theme of ceremony is one of gratitude expressed by human beings on behalf of all forms of life, and they complete the largest possible cycle of life, ultimately representing the cosmos in its specific realizations, becoming thankfully aware of itself."[14]

Cultural Identity

For the purposes of this paper we will use the terms "Native American" and "Indian" interchangeably, for Native peoples both in Canada and the United States. These terms will represent individuals and general populations. The question "who is an Indian?" is such a complex issue of cultural identity, history, geopolitics, and colonial classification that we will only touch on it here. "Native American identity has rarely been understood in its cultural and social setting in mainstream America."[15] But what appears to be even more difficult for Euro-Americans to understand is the critical *ecological* context of cultural identity. This identity has been and continues to be severely impacted by the social conflict and environmental degradation created by Euro-American colonialism. Today, the indigenous question is the struggle of indigenous peoples for self-determination and control over their territories and resources. "Tribal sovereignty is necessarily concerned with the identities of individual Indians who comprise the body politic."[16] So one begins to see that Indian identity, in addition to being a personal understanding of one's heritage and sense of self, has social, cultural, ecological, and political dimensions. "We must also recognize that Indian identity as it is actually realized in individual Indian lives is neither static over time or across situations nor necessarily inherent to Indian personhood."[17] Thus, the question of who is an Indian grows in complexity.

Today, for the first time in human history, besides a global ecological crisis, we witness an indigenous global ethnic question.[18] This ongoing crisis is reflected with its own peculiarities of time, space, and juridical and ecosociopolitical aspects in North America at the local, regional, and continental levels. As a result of special treaty agreements between Native Americans and the federal government, a unique historical and contemporary factor of the Native American indigenous question is that Native American tribes are nations. That is, they can claim sovereign legal and political status. In this regard, "unless authorized by federal law or affected, altered, or diminished by tribal law, Native American nations (or American Indian tribes) retain their sovereign powers, thus states (and provinces in Canada) lack civil or criminal jurisdiction over Indians within 'Indian Country'."[19] These sovereign powers, however, are inherently limited.

> The sovereignty of Indian "nations" has been tailored to the colonial interests of America insofar as so-called "external" powers of sovereignty (e.g., rights to make treaties, regulate immigration, print money, etc.) have been "extinguished" by congressional fiat, while the so-called "internal" powers of sovereignty (e.g., rights to determine citizenship, regulate elections, tax, etc.) remain.[20]

Often even the "internal powers" of Indian sovereignty are disregarded by non-Native communities, states, counties, and courts. So, who has the authority to define and assert sovereignty? Likewise, who has the right to assign Indian identity?

For our purposes here, we define Native Americans as anyone who can trace their ancestral lineage back to precontact Native nations and who personally identifies as an Indian. Because this chapter specifically addresses federally recognized tribes ("tribes," "First Nations," or "Native nations") and their responses to economic development on reservation lands, this group is the main community of Native Americans we discuss. It is important to note, however, that there are numerous problems with governmental definitions of Native Americans. Many Native Americans in North America (who are sometimes the traditional caretakers of sacred sites) have no federal recognition with the government: either they never had it or such recognition was terminated by the government. This means these individuals have no recognized rights, such as land rights, as First Nations peoples, in the eyes of those who control and monitor federal resources. In these cases, Native Americans respond to land threats through environmental and cultural preservation organizations that use public law and private methods and strategies, such as easements and private land trusts.[21]

Tribal Actors

Among the federally recognized tribes of the United States and Canada, we will focus on three types of actors: 1) tribal governments and leaders; 2) general tribal members; and 3) grassroots community activists. It is very important to differentiate between these actors because differences in their ideologies, goals, and practices lie at the root of much tribal conflict regarding economic development projects on reservation lands. "A distinction should be made between traditional native people and tribal governments. While some tribes have cultural committees and some respect traditional ways, not all elected or political tribal people are knowledgeable or can speak for the traditional cultural members of their nation."[22] In between tribal councils and traditional grassroots community activists (which are not always separate, obviously) is the general population of tribal members who are very concerned about jobs and improving their economic situation and want to protect the land for the future. Regarding environmental controversies on their lands, general tribal members are often torn about which direction to go and end up simply following the leadership of the tribal council. Through community education, however, this group also supports and contributes to grassroots efforts to protect their homelands from exploitation. In addition to, but linked to, the third actor, we will also discuss the role of Native nongovernmental organizations (NGOs) and institutions.

Historical Background

Like most continents, North America contains a vast array of microclimates and soil types, which contributes to a great diversity of ecosystems and bioregions. From the deserts of the southwestern United States to the subarctic of northern Canada and Alaska, North America has extreme biological and cultural differences. The forests of the Pacific Northwest and the rivers and prairies of the Great Plains at the heart of Turtle Island produce most of the world's timber and grain. The coastal rocky shores, bays, and inlets create rugged shores and productive fisheries. And the numerous north-south mountain ranges, most notably the Rockies, contain an amazing variety of natural metals, forests, and sacred places. The North American landscape was all Native lands, and many parts of it, including California and Nevada, are still considered Native lands because they were not officially ceded to the U.S. government in treaties.[23]

From the time of first contacts by European colonists to the late 1800s, already over 90 percent of Turtle Island native lands in the area to become the United States were taken from the original inhabitants through expropriation, genocide, and ecocide.[24] By 1887 Indians owned about 140 million acres of land in the United States, already a fraction of the roughly 2,100 million acres of U.S. land. The amended Dawes Act of 1887 provided a mechanism that allowed 90 million acres to pass to non-Indian ownership in forty-five years. In 1977 A. T. Anderson, special assistant of the American Indian Policy Review Commission, noted that Indians own more than 50 million acres of land.[25] Despite having been "tremendously reduced in size from their aboriginal extent, tribal lands still constitute an enormous land base."[26] Fifty out of two thousand million acres would hardly be considered "enormous" by any standards except by those who want to minimize Indian land control.

United States Indian reservations and Canadian Indian reserves are held "in trust" for the tribes by the U.S. and Canadian governments. This "trust relationship" is fraught with difficulties for Indian communities. For example, how can a Native nation be truly sovereign when another federal government ultimately holds the title to the land and oversees all tribal activities?[27] Underlying this particular type of land tenure we find central elements of two related but different environmental histories: one aims to restrengthen, reestablish, and re-indigenize the tradition of harmony with Mother Earth; the other dramatically depicts the overwhelming colonial and neocolonial socioeconomic and political forces that disrupt fundamental environmental and ecological balances—balances that historically existed not so long ago in North America.

The lands and tribal resources we are concerned with are approximately three hundred reservations in the United States, which cover about 55 million acres. This is 7 percent of all federal lands[28] and only 4 percent of the total amount of land in the United States.[29] In Canada there are approximately 2,300 reserves that cover 2.7 million hectares of land,[30] which is less than 1 percent of all Canadian lands.[31] We are again referring to a fraction of the original tribal territories of Turtle Island. Whenever discussing Native American environmental issues, one of the first questions that arises is, "who owns the land and how did that happen, historically?"

If we look back even one hundred years, we can see that Native American lands have been continuously exploited by non-native, usually governmental and private interests. As Judith Nies points out, the *real* American myth is that government is "an invasion into the individual resourcefulness of the Western pioneers." Referring to the coal strip mining of Navajo and Hopi lands, she exposes that "in reality, the government and big business made it all happen."[32] The development juggernaut of this government-business partnership is concerned with the economic gain made from extracting mineral, forest, fish and wildlife, energy, and other resources from tribal lands and peoples.[33] Additionally, Native lands are increasingly seen as endpoint depositories for the waste generated by non-native Americans and Canadians. The question of who, ultimately, controls the land is probably one of the most important questions on the minds of Native peoples regarding their environment. "The story that has not yet emerged is about the syndrome in which transnational corporations take and exploit indigenous lands with the cooperation of host governments."[34]

The Dawes Act of 1887,[35] the Burke Act of 1906,[36] the termination of federal-Indian trust relationships in the late 1920s and 1950s, and Indian assimilation and relocation policies of the 1950s and 1960s[37] may reappear as "old wines in new bottles." This reappearing may be in part identified, as Anishinabe activist Winona LaDuke suggests, in the recent heavy investment in Native American environmental issues by the federal government—"advising tribes on options for nuclear waste storage and supporting development of new federally funded environmental initiatives in Indian country." In addition, LaDuke carefully notes, and warns, that "millions of federal dollars are playing a major role in what may be one of the biggest territorial and environmental battles in North America—one that may pit Indian against Indian."[38]

At the heart of tribal conflicts regarding economic development projects on Native lands are the dual tribal goals of increasing economic self-sufficiency for the tribe and protecting the natural and cultural resources for future generations. Attaining one goal means decreasing unemployment rates by providing jobs to tribal members, which usually greatly improves the social climate of the tribe by decreasing poverty. For example, when the employment rate improved on the Turtle Mountain Band of Chippewa Indian reservation in North Dakota, there was a greater sense of self-worth in the individuals and the community, which motivated people to address other problems, such as alcoholism, abuse, health and nutrition, and overall community well-being.[39] The quality of tribal jobs, however, makes all the difference. If the only type of work available is mining uranium, such as what happened to the Navajo in the 1950s, 1960s, and 1970s, then the tribe has to reconsider seriously its priorities for how to increase employment for their people. But that is the question: does the tribal council really want to increase employment for their people, or personally benefit from development contracts? Sadly, greed can creep into the lives of anyone, and tribal councils certainly aren't immune. "In 1966, the Hopi and Navajo tribal councils—not to be confused with the general tribal population—signed strip-mining leases with a consortium of twenty utilities that had designed a new coal-fired energy grid for the urban Southwest."[40] To understand why a council will make such a decision, one has to understand the colonial history of a nation and the psychological effects that has had on a culture. "When you lose that sense of place and who you are, you make room for other things, such as greed. You get insecure, you fill your life up with material goods or certain kinds of obsessions. The history of the West is characterized by people who are obsessed with control."[41]

Concerns of Native Americans Regarding the Environment

Environmental Issues in Indian Country

Based on prior work and research for this chapter, we have gained an overview of environmental issues in Indian country. This overview provides initial evidence of the alarming extent, degree, and depth of environmental concerns in Native North America. The overview, in short, indicates how key basic irreplaceable components of life (air, water, land/soil) are being seriously polluted and/or destroyed, within reservations and in adjacent areas, mainly by outside forces: federal and state policies and actions and resource extractive activities by global developers. These forces have different effects on reservations because each reservation or reserve has different types of resources (natural, human, economic, technological). The scenario becomes even more critical in situations where numerous Native tribes have no federal recognition. These communities are involved in an ongoing struggle for federal recognition and tribal sovereignty. In other words, these Native nations are struggling, even at the dawn of the twenty-first century, for control over their basis for subsistence, reproduction, and identity.

We have tentatively grouped the contemporary environmental problems in Indian Country under the following basic comprehensive categories: air, community, federal recognition, forest/timberlands, land/soil and groundwater, land rights, legislative, sacred sites/burials, subsistence, water.[42] These categories are somewhat arbitrary. However, they reflect how environmental issues in Indian Country are being shaped. In reality, one environmental issue relates to other environmental issues. For example, it is not easy to separate land/soil issues from groundwater concerns, or treaty rights to hunt and fish from concerns about industrial contamination of traditional foods.

As development accelerated throughout the nineteenth and twentieth centuries in North America, resource extractive and related activities (monocrop agriculture, energy development, logging, mining, oil exploration/exploitation, fishing) have intensified and enlarged in scale. This in turn has had a major impact upon the environment at large (air, water, lakes, rivers, coastal waters, ocean, groundwater, soil, biological diversity—human beings included). Coupled with economic globalization and trade, today the environmental question in the United States is an international question. Within this long-term scenario of economic change and ecological decline in North America, two major stages signal a transition in tribal history. This transition is closely connected to Native American environmental history within and adjacent to reservations. Mathew Snipp, Cherokee/Choctaw sociologist, encapsulates these stages in two key, heuristically useful categories: "captive nations" and "internal colonies." Natural resource exploitation inside the reservation for consumption *outside* the reservation is the key element of this transition:

> This transition is significant because it represents a basic restructuring of the tribe's relationship with the U.S. economy. Framing this transition, the terms "captive nations" and "internal colonies" are a pair of simple, though heuristically useful categories for delineating two major stages of tribal development. The expression "captive nations" defines the status of American Indian tribes prior to the development of tribal resources for non-tribal consumption. For those tribes without

resources or development, "captive nationhood" reflects their existing relationship with non-Indian society. For tribes in the midst of development, their situation can be plausibly compared with the conditions associated with internal colonialism. The term "internal colony," in its conventional usage, is a new status for many tribes as the resources they harbor become more valuable and sought after.[43]

The relationship between Native nations and the U.S. and Canadian governments, based on the issue of land, has always been a primary concern among tribes. Today, land continues to be a central concern. However, in addition to the land encroachment issue, we have to add a series of major environmental threats to the basis of life reproduction within reservations.

Grassroots Organizations and Efforts

The environmental consequences of resource exploitation for consumption outside the reservation are leaving harmful long-term imprints on reservations environments, particularly in this century. Dams, industrial pollution, logging, mineral mining, uranium mining, radioactive waste dumps, and agri-business are causing serious long-term side effects that put at high risk the survival and reproduction of tribes, as well as those resources necessary for future Native American generations. It is the seriousness of these environmental threats that have, in large part, favored the creation of Native American grassroots organizations. These groups aim to respond to both the issue of sovereignty and to those forces, political and economic, posing a threat to current and future Native American generations and to life at large. These new indigenous grassroots organizations are also proposing innovative sustainable indigenous alternatives to production as well as to enhance their environments.[44] Unlike their white environmentalist counterparts, most of these grassroots organizations face severe financial constraints, lack of facilities and basic technology, and limited resources. We are witnessing a growing number of grassroots Native American organizations concerned with the environment, in particular with their immediate environment and resources within their original territories. What follows is an overview of one grassroots organization, the Indigenous Environmental Network.

The Indigenous Environmental Network

The Indigenous Environmental Network (IEN) was born ten years ago, in 1990, during a Native American environmental gathering focused on toxic dumping within native lands. At that time, Diné CARE (Citizens against Ruining Our Environment), a grassroots Navajo environmental group, invited a small group of about three hundred indigenous peoples from all over Turtle Island to come together in the Diné (Navajo) community of Dilkon located on the Navajo Nation in Arizona. This gathering formed the initial network committed to opposing toxic dumping on Native lands. The IEN was officially formed as a national grassroots organization during the 1991 gathering held in South Dakota near the sacred Bear Butte. This gathering was hosted by the Native Resource Coalition (NRC) and the Good Road Coalition, both Lakota community organizations fighting toxic landfills. Additionally, the NRC works to protect their lands and waters from incinerators, mining of minerals, and protection of water rights. The IEN is an alliance of grassroots indigenous peoples whose mission is "to protect the sacredness of Mother Earth from contamination and exploitation by strengthening, maintaining, and respecting the traditional teachings and the natural laws.[45]

In terms of the background of IEN members, their stories are embedded within "grassroots activism, confrontation and community organizing"[46] and, equally importantly, they "were staking out a new position in the histories of both the Native movement for sovereignty, and the environmental movement for a cleaner earth." In fact, some IEN leaders emerged from the activism of the American Indian Movement (AIM) in the 1970s but wanted to be less reactive and more proactive and strategic about addressing important issues in Indian country.[47] The creation of the IEN also coincided with the emerging environmental justice movement of the early 1990s. Indigenous leadership built upon and added critical voices to the growing multicultural resistance to environmental racism.

IEN's unifying principles. The IEN's unifying principles are based on a hemispheric breadth and historical understanding: "the Indigenous Peoples of the Americas have lived for over 500 years in confrontation with an immigrant society that holds an opposing world view. As a result we are now facing an environmental crisis which threatens the survival of all natural life." The following are some of the IEN's central unifying principles: (a) unified action, sharing of information, and working together with mutual respect, (b) assert our sovereignty and jurisdictional rights through the application of our traditional laws and recognizing our traditional forms of leadership of our indigenous nations, (c) stand on principles of empowering and supporting each other to take direct, informed action and affect our ability to protect our lands from contamination and exploitation, (d) by attempting to fulfill our responsibility to defend our mother earth we are assuring the survival of our unborn generations.

Environmental code of ethics. The IEN is based on five central points. In their own words, they are:

(a) as Indigenous Peoples, we speak for ourselves, no one else is authorized to speak on our behalf. Environmental groups have no right to represent Indigenous People. We represent ourselves; (b) We will always stand by the strongest position in defense of Traditional Natural Law; (c) We will support Indigenous People's rights to self-determination; (d) We will not make accommodations for, or deals with, polluters; (e) We support basic principles of environmental justice, including the rights of people to a clean environment regardless of race, economic position, gender, or national identity. Violations of environmental justice we understand to be violations of International Law, the Universal Declaration of Human Rights, and the United Nations Convention on Genocide.

Goals. The IEN's goals are embedded in a holistic indigenous worldview and are hemispheric, that is, embracing the indigenous peoples of the Americas. Their environmental advocacy involves the local, regional, national, and international. Central to the IEN's goals is the proposal of environmentally sound alternatives. These goals are:

(a) Educate and empower indigenous grassroots people to address and develop strategies for the protection of our environment; (b) re-affirm our traditional and natural laws as Indigenous Peoples; (c) recognize, support, promote environmentally sound lifestyles and economic livelihoods; (d) commitment to influence all politics that affect our people on a local, regional, national, and international level; (e) to include youth and elders in all levels of IEN activities; and (f) protect our rights to practice our spiritual beliefs.

Governing structure and membership. The IEN is governed by a national council of Indigenous grassroots organizations and individuals. The IEN member organizations and individuals include: Circle of Indigenous Youth, Diné Citizens against Ruining Our Environment (CARE), International Indian Treaty Council, Indigenous Women's Network (IWN), Columbia River Alliance for Economic and Environmental Education, New Mexico Alliance, Native Resource Coalition, Concerned Mescalero Citizens, Alaska Regional IEN, Oklahoma Regional IEN, Indian Toxics Campaign-Greenpeace, Great Lakes Regional IEN, Elderly Representatives, and individual representation.

Zoltan Grossman notes that part of the IEN's success is attributed to the fact that its foundation lies among traditional tribal members and its emphasis is on leadership from both elders and youth: "IEN is governed partly by an Elders Council. IEN's Youth Council not only tries to solicit youth involvement, but tries to make environmental issues relevant to the urban-based culture of many Native youth."[48]

"Protecting Mother Earth" conferences. The IEN's annual "Protecting Mother Earth" conferences (PMECs) may be understood as IEN's yearly summits. They are hosted by and held at a different Native nation each year. They are unique massive gatherings where attendants participate in a series of environmental workshops and plenaries, in addition to other culturally related activities, such as sweat lodges and talking circles. There have been ten annual Protecting Mother Earth conferences. One of us has attended four of the conferences and we both attended the ninth annual IEN PMEC, which was held in northern California, at Mount Shasta, Buckskin Family Camp, Fall River Mills, 2–5 August 1998.[49] In the presence of Mount Shasta, Mount Lassen, and Medicine Lake, the daily social environment of this gathering was marked by respect and solidarity. The opening and closing of the event was blessed by Native rituals and ceremonies. More than one thousand attendants camped and shared the series of workshops, plenaries, and food provided by the organizers. Since 1992, the theme for each year's gathering has been different, highlighting a pressing Native American regional environmental issue, with a call to action and engendering public support. The most recent conference, the tenth, was held at Mount Taylor at the Laguna Pueblo in New Mexico, not far from the Jackpile mine, one of the largest open-pit uranium mines in the world and a U.S. federal superfund site. This conference was hosted, like the first Protecting Mother Earth Conference, by Diné CARE and its theme was "Uranium and Indigenous Peoples."

The IEN's national office is concerned with a wide range of environmental issues. Among the most urgent are: toxic landfills and illegal dumping in native lands; toxic incinerators; chemical run-off from agricultural activities; toxin-producing industries and companies; air pollution from remote and local areas; water quality and water protection; clearcutting of forests; mining activities; nonrenewable resource extractions; leaking nuclear storage tanks (above- and below-ground); tribal environmental and natural resource management; tourism and recreation pollution; military toxins and facilities; environmental health; treaty rights; and rights to fish, hunt, and gather.

The IEN is an excellent example of the power of indigenous peoples united to protect the earth from the onslaught of environmentally damaging economic development projects. Through community education, regional organizing, strategic research, and cross-cultural collaboration, the IEN represents a significant and powerful voice in international environmentalism and human rights. Anyone who believes that native environmentalism is based in romanticism should attend one of their conferences to learn about the technical, scientific, political, economic, and spiritual dimensions of continuing the right

Figure 3. Laguna Pueblo Reservation, New Mexico, with Jackpile uranium mine tailings on the upper left. (Photograph Melissa Nelson)

and responsibility to resist the exploitation of life and to participate in creation in a harmonious way.

Nuclear Waste: The Last Frontier?

The Mescalero Apache Tribe and Ward Valley

Due to a series of major colonial policies—genocidal and ecocidal—it has been extremely difficult for Native Americans to exercise their fundamental right to be who they are, be related to their ancestral lands, and keep balance with all living beings. Since the 1950s, one of the most recent insidious threats to Native lands is pollution, in particular that generated by uranium mining, the nuclear industry, and nuclear testing. The result of nuclear-related activities (for civilian or military purposes) is the growing accumulation of radioactive waste.

> Today, nearly all of the U.S. civilian nuclear reactors constructed in the late 1950s and 1960s have been shut down, including the first Shippingport unit. However, the legacy of their atomic power, and that of the 109 units currently operating, remains in the form of spent, or used-up, radioactive fuel.[50]

The issue of nuclear waste disposal, in the case of the United States, involves three major actors: the U.S. government, the nuclear industry, and Native American tribes. In the case of the U.S. government, among other aspects central to the U.S. nuclear program, it is worth noting that the government promised the nuclear industry that it would dispose of the spent fuel. But the United States, because of political concerns, does not have a program in place for the disposal of spent radioactive fuel.

Spent radioactive fuel accumulation is growing yearly. It is estimated that by 2020, the existing 111 nuclear power plants will have generated between 79,000 and 106,000 metric tons (MT) of high level hazardous waste.[51] In 1994 "the national spent fuel inventory has grown to over 23,681 metric tons (MT) of uranium, plutonium, and other radioactive byproducts, and nearly 97% of the current inventory is stored at reactor sites, mainly in the eastern half of the U.S."[52] The scale of the danger of radioactivity levels is generated mainly by commercial and Department of Energy (DOE) radioactive wastes.

Of the total estimated inventories of commercial and DOE radioactive wastes, spent fuel accounts for 95.8% of total radioactivity at only 0.19% of total volume. This level of radioactivity is of incomparable magnitude and danger, and its storage has been subject to both national security and health concerns. Safe storage of such highly radioactive material for a time period that is literally an eternity is the challenge being presented to Native American nations by the federal government.[53]

Since 1990, through its federal nuclear spent fuel policy and the Nuclear Waste Negotiator (NWN) office, the federal government has searched for "volunteers" among Indian tribes and state units of government for hosting temporary waste storage. "The federal government and the nuclear industry have made over one hundred proposals to store nuclear waste on Indian reservations."[54] The storage program is known as Monitored Retrievable Storage (MRS). This is a program to store nuclear waste "temporarily" until a "permanent" site can be established at Yucca Mountain, Nevada.[55] Not even one of the fifty states of the Union is interested in hosting temporary waste storage. In that context, two related factors are important: Indian lands and Indian sovereignty. In the view of the Indigenous Environmental Network (IEN), the U.S. Nuclear Waste Negotiator targeted Indian lands primarily because tribal sovereign status exempts tribes from many state and local environmental laws and policies.

Tribal sovereignty is being revisited, and isolated, impoverished, and politically vulnerable tribes are being targeted and enticed by the prospect of receiving special federal feasibility assessment grants.[56] The major reason for the unusual federal attention to the tribal sovereignty issue is not only the sovereignty that tribal governments have over environmental regulations, but also the power that some of these governments have in circumventing the consensus of the tribal members concerning economic development and land exploitation. J. D. Erickson, D. Chapman, and R. E. Johnny provide further detail on the connection between tribal sovereignty and MRS:

> While constitutions, corporate charters, and law codes vary widely among tribes, the sovereign system of Indian nations as a whole, shaped through years of court cases and federal law, has effectively provided a loophole for studying, and possibly siting, an MRS [Monitored Retrievable Storage] facility in Indian Country.[57]

Given the serious implications that tribal council decisions will have for the futures of present and future generations of Native Americans, some important questions need to be raised regarding the "sovereignty from above/below" issue in relation to MRS.[58] Who is exercising sovereignty within tribes? Do tribal members have an appropriate mechanism for the proper exercise of sovereignty? Does the sovereignty exercised by some tribes reflect some of the problems (corruption, abuse of power, physical threats, mismanagement of resources, unsustainable development policies) common to most Western governments? Why have some tribal councils adopted this "sovereignty from above" method of leadership? Are tribes in a position to exercise "sovereignty from below"? "Sovereignty from below" would be characterized by the full participation of tribal members in the decision-making process of issues relevant to the tribe, without external or internal interference of practices that do not resemble the most democratic, traditional process of decision making.

It is not the intention of this chapter to answer the questions posed above. However, the two case studies presented below will provide some elements for a study to be done somewhere else. The studies of the Mescalero Apache and Ward Valley will focus on the concerns outlined in the first section of this chapter: the interaction and power relations of the three major tribal actors (leaders, general members, community activists) and how they respond to and negotiate with the U.S. government and the nuclear industry regarding nuclear waste storage proposals on their native land.

Case Study 1: The Mescalero Apache Tribe, New Mexico

The case of the Mescalero Apache Tribe illustrates the sociopolitical conditions in which a serious problem generated outside the tribe, in this case high-level nuclear waste, is proposed as a viable "development project" by both the U.S. government and the nuclear industry. A serious environmental issue, such as nuclear waste, has put on trial key aspects of the political structure of the tribe, the role and ideology of the Tribal Council on nuclear waste storage, in particular, and development, in general. For instance, the Tribal Council and tribal members have had to participate and interact in a difficult decision-making process to consider or reject nuclear waste storage within the tribe and reflect upon the cohesiveness of tribal development alternatives with their fundamental ecospiritual and cosmological beliefs and traditions. Underlying this case, among other aspects, is the question of how colonization, including internal colonization (mind, body, heart, and spirit), might have eroded the underlying foundation of tribal life.

Brief socioeconomic background. The Mescalero Apache Tribe is located in the southwestern part of New Mexico, two hundred miles from Albuquerque, New Mexico, and one hundred miles from El Paso, Texas. Originally established near Fort Stanton by a treaty in 1873, today's Mescalero Apache Reservation covers over 460,678 acres in the Sierra and Sacramento mountains. This reservation is tribally managed Trust Land. It contains timber, pastures, and crop land. The bulk of tribal income comes from timber sales, with individuals often involved with cattle production or farming. The tribe also owns and operates several profitable enterprises, including the Inn of the Mountain Gods, a luxury resort, and Ski Apache. The current Mescalero Apache reservation population is about 2,695—of this total, 2,526 are Indian.

According to two tribal members and a councilman of the Mescalero Apache Tribe, there is an unemployment rate of over 60 percent in the tribe. Only 12 percent of the tribal members are employed year-round on the reservation by the tribe, the Indian Health Service, or the U.S. Forest Service. Others are employed seasonally at the tribe's Ski Apache or the five-star Inn of the Mountain Gods. The ski resort and the hotel bring the tribe about $6 million per year. Approximately one-quarter of the tribal members are fruit growers in the southern part of the reservation, but their income is also seasonal.

The politics of monitored retrievable storage (MRS) and the Mescalero Apache Tribe. What are the environmental policy guidelines of the Mescalero Apache Tribal Council (MATC)? What is the socioeconomic, environmental, and political assessment that led the MATC to opt for the monitored retrievable storage alternative? What other indigenous development alternatives might have been considered and can be considered by the Tribal Council? Is MRS coherent with the Mescalero ecological-spiritual traditional values, and therefore something worth considering by the Mescalero Tribe? Why did the MATC, despite it's involvement in MRS negotiations over three years, not provide the necessary information, or favor wide discussion, among tribal members on MRS and nuclear waste–related issues? These are important questions that deserve further scrutiny in another study. Nevertheless, the decision of the Tribal Council to apply for federal grants provided by the Nuclear Waste Negotiator office to study the possibility of constructing an MRS site on tribal land has raised two major opposing views.

The majority of tribes in Indian country do not seem to be interested in issues related to nuclear waste, in particular, to issues about MRS. In 1991, the NWN office invited 573 tribal leaders to apply for feasibility study grants related to MRS sites. Only nineteen applications were submitted. Six of these applicants withdrew under tribal opposition—two before the grant was awarded, two after being awarded the grant (although they later returned the $100,000), and two during Phase II. In New Mexico, of twenty-two tribes, the Mescalero Apache Tribe was the only one that applied for the NWN feasibility study grants. Their application moved successfully through the three phases involved.[59] Of the tribes originally targeted as MRS sites, all but three have withdrawn.

The Tribal Council's structure and ideology. It is important to pay attention to the position of the Tribal Council president, and to the potential power he or she has in this position, within the internal organizational structure of the MATC, as well as in connection to other tribes or tribal-related institutions. The Tribal Council (on behalf of its tribal members) decided, *post factum,* to pursue a feasibility grant, negotiate an agreement, and allocate grant money. According to many community activists, the Council took these actions without sufficient consultation with tribal members and did not provide the community with the necessary information for an adequate study of MRS.

Neither the way the Tribal Council is elected nor how it operates guarantees a transparent election process or fluid communication on matters highly relevant to the tribe as a whole. Erickson, Chapman, and Johnny, in their study of the Mescalero Apache, note that: "whether the tribal council president Wendell Chino's unmarred election record is legitimate has been subject to debate. Elections are coordinated by an election committee appointed by Chino, and votes have always been counted in secrecy, despite tribal opposition."[60] Chino was tribal council president for more than thirty-five years.[61] In a position of substantial power, he appointed all key tribal posts, including election, voting, and housing officials. "His power as president is also deeply rooted in the tribe's BIA [Bureau of Indian Affairs] approved constitution. The president serves in the legislative and executive departments, appoints judiciary members, and holds the court of appeals. In particular, the president establishes committees, acts as contracting officer, holds veto power, grants pardons, and directs the tribal police."[62] It is in the context of the above web of power that the Tribal Council made the decision to study MRS, pursue a negotiated agreement, and allocate grant money and benefits. Equally important is the fact that such a decision is "ultimately at the discretion of the Mescalero tribal council and in particular subject to the influence of (former) tribal council president, Wendell Chino."[63]

One of the central premises of American policies of assimilation, besides the assumption that Indians were culturally inferior, was that Indians had to fit into the Euro-American model. This process of assimilation, of becoming who you are not, has been supported by three main goals: 1) Native Americans should become "advanced" agriculturally; 2) they must adopt the concept and practice of private property land ownership; and 3) Native Americans must become innovative and business-oriented within the capitalistic system. A brief selection of various statements made by Chino and other tribal council members provides some insight into the ideology behind signing up for the MRS program. Erickson, Chapman, and Johnny quote a paragraph of a letter from Wendell Chino to David Leroy, formerly with the NWN. In the paragraph, the tribe's president describes the Tribal Council motives to study MRS:

> First, because we were asked to consider it by the United States Government; second, because there appears to be an opportunity to operate an MRS facility on a sound commercial basis; and third, because we can bring to such a program our strong traditional values that favor protecting the earth.[64]

At the U.S. DOE-sponsored Fifth Annual International High-Level Radioactive Waste Management Conference, held in Las Vegas, tribal vice president Fred Peso stated that "[we] want to tell an encouraging story of private enterprise, tribal initiative, and corporate courage." Then Peso added: "the Mescaleros can bear this waste storage responsibility because of our strong traditional values that favor protection of the Earth. We can serve as reliable, trustworthy and responsible guardians of the nation's spent fuel."[65] Moving further and beyond the initiative of the NWN, Peso noted, at the same conference:

> I believe the Nuclear Waste Negotiator effort can be considered successful, even if the outcome is different than anyone expected. If we had never received David Leroy's invitation, today we wouldn't be considering a private nuclear waste storage facility with 33 partners. We wouldn't have learned that there was a market for spent nuclear fuel storage, and that there was a business opportunity for us.[66]

Tactics of intimidation, abuse of power, and manipulation have been used by the MATC against tribal members who are against an MRS site and nuclear waste on Mescalero land. "The few tribal members who initially spoke out publicly against the Tribe's MRS studies have all since been fired from their reservation jobs, some of which were federal positions with the BIA."[67] Regarding tribal officials' tactics related to the second ballot—favorable to MATC MRS goals—it is worth noting the comments of New Mexico Attorney General Tom Udall: "it appears to me that the tribal leadership has strong-armed members to get this result."[68]

The Nuclear Waste Negotiator and the nuclear power industry. Radioactive waste accumulation at nuclear plants and the promise of the federal government to take care of the nuclear waste have motivated the nuclear industry and the government to explore two strategies: a short-term one of creating reactor storage systems (or MRS) that will hold the waste temporarily while a long-term, permanent nuclear waste storage site at Yucca Mountain, Nevada, is finally constructed. The Yucca Mountain proposed nuclear dump site is running over twelve years behind schedule. Additionally, stockpiles of nuclear waste at utility plants across the country are either reaching or have already exceeded storage capacities.

Given the fact that the federal government is far behind schedule on the Yucca Mountain site and given the slow MRS process, nuclear utilities "have banded together to pursue a private-sector waste facility."[69] The nuclear industry sector has targeted, among others, the Mescalero Apache Tribal Council.

The Mescalero Apache Tribe has already completed Phase I ($100,000 in 1991) and Phase II-A ($200,000) of the MRS program and was a II-B ($2.8 million) applicant. This last phase would continue feasibility studies and enable the tribe to initiate educational

outreach, enter formal negotiations, identify potential sites, and commence an environmental assessment. Phase II-B, as part of the MRS
program, has met with opposition: financial, with the budget cancel-
lation of Phase II-B by Congress in 1993; sociopolitical; grassroots;
congressional; gubernatorial (the New Mexico governor); and from
various other actors with different interests. This has encouraged a
group of thirty-three nuclear utilities (organized around Northern
States Power, or NSP) and a Minnesota utility to work together with
the MATC toward establishing a private MRS site. The first step in
that direction has been the agreement signed early in 1994 by the
MATC with the NSP.[70]

New Mexico state and congressional response to nuclear waste.
Over the years, resistance to and organization and protest against the
MRS Program on Mescalero Apache land have grown. This resistance
has come from tribal members, Mescalero grassroots environmental
organizations, most communities neighboring the Mescalero tribe, the
New Mexico state legislature, congressional representatives, and various Native American environmental organizations, such as the IEN.
At the congressional level, New Mexico's Senator Pete Domenici
(R-NM) and Senator Jeff Bingaman (D-NM)[71] are opposed to an MRS
site in New Mexico and have led a successful campaign to cut further
funding of the MRS program. Their recommendation is that nuclear
waste be stored closer to its point of origin, in states where nuclear
reactors are located. At the state level, Governor Bruce King has been
opposed to MRS studies from the outset. He contends that his state
has done more than its share to address the nation's nuclear waste
problem through its Waste Isolation Pilot Project (WIPP).[72]

Grassroots tribal responses to nuclear waste. Tribal members' opposition to MRS studies is very significant. A great majority disagree
with the MATC in this particular regard. Erickson, Chapman, and
Johnny note that "Francine Magoosh and other tribal members estimate as much as 95% of the tribe opposes the MRS studies."[73] Native
American opposition to an MRS site in Mescalero Apache land can be
identified within and outside the Mescalero Apache tribe. It is at this
level that the issue of "sovereignty from below" is being revitalized
and, consequently, the "sovereignty from above" exercised by the
federal government and the MATC around nuclear industry interests
is being questioned. In the short-term shadow provided by meager
NWN grants ($380,000) and the promise of $50 million a year in

lease payment business, ten members of the MATC have made efforts to join and support "sovereignty from above." These council members seemed not to have asked themselves: why didn't even one state in the Union sign up to host nuclear waste generated by the nuclear industry and the government? In other words, MRS sites and nuclear waste are *not* the kind of profitable business states want. Behind such state decisions, many communities and counties are beginning to exercise "sovereignty from below" to put a halt to further environmental disaster and communal decay caused by the nuclear industry.

A significant number of the Mescalero Apache tribe has strongly opposed nuclear waste on tribal lands. In the early 1990s, this opposition was led by local community activists Francine Magoosh, Joe Geronimo, and Donna Lynn Torrez, who worked closely with the IEN, and others. They were very concerned with the potential for human error in transporting and storing nuclear waste on their lands and were very active in educating themselves and other tribal members about the potential consequences of hosting an MRS site.[74] The success of their educational efforts was partially shown by the 490 members who voted on 31 January 1995 to halt further negotiations with nuclear utilities to host the proposed private sector nuclear waste storage on Mescalero Apache land.

In 1994, Rufina Marie Laws, a Mescalero Apache educator and founder of the group Humans against Nuclear Waste Dumps (HANDS) stressed:

> The Mescalero Apache people have been diabolically and deliberately excluded. At the same time, the tribe is actively being obligated to agreements and contracts without the input and consensus of the people. Many tribal members are opposed to siting nuclear waste storage on our homeland, for they believe it will be a violation of our sacred land and sacred mountain, Sierra Blanca.[75]

On another occasion, following the successful vote that decided to halt further negotiations with nuclear utilities, Laws not only noted in public the fact that former MATC president Wendell Chino appointed all key tribal posts, including election, voting, and housing officials, but also stressed that "we don't have any checks and balances in our tribal constitution. And the tribal council is just a rubber stamp."[76]

The group Apache Stronghold was created after the results of a second ballot on 9 March 1995 (the measure passed 593 to 372) where the decision was in favor of continuing negotiations with the nuclear utility companies. This group, like HANDS, is located on the Mescalero Reservation. The central goal of Apache Stronghold is to work against the proposed nuclear storage facility. "The group is rapidly expanding membership, despite the threat of being blackballed from tribal employment, housing and other MATC-controlled services."[77] Abraham Chee, member of Apache Stronghold, expressed his concern about the coherence between elders and traditions in the ongoing MRS/nuclear waste debate:

> The main reason I'm against this is because of my kids: I want them to have what I have had growing up. . . . It upsets me that Wendell Chino is an elder and supports this. He should know our traditions. Nuclear waste is against our traditions. The people voted "No" the first time. The things that we Apache people pray to are our land, the trees, the sky. We learned this from our parents and our grandparents. We need to keep carrying these traditions on. I guess those who want this nuclear waste don't know what our grandparents fought for.[78]

Besides Mescalero Apache grassroots environmental organizations and individuals, the Indigenous Environmental Network (IEN) and the National Environmental Coalition of Native Americans (NECONA), among others, have expressed concerns about the dangers of MRS siting or any nuclear waste disposal on Indian lands. The IEN and NECONA are very active in encouraging Native nations to declare themselves Nuclear Free Zones (NFZs).[79] Finally, communities adjacent to Mescalero Apache land "adopted formal resolutions against an MRS siting and gathered thousands of signatures on petitions."[80] It is important to note the high level of opposition *outside* the reservation to the MRS site at the Mescalero Apache reservation. "But local and state opposition [wasn't] successful in breaking off negotiations; the tribe had a collective change of heart reportedly after an anti-nuke scolding by tribal elders, and voted to reject the plan."[81] It was most likely a combination of opposition from within and outside the reservation that finally led tribal members to vote against the nuclear waste storage in January 1995.[82] As we saw from the second 1995 vote mentioned above, however, this victory for the dump opposition was short-lived: "Within two months, following an intense lobbying effort reputedly by people who controlled access to reservation housing and jobs, and after contemplating as much as $1 billion over 40 years, the voters reversed themselves."[83]

About one year later, in April 1996, despite the Tribal Council's tenacious search to find avenues and achieve resolution for the construction of an MRS site, the first lines of a *Rocky Mountain News* article noted that "an Apache tribe and a consortium of utilities said Thursday that they were dropping their five-year effort to store radioactive fuel rods from the nation's nuclear power plants on tribal land."[84] It is important to realize that the MRS story on Mescalero Apache land has probably not ended. So long as there is outside political pressure and large financial enticements for storage from the nuclear power industry and the government and so long as there is high unemployment and economic difficulties on the Mescalaro reservation, the incentive on the part of the Tribal Council to bring jobs and money via MRS will be strong. The MRS story at the Mescalero Apache reservation, although currently nonactive, is still unfolding as different tribal actors, from above and below, assert their powers and values.

Case Study 2: Ward Valley, California

In the southeast Mojave Desert of California, about twenty miles west of the Colorado River, lies a large valley that is part of the ancestral homelands of five local California Indian tribes—the Fort Mojave, Chemehuevi, Cocopah, Quechan, and Colorado River Indian Tribes. This place, Ward Valley, is sacred to all of these tribes. But it is currently owned by the federal government and administered by the U.S. Bureau of Land Management (BLM). It is also critical habitat for the endangered desert tortoise. Ward Valley has been proposed as the site for a low-level radioactive waste dump. It is a classic example of environmental racism, that is, of colonial plans to exploit and pollute Native lands by the economic alliance of big business (nuclear power industry) and the State of California (California Department of Health Services—DHS). US Ecology, the green-washed name of the private nuclear dump contractor, provided former California governor Pete Wilson $500,000 to purchase federal BLM land at Ward Valley to build the proposed radioactive waste dump. In 1993, former Department of the Interior (DOI) secretary Manual Lujan had committed the DOI to the transfer. "In response to Lujan's action, the BAN Waste Coalition and the Fort Mojave, Chemehuevi and Colorado River Indian Tribes sued Lujan to stop the land transfer, using the protections of the Endangered Species Act."[85] In the spring of 1998, "the Justice

and Interior departments concluded that California's health department lacks authority and is ineligible to purchase the land."[86] The
State of California rejected the federal government's conclusions and,
with the support of US Ecology, filed a lawsuit against the DOI to try
to protect its illegal transfer and plans to store nuclear waste in Ward
Valley. Several of the top Democratic leaders in the California legislature "concluded that DHS has no authority to enter into contract to
purchase land and would have to undergo further legislative and administrative approval to legally acquire the 1,000 acres site for the
dump."[87]

The Colorado River Native Nations Alliance (CRNNA), made up
of five federally recognized tribes in the Ward Valley area, has been
opposing this dump for more than a decade. The tribes of CRNNA are
still opposing this dump on the grounds that their land is sacred and to
protect their land and water rights. They have cited numerous environmental protection laws, such as the Endangered Species Act, National
Environmental Policy Act, Clean Water Act, and President Clinton's
Executive Orders regarding the protection of Native American Sacred
Sites[88] and Environmental Justice,[89] to illustrate how ill-conceived the
proposed dump is. "Fighting back tears, Nora Helton, Chairwoman of

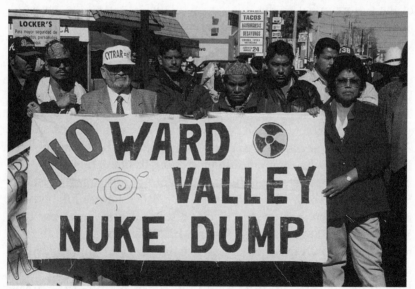

*Figure 4. Ward Valley protest action in front of the U.S. Embassy in
Juarez, Mexico, 1998. (Photograph Philip Klasky)*

the Fort Mojave Indian Tribe, vowed that the *Pipa Aha Macav,* or Keepers of the River, would defend their sacred lands against nuclear poisons."[90]

In late spring of 1998, the DOI suspended the current Supplemental Environmental Impact Statement (SEIS) because of the California legislature's findings and a 113-day occupation of Ward Valley by environmentalists and Native American tribes. CRNNA and connected environmental groups, such as BAN Waste Coalition and Save Ward Valley, conducted this 113-day grassroots occupation at the entrance to Ward Valley as a direct protest to proposed tritium tests by the DOI and the State of California. "These tests and the SEIS were vulnerable to influence and bias on the part of dump proponents."[91] The occupation had numerous benefits, the main one being the cessation of the tritium tests. Additionally, there was much media attention, coalition-building, and public education, and the Bureau of Land Management rescinded its notice to move the resistance camp.[92]

On 2 April 1999, a U.S. District Court judge ruled *against* the Ward Valley dump proponents (former California State governor Pete Wilson and US Ecology) whose lawsuit was against the U.S. Interior Department for refusing to transfer land to them for the dump site. Faced with the strong force of the Colorado River Native Nations Alliance and environmental coalitions and their victory in this federal ruling, US Ecology president Joe Nagel finally admitted, "I think the Ward Valley dump is dead."[93]

Both US Ecology and Governor Gray Davis immediately announced that they would not appeal this federal ruling regarding the Ward Valley land transfer. Governor Davis proposed looking at other alternatives for waste disposal in California. Then, US Ecology reversed their position and appealed the decision. Activists are still concerned with this project because Governor Davis refuses to withdraw the state's application to the U.S. Department of the Interior to transfer the federal land at Ward Valley to the state for the dump site. But, in a turn toward good news, in September 1999 the BLM issued a formal decision terminating any actions regarding the dump project by denying the State of California's request for sale of Ward Valley. These victories are very encouraging, yet Governor Davis has not officially terminated plans to purchase Ward Valley for the dump.

In response to all of the protests to the dump, in the fall of 1999 Governor Gray Davis created an advisory panel to look at alternatives

Figure 5. Sunrise Ceremony at Ward Valley. (Photograph Jim Bruggers)

to the Ward Valley site. His panel, unfortunately, is heavily stacked with pro-nuclear industry representatives. They outnumber representatives of environmental groups and Native American tribes by three to one. Members of BAN Waste Coalition criticized this panel's composition and "called for more balance with the addition of experts from public interest organizations."[94] These dump opponents have also pointed out that there are some significant conflicts of interest within this panel and have informed Governor Davis's office that this panel must find a new site and take Ward Valley off the table once and for all. Through his press secretary, Davis's office responded with a statement indicating that the governor is opposed to the Ward Valley dump site. But, until Governor Gray Davis makes a direct statement himself, resistance by the Colorado River Native Nations Alliance and environmental activists will continue.

As an example of Native resistance to outside economic development that damages the local environment, Ward Valley has many central elements: first, this radioactive dump is being proposed by the classic combination of a major industry interest and a governmental agency (where politicians are coerced to waive environmental laws in the project review process); second, this land is sacred ground to five local tribes who oppose the illegal poisoning of their traditional homelands on the basis that it would violate their religious freedom, cultural heritage, and environmental health; third, Ward Valley is critical habitat for the endangered desert tortoise and is near one of the largest freshwater sources for southern California and the Southwest; and fourth, resistance to the dump is fueled by cross-cultural collaboration with non-native environmentalists, cultural activists, and nonviolent protesters who adamantly oppose degradation of environmental quality on the basis that the land has, in addition to it's ecological value, spiritual and cultural significance. These facts help to build stronger resistance from the environmental movement and local citizens who ally themselves with the Native Nations Alliance to oppose the proposed dump. And finally, the proposed radioactive dump site at Ward Valley has been such a blatant case of environmental racism that the Environmental Protection Agency's National Environmental Justice Advisory Council (NEJAC) found that the proposed radioactive waste dump in Ward Valley "could adversely affect the sacred lands, environment and natural resources of the tribes."[95] NEJAC recommended that EPA officials "meet with the tribes and that an environmental justice impact analysis regarding the health, social, and economic impacts on the tribes should be conducted."[96] An unprecedented NEJAC resolution, in June 1998, called for a halt to the project. Additionally, the local tribes have themselves initiated economic development on their lands by growing and exporting food crops. If the dump project were to go through, the Colorado River could be contaminated with radioactive waste. As tribal council member Sonia Stone Chavez of the Colorado River Indian Tribes stated at a protest at the EPA building in San Francisco: "Our Native Nations Alliance would not be the only ones to suffer from this contamination, the whole country would feel it."[97]

To address the threat of nuclear waste storage and other energy resource issues on reservation lands, one must ask, "why are we generating all of this waste in the first place?" If it is not placed at one site, it will be placed at another. As a response to this question, members of the Indigenous Environmental Network have organized an annual day of rest for Mother Earth—"Unplug America"—on October 13. On this day, everyone is encouraged to "unplug" for a day by not using electricity and to reexamine our energy consumption habits. Decreasing our energy use is one way to minimize the pressure to exploit energy resources on Indian lands.

It is environmentally racist for non-native outsiders to try to place toxic waste on Native homelands. Radioactive waste pollutes natural resources for many generations. But what could be lost would be not only those natural resources, but the endangered tribal cultural knowledge about how to use them sustainably. "Tribal healers are perishing and their wisdom vanishing as fast as endangered plants are going extinct."[98] Thus, threats to native lands are as much an issue of cultural preservation as they are of environmental degradation.

Conclusion

As our case studies illustrate, in the transition from "captive nations" to "internal colonies," Native American reservations and reserves are threatened from within and without by sociopolitical and economic forces. Threats come from within when tribal councils and tribal members, under the prevalent Western economic-political value system, opt for short-term economic gains. In this context "sovereignty from above" is exercised by both the federal government and tribal councils. Environmentally speaking, sacred homelands are degraded and, consequently, tribes as a whole suffer. For example, in both our case studies each tribe is threatened by the major environmental threat of radioactive waste. The next losers may be nearby non-Native American communities. Finally, taking into account the environmental record regarding uranium mining and related activities, temporary nuclear waste sites at nuclear power plants, cold war nuclear waste sites, and nuclear weapon tests, the issue becomes a potential transnational environmental threat to the reproduction of indigenous and non-indigenous communities at large, as well as to the basic resources for the reproduction of life.

There is a simple economic truth outlined by Winona LaDuke that lies at the heart of this issue regarding environmentally damaging economic development projects on Native American reservation lands. Natural law, as outlined in the creation stories and original instructions of most Native nations, states that one should never take more than one needs when harvesting or collecting something from the earth. A related indigenous natural law is the law of reciprocity: if one receives a gift, whether a fish from a river, a deer from a forest, or dinner from a friend, one should return that gift with another gift— another food item, physical objects like clothes, or a gift of nature (shell, stone, feather) as appreciation, an honoring gesture, or a song. This practice of giving and being given (as opposed to taking) is a central tenet of indigenous religious traditions. Western capitalism, on the other hand, which thoroughly dominates the world through economic globalization, is based on the belief that one should provide the least amount of input (investment) for the maximum amount of output (profit). Put another way, one takes as much as possible while investing the least amount of resources (natural, human, financial). As LaDuke points out, it is clear that Western capitalism is out of balance with natural law.[99] How contemporary Native American nations in North America address this dilemma is an important area of research that needs further analysis. Our two case studies briefly review some of the major concerns, issues, and actors involved in these types of negotiations.

It seems that when Native American tribes adopt the Western mode of economic development, they also adopt the "sovereignty from above" mentality. This change from traditional subsistence economic systems initiates the transition from "captive nations" to "internal colonies." At this point, the meaning of sovereignty can shift significantly. We begin to see variable interpretations of sovereignty based on the colonizers' motive of resource exploitation. At the tribal council level, it is of the utmost importance to assess the councils' infrastructure and organization, as well as their short- and long-term visions, and to recognize their coherence with the essence of Native American traditions and values. We want to avoid "old wines in new bottles," or governments and businesses using tribal councils to get around state and federal environmental regulations. This pervasive practice of exploiting reservation lands by imposing a skewed interpretation of sovereignty must be made more clear in the minds of general tribal members, who are the ones who often suffer the most from damaging development projects. As they become more informed about the power relations of tribal councils and the government-business alliance, grassroots tribal members can resist and protest environmentally damaging projects on their lands. We see this happening at the Mescalero Apache reservation. At Ward Valley, we see the tribal councils of five nations honoring their traditional knowledge of protecting Mother Earth by opposing a nuclear dump site on their lands. There are several socioeconomic, historical, political, and ecospiritual factors that create this difference in tribal council support or opposition to outside economic development projects. In this chapter we have tried to point out some of these factors. One critical historical factor in the economic changes on reservations in the United States (that we can only mention here) is due to the Indian Reorganization Act of 1934: "Under the provisions of this act any tribe or the people of any reservation could organize themselves as a business corporation, adopt a constitution and bylaws, and exercise certain forms of self-government."[100] According to many traditionalists, this act enabled tribal members who were most affected by and concerned with Western modes of development, to put themselves in leadership roles and negotiate economic development deals on behalf of their tribes. As a result, the internal fragmentation of tribes and their goals was greatly exacerbated. Today, tribes are still dealing with the aftereffects of this change in leadership on reservations.[101] Janet McCloud poignantly and succinctly summarizes the situation:

> Tribal governments under the 1934 Indian Reorganization Act are not sovereign. First the US reduced us from an independent nation into a domestic dependent nation into a tribe, then into a federal agency, where our elected leadership acts as federal agents to legalize the exploitation and plunder the remaining lands and rights of our people. This is the final destruction to extinguish our internal sovereignty.[102]

As we enter the twenty-first century, Native American Nations are re-examining their pasts in order to prepare for the future. Many contemporary tribal movements include work to revitalize traditional cultural practices within a modern context. For example, Pueblo and Lakota farmers are restoring their traditional irrigation systems and practices of collecting rainwater and are conserving and planting heirloom seed varieties. They are also building solar-powered greenhouses, rammed-earth homes, and educational web sites. This process of restoring traditional practices is conversely a process of decolonizing oneself, spiritually, emotionally, physically, psychologically, and socially. For Native Americans to decolonize on a collective level, Onandaga faithkeeper Oren Lyons recommends that we no longer see ourselves as "members of a tribe" but as "citizens of a nation."[103] By doing this we are re-indigenizing ourselves, individually and collectively, and reclaiming our inherent sovereignty and responsibility to protect Mother Earth for future generations.

On a global scale, it is difficult to predict if indigenous nations will be able to restore and re-indigenize their lands, histories, and cultures and escape the neocolonialism of transnational capitalism. Yet, traditional land-based communities have survived numerous attempts at extermination and, today, persist and survive in isolated communities and places. Also, native communities that have been forced to give up some of their traditional ways are actively restoring their languages, ceremonies, stories, songs, and land-management practices through cultural revitalization, often in mixed-blood urban communities. By continuing and restoring land-based spiritual traditions, following the natural laws, and conducting ceremonies, we are maintaining our resistance to and immunity from the infectious greed of cannibalistic consumerism that is driving the world out of balance. As indigenous peoples, we pray for and work toward a vision of Native American sovereignty that is based on the best combination of traditional ecological knowledge, local economic systems, participatory decision-making processes, and modern sustainable technologies and practices. If we can create balance between all of these elements, then hopefully our children's grandchildren can again swim and drink freely in rivers and lakes without the threat of radioactive contamination.

Notes

1. Mandan tribal attorney Raymond Cross quoted in Paul VanDevelder, "A Coyote For All Seasons," *Native Peoples,* fall 1998, 45, 46, 48.
2. Jack D. Forbes, *Columbus and Other Cannibals* (Brooklyn: Autonomedia, 1992), 34.
3. Corbin Harney, Indigenous Environmental Network, Ninth Annual Protecting Mother Earth Conference, Buckskin Camp, California, 2–5 August 1998.
4. Forbes, *Columbus and Other Cannibals,* 27.
5. Joan Halifax, *The Fruitful Darkness: Reconnecting with the Body of the Earth* (New York: HarperCollins, 1993), 105.
6. Dennis Martinez, Indigenous Ecology and Cultural Restoration Workshop, The Cultural Conservancy and Society for Ecological Restoration, San Francisco, California, 23 September 1999.
7. K. H. Redford, "The Ecologically Noble Savage," *Orion Nature Quarterly* 9, no. 3 (1990): 25–29. Janis B. Alcorn, "Noble Savage or Noble State? Northern Myths and Southern Realities in Biodiversity Conservation," *Ethnoecologica* 2, no. 3 (1994): 7–19.
8. Frank Waters, *Book of the Hopi* (New York: Viking Press, 1963), 15–16.
9. Allen Kanner, "Romancing the Stone Age," in *Ecopsychology Newsletter* (California State University, Hayward, Ecopsychology Institute), 1994, 3.
10. See Gregory Cajete, *Look to the Mountain: An Ecology of Indigenous Education* (Durango: Kivaki Press, 1994); and John Bierhorst, *The Way of the Earth: Native America and the Environment* (New York: William Morrow, 1994).
11. Melissa Nelson, "Ecopsychology in Theory and Practice," in *Alexandria: The Journal of the Western Cosmological Traditions* (Grand Rapids, Mich.), 3 (1995).
12. See Gary Paul Nabhan, "Cultural Parallax: The Wilderness Concept in Crisis," in his *Cultures of Habitat: On Nature, Culture, and Story* (Washington, D.C.: Counterpoint Press, 1997). See also Winona LaDuke's and Dennis Martinez's articles in *Sierra Magazine,* November/December 1996; and Marcus Colchester, "Salvaging Nature: Indigenous Peoples, Protected Areas and Biodiversity Conservation," UNRISD Discussion Paper, DP 55, September 1994.
13. Thomas C. Blackburn and Kat Anderson, "Introduction: Managing the Domesticated Environment," in *Before the Wilderness: Environmental Management by Native Californians,* comp. and ed. Thomas C. Blackburn and Kat Anderson (Menlo Park, Calif.: Ballena Press, 1993), 19.
14. Vine Deloria, Jr., "Sacred Lands: The Sanctity of Lands Is the Foundation of Individual and Group Dignity," *Winds of Change,* autumn 1993, 36.
15. John A. Grim, "Cultural Identity, Authenticity, and Community Survival: The Politics of Recognition in the Study of Native American Religions," *American Indian Quarterly* 20, no. 3 (summer 1996): 353.
16. Joseph P. Gone, "So, Are You a Full Blood? Sovereignty, Status, and the Quest for an Authentic Indian Identity" (forthcoming, *Americans for Indian Opportunity*), 1.
17. Ibid., 8.
18. Vine Deloria Jr., *For This Land: Writings on Religion in America,* ed. James Treat (New York and London: Routledge, 1999); David Maybury-Lewis, "What Is the Future and Will It Work?" *Cultural Survival Quarterly,* summer-fall 1994, 1; Rodolfo

Stavenhagen, *The Ethnic Question* (Geneva: United Nations University Press, 1990); and Tirso Gonzales, "Political Ecology of Peasantry, the Seed and Non-Governmental Organizations in Latin America: A Study of Mexico and Peru, 1940–1995" (Ph.D. diss., University of Wisconsin-Madison, 1996).

19. J. D. Erickson, D. Chapman, and R. E. Johnny, "Monitored Retrievable Storage of Spent Nuclear Fuel in Indian Country: Liability, Sovereignty, and Socio-economics," *American Indian Law Review* 19, no. 1 (1994): 73–103.

20. Gone, "So, Are You a Full Blood?" 1.

21. Claire Cummings, "Saving Native Lands," in *Exchange* (Washington, D.C.: Land Trust Alliance), 1994.

22. Ibid.

23. For the case of California, see Bruce S. Flushman and Joe Barbieri, "Aboriginal Title: The Special Case of California," *Pacific Law Journal*, 1986, 391, 403; the Advisory Council on California Indian Policy Final Reports and Recommendations to the Congress of the U.S., pursuant to Public Law 102-416, Executive Summary, September 1997, 3; and R. F. Heizer, *The Eighteen Unratified Treaties of 1851–1852 between the California Indians and the United States Government* (Berkeley and Los Angeles: University of California Press, 1972), 33. For the case of the Shoshone in Nevada, see Steven J. Crum, *The Road on Which We Came: A History of Western Shoshone* (Salt Lake City: University of Utah Press, 1994), 124–47 and 176–83; and Jerry Mander, *In the Absense of the Sacred: The Failure of Technology and the Survival of the Indian Nations* (San Francisco: Sierra Club Books, 1991), 303–18.

24. This is a long and detailed sad story of land loss and devastation for Native nations. See Ward Churchill, *Struggle for the Land: Indigenous Resistance to Genocide, Ecocide, and Expropriation in Contemporary North America* (Monroe, Maine: Common Courage Press, 1993), 15–83; and Mander, *In the Absense of the Sacred*, 195–302.

25. Darcy McNickle, Mary E. Young, and Roger Buffalohead, "Captive Nations: A Political History of American Indians" (research report, 1977).

26. Charles Wilkinson, "Tribal Sovereignty in a Nutshell," World Wildlife web site: www.wwf.org/new/bridges/bb2.

27. See the cases *Johnson v. McIntosh,* 21 U.S. (8 Wheat.) 543 (1823), and *Cherokee Nation v. Georgia,* 30 U.S. (5 Pet) I (1831), for the political history of how independent Native nations became "domestic dependent nations" or "nations within a nation."

28. "Federal Lands in the Fifty States" (Washington, D.C.: National Geographic Society, Cartographic Division, 1996).

29. Winona LaDuke, "Native Environmentalism," *Cultural Survival Quarterly* 17, no. 4 (1994); also published in *Earth Island Journal,* summer 1993, 34–35.

30. Julian Burger, *Report from the Frontier: The State of the World's Indigenous Peoples,* Cultural Survival Report, 28 (London: Zed Books; Cambridge, Mass.: Cultural Survival, 1987), 203.

31. Indian control of lands is changing in Canada, as the new territory of Nunavut has recently been established. This entire territory of 770,000 square miles will be governed by the Inuits. See David Crary, "New Territory in Canada's Northland," *San Francisco Chronicle,* 28 March 1998; and *Native Peoples Magazine,* June-July 1999.

32. Judith Nies, "The Black Mesa Syndrome: Indian Lands, Black Gold," *Orion Magazine* 17, no. 3 (1998): 21.

33. Through the Human Genome Diversity Project and the "wealth" of traditional healing knowledge of tribal elders, indigenous knowledge and human cells and genes are now commodified and seen as a "resource" for capitalism.

34. Nies, "The Black Mesa Syndrome," 20.

35. The Dawes Act of 1887, or the "General Allotment Act," was a response of Congress to pressures from special interest groups by exploring ways to reduce Indian landholdings and force Indians to develop the lands they held. The Dawes Act was the device through which the government, fueled by special interests, hoped to accomplish this goal. Among the opponents of the act was Senator Teller of Colorado, who characterized an earlier version as "a bill to despoil the Indians of their land and to make them vagabonds on the face of the Earth" (McNickle, Young, and Buffalohead, "Captive Nations").

36. The Burke Act of 1906 further amended the Dawes Act to permit the Secretary of the Interior to bypass the trust period restrictions and issue "certificates of competency" to Indians declared by him to be 'competent.' As soon as the amendment became law, creditors and land buyers were on hand to help allottees make out applications and prepare the necessary affidavits showing competency in land matters and evidence of habits of civilized life. When the certificates were issued, these same people were present to purchase the land from the Indian owners. In this way and through other quasi-legal means, prime land passed into non-Indian ownership. Lush agricultural land, virgin timber, and mineral and water resources were taken eagerly. As William T. Hagan has observed: 'Severalty may not have civilized the Indian, but it definitely corrupted most of the white men who had any contact with it." (McNickle, Young, and Buffalohead, "Captive Nations").

37. Termination as official federal policy was supported by many Indian Affairs commissioners, most notably Dillon Myer and Glen Emmons. Senator Arthur Watkins of Utah also had a significant role in shaping the United States Indian policies of the 1950s and 1960s. Indian termination was accompanied by U.S. policies of Indian relocation where Indians were sent to urban centers as a way to acculturate and assimilate them into the dominant society.

38. LaDuke, "Native Environmentalism."

39. Women and Wellness Conference, Turtle Mountain Chippewa Indian Reservation, July 1996.

40. Nies,"The Black Mesa Syndrome," 19.

41. Greg Sarris, "The Truth Will Rise," in *Surviving in Two Worlds: Contemporary Native American Voices,* ed. Lois Crozier-Hogle and Darryl Babe Wilson (Austin: University of Texas Press), 228.

42. The "air" category is used to cover environmental issues related to air pollution from remote and local areas. The "community" category is used to highlight and embrace issues (nuclear waste, development policies, toxic waste dump, military exercises, forced relocation) that tend to have an affect upon tribal/reservation communities as a whole. The "federal recognition" category concentrates on the struggle for federal recognition by tribes. The "forest/timberlands" category pays attention to environmental issues that fall within or are related to forest and/or timberlands. The "land/soil and groundwater" category gathers issues having an impact on tribal land/ soil pollution/destruction, which might sometimes have a close relation to groundwater pollution.

43. C. Matthew Snipp, "The Changing Political and Economic Status of the American Indians: From Captive Nations to Internal Colonies," *American Journal of Economics and Sociology* 45, no. 2 (April 1986): 153–54.

44. See the programs of the Seventh Generation Fund, Arcata, California; the Traditional Native American Farmer's Association, Tesuque, New Mexico; Indigenous Peoples Restoration Network, Glendale, Oregon; the Sustainable Indigenous Communites Program of the Lannan Foundation; and the Indigenous Environmental Network.

45. Indigenous Environmental Network web site: www.alphacdc.com/ien/.

46. Zoltan Grossman, "History of the Indigenous Environmental Network," article available on the IEN web site: www.alphacdc.com/ien/.

47. Grossman, "History of the Indigenous Environmental Network"; and conversation with Tom Goldtooth, IEN National Coordinator, 14 January 2000.

48. Grossman, "History of the Indigenous Environmental Network."

49. The theme for the 1998 gathering was "Honoring Sacred Places."

50. Erickson, Chapman, and Johnny, "Monitored Retrievable Storage of Spent Nuclear Fuel," 73–103.

51. Indigenous Environmental Network web site: www.alphacdc.com/ien/

52. Erickson, Chapman, and Johnny, "Monitored Retrievable Storage of Spent Nuclear Fuel," 74.

53. Ibid., 75.

54. Philip M. Klasky, "Environmental Justice and the Proposed Ward Valley Nuclear Waste Dump," report to the Environmental Protection Agency, region IX (San Francisco: BAN Waste Coalition, 1998), 4.

55. Regarding the MRS program, the National Environmental Coalition of Native Americans (NECONA), under the leadership of Grace Thorpe, notes that "while problems with the permanent site cause long delays, the hosts of the 'temporary' will be risking their land and the future of their children for generations" (NECONA's web page, 1988).

56. Feasibility Assessment grants are made up of three phases. Successful grant applicants receive in Phase I a grant of $100,000. Phase II-A offers an additional $200,000 for continued education and feasibility studies. Phase II-B offered up to $2.8 million to continue feasibility studies and education outreach, enter formal negotiations, identify potential sites, and commence an environmental assessment.

57. Erickson, Chapman, and Johnny, "Monitored Retrievable Storage of Spent Nuclear Fuel," 83.

58. The explanatory power of the heuristic terms we proposed, "sovereignty/democratization from above" and "sovereignty/democratization from below," may be expanded by the work of John Brown Childs on globalization and democratization. For an introduction to Childs's work, read his "Globalization-from-Below," in *Global Visions: Beyond the New World Order*, ed. Jeremy Brecher, John Brown Childs, and Jill Cutler (Boston: South End Press, 1993).

59. See Suzanne Westerly, "Where the 'Atomic Age' Began: Grace Thorpe Honored Working for Nuclear Free Zones across America," in *News From Indian Country: The Independent Native Journal* (Los Alamos, N.M.), late October 1999.

60. Erickson, Chapman, and Johnny, "Monitored Retrievable Storage of Spent Nuclear Fuel," 90.

61. We want to acknowledge the recent passing of Wendell Chino in 1999. We send our condolences to his family and tribe. Although our case study analysis represents Chino in a somewhat negative light, we want to acknowledge his strong leadership in many other areas and his lifelong commitment to tribal issues.

62. Erickson, Chapman, and Johnny, "Monitored Retrievable Storage of Spent Nuclear Fuel," 90–91.

63. Ibid., 91.

64. Ibid.

65. Randel D. Hanson, "Nuclear Waste at Mescalero," *The Circle* 15, no. 8 (August 1994): 6–7.

66. Randel D. Hanson, "Indian Burial Grounds for Nuclear Waste," *Multinational Monitor* 16, no. 9 (September 1995).

67. Erickson, Chapman, and Johnny, "Monitored Retrievable Storage of Spent Nuclear Fuel," 92.

68. Hanson, "Indian Burial Grounds for Nuclear Waste."

69. Ibid.

70. Erickson, Chapman, and Johnny, "Monitored Retrievable Storage of Spent Nuclear Fuel," 98; Hanson, "Nuclear Waste at Mescalero"; Hanson, "Indian Burial Grounds for Nuclear Waste."

71. Grace Thorpe, leader of NECONA, notes in a paper that "as the number of tribes considering the MRS dwindled, pressure in Washington mounted. NECONA persuaded U.S. Senator Jeff Bingaman of New Mexico, who had been one of the moving forces behind the Radiation Exposure Compensation Act for uranium miners, to oppose the MRS on the energy and the appropriations committees. As a result Congress withheld funding for the program" (NECONA's web page, 1998, 3).

72. "The WIPP is currently expected to start a several year 'test phase' in which up to 4250 fifty-five gallon drums of high-level nuclear weapons waste will be accepted. WIPP is designed to store over six million cubic feet of this waste, quantities seemingly sufficient to 'unduly' burden New Mexico with additional nuclear waste at an MRS." Quoted in Erickson, Chapman, and Johnny, "Monitored Retrievable Storage of Spent Nuclear Fuel," 99.

73. Ibid., 91.

74. Based on conversation with Tom Goldtooth, IEN National Coordinator, national office, Bemidji, Minnesota, 14 January 2000.

75. Ibid., 2.

76. Ibid., 5.

77. Ibid., 6.

78. Ibid.

79. NECONA reports that, in total, seventy-five tribes are Nuclear Free Zones, both in the U.S and Canada (NECONA's web site, 1998).

80. Erickson, Chapman, and Johnny, "Monitored Retrievable Storage of Spent Nuclear Fuel," 99.

81. See Cherie Parker, "NSP's Skull Valley Duggery," in the *Twin Cities Reader,* January 1997.

82. See Shepard Krech III, *The Ecological Indian: Myth and History* (New York: W.W. Norton and Co., 1999), 222.

83. See ibid.; and "Nuclear Waste Dump Gets Tribe's Approval in Re-vote," *New York Times,* 11 March 1995.

84. Indigenous Environmental Network web site, 1998.

85. Ward Young, "Ward Valley Legal Update," *Save Ward Valley News* 6 (summer 1998): 3.

86. Michelle DeArmond, "Jackson Asks Clinton to Halt Desert Landfill," in *Press-Enterprise,* 16 June 1998.

87. Young, "Ward Valley Legal Update," 3.

88. On 24 May 1996, President Clinton signed Executive Order 13007, to "1) accommodate access to and ceremonial use of Indian sacred sites by Indian religious practitioners and 2) avoid adversely affecting the physical integrity of such sacred sites on federal lands."

89. On 11 February 1994, President Clinton signed Executive Order 12898: "Federal Actions to Address Environmental Justice in Minority Populations and Low-income Populations."

90. Philip M. Klasky, "Ward Valley: Saving a Storyscape," *Terrain* (Berkeley: Ecology Center), fall 1998, 19.

91. Philip M. Klasky, "Ward Valley: Steps toward Victory and the Challenges Ahead," *Save Ward Valley News* 6 (summer 1998): 2.

92. Ibid.

93. "Ruling Apparently Kills Ward Valley Nuclear Dump Plan," *Los Angeles Times,* 3 April 1999.

94. See Philip Klasky's 29 December 1999 "Ward Valley Update," to members of BAN Waste Coalition, San Francisco.

95. Ward Young and Philip M. Klasky, letter to coalition and supporters, Bay Area Nuclear Waste Coalition, 23 September 1998.

96. Klasky, "Ward Valley: Saving a Storyscape," 21.

97. Sonia Stone Chavez, at the Ward Valley protest and rally, San Francisco Environmental Protection Agency building, 17 October 1998.

98. See Lee Siegel, "Tribal Healers Dying Off: Scientist Fears Indian Wisdom May Become Lost," *Salt Lake Tribune,* 2 January 2000.

99. Winona LaDuke, "From Resistance to Regeneration: The Next 500 Years," *The Nonviolent Activist: Journal of The War Resisters League,* September-October 1992.

100. Vine Deloria, Jr., and Clifford Lytle, *The Nations Within: The Past and Future of American Indian Sovereignty* (New York: Pantheon, 1984), 5.

101. Because each Native nation is historically and sociologically different, it is important to note that the relationship between political leadership and spiritual leadership is very complex and needs to be addressed on a case-by-case basis. For example, in some tribes, these leadership roles are very separate, in others they are the same.

102. Janet McCloud, "Who's Sovereign?" 1 December 1980. See Indigenous Environmental Network web site: www.alphacdc.com/ien/.

103. Oren Lyons, "Spirituality, Reality, and the Dynamics of the Natural World" (plenary talk presented at the Indigenous Traditions and Ecology conference, Center for the Study of World Religions, Harvard University, 15 November 1997).

Liberative Ecologies

A Guest on the Table:
Ecology from the Yup'ik Eskimo
Point of View

ANN FIENUP-RIORDAN

Introduction

> There was a story about a goose telling a story. It was in the spring,
> when goose food becomes plentiful. . . . When the goose was coming it
> said, 'In the spring here, plants that had just thawed are so tasty. I am
> coming your way!' It knew that it would be hunted and caught by a
> human being. That is why the geese like to come here in the spring,
> because there are good-tasting foods for them. They use the truth about
> the story. Even if they know that they were going to be killed, they say
> that they will come back.[1]

Yup'ik Eskimos have a distinct view of their environment that governs
their action in the world. One aspect of this view is their attitude
toward animals, as well as their understanding of how animals view
them. Yup'ik people traditionally, and many today, view the relationship between hunter and prey as a cycle of reciprocity in which animals visit the human world where they are hosted and sent back to
return the following season. This return is not viewed as a necessary
response on the part of the animal guest but an intentional act.

Although respect for and attention to the needs of their animal
guests was fundamental, it would be a mistake to assume that the obligation to limit kills was a familiar concept to Yup'ik hunters. In fact,
the idea that animal populations are manageable through selective

hunting is antithetical to the Yup'ik view of animals as guests who return if given proper treatment and respect.

The Real People

> We call ourselves *Yupiit* or "Real People." In our language, *yuk* means "person" or "human being." Then we add *pik* meaning "real" or "genuine." We are the real people.[2]

Today close to twenty-five thousand Yup'ik Eskimos make their home in the Yukon-Kuskokwim delta of southwestern Alaska. The Bering Sea coast boasts abundant resources, including sea and land mammals, waterfowl, and fish. Prehistorically, this abundance supported the development and spread of Inuit culture, and some scholars have called the western coast of Alaska the "cradle of Eskimo civilization."[3]

Until the 1940s, the lack of commercial resources meant that non-Natives ignored southwestern Alaska. The elders of today were born into a world very much like that of their forebears, especially in their reliance on the harvest of fish and game. Rapid change has since come to coastal communities. The social reforms of the 1960s, the Alaska Native Claims Settlement Act in 1971, and the Alaska oil boom of the 1980s supported the establishment of fifty-seven modern villages between and along the Yukon and Kuskokwim Rivers, each with its own high school, corporation store, daily air service to the regional center of Bethel, electricity, television and telephone service, and, in some cases, indoor plumbing. Despite these changes, the Yup'ik language remains the first language of children born in coastal communities, and many traditions—especially dancing and elaborate community gift-giving—are living links to the past. Yup'ik people remain one of the most traditional groups of Native Americans, with an interest both in preserving their past and in carrying vital traditions into the future.

The harvest of fish and wildlife for local use also continues both a preferred and necessary activity in this isolated and economically underdeveloped region. Fish is the predominant food harvested by most coastal residents, with sea mammals and birds also important in the household economy. The dollar cost of replacing locally harvested fish and game by outside food stuffs is prohibitively high. In a 1986 study of three delta communities, the value of the subsistence harvest

varied from $7,800 per household in Alakanuk to $23,000 per household in Scammon Bay.[4]

Animals as Nonhuman Persons

Fish and wildlife are not only critical subsistence resources. The ongoing relationship between humans and animals is central to the
Yup'ik view of the world. For the Yupiit, society included both human
and nonhuman members. They extended personhood beyond the human domain and attributed it to animals as well. They did not believe
that only humans possessed immortal souls, in contrast to and dominant over the mute beasts that served them. On the contrary, the Yupiit
viewed the relationship between humans and animals as collaborative
reciprocity; the animals gave themselves to the hunters in response to
respectful treatment of them as persons (albeit nonhuman) in their
own right.

According to the Yup'ik view of the world, human and nonhuman
persons shared a number of fundamental characteristics. First, the
perishable flesh of both humans and animals belied the immortality of
their souls. All living things participated in an endless cycle of birth
and rebirth in which the souls of both animals and people were a part,
contingent on right thought and action by others as well as self.

Along with the belief in an essential spiritual continuity, the Yup'ik
people held that humans and animals alike possessed "awareness,"
which allowed individuals a sense of control over their destiny. From
the powerful bear to the small, apparently insignificant tundra lemming,
each was a thinking, feeling being. Animals were often depicted as
more sensitive and aware than their human counterparts. According to
Charlie David, "That was the way the old ones operated when they
totally respected the *ella* [universe]. . . . The land animals like the
ocean beings are very, very keen. Truly, they are aware of everything."[5]
This awareness was felt to be the product of experience. People
lacked a sense of self at birth. Gradually, however, they became aware
of their surroundings.

As they matured, both human and nonhuman persons received a
multitude of prescriptions for the culturally appropriate living of life.
Three related ideas underlie the elaborate detail of these rules: the
power of a person's thought, the importance of thoughtful action so as

not to injure another's mind, and the danger inherent in "following one's own mind." In all tasks undertaken, appropriate attitude was considered as important as action. Both humans and animals gave help to individual elders and tried to avoid their displeasure, because of the "power of the mind of the elders" to affect their future.[6]

The similarity between human and nonhuman persons created the common ground for their interaction. Just as human hunters were capable of conscious decisions as to what and where to hunt, animals were believed capable of conscious decisions that affected the success of individual hunters. Seals, fish, and birds were believed to disdain the approach of a hunter who seemed careless in either thought or action. The character of human conduct was an important factor in the interaction, yet was not sufficient to guarantee a hunter's success.

Jobe Nevak of Toksook Bay voiced the opinion that animal populations fluctuate because animals have their own worlds.[7]

> They used to say, "Sometimes there are fewer of this, and sometimes there are more." . . . There is a saying that animals have two worlds. First they live on our world, and then they disappear and live under there in their other world. . . . The mice population varies. . . . The fox population also varies. Sometimes there are lots and sometimes there are few. It's the same with all fur animals. They have two worlds.

Fundamental to these remarks is the idea that animals control their own destinies. When they are treated in ways they do not like, they do not return. On the other hand, if they receive proper treatment, including appropriate hunting, they will return in abundance.

> All the animals or birds decrease or increase when they want to. Although many are killed, they increase again. Many years ago we used to kill many geese. Geese don't decrease to extinction, they become plentiful again when they want to. Even the mink or any living creature that lives on the land decreases and increases when they want to.
>
> They know where they nest and go to their nesting ground. If they know their nesting ground is not good for nesting, they will find another spot.[8]

Although interaction between humans and nonhumans is made possible by their common possession of an immortal soul and a mind meriting respect, humans and animals are also clearly differentiated.

Within oral tradition, these differences are least evident in the *qulirat,* or traditional tales of the time "when the earth was thin" and animals often lifted up their beaks or muzzles, transforming themselves into human form. Charlie Friday of Hooper Bay told the story of a human boy who traveled with the geese on their fall migration:

> The geese brought him with them. When it was time, the grandfather did a *qaniqun* [shamanistic rite involving incantation] and taught him how to fly. When the boy learned to fly, he migrated with them. . . . They were like people across on the other side.[9]

Especially vivid accounts of animal and human interaction are tales describing humans visiting animal society and animals living within human society. Theresa Moses of Toksook Bay recounted another well-known traditional tale describing a young man who married a goose in human form and brought her to live among people:

> I used to hear lots of stories about the animals who wore clothing just like people. There was a story about a girl who wore a Canadian goose feather parka. When spring came, the woman would be out late. She would be smeared all over the face with mud from eating grasses. One day when it was melting out, she disappeared. She flew away with the geese.[10]

Even today, the treatment of animals in Yup'ik communities presupposes these shared aspects of personhood. Many believe that animals observe what is done to their carcasses and communicate with others of their kind. This conceptualization of animals as nonhuman persons underlies and sets the stage for everyday experience. An understanding of this view of the world can also help explain the miscommunication and talking past each other that characterizes many environmental issues in southwestern Alaska today.

Harvesting the Geese: The More Taken, the More Will Return

The distinctive treatment of animals as nonhuman persons meriting respect and acting intentionally toward their human hosts is a key feature differentiating at least some hunter-gatherers from small-scale agricultural and pastoral societies. It certainly differentiates many contemporary arctic and subarctic hunters from the non-Native biologists, sport hunters, and animal rights activists whose different views of animals conflict in Alaska and Canada today. At present, south-western Alaska is blessed with many animal species but cursed with many conflicts over how these animals should be managed. The fol-lowing pages focus on one such conflict—the debate over research and regulation of geese in general and black brant in particular—as a window into how different views of the environment shape action and attitude in the modern world.

In 1992 I was asked to carry out interviews with residents in six coastal Yup'ik communities. This modest research project was the "human dimension" of a larger National Science Foundation study of goose biology and ecology in the coastal wetlands adjacent to com-munities I have worked in as an anthropologist over the last twenty-five years. Although four nesting colonies of black brant have been the subject of intense biological research for more than a decade, no previous attempt had been made to work with local elders and com-munity leaders to ascertain their understanding of goose biology and ecology.

I was initially asked to do the work, but on reflection I thought better of it and requested that the grant be given to the local non-profit corporation, the Association of Village Council Presidents (AVCP), which subsequently employed village researchers to carry out the project. Although the AVCP hired me to help train local researchers and put together their final report,[11] the project was in Yup'ik hands from start to finish.

Interviews with coastal residents revealed a detailed understanding of the habits of goose populations. In the past, elders said, many geese nested in the muddy lowlands of the Bering Sea coast. "There were so many that in the fall people couldn't sleep because the geese made so much noise," recalled Mark Tom of Newtok.[12] These nesting geese produced thousands of eggs, the gathering of which was a major springtime harvesting activity. Mary Ann Sundown of Scammon Bay remembered: "When we went egg hunting, my mother used to tell us not to take all their eggs, but to leave an egg or two. It is true that they are like people. . . . They love their young which are precious to them."[13] Few people go egg hunting today. Paul John of Toksook Bay re-marked, "If they want eggs, they go to the store to go egg hunting. . . . They don't go egg hunting as much as they used to because of the chicken eggs."[14]

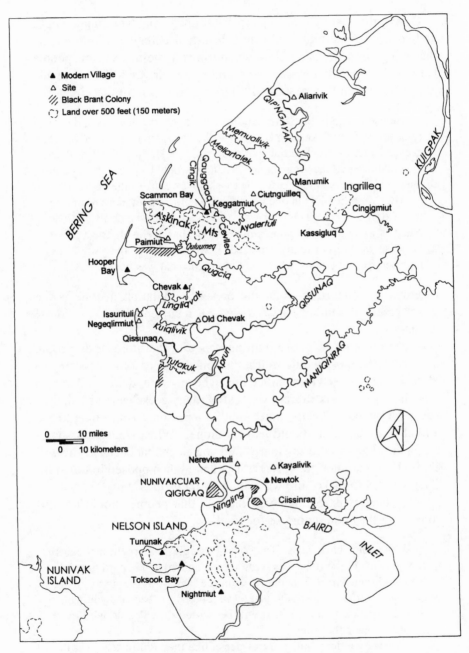

Figure 1. Modern villages and historic sites in the study area
(map prepared by Matt O'Leary, 1997)

During the nesting season people refrained from handling the eggs and goslings remaining in the nest, lest their parents avoid them and the young birds die. Later, however, during the molting season, people harvested geese in large numbers through goose drives. Mike Uttereyuk, Sr., of Scammon Bay described driving geese north of the village:

> We used to go to the coast and drive the geese downwards and stop right across from Scammon Bay. We walked in a semicircle to drive the geese. When we reached the spot, we would look at them and walk in the middle to part the group in half. Then we would let people go around them and free the other geese. That was how we drove the geese.
>
> After we killed lots in one year, there would be a lot more returning the next year. That was how it was. . . . Today, since we don't catch as much as we used to, the population of geese has declined. The amount of geese we kill is usually replaced. If we killed lots, they would be replaced by many more when they returned. That was how it was![15]

Uttereyuk's conclusion—that the present population decline is the direct result of limited harvests—was a recurrent theme in elders' testimony.

A central tenet of goose hunting was that the more birds people harvested, the more would return the following season: According to Michael John of Newtok: "Since I have been aware, there used to be a rule about geese. At different years after many geese were killed, they never decreased."[16] On the other hand, if a person wasn't going to use a food resource, they should leave it alone: "When we caught something, the elders would say to us, 'Did you catch that because you will eat it? If you are not going to eat it you are not supposed to touch it.' They wanted to make sure we abided by their rules."[17]

Mike Uttereyuk, Sr., recalled the rule that people should not kill something they could not use for food.

> White men have laws. The Yup'ik people had traditional laws, too. . . . One of the rules was if there is an animal that is hard to reach, we should not kill it. Whether it is on the land or in the ocean, if we can't get to it, . . . we should just leave it alone . . . because you won't be able to take it and eat it. It will be wasted. . . . People who lived before us made that rule. . . .
>
> Because we don't kill a lot of geese like they did in the past, the numbers have declined. Because white men are keeping a close eye on them. . . . They are making the goose population decrease.[18]

Uttereyuk's conclusion highlights a fundamental conflict between the Western scientific view of geese and that held by many contemporary Yupiit. Wildlife managers and biologists believe that overhunting and harvesting, in both Alaska and the Lower Forty-eight, are major factors contributing to the decline of goose populations along the Bering Sea coast.[19] For Uttereyuk and many of his generation the decline of the geese does not reflect overharvesting by Yup'ik hunters. Instead, it is limited harvests that insult the geese, causing them to go elsewhere.

Changes in Brant Nesting Grounds

Elders gave detailed accounts of the habits and habitat of black brant, based on years of personal observation. Brant inhabit the wetlands along the Bering Sea coast, an area rich in small grasses that form the staple of the brants' diet. They nest in four major colonies between Nelson Island and Scammon Bay, rather than in scattered single nests that they return to year after year. The population of these colonies declined an average 60 percent during the early 1980s. Biologists attribute this decline to both high harvest rates and high rates of nest destruction by arctic foxes.[20] Biologists report that since 1986 the population has been gradually increasing, although in some areas there has been a decline in females returning to nest, either because smaller goslings don't survive or because the colony, while recovering its size, prevents their return.[21]

Elders were asked to describe changes they had observed where geese nest and in their overall numbers. Some attributed these changes to spring flooding and nest destruction, noting that population fluctuations were often the result of changes in land and weather conditions. A common theme in their descriptions was that in the past many geese inhabited the muddy lowland, but since professional biologists and researchers began work in the area, the goose population has declined. Conversely, in coastal areas north of Scammon Bay, brant are increasing now that researchers and wildlife managers have stopped work in the area.

Many elders lay strong emphasis on the connection between increased human activity in the nesting grounds and declining numbers of geese. According to Nathan Kaganak of Scammon Bay:

At Mernualivik there used to be many black brant in the springtime when we go northward. We would pick eggs like we were picking wood from the ground. Then white people came to study the geese, and they became less. Now they don't nest at Mernualivik anymore.[22]

Like residents in villages to the north, Nelson Islanders also made the connection between increased human activity and changes in geese nesting areas, as well as a decline in their numbers. Theresa Moses of Toksook Bay noted:

When we used to go out egg hunting, many geese flew. They made it hard to look across the tundra because there were so many. Today, I don't know where that sight is.

I don't know why there is a decrease in the goose population. We who live on the coast don't play with them because we grew up with them. We leave them alone because they are our food. When they come they make our minds happy.[23]

Contrary to biologists' observations that the goose population has been steadily increasing since the mid-1980s, most Yup'ik men and women interviewed have seen an overall decline. They attribute this decline to a variety of factors: handling of goslings and eggs by biologists, increased noise and activity in the nesting grounds, and increased harvesting with modern technology. In the end, however, most Yup'ik observers believe that although changes in human activity set the stage, the geese are ultimately responsible for their own decline:

Sometimes we can't really blame anything and anyone for the decrease of geese. When they want to be fewer within a year they are fewer. We don't know why it happens, but the next year there are more. Even though a lot are killed, their numbers don't seem to change the following year.[24]

Many people deeply resent research and regulatory activity in the breeding grounds. Every elder interviewed spoke out against "Fish and Game," using this term comprehensively to include all non-Native biologists and state and federal wildlife managers working in the area. David Boyscout of Chevak reported:

The gathering grounds for geese are like sacred ground. No one should be there. . . . I would hunt there but not camp there. By summer I saw a tent pitched on that ground. All summer it was there. The next year, I checked that ground, there were no geese.[25]

Elders insisted that people should never handle either goose eggs or goslings. They maintain that handling the nest and its contents imparts a human smell that will "soak into the feathers" and scare adult birds away, leaving young birds prey to foxes, jaegers, and gulls. According to Thomas Akerelria of Scammon Bay: "Geese have their own world, their own awareness. If their eggs are handled, they won't go back to their eggs. They smell the scent of the people."[26]

Just as people attribute the decline in numbers of geese to the presence of "Fish and Game," the recent increase in geese is associated with "Fish and Game's" departure. Roy Henry of Scammon Bay stated, "Yes, I noticed the decrease for two to four years, and then they increased again because they are not bothered. There are no more Fish and Game people on the other side of our mountains."[27] Paul John of Toksook Bay agreed:

> There are rules towards the geese. When they are nesting, we should not scare them. If we don't need them right away, we leave them alone. Do not handle their eggs because, if we touch it and smear it with our hands, their mother will become scared and hesitant to tend her eggs. It will not go back to its eggs and they will not hatch. . . .
> We are not to play with them especially when they are goslings. When they hatch, they will grow and become our food. These rules were especially spoken to us a long time ago before the white people came.[28]

Even if biologists do not handle the geese, their presence disturbs them. Many residents believe that, by studying them, the biologists are "making the geese disappear."[29] Dick Lawrence of Toksook Bay testified, "When anyone makes a fuss over something, they don't increase. There used to be lots of caribou. Since the white people started keeping track of them, they disappeared. Same thing is happening with the geese."[30] Conversely, "when the geese had no one to keep an eye on them, there were so many."[31]

Underlying these statements is the Yup'ik understanding of geese as nonhuman persons, possessing awareness of their surroundings and capable of decisions as to where to nest and what to avoid. According to Eddie Bell of Hooper Bay, "They may be birds, but they have minds that work, too!"[32]

Because all animals, as nonhuman persons, are aware, they respond to human action. People are supposed to hunt what presents itself. This position is dramatically opposed to the non-Native view that re-

fraining from hunting will conserve resources and cause animal populations to increase. Michael John of Newtok spoke at length on this
issue:

> A long time ago I used to hear that nothing ever finishes. The prey,
> our food, is said to go into the ground. When they go underground, they
> decrease on the surface. After they seem to decrease, they will come
> back again.
>
> They also used to say that if a lot of something was killed, they
> won't decrease, but if they are not hunted, they will decrease. . . .
>
> Our land from the past has a law. The food from the land, also plants
> and fish, have laws for us. While they are available, we should gather
> without limits. There is also a saying: We should share the ones we
> have caught with our neighbors. That is what they used to say. . . .
>
> If we follow the rules of the past, the land's source of food, the fish,
> the geese, and birds won't be gone forever. . . . If we use the white
> people's rules, the food source won't increase.[33]

As significant as this fundamental conflict is—the conflict between
the non-Native view of geese as manageable wildlife and the Yup'ik
view of geese as persons possessing awareness and acting intentionally—many Yup'ik men and women also deeply resent the nonlocal control non-Native researchers and wildlife managers represent.
Their response to research and management activities not only reflects their perception of geese as other-than-human persons, but their
view of *themselves* as persons free to determine what occurs in their
homeland. Theresa Moses spoke with feeling:

> I am furious and can't stand it when the white people look after the
> geese. They act like they own the geese! I always think that it was a gift
> from God for all the people. I tell you the truth, my mind is unhappy
> about it. When I was growing up, we used to do what we wanted to do,
> abiding by our traditional laws. Now the white people come and handle
> the geese, going against the traditional laws.[34]

Mike Uttereyuk, Sr., comes to the point:

> Any person, whether white or nonwhite, should not boss us around
> when we hunt from the wild. Fish and Game are toying with us! Food
> from the wild has no boss. The people of Fish and Game may be intelli-
> gent, but they don't understand that our creator made it with no boss![35]

From the Yup'ik point of view, it is inappropriate to tell others what to do. Elders and parents can educate young people in proper behavior, but it is ultimately the individual's choice about how to live life. Thus, they resent the constraints of outside regulation as well as overt nonlocal interference and attempts at controlling them, "bossing them around" in their homeland. As Jorjean Charlie of Newtok put it, "The Yupiit were born on the land, and it belongs to them. They cannot tell their neighbors what to do. Fish and Game came and told us what not to do. That is what we are unthankful for."[36]

This objection to the presence of biologists is not a lightly held opinion, but is perceived to be based on experience. David Boyscout of Chevak testified, "I know the geese won't gather where people stay because I have experienced it. It happened in my presence. . . . They may not appreciate what I have to say, but it has to be spoken. That's how I feel." It will take a positive experience with biologists and game managers to change the opinion of Boyscout and others like him.

Conclusion

In southwestern Alaska today, many people continue to view humans and animals as sharing common personhood. Many see animals as sentient and aware of themselves and others (including hunters). Inappropriate human behavior may jeopardize animal harvests. Humans must show animals proper respect, which extends to taking an animal when it presents itself. The consequences of lack of respect are the animals' withdrawal. Many Yupiit believe that appropriately respectful humans cannot overhunt but can offend animals by not taking them when they offer themselves. As stated by Mike Uttereyuk, Sr.: "After we killed lots of geese in one year, there would be a lot more returning the next year. That was how it was. Today, since we don't catch as much as we used to, the population of geese has declined."[38] Biological research involving tagging birds and handling their eggs offends the sensitive geese, causing them to withdraw.

Biologists and wildlife managers in Alaska have had a difficult time accommodating their agendas to traditional hunting beliefs. To many, modern technology has effectively tilted the balance between humans and animals. The precontact use of stone arrow points, dog sleds, and kayaks is more appropriate to the Yup'ik worldview. Many Yup'ik people would answer that respect transcends technology.

Biologists defend their practices based on empirical evidence in their camps and study areas, which they invite villagers to visit. They say that they observe no adverse reaction by geese to their presence in the area. Yet villagers only rarely visit these camps as, by their very existence, the camps represent an unsolicited intrusion into their homeland. Some biologists hope that educating the local population will change peoples' minds in favor of their research programs. Yet education without collaboration, and in a situation where villagers have no control over the researchers' presence or agendas, rings hollow to local ears.

Along with articulating resistance, elders' testimony also presents possible solutions to this standoff. Some of those interviewed suggested how researchers might improve their work. Many said that it would be better if biologists took the time to listen to what villagers had to say. The consummate politician, Paul John, remarked:

> I like the work of the biologists. They try to make us understand, not hide things from us. . . . If we work together, it would be better. . . .
>
> I understand what biologists do. There are different kinds of biologists. Some stick with only what they know, they don't try to expand their knowledge. There are the others who want to learn more and expand their knowledge to help us. . . .
>
> I know some traditional Yup'ik rules. I often tell Fish and Game about these rules, but they don't listen.[39]

Elders suggested that researchers visit communities *before* studies are planned. Acceptable studies would pursue jointly determined research questions. Cooperative management of local resources has worked to ameliorate resource use conflicts in other parts of the Yukon-Kuskokwim region.[40] Comparable comanagement and collaboration in the planning and implementation of research projects may be necessary for village acceptance of biological research.

In fact, an emphasis on comanagement is beginning to characterize both sides of the debate. University of Alaska biologists have written to village councils indicating their desire to work more closely with community members. Community leaders like John Pingayak of Chevak, who led a demand for a moratorium on all biological research in the region, see advantages to continuing biological research in their areas but, like this project, under strict local control. For Pingayak, "What the scientists have been leaving out is the spiritual part of the land," and comanagement may provide the means to bring it back in.

Comanagement, as described by Pingayak and other village leaders, is not just a policy outcome but an attempt to renegotiate their relations with the outside world. The demand for comanagement is as much a statement of resistance as a statement of belief in a particular view of the world.[41] In their comments on the AVCP's goose ecology report, both University of Alaska-Fairbanks biologists and U.S. Fish and Wildlife representatives focused on the reliability of knowledge in a scientific paradigm and where elders' statements fit this paradigm. They saw a partial solution in education (narrowly defined) of community members, for example, taking people to research camps and letting them see that the geese are not being disturbed. They did not read the subtext of elders' complaints: "We want local control of our land and our lives." It is not just what the camps do that is objectionable, but the camps' very existence on ancestral lands. Perhaps more people do not come to the camps to be "educated" because, whatever their environmental impact, people do not want the camps there in the first place, unless under local control.

Yup'ik community members of all ages share this opposition to perceived encroachment on their homeland. For example, Nick Tom, Jr., of Newtok wrote an angry letter to the editor in the weekly Bethel newspaper *Tundra Drums* objecting to "Fish and Game" aerial surveys.[42] A month later Larson King, Natural Resource Director of the village of Mekoryuk, wrote objecting to the wooden bird-counting towers in nesting grounds, which were scaring away the birds, and concluded: "This will continue to happen if we let ourselves be run over by a system imposed on us which is not compatible to our lifestyle."[43] Local control of their land and their lives, many feel, is in greater jeopardy than the geese.

Over and over again, villagers' statements reflected their view that how things are done in their area is as important as what is accomplished. Sharing management of research projects is as important as any specific research policy decided on or results obtained. Researchers and those who fund them need to ask if what they learn from projects planned outside the community is worth the cost in terms of resentment and resistance on the local level. Conversely, research projects perceived as responsive to local concerns in all stages—planning, implementation, review—stand a much greater chance of eliciting community cooperation and support.

The stated goal of the goose ecology project was not only to allow scientists to hear elders' voices, but to depoliticize biology in southwestern Alaska and to explain the importance of science to the Yup'ik community. This ambitious goal was not met. Yet a beginning was made in better understanding the Yup'ik attitude toward both coastal ecology and biology and the non-Native scientists who engage in their study.

Notes

1. Mike Uttereyuk, Sr., Scammon Bay, in Ann Fienup-Riordan, *"Yagulget Qaillun Pilartat Nunaseng Ulerpagaaqan* (What the Birds Do When Their Places Are Flooded): Yup'ik Knowledge of Storm Surges and Goose Ecology" (Bethel, Alaska: Association of Village Council Presidents, 1997), 43. Elders' statements in this paper are from this report. Veronica Kaganak of Scammon Bay and Marie Meade of Anchorage provided translations of elders' comments.

2. Paul John, personal communication, 1985.

3. Ann Fienup-Riordan, *Eskimo Essays: Yup'ik Lives and How We See Them* (New Brunswick, N.J.: Rutgers University Press, 1990), 8.

4. Ann Fienup-Riordan, *When Our Bad Season Comes: A Cultural Account of Subsistence Harvesting and Harvest Disruption on the Yukon Delta,* Monograph Series, 1 (Aurora: Alaska Anthropological Association, 1986), 301–2.

5. Charlie David, interview with Marie Meade, 7 July 1994, *Agayuliyararput* Yup'ik Mask Exhibit Project, Anchorage Museum of History and Art, Anchorage, Alaska.

6. Fienup-Riordan, *Eskimo Essays,* 72–73.

7. Jobe Nevak, in Fienup-Riordan, *"Yagulget Qaillun Pilartat Nunaseng Ulerpagaaqan,"* 288–89.

8. Thomas Akerelria, Scammon Bay, in ibid., 78.

9. Charlie Friday, in ibid., 175.

10. Theresa Moses, in ibid., 312.

11. Fienup-Riordan, *"Yagulget Qaillun Pilartat Nunaseng Ulerpagaaqan."* This report has since been published in abbreviated form: *"Yagulget Qaillun Pilartat* (What the Birds Do): Yup'ik Eskimo Understanding of Geese and Those Who Study Them," *Arctic* 52, no. 1 (1999): 1–22.

12. Mark Tom, in Fienup-Riordan, *"Yagulget Qaillun Pilartat Nunaseng Ulerpagaaqan,"* 238.

13. Mary Ann Sundown, in ibid., 103.

14. Paul John, in ibid., 276, 280.

15. Mike Uttereyuk, Sr., in ibid., 42.

16. Michael John, in ibid., 257.

17. Xavier Simon, Scammon Bay, in ibid., 67.

18. Mike Uttereyuk, Sr., in ibid. 43–44.

19. James Sedinger, C. J. Lensink, D. H. Ward et al., "Current Status and Recent Dynamics of Black Brant *Branta bernicla* Breeding Population," *Wildlife* 44 (1993): 49–59.

20. J. H. Eisenhauer, "Nesting Ecology and Behavior of Pacific Brant in Alaska" (B.S. thesis, University of Lethbridge, Alberta, 1977); C. J. Lensink, *Numbers of Black Brant Nesting on the Yukon-Kuskokwim Delta Have Declined More Than 60 Percent,* U.S. Fish and Wildlife Service Res. Information Bulletin, 1987, 87–126; and James Sedinger, D. H. Ward, and D. Welsh, "The Status and Biology of Geese Nesting at Tutakoke, 1985: A Progress Report," unpublished report, U.S. Fish and Wildlife Service, 1985.

21. Sedinger, Lensink, Ward et al., "Current Status and Recent Dynamics of Black

Brant *Branta bernicla* Breeding Population."

22. Nathan Kaganak, in Fienup-Riordan, *"Yagulget Qaillun Pilartat Nunaseng Ulerpagaaqan,"* 87.

23. Theresa Moses, in ibid., 309.

24. Charlie Friday, Hooper Bay, in ibid., 173.

25. David Boyscout, in ibid., 123.

26. Thomas Akerelria, in ibid., 79.

27. Roy Henry, in ibid., 52–55.

28. Paul John, in ibid., 279.

29. Eddie Bell, Sr., Hooper Bay, in ibid., 213.

30. Dick Lawrence, in ibid., 298.

31. Albert Therchik, Toksook Bay, in ibid., 321.

32. Eddie Bell, in ibid., 213.

33. Michael John, in ibid., 258–59.

34. Theresa Moses, in ibid., 31.

35. Mike Uttereyuk, Sr., in ibid. 41.

36. Jorjean Charlie, in ibid., 250.

37. David Boyscout, in ibid., 123.

38. Mike Uttereyuk, Sr., in ibid. 42.

39. Paul John, in ibid., 278.

40. Dan Albrecht, "Co-management as Transaction: The Kuskokwim River Salmon Management Working Group" (M.A. thesis, McGill University, 1990).

41. Joseph Spaeder, "Cooperative Management in a Landscape of Resistance: The Evolution of Decentralized Institutions for Wildlife Management in Western Alaska" (research prospectus, Graduate Group in Ecology, University of California-Davis).

42. Nick E. Tom, Jr., "Fish and Game More Disturbing to Geese than Newtok," letter to the editor, *Tundra Drums* (Bethel), 7 November 1996, A4.

43. Larson King, "It's No Wonder Black Brant Are Gone," letter to the editor, *Tundra Drums* (Bethel), 5 December 1996, A4.

Learning from Ecological Ethnicities: Toward a Plural Political Ecology of Knowledge

PRAMOD PARAJULI

Among the Indian ethnic groups of Latin America (there are about 200), this *tortured body* and another body, the *altered earth,* represent a beginning, a rebirth of the will to *construct a political association.* A unity born of hardship and resistance to hardship is the historical locus, the collective memory of the social body, where a will that neither confirms nor denies this writing of history originates. "Today, at the hour of our awakening, we must be our own historians."

—Michel de Certeau[1]

We are establishing village republics (*nate-na-raj* as the people call it here) in the true spirit of democracy, equity and fraternity following the Gandhian tenets to the extent possible. The village republics of ours are not islands in wilderness, they comprise the smallest circle amongst the ever-expanding circles in the open sea. We believe that life in its totality and vivacity can be perceived, experienced and realized only in the microcosms of community and family. It is the community and community alone—not the formal state in any case—which can save the earth for humankind and other forms of life.

—B. D. Sharma, leader, Movement for
Tribal Self-Rule, India[2]

The indigenous rebellion is now a rock which hits once and
again the great dome of power or money. . . . The rocks do
not die. At most they become smaller rocks.
    —Subcomandante Marcos, Zapatista Movement[3]

W hy is there unmistakable convergence between the nature of ecological extraction from a specific ecoregion and the degree of ethnic
subordination within it? What do such ethno-ecological spaces sig-
nify in a globalized world? Through the notion of ecological ethnicity,
I will explicate what this particular relationship between economy
and ethnicity constitutes and what its peculiar characteristics are today. Ecological ethnicity refers not only to about 500 million indigenous populations of the world, but also to peasants, fisherfolk, forest
dwellers, nomadic shepherds, and a host of other people who share
similar predicaments, including being marginalized in the process of
what I call the global motion of capital.[4] Ecological ethnicities have
become distinct today because they maintain the rhythm of circularity
and regenerative cycles of nature's economy by cultivating appropriate
cosmovisions, observing related rituals, and practicing prudence in
the ways they care about nature, harvest from nature, nurture nature,
and in turn are nurtured.[5] There is nothing romantic or exceptional
about their worldviews or practices. What might seem exceptional in
our eyes is that among them, nature cannot be distinguished from
everyday production and consumption, livelihoods and survival,
rituals and festivities, inhabitation, or a sense of place. What is in nature is directly experienced and lived through plants, crops, and other
sources of sustenance, an interaction mediated through rituals associated with production, collection, preparation, and distribution of food.
In the most primal sense, it is through the search for food, nutrition,
and medicine that ecological ethnicities communicate with nature.[6]

I depart from identifying these people simply as "ecosystem
people," because this notion locates people within definite, and somewhat arbitrary, units of the natural world, creating the impression that
each functions like an organic machine. I agree with Gary Nabhan
when he uses the phrase "cultures of habitat" to show that each place
fosters enduring habits and worldviews among its inhabitants. I am
not so concerned about whether ecological ethnicities occupy one or
more ecosystems; rather, I am referring to the depth of interaction and

interdependence between the human and the nonhuman worlds within a widely defined ecoregion. Thus, the notions evoked by such terms as "habitat," "inhabitation," and "cultures of habitat" capture more accurately what I have in mind. A good practice of inhabitation implies right and wrong ways of interaction among humans in a society and between humans and nonhumans in a larger biotic community. As Gary Snyder echoes, "doing things right means living as though your grandchildren would also be alive, in this land."[7]

As I elaborate in this chapter, the notion of ecological ethnicity has a strong political ring to it. Although ecological ethnicities might internally have inequitable social relations with respect to gender, religion, caste, tribe, or language, these internal distinctions do not separate them, or situate them in an antagonistic relationship to each other. Despite their differences in social relational terms, they share an ecosystem loosely defined as watersheds, foodsheds, seedsheds, or bioregions. Because they share the same place for inhabitation, they belong to a community, despite their antagonistic relationships within it. The sense of community further intensifies if seemingly antagonistic groups are involved in a common struggle with an outsider. As much as their ecosystem is a source of conflict and struggle, it is also the source of unity and identity. What seems common in all these "geographies of difference" is a distinct geographical and ethnic makeup, resulting in potential for varying degrees of political autonomy.[8] At the end of this chapter, I outline some implications of this possibility for governance at the community level and for ecological citizenship.

From Protest to Proposal

I also use the notion of ecological ethnicity to show that these groups of people are not merely victims of global capitalism; they are active subjects with their own symbolic productivities and social movement strategies. Consequently, they have shifted from a phase of "protest" to a phase in which protests are accompanied by proactive "proposals." As evident within some ecological movements in India, these proposals offer alternative ways of envisioning social reality and choosing appropriate technologies. The difference between phases of protest and proposal is noteworthy. In a "protest" phase, ethno-ecological actors might be aware of the adverse impact of existing policies in their lives, but their responses in defending themselves are limited. The struggles in this phase try to implement policies, such as constitutional provisions that protect *adivasis,*[9] against illegal transfer of land and development projects that did not have proper environmental assessments. In short, these are protests that strive to achieve fair and equitable opportunities granted by the existing laws of the land. In the "proposals" phase, these movements go beyond demands made in keeping with existing laws and propose alternative programs that are based on indigenous knowledge systems, technologies of production, consumption, and patterns of social distribution. Usually, such alternatives are rooted in the history, ecology, and economy of the respective communities.

While sharpening their own locally specific knowledge claims, indigenous peoples are forming alliances with a diversity of social actors. Examples abound. I will refer to the convergence taking place between ecological and other social justice movements,[10] or in particular, between indigenous peoples' concerns about issues of biotechnology and biodiversity.[11] There is an emerging convergence between local movements claiming biotic wealth, anthropologists advocating traditions of peasant knowledge, and grassroots challenges to green revolution technologies, biotechnologies, and patent regimes.[12] In India, there are attempts to bring together actors of various movements, such as peasants, fisherfolk, women, agricultural laborers, and Adivasis. During the last decade, some of these attempts have given birth to larger umbrella organizations, such as the Bharat Jan Andolan (Indian Peoples' Movement), Bharat Jan Vikas Andolan (Indian Movement for Peoples' Development), and Stri Mukti Sammelan (Women's Liberation Conferences). Mobilization and network on specific issues, such as displacement, minimum wages, employment guarantees, gender issues, and tribal rights over forest lands, are more common and effective. Given the incredibly complex ecological and linguistic mosaic of India, such efforts are not and have not been easy.[13] Yet, in their own mini-spaces and in a gradual evolution, a parallel political ecology of knowledge is in the making. I highlight three trends: 1) ethno-ecological spaces as "geographies of difference" within the new global order; 2) a moral ecology of using nature and redefining environmentalism for ecological ethnicities; and 3) a move from the state and civil society to community as the locus of self-governance.

Historically, various constituencies within ecological ethnicities might be "residual" elements of the Indian social formation. But today, they can be considered as "emergent" social movement actors. Today, if the global motion of capital is the "dominant" form, the subsistence or nonmarket forms of peasant ecologies are "residual" forms. Social movements have articulated the residual forms into emergent ones. As Raymond Williams has shown, emergent forms are new meanings, new practices, and experiences that are continually being created in history. In contrast to emergent forms, residual forms are experiences, meanings, and values that cannot be verified or cannot be expressed in terms of the dominant culture because they are the residues of the previous social formations.[14] I have used the categories of "residual" and "emergent" to describe cultures at the margins of global capitalism, and these are relevant only when we look at reality from the center of capitalism. Those who have not entered the grid of capitalist time might not always have a linear view of history. Nevertheless, the delicate pedagogical and cognitive shift that is taking place while groups are transitioning from residual to emergent formations is the key characteristic of contemporary ethno-ecological movements.

The Mosaic of Ecological Ethnicities

In the opening quote above, Michel de Certeau characterizs the predicament of the indigenous peoples of Latin America through the twin metaphor of "tortured bodies" and "altered earth." Globally also, the immediate human toll of environmental destruction has usually been disproportionately born by the people who are least able to cope with it. The metaphor of "altered earth" signifies the crisis of nature and survival caused by biophysical limits to unlimited extraction. The metaphor of "tortured bodies" signifies the crisis of social justice resulting from the ways ecological costs are unevenly born by those who are rich in nature's wealth, including biodiversity and diversity of cultural forms. Since ecological ethnicities also constitute the cheapest and most expendable labor force for capitalist enterprises, they are also the most exploited in the labor market. The crisis of nature and the crisis of social justice are thus entangled in these communities.

And the numbers of "tortured bodies" are growing. Globally, over 500 million indigenous people, many of whom inhabit the world's remaining rainforests, coastal areas, deserts, and hilly and mountainous terrain, are pressed to extinction when forests are logged, large dams are built, and minerals are extracted. Over one million of these people will be displaced by economic and environmental programs within the next decade. For example, all nuclear weapons that have been tested by the United States have been detonated in the lands of indigenous peoples, with over six hundred tests within the Shoshone nation alone. Two-thirds of the uranium resources within the borders of the United States lie under native reservations. In North America, Native Americans produced 10 percent of the all federally controlled uranium in 1975. In Australia, three out of four of the largest uranium deposits are in Aborigine lands. Worldwide, 70 percent of the uranium resources are contained on indigenous lands.[15] Environmental racism is increasingly evident in U.S. urban neighborhoods. In one estimate, 60 percent of African American and Latino communities and over 50 per cent of Asian/Pacific islanders and Native Americans live in areas with one or more uncontrolled toxic waste sites. There is clear evidence that race plays the decisive role in the location of dirty industries and toxic dumps. Communities where people of color reside are deliberately targeted for receiving the "effluents of the affluent."[16]

Today, India is perhaps the best place to look for people embodying the double burden of "tortured bodies" and "altered earth." The last five decades of development have accelerated social polarization to such an extent that, for many, the issue is no less than "right to life," and for the few, the issue is "right to property."[17] As a result, increasing numbers of India's citizens are being pushed off their land and into the vagaries of a disorganized labor market that is neither stable nor disciplined by labor laws and trade union organizations. Their rights over resources have been violated and their access to any means of production is diminishing. Although this new form of marginalization builds upon and perpetuates other relations of domination and discrimination—including gender, caste, ethnicity, and class—in Indian society today, these are intertwined with the issues of ecology, survival, and the "deadly war over resources." In turn, ecological ethnicities have begun to search for their own traditions of knowledge, technologies of using nature, and modes of governance.[18]

The Adivasi belt of central India, comprising the Jharkhand region, the Narmada valley, and the tribal belt of Madhya Pradesh, offers the most striking case. There Adivasis are facing the "crisis of nature" because the fast speed of the extractive economy has outpaced the biophysical time needed for renewal and replenishment. They also face a "crisis of justice" because they are not properly compensated for the ecological costs they bear for industries, mining, and construction of large dams.[19] As the modern economy extracts more from the ecosystems of ecological ethnicities, natural resources are depleted and cause the crisis of survival. As Madhav Gadgil and Ramachandra Guha have shown, the history of capitalism can be traced as a "resource transfer," from the resource- and labor-rich ecoregions to those which are poor in resources but have purchasing power through the market economy.[20] The chain of resource transfer extends from the local to the global scale. While the rich, worldwide industrial economies consume as well as garner profits from natural resources, the non-industrial economies pay both by supplying the resources and labor cheaply and by disposing of the waste. This is unavoidable when a large portion of India's basic commodities is already produced for export, and the thrust of globalization is to accelerate this even further. Already, 33 percent of plywood, 84 percent of coffee, 38 percent of fish, 47 percent of bauxite and aluminum, 40 percent of iron ore, and 46 percent of crude oil are produced mostly in the non-industrial South to export to the industrial North.[21]

Such an export-driven economy makes it possible for the richer one-fifth of the world's population to consume four-fifths of the world's resources, while the poorer four-fifths world consume only one-fifth of the world's resources. These practices have created several levels of inequity. First, most of the resources used by the richer one-fifth do not meet the needs of humanity as a whole; they are used for making luxury products. In fact, such use deprives the social majorities of the very basis for survival. Second, resources are extracted primarily by displacing or polluting the habitats of poorer peoples who do not consume those commodities. Third, ethno-ecological communities have been made the sites for dumping toxic materials and other waste produced by the overconsumption of the richer one-fifth. What is left for the host communities is infertile soil surface, abandoned pits, and water and soil contaminated with heavy metals. Let me now turn to the immediate crisis brought about by the globalization of the economy to the lives of ecological ethnicities.

When Economic Time Outdoes Biological Time: Life in the Whirlwind of Globalization

Ecologically speaking, the fast pace of globalization is doomed because it needs to operate much faster than the biological process of regeneration and renewal. When economic time outdoes biological time, the accumulation of capital itself produces development and underdevelopment as mutually determining moments of capitalism.[22] Not only does this combined movement perpetuate class, caste, race, and gender inequities, it also creates regional and spatial inequalities. For example, the low wage is secured by playing the class-race-gender card in the formal labor economy; low prices on raw materials are also secured by not paying enough for the regeneration of resource-rich regions, such as Chiapas, Jharkhand, and the Amazon. Thus, contradictions that arise between the requirements of an extractive global economy and the regenerative needs of ecological ethnicities within the regions become increasingly irreconcilable.

Elsewhere I have identified the five-fold crises that ecological ethnicities are facing today, namely, the crises of nature, social justice, survival, knowledge and identity, and governance.[23] These crises are not necessarily new but have been further perpetuated because the global market continues its uneven encompassing of other economies and cultures. Crisis looms large today because the scale of extraction has already exceeded ecosystem capacity. Ethno-ecological movements suggest that economy can and should only be a subsystem of an ecosystem. Thus, their search is for the optimal scale of the macro economy relative to the environment. Not surprisingly, the demand for local self-governance is primarily about having power to decide whether, how, and how much to use natural resources.

Looking into attempts made by peasants to produce, use, and exchange their own seeds in opposition to the transnational seed companies is a matter of some urgency. In India, for example, recovery of the seeds is done through a quiet movement called Navadanya—an organization named after the Sanskrit word for "nine seeds." In the Andes, several grassroots peasant organizations inspired by Proyecto Andino Tecnologias Campesinas (PRATEC) are revitalizing the age-old practice of exchanging seeds and cultivating biodiversity in the *chakra*s (the farm fields).[24] In other parts of India, unlettered peasants have not only stopped paper factories that pollute the river or use their commons for monocultured plantations, but they have stopped large dams from being built. The way Mayan peasants of Chiapas are protecting *ejido* lands and *milpa* agriculture in defiance of the North American Free Trade Agreement (NAFTA) is another example of the resiliency of ecological ethnicities. Before the reform of 1991, Article 27 of the Mexican Constitution of 1917 obliged the state to redistribute land to those petitioners who fulfilled necessary legal requirements. The *ejido* land system consisted of individual plots and communal property, none of which could be legally sold, rented, or used as collateral until the 1991 reforms, which removed these specific provisions and opened the land for privatization. This constitutional amendment has been devastating to peasants, to the extent that it has ended the promise of agrarian reform that had been central to peasant and indigenous peoples' politics in Mexico.

The content and the spirit of these ethno-ecological movements are not merely about control over the outer structure of power, as if it were a war over tactics and strategies; they are about the very fabric of life and livelihoods, the very symbiosis between culture and nature. The micro-places where ecological ethnicities dwell cannot only be seen as "marginal," "displaced," or "annexed" into the larger body politic of incorporating "nation-states" or the encompassing "markets." These places are also "geographies of difference" which contain the seeds for regeneration and recovery. These are sites that are endowed with materiality of difference, as well as places where corresponding struggles and resistances are waged in order to reassert such differences. Such struggles do not aim merely to overcome groups' discrimination and marginalization. They are more about disengaging from dominating structures and might include choosing alternate technologies of production and consumption or, in short, other ways of being in and with the world.[25]

The Ethnosemiotics of Resistance

Ethno-ecological communities have undergone their own transformations as they have begun to articulate themselves vis-à-vis the national or global motion of capital and nation-states. They have taken on the double functions of critiquing social inequities within their own communities and regenerating some aspects of their own communities and cultures. Social movements are cognitive processes, and both the processes of critique and regeneration are built into them. As the globalization of the economy has intensified, the realization has grown that many share the five crises and that their place-specific ethnosemiotics might serve as an alternative to the semiotic expansion of capital.

Perhaps India's ecological ethnicities are coming out of the "growing pains" of development or sacrifice for nation-building; movements opposing large dams have shifted their focus from fighting for rehabilitation of those displaced to protesting the idea of the large dam itself. In this phase, affected people articulate alternatives to large dams based on indigenous forms of collecting, harvesting, and using water and of managing the use through community-based local water councils. People involved in the movements against large dams and social forestry programs have been able to establish connections between the larger context of developmental economics and economic policy and their own situation of destitution. At the same time, adversely affected people have begun to see why the elite of the country favor big technologies and why their own peasant-based technologies are undermined. Their physical displacement is then understood within the larger context of the delegitimization of their culture and traditions of knowledge. Thus, the movements have moved from a phase of merely critiquing inappropriate development models to seriously regenerating people's latent knowledge systems as alternatives.

This shift from "protest" to "proposal" came about only after a decades-long painful struggle to receive appropriate compensation for the negative impacts of development industry. The new phase of "active resistance" to development programs is distinct from two earlier phases. First was the phase of "passive consent," during which a vernacular critique of development might have been subsumed within the narrative of "sacrifice for nation-building." Next was the phase of "struggling for compensation," in which efforts were focused on seeking adequate environmental and social impact assessments and the implementation of rehabilitation programs for those who were to be displaced.

What then is the "ethnosemiotics" of this latest phase of resistance? In this phase, the urgent questions faced by these movements are many. What types of political and social organizations are required in order for communities to be self-reliant and organized? What model of development does not ask for their sacrifice for nation-building?

Most important, do ecological ethnicities have traditions of knowledge and technologies that could replace these inappropriate technologies? How can these alternative technologies enable ecological ethnicities to secure sustainable livelihoods? I will seek to answer these questions by discussing the ecological ethnicities' cosmovisions and the possibility of governance and ecological citizenship.

No Nature Apart: Ecological Ethnicities and Their Cosmovisions

For ecological ethnicities who eke out their livelihoods from nature's economy, the widely held ideas that "nature can be preserved in wilderness" and that "wilderness is what is untouched by humans" are simply untenable.[26] Historical examples clearly illustrate that this notion of nature is very much a cultural construct based on the culture-nature divide found in the Cartesian/Baconian tradition. Gary Nabhan calls this disjuncture between nature and culture an episode of cultural parallax:

> Parallax is the apparent displacement of an observed object due to the difference between two points of views. Simply put, it is the discrepancy between what you see out of the viewfinder and what the film sees through the lens. A cultural parallax, then, might be considered to be the difference in views Letween those who are actively participating in the dynamics of the habitats within their home range and those who view those habitats as "landscape" from the outside. As Leslie Silko has suggested, "so long as human consciousness remains within the hills, canyons, cliffs, and the plants, clouds and sky, the term landscape as it has entered the English language is misleading." A portion of territory the eye can comprehend in a single view does not correctly describe the relationship between a human being and his or her surroundings.[27]

The continuum of household-farm-forest found in the peasant economy does not allow such a parallax. To provide a glimpse of how Jharkhandi peasants relate to and use or abuse nature, let me provide a closer look at Jitpur, a settlement of about one hundred peasant households, mostly of Ghatwal peasants and some Santhal Adivasis, along the border of the Devghar and Giridih districts. Ghatwals consider themselves Hindus and are not officially included in the list of Scheduled Tribes of India. Yet their customs converge in many ways with those of the neighboring Santhals (who are Adivasis) especially in the ways they relate to nature. For example, their series of festivals starts with the Karam festival—one of the key festivals for all Adivasi groups in the region. Hindu Ghatwals observing the Karam festival illustrate the point that, given a common ecological makeup, both Adivasis and non-Adivasis share the same rituals and cosmovisions.

In Jitpur, the forest is not only the primary source of sustenance for their diet; it is also the most dependable assurance against agricultural failure due to the failure of the monsoon or to floods. Jhari, one of the Ghatwal youths I interviewed, remembers how the Chechali forest had fed them during a famine when he was eight or nine years old. The famine of 1978 was so bad, he told me, "that even the paddy seeds had to be brought from West Bengal." Throughout this period of extreme distress, people subsisted on *bel* (*Aegle marmelos*) and *mahuwa* (*Madhuca longifolia*). While the bel fruit was boiled and eaten, mahuwa flowers and fruit were eaten with *sattu* (ground corn mixed with chickpea flour). Then, they had sold some mahuwa flowers in the market and bought some grain, oil, and salt. In a pensive mood, Jhari shared with me his vision of what forest and farm mean to him:

> I do not know whether jungle and Jamin (land) are made by humans or by a superior being. But for us, both jungle and Jamin are good in themselves. I am surprised how every spot in the jungle is filled in. Then, I also went to work in the Chitra coal mine. I thought, we were making big holes in the land. It is natural law that somewhere it will be hilly and somewhere it will be plain. Somewhere there is water source. My guess is that *jungle jaminka chadar he* (forest is a shawl that covers the land). A true jungle is that one in which every species of trees that is possible in a climate is found. In our area, if a jungle does not have sal (*Shorea Robusta*), mahuwa (*Madhuca longifolia*), neem *(Azadirachta indica),* bel (*Aegle Mermelos*), kathal (*Artocarpus integri Folia*), badhal (*A. Lakoocha*) trees, how could it be a forest?

"Forest is the shawl that covers the land" is perhaps the most appropriate way of representing the peasant view of the connection between agricultural land and forest. What I find in the settlements of Jharkhand is that the nature we know "in the pure form" no longer exits. For the peasants, what exists is a continuum of farm and forest, commons and pastures. Unlike the fantasies of the urbanites and city-bred environmentalists who do not directly depend on nature's economy, the "wild" and "civilization" do not exist as distinct entities in peasant economy. Rather, human collectivities and the natural collectivities form parts of a whole, bound by a variety of functions and relationships. Historically, farming is perhaps the first step toward setting "humans apart from nature," if we take nature in the primordial sense. But from the peasant point of view, as I have pointed out elsewhere, clearing land for cultivation and growing crops is both "naturalizing culture" and "culturizing nature."[28]

For example, the mahuwa *(Madhuca longifolia)* tree has a specific function within the peasant ecology and economy of Jharkhand. Peasants believe that the mahuwa tree keeps the water level high and holds the soil very tightly, protecting the landscape from erosion. A higher water level makes the edible grasses grow, which then become fodder for cattle. That is why, when peasants take cattle for grazing in the jungle, cattle can graze in grasses and the cowherds are seen playing around the tree. If it is in season, they also collect mahuwa flowers while tending cattle. Both Ghatwal and Santal peasants have given ritual importance to the mahuwa tree. A Ghatwal girl must marry a mahuwa tree before she can marry her would-be husband. A mahuwa branch is always brought to the ritual altar. In the peasant tradition, nature is not an object but a world of complexity whose living components are a part of their ways of life and are often personified and defined in their respective cosmovisions.

Redefining Environmentalism: Toward a Moral Ecology of Nature Use

How can we appreciate the logic of peasant-based ecologies without giving into essentialism and romanticism? I suggest a notion of "moral ecology of nature use," which offers an alternative to the rampant "hit-and-run" ethic of environmental modernization or its antithesis, the "fencing off of wilderness areas" from human use. Let me summarize some characteristics of this environmentalism.

First, nature is simultaneously real, collective, and discursive. Thus, the theory and discourse about nature need to be naturalized, socialized, and deconstructed accordingly. We need to give adequate and equal attention to the discursive, material, social, and cultural dimensions of the human-environment interaction. This requires a balanced view that recognizes that nature has a solid biophysical dimension, while it is culturally and discursively constructed. The usual ideas that some environmental proposals are biocentric and some are ethnocentric, some are "nature-endorsing" and some are "nature-skeptical" are not adequate.

Second, there is a difference between how ecological ethnicities use and transform nature and how a capitalist mode of economy does so. For example, the technology used by a rural farmer to produce, collect, store, and distribute seed is very different from the way biotechnology and molecular technosciences transform the properties of nature, from recombinant DNA to gene mapping and nanotechnology. Even though both groups are actively using and sometimes abusing nature, the implications and impact they have are fundamentally different. Ecological ethnicities do certainly use and alter nature, but they do not alter and manipulate to the extent that it changes its very form and texture. Nature, plants, and animals, and other entities belong to a socioeconomic community subject to the same rules as humans. Winona LaDuke speaks of constant birth as the indicator of good life. Afro-Colombian peasants also talk about perpetual birth in the Pacific Coast as the sign of balance between humans and nature.[29]

Third, the relationship is mutual and based on nurturing. While Native Americans talk about the great natural law, Andean peasants speak of the delicate art of nurturing that connects humans and nonhumans in the relationship of mutuality. My mother and her friends in rural Nepal call the art of hospitality *dharma* and *punya,* a balance between good deeds and bad deeds. For them, the intricate web of human and nature is embedded in the three acts of *chalam* (use it), *jogam* (preserve it), and *bachham* (protect it). These are not fixed categories in space or time but are used complementarily as the situation demands.[30] For Native Americans, nature is a part of an intrinsic human experience; it is a way of self-realization. Lakota thinker Vine Deloria tries to capture the Native American nature-inclusive view of the world:

> If we could imagine a world in which human concerns were not the primary value, and we observed nature in the old Indian way, we would observe a plant (or a bird or animal) for a prolonged period of time. We would note what time of year the plant began to grow and green out; when it blossomed; when it bore fruit; how many fruits and seeds it produced; what animals and birds ate the fruits and when during matu-

ration process they appeared; what colors its leaves and fruits took on during the various parts of the growing season; whether it shed its leaves and needles and what birds and animals make use of them; and many other kinds of behavior of the plant. From these observations, we would come to understand both the plant and its life stages. By remembering the birds and animals who made use of the plant—and when they did so during the calendar year and when in terms of their own growth cycles—we would have a reasonable idea of how useful the plant would be for us.[31]

Finally, and this needs no reminder, any commitment to restructuring the economy also entails reinhabitating and renegotiating with the ecosystem. This entails governance at the local level, primarily originating with the power to decide how much nature to conserve and how much to use: in short, the need for a politics of nature use "appropriate to a place."[32] The watershed councils that have emerged all over the Pacific Northwest of the United States show that "local people can create a base of knowledge sufficient to manage lands, waters, habitat, natural areas, areas to be developed—and that if they can somehow achieve power to do so, they will often (but surely not always) rise to the task."[33]

Unlike the scientific model, I cannot and will not propose a universal model of the moral ecology of nature use. Local agricultural, forestry, or medicinal knowledge involves a context-specific, improvisational capacity rather than a coherent indigenous knowledge system among all ecological ethnicities. The knowledge is grounded on the local experience of use rather than on a cognitive system of logic and coherence. Thus, we can only talk about local models of land, knowledge, and production.[34] To put it simply, ecological and economic intersections, their interpretations, diagnoses of crisis, and resultant proposals are based on historical, linguistic, and cultural processes that retain certain place-bound specificities. This is what we are witnessing when foodsheds, watersheds, seedsheds, bioregionalism, and local currency systems are redefining boundaries of ecosystems as well as humans.

However, in the larger scheme of things, when thinking about regions such as Jharkhand or Chiapas or the Pacific Northwest, we need to cope with how places and spaces are to be created and represented. Ironically, the same place that claims regional identity as a hilly terrain, a sacred landscape, or a greener landscape also has to accept the fact that it was considered and represented as a backward place in the colonial as well as nationalist narratives. In the period of environmental modernization, the same places are regions brought under the management of profit-seeking ventures in biotechnology and pharmaceuticals.

Governing without Being Ruled: The Promise of Grassroots Governance

The field of politics for ecological ethnicities is the community, and not necessarily the civil society or the nation-state as one would usually suppose. A vigilant civil society or state is necessary and might be an effective forum from which to critique and mount pressure on the global and national systems. But the seeds of regeneration need the firm soil of community and culture, vernacular technology and agriculture, collectivities and memories. Ecological ethnicities might privilege ecology and community over state and civil society as the plausible site of governance for two basic reasons. First, ecology and community together can be the most appropriate base from which to interrogate global capitalism. Second, throughout ethno-ecological movements, ecology and community have been the source for regenerating what is lost and the site from which to envision alternatives. In other words, the twin notions of ecology and community simultaneously allow "critique" as well as "regeneration."

At this juncture, there are at least four kinds of proposals for governance. First is the global governance evidenced by the institutional trinity of large transnational corporations, the World Trade Organization (WTO), and the World Bank. These institutions, however, cannot generate ecological sustainability or greater democratic control to those lives, livelihoods, and identities that are rooted in their own natural and cultural economy. As long as some global governance will continue to legitimate the power of finance and global capital without social accountability, there is no hope that such a system of governance will create a more sustainable and democratic system for ecological ethnicities. Another equally plausible candidate is the global civil society, which has surfaced in the last decade as a potential actor in the national and international arenas, as exemplified in global summits, such as the WTO meeting in Seattle (1999), the Rio conference on the environment (1992), and many others.[35] Could this be the proper vehicle for ecological ethnicities to use in exercising political autonomy? As it is presently configured within the global economy and polity, global civil society has numerous vulnerabilities and dependencies. For a sound system of governance based on an ecosystem, what ecological ethnicities need is not merely to alter the mechanism of rule but to transform the "relations of ruling." As Partha Chatterjee suggests, communities rather than the state or civil society can alter that form of ruling because both the state and civil-social institutions have been enveloped within the narrative of capital.[36] Actually, an industrial mode of economy was firmly established and legitimized through the twin pillars of the state and civil society.

Although increasingly resilient in global negotiations, as civil society exists today in Europe or India, it is not a haven of democratic pluralism; it is not the space where every citizen can hope to attain freedom, individuality, and social justice. In fact, civil society has in most cases become the ideological cement in the structuring of contemporary nation-states, because states both frame civil society and occupy space within it. Ashis Nandy observes that in India, the state has come to dominate, not serve, civil society.[37] Most importantly, civil society cannot be a neutral arbiter in conflicts between communities and capital because it is a well-known domain for the market economy and civil law.

Third, there is the argument that nation-states should be rejuvenated as buffers between global economic institutions and local communities. Elsewhere, I have described the fragility of the nation-state's ability to encompass new identities and demands for autonomy as they are integrated into the global economy. What is needed is the basic strengthening of the ecoregional-based communities to assume the primary role in governance, on the basis of which the relative strengthening of the civil society, state, and even global institutions is conceivable. Alternatively, a system of governance at the level of an ecologically defined terrain holds the possibility for redefining the organization of production and consumption, technology and knowledge, lifestyles and aesthetics. The list of demands of the Zapatista Army of National Liberation (EZLN) is a case in point. These demands might seem modest, but their implications are far-reaching. The first demand is for land distribution programs, so that native people can have communal landholding in fertile lowland areas with guarantees of secure tenure.

The second demand is that communities have control over their means of production, including the use of land. Most importantly, the EZLN wants local-level, democratic decision making to be entrusted to the traditional leadership. And finally, the Zapatistas want the Mexican state to be comprised of multinationalities and their self-governing councils at all levels.[38]

Could it be, ironically, that the globalization of economy and governance has opened up the opportunity for new strategic alliances between the nation-states and the communities? Faced with a globalized economy, ecosystem-based production is "residual"; even some residue of nationalist planning and the protectionist role of the nation-state toward the weaker sections has served as a point of resistance. For example, the Zapatista movement in Chiapas, Mexico, evokes residual forms of state-peasant moral bonds against the onslaught of globalization. The movement is resurrecting the residual memories of *milpa* agriculture and the *ejido* system of land ownership, along with a fluid ideology of what it is to be Maya.[39] The Zapatistas remind the Mexican state of its social contract with its peasantry during the National Revolution of 1917. Accidentally, the guarantee of the *ejido* system was a central thread connecting indigenous peasantry to the Mexican nation-state. Similarly, the National Alliance for Tribal Self-Rule in India reminds the Indian state of the social contract between Adivasis and the Nehruvian state inscribed in the specific provisions of the Indian constitution and in guidelines in the *Panchsheel* on tribal development.[40] Such invocations of the moral economy of the nation-state then serve as a way of critiquing the march of globalized capital, and the state's subordination within it. As premised in the Multilateral Agreement on Trade, an unrestricted motion of global capital does not uphold any ethics of protection for these threatened peoples or abide by any national borders. Renato Ruggiero, the director-general of the WTO, aptly calls the agreement "the constitution for a single global economy."

It is crucial to note here that this is not an argument against the nation-state. A global civil society and a nation-state can and must act as a buffer between the imperatives of global capital and the regenerative needs of local communities. The social role of the state—public services, public security, and the well-being of all, particularly the vulnerable sectors of the population—must continue. States, tempered by social movements, can change course and play a constructive role in the delicate balance between economy and ecology. For example, the Indian parliament recently passed a law entitled the Provision of the Panchayats (Extension to Scheduled Areas Act 1996). The act states that every Gram Sabha (village assembly) will have the power, "to safeguard and preserve the traditions and customs of the people, their cultural identity, community resources and the customary mode of dispute resolution." This act heralds a new dimension in state-tribal relations of governance, taking them beyond the centralized state and planting them firmly in the heart of the community. If implemented fully, communities can resist, at least legally, the near total control of tribal areas and resources by the state and/or national and increasingly transnational capital. Time will tell if such a polity will be congruent with the mandates of the global economy. For now, this is definitely an arena of intense controversy and mobilization at the grassroots level.

Ecological Ethnicities as Citizens

What I am excited about is not so much that communities will achieve their due share of power (a worthwhile goal in itself), but that there exists the possibility of transforming the "relations of ruling" between global economy and local ecologies, states and ecological ethnicities. Contemporary ethno-ecological politics does not confront the state head on but weakens the system in question by creating counter-vailing bases of power. As the capacity of local communities for self-governance is strengthened, centralized power evaporates. The proposal of the Zapatista Movement in Chiapas, for example, is not to capture the Mexican state, but to democratize Mexican society based on three principles: 1) strengthening community; 2) respecting ethnic identity; and 3) exercising autonomous governance at the community level. Neither does the Alliance for Tribal Self-Rule in India aim to take over the Indian state. Instead, it aims at having a firm command over resources at the ecosystem level. Such claims of autonomy do not lead to either-or situations, but open up a different space for state-community relations.

Ethno-ecological movements defend a series of common values: they are based upon democratic equivalence between several groups; and they presuppose self-management regarding human relations and human's relationship with nature. What emerges is not another state, but a federation of self-managing communities. Here again, the central feature of emergent ethno-ecological politics is self-management of resources: land, forests, rivers, and other biotic wealth. In essence, what these communities aspire to are different social modes and different development alternatives (or even alternatives to development). Thus, indigenous politics recognizes and seeks a plurality of ways to organize autonomous units of governance.

The assertion of ecological ethnicities in governance has come at a juncture when the very legitimacy of nation-states to represent popular will has been most fragile. James Scott has shown that the edifice of the modern nation-state was the high modernist planned social order. Lenin, Nyerere, Nehru, and Truman were participants in the same theater of state-building, albeit for different purposes and in different contexts. Scott identifies four aspects of the modernist state that have created havoc in people's lives: first, the administrative ordering of nature and society; second, the robust confidence in scientific and technical progress; third, the authoritarian state that is willing and able to use the full weight of its coercive power to bring these high, modernist designs into being; and fourth, and most important, a disabled civil society that in some parts of the world lacks the capacity to resist the state's plans and programs of integration.[41]

With the globalization of the economy, the edifice of the state is also falling apart, if not becoming altered and reconstituted. Now the contradiction that is endemic in the state's conflicting roles as regulator of capital and as maintainer of unity and democracy within its territory is also affecting its ability to perform effectively. The state must choose between its obligations under international trade treaties and its responsibilities to protect and be responsive to its populace, who are expressing concern about unbridled and compulsive global capitalistic gain. Does this mean that there might be new opportunities for peoples' participation in governance? Is this an opening for grassroots organizations to fill the void left by the state's retreat? Or is this the move toward further erosion of civil society and communities? This is definitely a challenging but positive moment for civil society and communities. The notion of ecological ethnicity offers a suitable window to explore the depth, scope, and scale of this new opening.

Discussions about who governs and how nature is managed are crucial for ecological ethnicities because the eighteenth-century industrial worldview was made possible by a systematic reordering of nature as well as society. With the camera in the one hand and the microscope in the other, this worldview established an alliance between words and things, enabling one to see and say, define and manage. It integrated the individual and the biological in a discourse, while framing nature as landscape. As James Scott and many others have shown, the science of nature is more about governability—the art of bringing the myriad domains of life into sharper observation, planning, and control. Nature has then been made the object of expert knowledge, regularized, simplified, disciplined, managed, and planned.[42] The new move under the rubric of environmental modernization further intensifies the process, globally, that started about three hundred years ago in Europe.

Beyond the Interest Group: Inhabitation and Citizenship

A structure of governance for ecological ethnicities can revolve around the twin issues of ecology and democracy. While ecology can be considered a realm for self-organization and self-creation of life, democracy can be understood as self-governance at the level of ecoregions or communities. The starting point for the recovery of community is in preserving and restoring ecosystems. Cultivating commitments to foodsheds or watersheds can, as poet Gary Snyder hopes, create a different kind of citizenship—a citizenship "to become members of the deep, old biological communities of the land." Such citizenship is evident in the ways residents of the Mattole River watershed (most of them White men and women, by the way) made possible the return of king salmon in the streams following about fifteen years of restoration work.[43]

To appreciate these grassroots stirrings fully, I make a distinction between the "stakeholder or interest group" model of citizenship and the "place-based or inhabitant" model of citizenship. Despite the promise of people's participation, the stakeholder model relies on the articulation of interest groups, thus not allowing the common interest of the community to surface at all. It enfranchises only those with direct, vested interests, and so disenfranchises ecological ethnicities who tend to practice ownership in common rather than private property.

That form of individualistic ethic is in fact antithetical to the idea of
long-term ecological responsibility as part of a larger community.
Liberal democracy might encompass the security of individual interests, but it does so at the expense of the welfare of future generations or of nonhuman communities.[44] Liberal democracy that has been
reduced to a philosophy for the pursuit of private happiness, not for
public citizenship, does not suffice to undertake this task. Instead, an
ecological citizenship might require that we replace the market economy with moral ecology and a legal citizenship with an ecological
citizenship.

As David McClosky aptly comments, what is missing from this
model is the voice of the land itself. Overall, a stakeholder model is
anthropocentric. Instead, a place-based and inhabitant model of citizenship considers humans only as members of a wider community of
life, not as the top of the evolutionary chain. A watershed, a foodshed,
or a seedshed then becomes the true "council of the place." Place acts
as the common ground among its inhabitants and not as the interest
that divides them. On occasions, inhabitants may even have to go
against their own economic self-interests in order to give preference
to the common interest of a place, because inhabitants in a watershed,
foodshed, or a seedshed are primarily governed by the natural cycles
of energy flows within its different integrative parts.[45] The appeal of
the notion of foodsheds, writes Jack Kloppenburg, is "the graphic
imagery it evokes; streams of foodstuffs running into a particular locality, their flow mediated by the features of both natural and social
geography."[46]

An ecological citizen is a member of a community of persons who
considers herself morally accountable to the community comprised of
human and nonhuman communities as a whole. Given the insur-
mountable ecological crisis, the knowledge and skills to live well on
the earth are intrinsic to citizenship. Should we not consider the
failure to live well and balanced on earth an indication of the failure to
be a good citizen? In *A Sand County Almanac, and Sketches Here and
There,* Aldo Leopold stated that a "land ethic changes the role of
homo-sapiens from conqueror of the land to plain member and citizen
of it."[47] The conviction and behavioral commitment that land could be
viewed as a "collective organism" rather than as the "slave and servant" of human's greed is still alive, or recoverable, among ecological
ethnicities.

A community provides both the "hardware" and "software" for human relationships. As software, the community provides a sense of place and networks of connection and relations. As hardware, it facilitates arrangements for watersheds, riversheds, and foodsheds. Moreover, the promise of the community as the new organizing principle lies in the fact that community is Janus-faced. On the one hand, community is the site of remembering, restoring, and regenerating what was lost from the past. On the other, it is a site of constant critique, reform, and transformation of existing relations.[48] Yet, I am not trying to demonstrate that ethno-ecological communities are all harmonious and equal among and between themselves. Unity of a community does not mean unity in sameness. On the contrary, as Iris Young states, "our conception of social justice requires not the melting away of differences, but institutions that promote reproduction of and respect for group differences without oppression."[49] In the same vein, Bina Agarwal argues for the need of entitlement to land and property for South Asian women.[50] These are the precise critical spaces that all social movements utilize, both to critique the macro-structures of inequities in which they are embedded and to broaden and democratize micro-social relations within their own communities.

Concluding Remarks: Reknowing Ethnicity and Ecology

Ecologically speaking, Raymond Williams aptly noted, "resistance to capitalism is the decisive form of the necessary human defense." However, as I have indicated here, many resistances are futile because they are not informed or equipped by alternative worldviews or practices. That is why, except for bargaining with the dominant system, they cannot inform any immediate social practice or movement. Like the motion of global capital, Marxist and socialist models, for example, in matters of country and city, capital and community, centers and margins, continue and even intensify the same fundamental processes of degradation of environment and erosion of communities. Although the ecological crisis has attracted the attention, devotion, and energy of thousands of people all over the world, often its seriousness is underestimated, as if it were just another argument in the mainstream judicial system. Ecological ethnicities have gradually come out of that misplaced dream. If the legal victories for tribal self-rule in India and for the Zapatistas are any indication, it is time to think beyond the "relations of ruling" based upon the idea of development and integration of multiethnicities within the tight framework of the nation-state.

Today, the overlapping connection between ecology and ethnicity has also provoked responses of both suspicion and support. One response is the euphoric kind, in which ethnic movements are considered vectors of resistance to the excesses of nation-states and the institutional trinity of the World Bank, GATT, and the WTO. The second response has been to see ethnicity as a suspicious historical project, a kind of regressive resolution against the march of history, a source of social disintegration, violence, and terror, if not a retreat to backward times. This kind of reaction has come from both nationalist and Marxist observers. Yet, just because ethnicity does not fit in nicely with the formation of class or of nationality, this is insufficient reason to vilify ethnicity. One has to reckon with the fact that there are still ten thousand identity groups, based on ethnicity, linguistics, and religions, spread over 168 nation-states. Rather than ignoring them, in multiethnic countries such as India, Mexico, or the United States, a democratic state might have to create spaces for ecological and cultural citizenship. It is also starkly clear that ethnic concerns cannot be eliminated or subdued by violence in the nation-states, as has been done during the twentieth century. It is time to explore a new constitutive order, with a place for ethnic identity groups as coshapers of their polity, locally, regionally, nationally, and globally.[51]

As this chapter suggests, ethnic resurgence today is enriched by its inextricable connection with ecology. While addressing the immediate crises they are facing, several ethnic peasant and indigenous groups are engaged in creating pantribal, indigenous peoples' alliances, which are propelled by two tendencies. On the one hand, outsiders often look at these diverse ethnic groups as one entity, although they may be scattered geographically and have different histories. On the other, indigenous peoples have become aware of their common history of colonization and resistance, as well as of their deeply held differences. They are seeking affiliations and building networks on such diverse issues as biodiversity, territorial autonomy, recognition of their respective languages, and access to resources. This does not mean that their respective tribal worldviews and identities are disappearing or being subsumed within the larger entity. Instead, greater numbers of people are claiming that their supratribal consciousness operates collectively in global arenas, such as United Nations discourses on indigenous problems and forums on biodiversity, patent laws, and cultural diversity. Moreover, the indigenous movements are seeking alliances not only among indigenous ethnicities, but also with movements engaged in social justice, human rights, and ecological struggles and with cultural movements.

Are there dangers in my kind of optimism for ecological ethnicities? David Harvey warns us against such "militant particularisms" on the basis that "place here can function as a closed terrain of social control that becomes extremely hard to break (or break out of) once it achieves its particular permanence." There are individual as well as class interests involved in building and maintaining such places. He gives examples from the United States, where several isolated ethnic communities (lacking access to the rest of society, legal status, civil integration, and civil rights) provide docile bodies for the innumerable sweatshops run by the same ethnically distinct capitalist class. Examples abound of such sweatshops in New York, Los Angeles, and San Francisco in the United States, in immigrant enclaves in Europe, and in the corridors of Maquiladoras and the Free Trade Zones. In some circumstances, ethnic identity (even ecological ethnicities) can be the vehicle for manipulating a continuous flow of surplus extraction from resources and labor. David Harvey raises serious doubts about such politics. He thinks place-bound particularisms "do not necessarily give rise to militant politics. They can just as easily be the locus of political passivity or of collaboration and complicity with a dominant social order."[52]

With due respect to his astute observation, I think David Harvey falls short of appreciating the very central tenets of ecological ethnicities I outlined earlier. First, he does not consider the limits of anthropocentric notions implied in the usual theories of social transformation, nor is he aware that his views are centered on the nation-state. Second, he is utterly unaware that a healthy social movement is like a double-edged sword in that it critiques the present social relations as much as it regenerates them. To presume that such place-bound ethno-ecological politics would so easily lead to parochial, passive, and retrograde politics is a symptom of universalistic (including the so-called progressive) bias in his own theory. What is necessary today is to broaden our own understanding of how identities are formed and reconfigured when the global capitalist economy passes through new phases and changing dynamics.

One way of doing this is to overcome the nature-culture duality and look at the relationship between cultural and biological diversity. Let me ask this: Why are naturally diverse regions also culturally diverse? For example, why does Ecuador seem richer in both biota and cultural history than areas of equal size elsewhere? Why have the mountainous regions of the Himalayas and the Andes become abodes of biodiversity? Is this merely due to climatic conditions or have humans played a role in this? The question is urgent because the coexistence of cultural and biotic diversity within the same ecoregion is not an accident, but a fact. Gary Nabhan, among others, has illustrated that of the nine countries in which 60 percent of the world's remaining sixty-five hundred languages are spoken, six of them are also centers of megadiversity for flora and fauna: Mexico, Brazil, Indonesia, India, Zaire, and Australia. It is fair to say, Nabhan concludes, that wherever many cultures have coexisted within the same region, biodiversity has also survived.[53]

Yet, why is it that protecting biodiversity in the new global order has caused the cultural and linguistic extinction of the very people who nurtured this diversity throughout history? The biodiversity industry functions as though it would only survive if we put all biodiversity in a museum, in captivity, or in gene banks. Technocratic arrogance does not recognize that biodiversity will not survive without the co-evolving human diversity that is particular to that place, which also includes linguistic diversity, diversity in food and medicinal systems, and even in the ways we see how culture and nature intermingle. There is an organic link between human activity and what happens to nature, and "the most potent way of conserving biological diversity may be to protect the diversity of cultures that have stewarded the plant and animal communities on which our agriculture is based."[54]

Of course, the task of properly assessing the promise of ethno-ecological formations and attributing to them the roles they duly deserve is tremendous. For example, how are resistances to strip mining, a large dam, or the monoculture forestry organized? Are these protests useful? And if so, what are the culturally rooted notions about how the land should be used and what kinds of species a forest should have?

How are claims over land, forest, and water related to the territorial claims for political autonomy? And how have those notions been translated into the logistics of these movements? From what we see in the mainstream press, the struggle seems to be organized by trade unions within the mines that fight for compensation but do not oppose the mining as such. Peasants are struggling for access to land, but they do not mean to use it sustainably. Can we then assume that all of these conflicts will be resolved if adequate numbers of people who were displaced are employed or rehabilitated? Or would ecological ethnicities seek appropriate technologies for creating energy without mining coal, irrigating without large dams, cultivating biodiversity within their own farms without creating parks and sanctuaries, or restoring salmon without creating the bureaucracy of fisheries management? These technologies cannot simply be talked about in isolation from how the land, water, and forest are integrated into the overall fabric of their lives, and these communities have the right to decide regarding the use of and access to these resources.

Struggling to stay afloat in the rising tide of the global market and governmental institutions, ecological ethnicities are the victims of the last five hundred years' onslaught. Yet, they are a testimony to the most resilient and unique source of vital self-identity, armed not only with cultural but economic, political, and civilizational claims. Despite deep-rooted agony and injury, ecological ethnicities have remained resilient and have sustained their cultural memories. They have persisted to speak their languages, they have prevented capitalist accumulation through social sanctions, and despite all odds, they have kept alive the prudent technologies of harvesting nature. Most importantly, they have survived institutions of governance at the local level. This is the foundation that has led to their emergent social formation. They will not be silenced by the mere provision of more, or even handsome, opportunities in the global marketplace; they have become the "rocks" that are unassimilable by either the embrace of the nation-states or the magnetism of the global market.

Notes

1. See Michel de Certeau, *Heterologies: Discourses on the Other* (Minneapolis: University of Minnesota Press, 1986), 225.

2. See B. D. Sharma, *Globalization: The Tribal Encounter* (New Delhi: Har-Ananda Publications, 1996).

3. February 1998, e-mail communication.

4. I have introduced the notion of "ecological ethnicity" to explicate this particular phenomenon: see Pramod Parajuli, "Beyond Capitalized Nature: Ecological Ethnicity as a New Arena of Conflict in the Regime of Globalization," *Ecumene: A Journal of Environment, Culture and Meaning* 5, no. 2 (1998): 186–217; and "Ecological Ethnicity in the Making: Developmentalist Hegemonies and the Emergent Identities in India," *Identities* 3, no. 1-2 (1996): 15–59.

5. Also see my interpretation of the politics of knowledge implicit in these agro-ecological communities: Pramod Parajuli, "Discourse on Knowledge, Dialogue and Diversity: Peasant Cosmovision and the Science of Nature Conservation," *Worldviews: Environment, Culture, Religion* 1, no. 3 (1997): 189–210; and "How Can Four Trees Make a Jungle? Ecological Ethnicities and the Sociality of Nature," *Terra Nova: Nature and Culture* 3, no. 3 (1998): 15–31, special issue, *Wild and the World*. And, on the Andes, see Julio Valladolid and Frédérique Apffel-Marglin, "Andean Cosmovision and the Nurturing of Biodiversity," in this volume.

6. Recently, food has been brought back into the center of the discussion of peoples' relationship to land, their identities, and even their claim to localized forms of politics. For provocative statements, see Gary Paul Nabhan, *Cultures of Habitat: On Nature, Culture, and Story* (Washington, D.C.: Counterpoint, 1997); Jack Kloppenburg et al., "Coming in to the Foodshed," in *Rooted in the Land: Essays on Community and Place,* ed. William Vitek and Wes Jackson (New Haven: Yale University Press, 1996); and Francis Zimmermann, *The Jungle and the Aroma of Meats: An Ecological Theme in Hindu Medicine* (Berkeley and Los Angeles: University of California Press, 1987).

7. A passionate appeal for "bioregions" as a space for commitment and also as an organizational unit is found in Gary Snyder, "Coming into the Watershed," in *Changing Community, The Graywolf Annual,* vol. 10, ed. Scott Walker (Saint Paul: Graywolf Press, 1993), and *The Old Ways: Six Essays* (San Francisco: City Lights Books, 1977), 65. Also see *Reinhabiting a Separate Country: A Bioregional Anthology of Northern California,* ed. Peter Berg (San Francisco: Planet Drum Foundation, 1978). Through the Planet Drum Foundation, Berg and his colleagues have applied some of these ideas on watershed planning to California (see their website, www.planetdrum.org). In the same vein, the work of David McClosky of the Cascadia Institute in Seattle, of Freedom House in the Mettole River basin in northern California, and of Daniel Kemmis in the Northwest of the United States exemplifies this trend. I elaborate their ideas further in my discussion of ecological citizenship.

8. See Parajuli, "Beyond Capitalized Nature," and "Ecological Ethnicity in the Making"; Sharma, *Globalization;* and Pramod Parajuli and Smitu Kothari, "Struggling for Autonomy: Lessons from Local Governance," *Development: Seeds of Change* 41, no. 3 (1998): 18–29.

9. In India, the word *adivasi* is derived from two Sanskrit words: *adi* (original) and *vasi* (inhabitant). It denotes all Indian indigenous peoples (estimated to be around seventy million), whether they are included in the list of Scheduled Tribes or not.

10. The idea of linking ecological crisis with the crisis of social justice is now well developed. Whereas in the United States, the theme is expressed in the form of "environmental racism," in South Asia and other developing areas, social justice plays an even more central role. For some examples, See Smitu Kothari and Pramod Parajuli, "No Nature without Social Justice: A Plea for Cultural and Ecological Pluralism in India," in *Global Ecology: A New Arena of Political Conflict,* ed. Wolfgang Sachs (London: Zed Books, 1993), 224–39.; Madhav Gadgil and Ramachandra Guha, *Ecology and Equity: The Use and Abuse of Nature in Contemporary India* (London: Routledge, 1995); and Ramachandra Guha and Juan Martinez-Alier, *Varieties of Environmentalism: Essays North and South* (London: Earthscan, 1997). Indeed, an environmentalism of the South deserves serious attention beyond and distinct from the mainstream discourse of environmental modernization.

11. On the scientific critique of biotechnology from a feminist perspective, see *Biopolitics: A Feminist and Ecological Reader on Biotechnology,* ed. Ingunn Moser and Vandana Shiva (London: Zed Books, 1995). One of the leading champions against patent rights and monopolies of biotechnology has been the Canada-based Rural Advancement Foundation International (RAFI). Its publications, legal campaigns, and e-mail communications are available on their website (www.rafi.org). Winona LaDuke's essay "Indigenous Environmental Perspectives: A North American Primer," *Akwe:kon Journal* 9, no. 2 (1992): 52–70, on the other hand, offers a critique from a Native American perspective.

12. While a new genre of literature is highlighting the plight and promises of indigenous populations, some have preferred the notion of peasantry as the core of indigenous issues. For example, *The Spirit of Regeneration: Andean Culture Confronting Western Notions of Development,* ed. Frédérique Apffel-Marglin with PRATEC (London: Zed Books, 1998), portrays indigenous peoples of the Andes primarily as peasants. Gustavo Esteva, in "Hosting the Otherness of the Other: The Case of the Green Revolution," in *Decolonizing Knowledge: From Development to Dialogue,* ed. Frédérique Apffel-Marglin and Stephen A. Marglin (Oxford: Clarendon Press, 1996), 249–78, offers a peasant-centered perspective on Mexico. Both James C. Scott, in his *Seeing Like a State: How Certain Schemes to Improve the Human Condition Have Failed* (New Haven: Yale University Press, 1998), and Stephen A. Marglin, in "Farmers, Seedsman, and Scientists: System of Agriculture and Systems of Knowledge," in *Decolonizing Knowledge,* ed. Apffel-Marglin and Marglin, pose peasantry as having distinct ways of knowing and interpreting the world.

13. Parajuli, "Ecological Ethnicity in the Making," 43–44; Gail Omvedt, *Reinventing Revolution: New Social Movements and the Socialist Tradition in India* (Armonk, N.Y.: M. E. Sharpe, 1993).

14. The prolific writings of cultural Marxist Raymond Williams shed light on different dimensions of human agency and social structure, the delicate art of human consciousness, and the formation of social hegemonies. A rare phenomenon among Marxists, he also touches upon the sense of land, literature, and political expressions. See his *Marxism and Literature* (Oxford: Oxford University Press, 1977), and

Marxism and Interpretation of Culture (Oxford: Oxford University Press, 1981). The assertion that social movements might be the site where the "residual" evolves into "emergent" is entirely my own interpretation, based on how I saw the discursive terrain among ethno-ecological movements in India shifting from merely seeking equal opportunity to seeking autonomy.

15. An emergent global indigenous politics has revealed the many layers of racism implied in colonial and developmentalist politics of extraction. The issue of patents on medicinal herbs and seeds has further sharpened the divide between local use of and rights over resources and the claims of transnational companies. For a survey, see Al Gedicks, *The New Resource Wars: Native and Environmental Struggles against Multinational Corporations* (Boston: South End Press, 1993); and Jerry Mander, *In the Absence of the Sacred: The Failure of Technology and the Survival of the Indian Nations* (San Francisco: Sierra Club Books, 1991).

16. A major part of this analysis came to public notice through the work of sociologist Robert Bullard, which is now followed by many African Americans, Hispanic and Asian American writers, and many grassroots activists themselves. For initial documentation, see *Confronting Environmental Racism: Voices from the Grassroots,* ed. Robert D. Bullard (Boston: South End Press, 1993). Based on these sites of subaltern environmentalism, Giovanna Di Chiro furthers the idea of "ecology as community" in *Uncommon Ground: Toward Reinventing Nature,* ed. William Cronon (New York: W. W. Norton, 1995).

17. Sharma, *Globalization.*

18. Parajuli, "Discourse on Knowledge, Dialogue and Diversity."

19. Parajuli "Beyond Capitalized Nature."

20. Gadgil and Guha, *Ecology and Equity.*

21. Edward Goldsmith, "Global Trade and the Environment," in *The Case against the Global Economy,* ed. Jerry Mander and Edward Goldsmith (San Francisco: Sierra Club Books, 1996), 78–79; Parajuli, "Beyond Capitalized Nature," 206.

22. I. Altvater, "Ecological and Economic Modalities of Time and Space," in *Is Capitalism Sustainable? Political Economy and the Politics of Ecology,* ed. Martin O'Conner (New York: Guilford Press, 1994), 76–90.

23. Pramod Parajuli, "Tortured Bodies and Altered Earth: Ecological Ethnicities, Social Movements Learning and Civilizational Options in the Periphery" (unpublished book manuscript).

24. See *The Spirit of Regeneration,* ed. Apffel-Marglin with PRATEC; and Valladolid and Apffel-Marglin, "Andean Cosmovision," in this volume.

25. Frédérique Apffel-Marglin and Pramod Parajuli, "Geographies of Difference and the Resilience of Ecological Ethnicities: Place and the Motion of Global Capital," *Development: Seeds of Change* 41, no. 2 (1998): 16.

26. Parajuli, "How Can Four Trees Make a Jungle?"

27. See Nabhan, *Cultures of Habitat,* 157–58.

28. Parajuli, "How Can Four Trees Make a Jungle?"

29. A. Escobar, "After Nature: Steps to an Antiessentialist Political Ecology," *Current Anthropology* 40, no. 1 (1999): 1–30.

30. Parajuli, "How Can Four Trees Make a Jungle?"

31. Vine Deloria, "If You Think About It, You Will See That It Is True," *Revision* 18, no. 3 (1996): 42.

32. Freeman House, *Totem Salmon: Life Lessons from Another Species* (Boston: Beacon Press, 1999); Daniel Kemmis, *Community and the Politics of Place* (Norman: University of Oklahoma Press, 1990).

33. Donald Snow, as quoted in House, *Totem Salmon,* 199.

34. Nabhan, *Cultures of Habitat;* Parajuli, "How Can Four Trees Make a Jungle?"

35. Indeed, the visibility of nongovernmental organizations at global summits, such as those on the WTO (Seattle, 1999), women (Beijing, 1995), social development (Copenhagen, 1996), and the environment (Rio, 1992), has been impressive.

36. See Partha Chatterjee, *Nation and Its Fragments: Colonial and Postcolonial Histories* (Princeton: Princeton University Press, 1993).

37. See Ashis Nandy, *Plural Worlds: Ashis Nandy and the Post-Columbian Future,* special issue, *Emergences* 7/8 (1995–1996).

38. Pramod Parajuli, "The Other Vietnam? Zapatista Movement and the Ecological Critique of Capitalism" (manuscript).

39. George A. Collier and Elizabeth Lowry Quarantiello, *Basta! Land and Zapata Rebellion in Chiapas* (Oakland, Calif.: Food First Institute, 1994); June Nash, "The Reassertion of Indigenous Identity: Mayan Responses to State Intervention in Chiapas," *Latin American Research Review* 30 (1995): 7–39.

40. Sharma, *Globalization;* Parajuli, "Ecological Ethnicities in the Making."

41. Scott, *Seeing Like a State.*

42. See David Harvey, *Justice, Nature and the Geography of Difference* (Cambridge, Mass.: Blackwell Publishers, 1996), where he explains the logic of managing nature within the paradigm of environmental modernization. A more philosophical critique of the same is found in Canadian environmentalist Raymond A. Roger's *Nature and the Crisis of Modernity: A Critique of Contemporary Discourse on Managing the Earth* (Montreal: Black Rose Books, 1994).

43. House, *Totem Salmon.*

44. Ronald Engel, "Liberal Democracy and the Fate of the Earth," in *Spirit and Nature: Why the Environment Is a Religious Issue,* ed. Steven C. Rockefeller and John C. Elder (Boston: Beacon Press, 1992), 59–82.

45. David McClosky, "Watershed Democracy" (manuscript; Seattle: Cascadia Institute, 1998).

46. Kloppenburg et al., "Coming in to the Foodshed," 120.

47. Aldo Leopold, *A Sand Country Almanac, and Sketches Here and There* (London: Oxford University Press, 1949), 204.

48. Parajuli, "Tortured Bodies and Altered Earth."

49. Iris Young, *Justice and the Politics of Difference* (Princeton, N.J.: Princeton University Press, 1990), 47.

50. Bina Agarwal, *A Field of One's Own: Gender and Land Rights in South Asia* (Cambridge: Cambridge University Press, 1994).

51. Elise Boulding, "Ethnicity and the New Constitutive Orders," in *Global Visions: Beyond the New World Order,* ed. Jeremy Brecher et al. (Boston: South End Press, 1993), 213–15.

52. Harvey, *Justice, Nature and the Politics of Difference,* 304–24.

53. Nabhan, *Cultures of Habitat,* 37.

54. Ibid., 223.

Changing Habits, Changing Habitats: Melanesian Environmental Knowledge

MARY N. MACDONALD

Introduction

In the traditional communities of Melanesia,[1] that part of the South-west Pacific which includes the large island of New Guinea and many smaller islands, people responded to crucial points in the cycles of life by gathering to conduct rituals, rituals which would promote fruitful connections, encourage renewal, and chart a course for the future. Those of us who gather to discuss indigenous religions and ecology recognize that our planet is at a turning point and that human beings have a responsibility for its future. Our global situation echoes the situations in which Melanesian communities would turn to ritual. When, in the past, the land and the community lost their vitality, Melanesians knew what to do about it. For example, in highland New Guinea communities pigs would be killed and pork shared between the living and the ancestors. In our present environmental turning point no one way of knowing—not that of science, nor that of religion; not that of modernity, nor that of tradition—can speak with any assurance of the direction we should take amid the problems and possibilities of our time. Each, though, can help us to think about the human condition and the human habitat, the planet which we share with so many species. Each can help us review our habits, the customary ways in which we relate to all that constitutes our world.

Implicit in traditional practices and discourse are understandings of the world which sustained indigenous communities until recent times. Melanesian stories tell of the relationship of the land and its inhabitants while Melanesian rituals provide the means of sustaining the relationship. The cosmologies and ecologies which inform such narratives and rituals may offer insight into our present shared predicament or, at least, provide further perspectives on it. At the same time, Melanesian experiences of colonialism and postcolonialism highlight attitudes and problems which beset the global community. Anchored in local contexts, Melanesian views of the world have their limitations. We can look to them for suggestions, but we cannot expect them to give easy answers to complicated global questions. Yet, as I focus on traditional and changing ideas of place, relationships, and work, I suggest that the understanding of human responsibility for renewing the world, which we find in daily life, in ritual, and in myth, throughout Melanesia, is a helpful contribution to our reflection on the turn we are making in our habitation of planet Earth. I would construe the ethic of interdependence suggested by Melanesian narratives and rituals as consonant with the views of modern science, or, at least, not at odds with such views, even though expressed in different genre. However, there is no doubt that Melanesian narratives and rituals are at odds with the tale of modern markets and, therein, lies another point for our common reflection.

Traditional Melanesian knowledge of how to garden, fish, hunt, and gather medicinal materials while conserving local habitats is valuable. There are many reasons for conserving it. In the long term, though, what might be more valuable than particular areas of knowledge is an orientation toward the world which informs them. We could call this orientation an ethic of interdependence; in more concrete Melanesian terms it would be rendered as "give-and-take." Understanding relationships to land, people, and spirits in terms of mutual exchange, the peoples of the region have sustained their small-scale societies until today. In many of the more than one thousand languages in the region, the notions of transaction, which in English we would express as "buying" and "selling," are expressed by a single word to which a directional marker is added. That is, a reciprocal relationship is implied between givers and takers, between buyers and sellers.[2] Yet, the balanced reciprocity which traditional, largely egalitarian, subsistence economy societies were able to sustain is being disrupted with the incursion of resource-seeking multinational companies which do not have a long-term relationship to the land.

During the first week of October 1997, eight hundred thousand hectares of land in Indonesia were burning and millions of people in Indonesia, Malaysia, Papua New Guinea, and the Philippines were suffering the ill effects of the choking smog. The fires led to food shortages, and the smoke they produced prevented planes attempting to bring relief supplies from landing. In Irian Jaya which, like Papua New Guinea, was suffering a devastating drought, the worst in fifty years, the Red Cross reported that more than 270 people had died from starvation.[3] The fires and the drought, some would say, are not random occurrences but part of a global warming phenomenon which results, in part at least, from human choices, from failures in human responsibility. Moreover, the logging and mining operations which are causing catastrophic changes in habitats in the Asia-Pacific region result from choices made in other parts of the world to satisfy, as "economically" as possible, the needs and habits of people who live elsewhere. The indigenous logic of balanced "give-and-take" has not been able to prevail either with regard to overseas partners in trade or with regard to the human responsibility for Melanesian habitats.

Traditional Environmental Knowledge

Melanesians are expert gardeners whose subsistence economy depends on their knowledge of plants and soils and seasons, and on the techniques they have developed for making the most of their land. The highlanders of the large island of New Guinea were among the first people on earth to engage in intensive agriculture. In the Wahgi Valley of Papua New Guinea archaeologists have uncovered evidence of drainage channels and garden clearings, which they date to about nine thousand years ago. One could speculate on the change in orientation to the land which the agricultural breakthrough occasioned. From being dependent on the seasonal provision of game and plant foods, communities took more control of the food supply. However, human control was limited. Gardeners' awareness of their dependence on the weather, and on the good will of insects, is expressed in a multitude of gardening spells and rituals.

Melanesians who share forested areas with marsupials and birds know the habits of the various species. They have weapons and techniques for hunting game; they use bird plumes and animal fur in body

Figure 1. Dawn, Mararoko, Southern Highlands, Papua New Guinea. The People of this area are subsistence gardeners producing their own food and finding building materials in the forest. (Photograph Mary MacDonald)

decoration; they evoke the qualities of birds and animals in songs and spells. Similarly, people in coastal areas and in proximity to rivers understand the habits of fish and the ways of the ocean and streams; their rituals and myths express an understanding of sea creatures as kin. Not only do the forests and seas contribute food for the human diet, provide building materials for human habitations, and furnish medicinal products for the traditional pharmacopoeia. The living experience of rain forests and marine environments is an experience of the power and the precariousness of the human condition. The myths and rituals arising from that experience constitute a knowledge of the environment; they are traditional science.

A neighbor who grew up in Australia, and later lived and worked for eight years in Papua New Guinea, I admire the rich variety and complexity of Melanesian systems of knowledge. I also recognize the danger of forcing them into too simple a template.[4] In focusing on just three interrelated components of Melanesian life—place, relationships, and work—my intention is to explore traditional and changing ways of knowing. First, under the heading "traditional environmental knowledge," I shall comment on "traditional" experiences of place, relationships, and work. Then, under the heading "changing environmental knowledge," I shall discuss how encounter with industrialized nations and with Christianity has altered experiences of place, relationships, and work and has challenged traditional orientations to the world.

Place

A few years ago I visited a Kewa friend, Bernadet Kandi, whom I have known since 1973, in the area where she lives near Kagua in the Southern Highlands of Papua New Guinea. As we walked together, she pointed out places where events in her life had taken place. This was where she and her age-mates had taken part in courting parties. Here, her son had fallen into a pool and her husband had jumped in to rescue him. There, she had tilled a garden which produced huge sweet potatoes, much to the delight of her family.[5] When Kandi recalled things the two of us had done together she placed us in a landscape and, even, borrowing from Steven Feld's notion, to which I shall come shortly, of "soundscape," we might say, in a "tastescape." Thus, she remembered that we went down to Mararoko where Kauwanya and Mangalo gave us cassowary to eat; we sat on top of Rogomayo Mountain exhausted from the climb and "drank" sugar cane; we visited her parents in Wabi and chewed corn with them; we "ate" smoke from a large bamboo pipe with women in the Erave market.

Even without access to the journal I kept during the years I spent in the Southern Highlands, I would be able to place the events Kandi narrated in a chronological sequence. I would not, though, be sure of the years, and certainly not of the months. Kandi, if she wanted to, could surely do the same. Her cultural inclination, is, however, to know and recall her own life and mine spatially. She knows our biographies—experiences our lives—as relationship to particular locales: Mararoko to the south in the shadow of Mountain Sumale (Murray); Wabi in the grasslands to the north of the Erave River; Erave, a government post, in between the other places. Kandi also knew herself and myself and our relationship through food consumed, through the sensory experience of taste. The mention of cassowary wrapped in banana leaves and cooked in hot stones, corn roasted over coals, harsh tobacco inhaled from a shared pipe vividly evoke the situations and the people with whom we shared them. I could taste and smell them as she spoke. Through her telling we knew ourselves and constituted our lives through taste. We might say that it is a poetic and aesthetic way of knowing; it is also a knowing grounded in place and sensory experience.

Recounting experiences among the Kaluli, who live well to the west of the Kewa in the Southern Highlands and who inhabit a land of forests, rivers, and waterfalls, anthropologist and musicologist Steven Feld uses the notions of "soundscape" and "acoustemology" to embrace Kaluli modes of knowledge. The sounds and feels of water, he suggests, are important to the way the Kaluli locate themselves and know their world. The flow of water, summoned to consciousness in their songs, is homologous to the flow of human life. Trying to capture the Kaluli sense of place as heard and felt, he describes "a poetics of place." He observes of the poetic intensification of place memories:

The aesthetic power and pleasure of Kaluli songs emerges in part through their textual poesis of placename paths. Composed and performed by guests in ritual contexts to evoke tears from their hosts over memories of persons and places left behind, these songs can also be sung during work, leisure, and everyday activities by women and men as they move through and pass time in forest locales. In both ritual and everyday contexts, the songs are always reflective and contemplative, qualities enhanced in each instance by construction of a poetic cartography whose paradigmatic parallelism of path making and naming reveals how places are laminated to memories, biographies and feelings.[6]

What I notice in my friend Kandi's way of remembering and what Feld suggests about Kaluli ways of knowing is not, of course, peculiar to Melanesians. Attentiveness to places, to sounds, and to tastes is something we can all cultivate. In fact, though, while traditional communities are more likely to "know" through relationships to particular places, it is an attentiveness to particular times which structures modern worlds. For Melanesians, particular places and a community's land are the loci of the relationships and products that sustain life. In contrast, for someone raised in the industrialized world, land is not so much a ground of knowing as one of the four principal resources for economic development. While I note the contrasting perspectives, I do not want to exaggerate them. In areas of Papua New Guinea little affected by the outside world, I have seen people unnecessarily, and just for convenience sake, cut trees for firewood from places where erosion would surely follow. And, conversely, I know people whose work in industry even sharpens their sense of nature and place and commits them to environmental responsibility. All human beings in all cultures can answer, or refuse to answer, to place. One may know land in general and one may know it as an industrial resource; one may also know a particular land as home and, to borrow Deborah Bird Rose's term, know it as a "nourishing terrain."[7] How individuals and communities know the land affects the way they care for it.

The South Kewa of the Southern Highlands of Papua New Guinea, among whom I lived for several years in the 1970s, describe their cosmos as a number of linked communities. The Kewa cosmos includes the distant world of the sky people, the realms of spirits and ghosts, and the abode of the living. Today contact with the sky people is minimal, although it is said that long ago people could go back and forth between the sky and the earth. When mist clouds a settlement people say that the sky people have come to visit and, in traditional narratives, they tell of exchanges between the sky people and earth people. Yakili is the most important of the sky people and many Kewa equate him with the Christian God. Prior to missionary activity in the Southern Highlands, which began in the 1950s, regular offerings were made to him. Then there are the worlds of spirits and ghosts. Land spirits are found in trees and waterfalls and streams and they abound in the forest. Ghosts of the ancestors live in their ghost settlements which, it is thought, can be reached by following paths through the forest and entering caves or karst holes which lead to them. The Kewa clear their settlements and garden land from the forest and, by physical effort and ritual work, strive to keep the forest at bay. The Kewa cosmos is, then, a network of relationships and it is human "work," both practical and symbolic, which structures and sustains it.

The Kewa know the forest as a place of both opportunity and danger. After engaging in appropriate rituals men go there to hunt and to cut trees for building. Yet, people are apprehensive about what might happen in the forest. It is a place both attractive and awe-full, a numinous domain. Just as the settlement (*ada,* enclosure, also the word for house) is the home of human beings, so the forest is considered to be the home of a variety of spirits, some capricious and others belligerent, who are likely to cause trouble for people who trespass there. Ghosts, too, dwell in a realm which is reached by going into the forest. In the Kewa way of thinking about the world, the forest is the home of the spirits and the settlement is the home of human beings. Although in a general sense the terrain in which the community lives, hunts, and makes gardens is "home," human beings have cleared forest in order to make their particular home. As I mentioned, people are apprehensive about venturing into the forest. Accidents happen in the forest. Someone in a hurry falls into a karst hole, a person slips and cuts herself on a rock, a hunter is attacked by a cassowary. This way of conceiving of the relationship of human beings and forest differs from that of forest-dwelling people in other parts of Melanesia, and in places such as Sarawak, who experience the forest itself as home.

As intensive agriculturalists the Kewa share something of the attitude of those societies which have made the breakthrough to agriculture. Having for generations cleared land for subsistence gardens, it is perhaps not surprising that they will readily clear land for cash crops, such as coffee and cardamom. However, whereas their need for subsistence gardens was limited by how much the local community could consume, the "need" for cash cropping gardens, which are part of a global economy, is not. Learning that, until white settlement, Aboriginal Australians generally did not have gardens and depended for subsistence on the seasonal cycle of plants, the Kewa express surprise.

Surely, they suggest, people should make gardens so that they can stay in one place. Just as the Aborigines' relationship to their "country" is reinforced by their seasonal peregrinations and ritual enactments in that country, so for the Kewa a profound attachment to the land is reinforced in the act of gardening and the ritual work which accompanies it.

The Kewa say there are dangers associated with cutting down a tree. The spirit resident in the tree expresses anger and distress at being dislodged. Where will he go now? To compensate the spirit, people will offer him the smell of cooking marsupial meat to "eat" and point out another tree where he could take up residence. Proceeding by persuasion they give him something and take something from him. In this worldview the trees are homes, accommodating and protecting the "forest people," just as the settlement accommodates and protects its inhabitants. Trees may be cut to meet human needs for housing and firewood and fence posts, but, at the same time, it is recognized that to provide for human needs is to deprive other beings of their homes. In the traditional Kewa world the sense of injustice toward the trees and their residents is mitigated in the give-and-take of tree-cutting rituals.

The availability of land varies throughout Melanesia, some places being densely populated and others but sparsely so. Traditionally, there was little restriction on clearing land, but with the use of stone axes there was a limit to how much could be cleared. The introduction of the steel ax saw an increase in the amount of land cleared and in the size of pig herds which could be fed on the surplus tubers grown in the extended gardens.[8] Norms for how long land had to be unattended before someone else could use it and norms for the passing on of garden land varied from group to group. The pattern of tenure was that of usufruct, not of individual ownership. Today in Papua New Guinea about 97 percent of the land remains under traditional tenure; almost everyone has use of land. In contrast, across the border in Irian Jaya, much of the land has been used for resettlement of people from other parts of Indonesia who now outnumber the Melanesian inhabitants. Moreover, in both Papua New Guinea and Irian Jaya the expropriation of land for multinational mining companies has had deleterious ecological and social consequences, of which more shall be said.

As Melanesian tales tell of the shaping of the land—the placement of mountains, the cutting of rivers, the formation of ridges—they also reflect on the human condition and provide lessons on how to behave, and how not to behave, toward other people. Just as patterns for behavior toward siblings and spouses are told in tales and enacted in rituals so, too, they are "seen" in, and told from, the landscape. Stories of the mountains Giluwe and Sumale (Murray), located at the north and south, respectively, of Kewa territory, cast them as a husband and wife who argued and then went their separate ways, or as two suitors who quarreled over their affections for a third mountain called Ialibu. In the second story the disappointed Sumale stomps off to the south and now lives alone while Ialibu and Giluwe, poor Giluwe sporting broken teeth because Sumale punched him in the mouth, live side by side. Thus, a discourse on human experience and morality is taken from the landscape, and an attachment to the land is developed and sustained in the taking. Meeting Southern Highlanders in other parts of Papua New Guinea I have listened to their laments that they cannot see Sumale's head rising out of the clouds and have sympathized with their desire to be back near Ialibu and Giluwe in time for the pandanus harvest.

Relationships

As individual histories are mapped over familiar territories, so too the myth-histories of clans and village groups are played out within landscapes. The contours of the land and contours of lineage histories overlay each other in a synesthetic production which includes paths heard and felt, smelled and tasted, emotionally and visually apprehended.[9] When I myself think about a pig kill, a gathering in which pigs are killed and pork distributed—in the South Kewa form of the pig kill, sides of pork are exchanged for shells—I imagine the convergence of the paths along which the pigs and the shells have come. Indeed, the orators at pig kills spend hours telling where each shell and each side of pork has come from, who is now giving it to whom, who is deserving of praise for his generosity, and along which road the shell or side of pork will now go. Thus, ceremonial exchanges create maps in the mind. From yam exchanges and bride wealth distributions to large scale events, such as the *kula*, which links Trobriand Islanders to other island communities, and the various kinds of pig kill exchanges in the highlands, they enact the reciprocity which sustains and regenerates the social world. They engrave in one's mind and in one's sensory experiences the web of relationships within which one has identity.

The patterning of human relationships in Melanesia includes both patrilineal and matrilineal descent systems and both achieved and ascribed systems of leadership. Sometimes people from one area find it difficult to understand the social structures of those from another. What they don't find difficult to understand, though, is that each person is located within a social network and a traditional terrain and has intertwined obligations toward both. Loyalty to family, to clan, and to local residential group continues to be valued in Melanesia. For most people their own security depends on the mutuality of kin and alliance relationships. Very few people in Melanesia have pensions or retirement benefits. However, the introduction of a cash economy is now making it possible for some to live by a more individualistic ethic. In providing for oneself and one's immediate family with a superannuation scheme, one may even become free of traditional obligations.

Work

Traditionally, Melanesians have supported themselves by subsistence agriculture supplemented by hunting, gathering, and fishing. A few communities, such as the Yonggom living in sago swamps along the Ok Tedi River, now the site of a huge opencut mine, depend more on fishing and the processing of sago than on gardening. By and large, though, Melanesians are gardeners. The work of gardening has two aspects. On the one hand, gardening involves physical labor to clear land, to plant and tend crops, and to harvest produce. On the other hand, it involves ritual work to renew the fertility of the land and to ensure the success of the crop. The phrase "work for gardens" as often as not refers to ritual work.

The process of gardening is punctuated by symbolic words and actions which image the fruitful conjunction of male and female elements. Spells threaten insects and other predators and urge them to stay away. In places like the Trobriand Islands, so well known from the writings of Bronislaw Malinowski, specialists take responsibility for the major garden rituals.[10] Among the Kewa, on the other hand, the rituals are carried out by each set of gardeners, usually a husband and wife and children. The Kewa refer to the principal gardeners as the "father" and "mother" of the garden. Although most often they are spouses, they may be widowed brother and sister or unmarried siblings. They carry out the rituals which set a new phase of garden life in motion. Similarly, the two men who are leaders in the staging of a pig kill are the "father" and "mother." They are partners and parents who engender a new phase in the life of the community and in its herds of pigs. Thus, the idiom of generativity or parenting connects domains of experience as different, and as alike, as gardening and killing pigs.

Particular garden rituals need to be viewed within the larger context of ritual life. For example, the Huli of the Southern Highlands of Papua New Guinea locate ritual houses at points along a "root of the earth" which they conceive of as running from north to south and linking them with communities beyond their territory. Their mythico-ritual geography is based in territorial groupings called *hameigini* which occupy land associated with ancestors who are said to have emerged from underground. The ritual houses are located along the "root of the earth" at places where it comes close to the surface. Huli men go to the houses to offer pigs to the ancestors and to feed a giant python which is said to be entwined around the "root." Feeding the ancestor and the python are thought to replenish the fertility of the land and to promote the prosperity of the community. Even so, the Huli recognize that the physical and social worlds go through cycles of decline before they are again renewed. Just as Huli men carry out their rituals for the land and community of the clan, so do Huli men and women work ritually to nourish their family gardens. Both the rituals at the male cult houses and the rituals in the gardens follow the idiom of feeding; it is necessary to feed the land so that the land will feed the community.

Usually the combination of physical and symbolic work for gardens results in crops sufficient to feed local communities and their herds of pigs and to engage in food exchanges. Despite periodic droughts, such as the one which devastated crops in the highlands of New Guinea in 1997, hunger is much less a problem in Melanesia than in other parts of the world. Whether garden rituals are considered to be effective because they tap into an available life energy, or because they encourage commitment to the gardens, or because they facilitate a discourse about life, they are an integral part of what traditional Melanesia

Figure 2. The work of caring for pigs is accompanied by rituals to promote their growth. Here a woman smears white clay on a pig as she says words to encourage it to grow (Tiapoli, Southern Highlands, Papua New Guinea). (Photograph Mary MacDonald)

considers to be work. Garden rituals assert that human beings bear a responsibility for the fertility of the land and not just for its productivity. If people receive food from the land, they must return nourishment to the land. Echoing the idiom of give-and-take, garden rituals are a manifestation of the ethic which governs traditional life.

Changing Environmental Knowledge

In the past century Melanesia has come into relationship with traders, with colonial governments, and with missionaries. Cash economies, national states, local churches, and different approaches to knowing have resulted from these relationships. Some Melanesians sigh with nostalgia for the past; others cannot move fast enough into a new age. As in many areas of the world, the region's population has increased dramatically. The increase may be attributed to a lowering of infant mortality and increased life expectancy. In Irian Jaya it is also the result of immigration.[11] The population increase has skewed the relationship of human population to traditional habitat. Even apart from the pressures caused by foreign resource-gatherers, and the possibilities offered by new economic structures, the changed balance between human population and habitat necessitates changes in the ways that people understand and pursue their livelihood. The combination of increased human population and connection to an international economy in search of timber and minerals has altered the relationship between human communities and rain forest, between human communities and beloved mountains, between human communities and the communities of spirits and ghosts.

Place

Entering a village or town in Melanesia today, one is likely to see a church (in parts of Irian Jaya one may see a mosque and in parts of Fiji a Hindu temple), a health center, and some stores. Most Melanesians still eat from the garden and build with timber from the nearby forest. Store foods, such as canned meat and fish, supplement the diet; steel tools have made it easier to exploit forest resources. Those who live in the towns, which grew up as administrative posts during the colonial era, still identify with their home places and return periodically to the village. Urban workers who have little or no garden land and have to purchase produce in the market will refer to their pay check as their "garden," carrying a traditional idiom into a new economic situation. A road to town has been added to the mental map on which village people locate kin and friends, while those in town will make the new place familiar by applying to it place names from home. Despite emotional, social, and economic links to a traditional place, those who attend school, where they study history, and those who work in town, where clock and calendar determine their work schedule, experience themselves and others in new ways. Time plays an ever-increasing role in the ways that they conceptualize and recall knowledge.

Today some 90 percent of Melanesians are Christians. From first evangelization, which occurred in the late 1800s in some coastal and island areas but not until after World War II in the highlands of Irian Jaya and Papua New Guinea, until the 1970s, regions tended to be associated with particular Christian denominations. Catholicism, for example, embedded itself in the landscape and cultures of Bougainville and Anglicanism in what is now the Oro Province of Papua New Guinea. Building churches, schools, and health centers, providing a variety of services, offering new songs, stories, and rituals, Christian denominations established a physical and moral presence. They brought new knowledge which both competed with and complemented traditional knowledge.

Many Melanesians understood, and today understand, the message preached by missionaries as an extension of traditional loyalties into a larger field. Some resented, and still resent, Christian disparagement of traditional ways. Thus, while most Melanesians today acknowledge that they are Christian, this does not mean that they are completely comfortable with Christianity. Nor does it necessarily mean that they have abandoned traditional practices. With the inrush of hundreds of new Christian groups since the 1970s, the picture has become more complicated. Communities are now divided in their allegiances. For example, Catholic parents in the Sepik area will be appalled when their children join Pentecostal groups. For the parents Catholicism has become part of clan identity. Throughout Melanesia Christianity is conspicuous in spatial and temporal arrangements. Church buildings, sometimes several, dominate villages and the Christian calendar has come to punctuate the rhythm of community life.

Figure 3. A Christian prayer service in which participants cover the Bible with sweet-smelling flower petals to denote the sweetness of God's word (Mararoko, Southern Highlands, Papua New Guinea). (Photograph Mary MacDonald)

Relationships

The response to the intrusion of traders, colonial officers, and missionaries varied across Melanesia. Some were quickly despatched; others were welcomed. Christian narratives were invariably understood as corresponding to indigenous myths, and Christian rituals as supporting the economic endeavors of the newcomers. As time went on, Melanesians tried to establish with the foreigners the kind of reciprocal relationships which they had with allies and which they sustained through the exchange of goods. In some cases they were successful; in others they were not. In the classic cargo cults of the colonial period, myth and ritual were employed in searching for the goods, the "cargo," of equitable relationships. These cults, some of which continue, made use of Christian myth and ritual, mixed Christianity with indigenous practices, devised new ways of life, and, in some cases, reverted to what was understood to be strict tradition. Ostensibly the goal of cargo ritual is to obtain goods similar to those of the Europeans with whom the cultists have come in contact. Desire for the goods may be stated and understood in different ways: the goods may be desired because it is only right that black brother and white brother share in the same wealth; they may be desired so that, having appropriate items of exchange, Melanesians will be able to establish "give-and-take" relationships with the outsiders. In some cults the declared goal is a time and place of peace and reciprocity; in others it is the driving out of the Europeans who have disrupted traditional ways.

Over the long run Christianity has become a part of Melanesian identities and Melanesian landscapes. Of course, there are some Melanesians who follow only indigenous ways, there are some who are Muslim, some who are Hindu, and some who follow the Baha'i faith. There are even a few who claim to have no religion. I would suggest that one of the reasons that Christianity has found such an allegiance in Melanesia is that it articulates for a larger community an ideal that indigenous traditions already know. Melanesians describe ideal relationships in the language of kinship. The ideal is to behave toward the other person as though he or she were your brother or sister, your mother or father, your child. Every telling of a myth is an opportunity to think about the relationships which its plot negotiates; every ceremonial exchange is an opportunity to reinforce and rearrange relationships. Similarly, Christian stories provide the opportunity to think about relationships in a larger community. Not surprisingly, politicians in Melanesia frequently appeal to the Bible and to the image of Jesus as the ideal and universal brother as they strive to forge a sense of regional and national identity among people raised in small-scale societies with local loyalties.

Work

Today much of the work that is done in Melanesia is not for Melanesia. Gardeners still support their families by growing staple crops, such as sweet potatoes and taro. However, they are increasingly putting part of their garden land to cash crops, such as coffee and cardamom, thereby diverting their labors from the subsistence to the cash component of the economy. Perhaps the decision to grow both staples and cash crops is not a bad one if a balance can be maintained which ensures adequate nutrition to families from subsistence crops and provides a cash income which can be used to buy clothes and medicines, pay school fees, pay for transport to visit friends and family, participate in recreational activities, and so on. Yet, serious problems follow when desire for cash goods leads to mono-cropping for overseas markets and to neglect of food gardens.

Even more serious than the diversion of some land for cash cropping is the allocation of land to logging and mining operations. Resource-extracting companies focus on the potential return to their investors with little regard to advantages for Melanesian communities. By various means they convince governments that their provision of infrastructure (for example, roads they will use to carry their logs or minerals to the port) will assist the "developing" country. Seldom is there reciprocity. Most often the local landowners end up bitterly disappointed and the environment suffers.

We saw that traditional garden work is accompanied by garden ritual, which is also conceived of as a kind of work. In Christian communities in Melanesia, too, work is usually accompanied by prayer; it is thus set in a context larger than the immediate satisfaction of the needs and wants of the workers. As well as rituals being appropriated from Christianity, new rituals, including those labeled "cargo cults," have been developed. However, newly introduced works, such as logging and mining, are very different from the subsistence and even the cash-cropping labors of Melanesia. They are controlled by outsiders

and they lack a ritual component. Traditional work, points, in its accompanying ritual, to a relationship between the human being and his
or her habitat. The relationship may be characterized in some phases
as competitive and in others as cooperative. In either case there is
thought to be give-and-take between people and environment. The
new works of logging and mining are not predicated on such a relationship. I shall take the example of logging from Papua New Guinea
and an example of mining from Irian Jaya to suggest that these new
kinds of work, which violate the traditional morality of balanced
"give-and-take," have created a crisis in "knowing" in Melanesia.

Papua New Guinea holds the largest rain forest area remaining in
the Asia-Pacific region. Spread on either side of a central mountain
range which rises to over five thousand meters, it hosts a range of
microclimates and is home to an extraordinary diversity of plants, animals, reptiles, and insects. Until recent times slash-and-burn gardening was in balance with the ability of the forest to renew itself. Now,
both gardening and logging are contributing to the degradation of the
rain forest. There is concern about the long-term fertility and diversity
of the rain forest if these activities continue without control. If the
traditional ethic which recognizes the interdependence of human
community and habitat were to be invoked, it would suggest that
nothing should be taken unless the consequences are considered and
action taken to reciprocate for the loss. Likewise, if the biblical
covenant with all creation (Gen. 9:10), which today is part of the
storytelling repertoire of Melanesian communities, were to be taken
as a guide, it would suggest a responsibility for all of life. In fact,
though, ordinary Melanesians have been taken by surprise. Sad to say,
they have been exploited by outsiders with greater knowledge of
world markets and, even more sadly, by their own governments. Some
people do reflect on what is happening to their habitat via their telling
of traditional tales, but the forums of environmental decision making
are informed more by short-term economic expedience than by
tradition.

David Askin, an agricultural expert based in Papua New Guinea,
summarized Papua New Guinea's logging statistics for 1993 as
follows:

> During 1993, three million cubic meters of timber was exported at a
> value of K505 million.[12] Almost all of this was unprocessed logs, with
> Japan and Korea between them taking about 90% of the logs. A further

500,000 cubic meters of timber were cut for local processing. Taking a
total of about 3.5 million cubic meters of timber, and the forest producing about 30 cubic meters of timber per hectare, then at least 120,000
hectares of land were logged in that year. In the same year a mere 3.8
thousand hectares of land were planted.[13]

The logging companies are seeking to obtain high value tropical
timber at low prices. The companies are often aided in their quest by
local landowners who, persuaded by the prospect of "development"
for their regions, give them permission to take timber in expectation
of an inflow of cash and services.

The greed, the "taking without giving" ethic, which Askin rightly
attributes to the logging companies, also infects some landowners and
their representatives in the national government.[14] However, the payments landowners receive pale into insignificance beside the massive
gains of the companies. The traditional ethic of give-and-take is
threatened by the opportunities for quick gain to be found in the sale
of timber, some of it from species unique to Papua New Guinea. There
is a great need to raise awareness among people in rain forest areas
concerning the long-term consequences of gardening and logging.
Without education none of us can be expected to know how long it
takes the forest to regenerate and what we will lose by unregulated or
poorly regulated logging. We can hardly fault traditional environmental knowledge for failing to equip people to meet the challenge of the
loggers. However, the traditional insight that human beings have responsibility for the cycles of life provides a framework for considering what is to be done today. One could also interpret the traditional
role of ritual and the use of prayer by Melanesian Christians as providing an orientation in attitude toward the rain forest. To follow, for
example, the orientation implied in the traditional Kewa ritual of pla-
cating the resident spirit before cutting a tree, is to suggest that a disruption such as logging requires serious attention to consequences.
Perhaps, as we consider the dire straits of our home planet, we shall,
thinking along with indigenous people, come to see ritual, a pause in
which right relationships can be pondered and desired outcomes con-
templated, not as an optional practice but as a necessity for survival.

In 1967, two years before the so-called Act of Free Choice by
which The Netherlands ceded West Papua (Irian Jaya) to Indonesia,
Freeport-McMoran Copper and Gold Corporation, through its pre-
decessor corporation, initiated development of its Ertsberg mine in

Figure 4. Traditionally, wood has been used for building houses and as fuel for cooking fires. Today, with the export of timber, Papua New Guinea's rainforests are decreasing in extent (Maria Wepenyu, Mararoko, Southern Highlands, Papua New Guinea).
(Photograph Mary MacDonald)

the Dutch territory.[15] From the beginning there was tension between mine officials and indigenous Irianese, who resented the takeover of their land, including sites associated with Jo-Mun Nerek, the spirit of the Amungme people's ancestors. The Melanesian inhabitants also resented the resettlement of people from other parts of Indonesia in West Papua. When Papua New Guinea became independent in 1975, agitation for independence in Irian Jaya intensified. If the Melanesians of "East Papua" (i.e., those in the Australian-administered territories of Papua and New Guinea) could govern themselves, why not those in West Papua as well? In 1977, frustrated with the mining company's disrespect for sacred places and with their subjection to Indonesia, the Amungme people and the members of the pro-independence Papua Freedom Movement, blew up Freeport's pipeline to the coast. However, with the help of the Indonesian government Freeport was able to surmount the disruption and resume its operations.

After Freeport discovered a huge deposit of ore containing copper, gold, and silver in the Jayawijaya Mountain, it began, in 1988, to operate an opencut mine referred to as the Grasberg Mine. In 1991 Freeport signed a new contract with the Indonesian government adding 2.5 million hectares to its concession area. Most of the employees of the mine are brought in from other provinces of Indonesia and are Muslim. The indigenous peoples of Irian Jaya either follow traditional ways or are Christian, although, as in Papua New Guinea, many combine traditional practice and Christianity. The Amungme people feel that the Indonesian government treats them as inferior citizens in their own land and privileges settlers from other parts of the country. Freeport pays the Indonesian military to guard the mine. In violent conflicts between 1994 and 1996 it was obvious that the indigenous Melanesian peoples associate the mine with Indonesian oppression.

In 1996 in the United States District Court in the Eastern District for Louisiana Tom Beanal, a resident of Timika, Irian Jaya, and a leader of the Amungme Tribal Council, brought a complaint against Freeport-McMoran. The complaint, brought on behalf of himself and all others similarly situated, alleges human rights violation, environmental violations, and cultural genocide. The plaintiff submitted that

Freeport-McMoran, Inc. and Freeport-McMoran Copper and Gold, Inc. have systematically engaged in a corporate policy both directly and indirectly through third parties which has resulted in human rights violations against the Amungme Tribe and other Indigenous tribal people. Said actions include extra judicial killing, torture, surveillance and threats of death, severe physical pain and suffering by and through its security personnel employed in connection with its operation of the Grasberg mine.[16]

Environmental violations at the Grasberg Mine are said to include the release of mine tailings into the Ajkwa River and other streams resulting in the destruction of waterways, rain forest, and sago stands. In addition, it is claimed that the mining company has been responsible for the hollowing of mountains and the disruption of "the delicate ecosystem balance between the sea, the beaches, the swamp, the rain forest and the alpine areas within the Freeport mining concession." Whether a case concerning an operation in Irian Jaya will be heard in a U.S. court remains to be seen. The fact that it has been brought alerts people outside Irian Jaya to how indigenous people experience the work of mining as disruptive of place and relationships.

In writing of the work of an indigenous pastor/cargo cult leader, Zakheus Pakage (ca. 1920–1970), a young Irianese scholar and pastor, Benny Giay, describes his people's resistance to colonial expropriation of land.[17] Giay, like, the leader of whom he writes, is a Me from the Paniai region of Irian Jaya. Pakage, he says, rooted his visions of Christianity and development in the indigenous Me worldview. He and his followers came to believe that indigenous teachings and taboos, which emphasized the cultivation of relationships, were essentially the same as the message found in the Christian Bible. They asserted that the Bible, in the form of orally transmitted tradition, was already there before the missionaries arrived. Initially, Pakage sought to establish a reciprocity between indigenous wisdom and Christian wisdom. He also sought to integrate Dutch development plans with the work of local Me communities. In time, the Dutch government and the mission agency, CAMA (the Christian Missionary Alliance), with which Pakage worked, rejected the teachings he was promulgating and he was diagnosed as being mentally ill. His story is not unlike that of other cargo leaders. He may have been mentally ill, however that is to be defined. He was also sensitive to a nonreciprocal situation which denied the human dignity of the Me. Pakage's program captured, and continues to hold, the imagination of many Me. Remnants of his communities are to be found among those who today oppose Freeport-McMoran's mine and who fight for independence in Irian Jaya.

Conclusion

In describing traditional and changing ways of knowing the environment I have pointed to a crisis in knowledge in Melanesia. Elders lament that their children are growing up without the traditional skills of gardening and without the orientation to life of their ancestors. At the same time they lobby for more high schools so that their children will have the advantages of modern education. Meanwhile, most of those who have learned to read and write in church and government schools are not able to obtain the secure paid employment on which they had set their sights. Since the exploitation of natural resources offers jobs, even if these are only short-term, it is not surprising that many people are willing to cooperate with resource-extracting companies. Nor is it surprising that others, fighting to protect their land and their sacred places, oppose the companies. The disorientation caused by social and economic change, particularly in the past thirty years, is such that many people are caught between the old and the new. The world of land and relationships, sustained by physical and symbolic work, may still be the ideal, but it is under threat.

In the colonial period, as the first loggers and miners began transforming the landscape, Melanesians added Christian practices to their ritual repertoire. Since then, a dialogue between indigenous religion and Christianity has furnished ways of thinking about life and change. In the era of multinational mining and logging companies, the churches, which provide modern ritual specialists and teachers in Melanesia, are important players in the negotiation of ways of knowing that can link past and present and can move Melanesians toward solidarity with the global community of life. Organizations such as the Melanesian Council of Churches and the Melanesian Institute are in the forefront of those who challenge governments on both human rights abuses and environmental abuses. Various environmental organizations, notable among them the Melanesian Environmental Foundation, also play a prophetic role in negotiating the strange contemporary situation of work which lacks ritual and economic activities which lack reciprocity.

Can traditional wisdom address issues raised by confrontation with international business interests? Can a local ethic which emphasizes interdependence and reciprocity be carried into the arenas of national, regional, and global markets? Can innovative leaders apply the ethic of give-and-take, which has informed traditional social life and environmental knowledge, to modern circumstances? These are questions not only for Melanesia and not only for indigenous peoples. They affect all the peoples of the earth and, indeed, the earth itself. The challenge is to engage people at all levels of participation and decision making in the conversation about ecology. The awareness expressed in traditional lifeways, in ritual, and in myth, that human beings and other species share a common habitat and are part of a common moral order is a contribution which indigenous religions bring to the discussion of our global situation. Melanesian experiences of place, relationships, and work have changed dramatically in recent times. In moving from reflection on a traditional ethic of interdependence to analysis of the uneven relationships of indigenous communities and multinational companies, we recognize that we need spaces for conversation, for storytelling, and for ritual, in order to come to the knowledge which can sustain our global environment.

Notes

1. "Melanesia," literally, "black islands," is an ethnogeographic label for that part of the southwest Pacific which includes Irian Jaya (a province of Indonesia), Papua New Guinea (independent since 1975), the Solomon Islands (independent since 1978), New Caledonia (a French overseas territory), Vanuatu (the former New Hebrides, independent since 1980), Norfolk Island (an external territory of Australia), and Fiji (independent since 1970). The population of the region, estimated at more than seven million, includes not only indigenous Melanesians but also Indians (brought to Fiji to work in the sugar industry), French in New Caledonia, Indonesians in Irian Jaya, and Australians, including descendants of HMS Bounty mutineers, on Norfolk Island.

2. For example, in the Kewa language of the Southern Highlands of Papua New Guinea, *kaba* indicates one or the other side of an exchange relationship ("buying" or "selling") and prepositions indicate the direction.

3. *International Federation of Red Cross and Red Crescent Societies Weekly News,* 2 October 1997. By October 19 news reports put the number of the dead at more than five hundred.

4. In his contribution to this volume Simeon Namunu, from Misima in the Milne Bay Province of Papua New Guinea, provides an insider's point of view which acknowledges the value of traditional ecological practices and laments the failure of the modern nation-state to translate them into contemporary guidelines.

5. Julio Valladolid's paper describes agriculture and community life in the Andes where the sweet potato has been a staple for thousands of years. It is a relative newcomer to Melanesia, having been brought to the region through the voyages of the Spanish and Portuguese. Today it is the staple food for most highlanders of Papua New Guinea and Irian Jaya.

6. Steven Feld, "Waterfalls of Song," in Steven Feld and Keith H. Basso, *Senses of Place* (Santa Fe, N.M.: School of American Research Press, 1996), 114.

7. Deborah Bird Rose, *Nourishing Terrains: Australian Aboriginal Views of Landscape and Wilderness* (Canberra: Australian Heritage Commission, 1996).

8. On the regulation of pig herds through periodic pig kills, see Roy Rappaport, *Pigs for the Ancestors: Ritual in the Ecology of a New Guinea People,* rev. ed. (New Haven: Yale University Press, 1985).

9. On the notion of synesthesia, see Lawrence E. Sullivan, "Sound and Senses: Toward a Hermeneutics of Performance," *History of Religions* 26, no. 1 (1986): 1–33.

10. The classic account of the gardening rituals of the Trobriand Islands, in what is now the Milne Bay Province of Papua New Guinea, is Bronislaw Malinowski's *Coral Gardens and Their Magic* (London: Allen and Unwin, 1935). An account of Goodenough Island garden practices and rituals, which analyzes changes which occurred in the colonial period, is Michael W. Young's *Magicians of Manumanua* (Berkeley and Los Angeles: University of California Press, 1983). Goodenough Island, in the D'Entrecasteaux Islands group, is southeast of the Trobriand Islands, close to the mainland of Papua New Guinea.

11. Irian Jaya's 421,981 sq kms constitute 22 percent of Indonesia's total land area.

12. In November 1997, the PNG kina was worth about U.S.$ 0.66. It was more valuable in 1993.

13. David Askin, "Rainforest Destruction: Need and Greed in Papua New Guinea," *South Pacific Journal of Mission Studies* 15 (1995): 8–15.

14. See Justice Thomas Barnett, *The Barnett Report* (Hobart: Asia-Pacific Action Group, 1990). While preparing his report, in which he declared that the forestry sector was out of control and that mismanagement and corruption were widespread, Justice Barnett was stabbed outside his home in Port Moresby and almost died. In 1991, in response to his report, a new Forestry Act was passed in parliament. It was gazetted in 1992 and amended in 1993. Nevertheless, in a 1993 review the Melanesian Environmental Foundation reported, "The abuses exposed by the inquiry continue, and are even more entrenched and widespread than before." See Melanesian Environmental Foundation, "Take My Trees," in *Development and Environment,* ed. Hans-Martin Schoell, Point Series, no. 18 (Goroka, Papua New Guinea: Melanesian Institute, 1994).

15. Freeport-McMoran, Inc., and Freeport-McMoran Copper and Gold Corporation, incorporated in the State of Delaware, have their primary corporate domicile at 1615 Poydras Street, New Orleans.

16. United States District Court, Eastern Division for Louisiana, Civil Action, Case No: 96-1474, Section: SECT. K MAG. 3.

17. Benny Giay, "Zakheus Pakage and His Communities: Indigenous Religious Discourse, Socio-political Resistance, and Ethnohistory of the Me of Irian Jaya" (Ph.D. diss., Vrije Universiteit, Amsterdam, 1995).

Indigenous Education and Ecology: Perspectives of an American Indian Educator

GREGORY CAJETE

Introduction

This is a personal narrative, the perspective of an indigenous educator about indigenous education and ecology. My purpose is to present a broader, more inclusive view of the indigenous understanding of the natural world and the nature of teaching and learning about our place in that world. As such, this narrative does not presume to be an "objective" treatise, but rather, a culturally contexted and "subjective" perspective of indigenous ecological relationship. I present a view of the "indigenous" tempered by my experience as a Pueblo Indian, educator, artist, and environmentalist. I present a view of indigenous history, a sense of the present, and a vision of a possible future. I present a window into indigenous reality while at the same time offering a mirror through which Western-based environmental scholars may reflect upon their own insights on indigenous traditions and ecology.

As an American Indian educator, I focus the greatest portion of my professional work on the task of addressing the needs of American Indian students. This emphasis began over twenty-six years ago when I began working as a teacher at the Institute of American Indian Arts, a federally funded institution for the development of the artistic potential of young American Indian and Alaska Native people in Santa Fe, New Mexico. Today, much of the work I do in American Indian schools and communities is an attempt to re-enliven cultural sensibilities and an understanding of the tribally specific educational foundation that many Native people in America have been struggling to maintain or reintroduce. In my work as an educator and cultural historian, I attempt to facilitate rediscovery and revitalization of indigenous self-knowledge, community renewal, and environmental understanding. My work necessarily begins by helping to preserve these understandings among the very people who have given them birth, and that is indigenous people themselves.

I believe that indigenous forms of environmnetal knowledge present possibilities for the development of effective, sustainable, and place-oriented environmental education curricula. Therefore, in my own work as an indigenous educator, I create teaching contexts for integrating arts with culture, with science, and with communal and environmental sensibility in ways that get to the heart of the indigenous perspective. In my most recent work, I am finding that creating environmental curricula for children and their teachers about indigenous foods and gardening provides an effective way to re-enliven and apply the environmental sensibilities of Native people. I also find that the natural tendency to affiliate with nature is still alive in many students and, when given only a little encouragement, it yields a bountiful harvest. Indigenous gardening also helps to make conscious our relationship with Earth, and this is an essential step in the recovery of the natural sense of place that resides deep within each of us.

Ultimately, my work involves an exploration of the "deeper" dimensions of environmental awareness and the ways of "coming to know" and feel deeply connnected to one's place as expressed in indigenous life. It is a quest to recover a quality and context for contemporary life that is about and for sustainable ecological relationships to place. I advocate an approach to education that parallels the kind of environmental teaching and learning region-based indigenous peoples around the world have been applying for thousands of years. I believe the traditions of indigenous peoples reflect an ancient relationship to place, which provides insight into the development of the kind of environmnetal understanding needed to address the ecological challenges of the twenty-first century.

Central Purposes of Indigenous Education

The basic framework for indigenous education is an intimate and complex set of inner and outer place-oriented environmental relationships. It is this relationship to a place which the Acoma Pueblo poet Simon Ortiz refers to as "that place Indian people talk about." Place-oriented education forms the backdrop for the development of natural affiliation. This is not only a physical place with sun, wind, rain, water, lakes, rivers, and streams, but a spiritual place, a place of being and understanding. The sense of place is ever evolving and transforming through the life and relationship of all its participants. Humans naturally have a geographic sensibility and geographic imagination borne of millions of years of our species' interaction with places. Humans have always oriented themselves by establishing direct and personal relationship to places in the landscapes with which they have interacted. These places have also created us, since this sort of relationship building is really the result of processes of co-creation over long periods of time.

There is an ideal which traditionally oriented indigenous people strive for in the process of their teaching and their way of transferring the essence of who they are to each generation. This process is most often exemplified in the symbolic and actual lives of indigenous elders. In indigenous societies, elders are venerated, not simply because they are old, but because they are embodiments of an indigenous way of learning and understanding. This understanding is reflected in the ways that they carry themselves, in the ways that they speak, and in their ways of being who they are. Indigenous elders reflect an indigenous way of being affiliated with life.

In contrast, teaching about the reality of natural America as "place" is not the intent of modern education, which is designed to condition students to view nature and places as objects that can be manipulated through science and technology for human economic interests. Essentially, modern education conditions a "consumer consciousness," which in turn supports the notion that land without modern human habitation is devoid of real value and is therefore "empty" territory that becomes valuable only when it is bought, sold, developed, and inhabited.

An Indigenous Metaphor

Indigenous education is rooted not only in a sense for place but also in the development of a whole sense of being human. The Pre-Columbian Aztecs had a beautiful metaphor which describes the essential qualities and spirit of indigenous education. They said that a "complete" education had to address four interrelated processes within concentric rings of greater contexts of relationship. First, they believed that education should help individuals "find their face." That is simply to say that each individual should be transformed through the process of education and find that special "place" where resides one's unique qualities of self. For the Aztec, a key purpose of education was to help them find one's character, to help find one's identity, to help find one's true relationship with oneself, with one's community, and with the natural world. It is this process of searching for innate and important relationships that helps us define our "authentic" face. A second goal of a complete education was to help students "find their hearts," that is, to help individuals find that particular place within themselves where desire and motivation reside. Simply said, it is about searching for the passion that allows us to energize those things we feel are important. For the Aztec, "heart" reflected the essence of the soul. The third goal was to help individuals find that kind of work, that kind of foundation, that kind of vocation, that thing that would enable them to express most fully who they are. It is an education that helps them to express their individual faces, express their hearts, and express the authentic truthfulness of their being. All this was aimed at achieving a fourth goal of becoming "complete" as a man or as a woman. In earlier times this goal was embodied by the indigenous man and woman.

It is not only a complete man which makes the world, but a complete woman, and it is the interaction and the harmony of these two ways of being human which gives human life its song. So, the relative state of "completedness" may be said to be an ultimate purpose of indigenous education. The expression of such "completedness" is exemplified by the indigenous elder, represented in who the elder is and what he or she represents in the context of a tribal tradition. This is the expression of natural affiliation conditioned through the vehicle of indigenous education that is respectfully acknowledged by indigenous people in deference to the elderly. Tied to this deference to elders is the emphasis that many indigenous societies place on children as a vital part of indigenous community. It is really a concern for children which motivates indigenous education, since the ultimate purpose of such education is the transfer of a way of life and an accompanying worldview to the next generation.

What was the nature and context of indigenous education and its place in the expression of a sacred orientation to place among American Indian people? How is this environmental foundation of traditional indigenous education reflected in the art, the stories, the prayers, the ritual, and the self-identity of Indian people? How is the environmental foundation reflected in the philosophy and nature of ethics which Native people throughout the Americas have practiced and reflected in their understanding of the sacredness of the natural world? These are the essential questions that guide this narrative.

An Ensouled and Enchanted Land

The Americas are an ensouled geography and the relationship of Indian people to this geography embodies a sacred orientation to place that reflects the very essense of what may be called spiritual ecology. The traditional relationship and participation of Indian people with the American landscape includes not only the land itself but the very way in which they have perceived themselves and reality. Indian people through generations of living in America have formed, and have been formed by, the land. Indian kinship with this land, its climate, its soil, its water, its mountains, its lakes, its forests, its streams, its plants, and its animals, has literally determined the expressions of an American Indian theology. My use of the term theology obviously carries with it extensive baggage related to its Western usage. I use it here only as a shorthand frame of reference to reflect a spiritual perspective in which land figures prominently. Rather than losing the term because of problems of language and definition, I would like to reorient it toward considerations of place. The land is an extension of Indian thought and being. As one Pueblo elder states, "it is this place that holds our memories and the bones of our people . . . this is the place that made us!"

There is a metaphor that Pueblo people use which, when translated into English, means "that place that the People talk about." It is a metaphor that refers not only to a physical place but to a place of consciousness and an orientation to sacred ecology. Sacred orientation to place and space is a key element of the ecological awareness and intimate relationship Indians establish with their territory. Indian people have names for all of the places in their area that manifest important environmental features of the landscape. Indian languages are replete with environmentally derived references based on the kind of natural characteristics and experiences they have had living in relationship with their landscape.

Indian experience with the landscape of North America is indeed very ancient. Indian people have lived in this landscape for probably twenty thousand years or more. The North American landscape has been consecrated by the lives and communities of generations of Indian people. Indian people have a "long view" founded on an equally long experience with North America. This long view is reflected in another metaphor used by Tewa elders. The elders remind us of the importance of the long view when they say *pin peye obe,* "look to the mountain." They use this phrase to remind us that we need to look at things as if we are looking out from the top of a mountain. Through this metaphor, they emphasize the essential importance of seeing things in the much broader perspective of considering what we are doing for the generations that are yet to come. They remind us that in dealing with the landscape, we must think in terms of a ten-thousand-, twenty-thousand-, thirty-thousand-year relationship.

Pueblos depicted this sort of ecological understanding in many forms, one of which is the symbolic mythic figure called Kokopelli. Kokopelli is the seed carrier, the creative spirit of nature's fertility, of good fortune, culture, art, music, and dance. Kokopelli is a reflection of the procreative powers of nature and the creative powers of the human mind. Pueblos saw themselves as reflections of Kokopelli, as creative spirits in sacred interaction with natural places of the landscape, as bearers of unique gifts, and as planters of seeds. These perceptions of spiritual ecology related back to the guiding story shared by all Pueblos as a people who emerged from Earth's navel at the time of creation and began to journey through a sacred landscape. It was at that time in the remote past that the first people came to understand the meaning of their sacred relationship to Earth and to "that place that the People talk about."

Indigenous Windows into Natural Affiliation

Sacred orientation to place is a key concept of indigenous education. Indigenous peoples oriented themselves to their natural contexts. They honored their place and considered that they were situated in the center of a sacred space, and that sacred space had very distinct orientations. They recognized and named their directional relationships in terms of the natural and relational qualities associated with them. For instance, many American Indian tribes named the cardinal directions in a way that included a description of the way they naturally oriented themselves, such as referring to north as you are facing the sun, "to the right side of the sun rising"; south, "to the left side of the sun rising"; east, "to the sun rising"; and west, "to the sun setting." This is the way indigenous people metaphorically represent the physical qualities of directionality in their language. These qualities would be included with other qualities, such as colors, plants, animals, winds, kinds of thought, and features of the landscape of place they associated with each direction. Orientation is essential for indigenous people because each is a person of a place. Understanding orientation to place is essential in understanding what it is to be related. Many indigenous peoples recognize seven directions: the four cardinal directions, the above, the center, and the below. This way of viewing orientation creates a sphere of relationship founded on place and evolving through time and space. This is a deeply contexted and holistic reflection of relational orientation.

Art is another reflection of indigenous relational sensibility and education. For example, many ancient southwestern Mimbres pottery design motifs reflect the integration of humans with animals. The designs are completely integrated with one another and reflect the relationship which the Mimbres felt with regard to animals, plants, and nature. Primal symbols of nature also abound in contemporary Pueblo art which represent key features, elements, or foundations of their ecological relationships. One is the Pueblo cloud motif. This important symbol reflects the importance of water, the nature of water to flow in various states and cycles, and the ecological understanding of how water circulates in a semi-arid environment. Pueblo elders recognize many different kinds of rain. They understand that in their arid environment, rain is essential to vivifying the cycle of life, and hence, also essential for their survival. Pueblo elders watch clouds day in and day out. After centuries of such observation they began to discern the relationships and characteristics of clouds. They reflected on how water is intimately involved with the nature of clouds. They recognized all of the various kinds of rain that would be possible from particular kinds of clouds. And they prayed for the kinds of clouds that brought the qualities of water they needed. Whether it was snow, sleet, wind with rain, "baby" rain, grandfather rain, or mother rain, they honored the kinds of rains that brought them life.

Hunting and planting along with fishing and gathering are the food-procuring activities from which mythic tribal expressions derived. In many cultures such as the Pueblos, these orientations are represented in the evolution of traditional art designs, mythic themes, dance, and ritual. Indigenous traditional art forms are replete with designs that represent a people's relationship to the animals and plants that have given them life and given them identity. Included in this are the varieties of dance and ritual created by indigenous people to express and honor their collective sense of natural affiliation.

The understanding about ecological transformation gained from animals was portrayed in many forms among indigenous people, from art and song, dance, and story. Everywhere Indian people hunted, these traditions abounded. Each tribe reflected these understandings in their own unique cultural ways. Yet, core understandings were similar from tribe to tribe. The essential focus was relationship, the guiding sentiment was respect. The central intent revolved around honoring those entities that gave life to a people. Whether it was hunting in the Southwest or in the Far North, an intimate relationship between the hunter and the hunted was established. There was an ecological understanding that animals transformed themselves, and that while this may not be a literal transformation, it is an ecological reality. Animals eat other animals, and those animals that are eaten become a part of the substance of the other's life. This is the primary process of transformation of energy in the animal kingdom. Through observation and interaction with animals over generations, indigenous peoples understood that animals could teach us something about the essence of transformation.

Indigenous peoples created many kinds of symbolic ideals in reflecting about themselves and their relationship to animals. The essence of one such ideal is captured in the metaphoric construct of the "hunter of good heart." Hunting in and of itself is both a spiritual and an educational act. Hunting is one of those forty-thousand-year courses of study in which human beings have been involved. The hunter of good heart is really another kind of representation of the ideal of the complete man. Indeed, the hunter of good heart was a bringer of life to his people. He had to have not only a very intimate knowledge of the animals which he hunted, but also a deep and abiding respect for their nature, for their procreation, for their continuance as species. While he tracked the animal physically to feed himself and his family, he also tracked the animal ritually, thereby understanding at a deeper level his relationship with the animals he hunted. The hunted animal becomes one of the guides of relationship and community in indigenous education.

In the whole process of indigenous hunting, there is always a time for teaching. That time was often directly expressed when the hunter brought back his catch. A scene in many traditional American Indian-and Alaska Native communities is where a hunter returns from the hunt, says prayers of thanksgiving to the animals he has killed, and then gathers his extended family around him. He then tells the story of the animal that has been slain. He talks about the importance of maintaining the proper relationship to the animal that has given its life to perpetuate the life of the family and community. He expresses to his family why it is so important to continue to understand that life is sacred, and that animal life also begets human life through the sacrifice of its flesh to feed and clothe humans. He reminds all that one day we, as human beings, will provide the repayment of life through our own flesh for the purpose of perpetuating animal life. The necessity of sharing is also symbolically emphasized through the hunter sharing his catch with his extended family. These symbolic acts of respect and remembrance reinforce communal relationship to animals that gave life for a community's benefit. It is a way of remembering to remember relationship.

Another way of remembering to remember relationship occurs through the complex of animal dances found among indigenous people around the world. Animal dances are a commemoration of our continued relationship with the animal world. Indigenous dances are not only for renewal and opportunities for remembering to remember; they are also viewed by indigenous people as helping to maintain the balance of all essential relationships of the world. Such is the case with the Yurok White Deer Skin dance, which was performed to ensure the balance of the world from one year to the next. Indigenous people felt responsibility not only for themselves, but for the entire world around them. The world renewal ceremonies conducted by all indigenous people are reflections of this deep ecological sensibility and sense of responsibility.

Indigenous people created annual ceremonial cycles based on the belief that acknowledgment of the sources of a community's life must be made year in and year out. Ceremonial cycles are based on the understanding that people have to continue to remember and perpetuate essential ecological relationships through the life of individual tribal members and the generations that will follow. Once people break those cycles of remembering, they begin to forget essential life-sustaining relationships and they behave in the ways that have led to the ecological crisis we see today. And so, indigenous people dance the relationship of the people to animals as represented in their guiding story. They represent those symbols of their life in their art forms and in the things that they create in their daily life. These are also symbols that help them to maintain their tribal identity and assist in learning to be responsible for their essential life-affirming relationships. Such honoring and exploration of key relationships are equally reflected in the mythological complex of indigenous story making and telling.

The myths of indigenous peoples in North America are replete with animal characters. Indigenous peoples began to project their sense of what it was to live in reverent relationship into roles and characteristics of myths that they created. The Iroquois relate a myth in which Opossum, who was very conceited about his very elegant and bushy tail, was tricked into shaving his tail by Cricket and Hare. In reality we know that opossums have bald tails. But Opossum thought he would get a more glorious tail if he shaved his tail, and of course he didn't. This is a reflection of how we can get carried away by our own egotistical desires. The Paiutes relate a tale which describes the stealing of fire by Coyote after challenging powerful shamans who lived on an obsidian mountain. The shamans had captured the fire and kept it for themselves. They would not share it with the animals or the rest of the world. So the world remained in cold and darkness. Coyote and other animals challenged the shamans to a dance contest. Coyote and the shamans dance until all except Coyote fall asleep from exhaustion. Coyote then steals the last embers of the dance fire and runs away with the shamans in hot pursuit. As Coyote and the other birds and animals take turns running with the fire through the land, they shed light and warmth upon the dark frozen landscape. There are other myths about human relationships to animals, such as the well known Northwest Indian myth about the woman who married the bear. The relationships of bears and similarities of bears to human beings underlie the importance American Indian people place on treating bears respectfully. The role of birds, such as that of Raven in the creation of the first man and first woman, is related in a myth from the Eskimo which tells of the creation of first man from a pea pod. Each story is a complex of metaphors that teach the essential importance of proper relationship and respect for the natural world in that they illustrate the fact that all living things and natural entities have a role to play in maintaining the web of life.

The Pueblo Journey

In the Southwest, plants and agricultural ways of being became part of the way that Pueblo people expressed their essential relationships. Pueblo people learned how to cultivate corn in many different kinds of environments and developed many strains of corn which were drought resistant and grew under a variety of conditions. Corn, for Pueblo people, became a sacrament of life, a representation of life itself. It became a representation of the connection that Pueblo people feel toward the plant world. It is reflected in Pueblo art forms and in our ways of understanding ourselves as a people. Contemporary Hopi artists at times depict First Man and First Woman as perfect ears of corn being shrouded and guided by a Corn Mother who is a representation of the Earth Mother. Pueblo people express this intimate understanding and relationship by dancing for the perpetuation of corn. So, during the months of June, July, and August, grand corn dances occur among many Pueblo peoples in the Southwest. Indeed, until very recently, corn, beans, squash—all of the things which Pueblo people grew—were the physical foundation of Pueblo life and livelihood. These are the dances that Pueblo people continue today, representing themselves and their reflections of each other as a community of relationship. We are indeed related to one another in many, many different ways. As one Pueblo proverb relates,"we are all kernels on the same corn cob!"

The ancestors of Puebloan people have lived and hunted in New Mexico for ten thousand years or more, following herds of mastodon and bison retreating from the great glaciers of the north. Those first communities of Puebloan hunter-gatherers evolved and developed as simple communities comprised of no more than two or three extended families living together. They utilized everything within their environment. It was through this process of living that they began to understand the nature of sustaining themselves within the environments in which they lived. They evolved an understanding of how to use those things around them to cloth themselves, to create baskets, to create pottery, to sustain themselves in terms of food and shelter. Gradually, those communities became larger and more complex, and in those larger, more complex communities the understanding that one had to honor relationship, not only to each other, but to the environments which they depended upon for life, became even more important. In the stories Pueblo elders tell, the ancestors of the Pueblos journeyed many times and settled in many places. And each time they stopped, they established a relationship to the place in which they settled. They settled in places like Chaco Canyon, Mesa Verde, and Canyon de Chelly, and they learned from each of these places. They came to understand something about the essence of these natural places and something about the delicate environmental balance of nature in such places.

They settled by lakes and came to understand the nature of water and its importance and sanctity in an arid environment. They came to understand that water was one of the foundations for maintanance of life on Earth. They settled by mountains and came to understand the nature of mountains in terms of the way they provided a context, an environment in which Pueblo people and other living things could live. They depicted their understandings in many forms, one of which was the Kokopelli, an anthropomorphic symbol often depicted as a petroglyph among the thousands of petroglyphs which are found throughout the Southwest. Kokopelli is the seed carrier, the propagator of fertility, the carrier of good fortune, the carrier of culture, the bringer of music, the bringer of all of those things that are good and noble with regard to human beings.

Kokopelli is also a reflection of the procreative nature of life, a reflection of how life begets life, how life lives from other life. Each of us is a reflection of the Kokopelli in that we carry with us gifts, as did Kokopelli with his bag of seeds, his bag of very unique gifts. We are each planters of seeds, each of us has a creative sense, a creative spirit, each of us is a part of the procreative process of human consciousness and human life within the context of our communities and the world. The metaphoric symbol of Kokopelli provides us with eco-logical inspiration and a great sense of responsibility. Pueblo peoples, like all indigenous people, have a guiding story. In some versions of this guiding story it is related that humans now live in the fourth world, that there were three worlds before this, and in each of those worlds human beings had to learn something. They had to come to terms with an evolutionary task, to become "riper," in a sense, as human beings. Each world metaphorically represents a stage of natural evolution through which human beings learn how to become "more human."

Pueblo people believe that they emerged from an earth navel. It was a place of mountains looked upon lovingly by the sun and by the moon. It is believed that those first people were taught by certain animals and that their thoughts were guided by the evergreen tree of life. This was the place that people came to in this stage of our development, this stage of our being. This was "that place that the People talk about." Through guiding stories of creation, many American Indian tribes symbolize Earth as a feminine being to which all living things relate and the landscape as the contours of her great body. Indian people also represent these perceptions of life in relationship with the land in their oral traditions and through the symbols of art and ritual and the atti-tudes and activities that all Indians have traditionally practiced. It is through these symbols and by participating with the land in a kind of symbolic dance that Pueblo people have traditonally maintained the memory of our relationship to our places. Through traditional art forms, such as pottery, which are replete with designs based on our relationship to the land, its plants, and animals, Pueblo people have symbolized their sense of identity as a people of place. This continual establishing of relationship is not only for renewal and for remember-ing to remember who we are as a people, but it also is an attempt to perpetuate the spiritual ecology of the world as a whole. This is the complex of relationship, symbolism, attitude, and way of interacting with the land that comprises the Pueblo "theology of place."

There is no more complete example of this theology than that of traditional Pueblo farming. The Pueblo saying "corn is who we are" expresses the deep appreciation and relationship Pueblo feel for corn. Among the Pueblos, the domestication of plants and agricultural ways of being have been a part of the way we have expressed ourselves as a people since ancient times. We learned how to adapt the cultivation of corn to many of the varied ecological places of the Southwest. The varied strains of developed corn were a direct result of our collective ecological understanding of the places in which we have lived through the generations. Corn became a sacrament and symbol of our life and relationship with the land. So, corn and the other staple crops, such as beans, squash, and other plants that we grew, became metaphors for the sacred relationships we had established with the land. The grand corn dances performed as part of Puebloan ecologically based ceremonial cycles embody relationship a way of living and being with place. The corn dances and other dances and rituals that comprise the annual Pueblo ceremonial cycles are our way of enacting and maintaining, year in and year out, one generation to the next, our connection to and understanding of the spiritual ecology of place. Pueblo relational understandings revolving around corn are but one of many examples of indigenous ecology. Our practiced relationship to corn is a way of continuing to remember to remember what our relationship to our place is through our life and to perserve our view of life for each of the generations that will follow. Once we break these sacred cycles, we will begin to forget about sacred ecology and will collectively begin to do the kinds of things to the land that we are seeing today.

Community and Place in New Mexico

Today, among the Pueblo people of New Mexico, there are still numerous communal reflections of natural affiliation. The Pueblos are an ancient people. Puebloan peoples have continuously lived in the Southwest for ten thousand years or more. The place that is now called New Mexico is also sometimes called "the land of enchantment." The evocation of a feeling of enchantment is connected by some to the fact that New Mexico has been consecrated by the lives and the communities of so many Pueblo people. It is no accident that New Mexico has become a meeting place for many people. It is not only a place where geological and ecological regions intersect, but a meeting place of ideas, cultures, and ways of community. Pueblo people understood this and reflected on their understanding within the context of their communal perspective, their ways of understanding and expressing their relationships to each other and to "this place that Pueblo people talk about." As is true with other indigenous communities, the Pueblo elderly have been the first teachers in their communities. Their perspectives and their understanding of life have provided the foundation for the continuity of Pueblo cultures through time. And in their life they have reflected those understandings which can only really come as a part of long experience with living in a place and understanding it in very direct and intimate ways.

As mentioned earlier, children are the defining group of an indigenous community. Ultimately, the purpose of education is to transfer both culture and mind-set with a sense of spirit to the next generation. Among Pueblo people, children are valued because it is intimately understood that they are the carriers of Pueblo culture into the next generation. It is really a concern for children that motivates the collective enterprise of indigenous education. It is in the eyes, hearts, minds, and souls of a people's children that, ultimately, the essence of a culture will live or die. The teaching of Pueblo children is a sacred responsibility.

There are many ways of reflecting these essential understandings among indigenous peoples. Pueblo communities have a variety of linguistic metaphors reflecting essential ties to nature's cycles, natural phenomena, and the landscape that highlight this understanding. Among the Tewa-speaking Pueblos, some elders may be heard to say, "Look to the mountain, look to the mountain, look to the mountain," when giving advice to young people. They usually use this phrase in conjunction with telling youth that they need to look at things in a much broader perspective. The essential message of the metaphor is to emphasize the need to understand the ramifications of what you are doing into the next generation and every generation thereafter. People have to understand the repercussions of their actions and behavior with regard to the special perspective gained from looking from a mountain's perspective. This is an essential perspective of indigenous education that must be understood deeply. As stated earlier, indigenous education really is a ten-thousand-, a twenty-thousand-, a thirty-thousand-year strategic plan for how a people must learn to interact with natural environments that sustain their life as a people. It represents a way of thinking that goes far beyond a five- or ten-year strategic plan of modern mechanistic planning. Indeed, indigenous societies operate in terms of "generational" strategic plans. Indigenous education reflects such generational plans, which consider the longest human terms when developing communal contingencies. It is based on the reality that everything that humans do with regard to the environment affects everything else, and you can only understand this by educating for a perspective where you can see larger contexts of effects. This is where such metaphors lead indigenous consciousness. Tewa elders say, "Look to the mountain!" This metaphor and image of the great central mountain is evoked to remind us that we must think the highest thoughts and from a place of broad perspective when we reflect on our relationship to nature and our children. It is an image which engenders the need for farsighted vision and clarity when attempting to understand the true nature of our relationships to environments, "to those places that we talk about."

Final Thoughts: The Place of Indigenous Ecology in a Postmodern World

In reality, Native people throughout the Americas developed environmentally sound ways of living with the land. Traditionally, they understood deeply and venerably practiced the concept of sustainability within an environment. This way of sustainable living evolved into numerous ways of maintaining harmony at both individual and communal levels in dynamic balance with the places in which Indian people have lived in North America. Our ceremonial traditions combined with practical ecological knowledge expressed our orientation to sacred ecology and formed the basis for a theology of place.

However, American Indian people today live a dual existence. At times, it resembles a kind of schizophrenia characterized by constantly trying to adapt ourselves to a mainstream social, political, and cultural system that is not our own. We are constantly faced with living in a larger society that does not really understand or respect our traditional life symbols, our ecological perspectives, our understanding of relationship to the land, our traditional ways of remembering to remember who we are. In many ways, modern society does not know how to respect "that place that the People talk about."

What is even more ironic is that, because of modern education and our constant relationships with the U.S. government, many Indian people have moved away from a practiced and conscious relationship with place. This has resulted in many Indian communities experiencing the kind of "existential" problems, such alcoholism, suicide, self-abuse, depression, and other social and spiritual ills that befall traditional peoples once they begin to lose their direct connection to their spiritual ecology. Tewa people call this state of schizophrenic like existence, *pingeh heh* ("split thought," or "thinking or doing things with only half your mind"). As an Indian educator, I believe that modern Indian education ultimately has to be about healing this split. But, it is not just the task of Indian people to heal this split in themselves. It is also the task of others who consider themselves people of place and thereby suffer the subsequent alienation from mainstream society, as do many Indian people. It has now become everyone's task to "look to the mountain." Indigenous people around the world express their understanding of place and of relationship through their forms of education.

Today, indigenous people around the world struggle with living in two worlds. Therefore, reflecting their understanding of themselves as a traditional people through their symbols, art, and education while surviving in a modern context presents special challenges. The traditional designs found on Pueblo pottery are a reflection not only of an earth-based art form but of a reflection of relationship to those things in this environment that give Pueblo people their life. Similar to other indigenous people, Pueblos developed sustainable agriculture patterns and lived off the bounty of the land. They understood the whole concept of sustainability and what it means to maintain ourselves within an environment. These understandings contributed to healthy living because Puebloan peoples believed that health, both at the individual and the communal level, was essential for maintaining a harmony and balance between themselves and the world around them. These relational traditions of reverence reflect the spiritual ecology that is the foundation of indigenous education. Yet, despite these traditional orientations, Pueblo people find it more difficult than ever before to maintain their ancestral relationships to place.

I am reminded of a sculpture of a former student of mine at the Institute of American Indian Arts. This young Pueblo woman created a clay piece which symbolized her feelings as a young Native woman attempting to be an artist, living in two worlds, trying to be traditional and also modern. The clay sculpture was an androgynous figure sitting in a forlorn position with its arms folded and hands wrung around each other in such a way that the whole form expressed extreme anxiety. To extend this sculptural metaphor of anxiety, the head of the figure had been split in half. Half of the face was drawn up in a smile and the other half drawn down in a frown. The artist's deeply felt sense of being split, torn as she was between diametrically opposed views of the world, captures the sense of fragmentation and the dilemma that we all face as modern people living in an ecologically schizophrenic world. She felt a sense of "splitedness" and incompleteness. Her sculpture is the counterpoint of the complete man and complete women who were the embodiment of the ideal goal of the indigenous education process. My sense as an indigenous educator is that indigenous education must now focus on the recovery of our sensibility for natural affiliation and on its nurturance in our children. The education of the twenty-first century has to be about healing this cultural and ecological split. However, healing this schizophrenia is not just the task of indigenous education, but the task of all education. Our quintessential educational task is that of reconnecting with our innate sense for natural affiliation.

Human interactive relationships with places give rise to and define human cultures and community. As we change our landscape and allow the self-serving will of economic capitalism to have sway over our view of the land, we also allow the natural landscape of mind and soul to be altered in the same measure. When we allow the curriculum in our schools to serve the will of the "marketplace," we also allow the landscape of students' minds to be altered. The price we pay for such "lack of consciousness" in deeply examining the guiding paradigms of our curricula is too high to calculate. Indeed, with each generation since the turn of the century, Americans have collectively become more materially affluent. At the same time, each generation of Americans has become significantly impoverished in terms of its collective and individual connection to places which form the biologic and geographic tapestry of America.

We must once again ask the perennial question, "what is education for?" Our collective answer to this ancient question carries with it consequences that are more profound now then they have ever been in the history of humankind. There is a saying that some Indian people relate when this sort of quintessential questions are posed. Variably translated, the saying simply states that it is time to go to "that place that the People talk about." This is not only a physical place; it is also a place of consciousness. It is the place of soul and natural orientation.

It is important to move beyond the idealization and patronization of indigenous knowledge, something that inadvertently can lead to marginalization of the most profound indigenous epistemologies regarding interaction of human beings and nature. Indigenous people must be supported in their collective attempts to restore their traditions while also recreating and revitalizing themselves in ways they feel are appropriate in contemporary society. One of the places where this can happen is in the area of indigenous-based environmental education. As indigenous peoples around the world assert themselves politically and economically, they are also beginning to explore and revive their ancient educational practices in conjunction with contemporary educational priorities.

Indigenous people have been touted as the spiritual leaders of the environmental movement. Such a designation is more symbolic than actual since most environmental education is still primarily a reaction to the shortcomings of mainstream Western education. Still, many environmental educators, writers, and philosophers advocate getting back to the basics of relationship to environment and also to each other within communities, paralleling the traditional practices of indigenous societies. This is appropriate since indigenous people around the world have much to share and much to give. They also remain exploited, oppressed, and are usually the people who suffer the greatest loss of self and culture when dealing with various development and educational schemes. In spite of this, indigenous groups around the world have a very important message, a message that is related in a number of ways to the evolving disciplines of eco-psychology and eco-philosophy. This narrative relates the connection between the rise of interest in "biophilia" and the process of indigenous education as "a curriculum of place." Such curricula of place are continuing to evolve among indigenous peoples and hold great promise for the new generation of environmental education models.

As you begin your journey to find this ancient indigenous mind-set, think about who you are and who you represent. Understand that each of us in our own small way is a vital link within the context of creating an educational process that allows for a sustainable way of living. Whether the role you play is large or small, know that it has an effect. As you look to and imagine climbing this primordial mountain, reflect on your own life and your own understanding of what it is to be educated. And, as you move from that mountain down the pathway to begin a renewed journey of ecological thought and action, think about the journey of your life in relationship to a "place." Keep in view the fact that your journey can be a very important part of the transformation of education that must take place in this next generation. It is the task of each of us to engender a vision of sustainable future for all children, to "Look to the mountain!"

Andean Cosmovision and the Nurturing of Biodiversity

JULIO VALLADOLID and
FRÉDÉRIQUE APFFEL-MARGLIN

Introducing the Work of PRATEC

Frédérique Apffel-Marglin

PRATEC (Andean Project of Peasant Technologies) was founded in 1987 by Grimaldo Rengifo. He immediately invited Eduardo Grillo, and they later (in 1989) invited Julio Valladolid to join them. These three men had spent their lives working for development. Rengifo was the director of a large Peruvian-Dutch development project, Grillo was the director general of the National Bureau of Agricultural Statistics and Research, and Valladolid was teaching plant genetics and physiology in the faculty of agronomy at the University of Huamanga in Ayacucho. Through its extension program, as well as through its research, that faculty was deeply involved in bringing the green revolution to the Peruvian countryside.

They are all three of native peasant background and they devoted themselves to development in the belief that this was the way to help their people. In the course of their professional activities, they eventually came to the conclusion that development—including sustainable development—itself was the problem. This realization did not come swiftly; it emerged slowly after a lifetime of professional activity in the service of development. At first they thought that things were not working because the methodologies that they used were faulty. They worked hard to devise better methodologies. They lived through many phases and fashions in development, including sustainable development. They tried everything available, always striving to capture the reality of Andean peasant agriculture and of peasant life in general. At long last they came to the conclusion that no methodology would ever deliver and that the problem lay in the very idea of development, sustainable or otherwise. It is at this juncture that they left their professional activities and their jobs and founded PRATEC, a nongovernmental organization. In other words, they deprofessionalized themselves.

They had come to the realization that development had failed. The evidence lay scattered throughout the Peruvian landscape in what some of their colleagues have called "the archaeology of development," namely, ruined infrastructures, abandoned to the elements after the project officials had left, uncared for by the peasants for whom they were intended, and left to deteriorate. The evidence also lay in their experience of repeated efforts to devise better methodologies and the final realization that within the professional perspective and constraints, it was impossible to approximate peasant reality and therefore make development relevant to their lives.

It is important to note that at some point in their professional experience, they felt that perhaps a better knowledge of peasant reality would be available outside of their immediate disciplines. They devoted themselves then to reading all they could in sociology, anthropology, history, and whatever other fields wrote on peasant life. They emerged from that experience feeling that peasant reality was being captured from a position outside of that reality.

They awoke to the reality of peasant life, to the incredible richness and diversity of cultivars that are grown in this ecologically extremely variable environment. The Andes are one of the eight world centers where agriculture first emerged, according to the great Soviet geneticist Nikolai Ivanovich Vavilov.[1] Agriculture has almost a ten-thousand-year pedigree there, and the peasants continue to grow an astounding variety of plants: many varieties of grains, including the nutritionally reknowned quinua; many varieties of tubers, of which the potato is very important, with some thirty-five-hundred different varieties collected mostly in the Andes; and about sixteen hundred varieties of maize.[2] A good farmer will typically harvest more than fifty varieties of potatoes from his fields. In spite of the introduction of green revolution hybrids and packages, the peasants continue to grow their native cultivars for their own and their friends' and relatives' subsistence. The hybrids are grown for the urban market.

The members of PRATEC began to dedicate their lives to articulating these discoveries so that their personal experiences could benefit others like themselves, that is, professionals and practitioners of rural development whose origins lay in the native peasantry. This effort at articulating both agricultural/cultural peasant practices and the epistemologies and ontologies embedded in development practices and more generally in modern Western knowledge was undertaken not as a professional activity. It was engaged in as their participation in what they saw was happening among the peasantry.

Since the 1950s (actually, much earlier, but the movement picked up momentum at that time) the peasantry has been engaged in what Peruvian anthropologist Enrique Mayer has called a "silent movement."[3] They have taken over the lands of the large landed properties, the *haciendas,* in direct action without forming political parties or syndicates.[4] With the agrarian reform of 1969, which simply made official what had been going on for a long time, namely, the economic debacle of the hacienda system as well as the takeover or buyout of these lands by Andean peasants, that peasant reappropriation of lands accelerated. The government tried to replace the hacienda system with government cooperative schemes. It only took twenty-five years to reveal the total debacle of that state scheme. Andean peasants are reappropriating these lands as well and organizing themselves in their own way, many of them forming *ayllu*s. The *ayllu* is a local group of related persons, and other nonhuman beings of the locality, the *pacha.* There, in their reconstituted *ayllu*s they cultivate the land in their own manner, evidence of the vibrancy of native practices and culture.

The members of PRATEC saw a reaffirmation of Andean agriculture and culture happening throughout the country and they wanted to participate in that action. Although in the academic division of labor, agriculture is the domain of agronomy and culture that of anthropology, PRATEC insists that the two form a seamless whole. For them, it was also totally out of the question to imagine themselves as some sort of leadership or vanguard of that historical movement. Such a posture in their eyes totally betrays the communitarian and egalitarian ethos of Andean peasants and embodies an uncharacteristic hubris. Furthermore, they attributed the success of peasants in reappropriating lands precisely to the manner in which they did it, through direct action, without creating formal parties or organizations. Not being farmers themselves, they saw their own way of participating in that agri/cultural resurgence and affirmation to be in efforts to pass on to others like themselves what they had learned and continued to learn, hoping thereby to stem the drain of young bright Andeans toward development and modernization. This would simultaneously weaken development efforts and strengthen Andean life. They chose to do this through direct action by creating a course in Andean agriculture and culture for professionals of rural development with roots in the native peasantry.

They first dedicated themselves to writing about Andean agriculture and culture, contrasting it to development and modern Western knowledge, since the existing literature in their eyes failed to convey Andean reality from within that reality. The action of writing is also to help others like themselves (professionals of rural development with origins in the Andean peasantry) to realize the distorting, if not blinding, effects of seeing the Andean world through the lenses of the categories of professional knowledge, and then to show them that world from the point of view of those living that world, so that they can enter it and become part of the collective action of making that world. In that effort, they attempt to show how the categories of knowledge, as well as the very notion of knowledge, used in the academic professions carry within themselves the reproduction of industrial capitalism's institutions and status quo.

The members of PRATEC speak of industrial capitalism as "the modern West," since this is how they experience it. They learned the knowledge at the university and for a long time bought its message of universality and objectivity. But they experienced it nonetheless as a foreign import. It initiated them to a world different from the one they came from. They are aware of the internal heterogeneity of "the modern West," as they are of the internal heterogeneity of "the Andean world." The contrast they speak of is one that they and many like them have experienced as university-trained persons of Andean origins. But it is only through their action of deprofessionalizing themselves and of acting and writing from within the Andean collectivities that they could come to know with clarity the impossibility of participating in the Andean collective actions from within the professions. This realization brought with it an understanding of the nature of the knowledge they were taught in school and at the university, which simultaneously allowed them to see the Andean world with greater clarity.

They speak of this double realization as the need to decolonize their minds in order to clearly see and participate in the Andean world. They share this double realization with others like them in a course they started teaching in 1990.

By deprofessionalizing themselves, the members of PRATEC freed themselves from the constraints of academic disciplines. They devoted themselves to the challenging task of writing on peasant agriculture and culture from an Andean point of view. For this, they drew not only on their personal experience of growing up in that life but on their lifetime experience of conversations with peasants throughout the Peruvian Andes. They also draw on the work of their associates—former graduates of their course—who, with the help of PRATEC, have formed centers throughout the Peruvian Andes where they work collaboratively with peasants (many of whom are their relatives) to strengthen Andean practices, such as the exchanges of native seeds and the rituals in which the peasants converse with the beings of the nonhuman world.[5] Such an endeavor is collective and collaborative. The members of PRATEC and their associates accompany the peasants and collectively make their world.

This path has necessitated their deprofessionalization since the professionalization of knowledge has made of knowledge a commodity as well as an individual pursuit. What is bought on the market, the academic market (as well as the industrial, military, and government markets), is an individual's ability to produce knowledge, and in order for this to be bought and sold on the market it must be held indivisibly by an individual, just like the labor of a person must be owned individually for it to become a commodity to be bought and sold on the market.[6]

The theoretical egalitarianism of "objective" knowledge—its vaunted epistemological egalitarianism—is precisely what makes this knowledge universal and frees it from particularity and place. But this feature hides the particular embeddedness of this knowledge in the institutions of modern Western industrial capitalism. Philosopher Kathryn Pyne Addelson's alternative view of knowledge, one based on collective action, means that knowledge emerges out of particular encounters and relationships in particular localities. This view of knowledge goes a long way toward re-embedding knowledge in the regenerative collective actions of local communities, human and nonhuman.

The explicit purposes of professional knowledge are clear enough: the advancement of knowledge. Such purposes, however, take for granted the nature and legitimacy of that knowledge and of its social organization. In the process, it veils the manner in which professional expert knowledge is embedded in institutions which are instruments of governance:

> The unquestioned right to know in terms of one's disciplinary concepts and methods is at the foundation of the cognitive authority of scientists and other professionals. It places them in the *local* sites of laboratory and field, not as participants but as "judging observers" who are themselves to be unjudged. The outcomes of their work extend beyond the boundaries of their disciplines, professions, and institutions. This is because the institutions in which professionals make and transmit knowledge are instruments of governance. In the broadest sense, the double participation of scientists and other researchers is a participation in the local activity as hidden agents of governance. Except in special circumstances, whether any particular professional wills it or not, the participation is in support of the existing social, political, and economic orders—loyalty to these things is embedded in the institutional folk concepts of profession and university.[7]

The deprofessionalization of the members of PRATEC meant not only that they abandoned the right to know the Andean world in terms of their disciplinary concepts and methods (and thus abandoned cognitive authority), it meant a total change in their lives.

Their writing emerges from their own affective bonding with Andean peasants, first experienced in their families and communities of origin and subsequently in a wider set of friendships with particular peasants and particular places. Their deprofessionalization meant that there was no longer a double participation for them; the world of which they write is their own world, to which they are emotionally bonded through a multitude of particular relations. In other words, writing of that world and living the lives of that world have become for them a unified field of action. This is precisely why they quit their jobs; they realized that, willy-nilly, in their professions, they were agents of governance, specifically the state's purpose of developing the country, which has brought along its share of environmental degradation. They joined the collective action of the Andean peasants engaged in retaking possession of lands and re-establishing their own forms of organization and practices. They took repossession of their Andean selves and ways of being by ceasing to practice the double participation that professional knowledge making had required of them. They speak of the Andean world, not as judging outsiders, but as ones bonded to that world. They write books and articles like professional knowledge makers do, not with the intent to add to the fund of knowledge of their professions, but as their chosen field of action. They write of the Andean world, not primarily as a world to *know,* but as a world to live in, to participate in, to be a part of, and to collectively make.

In order to clarify many of the issues discussed so far—the issue of the professional as a judging outsider, the professional's right to know using the concepts and tools of the profession, and, in general, the role of the professional as a hidden agent of governance—I will take the example of the assessment of PRATEC's work made by Enrique Mayer, a Peruvian anthropologist.[8] Mayer's remarks concern the ecological relevance or lack thereof of PRATEC's work. He starts out by stating how important he considers the PRATEC proposal to be:

> I invite you to consider the proposal of PRATEC to strengthen the *chacra* [the peasant's field] as a point of departure exceedingly interesting in the context of contemporary Peru. In it, I think one can find the germs of a project of investigation, the ideas of a program of technical, social and political action.[9]

He then goes on to contextualize PRATEC historically and points out how a "return to the roots" is eminently understandable given the failure of what the government tried to do with the agrarian reform of 1969, namely, liberate the productive forces of the country and modernize it. Instead, today, thirty years after the fact, Peru is gripped by economic, political, and social crises. Furthermore, the unforeseen and unwanted result of the reform has been the *campesinizacion* (the "peasanticization") of almost all of rural Peru. Mayer then proceeds to criticize PRATEC for not being scientific:

> I have read with care, attention and sympathy almost all the publications of this group of intellectuals [he cites publications from 1987 to 1991]. My verdict is that, lamentably, until now there is very little in what is published by them which has any scientific value.[10]

Mayer goes on to detail how PRATEC's work fails to test the factual truth of what their "informants" tell them, of not using quantitative measures, and of confusing peasants' articulation of their worldview with "our real knowledge of ecological processes":

> The mere assertion of a postulated harmony does not demonstrate the existence of healthy or balanced ecological processes. There is a confusion in asserting without explanation or analysis informants' statements as if they were factual material results. . . .
>
> They do not mention possible mechanisms that might be relevant in the explanation, nor are direct observations made in the field, nor quantitative measures with which one might begin to create some evaluative criteria. . . .
>
> To demonstrate that Andean culture (or Andean cosmovision) also supports balance adds nothing to our real knowledge about ecological processes.[11]

Mayer finds fault in PRATEC's work because it fails to use the conceptual and methodological tools of his profession. Mayer is clear where *real* knowledge lies: not with what peasants say and do, but with what the professional researcher can empirically verify using his methodological and other conceptual tools. Here is a clear example of professional knowledge having cognitive authority and being a judging outsider. Mayer wants PRATEC members to be scientific professionals of an empiricist bent and judges them negatively for failing to measure up to those criteria. In the process, he is blind to the different epistemology and ontology that PRATEC tries to articulate, partly through a contrast with modern Western knowledge. The contrast is necessary in order precisely to make clear that what they are talking about is *not* a better methodology to get at the "facts." In PRATEC's presentation of Andean peasants' worlds, wisdom arises out of mutual nurturance and conversations between all the beings of the locality, of the *pacha*. They prefer to use the Spanish word *saber*—which also means "knowledge" but shares the same root with *sabiduria*, "wisdom"—to "knowledge," because knowledge (*conocimiento*) is so associated with concepts and language. In their view wisdom arises from certain kinds of actions between particular beings, be they humans or nonhumans. In the Andean world the conversations and mutual acts of nurturance between humans and between humans and the other beings in the world, such as stones, stars, sun, moon, animals, mountains, rivers, plants, and many others, are ritual acts.

Mayer's role as an agent of governance reveals itself most clearly in the following sentences:

> The hypotheses must lead to an experimental work and a work of potential development which can be given back to the *comuneros* [members of peasant communities] in efficient and absorbable form.[12]

There is absolutely no doubt that Mayer has any intention of relinquishing cognitive authority to the Andean peasants. Their practices and views will be taken as hypotheses by the professionals, well chewed up methodologically, and then generously given back in easily absorbable and efficient development pills.

Mayer concludes his ambivalent assessment of PRATEC's work in the following way: "To refuse, due to purist principles, to practice certain forms of our professions is to fall in sectarianism and extreme positions which are less than useful in these times of crisis."[13] Mayer's own inability or unwillingness to deprivilege his own professional tools and point of view, that is, the privileged, unsituated, archimedean standpoint of empiricist social sciences, makes him blind to what PRATEC is doing. PRATEC is entering into the nondualist Andean world, one in which organism and environment are not separate, pitted one against the other, but one in which they make each other. The late Eduardo Grillo of PRATEC states this rather unambiguously:

> Science is founded on a clear separation and opposition between humans and nature and between the knowing subject and the known object. For science, culture is an exclusively human attribute and is precisely the quality that makes humans and nature different. . . .
>
> Here [in the Andean world], conversation cannot be reduced to dialogue, to the word, as in the modern western world but rather here conversation engages us vitally: one converses with the whole body. To converse is to show oneself reciprocally, it is to share, it is to commune, it is to dance to the rhythm which at every moment corresponds to the annual cycle of life. Conversation assumes all the complication characteristic of the living world. Nothing escapes conversation. Here there is no privacy. Conversation is inseparable from nurturance. For humans, to make *chacra,* that is to grow plants, animals, soils, waters, climates, is to converse with nature. But in the Andean-Amazonian world, all, not only humans, make and nurture the *chacra,* all nurture. The human *chacra* is not only made [or nurtured] by humans, rather all, in one way

or another, participate in the creation/nurturance of the human *chacra:* the sun, the moon, the stars, the mountain, the birds, the rain, the wind . . . even the frost and the hail.[14]

Grillo and Valladolid reject the scientific method because of its dualism and objectivity and what these bring with them. They speak of a world in which the human and nonhuman collectivities nurture and create each other. This is how Grimaldo Rengifo writes about conversation:

> One converses with the mouth, the hands, the sense of smell, vision, hearing, gestures, flowerings, the colors of the skin, the taste of the rain, the color of the wind, etc. Since all are persons, all speak. The potatoes, the llamas, the human community, the mountains, the rain, the hail, the *wakas* [deities] speak. Language is not a verbal representation which encapsulates the named person.[15]

Julio Valladolid's use of the verb "to converse" in the second part of this essay needs to be understood in the context of the corpus of PRATEC's work. Grillo's and Rengifo's quotes make it clear that they do not use the term "to converse" either metaphorically or literally (i.e., mountains, rivers, stones do not speak in the same linguistic medium that humans do).

Understanding such conversing as metaphoric or symbolic emerges from situating oneself within a form of knowledge based on a worldview that radically separates the knower from the known, the external from the internal world, the symbol from the symbolized, organism from environment. This form of knowledge is referred to as "representational thought," and it has characterized Western philosophy from the beginning, becoming prominent with modernity and post-Cartesian thought.[16]

Representational thought—which *is* modern thought—is thoroughly anthropocentric, while the Andean world is radically non-anthropocentric. Knowledge in the modern world consists of linguistic and conceptual representations in an individual's mind. The kind of conversing that Valladolid writes about in the second part of this essay should not be confused with the kind of conversations that modern human beings engage in, somehow imagining that mountains, rivers, or stones speak like humans do. The conversing that Valladolid writes about is not literal in this sense since it is not necessarily linguistic;

and, it is not conceptual but is nonetheless real. Alternatively, the term "conversing" should not be understood metaphorically.

Valladolid speaks of Andean agriculture as being ritual agriculture. Traditionally, modern scholarship has understood ritual action as having two distinguishable parts, belonging to the two radically distinct categories of "efficacious technical action" and "symbolic action." Ever since Bronislaw Malinowski's famous anthropological writings on the Trobriand Islanders of Melanesia in the early twentieth century, the separation between pragmatic, utilitarian action and symbolic action has become canonical. The explanations have differed since he wrote, but the dual optic has persisted. Malinowski even insisted on the fact that the natives themselves made the distinction, linguistically, between the two types of actions. It is clear that Malinowski wanted to impress upon his readers that the natives were not so benighted as to confuse the two. This optic required an explanation of the puzzling part, which he called the magical actions, and this has remained the bread and butter of many anthropologists to this day, although the term "magic" has generally been replaced by the term "ritual."[17]

Such a view takes for granted the modern cosmology which emerged in the sixteenth and seventeenth centuries, in which the material world was totally separated from the nonmaterial world, the latter aptly captured by the word "supernatural." Conversing with the water, the wind, the rocks, the frost, the sun, and so forth is generally understood as a metaphorical or symbolic action aimed at some supernatural entities conceived of as the spirit of the water, the wind, and so on. These spirits or what have you are designated as being part of the belief system of a people. These "beliefs" are held in the minds of the people. The physical, material world, on the other hand, is devoid of spirits, of any metaphysical aspect. This great emptying out of meaning from the world was one of the achievements of René Descartes. Descartes's philosophical distinction between *res cogitans* and *res extensa* was operationalized by Robert Boyle, the father of experimental science, a few decades later.[18] Boyle carved out a purely secular domain of knowledge bearing on an objectified material reality. All metaphysical considerations were relegated to a private realm held in people's minds and hearts. The division between perception and knowledge, on one side, and belief bearing on metaphysical or supernatural reality, on the other, quickly established itself, after

Boyle's successes with his air-pump experiments, as the reigning paradigm. The world of the Andean peasants, however, is not divided into a material reality and a nonmaterial reality. All the beings of the *pacha,* the humans, the earth, the water, the wind, the rocks, the stars, the animals, the plants, and so forth, share the same world. The *waka*s, or deities, are these beings. Rather than being "believed in," they are experienced, they are conversed with, and reciprocated with. The peasants nurture them and are in turn nurtured by them and this is done in ritual acts. As the French anthropologist Jean Pouillon remarks about the Dangaleat of Chad in Africa, the world for them, as for the Andean peasants, is not divided between a this-worldly reality and an otherworldly reality. The spirits are experienced rather than believed in.[19]

As the critics of science in the last twenty years or so have argued, it is in fact impossible to separate the material from the nonmaterial world. This modernist invention necessitates a total ontological breach—to use Charles Taylor's phrase[20]—between the mind and the rest of the world, Descartes's *res extensa.* Furthermore, with the carrying out of all the "thought experiments" of the early quantum physicists in the late twentieth century, it has now been established that the world, including the experimenter, is all interconnected.[21] As the philosopher and anthropologist Bruno Latour has pithily put it, "we have never been modern."[22] We just dreamed that we were, deluding ourselves that our nonhuman companions were just inert objects. We now know that we are not the dominators of an inert, machine-like nature, but part of an interconnected living whole. The terrible amnesia about what Bruce Wilshire calls our mimetic engulfment in the world is beginning to erode. Mimetic engulfment refers to that "primal level of experience in which we are immediately involved as one self in one community of beings with which we identify, and goodness is effective and vital involvement in the world."[23] This amnesia, created by modern cosmology and its dominance, not only generates a breach of faith with everything that is, but makes of the will and desire of humans the only relevant entity as regards human action. This is what engenders the dual optic that divides "efficacious pragmatic action" from those actions that Valladolid refers to as conversing with the beings of the *pacha,* nurturing them and letting oneself be nurtured by them. Anthropocentrism is the assertion that only human will matters, that the only actor is Man. No wonder that the dawn of the third millennium is witness to such terrible environmental devastation and the extinction of innumerable species of plants and animals. They have been sacrificed to our desires. Scientific knowledge has amassed the greatest amount of information and understanding about the "natural world" but, as Tzvetan Todorov asserted in the context of the conquest of America, "we suspect that destruction becomes possible precisely because of this understanding."[24] By objectifying and despiritualizing the world, by separating the heart from the mind, and the good from the true, this knowledge has been incapable —or unwilling—to grant to the nonhuman world the integrity it sometimes grants to (some) humans.

In a world where the integrity of nonhuman beings is to be respected as much as that of human beings, actions by humans cannot be taken unilaterally. This requires a reigning in of human will, desire, and interest. It also requires the training of the self to become nurturing, respectful, and morally responsible for the outcome of one's actions. The members of PRATEC took a further decisive step in their journey after they deprofessionalized themselves. They decided that they would no longer give priority to their will and desires but would submit to the authority of the *wakas*. Early in the 1990s they sought out a *maestro* (healer or shaman) whom they consult whenever a decision has to be made. The *maestro* prepares a *mesa* (altar), and they say that the *mesa* decides. They submit their will to that of the deities. They also found their tutelary deity and engage in pilgrimages, offerings, and other rituals as members of PRATEC. They of course also participate in many of the peasants' rituals. They schedule the units of their course according to the Andean ritual calendar. In doing so, they rejoined their hearts and souls to their minds. Deprofessionalization was a necessary but not a sufficient step on their journey.

Andean Cosmovision and the Nurturing of Biodiversity in the Peasant Chacra

Julio Valladolid

Andean peasant agriculture involves the ritual growing of cultivated plants and animals in the *chacra* (cultivated field) and the *ayllu*. By ritual growing, in the Andes we mean the feeling of love and respect that the peasants have, not only for their plants and animals, but also for the whole landscape that accompanies them in their nurturance of their fields, or *chacras*, which they consider to be members of their family, or *ayllu*.

The peasants' manner of "seeing," "feeling," and living their Andean landscape, that is, their perennial Andean worldview, nurtures life, making it heterogeneous for the well-being of all those who dwell in this landscape, or in nature. They do not try to homogenize it for the benefit of humans only, as individuals from industrialized societies often try to do.

Although I come from a peasant background and have been surrounded since childhood by expressions of Andean culture and agriculture, my training as a scientist—I was a professor engaging in active research in plant physiology and plant genetics at the University of Huamanga in Ayacucho for twenty-five years—made me blind and deaf to this Andean ritual agriculture. It has been a very long journey for me to be able to "see" and "feel" with Andean eyes and heart, a journey that began some fourteen years ago when I initiated my (then still informal) association with PRATEC. Since then, I have stopped my scientific pursuits and no longer try to teach peasants how to use science's discoveries. Now I walk through the *chacras*, accompanying the peasants and learning from them how to see and feel with Andean heart and eyes once again. I will come back in the last part of this essay to my own journey and some of the reflections it has generated.

The Andes: Biodiversity and Ritual Agriculture

When the Europeans arrived in the Andes five hundred years ago, they found that almost as many species of plants were cultivated here as were grown by all the agriculturists of Europe and Asia combined.[25] The Andean region was also one of the few original centers of agriculture and culture in the world. Archaeological evidence confirms that more than eight thousand years ago, the majority of the Andean food plants that we know today were already being cultivated.[26]

Here, the Andean peasant grew, and continues to grow with love and dedication, hundreds, and in some cases thousands, of ecotypes, races, and varieties of more than seventy species of food plants of Andean origin. The most eloquent examples are the potato and maize. The potato, an indispensable crop for human alimentation, is the object of study by the International Center of the Potato, which identified thirty-five hundred different native potato cultivars grown.[27] During the 1950s, the Cooperative Maize Research Program of the Agrarian University of La Molina-Lima collected sixteen hundred entries of maize that were grouped into forty-eight races. These make Peru the country with the greatest genetic variability of maize in the world.[28] The number of maize races in the Andean region is almost the same as the number of races in the rest of the world, and this in spite of the fact that the diversity of genes in the Andean races is less than the one ascertained for the races of maize in Central America, which possibly is the primary center for the origin of maize.

Whichever may be the center of origin of this important grain, what is certain is that in the pre-Hispanic period the Andean peasant grew, and still grows and conserves with love and dedication, the greatest diversity of races of maize in the world. One also counts by the hundreds the varieties of other Andean crops whose grains, roots, fruits, flowers, leaves, and tubers continue to be the basis of alimentation in the Andes.[29]

More than half of the food that is consumed in Peru today comes from the peasants' *chacra*s, and it is produced with the same knowledge of the Andean cultures that made it possible for the region to achieve excellent yields during the pre-Hispanic period. The peasants of today, like those of yesterday, know how to converse with the variations in the climate, whether in a year of excess rain or in years of severe drought. During the period of growth and development of their plants, they obtain, thanks to their cosmovision, sufficient harvest to be able to share it with their families, their *ayllu*s.

Phytogenetic Diversity and Variety in the Andes

The mountainous chain of the Andes, traversing as it does from south to north, close to the Pacific Ocean, with perpetual snows in the middle of a tropical zone, incorporates a great diversity of natural life zones. The central Andes have the greatest ecological density in the world. In the short distance of two hundred lineal kilometers, it is possible to find about 80 percent of the 103 zones of natural life that Leslie Rensselaer Holdridge has proposed for the whole planet.[30]

Associated with this highly varied geography, the oceanic current of cold waters known as the "Peruvian current," the equatorial oceanic countercurrent of warm water called "the current of el niño," the Pacific southern anticyclone, and the presence to the east of extensive tropical forests combine in the central Andes to determine a widely diverse climate. Here, we have eight of the eleven climates proposed for the whole world. The atmospheric weather in each natural life zone is extremely variable, both from one year to the next and between the months of a single year or even week to week within a single month.

The variability of the atmospheric weather is thus a striking characteristic of the Andean climate. Frequently in the *chacras*, violent hail storms, frosts, heat waves, and periods of drought or excessive rain happen in the very middle of the growth cycle of the crops. During a millennium of experience, the peasants have learned to converse and share with the diversity and variability of the climate in order to obtain crops, whatever the type of year.

For some scholars of all things Andean (*lo Andino*), the varied terrain as well as the great variability in the weather would be sufficient reason to explain the great phytogenetic diversity and variability. For others, in addition to the varied terrain and the factors that determine the weather, it is necessary to take note of the great capacity of the phytogenetic material itself to produce mutations and natural recombinations and the morphological and functional characteristics of the plants themselves that also favor their intra- and interspecies variability.

Still, these considerations from the natural sciences do not fully explain the considerable number of species and the high number of varieties within each species that the Andean peasant cultivates. One cannot ignore—and, even less, not recognize—that it is the way the peasants of the Andes "see" and "feel" their world, that is, their own cosmovision, which in great part has made possible the fact that we now have such diversity and variety of plants and crops. The genetic richness of these species is owed in great part to a cosmovision that nurtures diversity and variability in the whole of life, on the basis of the peasants' *chacra*.

The Perennial Andean Worldview

The way a culture sees and feels the world is more readily revealed when one takes into account the circumstances that surround that culture, and this can be expressed better in the culture's own language, which is itself part of that worldview that includes and reflects the circumstances of those who share the same understanding. The Andean cultures have only oral languages, for example, Quechua and Aymara, which are languages for conversing, not for writing. The simple fact of writing freezes the flow of life, intertwined with its particular circumstances, which is an essential aspect of how peasants feel their everyday world. To express this worldview in written form and in a foreign language can only be an approximation.

Conscious of those limitations, we will start with nurturance in the *chacra,* which has always been and continues to be the principal activity of Andean peasants around which their whole world revolves.

Imana kaspapas . . . allpana, qaqana kawsayna, uywana kaspapas . . . lliwmi parlaypaq parlan,waqan, tusun ima . . . almaqunapas hinallapin muyunku, maymi kasqampi . . . paykunatapas qayakunchikmi. . . .

(Whatever little thing, earth, rock, plant, animals, they say that all speak, cry, dance . . . even the dead, they say, do not go far, they stay in their places . . . that is why to the soul we call. . . .)

These are the words of a peasant from Ayacucho, explaining that whatever surrounds him has life. It is not only that every thing is alive, but that every thing is a person with whom one converses and shares, equally.[31]

The following songs to the maize and the llama show this equality and the shared love and respect:

Song to the Maize
With the incandescent reflection
golden beard of Father Sun.
The Holy Mother Earth
gives fruit
to the maize of gold.
The maize of gold
gives life to all,
to the *wawas* [babies]
to the *pichones* [very young birds]
to the maidens
to the youths
to the grannies
to the old men
in this world.[32]

Song to the Llama
Let us go brother, let us go fellow countryman,
Our maize has failed us,
our potatoes, let us go to the quechua [the Quechua region]
You will enter bravely,
You will walk vigorously,
You are my father,
You are my mother,
You clothe me,
You feed me,
Without you they would have no life
these your children.[33]

In this worldview humans are the equals of the maize, the llama, the mountains, the stars, rocks, lakes, the departed who are also alive, and so on. All are nature; humans do not feel alienated from her, nor superior to her. Humans are not distant from nature, they are part of nature.

Humans feel that all are their *ayllu,* a Quechua word that in its broadest sense refers to the family that extends beyond just the human relatives. The rocks, the rivers, the sun, the moon, the plants, the animals are also members of the *ayllu.* All those that are found in the territory where they live in community are their *ayllu.*

Communitarian life is another characteristic of the Andean worldview. During the cultivation of the *chacra* one lives fully—by means of joyful *ayni* and *minka* (communal labor), conversing and sharing in community—in *ayllu.* One feels that all the members of one's *ayllu* are children of Pachamama (Mother Earth), toward whom one feels a love and respect equivalent to the love and respect a child feels for a mother.

In the testimonies of the Aymara peasants of the community of Conima, Puno, this feeling of deep love and respect for Pachamama is present. Before initiating the *qhollitaki mayt'asina,* or preparation of the field for planting, they deposit a few coca leaves for Pachamama —an action called *chillt'asina* or *k'intasina* in the Aymara tongue— saying: "Pachamama, Holy Earth, please pardon us, please excuse us. . . . Thus saying, we kiss her on our knees."[34]

All feel that they are children of Pachamama. When asked, "who are the children of Pachamama?" Don Jesus Urbano Rojas, a peasant from Ayacucho, answers: "All, all of us are the children. . . . I myself am the child of my parents, may they rest in peace, but I am also the child of Pachamama . . . (just like) the potato, the ullucu, the maize."[35] Since all are children of Pachamama, all are brothers and sisters, relatives, and together they grow the cultivated plants in their multiple and dispersed small fields, or *chacra*s.

All the relatives that comprise the *ayllu* (mountains, stones, animals, stars, ancestors, sun, moon) nurture the *chacra*. All are *chacareros*. This is another characteristic of the Andean worldview that cannot be understood unless one starts from the nurturing of the *chacra* along with the whole *ayllu*. Even the wind, the frost, the hail, the insects are part of the *ayllu*. From the point of view of modern agriculture, which prioritizes efficiency and profitability, those elements of climate are the principal factors that limit agricultural production in the Andes. Meanwhile, in their potato fields, the peasants plant a furrow for the hail, another one for the frost, another for insects, because they feel that, as members of the *ayllu*, these also have to eat, and they do not worry when the frost lightly burns the leaves of their crops. They say: "The frost has come to take its portion." When a strong hailstorm causes heavy damages, they do not blame the hail alone. They feel that it is everyone's fault, for having lost the harmony in the *ayllu* through fighting, conflicts, abortions, and the like. In this view, the hail is a warning. It is a sign that tells us that it is time again to harmonize the *ayllu* through ritual.

Ritual action in the Andes is an expression of utmost respect and love for the *waka*s, or Andean deities, who are considered to be members of the *ayllu* and who, in a specific time and place, facilitate the flow of life in the *ayllu*. The ritual offerings to the *waka*s are expressions of love and respect equal to those shown to a member of the family, rather than manifestations of adoration or supplication, as in other cultures.

The *waka*s are not always, or solely, *waka*s; they emerge charismatically in their proper time and place, in their own way. They are not adored or prayed to. One converses with them and ritually shares the harvest from the *chacra* with them. One sings to them, dances for them, just as one would do for any other relative of the *ayllu*, in terms of equivalency.

In the nurturance of harmony in the *ayllu* in which all its members participate, and that is based in the *chacra*, everything is important. From the smallest cricket to the majestic Apu Huanshan (the protector mountain with an altitude of 6,400 meters, located in the Cordillera Blanca in Ancash), all are important.

The *waka*s are: the Apus, or protector mountains; Pachamama; the *puquios* (springs or water sources); the lightning, stones, plants, animals, and the *runas* (human beings). Everything is *waka* in its time and place, including Jesus Christ, the Virgin Mary, and the saints of the Catholic religion, which were adopted as *waka*s when they arrived. Today, the peasants also converse, share, and nurture the *chacra* with them; they have all become *chacareros*.

In order to clarify—though this is only an approximation of other characteristics of the Andean worldview—we will consider that nature includes everyone and presents itself under three modalities:[36]

- The community of the *waka*s, or deities
- The community of humans
- The community of the *sallqa,* or nature.

Sallqa is a Quechua word that refers to all that is wild. Since humans and the *waka*s are also nature, we use the term *sallqa* to indicate the remaining parts of nature that in certain specific moments are neither *waka*s nor humans. The *waka*s arise spontaneously and charismatically in order to contribute to facilitating the flow of life and to nurture harmony in the *ayllu*. They then can return to being either *sallqa* or *runa*. The Quechua term *runa* refers to the human person but goes beyond just the human. The *runa* can be *sallqa* or *waka* without ceasing to be a human being.

We find this characteristic changeability in pre-Hispanic Andean ceramics from the Muchik region.[37] The Andean *maestro* or *paco* (medicine man) can have a human form or transform himself into a deer-*paco* or a mountain-*paco* and vice versa. Thus, the *runa* can be *sallqa* or *waka;* the *sallqa* can be *waka* or *runa;* and the *waka* can be *runa* or *sallqa* (see fig. 1). We will call this characteristic of the Andean world "interpenetrability." Peasants today continue to experience this characteristic in their rites.

In a further manifestation of this interpenetrability, the *runa*s cannot only be *sallqa* or *waka*. Within them are nested other forms corresponding to the different phases of their lives. Thus, a child already lives the adult person, the elder he or she will become, while not ceasing to be a child and vice versa. In Cajamarca, in northern Peru, the majority of the peasants do not speak Quechua. Nevertheless, through the "badly spoken" Spanish language in which they express themselves, they reflect their Andean worldview; they have "andeanized" the Spanish language. This interpenetrability is expressed by a peasant from Cajamarca who, referring to her childhood, says, "in my tender" instead of "in my childhood," which would be grammatically correct in the language of the city dweller. When the peasant says "in my tender," we understand that the child she once was still lives within her, whereas when we say "in my childhood," we refer to a phase of life, childhood, which we have left behind and which will never come back. These two expressions, spoken in the same language, express different ways of seeing and living life. While the peasants experience interpenetrability, the individual in the city, who is closer to the modern Western worldview, lives a historic, lineal time, in which one phase cancels out another.

Figure 1. Oquetlupuk muchik. *Left to right: animal/shaman, mountain/shaman, person/shaman.*
(Photograph Julio Valladolid. From Peru: Presencia Milenaria; Exposicion Universal de Sevilla, 1992; *and* Moche: Culturas Precolombinas Arte y Tesoros del Peru; Exposicion creada por Jose Antonio Lavalle *[Banco de Credito del Peru en la Cultura, Lima, Peru, 1985])*

In the Andes, life is experienced as if we had always been *chacareros* (makers of *chacra*), and it cannot be otherwise, since the nurturing of the *chacra* has been and still is the most important activity for the peasants. When the indigenous chronicler Don Felipe Guaman Poma de Ayala drew Adam and Eve—who, according to the Bible, were the first human couple—he represents them planting. Adam is opening furrows with the *chaquitaklla* (foot hoe) and Eve deposits the seeds.[38] These are the practices that today are still followed by the peasants: the woman plants the seeds in the furrows opened by the man with the *chaquitaklla*.

The Diversity and Variability of Plants in the *Chacra*

The peasants grow diverse and variable cultivated plants in their multiple and diverse *chacras*. The plants and animals that they nurture with dedication and love are members of their families. When the small shoots emerge in the *chacra,* they are their children; when they flower, they are companions with whom they dance and to whom they sing; and when they give fruit at the time of the harvest, they are their mothers. Andean peasant agriculture is this nurturance, full of feelings as for their own family. It is, in essence, a ritual agriculture in filigree. It is ritual because one constantly asks permission from the *wakas* (deities) as a sign of respect, and it is in filigree work because the Andean knowledge of nurturing plants and animals expresses itself in the smallest details in each specific instance and not in the more general aspects of the cultivating practices.

The peasants know that one converses with the Andean climate, through all its variability, by planting a mix of diverse species and varieties of plants. One plants the same mix—be it a mix of grains, such as maize and quinoa, or a mix of tubers, such as potato with oca, ullucu, or *mashwa*—in different places and at different times during the planting season, thereby insuring that some harvest will be obtained whatever the weather may be that particular year.

During the year—*wata,* in Quechua—there are two clearly differentiated seasons: one is cold and dry (*usyai uku* or *ch'aliy uras*); the other is warm and rainy (*puquy uku* or *paray uras*) and is the time plants grow in the *chacras*. During the warm season, there are frequent dry spells and excesses of rain, as well as hail and frost, with whom the peasants also converse and share the fruits of the *chacra*.

The following table summarizes in a sequential manner some of the knowledge used by the peasants to ritually nurture in their *chacra*s the diversity and variability of their plants.

Nurturing Heterogeneity in the Andean Chacra

1. A continuous conversation with the climate and the soil through indicators, or *lomasas,* in order to know under what weather conditions and in what type of soil the crops will grow. Peasants understand hundreds of indicators, of which the following are but a few examples.

1.1. Weather indicators:

1.1.1. Heavenly bodies: the rising and setting of the sun (*Taita Inti*) during the *wata,* or year; the phases of the moon (*Mama Quilla*); the greater or lesser brilliance of the stars of the Andean constellations of the Suchu or Colca (the Pleiades), the Amaru (Scorpius), and the Chacata (Andean Cross), which is not the Southern Cross but a much larger square cross that includes the latter.

1.1.2. Plants: the time of flowering as well as the quantity of flowers of certain wild plants, such as the columnar cactus called *sankay* (*Trichocereus* sp). An abundance of flowers indicates a rainy year (*puquy wata*); a scarce number of flowers indicates a year of little rain (*usyai wata*).

1.1.3. Animals: Changes in the coloring of the skin of toads. A dark coloring indicates a rainy year; a clear coloring a year of scant rain.

1.1.4. Atmospheric phenomena: The direction and color of the winds; the taste of the rain; the color of the cloudscape; the presence and numbers of rainbows.

1.1.5. Dreams: To dream of fire indicates that there will be periods of drought.

1.2. Soil indicators:

In the community of Chetilla in Cajamarca, if a wild plant called *chupica kewa* appears in the *chacra,* it is a sign that the soil is asking for a rest. If other wild gramineous plants grow in a fallow field, it is a sign that it is asking to be cultivated.

2. Various forms of nurturing the soil according to the weather and soil indicators and through the use of appropriate tools, such as the *chaquitaklla* (foot hoe):

2.1. In a year of scant rain (*usyai wata*) in the higher altitudes zones, where normally it rains more, the cultivated area is enlarged, that is, the "crops climb," and the furrows in the *chacra* are dug diagonally to the slope of the land in order to make the best use of humidity during a year of poor rains.

2.2. For a rainy year (*puquy wata*), the planted area is increased in the lower regions, where generally it rains less than in the high altitudes, that is, the "crops come down," and in the *chacra*s the furrows follow the slope of the land in order to avoid pools of water, but the furrows are short and alternate (the *huaccho* system) to avoid eroding the soil.

3. Different ways of growing plants in the *chacra:*

3.1. Planting a mix of species and varieties of crops in the same field in order to widen the genetic base, so that the planting of varieties resistant to drought and frost mixed with varieties resistant to excesses of humidity insures a sufficient level of products to feed the *ayllu* in either a dry year or a wet year.

3.1.1. Planting a mix of varieties of the same species—for example, a variety of potato—allows for a greater intraspecies genetic variability so that, as a result of the spontaneous genetic recombinations that occur naturally, new varieties appear and thus enrich the biodiversity of this one species.

3.1.2. The planting in the same *chacra* of "associations of mixed crops"—for example, the planting in strips of a mix of varieties of maize, alternating with rows (*shaiguas*) of mixes of quinoa ecotypes (*chenopodium quinoa*)—increases the genetic base of the species grown in the *chacra*.

3.2. Utilizing a very broad range of knowledge to plant the same crop at different times in multiple and dispersed *chacra*, situated at different altitudes:

3.2.1. Planting the same crop at different times:

   a) Within one agricultural year: for example, the community of Qasanqay in Ayacucho district does four plantings of potato in close succession:

      1. Very early planting, or *michka,* in irrigated *chacra*s;

2. Early planting (*naupa tarpuy*);

3. Intermediary planting (*chaupi tarpuy*);

4. Late planting (*quipa tarpuy*);

b) In a sequence of several years, through *laime*s or *aynoka*s—crop rotations that include fallow periods for the soil in areas generally situated in the higher altitudes.

3.2.2. Planting of the same crop at different altitudes:

a) Planting in different natural regions: for example:
The peasant community of Qasanqay in Ayacucho district has three altitudinally naturally different regions:

1. The Quechua region (3,100–3,200 meters above sea level), where associations of a mix of Andean grains are primarily grown, for example, mixes of maize with quinoa (*chenopodium quinoa*) and amaranth (*amaranthus caudatus*).

2. The Suni region (3,400–3,800 meters above sea level), where primarily the associations of mixes of Andean tubers, such as potato with oca (*oxalis tuberosa*), ullucu (*ullucus tuberosus*), and *mashwa* or *isaño* (*tropaeolum tuberosum*), are grown.

3. The Puna region (3,800–4,200 meters above sea level), where natural pastures grow that are also mixes of diverse species and varieties of grasses, which constitute the basis of the cattle's alimentation during the warm and rainy season (*puquy uku*).

b) Planting in different places and altitudes within the same natural region: for example:
In Qasanqay, each peasant plants on average three *chacra*s of maize in the Quechua region and four *chacra*s of potatoes in the Suni region.

4. Different forms of nurturing domestic animals are coordinated with the growing of crops with rotational and vertical pasturing within the different natural regions of the peasant community. For example, in Qasanqay in Ayacucho, during the warm, rainy season of the year (*puquy uku*), the cattle "climb" from the Quechua region to the Puna region where the natural pasture lands are found, and they "come down" to the Suni and Quechua regions for the cold, dry season (*usyai uku*). Furthermore, the manure of the cattle is the

principal source of fertilizer for the *chacra*s, mostly those of potato.

5. Different skills for processing, storing, conserving, and using the harvested fruits:

5.1. Of vegetable origin: for example:

5.1.1. Dehydration of tubers that then can be stored for several years:

    a) Of the bitter potato to obtain *chuño;*

    b) Of the sweet potato to make *cocopa;*

    c) Of the oca to obtain *caya;*

    d) Of the ullucu to obtain *ligli;*

5.1.2. "De-bittering" of Andean grains, such as *tarwi* or *chocho* (*lupinus mutabilis*) and quinoa.

5.2. Of animal origin:

For example, the dehydration of llama meat to obtain *charqui.*

Figure 2. Ritual to call the souls of the Ispallas (first
fruits of the chacra) *to increase the diversity in the* chacra.
(Photograph courtesy Associación Paqalqu, Puno)

6. A continuous conversation, through the indicators and ritual sharing, with all the relatives of the *ayllu*—such as the protector Apus, the *qochas* (ponds and lakes), the stars, the stones, the crickets—in order to create the organicity that facilitates the nurturance of the diversity and variability in the *chacra*s, through joyful *aynis* and *minkas* (communal labor) where people dance and eat well.

As all nurture the *chacra,* all share in its fruits; all are thankful for the harvests, and each time that an act of nurturance of plants or animals takes place, people respectfully ask permission of Mother Earth (Pachamama), requesting the protection and accompaniment of the Apus (protector mountains). Don Jesus Urbano Rojas, a peasant from Ayacucho, tells how he and his father grew *chacra*s of potato in Huanta:

> To begin the work we did the *pagapu* (gift of an offering) to Pachamama . . . another offering we did before the hilling of the potato plants

Figure 3. Ritual to the Ispallas, 2 February, Conima, Puno.
(Photograph courtesy Associación Chuyma Aru)

and then also when harvesting the first trial potatoes and then again to give thanks for the harvest.[39]

Don Modesto Machaca of the peasant community of Quispillacta, Ayacucho, says the following:

> . . . to open a chacra I have to ask permission of Pachamama so that she will let me work this soil . . . besides offering coca leaves and some liquor, I tell her . . . this land, I will cultivate her with love, without mistreating her, and the fruits that she will give me, we will all eat . . . we will even taste them.[40]

These two testimonies clearly express the love that the peasants feel in the depths of their hearts for their mother earth, Pachamama. Andean peasant agriculture *is* this profound feeling.

Some Reflections

To know, to understand, to grasp, to realize—concerns born of my scientific training—that Andean peasant agriculture is this feeling of profound love and respect for Pachamama was very difficult. Even more so was to see, feel, and experience it myself in spite of the fact that I come from a peasant background and have always been surrounded by expressions of Andean culture and agriculture.

As an agronomist, professionally trained to "manage" crops according to criteria of efficacy and profitability, I had to travel a very long journey, first as a university professor doing scientific experimental research in the genetics and physiology of plants of Andean origin, at the start, in an analytic manner—that is looking at each species of plant separately—and later utilizing the systems approach, integrating the plants into systems of agricultural production. I continued my journey, trying to test and teach this knowledge in the *chacra*s of the peasants, and I realized the limited results thus obtained. During this past decade, I have simply walked through the *chacra*s, accompanying the peasants without trying to teach them what they know very well, namely, Andean peasant agriculture, with no desire to lead them, and with even less sense that I have any sort of expertise. I walk, trying again to see in the perennial Andean way, what before I was looking at only from the point of view of formal science.

There is no place for feeling in science. The knowledge produced by science is constituted by rational and objective concepts, which, in the case of modern agriculture, are used for the efficient and profitable management of crops and not for feelings of respect and love, which is what characterizes the nurturance of plants and animals in the whole Andean landscape.

Native original cultures have worldviews similar to that of the Andean one. These are cultures that love and respect nature, and in their different languages they refer to her as "mother nature." One of the few cultures that destroys nature, mostly through environmental pollution, is the industrial culture of the modern West, whose main religions, interestingly, are monotheistic: Christianity and Judaism. Science, which is one of the pillars of such societies, depends on business, on economic gain, where the criteria of productivity, efficacy, competition, profitability, and standardized quality are given primacy. Globalization, which is the new name by which world development projects, based on the notion of a continuous progress, present themselves, is the latest reigning dogma.

In such a context, knowledge produced by science is the only valid knowledge, whereas the knowledge of other cultures is either not valid or does not exist. Science becomes the new fundamentalist monotheistic religion of the individual in industrialized societies, which are the ones that most pollute the environment, destroying nature in their excessive desire to have always more economic profitability to support their hunger for power.

The millenarian Andean culture has always nurtured the diversity and variability of life on the basis of the *chacra,* thus enriching biodiversity, and with it, the regeneration and sustainability of nature and of life itself in the Andes. At this point in time we cannot fail, once again, to see and consider as a life alternative the wisdom of the original indigenous cultures of the world.

Notes

1. See Shiv Visvanathan, "Footnotes to Vavilov: An Essay on Gene Diversity," in *Decolonizing Knowledge: From Development to Dialogue,* ed. Frédérique Apffel-Marglin and Stephen A. Marglin, 306–39 (Oxford: Clarendon Press, 1996). See also Jack Kloppenburg, Jr., *First the Seed: The Political Economy of Plant Biotechnology, 1492–2000* (Cambridge: Cambridge University Press, 1988), for a discussion of the Vavilov Centers of Diversity.

2. Julio Valladolid Rivera, "Agricultura Campesina Andina: Crianza de la diversidad de la vida en la chacra," in *Crianza Andina de la Chacra* (Lima: PRATEC, 1994).

3. Enrique Mayer, personal communication, 14 December 1995.

4. Two Marxist parties, the Confederacion Campesina del Peru (CCP) and the Confederacion Nacional Agraria (CNA), arrogated to themselves the leadership of a peasant movement with the intention of establishing communal landholding. The silent movement Mayer and PRATEC speak of refers to the direct action of Andean peasants inspired by their native culture and modes of relating to land (the re-creation of the *ayllu*). According to Danish anthropologist Soren Hvalkof (personal communication), the CCP and the CNA never succeeded in their aims. I am grateful to Soren for this information.

5. As of January 2000, there are fourteen such centers for biodiversity and the strengthening of the Andean Chacra.

6. Frédérique Apffel-Marglin, "Rationality, the Body and the World: From Production to Regeneration," in *Decolonizing Knowledge,* ed. Apffel-Marglin and Marglin.

7. Kathryn Pyne Addelson, *Moral Passages* (New York and London: Routledge, 1994), 161.

8. Enrique Mayer, "Recursos naturales, medio ambiente, tecnología y desarrollo," in *Peru: El problema agrario en debate, SEPIA V,* ed. Oscar Dancourt, Enrique Mayer, and Carlos Monge, 479–532 (Lima: CAPRODA; SEPIA, [1994]). Mayer now teaches in the anthropology department of Yale University. I am grateful to Tirso Gonzales for sending me this article of Mayer's.

9. Ibid., 513. My translation.

10. Ibid., 514.

11. Ibid., 514–15.

12. Ibid., 517.

13. Ibid.

14. Eduardo Grillo Fernandez, "Desarrollo o Descolonizacion en los Andes," in *Desarrollo o Descolonizacion en los Andes?* (Lima: PRATEC, 1994), 34, 35; cited in Frédérique Apffel-Marglin with PRATEC, *The Spirit of Regeneration: Andean Culture Confronting Western Notions of Development* (London: Zed Books, 1998), 24. Grillo and other PRATEC members often use the phrase "Andean-Amazonian." Some have criticized such inclusiveness, but its use can be defended by pointing out that at the rather general level at which PRATEC members speak, their principles apply to both regions, which are otherwise quite differentiated. The Andean world is itself a diverse one made up of various ethnicities. In this diversity, PRATEC members focus on some generally shared cosmological traits.

15. Grimaldo Rengifo, *Desarrollo o Descolonizacion en los Andes?* (Lima: PRATEC, 1994).

16. Carol Bigwood, *Earth Muse: Feminism, Nature, and Art* (Philadelphia: Temple University Press, 1993), 28.

17. Bronislaw Malinowski, *Coral Gardens and Their Magic*, 2 vols. (Bloomington: Indiana University Press, 1965); Stanley J. Tambiah, "The Magical Power of Words," in his *Culture, Thought, and Social Action: An Anthropological Perspective* (Cambridge, Mass.: Harvard University Press, 1985), 17–60.

18. Steven Shapin and Simon Schaffer, *Leviathan and the Air-Pump: Hobbes, Boyle, and the Experimental Life* (Princeton, N.J.: Princeton University Press, 1985).

19. Jean Pouillon, "Remarks on the Verb 'to Believe'," in *Between Belief and Transgression: Structuralist Essays in Religion, History, and Myth*, ed. Michel Izard and Pierre Smith (Chicago: University of Chicago Press, 1982), 8.

20. Charles Taylor, *Sources of the Self: The Making of Modern Identity* (Cambridge, Mass.: Harvard University Press, 1989).

21. Arthur Zajonc, *Catching the Light: The Intertwined History of Light and Mind* (New York: Bantam Books, 1993).

22. Bruno Latour, *We Have Never Been Modern*, trans. Catherine Porter (Cambridge, Mass.: Harvard University Press, 1993).

23. Bruce Wilshire, *The Moral Collapse of the University: Professionalism, Purity, and Alienation* (Albany: State University of New York Press, 1990), 39.

24. Tzvetan Todorov, *The Conquest of America* (Cambridge, Mass.: Harvard University Press, 1984), 127.

25. National Research Council, *Lost Crops of the Incas: Little Known Plants of the Andes with Promise for Worldwide Cultivation* (Washington, D.C.: National Academy Press, 1989).

26. D. Bonavia, "De la caza a la agricultura," in *Peru hombre e historia, de los origenes al siglo XV* (Lima: Edubanco, 1991); F. Silva-Santisteban, "El mundo Andino: De la caza a las tecnologias agropecuarias," *Cuadernos de Historia* (Lima) 11 (1990); P. Kaulicke, "La agricultura en el Peru Pre-hispanico: Su origen," *Boletin de Lima* 7, no. 40 (1985); and M. Vallejos, "Origen y desarollo de la agricultura en el Peru prehispanico," *Revista Ciencia Interamericana* 19, no. 1 (1978): 21–24.

27. Z. Human, "Conservacion de recursos fitogeneticos en el Centro Internacional de la Papa," *Diversity* 7, no. 1-2 (1991).

28. Ch. A. Manrique, *El Maiz en el Peru* (Lima: Fondo del libro del Banco Agrario, 1995).

29. Mario Tapia and Nicolas Mateo, "Andean Phytogenetic and Zootechnic Resources," in *Mountain Agriculture and Crop Genetic Resources*, ed. K. Lu. Riley et al. (New Delhi: Oxford IBH Publishing Co., 1990).

30. ONERN, *Mapa Ecologico del Peru: Guia Explicativa* (Lima: National Office of Evaluation of Natural Resources, 1976).

31. M. Machaca, "Vigencia y continuidad de la cultura y agricultura Andina en Quispillacta Ayacucho" (thesis, Faculty of Agronomy, National University of San Cristobal de Huamanga, Ayacucho, Peru, 1991).

32. "Song to the Maize," by Primitivo Evanan Poma, a peasant from Sarhua, Ayacucho, Peru).

33. Song of the llama herders of the community of Cotay-Huancavelica, cited in O. T. Espinoza, "Alpacas y Llamas: Cotay-Huancavelica" (thesis, Faculty of Agron-

omy, National University of San Cristobal de Huamanga, Ayacucho, Peru, 1996).

34. N. Chambi Pacoricona, "La religiosidad Aymara en el Pueblo Aymara en el Pueblo Andino de Conima-Puno" (thesis, course in Andean Peasant Agriculture, PRATEC/National University of San Cristobal de Huamanga, Ayacucho, Peru, 1991).

35. J. Urbano Rojas and P. Macera, *Santero y Caminante: Santoruraj-Nanpurej* (Lima: Editorial Apoyo, 1992).

36. Eduardo Grillo Fernandez, "La cosmovision Andina de siempre y la cosmologia Occidental moderna," in *Desarrollo o Descolonizacion en los Andes?* (Lima: PRATEC, 1994).

37. V. A. Rodriguez Suy Suy, *Los Pueblos Muchik en el Mundo Andino de Ayer y Siempre* (Lima: PRATEC, 1997).

38. F. Guaman Poma de Ayala, *Nueva Cronica y Buen Gobierno* (1615; Paris: Ethnological Institute, University of Paris, 1936).

39. Urbana and Macera, *Santero y Caminante: Santoruraj-Nanpurej.*

40. Machaca, "Vigencia y continuidad de la cultura y agricultura Andina en Quispillacta Ayacucho."

Select Bibliography

Abimbola, W. "Ifa: A West African Cosmological System." In *Religion in Africa: Experience and Expression*, ed. Thomas D. Blakeley, Walter E. A. vanBeek, and Dennis L. Thomson, 101–16. London: James Currey, 1994.

Abram, David. *The Spell of the Sensuous: Perception and Language in a More-than-Human World*. New York: Vintage Books, 1997.

Achebe, Chinua. *Things Fall Apart*. London: Heinemann, 1958.

Adams, Carol, ed. *Ecofeminism and the Sacred*. New York: Continuum, 1993.

Agarwal, Anil, et al. "Technology Control, Global Warming, and Environmental Colonialism: The WRI Report." *Social Action* 41 (January-March 1991).

———, eds. *The State of India's Environment 1982: A Citizens' Report*. New Delhi: Centre for Science and the Environment, 1982.

Agarwal, Bina. *A Field of Their Own: Gender and Land Rights in South Asia*. Cambridge: Cambridge University Press, 1994.

Alam, Javeed. "Fragmented Culture and Strangulated Existence: Jharkhand's Culture Encounter with the Modern." In *Continuity and Change in Tribal Society*, ed. Mrinal Miri, 11–22. Shimla: Indian Institute of Advanced Study, 1993.

Albanese, Catherine L. *Nature Religion in America: From the Algonkian Indians to the New Age*. Chicago: University of Chicago Press, 1990.

Alcorn, Janis. "Noble Savage or Noble State? Northern Myths and Southern Realities in Biodiversity Conservation." *Etnoecologica* 11, no. 3 (1994): 7–19.

Allaby, Michael. *The Concise Oxford Dictionary of Ecology*. Oxford: Oxford University Press, 1994.

Allan, William. *The African Husbandman*. Edinburgh: Oliver and Boyd, 1965.

Alpers, Antony. *Maori Myths and Tribal Legends.* Auckland: Longman Paul, 1964.

Alvarado, Elvia. *Don't Be Afraid Gringo: A Honduran Gringo Speaks from the Heart: The Story of Elvia Alvarado.* Trans. Medea Benjamin. New York: Harper and Row, 1987.

Amadiume, Iffi. *Female Husbands Male Daughters.* London: Zed Press, 1988.

"Amazon Indian Fights Oil Exploration, Dallas Company Defends Rain Forest Project as Safe." *Dallas Morning News,* 27 April 1992, 15A.

Amiotte, Arthur. "The Call to Remember." *Parabola* 17, no. 3 (1992): 29–34.

Amte, Baba. *Cry, the Beloved.* Chandrapur, Maharashtra, India: Maharogi Sewa Samiti, 1989.

Andel, Tj. H. van. "The Orinoco Delta." *Journal of Sedimentary Petrology* 37, no. 2 (1967): 297–310.

Anderson, J. W. *Fur Trader's Story.* Toronto: Ryerson, 1961.

Anderson, Robert S., and Walter Huber. *The Hour of the Fox, Tropical Forest, the World Bank, and Indigenous People in Central India.* Seattle: University of Washington Press, 1988.

Anthropology Resource Center (ARC). "Transnational Corporations and Indigenous Peoples." *ARC Newsletter* 5, no. 3 (1981).

Apffel-Marglin, Frédérique. "Introduction: Knowledge and Life Revisited." In *The Spirit of Regeneration : Andean Culture Confronts Western Notions of Development,* ed. Frédérique Apffel-Marglin, with PRATEC. London: Zed Books, 1998.

Apffel-Marglin, Frédérique, and Pramod Parajuli. "Geographies of Difference and the Resilience of Ecological Ethnicities: Place and the Motion of Global Capital." *Development: Seeds of Change* 41, no. 2 (1998): 14–21.

Apffel-Marglin, Frédérique, and Stephen Marglin, eds. *Decolonizing Knowledge: From Development to Dialogue.* Oxford: Oxford University Press, 1994.

———. *Dominating Knowledge: Development, Culture, and Resistance.* Oxford: Oxford University Press, 1990.

ARCO Report. "Environment, Health and Safety Report: Ecuador Rain Forest," updated 1995. <http://www.arco.com/corporate/ehs/earth/ecuador. htm> (cited 24 September 1999).

———. "Villano: Seeking Common Ground. A New Approach to Oil Development in the Tropical Rainforest of Ecuador," updated 1999. <http:// www.arco.com/corporate/reports/villano/villano1.htm> (cited 24 September 1999).

Areeparampil, Mathew. "Displacement Due to Mining in Jharkhand." *Economic and Political Weekly,* 15 June 1996, 1524–28.

Arizpe, Lourdes. "Chiapas: The Basic Problems." *Identities* 3, no. 1-2 (1995): 119–33.

Arnold, Guy. "Nomadic Penan of the Upper Rejang (Plieran), Sarawak." *Journal of the Malayan Branch of the Royal Asiatic Society* 31, pt. 1, no. 181 (1958): 40–82.

Asad, Talal. "Are There Histories of Peoples without Europe?" *Comparative Studies in Society and History* 29 (1987): 594–607.

Askin, David. "Rainforest Destruction: Need and Greed in Papua New Guinea." *South Pacific Journal of Mission Studies* 15 (1995): 8–15.

Associated Press. "Ecuador Indians Regain Title to Amazon Forest." *Milwaukee Sentinel,* 20 June 1992.

————. "Great Whale Project on Cree Land Collapses." *News from Indian Country* 23 (1994).

Aug, Lisa. "Humans and the Earth." *Turtle Quarterly* 3, no. 2 (1989).

Ayala Lafée, Cecilia. "La etnohistoria prehispánica Guaiqueri." *Antropológica* 82 (1994-1996): 5–128.

Bagamaspad, A., and Z. H. Pawid. *A People's History of Benguet.* Baguio City: Baguio Printing and Publishing Company, Inc., 1985.

Bagchi, Saugata. "Harming Trees, Hurting Tribals." *Inter Press Service,* 18 March 1991.

Baker, Rob. "A Canoe against the Mainstream: Preserving the Navajo Way. An Interview with Peterson Zah." *Parabola* 14, no. 2 (1989): 53–60.

Balee, William. *Footprints of the Forest: Ka'apor Ethnobotany—The Historical Ecology of Plant Utilization by an Amazonian People.* New York: Columbia University Press, 1994.

Barber, Karen. *I Could Speak Until Tomorrow.* Washington, D.C.: Smithsonian Institution Press, 1990.

Barlow, Cleve. *Tikanga Whakaaro: Key Concepts of Maori Culture.* Auckland: Oxford University Press, 1991.

Barra, G. *Kikuyu Proverbs.* Nairobi: Kenya Literature Bureau, 1939.

Barral, Basilio M. de. *Los indios Guaraúnos y su cancionero.* Biblioteca Missionalia Hispánica, 15. Madrid: Concejo Superior de Investigaciones Cientificas, Departamento de Misionologia Española.

Barreiro, Jose. "Indigenous Peoples Are the 'Miner's Canary' of the Human Family." In *Learning to Listen to the Land,* ed. Bill Willers. Washington, D.C.: Island Press, 1991.

Barret, Leonard. "African Religions in the Americas: The Island in Between." In *African Religions: A Symposium,* ed. Nowell S. Booth, 185. New York: Nok Publishers, 1977.

Barsh, R. L. "An Advocate's Guide to the Convention on Indigenous and Tribal Peoples." *Oklahoma City University Law Review* 15 (1990): 209–53.

Baviskar, Anita. "Fate of the Forest: Conservation and Tribal Rights." *Economic and Political Weekly,* 17 September 1994.

Bearskin, Job. "Dialogue with Job Bearskin." Legal briefing notes, in the possession of the author. Two pages typescript, 1972-73.

Beck, Peggy, and Anna Lee Walters. *The Sacred.* Tsaile: Navajo Community College Press, 1977.

Becker, Marc. "Nationalism and Pluri-Nationalism in a Multi-Ethnic State: Indigenous Organizations in Ecuador." Paper presented to the Mid-America Conference on History, 17–19 September, University of Kansas, 1992. <http://ukanaix.cc.ukans.edu/ftp/pub/history/articles/ecuador.txt> (cited 24 September 1999).

Belcher, Martha, and Angela Gennino, eds. *Southeast Asia Rainforests: A Resource Guide and Directory.* San Francisco: Rainforest Action Network, 1993.

Bell, Diane. *Daughters of the Dreaming.* 2d ed. Minneapolis: University of Minnesota Press, 1993.

———. "Desperately Seeking Redemption." *Natural History* 106, no. 2 (1997).

———. *Ngarrindjeri Wurruwarrin: A World That Is, Was, and Will Be.* North Melbourne: Spinifex Press, 1998.

Bennett, Bradley C. "Plants and People of the Amazonian Rainforests: The Role of Ethnobotany in Sustainable Development." *BioScience* 42, no. 8 (1992): 599–608.

Bennett, D. "Stepping from the Diagram: Australian Aboriginal Cultural and Spiritual Values Relating to Biodiversity." In *Cultural and Spiritual Values of Biodiversity,* ed. Darrell Addison Posey. United Nations Environment Programme (UNEP). Global Biodiversity Assessment. Nairobi: UNEP, 1998.

Berger, Mr. Justice Thomas R. *A Long and Terrible Shadow.* Vancouver: Douglas and McIntyre, 1991.

———. *Northern Frontier, Northern Homeland: The Report of the Mackenzie Valley Pipeline Inquiry.* Vol. 1. Ottawa: Ministry of Supply and Services Canada, 1977.

Berglund, Axel-lvar. *Zulu Thought-Patterns and Symbolism.* Bloomington: Indiana University Press, 1989.

Berkes, Fikret, ed. *James Bay Forum: Public Hearings on the James Bay Project Held in Montreal, April, 1973.* Montreal: The James Bay Committee, 1973.

Berkhofer, Robert F. *The White Man's Indian: Images of the Indian from Columbus to the Present.* New York: Vintage Books, 1979.

Bernbaum, Edwin. "Sacred Mountains." *Parabola* 13, no. 4 (1988): 12–18.

Berreman, Gerald D. "Chipko: A Movement to Save the Himalayan Environment and People." In *Contemporary Indian Tradition: Voices on Na-*

ture and the Challenge of Change, ed. Carla Borden, 239–66. Washington, D.C., and London: Smithsonian Institution Press, 1989.

Berry, Thomas. *The Dream of the Earth*. San Francisco: Sierra Club Books, 1998.

———. "The Viable Human." In *Environmental Philosophy,* ed. Michael E. Zimmerman et al., 171–81. Englewood Cliffs, N.J.: Prentice Hall, 1993.

Best, Elsdon. *Spiritual and Mental Concepts of the Maori*. Dominion Museum Monograph, no. 2. Wellington: Government Printer, 1973.

———. *Maori Religion and Mythology*. Part 1. Wellington: Government Printer, 1924.

Bidney, D. "Cultural Relativism." In *International Encyclopaedia of the Social Sciences*, ed. David L. Sills. New York: Macmillan, 1968.

Bierhorst, John. *The Way of the Earth: Native America and the Environment*. New York: William Morrow, 1994.

Biesele, Megan, et al. "Hunters, Clients and Squatters: The Contemporary Socioeconomic Status of Botswana Basarwa." *African Study Monographs* 9, no. 3 (1989): 109–51.

Bishop, Charles A. "The Emergence of Hunting Territories among the Northern Ojibwa." *Ethnology* 9 (1970).

Bishop, Charles A., and Toby Morantz, eds. *Who Owns the Beaver? Northern Algonquian Land Tenure Reconsidered*. Special issue, *Anthropologica* (Ontario) 28, no. 1-2 (1986).

Blackburn, Thomas, and Kat Anderson. "Introduction: Managing the Domesticated Environment." *Before the Wilderness: Environmental Management by Native Californians*, comp. and ed. Thomas C. Blackburn and Kat Anderson. Menlo Park, Calif.: Ballena Press, 1993.

Blaikie, Piers. "Changing Environments or Changing Views? A Political Ecology for Developing Countries." *Geography* 80, no. 3 (1995): 203–14.

Boas, Franz. *Keresan Texts*. New York: American Ethnological Society, 1928.

Boff, Leonardo. *Cry of the Earth, Cry of the Poor*. Maryknoll, N.Y.: Orbis Books, 1997.

Booth, Annie L., and Harvey M. Jacobs. "Ties That Bind: Native American Beliefs As a Foundation for Environmental Consciousness." *Environmental Ethics* 12 (1990): 27–44.

Bosu-Mullick, Sanjay. "Jharkhand Movement: A Historical Analysis." In *Continuity and Change in Tribal Society*, ed. Mrinal Miri. Shimla: Indian Institute of Advanced Study, 1993.

Botengan, Kate. "Bontoc Concepts on Sickness and Death." In *Filipino Tribal Religious Experience,* ed. Henry W. Kiley. Quezon City: Giraffe Books, 1994.

Boulding, Elise. "Ethnicity and the New Constitutive Orders." In *Global Visions*, ed. J. Brecher et. al. Boston: South End Press, 1993.

Broad, Robin, and John Cavanagh. *Plundering Paradise: The Struggle for the Environment in the Philippines*. Berkeley and Los Angeles: University of California Press, 1993.

Brokensha, David, Dennis Warren, and Oswald Werner, eds. *Indigenous Knowledge Systems and Development*. Washington, D.C.: University Press of America, 1980.

Brosius, J. Peter. "Bornean Forest Trade in Historical and Regional Perspective: The Case of Penan Hunter-Gatherers of Sarawak." In *Society and Non-Timber Products in Tropical Asia*, ed. J. Fox, 13–26. Occasional Papers: Environmental Series, no. 19. Honolulu: East-West Center, 1995.

———. "Contrasting Subsistence Ecologies of Eastern and Western Penan Foragers (Sarawak, East Malaysia)." In *Tropical Forests, People, and Food: Biocultural Interactions and Applications to Development*, ed. C. M. Hladik et al. Man and the Biosphere Series, 13. Paris: UNESCO; Carnforth, U.K., and Pearl River, N.Y.: Parthenon Publishing Group, 1993.

———. "Endangered Forest, Endangered People: Environmentalist Representations of Indigenous Knowledge." *Human Ecology* 25, no. 1 (1997): 47–69.

———. "Foraging in Tropical Rainforests: The Case of the Penan of Sarawak, East Malaysia (Borneo)." *Human Ecology* 19, no. 2 (1991): 123–50.

———. "Perspectives on Penan Development in Sarawak." *Sarawak Gazette* 119, no. 1519 (1992): 5–22.

———. "Prior Transcripts, Divergent Paths: Resistance and Acquiescence to Logging in Sarawak, East Malaysia." *Comparative Studies in Society and History* 39, no. 3 (1997): 468–510.

———. "River, Forest and Mountain: The Penan Geng Landscape." *Sarawak Museum Journal*, n.s., 36, no. 57 (1986): 173–84.

Brosius, J. Peter, Anna Tsing, and Charles Zerner. "Representing Communities: Histories and Politics of Community-Based Resource Management." *Society and Natural Resources* 11, no. 2 (1998): 157–68.

Brosted, Jens, et al. *Native Power: The Quest for Autonomy and Nationhood of Indigenous Peoples*. New York: Columbia University Press, 1985.

Brown, Jennifer S. H., and Robert Brightman. *The Orders of the Dreamed: George Nelson on Cree and Northern Ojibwa Religion and Myth, 1823*. Winnipeg: University of Manitoba Press, 1988.

Brown, Joseph Epes, ed. *The Sacred Pipe: Black Elk's Account of the Seven Rites of the Oglala Sioux*. Norman: University of Oklahoma Press, 1953.

Bruchac, Joseph. "The Storytelling Seasons: Some Reflections on Native American Storytelling Traditions." *Parabola* 14, no. 2 (1989): 87–92.

Brush, Stephen, and Doreen Stabinsky, eds. *Valuing Local Knowledge: Indigenous People and Intellectual Property Rights*. Washington, D.C.: Island Press, 1996.

Brysk, Alison. "Acting Globally: Indian Rights and International Politics in Latin America." In *Indigenous People and Democracy in Latin America*, ed. Donna Lee Van Cott. New York: St. Martin's Press, in association with the Inter-American Dialogue, 1994.

Bullard, Robert, ed. *Confronting Environmental Racism: Voices from the Grassroots*. Boston: South End Press, 1993.

Burger, Julian. *The Gaia Atlas of First Peoples: A Future for the Indigenous World*. New York: Anchor Books, 1990.

———. *Report from the Frontier: The State of the World's Indigenous Peoples*. London: Zed Books; Cambridge, Mass.: Cultural Survival, 1987.

Burman, Roy. "Indigenous and Tribal People, Global Hegemonies and the Constitution of India." *Mainstream* (New Delhi), 9 May 1992.

———. *Report of the Study Group on Land Holding Systems in Tribal Areas*. New Delhi: Government of India, 1987.

Burrows, Charles Kekuewa Pe'ape'a Makawalu. "Hawaiian Conservation Values and Practices." In *Conservation Biology in Hawai'i*, ed. Charles Stone and Danielle Stone. Honolulu: University of Hawai'i Cooperative National Park Resources Studies Unit, 1989.

Butenhko, J., and J. P. Barbot. "Características geotécnicas de los sedimentos marinos costafuera del Delta del Orinoco." *Fourth Latin American Geological Congress Trinidad and Tobago* 1 (1979): 144–54.

Cajete, Gregory A. *Look to the Mountain: An Ecology of Indigenous Education*. Durango, Colo.: Kivaki Press, 1994.

Callicott, J. Baird. "American Indian Land Wisdom? Sorting Out the Issues." In *In Defense of the Land Ethic: Essays in Environmental Philosophy*, ed. J. Baird Callicott. Albany: State University of New York Press, 1989.

———. *Earth's Insight: A Survey of Ecological Ethics from the Mediterranean Basin to the Australian Outback*. Berkeley and Los Angeles: University of California Press, 1994.

———. "Traditional American Indian and Traditional Western European Attitudes toward Nature: An Overview." In *Environmental Philosophy*, ed. R. Elliot and A. Gare. Milton Keynes: Open University Press, 1983.

Calow, Peter, and Geoffrey Pitts. *The Rivers Handbook: Hydrological and Ecological Principles*. Oxford: Blackwell Scientific Publications, 1992.

"Campaigns: Keeping Hydro-Quebec at Bay." *Ecologist* 24, no. 2 (1994).

Campbell, Joseph. *The Way of the Animal Powers*. London: Summerhill Press; San Francisco: Harper and Row, 1983.

Carlsen, Robert, and Martin Prechtel. "The Flowering of the Dead: An Interpretation of Highland Maya Culture." *Man* 26 (1991): 23–42.

Carlson, John B., and B. Sascha. "America's Ancient Skywatchers." *National Geographic* 177, no. 3 (1990): 76–107.

Caruso, Andrea, and Kevin Russell. "Journey to Borneo and the Resistance of the Penan." *Earth First!* 12, no. 7 (1992): 14.

Castells, Manuel. *The Power of Identity.* Vol. 2 of *The Information Age: Economy, Society and Culture.* London: Blackwell Publishers, 1997.

Center for Economic and Social Rights. *Rights Violations in the Ecuadorian Amazon: The Human Consequences of Oil Development.* New York: CESR, 1994.

Centre for Science and Environment. *The State of India's Environment 1984–85: The Second Citizen's Report.* New Delhi: Centre for Science and Environment, 1985.

Chagnon, Napolean. *Yanomamö: The Fierce People.* Fort Worth, Tex.: Holt Rinehart and Winston, 1983.

Chambers, Robert. "Microenvironments Unobserved." *Gatekeeper Series,* no. 22, 6–7. London: International Institute for Environment and Development, 1990.

———. *Volta Resettlement Experience.* London: Pall-Mall Press, 1970.

Chartier, Clem. "Malaysia: Logging Greatest Threat to Indigenous Peoples of Sarawak." *Statement to the UN Working Group on Indigenous Populations. International Work Group for Indigenous Affairs Newsletter* 51-52 (1987).

Chatchawan, Tongdeelert, and Larry Lohmann. "The Traditional Muang Faai Irrigation System of Northern Thailand." *Ecologist* 21, no. 2 (1991): 101–6.

Chavers, Dean. "There Is Evidence of Racism; We Must Expose It." *Indian Country Today,* 12 January 1998, A5.

Chay, Rigoberto Queme. "The Corn Men Have Not Forgotten Their Ancient Gods." In *Story Earth: Native Voices on the Environment,* comp. Inter Press Service. San Francisco: Mercury House, 1993.

Circles, Lone Wolf. *Full Circle: A Song of Ecology and Earthen Spirituality.* St. Paul, Minn.: Llewellyn New Times, 1991.

Clarkson, Linda, Vern Morrissette, and Gabriel Regallet. *Our Responsibility to the Seventh Generation: Indigenous Peoples and Sustainable Development.* Winnipeg: International Institute for Sustainable Development, 1992.

Clay, Jason. *Indigenous Peoples and Tropical Forests: Models of Land Use and Management from Latin America.* Cambridge, Mass.: Cultural Survival, 1988.

Cliffe, Lionel. "The Conservation Issue in Zimbabwe." *Review of African Political Economy* 42 (1988): 48–58.

Clifton, James A. *The Invented Indian: Cultural Fictions and Government Policies.* New Brunswick and London: Transaction Publishers, 1990.

Cohen, David William, and E. S. Atieno Odhiambo. *Siaya: The Historical Anthropology of an African Landscape.* London: John Currey, 1989.

Colchester, Marcus, and Larry Lohmann, eds. *The Struggle for Land and the Fate of the Forests*. Penang, Malaysia: World Rainforest Movement, 1993.

Collier, George A., and Elizabeth L. Quaratiello. *Basta! Land and the Zapatista Rebellion in Chiapas*. Oakland, Calif.: Food First, 1994.

Comaroff, Jean. *Body of Power, Spirit of Resistance: The Culture and History of a South African People*. Chicago: University of Chicago Press, 1985.

Comaroff, Jean, and John Comaroff. *Of Revelation and Revolution. Christianity, Colonialism, and Consciousness in South Africa*. Vol. 1. Chicago: University of Chicago Press, 1991.

Comaroff, John, and Jean Comaroff. *Ethnography and the Colonial Imagination*. Boulder, Colo.: Westview Press, 1992.

Conklin, Harold. *Ethnographic Atlas of Ifugao*. London: Yale University Press, 1980.

Conti, A. "Capitalist Organization of Production through Non-Capitalist Relations: Women's Role in Pilot Resettlement in Upper Volta." *Review of African Political Economy* 15-16 (1979): 75–92.

Cooper, Glen, et al. "Cree Stories." *Northeast Indian Quarterly* 8, no. 4 (1991): 30–33.

Courlander, Harold. *The Fourth World of the Hopi*. Albuquerque: University of New Mexico Press, 1987.

Cowan, James. "Aboriginal Solitude." *Parabola* 17, no. 1 (1992): 62–67.

Crarys, David. "New Territory in Canada's Northland," *San Francisco Chronicle*, 28 March 1998, and *Native Peoples Magazine*, June-July 1999.

Cree School Board. *James Bay Day*. Mistassini: Cree School Board, 1991.

Crocker, Jon Christopher. *Vital Souls: Bororo Cosmology, Natural Symbolism, and Shamanism*. Tucson: University of Arizona Press, 1985.

Cronon, William. *Changes in the Land: Indians, Colonists, and the Ecology of New England*. New York: Hifland Wang, 1983.

Cronyn, George W., ed. *American Indian Poetry*. New York: Ballantine Books, 1991.

Crosby, Alfred, Jr. *The Columbian Exchange: Biological and Cultural Consequences of 1492*. Westport: Greenwood Press, 1972.

———. *Ecological Imperialism: The Biological Expansion of Europe, 900–1900*. New York: Cambridge University Press, 1991.

Cummings, Claire. "Saving Native Lands." *Exchange: Journal of the Land Trust Alliance* (Washington, D.C.) 13 (1994).

Cunningham, A. B. *Ethics, Ethnobiological Research, and Biodiversity*. Gland, Switzerland: WWF-World Wide Fund for Nature, 1993.

Curran, W. Tees, and H. A. Calkins. *In Canada's Wonderful Northland: A Story of Eight Months of Travel by Canoe, Motorboat, and Dog-Team on the Northern Rivers and along the New Quebec Coast of Hudson Bay*. New York: G. P. Putnam's Sons, 1917.

Daley, Herman. *Development beyond Growth*. Boston: Beacon Press, 1995.

Dalmia, Yashodhara. *The Painted World of the Warlis: Art and Ritual of the Warli Tribes of Maharashtra*. New Delhi: Lalit Kala Akademi, 1988.

Daneel, Marthinus L. "African Independent Churches Face Challenge of Environmental Ethics." *Missionalia* 21, no. 3 (1993): 31–32.

———. "The Growth and Significance of Shona Independent Churches." In *Christianity South of the Zambezi*, vol. 2, ed. M. F. C. Bourdillon. Gwelo, Rhodesia: Mambo Press, 1977.

Davis, Mary, ed. *Native America in the Twentieth Century: An Encyclopedia*. New York: Garland Publishing, 1994.

Davis, Wade. "Death of a People: Logging in the Penan Homeland. " In *State of the Peoples: A Global Human Rights Report on Societies in Danger*, ed. Marc S. Miller. Boston: Beacon Press, 1993.

———. "Vanishing Cultures." *National Geographic* 196, no. 2 (1999): 64–76.

Day, David. *The Whale War*. San Francisco: Sierra Club Books, 1987.

de Certeau, Michel. *Heterologies: Discourse on the Other*. Minneapolis: University of Minnesota Press, 1986.

———. *The Practice of Everyday Life*. Berkeley and Los Angeles: University of California Press, 1984.

de los Reyes, Angelo J., and Aloma M. de los Reyes, eds. *Igorot: A People Who Daily Touch the Earth and the Sky*. Vol. 3, *Contemporary Life and Issues*. Baguio City: Cordillera Schools Group, 1987.

Deloria, Vine. *Denedeh: A Dene Celebration*. Toronto: McClelland and Stewart, 1984.

———. *For This Land: Writings on Religion in America*. New York: Routledge, 1999.

———. "If You Think About It, You Will See That It Is True." *Revision* 18, no. 3 (1996): 37–44.

———. "Sacred Lands: The Sanctity of Lands Is the Foundation of Individual and Group Dignity." *Winds of Change* 36 (autumn 1993).

Deloria, Vine, and Clifford M. Lytle. *The Nations Within: The Past and Future of American Indian Sovereignty*. New York: Pantheon, 1984.

Denevan, William M. "The Pristine Myth: The Landscape of the Americas in 1492." *Annals of the Association of American Geographers* 82 (1992): 369–85.

Descola, Philippe. "From Scattered to Nucleated Settlement: A Process of Socioeconomic Change among the Achuar." In *Cultural Transformations and Ethnicity in Modern Ecuador*, ed. Norman E. Whitten, Jr. Urbana: University of Illinois Press, 1981.

————. *The Spears of Twilight.* Trans. J. Lloyd. New York: New Press/ Harper Collins Publishers, 1996.

Dickason, Olive Patricia. *Canada's First Nations: A History of Founding Peoples from Earliest Times.* Toronto: McClelland and Stewart, 1992.

Dinham, Barbara, and Colin Hines. *Agribusiness in Africa.* London: Earth Resources, 1982.

Dobkin de Rios, Marlene, and Michael Winkelman. "Shamanism and Altered States of Consciousness: An Introduction." In *Shamanism and Altered States of Consciousness,* ed. Marlene Dobkin de Rios and Michael Winkelman. *Journal of Psychoactive Drugs* 21, no. 1 (1992).

Driben, Paul, and Donald J. Auger. *The Generation of Power and Fear: The Little Jackfish River Hydroelectric Project and the Whitesands Indian Band.* Research Report no. 3. Thunder Bay: Lakehead University Centre for Northern Studies, 1989.

Dudley, Michael Kioni. "Traditional Native Hawaiian Environmental Philosophy." In *Ethics, Religion and Biodiversity: Relations between Conservation and Cultural Values,* ed. Lawrence Hamilton. Cambridge: The White Horse Press, 1993.

Dudley, Michael Kioni, and Keoni Kealoha Agard. *Man, Gods, and Nature.* Honolulu: Na Kane o Ka Malo Press, 1990.

Duffy, R. Quinn. *The Road to Nunavut: The Progress of the Eastern Arctic Inuit since the Second World War.* Montreal: McGill-Queen's University Press, 1988.

Dumia, Manuel. *The Ifugao World.* Quezon City: New Day Publishers, 1979.

Dumont, James. "Journey To Daylight-land: Through Ojibwa Eyes." *Laurentian University Review* 8, no. 2 (1976).

Duncan, R. C. *Melanesian Forestry Sector Study.* Canberra: Centre for Development Studies, The Australian National University, 1996.

Durán, Fray Diego. *Historia de las Indias de Nueva España e Islas de Tierra Firme,* paleographic ed. of the Madrid manuscript, 1570–1579, with introduction, notes and vocabulary by Angel María Garibay K. 2 vols. México: Editorial Porrúa, 1967.

Durning, Alan. *Guardians of the Land: Indigenous Peoples and the Health of the Earth.* Washington, D.C.: Worldwatch, 1993.

Dye, Tom, and David Steadman. "Polynesian Ancestors and Their Animal World." *American Scientist* 78, no. 3 (1990): 207–15.

Edgerton, Robert. *Sick Societies: Challenging the Myth of Primitive Harmony.* New York: Free Press, 1992.

Edwards, J., and M. Palmers, eds. *Holy Ground: The Guide to Faith and Ecology.* Bilkington Press, 1997.

Egan, Kieran. *Teaching as Story Telling.* Chicago: University of Chicago Press, 1989.

Eichstaedt, Peter. *If You Poison Us: Uranium and Native Americans*. Santa Fe, N.Mex.: Red Crane, 1994.

Eisen, P. "ARCO Wins Second Exploration Block in Ecuador after Two-Year Wait." *Oil Daily* 48, no. 80 (1998).

Eisenhauer, J. H. "Nesting Ecology and Behavior of Pacific Brant in Alaska." B.S. thesis, University of Lethbridge, Alberta, 1977.

Elder, John, and Hertha D. Wong, eds. *Family of Earth and Sky: Indigenous Tales of Nature from around the World*. Boston: Beacon Press, 1994.

Eliade, Mircea. *The Sacred and the Profane: The Nature of Religion*. Trans. Willard R. Trask. New York: Harcourt, Brace, 1959.

Engel, Ronald. "Liberal Democracy and the Fate of the Earth." In *Spirit and Nature: Why the Environment Is a Religious Issue*, ed. Steven C. Rockfeller and John C. Elder, 59–82. Boston: Beacon Press, 1992.

Enloe, Cynthia. *The Politics of Pollution in Comparative Perspective: Ecology and Power in Four Nations*. New York: Longman, 1975.

Enthoven, R. E. *Tribes and Castes of Bombay*. Vol. 3. Bombay: Government Central Press, 1922.

Erdoes, Richard, and Alfonso Ortiz. *American Indian Myth and Legends*. New York: Pantheon Books, 1984.

Esber, George S., Jr. "Shortcomings of the Indian Self-Determination Policy." In *State and Reservation: New Perspectives on Federal Indian Policy*, ed. George Pierre Castile and Robert L. Bee, 212–23. Tucson: University of Arizona Press, 1992.

Escobar, Arturo. "After Nature: Steps to an Antiessentialist Political Ecology." *Current Anthropology* 40, no. 1 (1999): 1–30.

Esquillo, Ruth. "Community Action on Forest Preservation: The Case of San Fernando, Bukidnon." Thesis, Department of Sociology/Anthropology, Ateneo De Manilla University, 1992.

Esteva, Gustavo, and Madhu Sarin Prakash. *Grassroots Postmodernism: Beyond Global Thinking to Indigenous Knowledge*. London: Zed Books, 1998.

———. *Grassroots Postmodernism: Remaking the Soil of Cultures*. London: Zed Books, 1997.

Evatt, Elizabeth. *Review of the Aboriginal and Torres Strait Islander Heritage Protection Act 1984*. Canberra: Australian Government Publishing Service, 1996.

Evernden, Neil. *The Natural Alien: Humankind and the Environment*. Toronto: University of Toronto Press, 1993.

Faber, Daniel. *Environment under Fire: Imperialism and the Ecological Crisis in Central America*. New York: Monthly Review Press, 1993.

Fals-Borda, Orlando. "Social Movements and Political Power in Latin America." In *The Making of Social Movements in Latin America*, ed.

Arturo Escobar and Sonia Alvarez. Boulder, Colo.: Westview Press, 1992.

Faulstich, Paul. "Hawaiians Fight for the Rainforest." *Earth First!* 10, no. 5 (1990): 1, 7.

Fay, Chip, and Jim Barnes. "Mt. Apo Natives in Hot Water" *Earth First!* 10, no. 1 (1989): 9–10.

Feit, Harvey A. "Colonialism's Northern Cultures: Canadian Institutions and the James Bay Cree." In *On the Land: Confronting the Challenges to Aboriginal Self-Determination in Northern Quebec and Labrador*, ed. Bruce W. Hodgins and Kerri A. Cannon, 105–27. Toronto: Betelgeuse Books, 1995.

———. "The Construction of Algonquian Hunting Territories: Private Property as Moral Lesson, Policy Advocacy, and Ethnographic Error." In *Colonial Situations: Essays in the Contextualization of Ethnographic Knowledge. History of Anthropology,* vol. 7, ed. G. Stocking, Jr., 109–34. Madison: University of Wisconsin Press, 1991.

———. "Hunting and the Quest for Power: The James Bay Cree and Whitemen in the Twentieth Century." In *Native Peoples: The Canadian Experience,* 2d ed., ed. R. B. Morrison and C. R. Wilson, 181–223. Toronto: McClelland and Stewart, 1995.

Feld, Steven, and Keith H. Basso, eds. *Senses of Place.* Santa Fe, N.Mex.: School of American Research Press, 1996.

Fernandes, Walter. "Forests and Tribals: Informal Economy, Dependence and Management Traditions." In *Continuity and Change in Tribal Society,* ed. Mrinal Miri, 48–69. Shimla: Indian Institute of Advanced Study, 1993.

Fienup-Riordan, Ann. *Boundaries and Passages: Rule and Ritual in Central Yup'ik Oral Tradition.* Norman: University of Oklahoma Press, 1994.

———. *Eskimo Essays: Yup'ik Lives and How We See Them.* New Brunswick: Rutgers University Press, 1990.

———. *When Our Bad Season Comes: A Cultural Account of Subsistence Harvesting and Harvest Disruption on the Yukon Delta.* Monograph Series, 1. Aurora: Alaska Anthropological Association, 1986.

———. "Yazulget Qaillun Pilartat Nunaseng Ulerpagaaqan (What the Birds Do When Their Places are Flooded): Yup'ik Knowledge of Storm Surges and Goose Ecology." Bethel, Alaska: Association of Village Council Presidents, 1997.

Filer, Colin, ed. *The Political Economy of Forest Management in Papua New Guinea.* Monograph 32. Boroko, N.C.D.: National Research Institute of Papua New Guinea, 1997.

Fixico, Donald. *The Invasion of Indian Country in the Twentieth Century: American Capitalism and Tribal Natural Resources.* Niwot: University Press of Colorado, 1998.

Forbes, Jack. *Columbus and Other Cannibals.* Brooklyn: Autonomedia, 1992.

Ford, Daryll C. "A Creation Myth from Acoma." *Folk-Lore* 41 (1930): 359–87.

Forman, Charles. *The Island Churches of the South Pacific.* Maryknoll, N.Y.: Orbis Books, 1982.

Francis, Daniel. *The Imaginary Indian: The Image of the Indian in Canadian Culture.* Vancouver: Arsenal Pulp Press, 1993.

Francis, Daniel, and Toby Morantz. *Partners in Furs. A History of the Fur Trade in Eastern James Bay, 1600–1870.* Montreal: McGill-Queen's University Press, 1983.

Frantz, Klaus. *Indian Reservations in the United States.* Chicago: University of Chicago Press, 1999.

Freidel, David A., Linda Schele, and Joy Parker. *Maya Cosmos: Three Thousand Years on the Shaman's Path.* New York: Quill William Morrow, 1993.

Friedmann, John. *Empowerment: A Politics of Alternative Development.* Cambridge: Blackwell Publishers, 1992.

Friedmann, John, and Haripriya Rangan, eds. *In Defense of Livelihood: Comparative Studies in Environmental Action.* West Hartford, Conn.: Kumarian, 1993.

Gaba, C. *The Scriptures of an African People: Ritual Utterances of the Anlo.* New York: Nok Publishers, 1974.

Gadgil, Madhav, Fikret Berkes, and Carl Folke. "Indigenous Knowledge for Biodiversity Conservation." *Ambio* 22 (1993): 151–56.

Gadgil, Madhav, and Ramachandra Guha. *Ecology and Equity: The Use and Abuse of Nature in Contemporary India.* London: Routledge, 1995.

———. *This Fissured Land: An Ecological History of India.* Berkeley and Los Angeles: University of California Press, 1992.

García, Gregorio, Fray. *Origen de los Indios del Nuevo Mundo, 1607–1729.* Preliminary study by Franklin Pease G.Y. México: Fondo de Cultura Económica, 1981.

Garibay K., Angel María. *Teogonía e Historia de los Mexicanos: Tres Opúsculos del Siglo* XVI. México: Editorial Porrúa, 1965.

Gaspar, Karl. *A Peoples' Option to Struggle for Creation.* Quezon City: Claretian Publications, 1990.

Gedicks, Al. *The New Resource Wars: Native and Environmental Struggles against Multinational Corporations.* Boston: South End Press, 1993.

Gerstin, J. "No Permanent Condition: The Rainforests of Africa." In *Lessons of the Rainforest,* ed. Suzanne Head and Robert Heinzman. San Francisco: Sierra Club Books, 1990.

Geyshick, Ron, and Judith Doyle. *Te Bwe Win (Truth).* Toronto: Impulse Editions, Summerhill Press, 1989.

Giay, Benny. "Zakheus Pakage and His Communities: Indigenous Religious Discourse, Sociopolitical Resistance, and Ethnohistory of the Me of Irian Jaya." Ph.D. diss., Vrije Universiteit, Amsterdam, 1995.

Goetz, Delia, and Sylvanus Morley. *Popol Vuh: The Sacred Book of the Ancient Quiche Maya*. Norman: University of Oklahoma Press, 1983.

Goffman, Erving. *Frame Analysis: An Essay on the Organization of Experience*. Boston: Northeastern University Press, 1986.

Gomez-Pompa, Arturo, and Andrea Kaus. "Taming the Wilderness Myth." *Bioscience* 42, no. 4 (1992): 271–79.

Goodenough, Erwin. *The Psychology of Religious Experiences*. New York: Basic Books, 1965.

Gordon, Greg. "Huanorani Fight Oil Companies." *Earth First!* 7, no. 1 (1991): 8.

Gossen, Gary, ed. *Symbol and Meaning beyond the Closed Community: Essays in Mesoamerican Ideas*. Studies on Culture and Society, 1. New York: Institute for Mesoamerican Studies, The University at Albany, State University of New York, 1986.

Gottlieb, Roger. *This Sacred Earth: Religion, Nature, Environment*. New York: Routledge, 1996.

Gough, Robert P. W. "A Cultural-Historical Assessment of the Wild Rice Resources of the Sokaogon Chippewa." An Analysis of the Socio-Economic and Environmental Impacts of Mining and Mineral Resource Development on the Sokaogon Chippewa Community. Madison, Wis.: COACT Research, Inc., 1980.

Government of India. *The National Forest Policy*. New Delhi: Government of India, 1988.

———. *Report of the Bombay Forest Commission 1887*. Vols. 1–4. Government Central Press, 1887.

Grand Council of the Cree (of Quebec). *Fighting for Our Future*. Broadsheet newspaper, 8 pages, Supplement to the *Hill Times*, 1 August 1991.

Greaves, Tom, ed. *Intellectual Property Rights for Indigenous Peoples: A Sourcebook*. Oklahoma City: Society for Applied Anthropology, 1994.

Greenhouse, Linda. "Court Denies Indian Authority in Alaska Case." *New York Times*, 26 February 1998, A16.

Grillo Fernandez, Eduardo. "Sabiduria Andino-Amazonica y Conocimiento Cientifico." *Revista Peruana de Epidemiologia* 7, no. 2 (1994): 34–35.

Grim, John A. "Cultural Identity, Authenticity, and Community Survival: The Politics of Recognition in the Study of Native American Religions." *American Indian Quarterly* 20, no. 3 (summer 1996): 353.

Grinde, Donald A., Jr., and Bruce E. Johansen. *Ecocide of Native America: Environmental Destruction of Indian Lands and Peoples*. Santa Fe, N.Mex.: Clear Light Publishers, 1995.

Grumbine, Edward. *Ghost Bears: Exploring the Biodiversity Crisis.* Washington, D.C.: Island Press, 1992.

Guha, Ramachandra. "Forestry Debate and Draft Forest Act: Who Gains, Who Loses?" *Economic and Political Weekly,* 20 August 1994.

———. *The Unquiet Woods: Ecological Change and Peasant Resistance in the Himalaya.* Berkeley and Los Angeles: University of California Press, 1989.

Guha, Ramachandra, and Juan Martinez-Alier. *Varieties of Environmentalism: Essays North and South.* London: Earthscan, 1997.

Guthrie, Daniel. "Primitive Man's Relationship to Nature." *Bioscience* 21 (1971).

Hadjor, Kofi Buenor. *Africa in an Era of Crisis.* Trenton, N.J.: African World Press, 1990.

Hallman, David G. *Ecotheology: Voices from South and North.* Maryknoll, N.Y.: Orbis Books, 1994.

Hallowell, Alfred Irving. *Contributions to Anthropology: Selected Papers of A. Irving Hallowell.* Chicago: University of Chicago Press, 1976.

Hallowell, Alfred Irving, and Jennifer S. H. Brown. *The Ojibwa of Berens River, Manitoba: Ethnography into History.* Fort Worth: Harcourt Brace Jovanovich College Publishers, 1992.

———. "Ojibwa Ontology: Behavior and World View." In *Culture in History,* ed. Stanley Diamond. New York: Columbia University Press, 1960.

Hamilton, Lawrence S., ed. *Ethics, Religion and Biodiversity: Relations between Conservation and Cultural Values.* Cambridge: The White Horse Press, 1993.

Hanbury-Tension, Robin. "No Surrender in Sarawak." *New Scientist,* 1 December 1990.

Hanratty, Dennis Michael. *Ecuador: A Country Study.* Washington, D.C.: Federal Research Division, Library of Congress, 1991.

Haraway, Donna. *Primate Visions: Gender, Race and Nature in the World of Modern Science.* London: Routledge, 1989.

Hardiman, David. *Peasant Resistance in India: 1858–1914.* Oxford: Oxford University Press, 1992.

———. "Power in the Forest: The Dangs, 1820–1940." In *Subaltern Studies,* vol. 7, ed. D. Arnold et al. Delhi: Oxford University Press, 1994.

Harner, Michael. *Hallucinogens and Shamanism.* New York: Oxford University Press, 1973.

———. *The Jívaro: People of the Sacred Waterfalls.* Garden City, N.Y.: Doubleday/Natural History Press, 1972.

Harris, Marvin. *The Nature of Cultural Things.* New York: Random House, 1964.

Harrison, Paul. *The Greening of Africa.* London: Penguin, 1987.

Harrison, Robert Pogue. *Forests: The Shadow of Civilization*. Chicago: University of Chicago Press, 1992.

Harrisson, Tom. "Notes on some Nomadic Punans." *Sarawak Museum Journal* 5, no. 1 (1949): 130–46.

Harvey, David. *Justice, Nature and the Geography of Difference*. London: Blackwell Publishers, 1996.

Hawthorne, Harry Bertram, ed. *A Survey of the Contemporary Indians of Canada*. Ottawa: Department of Indian Affairs and Northern Development, 1967.

Hay, P. R. "Vandals at the Gate: The Tasmanian Greens and the Perils of Sharing Power." In *Green Politics Two*, ed. Wolfgang Rüdig, 86–110. Edinburgh: Edinburgh University Press, 1992.

Headland, Thomas. "Revisionism in Ecological Anthropology." *Current Anthropology* 38, no. 4 (1997): 605–30.

Hecht, Susanna B., and Alexander Cockburn. *Fate of the Forest: Developers, Destroyers and Defenders of the Amazon*. London: Verso, 1989.

Hedge, Pandurang. "The Appiko Movement: Forest Conservation in Southern India." *Cultural Survival Quarterly* 13, no. 2 (1989): 29–30.

Heinen, H. Dieter. "El abandono de un ecosistema: el caso de los morichales del Delta del Orinoco." *Antropológica* 81 (1994-1996): 3–36.

———. "The Early Colonization of the Lower Orinoco and Its Impact on Present-Day Indigenous Peoples." *Antropológica* 78 (1992): 51–86.

Heinen, H. Dieter, Jose San Jose, Hortensia Caballero Arias, and Ruben Montes. "Subsistence Activities of the Warao Indians and Anthropogenic Changes in the Orinoco Delta Vegetation." *Scientia Guaianae* 5 (1995): 312–34.

Henare, Manuka, and Bernard Kemot. "Maori Religion: The Spiritual Landscape." In *Can Humanity Survive? The World's Religions and the Environment*, ed. James Veitch, 205–15. Auckland: Awareness Book Co., 1996.

Hendricks, Janet Wall. *To Drink of Death: The Narrative of a Shuar Warrior*. Tucson: University of Arizona Press, 1993.

———. "Symbolic Counterhegemony among the Ecuadorian Shuar." In *Nation States and Indians in Latin America*, ed. Joel Sherzer and Greg Urban. Austin: University of Texas Press, 1991.

Hernandez, Raymond. "In a Shift, State Won't Try to Tax Sales on Indian Reservations." *New York Times*, 23 May 1997, A27.

Heyden, Doris. *The Eagle, the Cactus, the Rock: The Roots of Mexico—Tenochtitlan's Foundation Myth and Symbol*. BAR International Series, 484. Oxford: B.A.R., 1989.

Hiebert, P. G. *Anthropological Insights for Missionaries*. Grand Rapids, Mich.: Baker Books, 1985.

688 — *Indigenous Traditions and Ecology*

Hill, Norbert, ed. "Words of Power: Voices from Indian America." In *American Indian Science and Engineering Society*. Golden, Colo.: Fulcrum Publishing, 1994.

Hinga, Teresia. "The Gikuyu Theology of Land and Environmental Justice." In *Women Healing Earth: Third World Women on Ecology, Feminism, and Religion*, ed. Rosemary Radford Ruether. Maryknoll, N.Y.: Orbis Books, 1996.

Hirsch, Philip, and Larry Lohmann. "The Contemporary Politics of Environment in Thailand." *Asian Survey* 29, no. 4 (1989): 439–51.

Hitchcock, Robert K., and John D. Holm. "Bureaucratic Domination of Hunter-Gatherer Societies: A Study of the San in Botswana." *Development and Change* 24, no. 2 (1993): 305–38.

Hobson, Geary, ed. *The Remembered Earth*. Albuquerque: Red Earth Press, 1979.

Hornborg, Alf. "Environmentalism, Ethnicity and Sacred Places: Reflections on Modernity, Discourse and Power." *Canadian Review of Sociology and Anthropology* 31, no. 3 (1994): 245–67.

Horton, Robin. "The Kalabari Worldview: An Outline and Interpretation." *Africa* 32, no. 3 (1962): 197–220.

———. *The Patterns of Thought in Africa and the West*. New York: Cambridge University Press, 1993.

House, Freeman. *Totem Salmon: Life Lessons from Another Species*. Boston: Beacon Press, 1999.

Huehne, W. H. "A Doctor among 'Nomadic' Punans." *Sarawak Museum Journal* 9, no. 13-14 (1959): 195–202.

Hughes, J. Donald. *American Indian Ecology*. El Paso: Texas Western Press, 1983.

Hultkrantz, Åke. *Native Religions of North America*. New York: Harper and Row, 1987.

———. "Ecology." In *The Encyclopedia of Religion*, ed. Mircea Eliade, 4: 581–85. New York: Macmillan, 1987.

Hurst, Philip. *Rainforest Politics: Ecological Destruction in South East Asia*. London: Zed Books, 1990.

Hurtado, Osvaldo. *Political Power in Ecuador*. Trans. N. D. Mills, Jr. Boulder, Colo.: Westview Press, 1985.

Hyman, Jacqueline. "Conflicting Perceptions of Exchange in Indian-Missionary Contact." M.A. thesis, McGill University, Department of Anthropology, 1971.

Ilogu, Edmund. "The Land is Sacred." In *Traditional Religion in West Africa*, ed. E. A. Adegbola. Ibadan: Daystan Press, 1983.

Indigenous Environmental Network. Web site: www.ienearth.org.

Inglis, Julian T., ed. *Concepts and Cases: Traditional Ecological Knowl-*

edge. Ottawa: International Program on Traditional Ecological Knowledge, Canadian Museum of Nature, 1993.

Innis, Harold. *The Fur Trade in Canada*. Toronto: University of Toronto Press, 1970.

Inter Press Service. *Story Earth: Native Voices on the Environment*. San Francisco: Mercury House, 1993.

International Treaty Council. "International NGO Conference on Discrimination against Indigenous Populations in the Americas." In *Treaty Council News* 1, no. 7 (1977).

Irwin, James. *An Introduction to Maori Religion*. Special Studies in Religions, 4. Bedford Park, South Australia: Australian Association for the Study of Religions, 1984.

Iyam, David Uru. *The Broken Hoe: Cultural Reconfiguration in Biase, Southern Nigeria*. Chicago: University of Chicago Press, 1995.

Jaakko Poyry Oy. *Thai Forestry Sector Master Plan*. 6 Vols. Helsinki: Finnish International Development Agency, Ministry for Foreign Affairs, 1993.

Jackson, Michael. *Barawa and the Ways Birds Fly in the Sky*. Washington, D.C.: Smithsonian Institute Press, 1986.

Jacobs, Jane. "Earth Honoring: Western Desires and Indigenous Knowledges." In *Writing Women and Space: Colonial and Postcolonial Geographies*, ed. Alison Blunt and Gilliam Rose. New York: Guilford Press, 1994.

Jaimes, M. Annette, ed. *The State of Native America*. Boston: South End Press, 1992.

Jenness, Diamond. *The Indians of Canada*. National Museum of Canada Bulletin, 65. Ottawa: F. A. Acland, 1932.

Jochnick, Chris. "Amazon Oil Offensive." *Multinational Monitor* 16, no. 1-2 (1995): 12–16.

Johansen, J. Prytz. *Studies in Maori Rites and Myths*. Copenhagen: Ejnar Mungksgaard, 1958.

Johnson, Elliott. *Royal Commission into Aboriginal Deaths in Custody. National Report: Overview and Recommendations*. Canberra: Australian Government Publishing Service, 1991.

Johnson, M. "Documenting Dene Traditional Ecological Knowledge." *Akwe:kon Journal*, summer 1992, 72–79.

———. *Lore: Capturing Traditional Environmental Knowledge*. Hay River: Dene Cultural Institute/IDRC, 1992.

Johnson, Trebbe. "The Four Sacred Mountains of the Navajos." *Parabola* 13, no. 4 (1988): 40–47.

Jonaitis, Aldona, ed. *Chiefly Feasts: The Enduring Kwakiutl Potlatch*. Seattle: University of Washington Press; New York: American Museum of Natural History, 1991.

Juma, Calestous. *Biological Diversity and Innovation: Conserving and Utilizing Genetic Resources in Kenya.* Nairobi: African Centre for Technology Studies, 1989.

————, and J. B. Ojwang, eds. *Innovation and Sovereignty: The Patent Debate in African Development.* Nairobi: African Centre for Technology Studies, 1989.

Kaho'olawe Island Conveyance Commission. *Kaho'olawe Island: Restoring a Cultural Treasure. Final Report of the Kaho'olawe Island Conveyance Commission to the Congress of the United States.* Wailuku, Hawaii: The Commission, 1993.

Kalu, Ogbu. *The Embattled Gods: Christianization of Igboland, 1841–1991.* Lagos and London: Minaj Publishers, 1996.

Kalyalya, Denny, et al., eds. *Aid and Development in Southern Africa: Evaluating a Participatory Learning Process.* Trenton, N.J.: Africa World Press, 1988.

Kamma, Freerk Ch. *Koreri: Messianic Movements in the Biak-Numfor Culture Area.* 's-Gravenhage: Martinus Nijhoff, 1972.

Kampen, M. E. *The Religion of the Maya.* Iconography of Religions, section 11, fasc. 4. Leiden: Brill, 1981.

Kane, Joe. *Savages.* New York: Random House, 1995.

Kanner, Allen. "Romancing the Stone Age." *Ecopsychology Newsletter* (Ecopsychology Institute, California State University-Hayward), no. 3 (1994).

Kanogo, Tabitha M. *Squatters and Roots of Mau Mau.* London: James Currey, 1987.

Kawharu, Ian Hugh. "Land as Turangaweewae: Ngati Whatua's Destiny at Orakei." In *He Matapuna: Some Maori Perspectives.* Wellington: New Zealand Planning Council, 1979.

Kedit, Peter M. "An Ecological Survey of the Penan." *Sarawak Museum Journal* (special issue no. 2) 30, no. 51 (1982): 225–79.

————. *Gunong Mulu Report: A Human-Ecological Survey of Nomadic/ Settled Penan within the Gunong Mulu National Park Area, Fourth/ Fifth Division, Sarawak.* Sarawak Museum Field Report Series, no. 1. Kuching: Sarawak Museum, 1978.

Keesing, Roger M. *Custom and Confrontation. The Kwaio Struggle for Cultural Autonomy.* Chicago: University of Chicago Press, 1992.

————. "Rethinking Mana." *Journal of Anthropological Research* 40 (1984): 137–56.

Keith, Robert F., and Alan Saunders, eds. *A Question of Rights. Northern Wildlife Management and the Anti-Harvest Movement—National Symposium on the North.* Ottawa: Canadian Arctic Resources Committee, 1989.

Kenny, Chris. *It Would Be Nice If There Was Some Women's Business*. Potts Point: Duffy and Snellgrove, 1996.

Kensinger, Kenneth. "The Body Knows: Cashinahua Perspectives on Knowledge." *Acta Americana* 1, no. 2 (1994): 7–14.

King, Larson. "It's No Wonder Black Brant are Gone." *Tundra Drums* (Bethel, Alaska), 5 December 1996, A4.

King, Victor. *The Peoples of Borneo*. Oxford: Blackwell Publishers, 1993.

Kinsley, David. *Ecology and Religion: Ecological Spirituality in Cross-Cultural Perspective*. Englewood Cliffs, N.J.: Prentice Hall, 1995.

Kirby, Andrew. *Power/Resistance: Local Politics and the Chaotic State*. Bloomington: Indiana University Press, 1993.

Klasky, Philip M. "Environmental Justice and the Proposed Ward Valley Nuclear Waste Dump." *Report to the Environmental Protection Agency*, Region 9, no. 4. San Francisco: BAN Waste Coalition, 1998.

Klee, Gary. *World Systems of Traditional Resource Management*. New York: John Wiley and Sons, 1980.

Klein, Cecelia. *The Face of the Earth: Frontality in Two-Dimensional Mesoamerican Art*. New York: Garland Publications, 1976.

Kloos, Helmut. "Development, Drought, and Famine in the Awash Valley of Ethiopia." *African Studies Review* 25, no. 4 (1982): 21–48.

Kloppenburg, Jack, et al. "Coming into the Foodshed." In *Rooted in the Land: Essays in Community and Place*, ed. William Vitek and Wes Jackson. New Haven: Yale University Press, 1997.

Kocherry, Thomas, and Thankappan Achary. "Fishing for Resources: Indian Fisheries in Danger." *Cultural Survival Quarterly* 13, no. 2 (1989): 31–33.

Korp, Maureen. "Before Mother Earth: The American Indian Earth Mound." *Studies in Religion/ Sciences Religieuses* 19, no. 1 (1990): 17–25.

Kothari, Rajni. *Rethinking Development: In Search of Humane Governance*. Delhi: Ajanta Publications, 1990.

Kothari, Smitu. "On Displacement." *Economic and Political Weekly*, 15 June 1996.

LaChapelle, Dolores. *Earth Wisdom*. Silverton, Colo.: Finn Hill Arts, 1978.

———. *Sacred Land, Sacred Sex: Rapture of the Deep*. Silverton, Colo.: Kivakf Press, 1992.

LaDuke, Winona. *All Our Relations: Native Struggles for Land and Life*. Cambridge, Mass.: South End Press, 1999.

———. "Hydro Quebec Fears Cree Activists." *Earth First!* 13, no. 7 (1993).

———. "Indigenous Environmental Perspectives: A North American Primer." *Akwe:kon Journal* 9, no. 2 (1992): 52–70.

———. "Native Environmentalism." *Cultural Survival Quarterly* 17, no. 4 (1994).

————. "Traditional Ecological Knowledge and Environmental Futures." In *Endangered Peoples: Indigenous Rights and the Environment*. Niwot: University Press of Colorado. Special issue of *Colorado Journal of International Environmental Law and Policy* 5 (1994).

Lame Deer, John (Fire), and Richard Erdoes. *Lame Deer: Seeker of Visions*. New York: Washington Square Press, 1972.

Lang, Julian. "The Basket and World Renewal." *Parabola* 16, no. 3 (1991): 82–85.

Langub, Jayl. "Background Report on Potential for Agricultural and Social Extension Service in the Penan Community of Belaga District." *Sarawak Gazette* 100, no. 1395 (1974): 93–96.

————. "A Journey through the Nomadic Penan Country." *Sarawak Gazette* 117, no. 1514 (1990): 5–27.

————. "Some Aspects of Life of the Penan." *Sarawak Museum Journal* (special issue no. 4, pt. 3) 40, no. 61 (1989): 169–84.

Lawrence, Peter. *Road Belong Cargo: A Study of the Cargo Movement in the Southern Madang District, New Guinea*. Melbourne: Melbourne University Press, 1964.

Lensink, C. J. *Numbers of Black Brant Nesting on the Yukon-Kuskokwim Delta Have Declined More than 60 Percent*. Information Bulletin, U.S. Fish and Wildlife Service Res., 1987, 87–126.

Leopold, Aldo. *A Sand Country Almanac and Sketches Here and There*. London: Oxford University Press, 1949.

Leskien, Dan, and Michael Flitner. "Intellectual Property Rights and Plant Genetic Resources: Options for a *Sui Generis* System." *Issues in Genetic Resources* (Rome: International Plant Genetic Resources Institute), 6 (1997).

Linden, Eugene. "Lost Tribes, Lost Knowledge." *Time Magazine,* 23 September 1991.

Liswanso, Mufalo, ed. *Voices of Zambia*. Lusaka: NECZam Press, 1971.

Livingstone, L. *Poverty in Africa*. New York: Oxford University Press, 1988.

Lockhead, James. "The Sarawak Campaign: Perspectives for Discussion." *Earth First!* 13, no. 1 (1992): 18.

Lohmann, Larry. "Green Orientalism." *Ecologist* 23, no. 6 (1993): 202–4.

————. "Land, Power and Forest Colonization in Thailand." In *The Struggle for Land and the Fate of the Forests*, ed. Marcus Colchester and Larry Lohmann. London: Zed Books, 1993.

————. "Peasants, Plantations and Pulp: The Politics of Eucalyptus in Thailand." *Bulletin of Concerned Asian Scholars* 23, no. 4 (1991): 3–17.

————. "Visitors to the Commons: Approaching Thailand's 'Environmental' Struggles from a Western Starting Point." In *Ecological Resistance Movements: The Global Emergence of Radical and Popular Environ-*

mentalism, ed. Bron Raymond Taylor. Albany: State University of New York Press, 1995.

Luangaramsri, Pinkaew, and Noel Rajesh, eds. *The Future of People and Forests in Thailand after the Logging Ban.* Bangkok: Project for Ecological Recovery, 1992.

Luhrmann, T. "The Resurgence of Romanticism: Contemporary Neopaganism, Feminist Spirituality and the Divinity of Nature." In *Environmentalism: The View from Anthropology,* ed. Kay Milton, 219–32. London: Routledge, 1993.

Lyons, Oren. "Our Mother Earth." *Parabola* 6, no. 1 (1981): 91–93.

MacGregor, Roy. *Chief: The Fearless Vison of Billy Diamond.* Markham: Viking Penguin, 1989.

Maddox, Marion. "Sticks and Stones: Religious Freedom, State Neutrality and Indigenous Heritage Protection." In *Proceedings of the Australian Political Studies Association,* ed. George Crowder. Adelaide: Department of Politics, Flinders University of South Australia, 1997.

Mainwaring, Scott. *The Catholic Church and Politics in Brazil, 1916–1985.* Stanford: Stanford University Press, 1986.

Malinowski, Bronislaw. *Coral Gardens and Their Magic.* London: Allen and Unwin, 1935.

Maller, Peter. "Mole Lake Expect Allies in Mine Fight." *Milwaukee Sentinel,* 16 June 1994.

Malville, J. McKim, and Claudia Putnam. *Prehistoric Astronomy in the Southwest.* Boulder, Colo.: Johnson Books, 1991.

Mander, Jerry. *In the Absence of the Sacred.* San Francisco: Sierra Club Books, 1991.

———, and Edward Goldsmith, eds. *The Case against the Global Economy.* San Francisco: Sierra Club Books, 1989.

Marcus, Joyce, and Kent Flannery. *Zapotec Civilization: How Urban Society Evolved in Mexico's Oaxaca Valley.* London: Thames and Hudson, 1996.

Martin, Calvin. *Keepers of the Game: Indian-Animal Relationships and the Fur Trade.* Berkeley and Los Angeles: University of California Press, 1978.

Martin, E. "The Last Mountain." *American Forests,* March-April 1993, 44–54.

Masty, David, Sr. "Traditional Use of Fish and Other Resources of the Great Whale River Region." *Northeast Indian Quarterly* 8, no. 4 (1991).

Mathews, John Joseph. *Talking to the Moon.* Norman: University of Oklahoma Press, 1945.

Mato, Daniel. "The Indigenous Uprising in Chiapas: The Politics of Institutionalized Knowledge and Mexican Perspectives." *Identities* 3, no. 1-2 (1996): 205–18.

Matowanyika, Joseph Zano Z. "Resource Management and the Shona People in Rural Zimbabwe." In *Indigenous Peoples and Sustainability: Cases and Actions*, ed. Darrell Addison Posey and Graham Dutfield, 257–66. Utrecht: IUCN and International Books, 1997.

Matthews, Washington. *Navajo Legends*. Boston: American Folklore Society, 1897.

Matthiessen, Peter. "Native Earth." *Parabola* 6, no. 1 (1981): 6–17.

Maull, Samuel. "Ecuadorian Tribes Sue Texaco, Inc." *News from Indian Country* 7, no. 22 (1993).

Maybury-Lewis, David. *Indigenous Peoples, Ethnic Groups, and the State.* Cultural Survival Studies in Ethnicity and Change. Boston: Allyn and Bacon, 1997.

Mbilinyi, Marjorie. "Structural Adjustment, Agri-Business and Rural Women in Tanzania." In *The Food Question: Profits versus People?* ed. Henry Bernstein, B. Crow, M. Mackintosh, and C. Martin, 111–24. London: Earthscan, 1990.

Mbiti, John. *Introduction to African Religion*. New York: Heinemann, 1991.

McCloskey, David. "Watershed Democracy." Draft. Seattle: Cascadia Institute, 1998.

McCloud, William Christie. "Conservation among Primitive Hunting Peoples." *Scientific Monthly* 43 (1939).

McCutcheon, Sean. *Electric Rivers: The Story of the James Bay Project.* Montreal: Black Rose, 1991.

McGaa, Ed (Eagle Man). *Mother Earth Spirituality: Native American Paths to Healing Ourselves and Our World.* Toronto: Harper, 1990.

McGee, Jon. *Life, Ritual, and Religion among the Lacandon Maya.* Belmont, Calif.: Wadsworth Publishing Company, 1990.

McNeil, Donald G., Jr. "In Bushmanland, Hunters' Tradition Turns to Dust." *New York Times* 13 November 1997, A3.

McNeley, James K. *Holy Wind in Navajo Philosophy.* Tucson: University of Arizona Press, 1981.

McPherson, Dennis H., and J. Douglas Rabb. *Indian from the Inside: A Study in Ethno-Metaphysics.* Thunder Bay, Ontario: Lakehead University, 1993.

McPherson, Robert. *Sacred Land, Sacred View: Navajo Perceptions of the Four Corners Region.* Provo, Utah: Brigham Young University, Charles Redd Center for Western Studies, 1992.

Mead, Greg. *A Royal Omission: A Critical Summary of the Evidence Given to the Hindmarsh Island Royal Commission with an Alternative Report.* Adelaide: Greg Mead, 1995.

Mehra, J. D. "A Worldview of Indian Tribes." In *Tribal Heritage of India*, ed. Shyama Charan Dube. New Delhi: Vikas Publishing House, 1977.

Mehra, O. P. "Foreword." In *The Tribes in Maharashtra*, ed. G. M. Gare and M. B. Aphale. Pune: Tribal Research Institute, 1968.

Melmer, David. "The Decision: U.S. Supreme Court Rules in Favor of States' Rights." *Indian Country Today*, 4 April 1996, A1, A2.

Melone, Michelle A. "The Struggle of the Seringueiros: Environmental Action in the Amazon." In *In Defense of Livelihood*, ed. John Friedmann and Haripriya Rangan, 106–26. West Hartford, Conn.: Kumarian, 1993.

Melucci, Alberto. *Nomads of the Present*. Philadelphia: Temple University Press, 1989.

Menchu, Rigoberta, and Elizabeth DeBray. *Rigoberta Menchu: An Indian Woman in Guatemala*. New York: Verso, 1996.

Merchant, Carolyn. *The Death of Nature: Women, Ecology and the Scientific Revolution*. London: Wildwood House, 1982.

Miyoshi, Masao. "Sites of Resistance in Global Economy." *Boundary 2* 22, no. 1 (1991): 61–84.

Molutsi, Patrick. "Environment and Peasant Consciousness in Botswana." *Review of African Political Economy* 42 (1988): 40–47.

Momaday, N. Scott. "A First American Views His Land." *National Geographic* 150, no. 1 (1976).

———. "The Man Made of Words." In *Indian Voices: The First Convocation of American Indian Scholars*, ed. Rupert Costo. San Francisco: Indian Historian Press, 1970.

Monbiot, George. "Brazil: Land Ownership and the Flight to Amazonia." In *The Struggle for Land and the Fate of the Forests*, ed. Marcus Colchester and Larry Lohmann. Penang, Malaysia: World Rainforest Movement, 1993.

Monet, Don, and Skanu'u (Ardythe Wilson). *Colonialism on Trial: Indigenous Land Rights and the Gitksan and Wet'suwet'en Sovereignty Case*. Philadelphia: New Society Publishers, 1992.

Montejo, Victor. "In the Name of the Pot, the Sun, the Broken Spear, the Rock, the Idol, ad infinitum and ad nauseum: An Exposé of Anglo Anthropologists Obsessions with and Invention of Mayan Gods." *Wicazo SA Review* 9, no. 1 (1993).

Moquin, Wayne, and Charles Van Doren, eds. *Great Documents in American Indian History*. New York: Praeger Publishers, 1973.

Morrison, Alvin H. "The Spirit of the Law versus the Storm Spirit: A Wabanaki Case." In *Papers of the Thirteenth Algonquian Conference*, ed. W. Cowan. Ottawa: Carleton University, 1982.

Morrow, David J. "Making Good on the Great Alaskan Windfall." *New York Times* 15 November 1996, D1.

Morse, Bradford W. *Aboriginal Peoples and the Law: Indian, Metis and Inuit Rights in Canada*. Ottawa: Carleton University Press, 1985.

Morse, Bradford W., and Thomas R. Berger. *Sardar Sarovar: Report of the Independent Review*. Ottawa: Resources Future International, Inc., 1992.

Moser, Irene, and Vandana Shiva, eds. *Biopolitics: A Feminist and Ecological Reader on Biotechnology*. London: Zed Books, 1995.

Mowat, Farley. *Rescue the Earth! Conversations with the Green Crusaders*. Toronto: McClelland and Stewart, 1990.

Moyo, S., et al. *The Southern African Environment: Profiles of the SADC Countries*. London: Earthscan, 1993.

Munda, Ram Dayal. "Tribal Autonomy Question in India: Lessons from Jharkhand." Draft. Syracuse, N.Y.: Syracuse University, 1995.

Murton, Brian. "South Asia." In *World Systems of Traditional Resource Management*, ed. Gary Klee. New York: Halsted Press Books, 1980.

Myerhoff, Barbara G. *Peyote Hunt*. Ithaca: Cornell University Press, 1974.

Myers, Norman. *The Primary Source: Tropical Forests and Our Future*. New York: W. W. Norton, 1992.

―――. "Threatened Biotas: 'Hotspots' in Tropical Forests." *Environmentalist* 8, no. 3 (1988).

Nabhan, Gary Paul. *Cultures of Habitat: On Nature, Culture, and Story*. Washington, D.C.: Counterpoint, 1997.

―――. *Enduring Seeds: Native American Agriculture and Wild Plant Conservation*. Berkeley, Calif.: North Point Press, 1996.

Nabokov, Peter, and Margaret MacLean. "Ways of Indian Running." *CoEvolution* 26 (summer 1980).

Nandy, Ashis. "Shamans, Savages, and the Wilderness: On the Audibility of Dissent and the Future of Civilizations." *Alternatives* 14 (1989): 263–77.

Nash, June. "The Reassertion of Indigenous Identity: Mayan Responses to State Intervention in Chiapas." *Latin American Research Review*, 1994, 7–39.

National Research Council. *Lost Crops of the Incas: Little-Known Plants of the Andes with Promise for Worldwide Cultivation*. Washington, D.C.: National Academy Press, 1989.

Needham, Rodney. "Penan and Punan." *Journal of the Malayan Branch, Royal Asiatic Society* 27, no. 1 (1954): 73–83.

―――. "Punan-Penan." In *Ethnic Groups of Insular Southeast Asia*. Vol. 1, *Indonesia, Andaman Islands, and Madagascar*, ed. Frank M. Lebar. New Haven, Conn.: Human Relations Area Files Press, 1972.

Neihardt, John G. *Black Elk Speaks*. New York: Pocket Books, 1972.

Nelson, Melissa. "Ecopsychology in Theory and Practice." *Alexandria: Journal of the Western Cosmological Traditions*. Grand Rapids, Mich.: Phranes Press, 1995.

Nelson, Richard K. *Make Prayers to the Raven: A Koyukon View of the Northern Forest*. Chicago: University of Chicago Press, 1983.

Ngidio, Robert. "Conserving Biodiversity: The Case of the Ifugao Farming System." *People, Earth and Culture.* Los Banos: Philippine Council for Agriculture, Forestry and Natural Resources Research and Development, and National Commission for Arts and Culture, 1998.

Nicolaisen, Johannes. "The Penan of Sarawak: Further Notes on the Neo-Evolutionary Concept of Hunters." *Folk* 18 (1976): 205–36.

———. "The Penan of the Seventh Division of Sarawak: Past, Present and Future." *Sarawak Museum Journal* 24, no. 45 (1976): 35–61.

Nies, Judith. "The Black Mesa Syndrome: Indian Lands, Black Gold." *Orion Magazine* 17, no. 3 (1999): 21.

Nollman, Jim. *Spiritual Ecology.* New York: Bantam Books, 1990.

North American Congress on Latin America. "Ecuador: Oil Up for Grabs." *NACLA's Latin America and Empire Report* 9, no. 8 (1975).

Northern Land Council. *Ecopolitics IX: Perspectives on Indigenous Peoples' Management of Environmental Resources.* Casuarina: Northern Land Council, 1996.

Obadina, Elizabeth. "Ageing." *New Internationalist* 264 (1995): 16–17.

Obiechin, Emmanuel. *Culture, Tradtion and Society in West African Novels.* Cambridge: Cambridge University Press, 1975.

Ojo, G. J. Afolabi. *Yoruba Culture: A Geographical Analysis.* London: University of London Press, 1966.

Ole Parkipuny, M. S. "The Ngorongoro Crater Issue: The Point of View of the Indigenous Maasai Community of Ngorongoro." In *Paper for the International Congress on Nature Management and Sustainable Development,* 6–9 December. Groningen, the Netherlands: University of Groningen, 1988.

Olsen, Dale A. *Music of the Warao of Venezuela: Song People of the Rain Forest.* Gainesville: University Press of Florida, 1996.

Olson, Paul A., ed. *The Struggle for the Land: Indigenous Insight and Industrial Empire in the Semiarid World.* Lincoln: University of Nebraska Press, 1990.

Olupona Jacob. *Kingship, Religion, and Rituals in a Nigerian Community.* Stockholm: Almqvist and Wiksell International, 1991.

Omengan, Elizabeth, and F. Dumondon. "Holok: Forest Plants, Rice Pests and Ifugao Gods." Montanosa Research and Development Center Occasional Papers. Sagada: MRDC, July 1989.

Omvedt, Gail. *Reinventing Revolution: New Social Movements and the Socialist Tradtion in India.* New York: M. E. Sharpe, 1993.

OPIP. "Declaration of the Quichua and Shuar Nations before the Government, ARCO, and International Opinion." *Voz de la CONFENIAE* 10, no. 2 (1994): 5.

Opoku, K. A. *West African Traditional Religion.* Lagos: FEP International Pvt., 1978.

Orbell, Margaret. *The Natural World of the Maori*. Auckland: Collins, in association with David Bateman, 1985.

Ortiz, Alfonso. *The Tewa World*. Chicago: University of Chicago Press, 1969.

Ottenberg, Simon. *Leadership and Authority in an African Society*. Seattle: University of Washington Press, 1971.

Overholt, Thomas W., and J. Baird Callicott. *Clothed-in-Fur and Other Tales: An Introduction to an Ojibwa World View*. Lanham, Md.: University Press of America, 1982.

Pachamama Alliance. Web site <http://www.pachamama.org/> (cited 24 September 1999).

———. "Santiago's Message: State of the World Forum, 28 October 1998." <http://www.pachamama.org/updates/santiago_message.htm> (cited 24 September 1999).

Pandam, Rafael. "Statement of the Confederation of Indigenous Nationalities of Ecuador." In *Rights Violations in the Ecuadorian Amazon*. New York: Center for Economic and Social Rights, 1994.

Parajuli, Pramod. "Beyond Capitalized Nature: Ecological Ethnicity as a New Arena of Conflict in the Regime of Globalization." *Ecumene: A Journal of Environment, Culture, and Meaning* 5, no. 2 (1998): 186–217.

———. "Discourse on Knowledge, Dialogue and Diversity: Peasant Cosmovision and the Science of Nature Conservation." *Worldviews: Environment, Culture, and Religion* 1, no. 3 (1997): 189–210.

———. "Ecological Ethnicity in the Making: Developmentalist Hegemonies and the Emergent Identities in India." *Identities* 3, no. 1-2 (1996): 15–59.

———. "How Can Four Trees Make a Jungle?: Ecological Ethnicities and the Sociality of Nature." *Terra Nova: Nature and Culture* 3, no. 3 (1998): 15–31.

———. *Tortured Bodies and Altered Earth: Ecological Ethnicities in the Regime of Globalization*. Lanham, Md.: Rowman and Littlefield Publishers, 2000 (forthcoming).

Parajuli, Pramod, and Smitu Kothari. "Struggling for Autonomy: Lessons from Local Governance." *Development: Seeds of Change* 41, no. 3 (1998): 18–29.

Parrinder, Geoffrey. *African Traditional Religion*. 3d ed. London: Sheldon Press, 1974.

Pashagumiskum, Nellie. "In Memory of Joab Bearskin." *The Northland* 46, no. 2 (1989-90): 7.

Patkar, Medha. "The Strength of a People's Movement." *India International Centre Quarterly* 19, no. 1-2 (1992): 273–99.

———. "The Struggle for Participation and Justice: A Historical Narrative." In *Toward a Sustainable Development? Struggling over India's Narmada*

River, ed. William F. Fisher, 157–76. London: M. E. Sharpe, 1995.

Patterson, John. "Maori Environmental Virtues." *Environmental Ethics* 16, no. 4 (1994): 397–409.

Peet, Richard, and Michael Watts. *Liberation Ecologies: Environment, Development, Social Movements*. New York: Routledge, 1996.

Pei, Shengji. "Managing for Biological Diversity Conservation in Temple Yards and Holy Hills: The Traditional Practices of the Xishuangbanna Dai Community, Southwest China." In *Ethics, Religion and Biodiversity*, ed. Lawrence S. Hamilton. Cambridge: The White Horse Press, 1993.

Pele Defense Fund. "Pele Victory." *Earth First!* 14, no. 5 (1994): 13.

Peluso, Nancy Lee. *Rich Forest, Poor People: Resource Control and Resistance in Java*. Berkeley and Los Angeles: University of California Press, 1992.

Pemberton, John. *On the Subject of "Java."* Ithaca, N.Y.: Cornell University Press, 1994.

Penan leaders. "Malaysian Army Attacks Penan." *Earth First!* 14, no. 2 (1993): 1, 25.

Pere, Rangimarie Rose. *Ako: Concepts and Learning in the Maori Tradition*. Hamilton: University of Waikato, Department of Sociology, 1982.

Pereira, W., and A. K. Gupta. "A Dialogue on Indigenous Knowledge." *Honey Bee* 4 (1993): 6–10.

Perez, Gabina. *North American Native Workshop on Environmental Justice*. Denver: Iliff School of Theology, 1995.

Perlin, John. *A Forest Journey: The Role of Wood in the Development of Civilization*. Cambridge, Mass.: Harvard University Press, 1989.

Pezzoli, Keith. *Human Settlements and Planning for Ecological Sustainability: The Case of Mexico City*. Cambridge, Mass.: MIT Press, 1998.

———. "Sustainable Livelihoods in an Urban Milieu: A Case Study from Mexico City." In *In Defense of Livelihood*, ed. John Friedmann and Haripriya Rangan, 127–54. West Hartford, Conn.: Kumarian, 1993.

Pike, Kenneth. *Language in Relation to a Unified Theory of the Structure of Human Behavior*. The Hague: Mouton, 1967.

Plant, Christopher, and Judith Plant. *Turtle Talk: Voices for a Sustainable Future*. Philadelphia: New Society Publishers, 1990.

Platvoet, Jan, James Cox, and Jacob Olupona, eds. *The Study of Religions in Africa: Past, Present, and Prospects*. Cambridge: Roots and Branches, 1996.

Pomedli, Michael M. "The Concept of Soul in the Jesuit Relations: Were There Any Philosophers among the North American Indians?" *Laval Théologique et Philosophique* 41, no. 1 (1985).

———. *Ethnophilosophical and Ethnolinguistic Perspectives on the Huron Indian Soul*. Lewiston, N.Y.: The Edwin Mellen Press, 1991.

Pommersheim, Frank. "The Crucible of Sovereignty: Analyzing Issues of Tribal Jurisdiction." *Arizona Law Review* 31 (1989): 329–63.

Ponte, J. Veronica. "Contributions of the Warao Indians to the Ichthyology of the Orinoco Delta." *Scientia Guainae* 5 (1995): 371–92.

Porterfield, K. Marie. "City Admits Racism Exists." *Indian Country Today,* 12 January 1998, B1.

Portillo, Miguel Leon. *Aztec Thought and Culture.* Norman: University of Oklahoma Press, 1963.

Posey, Darrell Addison. "Cultivating the Forest of the Amazon: Science of the Mebengokre." *Orion Nature Quarterly* 9 (1990): 16–23.

———, ed. *Cultural and Spiritual Values of Biodiversity.* United Nations Environment Programme (UNEP). Global Biodiversity Assessment. Nairobi: UNEP, 1998.

———. "Indigenous Management of Tropical Forest Ecosystems: The Case of the Kayapo Indians of the Brazilian Amazon." *Agroforestry Systems* 3 (1985): 139–58.

———. *Indigenous Peoples and Traditional Resource Rights: A Basis for Equitable Relationships?* Oxford: Green College Centre for Environmental Policy and Understanding, 1995.

———. "The Kayapo: The Role of Intellectual Property in Resource Management in the Brazilian Amazon." In *Indigenous Peoples and Sustainability: Cases and Actions,* ed. Darrell Addison Posey and Graham Dutfield, 240–54. Utrecht: IUCN and International Books, 1997.

———. "Protecting Indigenous Peoples' Rights to Biodiversity." *Environment* 38, no. 8 (1996).

Posey, Darrell Addison, and Graham Dutfield. *Beyond Intellectual Property: Toward Traditional Resource Rights for Indigenous Peoples and Local Communities.* Ottawa: International Development Research Centre, 1996.

Posluns, Michael. *Voices from the Odeyak.* Toronto: NC Press, 1993.

Powers, William K. *Yuwipi.* Lincoln: University of Nebraska Press, 1982.

Prabhu, Pradip. "The Bhutali Phenomenon." *Socialist Health Review* (Bombay), 1988.

———. "Forest Legislation Pre-Independence." *Legal Resources for Social Action* (Madras), 1982.

Preston, Richard. *Cree Narrative: Expressing the Personal Meaning of Events.* Canadian Ethnology Service, Paper no. 30. Ottawa: National Museum of Man, 1975.

Prill-Brett, June. *Coping Strategies in the Bontok Highland Agroecosystem: The Role of Ritual.* Baguio City: Cordillera Studies Center, 1997.

Prins, Harald E. L. "Neo-traditions in Native Communities: Sweat Lodge and Sun Dance among the Micmac Today." In *Actes du Vingt-cinquième*

Congrès des Algonquinistes, ed. W. Cowan. Ottawa: Carleton University, 1994.

Project for Ecological Recovery. *Survey Report for the Pak Mun Area.* Bangkok: Project for Ecological Recovery, 1993.

Puwáinchir, M. "The Voice of the Ecuadorian Amazon." *Grassroots Development* 16, no. 2 (1992): 40.

Rae, Eleanor. *Women, the Earth, the Divine.* Maryknoll, N.Y.: Orbis Books, 1994.

Rafael, Vicente. *Contracting Colonialism: Translation and Christian Conversion in Tagalog Society under Early Spanish Rule.* Ithaca, N.Y.: Cornell University Press, 1988.

Rainforest Action Network. "Biggest Demo in Hawaii's History Protests Puna Destruction." *World Rainforest Report* 6, no. 2 (1990): 5.

———. "Crackdown in Malaysia." *Earth Island Journal* 3, no. 1 (1988).

———. "Ecuador: ARCO, UNOCAL Drilling in Amazon." *World Rainforest Report*, January/March 1991.

———. "Action Alert 140: Ecuadorian Indians Take a Stand against Oil," updated 1998. <http://www.ran.org./ran/info_center/aa/aa140.html> (cited 24 September 1999).

———. "With the Penan at the Last Blockade." *Earth Island Journal* 4, no. 1 (1989).

Rajotte, Freda. *First Nations Faith and Ecology.* Toronto: Anglican Book Centre; Etobicoke, Ont.: United Church Publishing House; London: Cassell, 1998.

Ramirez-Faria, Carlos. *The Origins of Economic Inequality between Nations: A Critique on Western Theories of Development and Underdevelopment.* Cambridge, Mass.: Unwin-Hyman, 1990.

Ramphele, Mamphela, ed. *Restoring the Land: Environment and Change in Post-Apartheid South Africa.* London: Panos Institute, 1991.

Ranger, Terence. *Peasant Consciousness and Guerrilla War in Zimbabwe.* London: University of California Press, 1985.

Rappaport, Roy A. *Ecology, Meaning, and Religion.* Richmond, Calif.: North Atlantic Books, 1979.

———. *Pigs for the Ancestors: Ritual in the Ecology of a New Guinea People.* Rev. ed. New Haven: Yale University Press, 1985.

Ray, Arthur. *The Canadian Fur Trade in the Industrial Age.* Toronto: University of Toronto Press, 1990.

Ray, N. Introductory address in *Tribal Situation in India*, ed. K. Singh. Shimla: Indian Institute of Advanced Studies, 1995.

Razari, Hossein. "Financing Oil and Gas Projects in Developing Countries." *Finance and Development* 3, no. 2 (1996): 3.

Redford, Kent. The Ecologically Noble Savage. *Cultural Survival Quarterly* 15, no. 1 (1993): 46–48.

Redford, Kent, and Jane Mansour, eds. *Traditional Peoples and Biodiversity Conservation in Large Tropical Landscapes*. Arlington, Va.: The Nature Conservancy, 1996.

Reichel-Dolmatoff, Gerardo. *Amazonian Cosmos: The Sexual and Religious Symbolism of the Tukano Indians*. Chicago: University of Chicago Press, 1971.

Reid, Bill, and Robert Bringhurst. *The Raven Steals the Light*. Vancouver: Douglas and McIntyre, 1984.

Remedios, Avellino. *Mythos and Logos of the Warlis*. New Delhi: Concept Publishing Company, 1998.

Rengifo, Grimaldo Vasquez. "Educacion en Occidente Moderno y en la Cultura Moderna." *Desarrollo o Descolonizacion en los Andes?* 163–87. Lima: PRATEC, 1993.

Report of the Royal Commission on Aboriginal Peoples. Ottawa: The Commission, 1996.

Rich, E. E. "Trade Habits, Economic Motivation among the Indians of North America." *Canadian Journal of Economic and Political Science* 26, no. 1 (1960): 35–53.

Richards, Audrey. *Land, Labour and Diet in Northern Rhodesia*. London and New York: Oxford University Press, 1939.

Richards, P. "Alternative Strategies for the African Environment: Folk Ecology as a Basis for Community Oriented Agricultural Development." In *African Environment: Problems and Perspectives*, ed. P. Richards. London: International African Institute, 1975.

Richardson, Boyce. *Flooding Job's Garden*. Toronto: Canadian Broadcasting Company and National Film Board of Canada, 1991. Film.

———. *James Bay: The Plot to Drown the North Woods*. San Francisco: Sierra Club; Toronto: Clarke, Irwin and Company, 1972.

———. *Job's Garden*. Toronto: Tamarack Productions, 1974. Film.

———. "A Return to Job's Garden." In *On the Land: Confronting the Challenges to Aboriginal Self-Determination in Northern Quebec and Labrador*, ed. Bruce W. Hodgins and Kerry A. Cannon, 145–54. Toronto: Betelgeuse Books, 1995.

———. *Strangers Devour the Land*. Toronto: Douglas and McIntyre, 1991.

Riley, Murdoch. "Maori Healing and Herbal." *New Zealand Ethnobotanical Sourcebook*. Paraparaumu: Viking Sevenseas, 1994.

Rirash, M. A. "Camel Herding and Its Effect on Somali Literature." In *Camels in Development*, ed. A. Hjort af Ornas. Uppsala: Scandinavian Institute of African Studies, 1988.

Rivera, George. *Then and Now: Pojoaque Pueblo in Perspective*. Pojoaque Pueblo, N.Mex., 1992.

Rogers, E. S. *The Round Lake Ojibwa*. Occasional Paper, 5. Toronto: Royal

Ontario Museum, University of Toronto, Art and Archaeology Division, 1962.

Ross, Allan C. *Mitakuye Oyasin, 'We are All Related.'* Fort Yates: Bear Press, 1989.

Rossler, M. "Tongariro: First Cultural Landscape on the World Heritage List." *World Heritage Newsletter* 4 (1993): 15.

Roszak, Theodore. *The Voice of the Earth: An Exploration of Ecopsychology.* New York: Simon and Schuster/Touchstone, 1992.

Rothenberg, Jerome, ed. *Technicians of the Sacred.* Berkeley and Los Angeles: University of California Press, 1985.

Rousseau, Jerome. *Central Borneo: Ethnic Identity and Social Life in a Stratified Society.* Oxford: Clarendon Press, 1990.

Roy, S. C. "Oraon Religion and Custom." *Man in India* (Ranchi), 1928.

Rudel, T. K., and B. Horowitz. *Small Farmers and Land Clearing in the Ecuadorian Amazon.* New York: Columbia University Press, 1993.

Rudolph, Carol P. *Petroglyphs and Pueblo Myths of the Rio Grande.* Albuquerque: Avanyu Publishing Inc., 1990.

Ruether, Rosemary Radford. *Women Healing Earth: Third World Women on Ecology, Feminism, and Religion.* Maryknoll, N.Y.: Orbis Books, 1996.

Ryan, Lyndall, ed. "Secret Women's Business: Hindmarsh Island Affair." *Journal of Australian Studies* 48 (1996).

Sachs, Aaron. "Dying for Oil." *World Watch* 9, no. 3 (1996): 12–13.

———. "Upholding Human Rights and Environmental Justice." *State of the World.* Washington, D.C.: Worldwatch Institute, 1993.

Sachs, Wolfgang. "The Political Anatomy of Sustainable Development." *Interculture* 29, no. 1 (1996): 14–35.

———, ed. *Global Ecology: A New Arena of Political Conflict.* London: Zed Books; Atlantic Highlands, N.J.: Fernwood Publishers, 1993.

Sahabat Alam Malaysia. "Malaysia: Appeal by the Orang Ulu to Protect Their Lands, Forests and Resources." *IWGIA Newsletter* (Copenhagen) 53-54 (1988).

Sahagún, Fray Bernardino de. *Historia general de las cosas de Nueva España.* Ed. and notes Angel María Garibay K. 4 vols. México: Editorial Porrúa, S.A., 1956.

Salazar, Ernesto. "An Indian Federation in Lowland Ecuador." *IWGIA Newsletter* (Copenhagen) 28 (1977).

Sale, Kirkpatrick. *Dwellers in the Land: The Bioregional Vision.* San Francisco: Sierra Club Books, 1985.

Salisbury, Richard F. *A Homeland for the Cree.* Montreal: McGill-Queen's University Press, 1986.

Salzman, Philip Carl. "Fads and Fashions in Anthropology." *Anthropology Newsletter* 29, no. 5 (1988): 1, 32–33.

Sam-Cromarty, Margaret. *James Bay Memories: A Cree Woman's Ode to Her Homeland.* Lakefield, Ont.: Waapoone Publishing, 1992.

Sandner, Donald. *Navajo Symbols of Healing.* New York: Harcourt Brace Jovanovich, 1979.

Sanitsuda, Ekachai. *Behind the Smile: Voices of Thailand.* Bangkok: Bangkok Development Support Committee, 1990.

Save, K. J. *The Warlis.* Bombay: Padma Press, 1945.

Savyasaachi. *Tribal Forest Dwellers and Self Rule.* New Delhi: Indian Social Institute, 1998.

Sawyer, Suzanna. "The 1992 Indian Mobilization in Lowland Ecuador." *Latin American Perspectives* 24, no. 3 (1997): 65–83.

Sayen, Jamie, and Michael Posluns. "A History of James Bay Development." Broadsheet published by the Northeast Alliance to Protest James Bay, Cambridge, Mass., 1991.

Schele, Linda, and David Freidel. *A Forest of Kings: The Untold Story of the Ancient Maya.* New York: William Morrow and Company, 1990.

Schmink, Marianne, and Charles H. Wood. *Contested Frontiers in Amazonia.* New York: Columbia University Press, 1992.

Schodt, David W. *Ecuador: An Andean Enigma.* Boulder, Colo.: Westview Press, 1987.

Schoell, Hans-Martin, ed. *Environment and Development.* Point series, no. 18. Goroka, Papua New Guinea: Melanesian Institute, 1994.

Schrempp, Gregory. "Magical Arrows." *The Maori, the Greeks, and the Folklore of the Universe.* Madison: University of Wisconsin, 1992.

Schubert, Louis. "Environmental Politics in Asia." *Environmental Politics in the International Arena*, ed. Sheldon Kamieniecki, 239–55. Albany: State University of New York Press, 1993.

Scott, Colin H. "Property, Practice, and Aboriginal Rights among Quebec Cree Hunters." In *Hunters and Gatherers 2*, ed. Tim Ingold, David Riches, and James Woodburn, 35–51. New York: Berg, 1988.

———. "Science for the West, Myth for the Rest? The Case of James Bay Cree Knowledge Construction." In *Naked Science. Anthropological Inquiry into Boundaries, Power, and Knowledge*, ed. Laura Nader, 69–86. New York: Routledge, 1996.

Scott, James. *Weapons of the Weak: Everyday Forms of Peasant Resistance.* New Haven: Yale University Press, 1985.

Scott, William Henry. *Of Igorots and Independence.* Baguio City: ERA, 1993.

———. *On the Cordillera, A Look at the Peoples and Cultures of the Mountain Province.* Manila: MCS Enterprises, 1969.

———. *A Sagada Reader.* Quezon City: New Day Publishers, 1988.

Sedinger, James, D. H. Ward, and D. Welsh. "The Status and Biology of the

Geese Nesting at Tutakoke, 1985: A Progress Report." Unpublished Report. U.S. Fish and Wildlife Service, 1985.

Selcraig, Bruce. "Native Americans Join to Stop the Newest of the Indian Wars." *Sierra Magazine* 79, no. 3 (1994).

Selverston, Melina H. "The Politics of Culture: Indigenous Peoples and the State in Ecuador." In *Indigenous Peoples and Democracy in Latin America*, ed. Donna Lee van Cott. New York: St. Martin's Press, in association with the Inter-American Dialogue, 1994.

Setterberg, Fred, and Lonny Shavelson. *Toxic Nation: The Fight to Save Our Communities from Chemical Contamination*. New York: John Wiley and Sons, 1993.

Shah, Ganshyam. "Tribal Issues: Problems and Perspectives." In *Socio-Economic and Ecological Development*, ed. Buddhadeb Chaudhari. New Delhi: Inter India Publications, 1992.

Sharma, Pranjal. "Muddying the Waters." *India Today,* 15 February 1994.

Shiva, Vandana. *Ecology and the Politics of Survival: Conflicts over Natural Resources in India*. New Delhi: Sage Publications, 1991.

————. *Monocultures of the Mind*. London: Zed Books, 1993.

————. *Staying Alive: Women, Ecology and Development*. London: Zed Books, 1988.

Shiva, Vandana, et al. *The Seed Keepers*. New Delhi: Navdanya, 1995.

Sinclair, Douglas. "Land: Maori View and European Response." In *Te Ao Hurihuri: The World Moves On*, ed. Michael King. Wellington: Hicks Smith and Methuen, 1977.

Singh, Chhatrapati. *Common Property and Common Poverty: India's Forests, Forest Dwellers and the Law*. Delhi: Oxford University Press, 1986.

Singh, K. S., gen. ed. *People of India*. Vol. 18, *Dadra and Nagar Haveli*, ed. Faquir Chand and N. K. Sinha. Calcutta: Anthropological Survey of India; Bombay: Popular Prakashan, 1994.

Singh, Pradip. "Hill-Man-Spirit Complex of a Hill Tribe." In *Nature-Man-Spirit Complex in Tribal India*, ed. R. S. Mann. New Delhi: Concept Publishing House, 1981.

Sinha, Surajit. "Tribal Cult of Peninsular India." *Man in India* (Ranchi) 37 (1957).

Sitakant, Mahapatra. *Unending Rhythms, Oral Poetry of the Indian Tribes*. New Delhi: Inter India Publications, 1992.

Snipp, Matthew. "The Changing Political and Economic Status of the American Indians: From Captive Nations to Internal Colonies." *American Journal of Economics and Sociology* 45, no. 2 (1986): 153–54.

Snyder, Gary. "Coming into the Watershed." In *Changing Community: The Graywolf Annual Ten*, ed. Scott Walker. St. Paul, Minn.: Graywolf Press, 1992.

————. *The Old Ways*. San Francisco: City Light Books, 1977.

————. *The Practice of the Wild*. Berkeley: North Point Press, 1990.

South and Meso American Indian Rights Center. "Oil Destruction Set to Begin in Pastaza, Ecuador," updated 1998. <http://www.forest.org/gopher/ecuador/oiltobeg.txt> (cited 1 October 1999).

Southhall, Aidan William, and Michael Schatzbert, eds. *Small Urban Centres in Rural Development in Africa*. Madison: African Studies Program, University of Wisconsin, 1979.

Speck, Frank G. "Animals in Special Relation to Man." In *Naskapi: The Savage Hunters of the Labrador Peninsula*. Norman: University of Oklahoma Press, 1977.

————. "Family Hunting Territories and Social Life." *American Anthropologist*, spring 1915.

Stanner, W. E. H. *On Aboriginal Religion*. Oceania Monographs, 11. Sydney: University of Sydney, 1963.

Steen, Harold K., and Richard P. Tucker, eds. *Changing Tropical Forests: Historical Perspectives on Today's Challenges in Central and South America*. Durham, N.C.: Forest History Society, 1992.

Steller, Tirn. "Ecuador's Rain Forest Natives Struggle for Lands." *The Circle* 13, no. 5 (1992).

Stevens, Iris. *Report of the Hindmarsh Island Royal Commission*. Adelaide: The Royal Commission, 1995.

Stevens, Stanley F. *Claiming the High Ground: Sherpas, Subsistence, and Environmental Change in the Highest Himalaya*. Berkeley and Los Angeles: University of California Press, 1993.

————. *Conservation through Cultural Survival*. Washington, D.C.: Island Press, 1997.

Stevenson, Gil. "Haudenosaunee Nations and United Nations Begin Historic Environmental Collaboration." *Indian Country Today*, 27 July 1995, A2.

Stevenson, J. T. "Aboriginal Land Rights in Northern Canada." In *Contemporary Moral Issues*, ed. Wesley Cragg. Toronto: McGraw-Hill Ryerson, 1987.

Stock, R. "Environmental Sanitation in Nigeria." *Review of African Political Economy* 42 (1988): 19–31.

Stoll, David. "Evangelicals, Guerrillas, and the Army: The Ixil Triangle Under Rios Montt." In *Harvest of Violence: The Maya Indians and the Guatemalan Crises*, ed. Robert Carmack. Norman: University of Oklahoma Press, 1988.

Stott, Philip. "Mu'ang and Pa: Elite Views of Nature in a Changing Thailand." In *Thai Constructions of Knowledge*, ed. Manas Chitkasem and Andrew Turton, 142–54. London: University of London, 1991.

Strehlow, Theodor Georg Heinrich. *Songs of Central Australia.* Sydney: Angus and Robertson, 1971.

Sullivan, Lawrance E. *Icanchu's Drum: Orientation to Meaning in South American Religions.* New York: Macmillan, 1988.

Sundkler, Bengt. *Bantu Prophets in South Africa.* London: Oxford University Press, 1961.

Surplus People Project (South Africa). *Forced Removals in South Africa.* Surplus People Project Report, 1. Cape Town: Surplus People Project, 1983.

Survival International. "Ecuador: Indians Kill Bishop as Oil Companies Invade." *Urgent Action Bulletin,* August 1987.

Suzuki, David. *Time to Change.* Toronto: Allen and Unwin, 1994.

Suzuki, David, and Peter Knudtson. *Wisdom of the Elders: Honoring Sacred Native Visions of Nature.* New York: Bantam Books, 1992.

Swan, Brian, ed. *Smoothing the Ground.* Berkeley and Los Angeles: University of California Press, 1983.

Swan, James. *Sacred Places: How the Living Earth Seeks Our Friendship.* Santa Fe, N.Mex.: Bear and Company Publishers, 1990.

Swimme, Brian, and Thomas Berry. *The Universe Story: From the Primordial Flaring Forth to the Ecozoic Era: A Celebration of the Unfolding Cosmos.* San Francisco: HarperSanFrancisco, 1992.

Switkes, Glenn. "Amazon Indians' Movement Broadens." *Earth First!* 9, no. 5 (1989): 12.

Symington, D. *Report of the Aboriginal and Hill Tribes of Partially Excluded Areas in the Bombay Presidency.* Bombay: Central Government Press, 1938.

Tanner, Adrian. *Bringing Home Animals: Religious Ideology and Mode of Production of the Mistassini Cree.* St. John's: Institute of Social and Economic Research, Memorial University of Newfoundland, 1979.

Taube, Karl A. "The Teotihuacan Cave of Origin: The Iconography and Architecture of Emergence Mythology in Mesoamerica and the American Southwest." *RES: Anthropology and Aesthetics* 12 (1986): 51–82.

Tauli-Corpuz, Victoria. *The Asian Indigenous Peoples' Perspectives On Environment and Development.* New York: UN Conference on Environment and Development Publication, 1992.

Taylor, Bron, ed. *Ecological Resistance Movements.* Albany: State University of New York Press, 1995.

Taylor, Dorceta. "Can the Environmental Movement Attract and Maintain the Support of Minorities?" In *Race and the Incidence of Environmental Hazards: A Time for Discourse,* ed. Bunyan Bryant and Paul Mohai, 28–54. Boulder, Colo.: Westview Press, 1992.

Taylor, K. I. "Why Supernatural Eels Matter." In *Lessons of the Rainforest,* ed. Suzanne Head and Robert Heinzman. San Francisco: Sierra Club Books, 1990.

Tedlock, Dennis. *Popol Vuh: The Definitive Edition of the Mayan Book of the Dawn of Life and the Glory of Gods and Kings*. New York: A Touchstone Book, Simon and Schuster, 1996.

Tedlock, Dennis, and Barbara Tedlock. *Teachings from the American Earth*. New York: Liveright Publishing Corporation, 1992.

Teit, James Alexander. "The Jesup North American Expedition." In *The Lillooet Indians*, ed. Franz Boas, vol. 2, part 5. New York: G. E. Stechert, 1906.

Thwaites, Ruben Gold, ed. *Jesuit Relations and Allied Documents: Travels and Explorations of the Jesuit Missionaries in New France*. Vol. 1. New York: Pagent, 1959.

Tinker, George. "The Full Circle of Liberation." *Sojourners* (Washington, D.C.) 21 (October 1992): 12–17.

Tiwari, Rajiv. "India: Undermining the Himalaya." *Inter Press Service,* 6 November 1986.

Tobias, John L. "Protection, Civilization, Assimilation: An Outline History of Canada's Indian Policy." *Western Canadian Journal of Anthropology* 6, no. 2 (1976): 13–30.

Tom, Nick E., Jr. "Fish and Game More Disturbing to Geese than Newtok." *Tundra Drums* (Bethel, Alaska), 7 November 1996, A4.

Trenchard, E. "Rural Women's Work in Sub-Saharan Africa and the Implications for Nutrition." In *Geography of Gender*, ed. Janet Momsen and Janet Townsend, 53–72. Albany: State University of New York Press, 1987.

Trigger, Bruce G. *Natives and Newcomers*. Montreal: McGill-Queen's University Press, 1985.

Tuan, Yi-Fu. *Topophilia: A Study of Environmental Perception, Attitudes, and Values*. Englewood Cliffs, N.J.: Prentice Hall, 1974. Reprint, New York: Columbia University Press, 1990.

Tucker, Mary Evelyn, and John Grim, eds. *Worldviews and Ecology: Religion, Philosophy, and the Environment*. Lewisburg, Pa.: Bucknell University Press, 1993. Reprint, Maryknoll, N.Y.: Orbis Press, 1994.

Turner, Billie Lee, II. *The Earth As Transformed by Human Action: Global and Regional Changes in the Biosphere over the Past 300 Years*. New York: Cambridge University Press, 1991.

Turner, Terence S. "Anthropology and the Politics of Indigenous People's Struggles." *Cambridge Anthropology* 5, no. 1 (1977): 1–43.

————"The Role of Indigenous People in the Environmental Crisis: The Example of the Kayapó of the Brazilian Amazon." *Perspectives on Biological Medicine* 36 (1993): 3.

———. "The World Struggle to Save James Bay." In *Northeast Indian Quarterly* 8, no. 4 (1991).

Tyler, Hamilton. *Pueblo Gods and Myths*. Norman: University of Oklahoma Press, 1964.

Unidad Ecologiea Salvadorena. *The Proceedings of the People of Color Environmental Leadership Summit*. New York: UCC Commission on Racial Justice, 1992.

United Nations. *Universal Declaration on the Rights of Indigenous Peoples*. Draft. Geneva, Switzerland: Working Group on Indigenous Populations, 1989.

United Nations Conference on Environment and Development. *Agenda 21: The Earth Summit Strategy to Save our Planet*, ed. Daniel Sitarz. Boulder, Colo.: EarthPress, 1993.

United Nations Environment Programme. *The Biodiversity Agenda: Decisions from the Third Meeting of the Conference of the Parties to the Convention on Biological Diversity*. Buenos Aires, Argentina, 1996.

United States Energy Information Administration (EIA). "Ecuador," updated 2000. <http://www.eia.doe.gov/cabs/ecuador.html> (cited 24 September 1999).

Urquhart, Ian A. N. "Nomadic Punans and Pennans." In *The Peoples of Sarawak*, ed. Tom Harrisson. Kuching: Sarawak Museum, 1959.

———. "Some Notes on Jungle Punans in Kapit District." *Sarawak Museum Journal* 5, no. 13 (1951): 495–533.

Valladolid Rivera, Julio. "Agricultura Campesina Andina: Crianza de la diversidad de la vida en la chacra." In *Crianza Andina de la Chacra*. Lima: PRATEC, 1994.

van der Vlist, L., ed. *Voices of the Earth: Indigenous Peoples, New Partners and the Right to Self-determination in Practice*. Amsterdam: Netherlands Centre for Indigenous Peoples, 1994.

Vanucci, M. "Sacred Groves or Holy Forests." In *Concepts of Space, Ancient and Modern*, ed. Kapila Vatsayayan. New Delhi: Indira Gandhi Centre for the Arts, 1991.

Varese, Stefano. "The New Environmentalist Movement of Latin American Indigenous People." In *Valuing Local Knowledge: Indigenous People and Intellectual Property Rights*, ed. Stephen D. Brush and Doreen Stabinsky. Washington, D.C.: Island Press, 1996.

Vartak, H. G. *Report of Committee to Examine Difficulties Experienced by Scheduled Tribe Land Holders/Cultivators in Respect of Their Lands in the Working of Certain Acts*. Bombay: Government Press, 1972.

Vartak, V. D., and Madhav Gadgil. "Studies on Sacred Groves along Western Ghats from Maharashtra and Goa: Role of Beliefs and Folklores." In *Glimpses of Indian Ethnobiology*, ed. S. K. Jain. New Delhi: Oxford University Press and IBH, 1981.

Vecsey, Christopher T., and Robert W. Venables, eds. *American Indian Environments: Ecological Issues in Native American History.* Syracuse: Syracuse University Press, 1992.

Vennum, Thomas, Jr. *Wild Rice and the Ojibway People.* St. Paul: Minnesota Historical Society Press, 1988.

Ventocilla, Jorge, Heraclio Herrera, and Valerio Nunuz. *Plants and Animals in the Life of the Kuna.* Austin: University of Texas Press, 1995.

Vidharthi, L. P. *The Maler: A Study in Nature-Man-Spirit Complex of a Hill Tribe.* Allahabad: Bookland Pvt. Ltd., 1963.

Walker, Ranginui. "The Relevance of Maori Myth and Tradition." In *The Mauri Ora: Aspects of Maoritanga,* ed. Michael King. Wellington: Methuen, 1978.

Ward, Churchill. *Struggle for Land: Indigenous Resistance to Genocide, Ecocide, and Expropriation in Contemporary North America.* Monroe, Me.: Common Courage Press, 1993.

Warren, D. M., L. J. Slikkerveer, and D. Brokensha, eds. *The Cultural Dimension of Development: Indigenous Knowledge Systems.* London: Intermediate Technology Publications, 1995.

Wauthier, Claude. *The Literature and Thought of Modern Africa.* Trans. Shirley Kay. London: Heinemann Educational, 1978.

Weatherford, Jack. *Indian Givers: How the Indians of the Americas Transformed the World.* New York: Crown Publisher, Inc., 1988.

Weaver, Jace. *Defending Mother Earth: Native American Perspectives on Environmental Justice.* Maryknoll, N.Y.: Orbis Books, 1996.

Weiner, Daniel, and Richard Levin. "Land and Agrarian Transition in South Africa." *Antipode* 23, no. 1 (1991): 92–120.

Whaley, Rick, and Bresette Walter. *Walleye Warriors: An Effective Strategy against Racism and for the Earth.* Philadelphia: New Society, 1993.

Whitaker, Thomas, and Hugh Cutler. "Cucurbits from the Tehuacan Caves." *The Prehistory of the Tehuacan Valley.* Vol. 1, *Environment and Subsistence,* ed. Douglas Byers, 212–219. Austin: University of Texas Press, 1967.

White, Benjamin, Jr. "Kararao: A Dam Called War." *Earth First!* 9, no. 4 (1989): 15.

White, Leslie. *The Acoma Indians.* Washington, D.C.: Bureau of American Ethnology, 1932.

Whitten, Norman E., Jr. *Cultural Transformations and Ethnicity in Modern Ecuador.* Urbana: University of Illinois Press, 1981.

Wilbert, Johannes. *Mindful of Famine: Religious Climatology of the Warao Indians.* Cambridge, Mass.: Harvard University Center for the Study of World Religions, 1996.

———. *Mystic Endowment: Religious Ethnography of the Warao Indians.*

Cambridge, Mass.: Harvard University Center for the Study of World Religions, 1993.

Wilbert, Werner. "Bush-spirit Encounters in Warao Life and Lore." *Antropológica* 77 (1992): 63–92.

Willett, A. B. J. "Indigenous Knowledge and Its Implications for Agricultural Development and Agricultural Extension: A Case Study of the Vedic Tradition in Nepal." Ph.D. diss., Iowa State University, 1993.

Williamson, Ray A. *Living the Sky: The Cosmos of the American Indian.* Norman: University of Oklahoma Press, 1984.

Wilmer, Frank. *The Indigenous Voice in World Politics: Since Time Immemorial.* Newbury Park, Calif.: Sage Publications, 1993.

Wilson, E. O., and Frances Peter. *Biodiversity.* Washington, D.C.: National Academy Press, 1988.

Wilson, Ronald. *Bringing Them Home: Report of the National Inquiry into the Separation of Aboriginal and Torres Strait Islander Children and Their Families.* Sydney: Human Rights and Equal Opportunity Commission, 1977.

Wisner, B., and P. Mbithi. "Drought in Eastern Kenya: Nutritional Status and Farmer Activity." In *Natural Hazards, Local, National, Global,* ed. Gilbert F. White, 87–97. New York: Oxford University Press, 1974.

Wisner, Benjamin. *Power and Need in Africa.* London: Earthscan, 1988.

Witte, John. *Deforestation in Zaire: Logging and Landlessness,* ed. Marcus Colchester and Larry Lohmann. Penang, Malaysia: World Rainforest Movement, 1993.

Wood, Marion. *Spirits, Heroes, and Hunters from North American Indian Mythology.* New York: Shocken Books, 1982.

Woodward, A. E. *Aboriginal Land Rights Commission.* Second Report. Canberra: Australian Government Publishing Service, 1974.

World Bank. *Sub-Saharan Africa: From Crisis to Sustainable Growth.* New York: Oxford University Press, 1989.

World Commission on Environment and Development. *Food 2000.* London: Zed Press, 1987.

———. *Our Common Future.* New York: Oxford University Press, 1987.

World Rainforest Movement. "Declaration of the World Rainforest Movement." *IWGIA Newsletter* (Copenhagen) 59 (1989).

Worster, Donald. *The Wealth of Nature.* Oxford: Oxford University Press, 1993.

Wright, Ronald. *Stolen Continents: The New World through Indian Eyes.* London: Penguin Books, 1993.

Yachir, F. *Mining in Africa Today: Strategies and Prospects.* Tokyo: University Nations University Press; Atlantic Highlands, N.J.: Zed Books, 1988.

Yellowtail, Thomas, and Michael Fitzgerald. *Yellowtail: Crow Medicine*

Man and Sun Dance Chief: An Autobiography. Norman: University of
Oklahoma Press, 1991.

Yong, John. *Kokopeli.* Palmer Lake, Colo.: Filter Press, 1990.

Young, David, Grant Ingram, and Lise Swartz. *Cry of the Eagle.* Toronto:
University of Toronto Press, 1989.

Young, Michael. *Magicians of Manumanua.* Berkeley and Los Angeles:
University of California Press, 1983.

Yunupingu, J. G. Quoted in Australian Catholic Social Justice Council's
"Recognition: The Way Forward." In *Native Title Report: January-
June 1994.* Canberra: Australian Government Publishing Service, Ab-
original and Torres Strait Islander Social Justice Commissioner, 1995.

Notes on Contributors

Frédérique Apffel-Marglin is Professor of Anthropology at Smith College where she also codirects the Center for Mutual Learning. She has published the following books based on research in Orissa, India: *Wives of the God-King: The Rituals of the Devadasis of Puri* (Oxford University Press, 1985); *Purity and Auspiciousness in Indian Society,* edited with John Carman (E. J. Brill, 1985); *Dominating Knowledge: Development, Culture, and Resistance,* edited with Stephen A. Marglin (Oxford University Press, Clarendon Press, 1990); and *Decolonizing Knowledge: From Development to Dialogue,* edited with Stephen A. Marglin (Oxford University Press, Clarendon Press, 1996). She now collaborates with several NGOs in Peru and Bolivia and from that work has published *The Spirit of Regeneration: Andean Culture Confronting Western Notions of Development,* edited with PRATEC (Zed Books and St. Martins Press, 1998).

Diane Bell is a feminist anthropologist whose interests include the rights of indigenous women (particularly the Aboriginal people of Australia), indigenous land rights, human rights, indigenous religions, violence against women, and the writing of feminist ethnography. From 1989 to 1998, before joining the faculty of the George Washington University as Professor of Anthropology and director of the Women't Studies Program, she was the Henry R. Luce Professor of Religion, Economic Development and Social Justice at Holy Cross College, Worcester, Massachusetts. Her books include *Daughters of the Dreaming* (2d ed., University of Minnesota Press, 1993), *Generations: Grandmothers, Mothers, and Daughters* (Penguin, 1987), and *Law: The Old and the New,* with Pam Ditton (Canberra, 1984). Her most recent is the award-winning *Ngarrindjeri Wurruwarrin: A World That Is, Was, and Will Be* (Spinifex Press, 1998).

María Elena Bernal-García was born in Mexico City, obtaining her Ph.D. degree in Pre-Columbian art history from the University of Texas at Austin in 1993. Her studies included a minor at the B.A. level in cultural anthropology, and a minor in cultural linguistics at the Ph.D. level. After the experience of contributing with the Urban Design Commission of Pima County, Arizona, in 1986, she fused her interests in the Mesoamerican holy mountain and urban planning to study the symbolism of that icon in Mesoamerica's sacred geography and urbanscape. She is currently on the faculty of the Architecture and Art History Schools, Universidad Autónoma del Estado de Morelos, Cuernavaca, Morelos, México.

J. Peter Brosius is Associate Professor, Department of Anthropology, University of Georgia, and president of the Anthropology and Environment Section, American Anthropological Association. He is also affiliated with the Institute of Ecology, the Conservation and Sustainable Development Program, and the Environmental Ethics Program at the University of Georgia, and is an associate editor of the journal *Human Ecology*. Brosius has a long record of research and publication on ecological and environmental issues in Southeast Asia. Since 1992 his research has focused on transnational environmental politics in Sarawak, East Malaysia. He is currently completing a book entitled *Arresting Images: The Sarawak Rainforest Campaign and Transnational Environmental Politices*.

Gregory Cajete, Ph.D., is a Native American educator whose work is dedicated to honoring the foundations of indigenous knowledge in education. A Tewa Indian from Santa Clara Pueblo, New Mexico, he has lectured at colleges and universities in the United States, Canada, Russia, and Japan. He has taught at the Institute of American Indian and Alaska Native Arts for the past twenty-six years, where he also was the founding dean of the Center for Research and Cultural Exchange and chairman of Native American Studies. He is now an associate professor in the College of Education at the University of New Mexico and an adjunct professor in Native American Studies at the Institute of American Indian Arts. His books include *Look to the Mountain: An Ecology of Indigenous Education* (Kivaki Press, 1994) and *A People's Ecology: Explorations in Sustainable Living* (Clear Light Publishers, 1999).

Harvey A. Feit is Professor of Anthropology, McMaster University (Ph.D. McGill, 1979). His long-term research with James Bay Cree, studies of government indigenous policymaking, and studies of environmental and social movements focus on interpretations of nature, environmental and conservation practices, and postcolonial relationships. He is a former president of the Canadian Anthropology Society, North American editor of the *Cambridge Encyclopedia of Hunters and Gatherers* (1999), a Killam Postdoctoral Scholar, and cofounder of the Indigenous Studies Program at McMaster. He was senior social consultant with the Cree during negotiation and initial implementation of the James Bay and Northern Quebec Agreement and has consulted with indigenous peoples and governments across Canada, as well as in Alaska and Australia.

Ann Fienup-Riordan, an independent scholar, received the Ph.D. in cultural anthropology from the University of Chicago in 1989. She has lived, worked, and taught in Alaska since 1973. Her books include: *The Nelson Island Eskimo* (Alaska Pacific University Press, 1983); Eskimo *Essays* (Rutgers University Press, 1990); *The Real People and the Children of Thunder* (University of Oklahoma Press, 1991); *Boundaries and Passages* (University of Oklahoma Press, 1994); *Freeze Frame: Alaska Eskimos in the Movies* (University of Washington Press, 1995); and *The Living Tradition of Yup'ik Masks* (University of Washington Press, 1996). She was named 1991 Historian of the Year by the Alaska Historical Society and 1983 Humanist of the Year by the Alaska Humanities Forum. Since 1994 she has worked with the Anchorage Museum and the Yup'ik Cultural Center in Bethel curating the exhibit of Yup'ik masks *Agayuliyararput: Our Way of Making Prayer.*

Jack D. Forbes is Professor Emeritus of Native American Studies at the University of California, Davis. He is one of the cofounders of the emerging field of Native Studies and also of the indigenous-controlled higher education movement. He is the author of *Red Blood* (Theytus Books, 1997), *Only Approved Indians* (University of Oklahoma Press, 1995), and numerous other books. His web site is http://www.cougar.ucdavis.edu/nas.faculty/forbes.

Stephanie Fried is a specialist in Asian and Pacific issues at the Hawai'i office of Environmental Defense, a national nonprofit environmental organization with over 300,000 members throughout the United States. She is also a Visiting Fellow at the East West Center. The recipient of two Fulbright Fellowships for research in Indonesia, she has worked for indigenous communities in Indonesia and the Pacific Islands in support of their efforts to protect traditional territories and natural resources. In addition, she tracks and analyses multilateral and bilateral public finance and its impact upon the environment and human rights. Recent publications include: "Tropical Forests Forever? A Contextual Ecology of Bentian Rattan Agroforestry Systems," in C. Zerner, ed., *People, Plants, and Justice: The Politics of Nature Conservation* (Columbia University Press, 2000); and *Export Credit Agency Finance in Indonesia* (Environmental Defense, 2000; www.environmentaldefense.org).

Javier Galicia Silva, from Náhuatl, Mexico, has been a Rockefeller Fellow in Native American Studies, the University of California, Davis.

Angel Julián García Zambrano is a Venezuelan scholar with a B.A. in history from the Universidad de Los Andes who earned his M.A. and Ph.D. degrees in Latin American colonial art and urbanism from the University of New Mexico. After receiving Guggenheim and Fulbright Fellowships, he devoted himself to the study of sacred landscape and the settlement of Indian towns during the Early Colonial period. He has found key connections between flora, myth, and geography in Mesoamerican indigenous cultures. He is currently on the faculty of the Architecture and Art History Schools, Universidad Autónoma del Estado de Morelos, Cuernavaca, Morelos, México.

Tirso A. Gonzales (Peruvian Aymara) received his Ph.D. in sociology/rural sociology from the University of Wisconsin, Madison, with a dissertation entitled "Political Ecology of Peasantry, the Seed, and NGOs, in Latin America: A Comparative Study of Mexico and Peru, 1940–1955." He has been the principal researcher in the Pew project on biodiversity and indigenous peoples in Latin America under the direction of Jack Kloppenburg. His current research focuses, from an interdisciplinary perspective, on biodiversity, agrobiodiversity, indigenous peoples, biotechnology, and intellectual property rights. He is also analyzing the political economy and ecology of biodiversity in the Americas (North, Meso, and South). He is a University of California President's Postdoctoral Fellow associated with the Native American Studies Department at the University of California, Davis.

Tom Greaves is Professor of Anthropology at Bucknell University. Past president of the Society for Applied Anthropology and of the Society for the Anthropology of Work, Greaves has researched and written on cultural anthropology issues in the Andean world and, more recently, on the contemporary struggles of the indigenous groups of the United States and Canada, with a focus on intellectual, cultural, and environmental rights. He is the editor of and a contributor to *Intellectual Property Rights for Indigenous Peoples: A Sourcebook* (Society for Applied Anthropology, 1994).

John A. Grim is Professor of Religion at Bucknell University. As a historian of religions, he undertakes annual field studies in American Indian lifeways among the Apsaalooke/Crow peoples of Montana and the Swy-ahl-puh/Salish peoples of the Columbia River plateau in eastern Washington. Raised in the Missouri drift prairies of North Dakota, John went to the urban environs of the Bronx to study with Thomas Berry at Fordham University. He has published *The Shaman: Patterns of Religious Healing among the Ojibway Indians* (University of Oklahoma Press, 1983; 2d ed., 1987). With his wife Mary Evelyn Tucker, he has coedited *Worldviews and Ecology* (Orbis Books, 1994), and they are coeditors of the series "Religions of the World and Ecology." John is also president of the American Teilhard Association.

Manuka Henare teaches Māori development courses in the School of Business and Economics, The University of Auckland. He has taught in the School of Māori Studies, Victoria University of Wellington, on Māori religion, cosmology, traditional history, and the environment. He is currently finishing a major study of early-nineteenth-century (1820–1840) Māori religion, philosophy, and worldview—its coherence and flexibility to accommodate cultural, economic, and political developments. His academic background is in anthropology and history. For twenty-eight years, in his previous career in justice, peace, and development organizations, he traveled the Pacific Islands (Micronesia, Polynesia, and Melanesia) and Asia assessing human rights and development projects for both governmental and nongovernmental development programs. He also has a background in theology, and he was for nine years the national director of the New Zealand Catholic Bishops Conference Commission for Justice, Peace and Development.

Ogbu U. Kalu is an Igbo of southeastern Nigeria. He teaches at the University of Nigeria and holds a Ph.D. in history (University of Toronto), an M.Div. (Princeton Theological Seminary), and a D.D. (McGill University). Formerly, he was head of the Department of Religion, dean of the Faculty of the Social Sciences, and, most recently, director of the Institute of African Studies, University of Nigeria, Nsukka. His publications include *The History of Christianity in West Africa* (Longmans, 1981), *Embattled Gods: Christianization of Igboland, 1841–1991* (Minaj Publishers, 1996), and *Power, Poverty and Prayer: The Challenges of Poverty and Pluralism in African Christianity, 1960–1996* (Peter Lang, 2000).

Smitu Kothari is recognized as one of India's leading activists, working toward a non-party people's political movement for just, sustainable, and inclusive development in the country. He is an editor of the *Lokayan Bulletin* ("Dialogue of the People"), Delhi, and a contributing editor of the *People-Centered Development Forum*, New York. He has coedited *Out of the Nuclear Shadow*, with Zia Mian (Zed Books, 2001), and, with Harsh Sethi, *Rethinking Human Rights: Challenges for Theory and Action* (Lokayan, 1991) and *Voices from a Scarred City: The Delhi Carnage in Perspective* (Lokayan, 1985).

Mary N. MacDonald is originally from Australia. She worked for eight years as a teacher and researcher in Papua New Guinea. Since completing studies in the history of religions at the University of Chicago in 1988, she has taught at Le Moyne College in Syracuse, New York. Her current research focuses on Melanesian styles of Christianity. She is the author of *Local Religions* (Orbis Press, forthcoming) and *Mararoko: A Study in Melanesian Religion* (Peter Lang, 1991).

718   *Indigenous Traditions and Ecology*

Victor D. Montejo is Associate Professor of Native American Studies at the University of California, Davis. He is a Jakaltek Maya anthropologist active in issues of human rights and indigenous movements. He is the author of *Testimony: Death of a Guatemalan Village* (Curbstone Press, 1987), *Popol Vuh: The Sacred Book of the Mayas* (a version for young readers), *Q'anil: The Man of Lightning* (Fundacion Yax Te, 1999), *The Bird Who Cleans the World and Other Mayan Fables* (Curbstone Press 1991), and *Voices from Exile: Violence and Survival in Modern Maya History* (University of Oklahoma Press, 1999).

Simeon B. Namunu is a minister of the United Church in Papua New Guinea. He graduated with a Diploma in Theology in 1978, Bachelor of Divinity in 1983, and Bachelor of Arts with Honours in 1996. He has served in his church in various capacities as chaplain for various educational institutions, pastor of circuits, and bishop of a region of the United Church for six years. He served as the assistant director and a member of the faculty of the Melanesian Institute in Goroka, Papua New Guinea. He is presently serving as minister of the Reverend Sione Kami Memorial Church in Port Moresby.

Melissa K. Nelson, Ph.D., is executive director of the Cultural Conservancy, a San Francisco-based Native American nonprofit organization dedicated to the preservation and revitalization of indigenous communities and their ancestral lands. She is a writer, researcher, educator, and activist in the areas of cultural ecology, indigenous knowledge, native land rights, and cultural preservation. She teaches ecological studies at the California Institute of Integral Studies. She is a member of the Turtle Mountain band of Chippewa Indians.

Richard Nelson is a cultural anthropologist and writer who lives in Alaska. His books *Make Prayers to the Raven* (University of Chicago Press, 1983), *Shadow of the Hunter* (University of Toronto Press; University of Chicago Press, 1980), *Hunters of the Northern Ice* (University of Chicago Press, 1969), and *Hunters of the Northern Forest* (University of Chicago Press, 1973; 2d ed., 1986) describe relationships to the natural world among the Inupiaq Eskimos, Koyukon Indians, and Gwich'in Indians. He also wrote *Heart and Blood: Living with Deer in America* (A. A. Knopf, 1997) and *The Island Within* (North Point Press, 1989), which received the John Burroughs Award for nature writing.

Pramod Parajuli is a faculty member of the Global Ecology Program of the International Honors Program, Boston, Massachusetts. His research interests are in analyzing the intersection of social movements, ecology, and traditions of knowledge among ecological ethnicities—peasants, indigenous peoples, rural peasants, fisherfolk. He has recently completed a book manuscript entitled *Tortured Bodies and Altered Earth: Ecological Ethnicities in the Regime of Globalization.* He is actively involved in various ethno-ecological movements and movements for sustainable livelihoods in Nepal, his home country, and in India.

Darrell Addison Posey, Ph.D., is director of the Programme for Traditional Resource Rights of the Oxford Centre for the Environment, Ethics and Society at Mansfield College, University of Oxford. He is also Professor of Biological Sciences at the Federal University of Maranhao, Brazil, and scientific director of the Institute for Ethnobiology of the Amazon, Belem, Brazil. Dr. Posey is a founder and past president of the International Society for Ethnobiology and recipient of the United Nations' Environmental Programme's "Global 500" Award. His most recent books include: *Cultural and Spiritual Values of Biodiversity* (Intermediate Technology and UNEP, 1999); and, with Graham Dutfield, *Beyond Intellectual Property Rights: Toward Traditional Resource Rights for Indigenous Peoples and Local Communities* (International Development Research Centre, 1996) and *Traditional Resource Rights* (IUCN—the World Conservation Union, 1996).

Pradip Prabhu is an advocate and activist working for the past twenty-five years with the Kashtakari Sanghatna, a popular mass organization of landless and marginal farmers from the Warli, Kokna, Katkari, Thakur, and Koli tribal peoples of India. After receiving an undergraduate degree in philosophy, he earned a masters degree in business management. While working toward a doctorate, he became closely involved with the Warlis. Events in the tribal areas led him to put his doctoral studies on hold while he completed a masters in law. Activism continuously forces him toward new academic pursuits in an effort to learn from history to understand the present.

Leslie E. Sponsel earned the B.A. in geology from Indiana University and the M.A. and Ph.D. in anthropology from Cornell University. He is Professor of Anthropology at the University of Hawai'i, where he directs the Ecological Anthropology Program and teaches courses on historical, cultural, and spiritual aspects of human ecology as well as peace studies and human rights. For four years he served as chair of the Commission for Human Rights and the subsequent permanent Committee for Human Rights of the American Anthropological Association. He is the editor of *Indigenous Peoples and the Future of Amazonia: An Ecological Anthropology of an Endangered World* (University of Arizona Press, 1995) and *Endangered Peoples of Southeast and East Asia: Struggles to Survive and Thrive* (Greenwood Publishing Group, 2000). He is editor of the forthcoming *Sanctuaries of Culture and Nature: Sacred Places and Biodiversity Conservation.*

Victoria Tauli-Corpuz established in 1996 the Indigenous Peoples' International Centre for Policy Research and Advocacy (Tebtebba Foundation, Inc.), an NGO helping indigenous peoples to articulate and project their own views and positions on issues directly affecting them. From 1987 to 1995 she was the founder and executive director of the Cordillera Women's Education and Resource Center, Inc., an NGO engaged in raising social and feminist awareness of indigenous women in the Cordillera and helping them strengthen sustainable indigenous agroforestry projects and other natural resource management practices. In 1996 she helped organize and convene the indigenous women's caucus during the United Nations' fourth World Conference on Women. She has published several articles on globalization and indigenous peoples and is one of the leading indigenous activists lobbying for the adoption by the UN of the "Declaration on the Rights of Indigenous Peoples."

Ellen Trevorrow, from Ngarrindjeri, Australia, and her husband Tom run Camp Coorong, a cross-cultural race relations educational camp on Ngarrindjeri lands in southeast Australia. Ellen is a traditional weaver.

Tom Trevorrow, from Ngarrindjeri, Australia, and his wife Ellen run Camp Coorong, a cross-cultural race relations educational camp on Ngarrindjeri lands in southeast Australia. He has worked on environmental issues all his life. He is chair of the Ngarrindjeri Lands and Progress Association and a member of the Ngarrindjeri Treaty Committee and the Ngarrindjeri Native Title Committee.

Julio Valladolid is a native of Huancayo, Peru, an agronomist with graduate studies in the genetic improvement of plants. He is Emeritus Professor, Faculty of Agricultural Sciences, San Cristobal National University, Huamanga, in Ayacucho, Peru. He has published in the areas of the physiology of Andean crops and Andean peasant agriculture. He is currently working within the organization Andean Project of Peasant Technologies (PRATEC), dedicated to the revalorization of Andean culture.

Werner Wilbert is a member of the Departamento Antropología, Instituto Venezolano de Investigaciones Científicas, in Caracas, Venezuala. He has been a senior research associate at the Instituto Caribe de Antropologia y Sociologia, Fundacion La Salle, Caracas, Venezuela and a senior fellow at the Center for the Study of World Religions, Harvard Divinity School. He has been active in ethnobotanical studies among Warao peoples, describing their telluric, cultural, and value systems to unveil a world order of balanced complementary diversity. He is the author of *Fitoterapia Warao: Una teoria pneumica de la salud, la enfermedad y su tratamiento* (Fundacion La Salle de Ciencias Naturales, Instituto Caribe de Antropologia y Sociologia, 1996).

Index